PRINCIPLES OF COMPUTER ARCHITECTURE

Miles J. Murdocca

Department of Computer Science
Rutgers University
New Brunswick, NJ

Vincent P. Heuring

Department of Electrical and Computer Engineering
University of Colorado
Boulder, CO

Prentice Hall
Upper Saddle River, NJ 07458

Library of Congress Cataloging-in-Publication Data

Murdocca, Miles.

Principles of computer architecture/ Miles J. Murdocca, Vincent P. Heuring.

p. cm

ISBN 0-201-43664-7

1. Computer architecture. I. Heuring, Vincent P. II. Title.

QA76.9.A73 M86 2000

004.2'2--dc21 99-046113

CIP

Editor-in-chief: *Marcia Horton*
Publisher: *Tom Robbins*
Acquisitions editor: *Eric Frank*
Director of production and manufacturing: *David W. Riccardi*
Executive managing editor: *Vince O'Brien*
Managing editor: *David George*
Editorial supervision/Page composition: *Scott Disanno*
Cover director: *Jayne Conte*
Cover: *Bruce Kenselaar*
Marketing manager: *Danny Hoyt*
Manufacturing buyer: *Pat Brown*
Editorial assistant: *Jenni DiBlasi*

Credit to:
Bob Van Ess
420 S. Main Street
Hughesville, PA 17737
bobvaness@usa.net
http://home.ptd.net/~drbob

The author and publisher of this book have used their best efforts in preparing this book. These efforts include the development, research, and testing of the theories and programs to determine their effectiveness. The author and publisher shall not be liable in any event for incidental or consequential damages in connection with, or arising out of, the furnishing, performance, or use of these programs.

Printed in the United States of America

10 9 8 7 6 5 4 3 2

ISBN 0-201-43664-7

Prentice-Hall International (UK) Limited, *London*
Prentice-Hall of Australia Pty. Limited, *Sydney*
Prentice-Hall Canada, Inc., *Toronto*
Prentice-Hall Hispanoamericana, S.A., *Mexico*
Prentice-Hall of India Private Limited, *New Delhi*
Prentice-Hall of Japan, Inc., *Tokyo*
Prentice-Hall (Singapore) Pte., Ltd., *Singapore*
Editora Prentice-Hall do Brazil, Ltda., *Rio de Janeiro*

For Ellen, Alexandra, and Nicole

and

For Gretchen

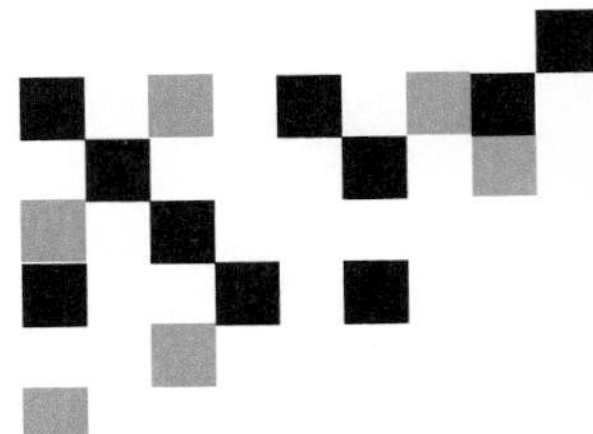

TABLE OF CONTENTS

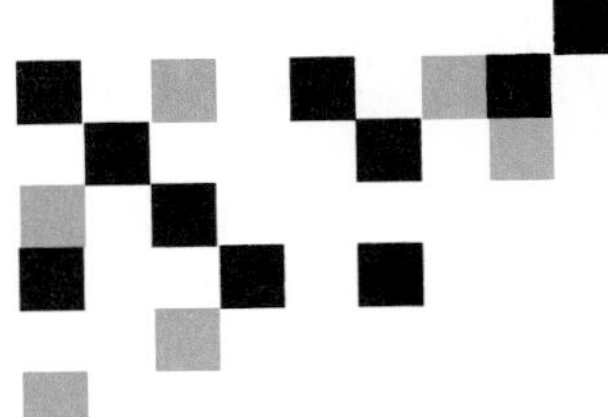

PREFACE

About the Book

Our goal in writing this book is to expose the inner workings of the modern digital computer at a level that demystifies what goes on inside the machine. The only prerequisite to *Principles of Computer Architecture* is a working knowledge of a high-level programming language. The breadth of material has been chosen to cover topics normally found in a first course in computer architecture or computer organization. The breadth and depth of coverage have been steered to place the beginning student on a solid track for continuing studies in computer-related disciplines.

In creating a computer architecture textbook, the technical issues fall into place fairly naturally, and it is the organizational issues that bring important features to fruition. Some of the features that received the greatest attention in *Principles of Computer Architecture* include the choice of the instruction set architecture (ISA), the use of case studies, and a voluminous use of examples and exercises.

THE INSTRUCTIONAL ISA

A textbook that covers assembly language programming needs to deal with the issue of which ISA to use: a model architecture, or one of the many commercial architectures. The choice impacts the instructor, who may want an ISA that matches a local platform used for student assembly language programming assignments. To complicate matters, the local platform may change from semester to semester: yesterday the MIPS, today the Pentium, tomorrow the SPARC. The authors opted for having it both ways by adopting a SPARC-subset for an instructional ISA, called "A RISC Computer" (ARC), which is carried through the mainstream of the book, and complementing it with platform-independent software tools that simulate the ARC ISA as well as the MIPS and x86 (Pentium) ISAs.

CASE STUDIES, EXAMPLES, AND EXERCISES

Every chapter contains at least one case study as a means for introducing the student to "real world" examples of the topic being covered. This places the topic in perspective, and in the authors' opinion, lends an air of reality and interest to the material.

We incorporated as many examples and exercises as we practically could, covering the most significant points in the text. Additional examples and solutions are available online, at the companion web site.

Coverage of Topics

Our presentation views a computer as an integrated system. If we were to choose a subtitle for the book, it might be "An Integrated Approach," which reflects high-level threads that tie the material together. Each topic is covered in the context of the entire machine of which it is a part, and with a perspective as to how the implementation affects behavior. For example, the finite precision of binary numbers is brought to bear in observing how many 1's can be added to a floating point number before the error in the representation exceeds 1. (This is one reason why floating point numbers should be avoided as loop control variables.) As another example, subroutine linkage is covered with the expectation that the reader may someday be faced with writing C or Java programs that make calls to routines in other high-level languages, such as Fortran.

As yet another example of the integrated approach, error detection and correction are covered in the context of mass storage and transmission, with the expectation that the reader may tackle networking applications (where bit errors and data packet losses are a fact of life) or may have to deal with an unreliable storage medium such as a compact disk read-only memory (CD-ROM).

Computer architecture impacts many of the ordinary things that computer professionals do, and the emphasis on taking an integrated approach addresses the great diversity of areas in which a computer professional should be educated. This emphasis reflects a transition that is taking place in many computer-related undergraduate curricula. As computer architectures become more complex, they must be treated at correspondingly higher levels of abstraction, and in some ways they also become more technology dependent. For this reason, the major portion of the text deals with a high-level look at computer architecture, while the appendices and case studies cover lower-level, technology-dependent aspects.

THE CHAPTERS

Chapter 1: Introduction introduces the textbook with a brief history of computer architecture, and progresses through the basic parts of a computer, leaving the student with a high-level view of a computer system. The conventional von Neumann model of a digital computer is introduced, followed by the system bus model, followed by a topical exploration of a typical computer. This chapter lays the groundwork for the more detailed discussions in later chapters.

Chapter 2: Data Representation covers basic data representation. One's complement, two's complement, signed magnitude, and excess representations of signed numbers are covered. Binary coded decimal (BCD) representation, which is frequently found in calculators, is also covered in Chapter 2. The representation of floating point numbers is covered, including the IEEE 754 floating point standard for binary numbers. The ASCII, EBCDIC, and Unicode character representations are also covered.

Chapter 3: Arithmetic covers computer arithmetic and advanced data representations. Fixed point addition, subtraction, multiplication, and division are covered for signed and unsigned integers. Nine's complement and ten's complement representations, used in BCD arithmetic, are covered. BCD and floating point arithmetic are also covered. High-performance methods such as carry-lookahead addition, array multiplication, and division by functional iteration are covered. A short discussion of residue arithmetic introduces an unconventional high-performance approach.

Chapter 4: The Instruction Set Architecture introduces the basic architectural components involved in program execution. Machine language and the fetch-execute cycle are covered. The organization of a central processing unit is detailed, and the role of the system bus in interconnecting the arithmetic/logic unit, registers, memory, input and output units, and the control unit is discussed.

Assembly language programming is covered in the context of the instructional ARC (A RISC Computer), which is loosely based on the commercial SPARC architecture. The instruction names, instruction formats, data formats, and the suggested assembly language syntax for the SPARC have been retained in the ARC, but a number of simplifications have been made. Only 15 SPARC instructions are used for most of the chapter, and only a 32-bit unsigned integer data type is allowed initially. Instruction formats are covered, as well as addressing modes. Subroutine linkage is explored in a number of styles, with a detailed discussion of parameter passing using a stack.

Chapter 5: Languages and the Machine connects the programmer's view of a computer system with the architecture of the underlying machine. System software issues are covered with the goal of making the low level machine visible to a programmer. The chapter starts with an explanation of the compilation process, first covering the steps involved in compilation, and then focusing on code generation. The assembly process is described for a two-pass assembler, and examples are given of generating symbol tables. Linking, loading, and macros are also covered.

Chapter 6: Datapath and Control provides a step-by-step analysis of a datapath and a control unit. Two methods of control are discussed: microprogrammed and hardwired. The instructor may adopt one method and omit the other, or cover both methods as time permits. The example microprogrammed and hardwired control units implement the ARC subset of the SPARC assembly language introduced in Chapter 4.

Chapter 7: Memory covers computer memory beginning with the organization of a basic random access memory, and moving to advanced concepts such as cache and virtual memory. The traditional direct, associative, and set associative cache mapping schemes are covered, as well as multilevel caches. Issues such as overlays, replacement policies, segmentation, fragmentation, and the translation lookaside buffer are also discussed.

Chapter 8: Input and Output covers bus communication and bus access methods. Bus-to-bus bridging is also described. The chapter covers various I/O devices commonly in use such as disks, keyboards, printers, and displays.

Chapter 9: Communication covers network architectures, focusing on modems, local area networks, and wide area networks. The emphasis is primarily on *network architecture*, with accessible discussions of protocols that spotlight key features of network architecture. Error detection and correction are covered in depth. The TCP/IP protocol suite is introduced in the context of the Internet.

Chapter 10: Trends in Computer Architecture covers advanced architectural features that have either emerged or taken new forms in recent years. The early part of the chapter covers the motivation for reduced instruction set computer (RISC) processors and the architectural implications of RISC. The latter portion of the chapter covers multiple instruction issue machines and very large instruction word (VLIW) machines. A case study makes RISC features visible to the programmer in a step-by-step analysis of a C compiler-generated SPARC program, with explanations of the stack frame usage, register usage, and pipelining. The chapter covers parallel and distributed architectures, and interconnection networks used in parallel and distributed processing.

Appendix A: Digital Logic covers combinational logic and sequential logic, and provides a foundation for understanding the logical makeup of components discussed in the rest of the book. Appendix A begins with a description of truth tables, Boolean algebra, and logic equations. The synthesis of combinational logic circuits is described, and a number of examples are explored. Medium scale integration (MSI) components such as multiplexers and decoders are discussed, and examples of synthesizing circuits using MSI components are explored.

Synchronous logic is also covered in Appendix A, starting with an introduction to timing issues that relate to flip-flops. The synthesis of synchronous logic circuits is covered with respect to state transition diagrams, state tables, and synchronous logic designs.

Appendix A can be paired with **Appendix B: Reduction of Digital Logic** which covers reduction for combinational and sequential logic. Minimization is covered using algebraic reduction, Karnaugh maps, and the tabular (Quine-McCluskey) method for single and multiple functions. State reduction and state assignment are also covered.

CHAPTER ORDERING

The order of chapters is created so that the chapters can be taught in numerical order, but an instructor can modify the ordering to suit a particular curriculum and syllabus. Figure P-1 shows prerequisite relationships among the chapters. Special considerations regarding chapter sequencing are detailed next.

Chapter 2 (Data Representation) should be covered prior to Chapter 3 (Arithmetic), which has the greatest need for the material on data representation. Appendix A (Digital Logic) and Appendix B (Reduction of Digital Logic) can be

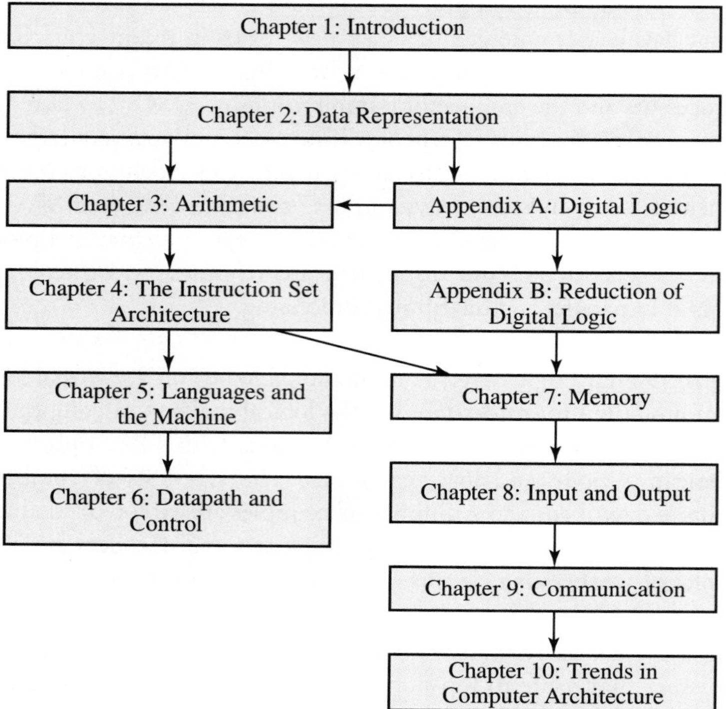

Figure P-1 Prerequisite relationships among chapters.

omitted if digital logic is covered earlier in the curriculum, but if the material is not covered, then the structure of some components (such as an arithmetic logic unit or a register) will remain a mystery in later chapters if at least Appendix A is not covered earlier than Chapter 3.

Chapter 4 (The Instruction Set Architecture) and Chapter 5 (Languages and the Machine) appear in the early half of the book for two reasons: (1) They introduce the student to the workings of a computer at a fairly high-level, which allows for a top-down approach to the study of computer architecture; and (2) it is important to get started on assembly language programming early if hands-on programming is part of the course.

The material in Chapter 10 (Trends in Computer Architecture) typically appears in graduate level architecture courses and should therefore be covered only as time permits, after the material in the earlier chapters is covered.

The Companion Web Site

A companion web site

`http://www.prenhall.com/murdocca`

pairs with this textbook. The companion web site contains a wealth of supporting material such as software, Acrobat slides, and errata. Solutions for all of the problems in the book and sample exam problems with solutions are also available for textbook adopters. (Contact your Prentice Hall representative if you are an instructor and need access to this information.)

SOFTWARE TOOLS

We provide an assembler and a simulator for the ARC and subsets of the assembly languages of the MIPS and x86 (Pentium) processors. Written as Java applications for easy portability, these assemblers and simulators are available via download from the companion web site.

SLIDES

All of the figures and tables in *Principles of Computer Architecture* have been included in an Adobe Acrobat slide presentation. A free-of-charge Acrobat reader is available from **`www.adobe.com`**.

EXAM PROBLEMS AND SOLUTIONS

The sample exam problems and solutions have been fully class tested. The problems are numerous enough to serve as exam and quiz problems, and to also serve as practice problems for review sessions at the instructor's discretion. The sample exam problems (which also include solutions) and the solutions to problems are available to instructors who adopt the book. (Contact your Prentice Hall representative for access to this area of the web site. We only ask that you do not place this material on a web site someplace else.)

IF YOU FIND AN ERROR

In spite of the best of the best efforts of the authors, editors, reviewers, and class testers, this book undoubtedly contains errors. Before reporting an error, check online at **`http://www.prenhall.com/murdocca`** to see if it has been catalogued. Error should be reported to `pocabugs@cs.rutgers.edu`. Please mention the chapter number where the error occurs in the `Subject:` header.

Credits and Acknowledgments

We did not create this book entirely on our own, and we gratefully acknowledge the support of many people for their influence in the preparation of the book and on our thinking in general. We first wish to thank our acquisitions editors, Paul Becker, Thomas Robbins, and Eric Frank, who had the foresight and vision to guide this book and its supporting materials through to completion. Donald Chiarulli was an important influence on an early version of the book, which was class-tested at Rutgers University and the University of Pittsburgh. Saul Levy, Donald Smith, Vidyadhar Phalke, Ajay Bakre, Jinsong Huang, and Srimat Chakradhar helped test the material in courses at Rutgers and provided some of the text, problems, and valuable explanations. Brian Davison and Shridhar Venkatanarisam worked on an early version of the solutions and provided many helpful comments. Irving Rabinowitz provided a number of problem sets. Larry Greenfield provided advice from the perspective of a student who is new to the subject, and he is credited with helping in the organization of Chapter 2. Blair Gabett Bizjak is credited with providing the framework for much of the material on local area networks. Ann Yasuhara provided text on Turing's contributions to computer science. William Waite, University of Colorado, Boulder, provided a number of the assembly language examples. Ann Root, University of Colorado, Boulder, did a superb job on the development of the supporting architecture simulation tools, which are available on the companion web site. The Rutgers University and University of Colorado student populations provided important proving grounds for the material, and we are grateful for their patience and recommendations while the book was under development.

We also wish to thank our reviewers, who were most helpful in suggesting changes to the manuscript, including Perry Alexander (University of Cincinnati), Thomas L. Casavant (University of Iowa Electrical and Computer Engineering Department), J. Kelly Flanagan (Brigham Young University (Dept. of Computer Science), Shelly Dalton Goggin, (University of Colorado at Denver), Nikrouz Faroughi, (California State University Sacramento, Computer Science Dept.), Mark Jones (Virginia Tech., Department of Electrical and Computer Engineering), Thuy T. Le (Adjunct Professor, Electrical Engineering Dept., San Jose State University and Senior Researcher, High Performance Computing Group, Fujitsu America, Inc.), Gary Lippman, Professor, California State University Hayward, Dept. of Mathematics and Computer Science), Walid Najjar (Colorado State University, Computer Science Dept.), William Hsu (San Francisco State University), Jyh-Charn (Steven) Liu (Computer Science Dept., Texas A&M University), David B. Wortman (University of Toronto, Dept. of Computer Science), and Janusz Zalerwski (University of Central Florida, Orlando, Florida - Dept. of Electrical and Computer Engineering).

I (M. J. M.) was encouraged by my parents Dolores and Nicholas Murdocca, my sister Marybeth, and my brother Mark. My wife Ellen and my daughters Alexandra and Nicole have been an endless source of encouragement and inspiration. I do not think I could have found the energy for such an undertaking without all of their support.

I (V. P. H.) wish to acknowledge the support of my wife Gretchen, who was exceedingly patient and encouraging throughout the process of writing this book.

There are surely other people and institutions who have contributed to this book, either directly or indirectly, whose names we have inadvertently omitted. To those people and institutions we offer our tacit appreciation and apologize for having omitted explicit recognition here.

Miles J. Murdocca
Rutgers University
murdocca@cs.rutgers.edu

Vincent P. Heuring
University of Colorado at Boulder
heuring@colorado.edu

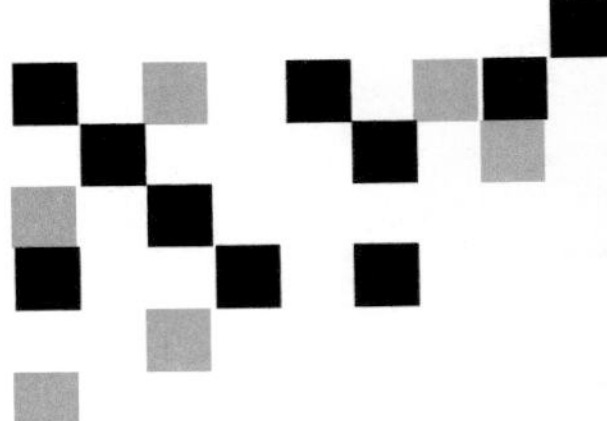

1 INTRODUCTION

1.1 Overview

Computer **architecture** deas with the functional behavior of a computer system as viewed by a programmer. This view includes aspects such as the sizes of data types (e.g., using 16 binary digits to represent an integer) and the types of operations that are supported (like addition, subtraction, and subroutine calls). Computer **organization** deals with structural relationships that are not visible to the programmer, such as interfaces to peripheral devices, the clock frequency, and the technology used for the memory. This textbook deals with both architecture and organization, with the term "architecture" referring broadly to both architecture and organization.

There is a concept of **levels** in computer architecture. The basic idea is that there are many levels, or views, at which a computer can be considered, from the highest level, where the user is running programs, or *using* the computer, to the lowest level, consisting of transistors and wires. Between the high and low levels are a number of intermediate levels. Before we discuss those levels, we will present a brief history of computing in order to gain a perspective on how it all came about.

1.2 A Brief History

Mechanical devices for controlling complex operations have been in existence since at least the 1500s, when rotating pegged cylinders were used in music boxes much as they are today. Machines that perform calculations, as opposed to simply repeating a predetermined melody, came in the next century.

Blaise Pascal (1623–1662) developed a mechanical calculator to help in his father's tax work. The Pascal calculator "Pascalene" contains eight dials that connect to a drum (Figure 1-1), with an innovative linkage that causes a dial to rotate one notch when a carry is produced from a dial in a lower position. A window is placed over the dial to allow its position to be observed, much like the

Figure 1-1 Pascal's calculating machine. (Reprinted with permission of the Department of Computer Science., University of Manchester.)

odometer in a car except that the dials are positioned horizontally, like a rotary telephone dial. Some of Pascal's adding machines, which he started to build in 1642, still exist today. It would not be until the 1800s, however, that someone would put the concepts of mechanical control and mechanical calculation together into a machine that we recognize today as having the basic parts of a digital computer. That person was Charles Babbage.

Charles Babbage (1791–1871) is sometimes referred to as the *grandfather* of the computer, rather than the father of the computer, because he never built a practical version of the machines he designed. Babbage lived in England at a time when mathematical tables were used in navigation and scientific work. The tables were computed manually, and, as a result, they contained numerous errors. Frustrated by the inaccuracies, Babbage set out to create a machine that would compute tables by simply setting and turning gears. The machine he designed could even produce a plate to be used by a printer, thus eliminating errors that might be introduced by a typesetter.

Babbage's machines had a means for reading input data, storing data, performing calculations, producing output data, and automatically controlling the operation of the machine. These are basic functions that are found in nearly every modern computer. Babbage created a small prototype of his **difference engine**, which evaluates polynomials using the method of finite differences. The success of the difference engine concept gained him government support for the much larger **analytical engine**, which was a more sophisticated machine that had a mechanism for **branching** (making decisions) and a means for programming, using punched cards in the manner of what is known as the **Jacquard pattern-weaving loom**.

The analytical engine was designed but was never built by Babbage because the mechanical tolerances required by the design could not be met with the technology of the day. A version of Babbage's difference engine was actually built by the Science Museum in London in 1991 and can still be viewed today.

It took over a century, until the start of World War II, before the next major thrust in computing was initiated. In England, German **U-boat** submarines were inflicting heavy damage on Allied shipping. The U-boats received communications from their bases in Germany using an encryption code which was implemented by a machine made by Siemens AG known as **ENIGMA**.

The process of encrypting information had been known for a long time, and even the United States president Thomas Jefferson (1743–1826) designed a forerunner of ENIGMA, though he did not construct the machine. The process of decoding encrypted data was a much harder task. It was this problem that prompted the efforts of Alan Turing (1912–1954), and other scientists in England in creating codebreaking machines. During World War II, Turing was the leading cryptographer in England and was among those who changed cryptography from a subject for people who deciphered ancient languages to a subject for mathematicians.

The **Colossus** was a successful codebreaking machine that came out of Bletchley Park, England, where Turing worked. Vacuum tubes store the contents of a paper tape that is fed into the machine, and computations take place among the vacuum tubes and a second tape that is fed into the machine. Programming is performed with plugboards. Turing's involvement in the various Collosi machine versions remains obscure due to the secrecy that surrounds the project, but some aspects of his work and his life can be seen in the Broadway play *Breaking the Code*, which was performed in London and New York in the late 1980s.

Around the same time as Turing's efforts, J. Presper Eckert and John Mauchly set out to create a machine that could be used to compute tables of ballistic trajectories for the U.S. Army. The result of the Eckert-Mauchly effort was the Electronic Numerical Integrator And Computer (**ENIAC**). The ENIAC consists of 18,000 vacuum tubes, which make up the computing section of the machine. Programming and data entry are performed by setting switches and changing cables. There is no concept of a stored program, and there is no central memory unit, but these are not serious limitations because all that the ENIAC needed to do was to compute ballistic trajectories. Even though it did not become operational until 1946, after the war was over, it was considered quite a success and was used for nine years.

After the success of ENIAC, Eckert and Mauchly, who were at the Moore School at the University of Pennsylvania, were joined by John von Neumann

(1903–1957), who was at the Institute for Advanced Study at Princeton. Together they worked on the design of a stored program computer called the **EDVAC**. A conflict developed, however, and the Pennsylvania and Princeton groups split. The concept of a stored program computer thrived, however, and a working model of the stored program computer, the **EDSAC**, was constructed by Maurice Wilkes, of Cambridge University, in 1947.

1.3 The von Neumann Model

Conventional digital computers have a common form that is attributed to von Neumann, although historians agree that the entire team was responsible for the design. The **von Neumann model** consists of five major components as illustrated in Figure 1-2. The **input unit** provides instructions and data to the system, which are subsequently stored in the **memory unit**. The instructions and data are processed by the **arithmetic and logic unit** (ALU) under the direction of the **control unit**. The results are sent to the **output unit**. The ALU and control unit are frequently referred to collectively as the **central processing unit (CPU)**. Most commercial computers can be decomposed into these five basic units.

The **stored program** is the most important aspect of the von Neumann model. A program is stored in the computer's memory along with the data to be processed. Although we now take this for granted, prior to the development of the stored program computer, programs were stored on external media, such as plugboards (mentioned earlier) or punched cards or tape. In the stored program computer, the

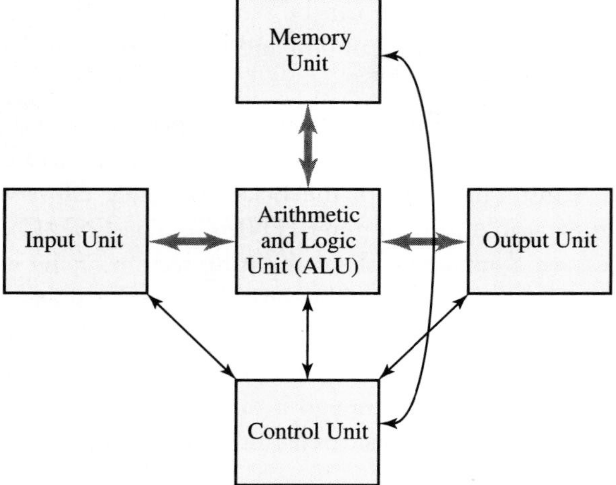

Figure 1-2 The von Neumann model of a digital computer. Thick arrows represent data paths. Thin arrows represent control paths.

program can be manipulated as if it is data. This gave rise to compilers and operating systems and makes possible the great versatility of the modern computer.

1.4 The System Bus Model

Although the von Neumann model prevails in modern computers, it has been streamlined. Figure 1-3 shows the **system bus model** of a computer system. This model partitions a computer system into three subunits: CPU, memory, and input/output (I/O). This refinement of the von Neumann model combines the ALU and the control unit into one functional unit, the CPU. The input and output units are also combined into a single I/O unit.

Most important to the system bus model, the communications among the components are by means of a shared pathway called the **system bus**, which is made up of the **data bus** (which carries the information being transmitted), the **address bus** (which identifies where the information is being sent), and the **control bus** (which describes aspects of how the information is being sent, and in what manner). There is also a **power bus** for electrical power to the components, which is not shown, but its presence is understood. Some architectures may also have a separate I/O bus.

Physically, buses are made up of collections of wires that are grouped by function. A 32-bit data bus has 32 individual wires, each of which carries one bit of data (as opposed to address or control information). In this sense, the system bus is actually a group of individual buses classified by their function.

The data bus moves data among the system components. Some systems have separate data buses for moving information to and from the CPU, in which case there is a **data-in** bus and a **data-out** bus. More often, a single data bus moves data in either direction, although never both directions at the same time.

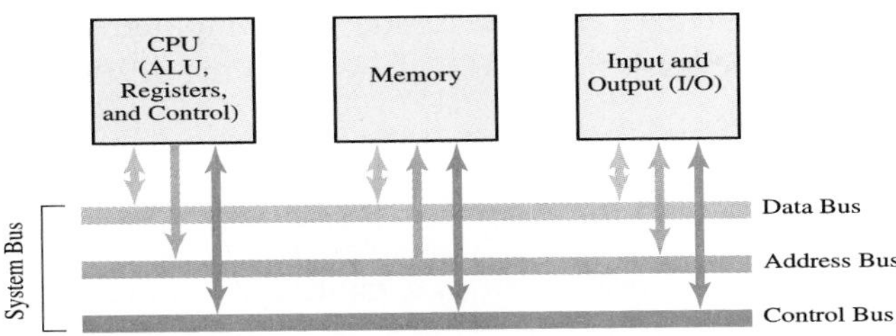

Figure 1-3 The system bus model of a computer system. (Contributed by Donald Chiarulli, Univ. Pittsburgh.)

If the bus is to be shared among communicating entities, then the entities must have distinguished identities: addresses. In some computers, all addresses are assumed to be memory addresses whether they are in fact part of the computer's memory or are actually I/O devices, while in others I/O devices have separate I/O addresses. (This topic of I/O addresses is covered in more detail in Chapter 8, Input, Output, and Communication.)

A **memory address,** or location, identifies a memory location where data is stored, similar to the way a postal address identifies the location where a recipient receives and sends mail. During a memory read or write operation, the address bus contains the address of the memory location where the data is to be read from or written to. Note that the terms "read" and "write" are with respect to the CPU: the CPU *reads* data from memory and *writes* data into memory. If data is to be read from memory, then the data bus contains the value read from that address in memory. If the data is to be written into memory, then the data bus contains the data value to be written into memory.

The control bus is somewhat more complex, and we defer discussion of this bus to later chapters. For now the control bus can be thought of as coordinating access to the data bus and to the address bus, and directing data to specific components.

1.5 Levels of Machines

As with any complex system, the computer can be viewed from a number of perspectives, or levels, from the highest "user" level to the lowest, transistor level. Each of these levels represents an abstraction of the computer. Perhaps one of the reasons for the enormous success of the digital computer is the extent to which these levels of abstraction are separate, or independent from one another. This is readily seen: A user who runs a word processing program on a computer needs to know nothing about its programming. Likewise a programmer need not be concerned with the logic gate structure inside the computer. One interesting way that the separation of levels has been exploited is in the development of upwardly compatible machines.

1.5.1 *UPWARD COMPATIBILITY*

The invention of the transistor led to a rapid development of computer hardware, and with this development came a problem of compatibility. Computer users wanted to take advantage of the newest and fastest machines, but each new computer model had a new architecture, and the old software would not run on the new hardware. The hardware/software compatibility problem became so serious that users often delayed purchasing a new machine because of the cost of rewriting the software to run on the new hardware. When a new computer was purchased, it would often sit unavailable to the target users for months while the old software and data sets were converted to the new systems.

In a successful gamble that pitted compatibility against performance, IBM pioneered the concept of a "family of machines" with its 360 series. More capable machines in the same family could run programs written for less capable machines without modifications to those programs—upward compatibility. Upward compatibility allows a user to upgrade to a faster, more capable machine without rewriting the software that runs on the less capable model.

1.5.2 *THE LEVELS*

Figure 1-4 shows seven levels in the computer, from the user level down to the transistor level. As we progress from the top level downward, the levels become less "abstract" and more of the internal structure of the computer shows through. We discuss these levels next.

User or Application Program Level

We are most familiar with the user, or application program level of the computer. At this level, the user interacts with the computer by running programs such as word processors, spreadsheet programs, or games. Here the user sees the computer through the programs that run on it, and little (if any) of its internal or lower-level structure is visible.

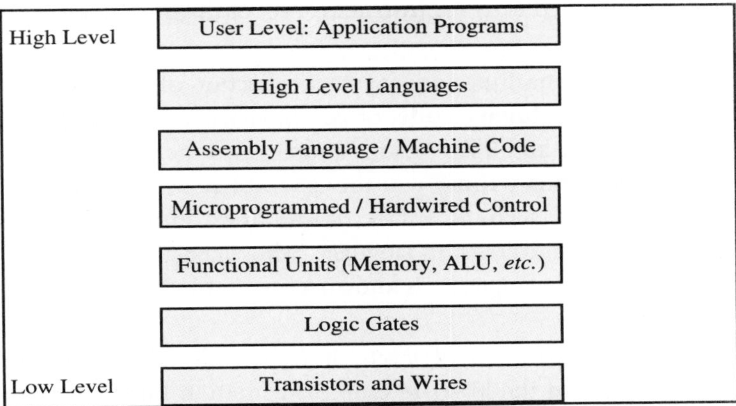

Figure 1-4 Levels of machines in the computer hierarchy.

High-Level Language Level

Anyone who has programmed a computer in a high-level language such as C, Pascal, Fortran, or Java has interacted with the computer at this level. Here, a programmer sees only the language and none of the low-level details of the machine. At this level, the programmer sees the data types and instructions of the high-level language but needs no knowledge of how those data types are actually implemented in the machine. It is the role of the **compiler** to map data types and instructions from the high-level language to the actual computer hardware. Programs written in a high-level language can be recompiled for various machines that will (hopefully) run the same and provide the same results regardless of the machine on which they are compiled and run. We can say that programs are compatible across machine types if written in a high-level language, and this kind of compatibility is referred to as **source code compatibility**.

Assembly Language/Machine Code Level

As pointed out previously, the high-level language level really has little to do with the machine on which the high-level language is translated. The compiler translates the source code to the actual machine instructions, sometimes referred to as **machine language** or **machine code**. High-level languages "cater" to the programmer by providing a certain set of presumably well-thought-out language constructs and data types. Machine languages look "downward" in the hierarchy and thus cater to the needs of the lower-level aspects of the machine design. As a result, machine languages deal with hardware issues such as registers and the transfer of data between them. In fact, many machine instructions can be described in terms of the register transfers that they effect. The collection of machine instructions for a given machine is referred to as the **instruction set** of that machine.

Of course, the actual machine code is just a collection of 1's and 0's, sometimes referred to as **machine binary code**, or just binary code. As we might imagine, programming with 1's and 0's is tedious and error prone. As a result, one of the first computer programs written was the **assembler**, which translates ordinary language **mnemonics** such as `MOVE Data, Acc`, into their corresponding machine language 1's and 0's. This language, whose constructs bear a one-to-one relationship to machine language, is known as **assembly language**.

As a result of the separation of levels, it is possible to have many different machines that differ in the lower-level implementation but that have the same instruction set, or sub- or supersets of that instruction set. This allowed IBM to design a product line such as the **IBM 360** series with guaranteed upward compatibility of machine code. Machine code running on the 360 Model 35 would run unchanged on the 360 Model 50, should the customer wish to upgrade to the more powerful machine. This kind of compatibility is known as "binary compatibility," because the binary code will run unchanged on the various family members. This feature was responsible in large part for the great success of the IBM 360 series of computers.

Intel Corporation has stressed binary compatibility in its family members. In this case, binaries written for the original member of a family, such as the 8086, will run unchanged on all subsequent family members, such as the 80186, 80286, 80386, 80486, and the most current family member, the Pentium processor. Of course this does not address the fact that there are other computers that present different instruction sets to the users, which makes it difficult to port an installed base of software from one family of computers to another.

The Control Level

It is the **control unit** that effects the register transfers described previously. It does so by means of **control signals** that transfer the data from register to register, possibly through a logic circuit that transforms it in some way. The control unit interprets the machine instructions one by one, causing the specified register transfer or other action to occur.

How it does this is of no need of concern to the assembly language programmer. The Intel 80x86 family of processors presents the same behavioral view to an assembly language programmer regardless of which processor in the family is considered. This is because each future member of the family is designed to execute the original 8086 instructions in addition to any new instructions implemented for that particular family member.

As Figure 1-4 indicates, there are several ways of implementing the control unit. Probably the most popular way at the present time is by "hardwiring" the control unit. This means that the control signals that effect the register transfers are generated from a block of digital logic components. Hardwired control units have the advantages of speed and component count, but until recently were exceedingly difficult to design and modify. (We will study this technique more fully in Chapter 9.)

A somewhat slower but simpler approach is to implement the instructions as a **microprogram**. A microprogram is actually a small program written in an even lower-level language, and implemented in the hardware, whose job is to interpret the machine language instructions. This microprogram is referred to as **firmware** because it spans both hardware and software. Firmware is executed by a **microcontroller**, which executes the actual microinstructions. (We will also explore microprogramming in Chapter 9.)

Functional Unit Level

The register transfers and other operations implemented by the control unit move data in and out of "functional units," so called because they perform some function that is important to the operation of the computer. Functional units include internal CPU registers, the ALU, and the computer's main memory.

Logic Gates, Transistors, and Wires

The lowest levels at which any semblance of the computer's higher-level functioning is visible are at the **logic gate** and **transistor** levels. It is from logic gates that the functional units are built, and from transistors that logic gates are built. The logic gates implement the lowest-level logical operations upon which the computer's functioning depends. At the very lowest level, a computer consists of electrical components such as transistors and wires, which make up the logic gates, but at this level the functioning of the computer is lost in details of voltage, current, signal propagation delays, quantum effects, and other low-level matters.

Interactions between Levels

The distinctions within levels and between levels are frequently blurred. For instance, a new computer architecture may contain floating point instructions in a full-blown implementation, but a minimal implementation may have only enough hardware for integer instructions. The floating point instructions are **trapped**[1] prior to execution and replaced with a sequence of machine language instructions that imitate, or **emulate** the floating point instructions using the existing integer instructions. This is the case for **microprocessors** that use optional floating point coprocessors. Those without floating point coprocessors emulate the floating point instructions by a series of floating point routines that are implemented in the machine language of the microprocessor, and frequently stored in a **ROM**, which is a read-only memory chip. The assembly language and

---

[1]Traps are covered in Chapter 6.

high-level language view for both implementations is the same except for execution speed.

It is possible to take this emulation to the extreme of emulating the entire instruction set of one computer on another computer. The software that does this is known as an **emulator** and was used by **Apple Computer** to maintain binary code compatibility when Apple began employing Motorola PowerPC chips in place of Motorola 68000 chips, which had an entirely different instruction set.

The high-level language level and the firmware and functional unit levels can be so intermixed that it is hard to identify what operation is happening at which level. The value in stratifying a computer architecture into a hierarchy of levels is not so much for the purpose of classification, which we just saw can be difficult at times, but rather simply to give us some focus when we study these levels in the chapters that follow.

The Programmer's View—The Instruction Set Architecture

As described in the preceding discussion of levels, the assembly language programmer is concerned with the assembly language and functional units of the machine. This collection of instruction set and functional units is known as the **instruction set architecture** (ISA) of the machine.

The Computer Architect's View

On the other hand, the computer architect views the system at all levels. The architect that focuses on the design of a computer is invariably driven by performance requirements and cost constraints. Performance may be specified by the speed of program execution, the storage capacity of the machine, or a number of other parameters. Cost may be reflected in monetary terms, or in size or weight, or power consumption. The design proposed by a computer architect must attempt to meet the performance goals while staying within the cost constraints. This usually requires trade-offs between and among the levels of the machine.

1.6 A Typical Computer System

Modern computers have evolved from the great behemoths of the 1950s and 1960s to the much smaller and more powerful computers that surround us today. Even with all of the great advances in computer technology that have been made in the past few decades, the five basic units of the von Neumann model are still distinguishable in modern computers.

Figure 1-5 shows a typical configuration for a desktop computer. The input unit is composed of the **keyboard**, through which a user enters data and commands. A **video monitor** comprises the output unit, which displays the output in a visual form. The ALU and the control unit are bundled into a single microprocessor that serves as the CPU. The memory unit consists of individual memory circuits and also a **hard disk** unit, a **diskette** unit, and a **CD-ROM** (compact disk read-only memory) device.

As we look deeper inside of the machine, we can see that the heart of the machine is contained on a single **motherboard**, similar to the one shown in Fig-

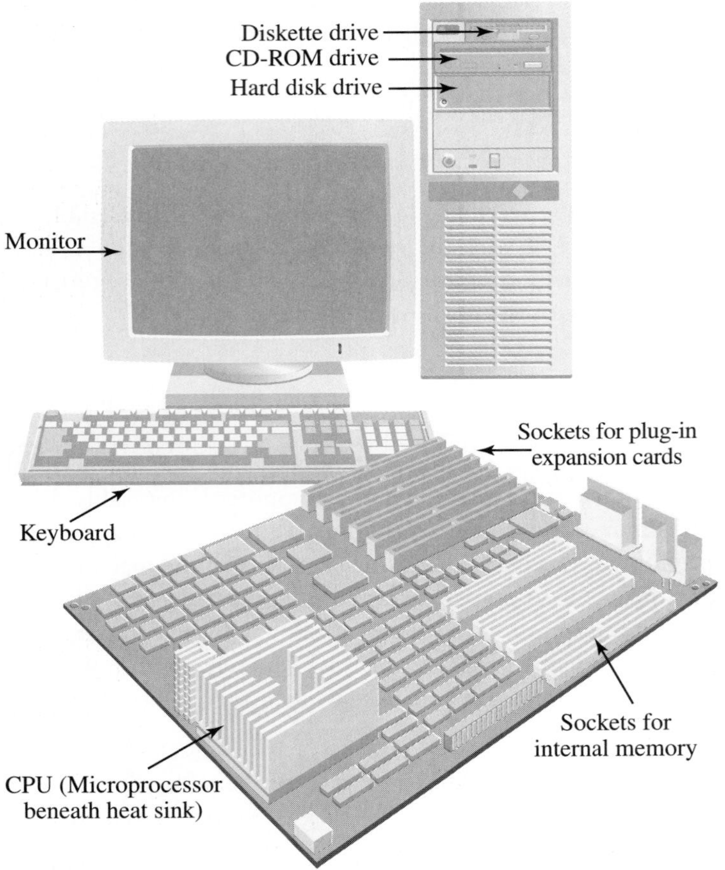

Figure 1-5 A desktop computer system.

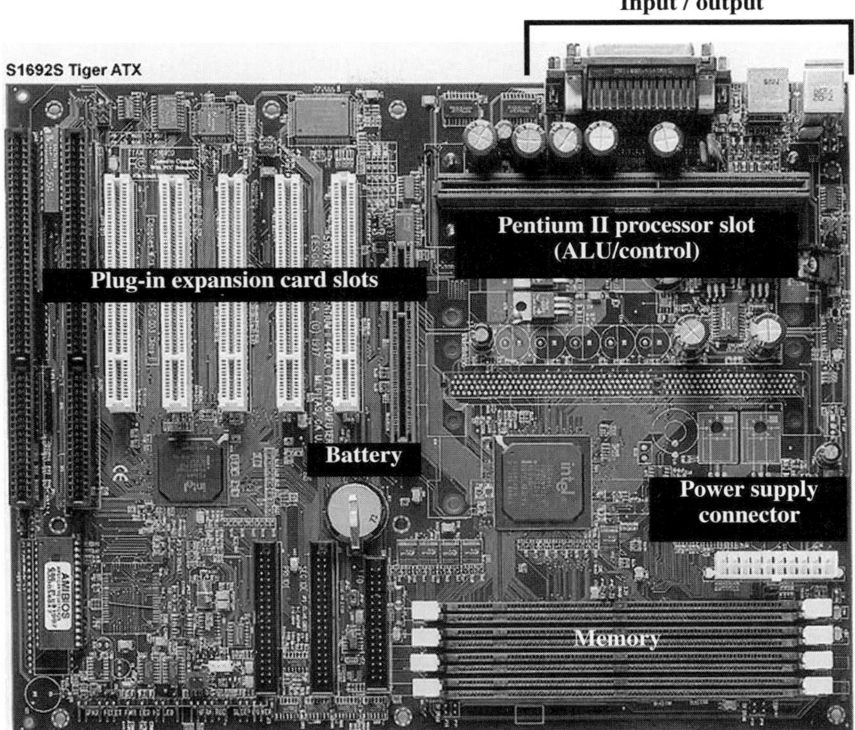

Figure 1-6 A Pentium II-based motherboard. (Source: TYAN Computer, http://www.tyan.com.)

ure 1-6. The motherboard contains **integrated circuits** (ICs), plug-in expansion card slots, and the wires that interconnect the ICs and expansion card slots. The input, output, memory, and ALU/control sections are highlighted as shown. (We will cover motherboard internals in later chapters.)

1.7 Organization of the Book

We explore the inner workings of computers in the chapters that follow. Chapter 2 covers the representation of data, which provides background for all of the chapters that follow. Chapter 3 covers methods for implementing computer arithmetic. Chapters 4 and 5 cover the instruction set architecture, which serves as a vehicle for understanding how the components of a computer interact. Chapter 6 ties the earlier chapters together in the design and analysis of a control unit for the instruction set architecture. Chapter 7 covers the organization of memory units and memory management techniques. Chapter 8 covers input, output, and communication. Chapter 9 covers advanced aspects of single-CPU systems (which might have more than one processing unit). Chapter 10 covers advanced aspects of multiple-CPU systems, such as parallel and distributed architectures and network architectures. Finally, in Appendices A and B, we look into the design of digital logic circuits, which are the building blocks for the basic components of a computer.

1.8 Case Study: What Happened to Supercomputers?

[Note from the authors: The following contribution comes from Web page http://www.paralogos.com/DeadSuper created by Kevin D. Kissell at kevink@acm.org. Kissell's Web site lists dozens of supercomputing projects that have gone by the wayside. (See Figure 1-7[2] for a historical look at the earliest supercomputer technology.) One of the primary reasons for the near-extinction of supercomputers is that ordinary, everyday computers achieve a significant fraction of supercomputing power at a price that the common person can afford. The price-to-performance ratio for desktop computers is very favorable due to low costs achieved through mass market sales. Supercomputers enjoy no such mass markets and continue to suffer very high price-to-performance ratios.

Following Kissell's contribution is an excerpt from an *Electrical Engineering Times* article that highlights the enormous investment in everyday microprocessor development, which helps maintain the favorable price-to-performance ratio for low-cost desktop computers.]

The Passing of a Golden Age?

From the construction of the first programmed computers until the mid 1990s, there was always room in the computer industry for someone with a clever, if sometimes challenging, idea on how to make a more powerful machine. Computing became strategic during the Second World War, and remained so during the Cold War that followed. High-performance computing is essential to any modern nuclear weapons program, and a computer technology "race" was a logical corollary to the arms race. While powerful computers are of great value to a number of other industrial sectors, such as petroleum, chemistry, medicine, aeronautical, automotive, and civil engineering, the role of governments, and particularly the national laboratories of the US government, as catalysts and incubators

---

[2]Figure courtesy of Manchester University. The history of the Manchester Mark I is chronicled at http://www.computer50.org.

Figure 1-7 The Manchester University Mark I, made operational on June 21, 1948. (Not to be confused with the Harvard Mark I, donated to Harvard University by IBM in August 1944.) (Reprinted with permission of the Department of Computer Science., University of Manchester.)

for innovative computing technologies can hardly be overstated. Private industry may buy more machines, but rarely do they risk buying those with single-digit serial numbers. The passing of Soviet communism and the end of the Cold War brought us a generally safer and more prosperous world, but it removed the *raison d'etre* for many merchants of performance-at-any-price.

Accompanying these geopolitical changes were some technological and economic trends that spelled trouble for specialized producers of high-end computers. Microprocessors began in the 1970s as devices whose main claim to fame was that it was possible to put a stored-program computer on a single piece of silicon. Competitive pressures, and the desire to generate sales by obsoleting last year's product, made for the doubling of microprocessor computing power every 18 months, Moore's celebrated "law." Along the way, microprocessor designers borrowed almost all the tricks that designers of mainframe and numerical supercomputers had used in the past: storage hierarchies, pipelining, multiple functional units, multiprocessing, out-of-order execution, branch prediction, SIMD processing, speculative and predicated execution. By the mid 1990s, research ideas were going directly from simulation to implementation in microprocessors destined for the desktops of the masses. Nevertheless, it must be noted that most of the gains in raw performance achieved by microprocessors in the preceding decade came not from these advanced techniques of computer architecture, but from the simple speedup of processor clocks and quantitative increases in processor resources made possible by advances in semiconductor technology. By 1998, the CPU of a high-end Windows-based personal computer was running at a higher clock rate than the top-of-the-line Cray Research supercomputer of 1994.

It is thus hardly surprising that the policy of the US national laboratories has shifted from the acquisition of systems architected from the ground up to be supercomputers to the deployment of large ensembles of mass-produced microprocessor-based systems, with the ASCI project as the flagship of this activity. As of this writing, it remains to be seen if these agglomerations will prove to be sufficiently stable and usable for production work, but the preliminary results have been at least satisfactory. The halcyon days of supercomputers based on exotic technology and innovative architecture may well be over.

Invest or die: Intel's life on the edge[3]

By Ron Wilson and Brian Fuller

SANTA CLARA, Calif.—With about $600 million to pump into venture companies this year, Intel Corp. has joined the major leagues of venture-capital firms. But the unique imperative that drives the microprocessor giant to invest gives it influence disproportionate to even this large sum. For Intel, venture investments are not just a source of income; they are a vital tool in the fight to survive.

Survival might seem an odd preoccupation for the world's largest semiconductor company. But Intel, in a way all its own, lives hanging in the balance. For every new generation of CPUs, Intel must make huge investments in process development, in buildings and in fabs—an investment too huge to lose.

Gordon Moore, Intel chairman emeritus, gave scale to the wager. "An R&D fab today costs $400 million just for the building. Then you put about $1 billion of equipment in it. That gets you a quarter-micron fab for maybe 5,000 wafers per week, about the smallest practical fab. For the next generation," Moore said, "the minimum investment will be $2 billion, with maybe $3 billion to $4 billion for any sort of volume production. No other industry has such a short life on such huge investments."

---

[3]Copyright © 1998 CMP Media Inc. Reprinted from *Electronic Engineering Times* with permission.

Much of this money will be spent before there is a proven need for the microprocessors the fab will produce. In essence, the entire $4 billion per fab is bet on the proposition that the industry will absorb a huge number of premium-priced CPUs that are only somewhat faster than the currently available parts. If for just one generation that didn't happen—if everyone judged, say, that the Pentium II was fast enough, thank you—the results would be unthinkable.

"My nightmare is to wake up some day and not need any more computing power," Moore said.

■ SUMMARY

Computer architecture deals with those aspects of a computer that are visible to a programmer, while computer organization deals with those aspects that are at a more physical level and are not made visible to a programmer. Historically, programmers had to deal with every aspect of a computer – Babbage with mechanical gears and ENIAC programmers with plugboard cables. As computers grew in sophistication, the concept of levels of machines became more pronounced, allowing computers to have very different internal and external behaviors while managing complexity in stratified levels. The single most significant development that makes this possible is the stored program computer that is embodied in the von Neumann model. It is the von Neumann model that we see in most conventional computers today.

■ Further Reading

The history of computing is filled with interesting personalities and milestones. (Anderson, 1991) gives a short, readable account of both during the last century. (Bashe et al., 1986) give an interesting account of the IBM machines. (Bromley, 1987) chronicles Babbage's machines. (Ralston and Reilly, 1993) give short biographies of the more celebrated personalities. (Randell, 1982) covers the history of digital computers. A very readable Web-based history of computers by Michelle A. Hoyle can be found at http://www.ifi.unizh.ch/se/people/hoyle/Lecture/. (Swade, 1993) covers a readable version of the method of finite differences as it appears in Babbage's machines and the version of the analytical difference engine created by the Science Museum in London. (Tanenbaum, 1999) is one of a number of texts that popularizes the notion of levels of machines.

Anderson, Harlan, Dedication address for the Digital Computer Laboratory at the University of Illinois, April 17, 1991, as reprinted in *IEEE Circuits and Systems: Society Newsletter*, **2**, no. 1, pp. 3–6 (March 1991).

Bashe, Charles J., Lyle R. Johnson, John H. Palmer, and Emerson W. Pugh, *IBM's Early Computers*, The MIT Press (1986).

Bromley, A. G., "The Evolution of Babbage's Calculating Engines," *Annals of the History of Computing*, **9**, pp. 113–138 (1987).

Randell, B., *The Origins of Digital Computers*, 3/e, Springer-Verlag (1982).

Ralston, A. and E. D. Reilly, eds., *Encyclopedia of Computer Science*, 3/e, van Nostrand Reinhold (1993).

Doron D. Swade, "Redeeming Charles Babbage's Mechanical Computer," *Scientific American*, **268**, no. 2, pp. 86–91 (Feb. 1993).

Tanenbaum, A., *Structured Computer Organization*, 4/e, Prentice Hall (1999).

PROBLEMS

1.1 Moore's law, which is attributed to Intel founder Gordon Moore, states that computing power doubles every 18 months for the same price. An unrelated observation is that floating point instructions are executed 100 times faster in hardware than via emulation. Using Moore's law as a guide, how long will it take for computing power to improve to the point that floating point instructions are emulated as quickly as their (earlier) hardware counterparts?

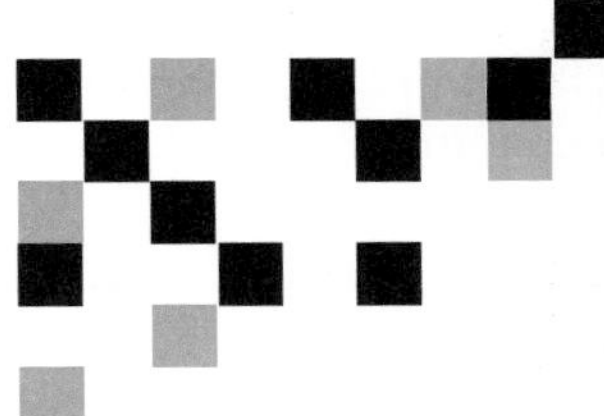

2

DATA REPRESENTATION

2.1 Introduction

In the early days of computing, there were common misconceptions about computers. One misconception was that the computer was only a giant adding machine performing arithmetic operations. Computers could do much more than that, even in the early days. The other common misconception, in contradiction to the first, was that the computer could do "anything." We now know that there are indeed classes of problems that even the most powerful imaginable computer finds intractable with the von Neumann model. The correct perception, of course, is somewhere between the two.

We are familiar with computer operations that are non arithmetic: computer graphics, digital audio, even the manipulation of the computer mouse. Regardless of what kind of information is being manipulated by the computer, the information must be represented by patterns of 1's and 0's (also known as "on-off" codes). This immediately raises the question of how that information should be described or represented in the machine—this is the **data representation**, or **data encoding**. Graphical images, digital audio, or mouse clicks must all be encoded in a systematic, agreed-upon manner.

We might think of the decimal representation of information as the most natural when we know it the best, but the use of on-off codes to represent information predated the computer by many years, in the form of Morse code.

This chapter introduces several of the simplest and most important encodings: the encoding of signed and unsigned fixed point numbers, real numbers (referred to as **floating point numbers** in computer jargon), and the printing characters. We shall see that in all cases there are multiple ways of encoding a given kind of data, some useful in one context, some in another. We will also take an early look at computer arithmetic for the purpose of understanding some of the encoding schemes, though we will defer details of computer arithmetic until Chapter 3.

In the process of developing a data representation for computing, a crucial issue is deciding how much storage should be devoted to each data value. For example, a computer architect may decide to treat integers as being 32 bits in size, and to implement an ALU that supports arithmetic operations on those 32-bit values that return 32-bit results. Some numbers can be too large to represent using 32 bits, however, and in other cases, the operands may fit into 32 bits, but the result of a computation will not, creating an **overflow** condition, which is described in Chapter 3. Thus, we need to understand the limits imposed on the accuracy and range of numeric calculations by the finite nature of the data representations. We will investigate these limits in the next few sections.

2.2 Fixed Point Numbers

In a fixed point number system, each number has exactly the same number of digits, and the "point" is always in the same place. Examples from the decimal number system would be 0.23, 5.12, and 9.11. In these examples, each number has 3 digits, and the decimal point is located two places from the right. Examples from the **binary** number system (in which each digit can take on only one of the values 0 or 1) would be 11.10, 01.10, and 00.11, where there are 4 binary digits and the binary point is in the middle. An important difference between the way that we represent fixed point numbers on paper and the way that we represent them in the computer is that when fixed point numbers are represented in the computer *the binary point is not stored anywhere*, but only assumed to be in a certain position. One could say that the binary point exists only in the mind of the programmer.

We begin coverage of fixed point numbers by investigating the range and precision of fixed point numbers, using the decimal number system. We then take a look at the nature of number bases, such as decimal and binary, and how to convert between the bases. With this foundation, we then investigate several ways of representing negative fixed point numbers, and take a look at simple arithmetic operations that can be performed on them.

2.2.1 *RANGE AND PRECISION IN FIXED POINT NUMBERS*

A fixed point representation can be characterized by the **range** of expressible numbers (that is, the distance between the largest and smallest numbers) and the **precision** (the distance between two adjacent numbers on a number line). For the preceding fixed-point decimal example, using three digits and the decimal point placed two digits from the right, the range is from 0.00 to 9.99 inclusive of the endpoints, denoted as [0.00, 9.99], the precision is .01, and the **error** is 1/2 of the difference between two "adjoining" numbers, such as 5.01 and 5.02, which have a difference of .01. The error is thus .01/2 = .005. That is, we can represent any number within the range 0.00 to 9.99 to within .005 of its true or precise value.

Notice how range and precision trade off: With the decimal point on the far right, the range is [000, 999] and the precision is 1.0. With the decimal point at the far left, the range is [.000, .999] and the precision is .001.

In either case, there are only 10^3 different decimal "objects," ranging from 000 to 999 or from .000 to .999, and thus it is possible to represent only 1000 different items, regardless of how we apportion range and precision.

There is no reason why the range must begin with 0. A 2-digit decimal number can have a range of [00, 99] or a range of [–50, +49], or even a range of [–99, +0]. The representation of negative numbers is covered more fully in Section 2.2.6.

Range and precision are important issues in computer architecture because both are finite in the implementation of the architecture, but are infinite in the real world, and so the user must be aware of the limitations of trying to represent external information in internal form.

2.2.2 *THE ASSOCIATIVE LAW OF ALGEBRA DOES NOT ALWAYS HOLD IN COMPUTERS*

In early mathematics, we learned the associative law of algebra:

$$a + (b + c) = (a + b) + c$$

As we will see, the associative law of algebra does not hold for fixed point numbers having a finite representation. Consider a 1-digit decimal fixed point representation with the decimal point on the right, and a range of [–9, 9], with $a = 7$, $b = 4$, and $c = -3$. Now $a + (b + c) = 7 + (4 - 3) = 7 + 1 = 8$. But $(a + b) + c = (7 + 4) - 3 = 11 - 3$. However the intermediate result of 11 is outside the range of our number system! We have overflow in an intermediate calculation, but the final result would have been within the number system. This is every bit as bad because the final result will be wrong if an intermediate result is wrong.

Thus we can see by example that the associative law of algebra does not hold for finite-length fixed point numbers. This is an unavoidable consequence of this form of representation, and there is nothing practical to be done except to detect overflow wherever it occurs, and either terminate the computation immediately and notify the user of the condition, or, having detected the overflow, repeat the computation with numbers of greater range. (The latter technique is seldom used except in critical applications.)

2.2.3 *RADIX NUMBER SYSTEMS*

In this section, we learn how to work with numbers having arbitrary bases, although we will focus on the bases most used in digital computers, such as base 2 (binary) and its close cousins base 8 (octal) and base 16 (hexadecimal.)

The **base**, or **radix**, of a number system defines the range of possible values that a digit may have. In the base 10 (decimal) number system, one of the 10 values 0, 1, 2, 3, 4, 5, 6, 7, 8, 9 is used for each digit of a number. The most natural system for representing numbers in a computer is base 2, in which data is represented as a collection of 1's and 0's.

The general form for determining the decimal value of a number in a radix k fixed point number system is as follows:

$$\text{Value} = \sum_{i=-m}^{n-1} b_i \cdot k^i$$

The value of the digit in position i is given by b_i. There are n digits to the left of the radix point and there are m digits to the right of the radix point. This form of a number, in which each position has an assigned weight, is referred to as a **weighted position code**. Consider evaluating $(541.25)_{10}$, in which the subscript 10 represents the base. We have $n = 3$, $m = 2$, and $k = 10$:

$$5 \times 10^2 + 4 \times 10^1 + 1 \times 10^0 + 2 \times 10^{-1} + 5 \times 10^{-2} =$$

$$(500)_{10} + (40)_{10} + (1)_{10} + (2/10)_{10} + (5/100)_{10} = (541.25)_{10}$$

Now consider the base 2 number $(1010.01)_2$ in which $n = 4$, $m = 2$, and $k = 2$:

$$1 \times 2^3 + 0 \times 2^2 + 1 \times 2^1 + 0 \times 2^0 + 0 \times 2^{-1} + 1 \times 2^{-2} =$$

$$(8)_{10} + (0)_{10} + (2)_{10} + (0)_{10} + (0/2)_{10} + (1/4)_{10} = (10.25)_{10}$$

This suggests how to convert a number from an arbitrary base into a base 10 number using the **polynomial method**. The idea is to multiply each digit by the weight assigned to its position (powers of two in this example) and then sum up the terms to obtain the converted number. Although conversions can be made among all of the bases in this way, some bases pose special problems, as we will see in the next section.

Note: In these weighted number systems we define the bit that carries the most weight as the **most significant bit (MSB)**, and the bit that carries the least weight as the **least significant bit (LSB)**. Conventionally the MSB is the left-most bit and the LSB the rightmost bit.

2.2.4 *CONVERSIONS AMONG RADICES*

In the previous section, we saw an example of how a base 2 number can be converted into a base 10 number. A conversion in the reverse direction is more involved. The easiest way to convert fixed point numbers containing both integer and fractional parts is to convert each part separately. Consider converting $(23.375)_{10}$ to base 2. We begin by separating the number into its integer and fractional parts:

$$(23.375)_{10} = (23)_{10} + (.375)_{10}$$

Converting the Integer Part of a Fixed Point Number—The Remainder Method

As suggested in the previous section, the general polynomial form for representing a binary integer is

$$b_i \times 2^i + b_{i-1} \times 2^{i-1} + \ldots + b_1 \times 2^1 + b_0 \times 2^0$$

If we divide the integer by 2, then we will obtain

$$b_i \times 2^{i-1} + b_{i-1} \times 2^{i-2} + \ldots + b_1 \times 2^0$$

with a remainder of b_0. As a result of dividing the original integer by 2, we discover the value of the first binary coefficient b_0. We can repeat this process on the remaining polynomial and determine the value of b_1. We can continue iterating the process on the remaining polynomial and thus obtain all of the b_i. This process forms the basis of the **remainder method** of converting integers between bases.

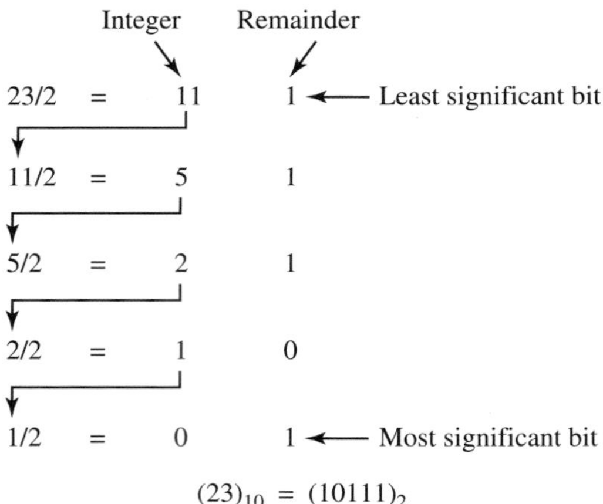

Figure 2-1 A conversion from a base 10 integer to a base 2 integer using the remainder method.

We now apply the remainder method to convert $(23)_{10}$ to base 2. As shown in Figure 2-1, the integer is initially divided by 2, which leaves a remainder of 0 or 1. For this case, 23/2 produces a quotient of 11 and a remainder of 1. The first remainder is the least significant **b**inary dig**it** (**bit**) of the converted number (the rightmost bit). In the next step 11 is divided by 2, which creates a quotient of 5 and a remainder of 1. Next, 5 is divided by 2, which creates a quotient of 2 and a remainder of 1. The process continues until we are left with a quotient of 0. If we continue the process after obtaining a quotient of 0, we will only obtain 0's for the quotient and remainder, which will not change the value of the converted number. The remainders are collected into a base 2 number in the order shown in Figure 2-1 to produce the result $(23)_{10} = (10111)_2$. In general, we can convert any base 10 integer to any other base by simply dividing the integer by the base to which we are converting.

We can check the result by converting it from base 2 back to base 10 using the polynomial method:

$$
\begin{aligned}
(10111)_2 &= 1 \times 2^4 + 0 \times 2^3 + 1 \times 2^2 + 1 \times 2^1 + 1 \times 2^0 \\
&= 16 + 0 + 4 + 2 + 1 \\
&= (23)_{10}
\end{aligned}
$$

At this point, we have converted the integer portion of $(23.375)_{10}$ into base 2.

Converting the Fractional Part of a Fixed Point Number—The Multiplication Method

The conversion of the fractional portion can be accomplished by successively multiplying the fraction by 2 as described next.

A binary fraction is represented in the general form

$$b_{-1} \times 2^{-1} + b_{-2} \times 2^{-2} + b_{-3} \times 2^{-3} + \ldots$$

If we multiply the fraction by 2, then we will obtain

$$b_{-1} + b_{-2} \times 2^{-1} + b_{-3} \times 2^{-2} + \ldots$$

We thus discover the coefficient b_{-1}. If we iterate this process on the remaining fraction, then we will obtain successive b_i. This process forms the basis of the **multiplication** of converting fractions between bases. For the example used here (Figure 2-2), the initial fraction $(.375)_{10}$ is less than 1. If we multiply it by 2, then the resulting number will be less than 2. The digit to the left of the radix point will then be 0 or 1. This is the first digit to the right of the radix point in the converted base 2 number, as shown in the figure. We repeat the process on the fractional portion until we are either left with a fraction of 0, at which point only trailing 0's are created by additional iterations, or we have reached the limit of precision used in our representation. The digits are collected and the result is obtained: $(.375)_{10} = (.011)_2$.

For this process, the multiplier is the same as the target base. The multiplier is 2 here, but if we wanted to make a conversion to another base, such as 3, then we would use a multiplier of 3.[1]

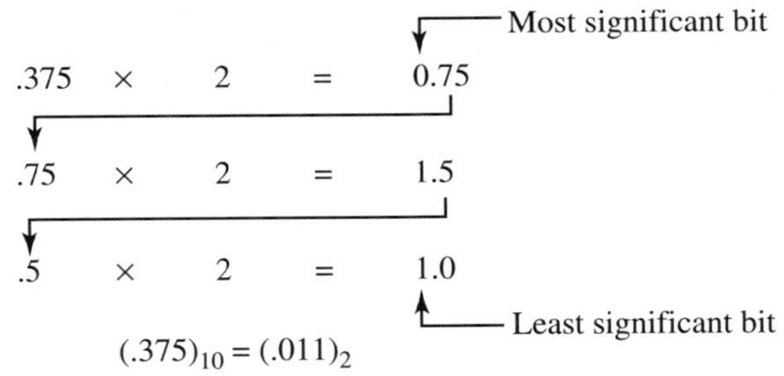

Most significant bit

.375 × 2 = 0.75

.75 × 2 = 1.5

.5 × 2 = 1.0

Least significant bit

$(.375)_{10} = (.011)_2$

Figure 2-2 A conversion from a base 10 fraction to a base 2 fraction using the multiplication method.

[1] Alternatively, we can use the base 10 number system and also avoid the conversion if we retain a base 2 representation, in which combinations of 1's and 0's represent the base 10 digits. This is known as binary coded decimal (BCD), which we will explore later in the chapter.

We again check the result of the conversion by converting from base 2 back to base 10 using the polynomial method as follows:

$$(.011)_2 = 0 \times 2^{-1} + 1 \times 2^{-2} + 1 \times 2^{-3} = 0 + 1/4 + 1/8 = (.375)_{10}$$

We now combine the integer and fractional portions of the number and obtain the final result:

$$(23.375)_{10} = (10111.011)_2$$

Nonterminating Fractions

Although this method of conversion will work among all bases, some precision can be lost in the process. For example, not all terminating base 10 fractions have a terminating base 2 form. Consider converting $(.2)_{10}$ to base 2 as shown in Figure 2-3. In the last row of the conversion, the fraction .2 reappears, and the process repeats *ad infinitum*. As to why this can happen, consider that any nonrepeating base 2 fraction can be represented as $i/2^k$ for some integers i and k. (Repeating fractions in base 2 cannot be so represented.) Algebraically,

$$2^k = i \times 5^k/(2^k \times 5^k) = i \times 5^k/10^k = j/10^k$$

where j is the integer $i \times 5^k$. The fraction is thus nonrepeating in base 10. This hinges on the fact that only nonrepeating fractions in base b can be represented as i/b^k for some integers i and k. The condition that must be satisfied for a nonrepeating base 10 fraction to have an equivalent nonrepeating base 2 fraction is:

$$i/10^k = i/(5^k \times 2^k) = j/2^k$$

$$.2 \times 2 = 0.4$$
$$.4 \times 2 = 0.8$$
$$.8 \times 2 = 1.6$$
$$.6 \times 2 = 1.2$$
$$.2 \times 2 = 0.4$$

$\vdots$

Figure 2-3 A terminating base 10 fraction that does not have a terminating base 2 form.

where $j = i/5^k$, and 5^k must be a factor of i. For one digit decimal fractions, only $(.0)_{10}$ and $(.5)_{10}$ are nonrepeating in base 2 (20% of the possible fractions); for two digit decimal fractions, only $(.00)_{10}$, $(.25)_{10}$, $(.50)_{10}$, and $(.75)_{10}$ are nonrepeating (4% of the possible fractions); etc. There is a link between relatively prime numbers and repeating fractions, which is helpful in understanding why some terminating base 10 fractions do not have a terminating base 2 form. (Knuth, 1981) provides some insight in this area.

Binary versus Decimal Representations

While most computers use base 2 for internal representation and arithmetic, some calculators and business computers use an internal representation of base 10, and thus do not suffer from this representational problem. The motivation for using base 10 in business computers is not entirely to avoid the terminating fraction problem, however, but also to avoid the conversion process at the input and output units which historically have taken a significant amount of time.

Binary, Octal, and Hexadecimal Radix Representations

While binary numbers reflect the actual internal representation used in most machines, they suffer from the disadvantage that numbers represented in base 2 tend to need more digits than numbers in other bases (why?), and it is easy to make errors when writing them because of the long strings of 1's and 0's. We mentioned earlier in the chapter that base 8, **octal radix**, and base 16, **hexadecimal radix**, are related to base 2. This is due to the three radices all being divisible by 2, the smallest one. We show that converting among the three bases 2, 8, and 16 is trivial, and there are significant practical advantages to representing numbers in these bases.

Binary numbers may be considerably wider than their base 10 equivalents. As a notational convenience, we sometimes use larger bases than 2 that are even multiples of 2. Converting among bases 2, 8, or 16 is easier than converting to and from base 10. The values used for the base 8 digits are familiar to us as base 10 digits, but for base 16 (hexadecimal) we need six more digits than are used in base 10. The letters A, B, C, D, E, F or their lower-case equivalents are commonly used to represent the corresponding values (10, 11, 12, 13, 14, 15) in hexadecimal. The digits commonly used for bases 2, 8, 10, and 16 are summarized in Figure 2-4. In comparing the base 2 column with the base 8 and base 16 columns, we need three bits to represent each base 8 digit in binary, and we need four bits to represent each base 16 digit in binary. In general, k bits are needed to

Binary (base 2)	Octal (base 8)	Decimal (base 10)	Hexadecimal (base 16)
0	0	0	0
1	1	1	1
10	2	2	2
11	3	3	3
100	4	4	4
101	5	5	5
110	6	6	6
111	7	7	7
1000	10	8	8
1001	11	9	9
1010	12	10	A
1011	13	11	B
1100	14	12	C
1101	15	13	D
1110	16	14	E
1111	17	15	F

Figure 2-4 Values for digits in the binary, octal, decimal, and hexadecimal number systems.

represent each digit in base 2^k, in which k is an integer, so base $2^3 = 8$ uses three bits and base $2^4 = 16$ uses four bits.

In order to convert a base 2 number into a base 8 number, we partition the base 2 number into groups of three starting from the radix point, and pad the outermost groups with 0's as needed to form triples. Then we convert each triple to the octal equivalent. For conversion from base 2 to base 16, we use groups of four. Consider converting $(10110)_2$ to base 8:

$$(10110)_2 = (010)_2\,(110)_2 = (2)_8\,(6)_8 = (26)_8$$

Notice that the leftmost two bits are padded with a 0 on the left in order to create a full triplet.

Now consider converting $(10110110)_2$ to base 16:

$$(10110110)_2 = (1011)_2\,(0110)_2 = (B)_{16}\,(6)_{16} = (B6)_{16}$$

(Note that B is a base 16 digit corresponding to 11_{10}. B is not a variable.)

The conversion methods can be used to convert a number from any base to any other base, but it may not be very intuitive to convert something like $(513.03)_6$

to base 7. As an aid in performing an unnatural conversion, we can convert to the more familiar base 10 form as an intermediate step, and then continue the conversion from base 10 to the target base. As a general rule, we use the polynomial method when converting *into* base 10, and we use the remainder and multiplication methods when converting *out* of base 10.

2.2.5 *AN EARLY LOOK AT COMPUTER ARITHMETIC*

We will explore computer arithmetic in detail in Chapter 3, but for the moment, we need to learn how to perform simple binary addition because it is used in representing signed binary numbers. Binary addition is performed similar to the way we perform decimal addition by hand, as illustrated in Figure 2-5. Two binary numbers A and B are added from right to left, creating a sum and a carry in each bit position. Since the rightmost bits of A and B can each assume one of two values, four cases must be considered: 0 + 0, 0 + 1, 1 + 0, and 1 + 1, with a carry of 0, as shown in the figure. The carry into the rightmost bit position defaults to 0. For the remaining bit positions, the carry into the position can be 0 or 1, so that a total of eight input combinations must be considered as shown in the figure.

Notice that the largest number we can represent using the eight-bit format shown in Figure 2-5 is $(11111111)_2 = (255)_{10}$ and that the smallest number that can be represented is $(00000000)_2 = (0)_{10}$. The bit patterns 11111111 and 00000000 and all of the intermediate bit patterns represent numbers on the closed interval from 0 to 255, which are all positive numbers. Up to this point we have considered only unsigned numbers, but we need to represent signed numbers as well, in which (approximately) one half of the bit patterns is assigned to positive numbers and the other half is assigned to negative numbers. Four common representations for base 2 signed numbers are discussed in the next section.

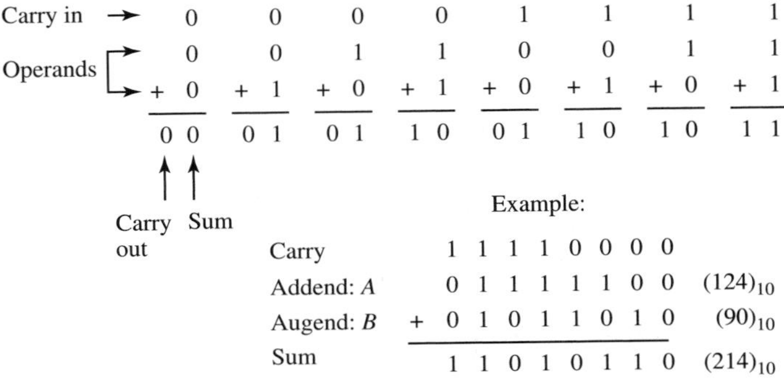

Figure 2-5 Example of binary addition.

2.2.6 *SIGNED FIXED POINT NUMBERS*

Up to this point we have considered only the representation of unsigned fixed point numbers. The situation is quite different in representing *signed* fixed point numbers. There are four different ways of representing signed numbers that are commonly used: sign magnitude, one's complement, two's complement, and excess notation. We will cover each in turn, using integers for our examples. Throughout the discussion, the reader may wish to refer to Table 2-1, which shows for a 3-bit number how the various representations appear.

Decimal	Unsigned	Sign Mag.	1's Comp.	2's Comp.	Excess 4
7	111	–	–	–	–
6	110	–	–	–	–
5	101	–	–	–	–
4	100	–	–	–	–
3	011	011	011	011	111
2	010	010	010	010	110
1	001	001	001	001	101
+0	000	000	000	000	100
–0	–	100	111	000	100
–1	–	101	110	111	011
–2	–	110	101	110	010
–3	–	111	100	101	001
–4	–	–	–	100	000

Table 2-1: 3-Bit Integer Representations

Signed Magnitude

The **signed magnitude** (also referred to as **sign and magnitude**) representation is most familiar to us as the base 10 number system. A plus or minus sign to the left of a number indicates whether the number is positive or negative as in $+12_{10}$ or -12_{10}. In the binary signed magnitude representation, the leftmost bit is used for the sign, which takes on a value of 0 or 1 for + or – , respectively. The remaining bits contain the absolute magnitude. Consider representing $(+12)_{10}$ and $(-12)_{10}$ in an eight-bit format:

$$(+12)_{10} = (00001100)_2$$

$$(-12)_{10} = (10001100)_2$$

The negative number is formed by simply changing the sign bit in the positive number from 0 to 1. Notice that there are both positive and negative representations for zero: 00000000 and 10000000.

There are eight bits in this example format, and all bit patterns represent valid numbers, so there are $2^8 = 256$ possible patterns. Only $2^8 - 1 = 255$ different numbers can be represented, however, since +0 and −0 represent the same number.

We will make use of the signed magnitude representation when we look at floating point numbers in Section 2.3.

One's Complement

The **one's complement** operation is trivial to perform: Convert all of the 1's in the number to 0's, and all of the 0's to 1's. See the fourth column in Table 2-1 for examples. We can observe from the table that in the **one's complement** representation the leftmost bit is 0 for positive numbers and 1 for negative numbers, as it is for the signed magnitude representation. This negation, changing 1's to 0's and changing 0's to 1's, is known as **complementing** the bits. Consider again representing $(+12)_{10}$ and $(-12)_{10}$ in an eight-bit format, now using the one's complement representation:

$$(+12)_{10} = (00001100)_2$$

$$(-12)_{10} = (11110011)_2$$

Note again that there are representations for both +0 and −0, which are 00000000 and 11111111, respectively. As a result, there are only $2^8 - 1 = 255$ different numbers that can be represented even though there are 2^8 different bit patterns.

The one's complement representation is not commonly used. This is at least partly due to the difficulty in making comparisons when there are two representations for 0. There is also additional complexity involved in adding numbers, which is discussed further in Chapter 3.

Two's Complement

The two's complement is formed in a way similar to forming the one's complement: complement all of the bits in the number, but then add 1, and if that addition results in a carry-out from the most significant bit of the number, discard the carry-out. Examination of the fifth column of Table 2-1 shows that in the **two's complement** representation, the leftmost bit is again 0 for positive numbers and is 1 for negative numbers. However, this number format does not have the unfortunate characteristic of signed-magnitude and one's complement representations: It has only one representation for zero. To see that this is true, consider forming the negative of $(+0)_{10}$, which has the bit pattern

$$(+0)_{10} = (00000000)_2$$

Forming the one's complement of $(00000000)_2$ produces $(11111111)_2$ and adding 1 to it yields $(00000000)_2$, thus $(-0)_{10} = (00000000)_2$. The carry-out of the leftmost position is discarded in two's complement addition (except when detecting an overflow condition). Since there is only one representation for 0, and since all bit patterns are valid, there are $2^8 = 256$ different numbers that can be represented.

Consider again representing $(+12)_{10}$ and $(-12)_{10}$ in an eight bit format, this time using the two's complement representation. Starting with $(+12)_{10} = (00001100)_2$, complement, or negate the number, producing $(11110011)_2$. Now add 1, producing $(11110100)_2$, and thus $(-12)_{10} = (11110100)_2$:

$$(+12)_{10} = (00001100)_2$$

$$(-12)_{10} = (11110100)_2$$

There is an equal number of positive and negative numbers provided zero is considered to be a positive number, which is reasonable because its sign bit is 0. The positive numbers start at 0, but the negative numbers start at −1, and so the magnitude of the most negative number is one greater than the magnitude of the most positive number. The positive number with the largest magnitude is +127, and the negative number with the largest magnitude is −128. There is thus no positive number that can be represented that corresponds to the negative of −128. If we try to form the two's complement negative of −128, then we will arrive at a negative number, as follows:

$$(-128)_{10} = (10000000)_2$$

$$\Downarrow$$

$$\begin{array}{r} 01111111 \\ +\quad 1 \\ \hline (10000000)_2 \end{array}$$

The two's complement representation is the representation most commonly used in conventional computers, and we will use it throughout the book.

Excess Representation

In the **excess** or **biased** representation, the number is treated as unsigned but is "shifted" in value by subtracting the bias from it. The concept is to assign the smallest numerical bit pattern, all zeros, to the negative of the bias, and assign the remaining numbers in sequence as the bit patterns increase in magnitude. A convenient way to think of an excess representation is that a number is represented as the sum of its two's complement form and another number, which is known as the "excess," or "bias." Once again, refer to Table 2-1, the rightmost column, for examples.

Consider again representing $(+12)_{10}$ and $(-12)_{10}$ in an eight-bit format but now using an excess 128 representation. An excess 128 number is formed by adding 128 to the original number and then creating the unsigned binary version. For $(+12)_{10}$, we compute $(128 + 12 = 140)_{10}$ and produce the bit pattern $(10001100)_2$. For $(-12)_{10}$, we compute $(128 + -12 = 116)_{10}$ and produce the bit pattern $(01110100)_2$:

$$(+12)_{10} = (10001100)_2$$

$$(-12)_{10} = (01110100)_2$$

Note that there is no numerical significance to the excess value: It simply has the effect of shifting the representation of the two's complement numbers.

There is only one excess representation for 0, since the excess representation is simply a shifted version of the two's complement representation. For the previous case, the excess value is chosen to have the same bit pattern as the largest negative number, which has the effect of making the numbers appear in numerically sorted order if the numbers are viewed in an unsigned binary representation. Thus, the most negative number is $(-128)_{10} = (00000000)_2$ and the most positive number is $(+127)_{10} = (11111111)_2$. This representation simplifies making comparisons between numbers, since the bit patterns for negative numbers have numerically smaller values than the bit patterns for positive numbers. This is important for representing the exponents of floating point numbers, in which exponents of two numbers are compared in order to make them equal for addition and subtraction. We will explore floating point representations in Section 2.3.

2.2.7 *BINARY CODED DECIMAL*

Numbers can be represented in the base 10 number system while still using a binary encoding. Each base 10 digit occupies four bit positions, which is known as **binary coded decimal (BCD)**. Each BCD digit can take on any of 10 values. There are $2^4 = 16$ possible bit patterns for each base 10 digit, and as a result, six bit patterns are unused for each digit. In Figure 2-6, there are four decimal significant digits, so $10^4 = 10{,}000$ bit patterns are valid, even though $2^{16} = 65{,}536$ bit patterns are possible with 16 bits.

Although some bit patterns are unused, the BCD format is commonly used in calculators and in business applications. There are fewer problems in representing terminating base 10 fractions in this format, unlike the base 2 representation. There is no need to convert data that is given at the input in base 10 form (as in a calculator) into an internal base 2 representation, or to convert from an internal representation of base 2 to an output form of base 10.

Performing arithmetic on signed BCD numbers may not be obvious. Although we are accustomed to using a signed magnitude representation in base 10, a different method of representing signed base 10 numbers is used in a computer. In the **nine's complement** number system, positive numbers are represented as in ordinary BCD, but the leftmost digit is less than 5 for positive numbers and is 5 or greater for negative numbers. The nine's complement negative is formed by subtracting each digit from 9. For example, the base 10 number +301 is represented as 0301 (or simply 301) in both nine's and ten's complement as shown in Figure 2-6a. The nine's complement negative is 9698 (Figure 2-6b), which is obtained by subtracting each digit in 0301 from 9.

The **ten's complement** negative is formed by adding 1 to the nine's complement negative, so the ten's complement representation of −301 is then 9698 + 1 =

(a)	0 0 0 0	0 0 1 1	0 0 0 0	0 0 0 1	$(+301)_{10}$	Nine's and ten's complement
	$(0)_{10}$	$(3)_{10}$	$(0)_{10}$	$(1)_{10}$		
(b)	1 0 0 1	0 1 1 0	1 0 0 1	1 0 0 0	$(-301)_{10}$	Nine's complement
	$(9)_{10}$	$(6)_{10}$	$(9)_{10}$	$(8)_{10}$		
(c)	1 0 0 1	0 1 1 0	1 0 0 1	1 0 0 1	$(-301)_{10}$	Ten's complement
	$(9)_{10}$	$(6)_{10}$	$(9)_{10}$	$(9)_{10}$		

Figure 2-6 BCD representations of 301 (a) and –301 in nine's complement (b) and ten's complement (c).

9699 as shown in Figure 2-6c. For this example, the positive numbers range from 0 to 4999 and the negative numbers range from 5000 to 9999.

2.3 Floating Point Numbers

The fixed point number representation, which we explored in Section 2.2, has a fixed position for the radix point and a fixed number of digits to the left and right of the radix point. A fixed point representation may need a great many digits in order to represent a practical range of numbers. For example, a computer that can represent a number as large as a trillion[2] maintains at least 40 bits to the left of the radix point since $2^{40} \approx 10^{12}$. If the same computer needs to represent one trillionth, then 40 bits must also be maintained to the right of the radix point, which results in a total of 80 bits per number.

In practice, much larger numbers and much smaller numbers appear during the course of computation, which places even greater demands on a computer. A great deal of hardware is required in order to store and manipulate numbers with 80 or more bits of precision, and computation proceeds more slowly for a large number of digits than for a small number of digits. Fine precision, however, is generally not needed when large numbers are used, and conversely, large numbers do not generally need to be represented when calculations are made with small numbers. A more efficient computer can be realized when only as much precision is retained as is needed.

2.3.1 *RANGE AND PRECISION IN FLOATING POINT NUMBERS*

A **floating point** representation allows a large range of expressible numbers to be represented in a small number of digits by separating the digits used for *precision* from the digits used for *range*. The base 10 floating point number representing Avogadro's number is as follows:

$$+6.023 \times 10^{23}$$

Here, the range is represented by a power of 10, 10^{23} in this case, and the precision is represented by the digits in the fixed point number, 6.023 in this case. In discussing floating point numbers, the fixed point part is often referred to as the

[2]In the American number system, which is used here, a trillion = 10^{12}. In the British number system, this is a "million million," or simply a "billion." The British "milliard," or a "thousand million," is what Americans call a "billion."

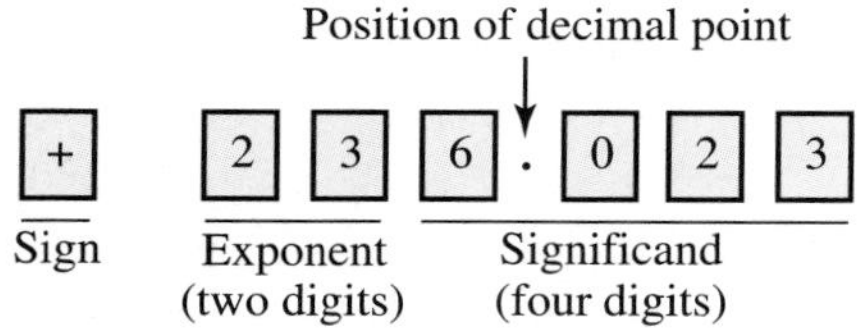

Figure 2-7 Representation of a base 10 floating point number.

mantissa, or **significand** of the number. Thus, a floating point number can be characterized by a triple of numbers: sign, exponent, and significand.

The range is determined primarily by the number of digits in the exponent (two digits are used here) and the base to which it is raised (base 10 is used here) and the precision is determined primarily by the number of digits in the significand (four digits are used here). Thus the entire number can be represented by a sign and 6 digits, two for the exponent and four for the significand. Figure 2-7 shows how the triple of sign, exponent, significand might be formatted in a computer. Notice how the digits are packed together with the sign first, followed by the exponent, followed by the significand. This ordering will turn out to be helpful in comparing two floating point numbers. The reader should be aware that the decimal point does not need to be stored with the number as long as the decimal point is always in the same position in the significand. (This will be discussed in Section 2.3.2.)

If we need a greater range, and if we are willing to sacrifice precision, then we can use just three digits in the fraction and have three digits left for the exponent without increasing the number of digits used in the representation. An alternative method of increasing the range is to increase the base, which has the effect of increasing the precision of the smallest numbers but decreasing the precision of the largest numbers. The range/precision trade-off is a major advantage of using a floating point representation, but the reduced precision can cause problems, sometimes leading to disaster, an example of which is described in Section 2.4.

2.3.2 *NORMALIZATION AND THE HIDDEN BIT*

A potential problem with representing floating point numbers is that the same number can be represented in different ways, which makes comparisons and arithmetic operations difficult. For example, consider the following numerically equivalent forms:

$$3584.1 \times 10^0 = 3.5841 \times 10^3 = .35841 \times 10^4$$

In order to avoid multiple representations for the same number, floating point numbers are maintained in **normalized** form. That is, the radix point is shifted to the left or to the right and the exponent is adjusted accordingly until the radix point is to the left of the leftmost nonzero digit. So the rightmost number in the preceding equation is the normalized one. Unfortunately, the number zero cannot be represented in this scheme, so to represent zero an exception is made. The exception to this rule is that zero is represented as all 0's in the mantissa.

If the mantissa is represented as a binary, that is, base 2, number, and if the normalization condition is that there is a leading "1" in the normalized mantissa, then there is no need to store that "1" and in fact, most floating point formats do *not* store it. Rather, it is "chopped off" before packing up the number for storage, and it is restored when unpacking the number into exponent and mantissa. This results in having an additional bit of precision on the right of the number, due to removing the bit on the left. This missing bit is referred to as the **hidden bit**, also known as a **hidden 1**. For example, if the mantissa in a given format is .11010 after normalization, then the bit pattern that is stored is 1010—the leftmost bit is truncated, or hidden. We will see that the IEEE[3] 754 floating point format uses a hidden bit.

2.3.3 *REPRESENTING FLOATING POINT NUMBERS IN THE COMPUTER—PRELIMINARIES*

Let us design a simple floating point format to illustrate the important factors in representing floating point numbers on the computer. Our format may at first seem to be unnecessarily complex. We will represent the significand in signed magnitude format, with a single bit for the sign bit, and three hexadecimal digits for the magnitude. The exponent will be a 3-bit excess-4 number, with a radix of 16. The normalized form of the number has the hexadecimal point to the left of the three hexadecimal digits.

The bits will be packed together as follows: The sign bit is on the left, followed by the 3-bit exponent, followed by the three hexadecimal digits of the significand. Neither the radix nor the hexadecimal point will be stored in the packed form.

The reason for these rather odd-seeming choices is that numbers in this format can be compared for $=$, $\neq$, $\leq$, and $\geq$ in their "packed" format, which is shown in the following illustration:

---

[3]Institute of Electrical and Electronics Engineers.

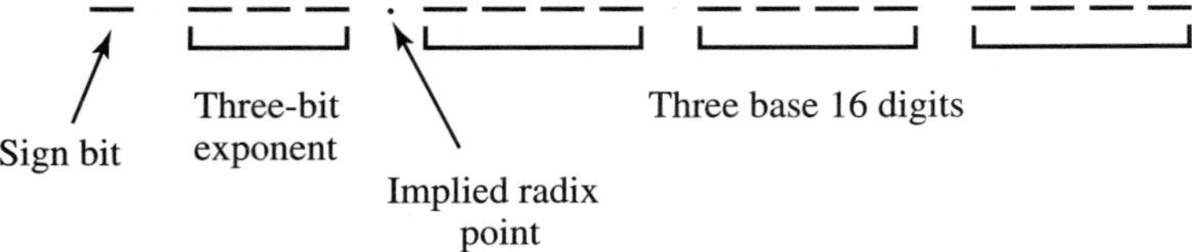

Consider representing $(358)_{10}$ in this format.

The first step is to convert the fixed point number from its original base into a fixed point number in the target base. Using the method described in Section 2.1.3, we convert the base 10 number into a base 16 number as follows:

	Integer	Remainder
358/16 =	22	6
22/16 =	1	6
1/16 =	0	1

Thus $(358)_{10} = (166)_{16}$. The next step is to convert the fixed point number into a floating point number:

$$(166)_{16} = (166.)_{16} \times 16^0$$

Note that the form 16^0 reflects a base of 16 with an exponent of 0 and that the number 16 as it appears on the page uses a base 10 form. That is, $(16^0)_{10} = (10^0)_{16}$. This is simply a notational convenience used in describing a floating point number.

The next step is to normalize the number:

$$(166.)_{16} \times 16^0 = (.166)_{16} \times 16^3$$

Finally, we fill in the bit fields of the number. The number is positive, and so we place a 0 in the sign bit position. The exponent is 3, but we represent it in excess 4, so the bit pattern for the exponent is computed as follows:

$$
\begin{array}{lrl}
 & 0\ 1\ 1 & (+3)_{10} \\
\text{Excess 4} & +\ 1\ 0\ 0 & (+4)_{10} \\
\hline
\text{Excess 4 exponent} & 1\ 1\ 1 &
\end{array}
$$

Alternatively, we could have simply computed 3 + 4 = 7 in base 10, and then made the equivalent conversion $(7)_{10} = (111)_2$.

Finally, each of the base 16 digits is represented in binary as 1 = 0001, 6 = 0110, and 6 = 0110. The final bit pattern is as follows:

0	1 1 1	.	0 0 0 1	0 1 1 0	0 1 1 0
+	3		1	6	6
Sign	Exponent			Fraction	

Notice again that the radix point is not explicitly represented in the bit pattern, but its presence is implied. The spaces between digits are for clarity only and do not suggest that the bits are stored with spaces between them. The bit pattern as stored in a computer's memory would look like this:

0111000101100110

The use of an excess 4 exponent instead of a two's complement or a signed magnitude exponent simplifies addition and subtraction of floating point numbers (which we will cover in detail in Chapter 3). In order to add or subtract two normalized floating point numbers, the smaller exponent (smaller in degree, not magnitude) must first be increased to the larger exponent (this retains the range), which also has the effect of unnormalizing the smaller number. In order to determine which exponent is larger, we only need to treat the bit patterns as unsigned numbers and then make our comparison. That is, using an excess 4 representation, the smallest exponent is −4, which is represented as 000. The largest exponent is +3, which is represented as 111. The remaining bit patterns for −3, −2, −1, 0, +1, and +2 fall in their respective order as 001, 010, 011, 100, 101, and 110.

Now if we are given the bit pattern shown previously for $(358)_{10}$ along with a description of the floating point representation, then we can easily determine the number. The sign bit is a 0, which means that the number is positive. The exponent in unsigned form is the number $(+7)_{10}$, but since we are using excess 4, we must subtract 4 from it, which results in an actual exponent of $(+7 - 4 = +3)_{10}$. The fraction is grouped in four-bit hexadecimal digits, which gives a fraction of $(.166)_{16}$. Putting it all together results in $(+.166 \times 16^3)_{16} = (358)_{10}$.

Now suppose that only 10 bits are allowed for the fraction in the preceding example, instead of the 12 bits that group evenly into fours for hexadecimal digits. How does the representation change? One approach might be to round the fraction and adjust the exponent as necessary. Another approach, which we use here, is simply to truncate the least significant bits by **chopping** and avoid making adjustments to the exponent, so that the number we actually represent is

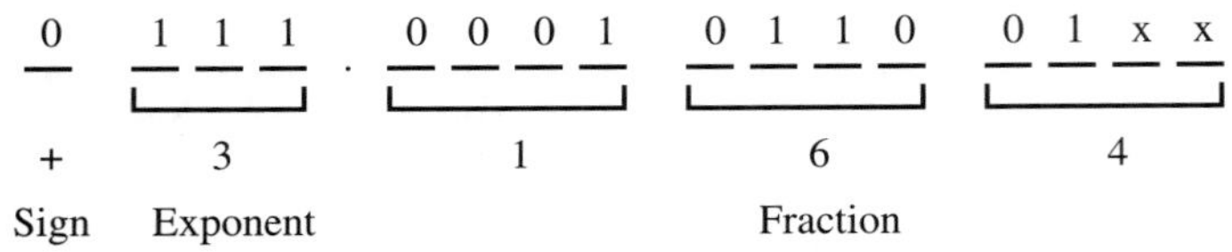

```
 0     1 1 1  .  0 0 0 1   0 1 1 0   0 1 x x
 _     _ _ _     _ _ _ _   _ _ _ _   _ _ _ _
       |___|     |_____|   |_____|   |_____|
 +       3          1         6         4
Sign  Exponent            Fraction
```

If we treat the missing bits as 0's, then this bit pattern represents $(.164 \times 16^3)_{16}$. This method of truncation produces a biased error, since values of 00, 01, 10, and 11 in the missing bits are all treated as 0, and so the error is in the range from 0 to $(.003)_{16}$. The bias comes about because the error is not symmetric about 0. We will not explore the bias problem further here, but a more thorough discussion can be found in (Hamacher et al., 1990).

We again stress that whatever the floating point format is, it must be known to all parties that intend to store or retrieve numbers in that format. The IEEE has taken the lead in standardizing floating point formats. The IEEE 754 floating point format, which is in nearly universal usage, is discussed in Section 2.3.5.

2.3.4 *ERROR IN FLOATING POINT REPRESENTATIONS*

The fact that finite precision introduces error means that we should consider how great the error is (by "error," we mean the distance between two adjacent representable numbers) and whether it is acceptable for our application. As an example of a potential pitfall, consider representing one million in floating point, and then subtracting one million 1's from it. We may still be left with a million if the error is greater than 1.[4]

---

[4]Most computers these days will let this upper bound get at least as high as 8 million using the default precision.

In order to characterize error, range, and precision, we use the following notation:

b	Base
s	Number of significant *digits* (not bits) in the fraction
M	Largest exponent
m	Smallest exponent

The number of significant digits in the fraction is represented by s, which is different from the number of bits in the fraction if the base is anything other than 2 (for example, base 16 uses four bits for each digit). In general, if the base is 2^k where k is an integer, then k bits are needed to represent each digit. The use of a hidden 1 increases s by one bit even though it does not increase the number of representable numbers. In the previous example, there are three significant digits in the base 16 fraction and there are 12 bits that make up the three digits. There are three bits in the excess 4 exponent, which gives an exponent range of $[-2^2$ to $2^2 - 1]$. For this case, $b = 16$, $s = 3$, $M = 3$, and $m = -4$.

In the analysis of a floating point representation, there are five characteristics that we consider: the number of representable numbers, the numbers that have the largest and smallest magnitudes (other than zero), and the sizes of the largest and smallest gaps between successive numbers.

The number of representable numbers can be determined as shown in Figure 2-8. The sign bit can take on two values, as indicated by the position marked with an encircled "A." The total number of exponents is indicated in position B. Note that not all exponent bit patterns are valid in all representations. The IEEE 754 floating point standard, which we will study shortly, has a smallest exponent of −126 even though the eight-bit exponent can support a number as small as

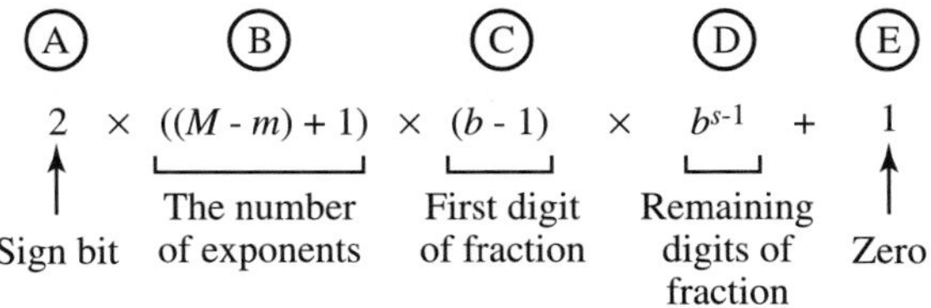

Figure 2-8 Calculation of the number of representable numbers in a floating point representation.

−128. The forbidden exponents are reserved for special numbers, such as zero and infinity.

The first digit of the fraction is considered next, which can take on any value except 0 in a normalized representation (except when a hidden 1 is used) as indicated by $(b-1)$ at position C. The remaining digits of the fraction can take on any of the b values for the base, as indicated by b^{s-1} at position D. If a hidden 1 is used, then position C is removed and position 4 is replaced with b^s. Finally, there must be a representation for 0, which is accounted for in position E.

Consider now the numbers with the smallest and largest magnitudes. The number with the smallest magnitude has the smallest exponent and the smallest nonzero normalized fraction. There must be a nonzero value in the first digit, and since a 1 is the smallest value we can place there, the smallest fraction is b^{-1}. The number with the smallest magnitude is then $b^m \cdot b^{-1} = b^{m-1}$. Similarly, the number with the largest magnitude has the largest exponent and the largest fraction (when the fraction is all 1's), which is equal to $b^M \cdot (1 - b^{-s})$.

The smallest and largest gaps are computed in a similar manner. The smallest gap occurs when the exponent is at its smallest value and the least significant bit of the fraction changes. This gap is $b^m \cdot b^{-s} = b^{m-s}$. The largest gap occurs when the exponent is at its largest value and the least significant bit of the fraction changes. This gap is $b^M \cdot b^{-s} = b^{M-s}$.

As an example, consider a floating point representation in which there is a sign bit, a two-bit excess 2 exponent, and a three-bit normalized base 2 fraction in which the leading 1 is visible; that is, the leading 1 is not hidden. The representation of 0 is the bit pattern 000000. A number line showing all possible numbers that can be represented in this format is shown in Figure 2-9. Notice that there is a relatively large gap between 0 and the first representable number, because the

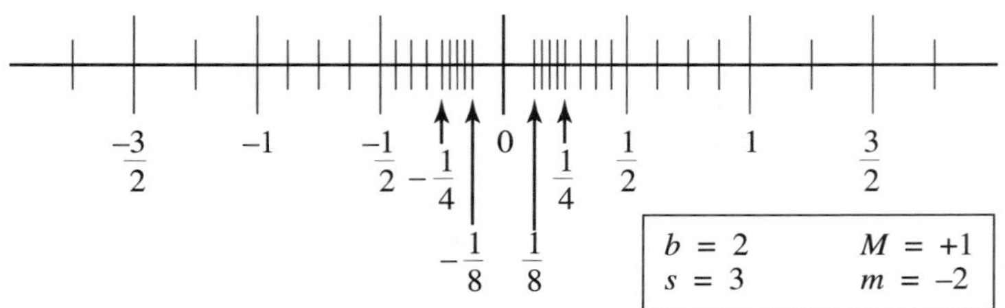

Figure 2-9 A number line showing all representable numbers in a simple floating point format.

normalized representation does not support bit patterns that correspond to numbers between 0 and the first representable number.

The smallest representable number occurs when the exponent and the fraction are at their smallest values. The smallest exponent is –2, and the smallest normalized fraction is $(.100)_2$. The smallest representable number is then

$$b^m \times b^{-1} = b^{m-1} = 2^{-2-1} = 1/8$$

Similarly, the largest representable number occurs when the exponent and the fraction are both at their largest values. The largest fraction occurs when the fraction is all 1's, which is a number that is 2^{-3} less than 1 since there are three digits in the fraction. The largest representable number is then

$$b^M \times (1 - b^{-s}) = 2^1 \times (1 - 2^{-3}) = 7/4$$

The smallest gap occurs when the exponent is at its smallest value and the least significant bit of the fraction changes, which is

$$b^m \times b^{-s} = b^{m-s} = 2^{-2-3} = 1/32$$

Similarly, the largest gap occurs when the exponent is at its largest value and the least significant bit of the fraction changes, whichis

$$b^M \times b^{-s} = b^{M-s} = 2^{1-3} = 1/4$$

The number of bit patterns that represent valid numbers is less than the number of possible bit patterns, due to normalization. As discussed earlier, the number of representable numbers consists of five parts, which take into account the sign bit, the exponents, the first significant digit, the remaining digits, and the bit pattern for 0. This is computed as follows:

$$2 \times ((M - m) + 1) \times (b - 1) \times b^{s-1} + 1$$

$$= 2 \times ((1 - (-2)) + 1) \times (2 - 1) - 2^{3-1} + 1$$

$$= 33$$

Notice that the gaps are small for small numbers and that the gaps are large for large numbers. In fact, the relative error is approximately the same for all numbers. If we take the ratio of a large gap to a large number, and compare that to the ratio of a small gap to a small number, then the ratios are the same:

$$\frac{\text{A large gap}}{\text{A large number}} \longrightarrow \frac{b^{M-s}}{b^M \times (1-b^{-s})} = \frac{b^{-s}}{1-b^{-s}} = \frac{1}{b^s - 1}$$

and

$$\frac{\text{A small gap}}{\text{A small number}} \longrightarrow \frac{b^{m-s}}{b^m \times (1-b^{-s})} = \frac{b^{-s}}{1-b^{-s}} = \frac{1}{b^s - 1}$$

The representation for a "small number" is used here, rather than the smallest number, because the large gap between zero and the first representable number is a special case.

EXAMPLE

Consider the problem of converting $(9.375 \times 10^{-2})_{10}$ to base 2 scientific notation. That is, the result should have the form $x.yy \times 2^E$. We start by converting from base 10 floating point to base 10 fixed point by moving the decimal point two positions to the left, which corresponds to the –2 exponent: .09375. We then convert from base 10 fixed point to base 2 fixed point by using the multiplication method:

$$
\begin{array}{lcccl}
.09375 & \times & 2 & = & 0.1875 \\
.1875 & \times & 2 & = & 0.375 \\
.375 & \times & 2 & = & 0.75 \\
.75 & \times & 2 & = & 1.5 \\
.5 & \times & 2 & = & 1.0
\end{array}
$$

so $(.09375)_{10} = (.00011)_2$. Finally, we convert to normalized base 2 floating point: $.00011 = .00011 \times 2^0 = 1.1 \times 2^{-4}$. ■

2.3.5 *THE IEEE 754 FLOATING POINT STANDARD*

There are many ways to represent floating point numbers, a few of which we have already explored. Each representation has its own characteristics in terms of range, precision, and the number of representable numbers. In an effort to improve software portability and ensure uniform accuracy of floating point calculations, the IEEE 754 floating point standard for binary numbers was developed (IEEE, 1985). There are a few entrenched product lines that predate the standard that do not use it, such as the IBM/370, the DEC VAX, and the Cray line, but virtually all new architectures generally provide some level of IEEE 754 support.

The IEEE 754 standard as described in this section must be supported by a computer *system*, and not necessarily by the hardware entirely. That is, a mixture of hardware and software can be used while still conforming to the standard.

2.3.5.1 Formats

There are two primary formats in the IEEE 754 standard: **single precision** and **double precision**. Figure 2-10 summarizes the layouts of the two formats. The single-precision format occupies 32 bits, whereas the double-precision format occupies 64 bits. The double precision format is simply a wider version of the single precision format.

The sign bit is in the leftmost position and indicates a positive or negative number for a 0 or a 1, respectively. The 8-bit excess 127 (*not* 128) exponent follows, in which the bit patterns 00000000 and 11111111 are reserved for special cases, as described later. For double precision, the 11-bit exponent is represented in

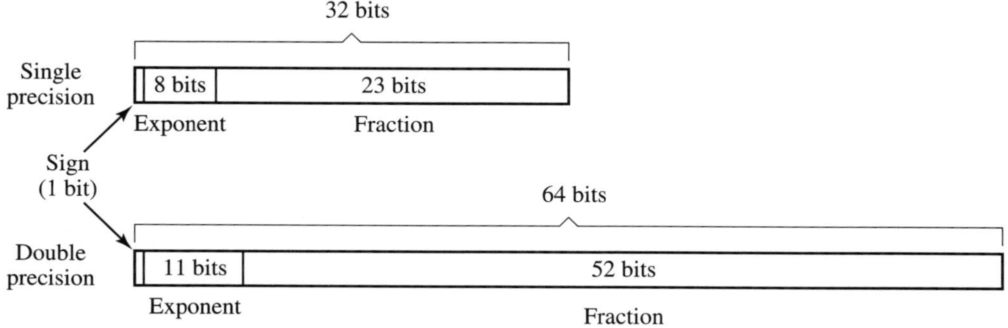

Figure 2-10 Single-precision and double-precision IEEE 754 floating point formats.

excess 1023, with 00000000000 and 11111111111 reserved. The 23-bit base 2 fraction follows. There is a hidden bit to the *left* of the binary point, which when taken together with the single-precision fraction forms a 23 + 1 = 24-bit significand of the form 1.fff...f where the fff...f pattern represents the 23-bit fractional part that is stored. The double-precision format also uses a hidden bit to the left of the binary point, which supports a 52 + 1 = 53 bit significand. For both formats, the number is normalized unless **denormalized** numbers are supported, as described later.

There are five basic types of numbers that can be represented. Nonzero normalized numbers take the form described previously. A so-called "clean zero" is represented by the reserved bit pattern 00000000 in the exponent and all 0's in the fraction. The sign bit can be 0 or 1, and so there are two representations for zero: +0 and −0.

Infinity has a representation in which the exponent contains the reserved bit pattern 11111111, the fraction contains all 0's, and the sign bit is 0 or 1. Infinity is useful in handling overflow situations or in giving a valid representation to a number (other than zero) divided by zero. If zero is divided by zero or infinity is divided by infinity, then the result is undefined. This is represented by the **NaN** (not a number) format in which the exponent contains the reserved bit pattern 11111111, the fraction is nonzero, and the sign bit is 0 or 1. A NaN can also be produced by attempting to take the square root of −1.

As with all normalized representations, there is a large gap between zero and the first representable number. The denormalized, "dirty zero" representation allows numbers in this gap to be represented. The sign bit can be 0 or 1, the exponent contains the reserved bit pattern 00000000 that represents −126 for single precision (−1022 for double precision), and the fraction contains the actual bit pattern for the magnitude of the number. Thus, there is no hidden 1 for this format. Note that the *denormalized* representation is not an *unnormalized* representation. The key difference is that there is only one representation for each denormalized number, whereas there are infinitely many unnormalized representations.

Figure 2-11 illustrates some examples of IEEE 754 floating point numbers. Examples (a) through (h) are in single precision format and example (i) is in double precision format. Example (a) shows an ordinary single precision number. Notice that the significand is 1.101, but that only the fraction (101) is explicitly represented. Example (b) uses the smallest single-precision exponent (−126) and example (c) uses the largest single-precision exponent (127).

	Value	Bit Pattern		
		Sign	Exponent	Fraction
(a)	$+1.101 \times 2^5$	0	1000 0100	101 0000 0000 0000 0000 0000
(b)	-1.01011×2^{-126}	1	0000 0001	010 1100 0000 0000 0000 0000
(c)	$+1.0 \times 2^{127}$	0	1111 1110	000 0000 0000 0000 0000 0000
(d)	+0	0	0000 0000	000 0000 0000 0000 0000 0000
(e)	–0	1	0000 0000	000 0000 0000 0000 0000 0000
(f)	$+\infty$	0	1111 1111	000 0000 0000 0000 0000 0000
(g)	$+2^{-128}$	0	0000 0000	010 0000 0000 0000 0000 0000
(h)	+NaN	0	1111 1111	011 0111 0000 0000 0000 0000
(i)	$+2^{-128}$	0	011 0111 1111	0000 0000 0000 0000 0000 0000 0000 0000 0000 0000 0000 0000 0000

Figure 2-11 Examples of IEEE 754 floating point numbers in single-precision format (a – h) and double-precision format (i). Spaces are shown for clarity only: They are not part of the representation.

Examples (d) and (e) illustrate the two representations for zero. Example (f) illustrates the bit pattern for $+\infty$. There is also a corresponding bit pattern for $-\infty$. Example (g) shows a denormalized number. Notice that although the number itself is 2^{-128}, the smallest representable exponent is still -126. The exponent for single-precision denormalized numbers is always -126, which is represented by the bit pattern 00000000 and a nonzero fraction. The fraction represents the magnitude of the number rather than a significand. Thus we have $+2^{-128} = +.01 \times 2^{-126}$, which is represented by the bit pattern shown in Figure 2-11g.

Example (h) shows a single-precision NaN. A NaN can be positive or negative. Finally, example (i) revisits the representation of 2^{-128} but now using double precision. The representation is for an ordinary double-precision number and so there are no special considerations here. Notice that 2^{-128} has a significand of 1.0, which is why the fraction field is all 0's.

In addition to the single-precision and double-precision formats, there are also **single extended** and **double extended** formats. The extended formats are not visible to the user, but they are used to retain a greater amount of internal precision during calculations to reduce the effects of roundoff errors. The extended formats increase the widths of the exponents and fractions by a number of bits that can vary depending on the implementation. For instance, the single extended format adds at least three bits to the exponent and eight bits to the fraction. The double extended format is typically 80 bits wide, with a 15-bit exponent and a 64-bit fraction.

2.3.5.2 Rounding

An implementation of IEEE 754 must provide at least single precision, whereas the remaining formats are optional. Further, the result of any single operation on floating point numbers must be accurate to within half a bit in the least significant bit of the fraction. This means that some additional bits of precision may need to be retained during computation (referred to as **guard bits**), and there must be an appropriate method of rounding the intermediate result to the number of bits in the fraction.

There are four rounding modes in the IEEE 754 standard. One mode rounds to 0, another rounds toward $+\infty$, and another rounds toward $-\infty$. The default mode rounds to the nearest representable number. Halfway cases round to the number whose low-order digit is even. For example, 1.01101 rounds to 1.0110 whereas 1.01111 rounds to 1.1000.

2.4 Case Study: Patriot Missile Defense Failure Caused by Loss of Precision

During the 1991–1992 Operation Desert Storm conflict between Coalition forces and Iraq, the Coalition used a military base in Dhahran, Saudi Arabia that was protected by six U.S. Patriot Missile batteries. The Patriot system was originally designed to be mobile and to operate for only a few hours in order to avoid detection.

The Patriot system tracks and intercepts certain types of objects, such as cruise missiles or Scud ballistic missiles, one of which hit a U.S. Army barracks at Dhahran on February 5, 1991, killing 28 Americans. The Patriot system failed to track and intercept the incoming Scud due to a loss of precision in converting integers to a floating point number representation.

A radar system operates by sending out a train of electromagnetic pulses in various directions and then listening for return signals that are reflected from objects in the path of the radar beam. If an airborne object of interest such as a Scud is detected by the Patriot radar system, then the position of a **range gate** is determined (see Figure 2-12), which estimates the position of the object being tracked during the next scan. The range gate also allows information outside of its boundaries to be filtered out, which simplifies tracking. The position of the object (a Scud for this case) is confirmed if it is found within the range gate.

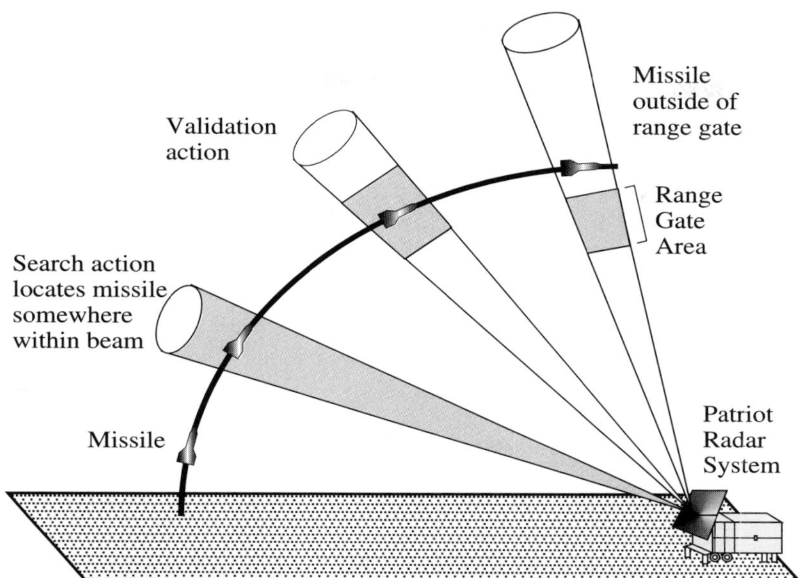

Figure 2-12 Effect of conversion error on range gate calculation.

The prediction of where the Scud will next appear is a function of the Scud's velocity. The Scud's velocity is determined by its change in position with respect to time, and time is updated in the Patriot's internal clock in 100 ms intervals. Velocity is represented as a 24-bit floating point number, and time is represented as a 24-bit integer, but both must be represented as 24-bit floating point numbers in order to predict where the Scud will next appear.

The conversion from integer time to real time results in a loss of precision that increases as the internal clock time increases. The error introduced by the conversion results in an error in the range gate calculation, which is proportional to the target's velocity and the length of time that the system is running. The cause of the Dhahran incident, after the Patriot battery had been operating continuously for over 100 hours, is that the range gate shifted by 687 m, resulting in the failed interception of a Scud.

The conversion problem was known two weeks in advance of the Dhahran incident as a result of data provided by Israel, but it took until the day after the attack for new software to arrive due to the difficulty of distributing bug fixes in a wartime environment. A solution to the problem, until a software fix could be made available, would have been simply to reboot the system every few hours which would have the effect of resetting the internal clock. Since field personnel were not informed of how long was too long to keep a system running, which was in fact known at the time from data provided by Israel, this solution was never implemented. The lesson for us is to be very aware of the limitations of relying on calculations that use finite precision.

2.5 Character Codes

Unlike real numbers, which have an infinite range, there is only a finite number of characters. An entire character set can be represented with a small number of bits per character. Three of the most common character representations, ASCII, EBCDIC, and Unicode, are described here.

2.5.1 *THE ASCII CHARACTER SET*

The American Standard Code for Information Interchange (**ASCII**) is summarized in Figure 2-13, using hexadecimal indices. The representation for each character consists of 7 bits, and all 2^7 possible bit patterns represent valid characters. The characters in positions 00–1F and position 7F are special control characters that are used for transmission, printing control, and other non textual purposes. The remaining characters are all printable and include letters, numbers, punctuation, and a space. The digits 0–9 appear in sequence, as do the upper- and lower-case letters.[5] This organization simplifies character manipulation. In order to change the character representation of a digit into its numerical value, we can subtract $(30)_{16}$ from it. In order to convert the ASCII character "5," which is in position $(35)_{16}$, into the number 5, we compute $(35 - 30 = 5)_{16}$. In order to convert an upper-case letter into a lower-case letter, we add $(20)_{16}$. For example, to convert the letter "H," which is at location $(48)_{16}$ in the ASCII table, into the letter "h," which is at position $(68)_{16}$, we compute $(48 + 20 = 68)_{16}$.

---

[5]As an aside, the character "a" and the character 'A' are different and have different codes in the ASCII table. The small letters like "a" are called **lower case**, and the capital letters like "A" are called **upper case**. The naming comes from the positions of the characters in a printer's typecase. The capital letters appear above the small letters, which resulted in the upper-case/lower-case naming. These days, typesetting is almost always performed electronically, but the traditional naming is still used.

00	NUL	10	DLE	20	SP	30	0	40	@	50	P	60	`	70	p
01	SOH	11	DC1	21	!	31	1	41	A	51	Q	61	a	71	q
02	STX	12	DC2	22	"	32	2	42	B	52	R	62	b	72	r
03	ETX	13	DC3	23	#	33	3	43	C	53	S	63	c	73	s
04	EOT	14	DC4	24	$	34	4	44	D	54	T	64	d	74	t
05	ENQ	15	NAK	25	%	35	5	45	E	55	U	65	e	75	u
06	ACK	16	SYN	26	&	36	6	46	F	56	V	66	f	76	v
07	BEL	17	ETB	27	'	37	7	47	G	57	W	67	g	77	w
08	BS	18	CAN	28	(	38	8	48	H	58	X	68	h	78	x
09	HT	19	EM	29	)	39	9	49	I	59	Y	69	i	79	y
0A	LF	1A	SUB	2A	*	3A	:	4A	J	5A	Z	6A	j	7A	z
0B	VT	1B	ESC	2B	+	3B	;	4B	K	5B	[	6B	k	7B	{
0C	FF	1C	FS	2C	´	3C	<	4C	L	5C	\	6C	l	7C	|
0D	CR	1D	GS	2D	-	3D	=	4D	M	5D	]	6D	m	7D	}
0E	SO	1E	RS	2E	.	3E	>	4E	N	5E	^	6E	n	7E	~
0F	SI	1F	US	2F	/	3F	?	4F	O	5F	_	6F	o	7F	DEL

NUL Null
SOH Start of heading
STX Start of text
ETX End of text
EOT End of transmission
ENQ Enquiry
ACK Acknowledge
BEL Bell
BS Backspace
HT Horizontal tab
LF Line feed
VT Vertical tab
FF Form feed
CR Carriage return
SO Shift out
SI Shift in
DLE Data link escape
DC1 Device control 1
DC2 Device control 2
DC3 Device control 3
DC4 Device control 4
NAK Negative acknowledge
SYN Synchronous idle
ETB End of transmission block
CAN Cancel
EM End of medium
SUB Substitute
ESC Escape
FS File separator
GS Group separator
RS Record separator
US Unit separator
SP Space
DEL Delete

Figure 2-13 The ASCII character code, shown with hexadecimal indices.

2.5.2 *THE EBCDIC CHARACTER SET*

A problem with the ASCII code is that only 128 characters can be represented, which is a limitation for many keyboards that have a lot of special characters in addition to upper- and lower-case letters. The Extended Binary Coded Decimal Interchange Code (**EBCDIC**) is an eight-bit code that is used extensively in IBM mainframe computers. Since seven-bit ASCII characters are frequently represented in an eight-bit modified form (one character per byte), in which a 0 or a 1 is appended to the left of the seven-bit pattern, the use of EBCDIC does not place a greater demand on the storage of characters in a computer. For serial transmission, however (see Chapter 8), an eight-bit code takes more time to transmit than a seven-bit code, and for this case the wider code does make a difference.

The EBCDIC code is summarized in Figure 2-14. There are gaps in the table, which can be used for application-specific characters. The fact that there are gaps in the upper- and lower-case sequences is not a major disadvantage because character manipulations can still be done as for ASCII, but using different offsets.

2.5.3 *THE UNICODE CHARACTER SET*

The ASCII and EBCDIC codes support the historically dominant (Latin) character sets used in computers. There are many more character sets in the world, and a simple ASCII-to-language-X mapping does not work for the general case, and so a new universal character standard was developed that supports a great breadth of the world's character sets, called **Unicode**.

Unicode is an evolving standard. It changes as new character sets are introduced into it, and as existing character sets evolve and their representations are refined. In version 2.0 of the Unicode standard, there are 38,885 distinct coded characters that cover the principal written languages of the Americas, Europe, the Middle East, Africa, India, Asia, and Pacifica.

The Unicode Standard uses a 16-bit code set in which there is a one-to-one correspondence between 16-bit codes and characters. Like ASCII, there are no complex modes or escape codes. While Unicode supports many more characters than ASCII or EBCDIC, it is not the end-all standard. In fact, the 16-bit Unicode standard is a subset of the 32-bit ISO 10646 Universal Character Set (UCS-4).

Glyphs for the first 256 Unicode characters are shown in Figure 2-15, according to Unicode version 2.1. Note that the first 128 characters are the same as for ASCII.

00	NUL	20	DS	40	SP	60	–	80		A0		C0	{	E0	\
01	SOH	21	SOS	41		61	/	81	a	A1	~	C1	A	E1	
02	STX	22	FS	42		62		82	b	A2	s	C2	B	E2	S
03	ETX	23		43		63		83	c	A3	t	C3	C	E3	T
04	PF	24	BYP	44		64		84	d	A4	u	C4	D	E4	U
05	HT	25	LF	45		65		85	e	A5	v	C5	E	E5	V
06	LC	26	ETB	46		66		86	f	A6	w	C6	F	E6	W
07	DEL	27	ESC	47		67		87	g	A7	x	C7	G	E7	X
08		28		48		68		88	h	A8	y	C8	H	E8	Y
09		29		49		69		89	i	A9	z	C9	I	E9	Z
0A	SMM	2A	SM	4A	¢	6A	‘	8A		AA		CA		EA	
0B	VT	2B	CU2	4B		6B	,	8B		AB		CB		EB	
0C	FF	2C		4C	<	6C	%	8C		AC		CC		EC	
0D	CR	2D	ENQ	4D	(	6D	_	8D		AD		CD		ED	
0E	SO	2E	ACK	4E	+	6E	>	8E		AE		CE		EE	
0F	SI	2F	BEL	4F	|	6F	?	8F		AF		CF		EF	
10	DLE	30		50	&	70		90		B0		D0	}	F0	0
11	DC1	31		51		71		91	j	B1		D1	J	F1	1
12	DC2	32	SYN	52		72		92	k	B2		D2	K	F2	2
13	TM	33		53		73		93	l	B3		D3	L	F3	3
14	RES	34	PN	54		74		94	m	B4		D4	M	F4	4
15	NL	35	RS	55		75		95	n	B5		D5	N	F5	5
16	BS	36	UC	56		76		96	o	B6		D6	O	F6	6
17	IL	37	EOT	57		77		97	p	B7		D7	P	F7	7
18	CAN	38		58		78		98	q	B8		D8	Q	F8	8
19	EM	39		59		79		99	r	B9		D9	R	F9	9
1A	CC	3A		5A	!	7A	:	9A		BA		DA		FA	|
1B	CU1	3B	CU3	5B	$	7B	#	9B		BB		DB		FB	
1C	IFS	3C	DC4	5C	·	7C	@	9C		BC		DC		FC	
1D	IGS	3D	NAK	5D	)	7D	'	9D		BD		DD		FD	
1E	IRS	3E		5E	;	7E	=	9E		BE		DE		FE	
1F	IUS	3F	SUB	5F	¬	7F	"	9F		BF		DF		FF	

STX	Start of text	RS	Reader Stop	DC1	Device Control 1	BEL	Bell
DLE	Data Link Escape	PF	Punch Off	DC2	Device Control 2	SP	Space
BS	Backspace	DS	Digit Select	DC4	Device Control 4	IL	Idle
ACK	Acknowledge	PN	Punch On	CU1	Customer Use 1	NUL	Null
SOH	Start of Heading	SM	Set Mode	CU2	Customer Use 2		
ENQ	Enquiry	LC	Lower Case	CU3	Customer Use 3		
ESC	Escape	CC	Cursor Control	SYN	Synchronous Idle		
BYP	Bypass	CR	Carriage Return	IFS	Interchange File Separator		
CAN	Cancel	EM	End of Medium	EOT	End of Transmission		
RES	Restore	FF	Form Feed	ETB	End of Transmission Block		
SI	Shift In	TM	Tape Mark	NAK	Negative Acknowledge		
SO	Shift Out	UC	Upper Case	SMM	Start of Manual Message		
DEL	Delete	FS	Field Separator	SOS	Start of Significance		
SUB	Substitute	HT	Horizontal Tab	IGS	Interchange Group Separator		
NL	New Line	VT	Vertical Tab	IRS	Interchange Record Separator		
LF	Line Feed	UC	Upper Case	IUS	Interchange Unit Separator		

Figure 2-14 The EBCDIC character code, shown with hexadecimal indices.

0000	NUL	0020	SP	0040	@	0060	`	0080	Ctrl	00A0	NBS	00C0	À	00E0	à
0001	SOH	0021	!	0041	A	0061	a	0081	Ctrl	00A1	¡	00C1	Á	00E1	á
0002	STX	0022	"	0042	B	0062	b	0082	Ctrl	00A2	¢	00C2	Â	00E2	â
0003	ETX	0023	#	0043	C	0063	c	0083	Ctrl	00A3	£	00C3	Ã	00E3	ã
0004	EOT	0024	$	0044	D	0064	d	0084	Ctrl	00A4	¤	00C4	Ä	00E4	ä
0005	ENQ	0025	%	0045	E	0065	e	0085	Ctrl	00A5	¥	00C5	Å	00E5	å
0006	ACK	0026	&	0046	F	0066	f	0086	Ctrl	00A6	¦	00C6	Æ	00E6	æ
0007	BEL	0027	'	0047	G	0067	g	0087	Ctrl	00A7	§	00C7	Ç	00E7	ç
0008	BS	0028	(	0048	H	0068	h	0088	Ctrl	00A8	¨	00C8	È	00E8	è
0009	HT	0029	)	0049	I	0069	i	0089	Ctrl	00A9	©	00C9	É	00E9	é
000A	LF	002A	*	004A	J	006A	j	008A	Ctrl	00AA	ª	00CA	Ê	00EA	ê
000B	VT	002B	+	004B	K	006B	k	008B	Ctrl	00AB	«	00CB	Ë	00EB	ë
000C	FF	002C	´	004C	L	006C	l	008C	Ctrl	00AC	¬	00CC	Ì	00EC	ì
000D	CR	002D	-	004D	M	006D	m	008D	Ctrl	00AD	–	00CD	Í	00ED	í
000E	SO	002E	.	004E	N	006E	n	008E	Ctrl	00AE	®	00CE	Î	00EE	î
000F	SI	002F	/	004F	O	006F	o	008F	Ctrl	00AF	¯	00CF	Ï	00EF	ï
0010	DLE	0030	0	0050	P	0070	p	0090	Ctrl	00B0	°	00D0	Ð	00F0	ð
0011	DC1	0031	1	0051	Q	0071	q	0091	Ctrl	00B1	±	00D1	Ñ	00F1	ñ
0012	DC2	0032	2	0052	R	0072	r	0092	Ctrl	00B2	²	00D2	Ò	00F2	ò
0013	DC3	0033	3	0053	S	0073	s	0093	Ctrl	00B3	³	00D3	Ó	00F3	ó
0014	DC4	0034	4	0054	T	0074	t	0094	Ctrl	00B4	´	00D4	Ô	00F4	ô
0015	NAK	0035	5	0055	U	0075	u	0095	Ctrl	00B5	µ	00D5	Õ	00F5	õ
0016	SYN	0036	6	0056	V	0076	v	0096	Ctrl	00B6	¶	00D6	Ö	00F6	ö
0017	ETB	0037	7	0057	W	0077	w	0097	Ctrl	00B7	·	00D7	×	00F7	÷
0018	CAN	0038	8	0058	X	0078	x	0098	Ctrl	00B8	¸	00D8	Ø	00F8	ø
0019	EM	0039	9	0059	Y	0079	y	0099	Ctrl	00B9	¹	00D9	Ù	00F9	ù
001A	SUB	003A	:	005A	Z	007A	z	009A	Ctrl	00BA	º	00DA	Ú	00FA	ú
001B	ESC	003B	;	005B	[	007B	{	009B	Ctrl	00BB	»	00DB	Û	00FB	û
001C	FS	003C	<	005C	\	007C	|	009C	Ctrl	00BC	1/4	00DC	Ü	00FC	ü
001D	GS	003D	=	005D	]	007D	}	009D	Ctrl	00BD	1/2	00DD	Ý	00FD	Þ
001E	RS	003E	>	005E	^	007E	~	009E	Ctrl	00BE	3/4	00DE	ý	00FE	þ
001F	US	003F	?	005F	_	007F	DEL	009F	Ctrl	00BF	¿	00DF	§	00FF	ÿ

NUL	Null	SOH	Start of heading	CAN	Cancel	SP	Space
STX	Start of text	EOT	End of transmission	EM	End of medium	DEL	Delete
ETX	End of text	DC1	Device control 1	SUB	Substitute	Ctrl	Control
ENQ	Enquiry	DC2	Device control 2	ESC	Escape	FF	Form feed
ACK	Acknowledge	DC3	Device control 3	FS	File separator	CR	Carriage return
BEL	Bell	DC4	Device control 4	GS	Group separator	SO	Shift out
BS	Backspace	NAK	Negative acknowledge	RS	Record separator	SI	Shift in
HT	Horizontal tab	NBS	Non-breaking space	US	Unit separator	DLE	Data link escape
LF	Line feed	ETB	End of transmission block	SYN	Synchronous idle	VT	Vertical tab

Figure 2-15 The first 256 glyphs in Unicode, shown with hexadecimal indices.

SUMMARY

All data in a computer is represented in terms of bits, which can be organized and interpreted as integers, fixed point numbers, floating point numbers, or characters. Character codes, such as ASCII, EBCDIC, and Unicode, have finite sizes and can thus be completely represented in a finite number of bits. The number of bits used for representing numbers is also finite, and as a result only a subset of the real numbers can be represented. This leads to the notions of range, precision, and error. The range for a number representation defines the largest and smallest magnitudes that can be represented and is almost entirely determined by the base and the number of bits in the exponent for a floating point representation. The precision is determined by the number of bits used in representing the magnitude (excluding the exponent bits in a floating point representation). Error arises in floating point representations because there are real numbers that fall within the gaps between adjacent representable numbers.

Further Reading

(Knuth 1981) provides a thorough treatment of computer arithmetic and algorithms. (Hamacher et al., 1990) provides a good explanation of biased error in floating point representations. The IEEE 754 floating point standard is described in (IEEE, 1985). The analysis of range, error, and precision in Section 2.3 was influenced by (Forsythe, 1970). The GAO report (U.S. GAO report GAO/IMTEC-92-26) gives a very readable account of the software problem that led to the Patriot failure in Dhahran. See http://www.unicode.org for information on the Unicode standard.

Forsythe, G. E., "*Pitfalls in Computation, or Why a Math Book Isn't Enough,*" The American Mathematical Monthly, **77**, no. 9, pp. 931-956 (Nov. 1970).

Hamacher, V. C., Z. G. Vranesic, and S. G. Zaky, *Computer Organization*, 3/e, McGraw Hill (1990).

IEEE, "*IEEE Standard for Binary Floating Point Arithmetic*," ANSI/IEEE Standard 754-1985. An early version also appears in IEEE COMPUTER, **14**, pp. 51-62 (Mar. 1981).

Knuth, D. E. *The Art of Computer Programming, vol 2, Semi-numerical algorithms*, 2/e, Addison-Wesley-Longman (1981).

U.S. General Accounting Office report GAO/IMTEC-92-26, "*Patriot Missile Defense: Software Problem Led to System Failure at Dhahran, Saudi Arabia,*", U.S. General Accounting Office, P.O. Box 6015, Gaithersburg, Maryland, 20877 (Feb. 1992).

PROBLEMS

2.1 Given a signed, fixed point representation in base 10, with three digits to the left and right of the decimal point,

(a) What is the range? (Calculate the highest positive number and the lowest negative number.)

(b) What is the precision? (Calculate the difference between two adjacent numbers on a number line. Remember that the error is 1/2 the precision.)

2.2 Convert the following numbers as indicated, using as few digits in the results as necessary.

(a) $(47)_{10}$ to unsigned binary

(b) $(-27)_{10}$ to binary signed magnitude

(c) $(213)_{16}$ to base 10

(d) $(10110.101)_2$ to base 10

(e) $(34.625)_{10}$ to base 4

2.3 Convert the following numbers as indicated, using as few digits in the results as necessary.

(a) $(011011)_2$ to base 10

(b) $(-27)_{10}$ to excess 32 in binary

(c) $(011011)_2$ to base 16

(d) $(55.875)_{10}$ to unsigned binary

(e) $(132.2)_4$ to base 16

2.4 Convert $.201_3$ to decimal.

2.5 Convert $(43.3)_7$ to base 8 using no more than one octal digit to the right of the radix point. Truncate any remainder by chopping excess digits. Use an ordinary unsigned octal representation.

2.6 Represent $(17.5)_{10}$ in base 3, then convert the result back to base 10. Use two digits of precision to the right of the radix point for the intermediate base 3 form.

2.7 Find the decimal equivalent of the four-bit two's complement number: 1000.

2.8 Find the decimal equivalent of the four-bit one's complement number: 1111.

2.9 Show the representation for $(305)_{10}$ using three BCD digits.

2.10 Show the ten's complement representation for $(-305)_{10}$ using three BCD digits.

2.11 For a given number of bits, are there more representable integers in one's complement two's complement, or are they the same?

2.12 Complete the following table for the 5-bit representations (including the sign bits) indicated. Show your answers as signed base 10 integers.

	5-bit signed magnitude	5-bit excess 16
Largest number		
Most negative number		
No. of distinct numbers		

2.13 Complete the following table using base 2 scientific notation and an eight-bit floating point representation in which there is a three-bit exponent in excess 3 notation (not excess 4) and a four-bit normalized fraction with a hidden 1. In this representation, the hidden 1 is to the left of the radix point. This means that the number 1.0101 is in normalized form, whereas .101 is not.

Base 2 scientific notation	Floating point representation Sign	Exponent	Fraction
-1.0101×2^{-2}			
$+1.1 \times 2^{2}$			
	0	001	0000
	1	110	1111

2.14 The IBM short floating point representation uses base 16, one sign bit, a seven-bit excess 64 exponent, and a normalized 24-bit fraction.

(a) What number is represented by the following bit pattern?

1 0111111 01110000 00000000 00000000

Show your answer in decimal. Note: The spaces are included in the number for readability only.

(b) Represent $(14.3)_6$ in this notation

2.15 For a normalized floating point representation, keeping everything else the same but

(a) decreasing the base will increase/decrease/not change the number of representable numbers.

(b) increasing the number of significant digits will increase/decrease/not change the smallest representable positive number.

(c) increasing the number of bits in the exponent will increase/decrease/not change the range.

(d) changing the representation of the exponent from excess 64 to two's complement will increase/decrease/not change the range.

2.16 For parts (a) through (e), use a floating point representation with a sign bit in the leftmost position, followed by a two-bit two's complement exponent, followed by a normalized three-bit fraction in base 2. Zero is represented by the bit pattern 0 0 0 0 0 0. There is no hidden 1.

(a) What decimal number is represented by the bit pattern 1 0 0 1 0 0?

(b) Keeping everything else the same but changing the base to 4 will increase/decrease/not change the smallest representable positive number.

(c) What is the smallest gap between successive numbers?

(d) What is the largest gap between successive numbers?

(e) There are a total of six bits in this floating point representation, and there are $2^6 = 64$ unique bit patterns. How many of these bit patterns are valid?

2.17 Represent $(107.15)_{10}$ in a floating point representation with a sign bit, a seven-bit excess 64 exponent, and a normalized 24-bit fraction in base 2. There is no hidden 1. Truncate the fraction by chopping bits as necessary.

2.18 For the following single-precision IEEE 754 bit patterns show the numerical value as a base 2 significand with an exponent (e g. 1.11×2^5).

(a) 0 10000011 01100000000000000000000

(b) 1 10000000 00000000000000000000000

(c) 1 00000000 00000000000000000000000

(d) 1 11111111 00000000000000000000000

(e) 0 11111111 11010000000000000000000

(f) 0 00000001 10010000000000000000000

(g) 0 00000011 01101000000000000000000

2.19 Show the IEEE 754 bit patterns for the following numbers:

(a) $+1.1011 \times 2^5$ (single precision)

(b) +0 (single precision)

(c) -1.00111×2^{-1} (double precision)

(d) –NaN (single precision)

2.20 Using the IEEE 754 single-precision format, show the value (not the bit pattern) of:

(a) The largest positive representable number (note: ∞ is not a number)

(b) The smallest positive nonzero number that is normalized

(c) The smallest positive nonzero number in denormalized format

(d) The smallest normalized gap

(e) The largest normalized gap

(f) The number of normalized representable numbers (including 0; note that ∞ and NaN are not numbers)

2.21 Two programmers write random number generators for normalized floating point numbers using the same method. Programmer A's generator creates random numbers on the closed interval from 0 to 1/2, and programmer B's generator creates random numbers on the closed interval from 1/2 to 1. Programmer B's generator works correctly, but Programmer A's generator produces a skewed distribution of numbers. What could be the problem with Programmer A's approach?

2.22 A hidden 1 representation will not work for base 16. Why not?

2.23 With a hidden 1 representation, can 0 be represented if all possible bit patterns in the exponent and fraction fields are used for nonzero numbers?

2.24 Given a base 10 floating point number (e g. $.583 \times 10^3$), can the number be converted into the equivalent base 2 form: $.x \times 2^y$ by separately converting the fraction (.583) and the exponent (3) into base 2?

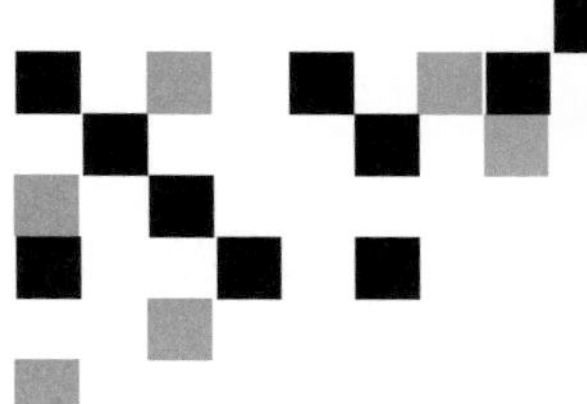

3

ARITHMETIC

3.1 Overview

In the previous chapter, we explored a few ways that numbers can be represented in a digital computer, but we only briefly touched upon arithmetic operations that can be performed on those numbers. In this chapter, we cover four basic arithmetic operations: addition, subtraction, multiplication, and division. We begin by describing how these four operations can be performed on fixed point numbers, and continue with a description of how these four operations can be performed on floating point numbers.

Some of the largest problems, such as weather calculations, quantum mechanical simulations, and land-use modeling, tax the abilities of even today's largest computers. Thus the topic of high-performance arithmetic is also important. We conclude the chapter with an introduction to some of the algorithms and techniques used in speeding arithmetic operations.

3.2 Fixed Point Addition and Subtraction

The addition of binary numbers and the concept of overflow were briefly discussed in Chapter 2. Here, we cover addition and subtraction of both signed and unsigned fixed point numbers in detail. Since the two's complement representation of integers is almost universal in today's computers, we will focus primarily on two's complement operations. We will briefly cover operations on 1's complement and BCD numbers, which have a foundational significance for other areas of computing, such as networking (for one's complement addition) and hand-held calculators (for BCD arithmetic.)

3.2.1 *TWO'S COMPLEMENT ADDITION AND SUBTRACTION*

In this section, we look at the addition of signed two's complement numbers. As we explore the *addition* of signed numbers, we also implicitly cover *subtraction* as well, as a result of the arithmetic principle:

$$a - b = a + (-b)$$

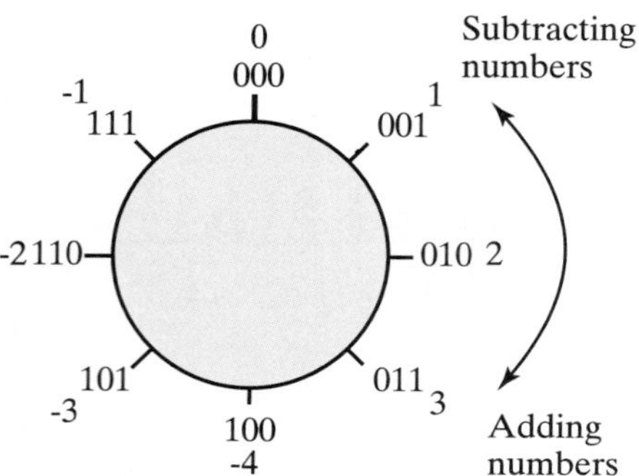

Figure 3-1 Number circle for 3-bit two's complement numbers.

We can negate a number by complementing it (and adding 1, for two's complement), and so we can perform subtraction by complementing and adding. This results in a savings of hardware because it avoids the need for a hardware subtractor. We will cover this topic in more detail later.

We will need to modify the interpretation that we place on the results of addition when we add two's complement numbers. To see why this is the case, consider Figure 3-1. With addition on the real number line, numbers can be as large or as small as desired—the number line goes to $\pm\infty$, so the real number line can accommodate numbers of any size. On the other hand, as discussed in Chapter 2, computers represent data using a finite number of bits and as a result can only store numbers within a certain range. For example, an examination of Table 2-1 shows that if we restrict the size of a number to, for example, 3 bits, there will only be eight possible two's complement values that the number can assume. In Figure 3-1 these values are arranged in a circle beginning with 000 and proceeding around the circle to 111 and then back to 000. The figure also shows the decimal equivalents of these same numbers.

Some experimentation with the number circle shows that numbers can be added or subtracted by traversing the number circle clockwise for addition and counterclockwise for subtraction. Numbers can also be subtracted by two's complementing the subtrahend and adding. Notice that overflow can only occur for addition when the operands ("addend" and "augend") are of the same sign. Furthermore, overflow occurs if a transition is made from +3 to −4 while proceeding around the number circle when adding, or from −4 to +3 while subtracting. (Two's complement overflow is discussed in more detail later in the chapter.)

Here are two examples of 8-bit two's complement addition, first using two positive numbers:

```
    0 0 0 0 1 0 1 0    (+10)10
+   0 0 0 1 0 1 1 1    (+23)10
    ---------------
    0 0 1 0 0 0 0 1    (+33)10
```

A positive and a negative number can be added in a similar manner:

```
                    0 0 0 0 0 1 0 1    (+5)10
                +   1 1 1 1 1 1 1 0    (−2)10
                    ---------------
Discard carry →(1)  0 0 0 0 0 0 1 1    (+3)10
```

The carry produced by addition at the highest (leftmost) bit position is discarded in two's complement addition. A similar situation arises with a carry out of the highest bit position when adding two negative numbers:

```
                    1 1 1 1 1 1 1 1    (−1)10
                +   1 1 1 1 1 1 0 0    (−4)10
                    ---------------
Discard carry →(1)  1 1 1 1 1 0 1 1    (−5)10
```

The carry out of the leftmost bit is discarded because the number system is **modular**—it "wraps around" from the largest positive number to the largest negative number as Figure 3-1 shows.

Although an addition operation may have a (discarded) carry-out from the MSB, this does not mean that the result is erroneous. The two preceding examples yield correct results in spite of the fact that there is a carry-out of the MSB. The next section discusses overflow in two's complement addition in more detail.

Overflow

When two numbers are added that have large magnitudes and the same sign, an **overflow** will occur if the result is too large to fit in the number of bits used in the representation. Consider adding $(+80)_{10}$ and $(+50)_{10}$ using an eight bit format. The result should be $(+130)_{10}$, however, as shown here, the result is $(-126)_{10}$:

$$
\begin{array}{rl}
0\,1\,0\,1\,0\,0\,0\,0 & (+80)_{10} \\
+\,0\,0\,1\,1\,0\,0\,1\,0 & (+50)_{10} \\
\hline
1\,0\,0\,0\,0\,0\,1\,0 & (-126)_{10}
\end{array}
$$

This should come as no surprise, since we know that the largest positive 8-bit two's complement number is $+(127)_{10}$, and it is therefore impossible to represent $(+130)_{10}$. Although the result 10000010_2 "looks" like 130_{10} if we think of it in unsigned form, the sign bit indicates a negative number in the signed form, which is clearly wrong.

In general, if two numbers of opposite signs are added, then an overflow cannot occur. Intuitively, this is because the magnitude of the result can be no larger than the magnitude of the larger operand. This leads us to the definition of two's complement overflow:

> *If the numbers being added are of the same sign and the result is of the opposite sign, then an overflow occurs and the result is incorrect. If the numbers being added are of opposite signs, then an overflow will never occur. As an alternative method of detecting overflow for addition, an overflow occurs if and only if the carry into the sign bit differs from the carry out of the sign bit.*
>
> *If a positive number is subtracted from a negative number and the result is positive, or if a negative number is subtracted from a positive number and the result is negative, then an overflow occurs. If the numbers being subtracted are of the same sign, then an overflow will never occur.*

3.2.2 *HARDWARE IMPLEMENTATION OF ADDERS AND SUBTRACTORS*

Up until now we have focused on algorithms for addition and subtraction. Now we will take a look at implementations of simple adders and subtractors.

Ripple-Carry Addition and Ripple-Borrow Subtraction

In Appendix A, a design of a four-bit ripple-carry adder is explored. The adder is modeled after the way that we normally perform decimal addition by hand, by summing digits in one column at a time while moving from right to left. In this

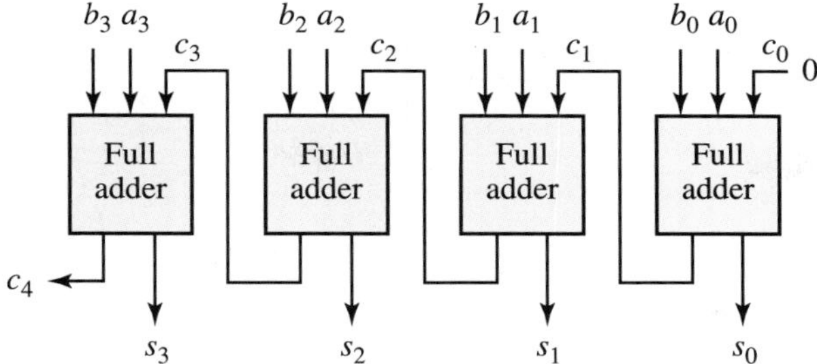

Figure 3-2 Ripple-carry adder.

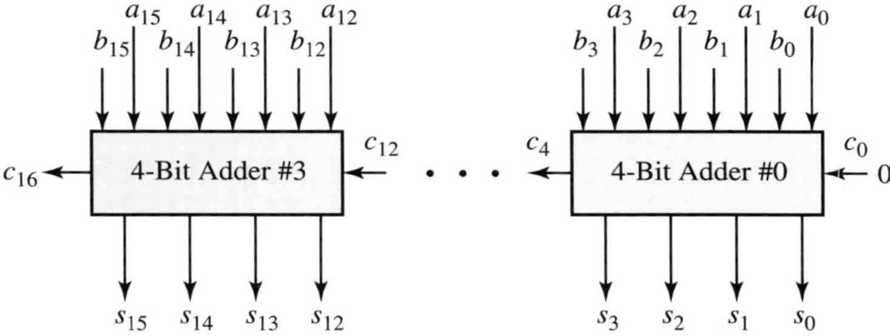

Figure 3-3 A 16-bit adder is made up of a cascade of four 4-bit ripple-carry adders.

section, we review the **ripple-carry adder** and then take a look at a **ripple-borrow subtractor**. We then combine the two into a single addition/subtraction unit.

Figure 3-2 shows a 4-bit ripple-carry adder that is developed in Appendix A. Two binary numbers A and B are added from right to left, creating a sum and a carry at the outputs of each full adder for each bit position.

Four 4-bit ripple-carry adders are cascaded in Figure 3-3 to add two 16-bit numbers. The rightmost full adder has a carry-in of 0. Although the rightmost full adder can be simplified as a result of the carry-in of 0, we will use the more general form and force c_0 to 0 in order to simplify subtraction later on.

Subtraction of binary numbers proceeds in a fashion analogous to addition. We can subtract one number from another by working in a single column at a time, subtracting digits of the **subtrahend** b_i, from the **minuend** a_i, as we move from right to left. As in decimal subtraction, if the subtrahend is larger than the minuend or there is a borrow from a previous digit, then a borrow must be propagated to the next most significant bit. Figure 3-4 shows the truth table and a "black-box" circuit for subtraction.

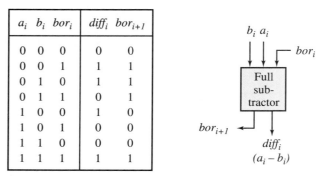

a_i	b_i	bor_i	$diff_i$	bor_{i+1}
0	0	0	0	0
0	0	1	1	1
0	1	0	1	1
0	1	1	0	1
1	0	0	1	0
1	0	1	0	0
1	1	0	0	0
1	1	1	1	1

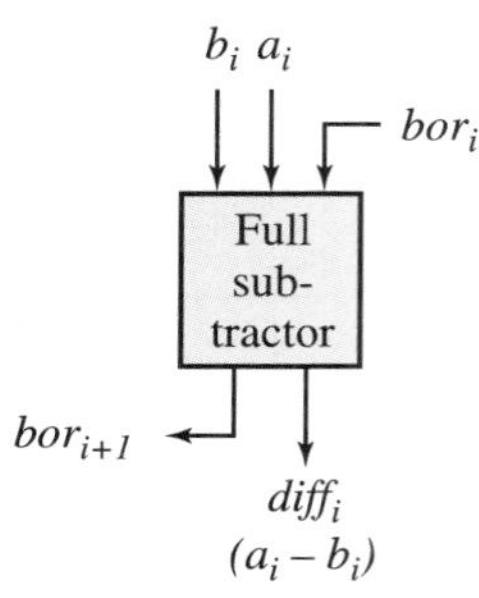

Figure 3-4 Truth table and schematic symbol for a ripple-borrow subtractor.

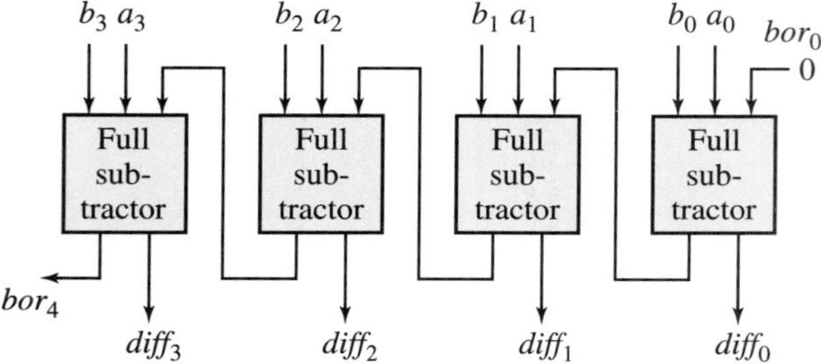

Figure 3-5 Ripple-borrow subtractor.

Full subtractors can be cascaded to form **ripple-borrow** subtractors in the same manner that full adders are cascaded to form ripple-carry adders. Figure 3-5 illustrates a four-bit ripple-borrow subtractor that is made up of four full subtractors.

As discussed previously, an alternative method of implementing subtraction is to form the two's complement negative of the subtrahend and *add* it to the minuend. The circuit that is shown in Figure 3-6 performs both addition and subtraction on four-bit two's complement numbers by allowing the b_i inputs to be complemented when subtraction is desired. An $\overline{\text{ADD}}$/SUBTRACT control line determines which function is performed. The bar over the ADD symbol indicates the ADD operation is active when the signal is low. That is, if the control line is 0, then the a_i and b_i inputs are passed through to the adder, and the sum is generated at the s_i outputs. If the control line is 1, then the a_i inputs are passed through to the adder, but the b_i inputs are one's complemented by the XOR gates before they are passed on to the adder. In order to form the two's complement negative, we must add 1 to the one's complement negative, which is

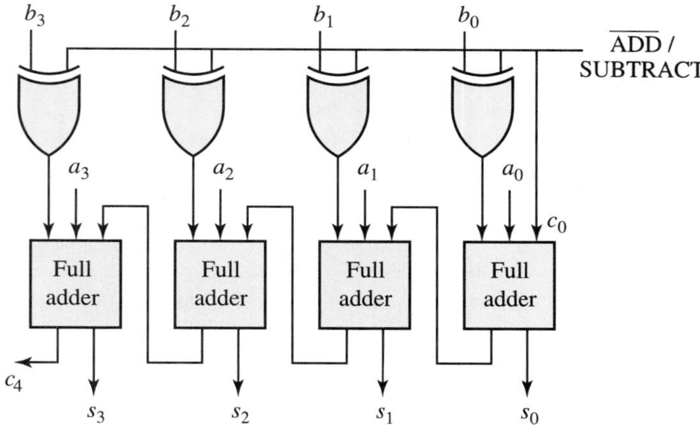

Figure 3-6 Addition / subtraction unit.

accomplished by setting the *carry_in* line (c_0) to 1 with the control input. In this way, we can share the adder hardware among both the adder and the subtractor.

3.2.3 *ONE'S COMPLEMENT ADDITION AND SUBTRACTION*

Although it is not heavily used in mainstream computing anymore, the one's complement representation was used in early computers. One's complement addition is handled somewhat differently from two's complement addition: the carry out of the leftmost position is not discarded but is added back into the least significant position of the integer portion, as shown in Figure 3-7. This is known as an **end-around carry**.

We can better visualize the reason that the end-around carry is needed by examining the 3-bit one's complement number circle in Figure 3-8. Notice that the number circle has two positions for 0. When we add two numbers, if we traverse through both −0 and +0, then we must compensate for the fact that 0 is visited twice. The end-around carry advances the result by one position for this situation.

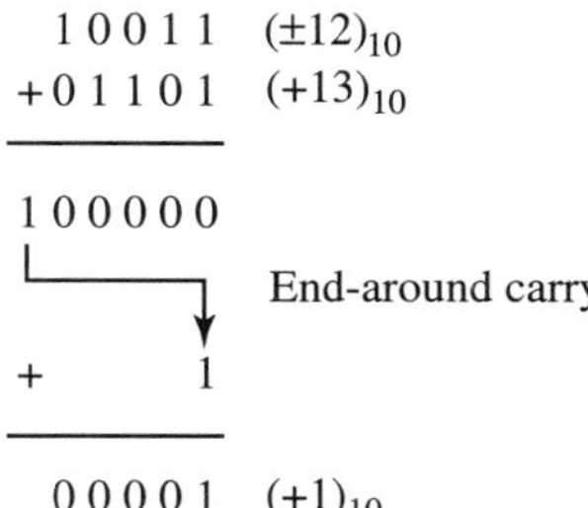

Figure 3-7 An example of one's complement addition with an end-around carry.

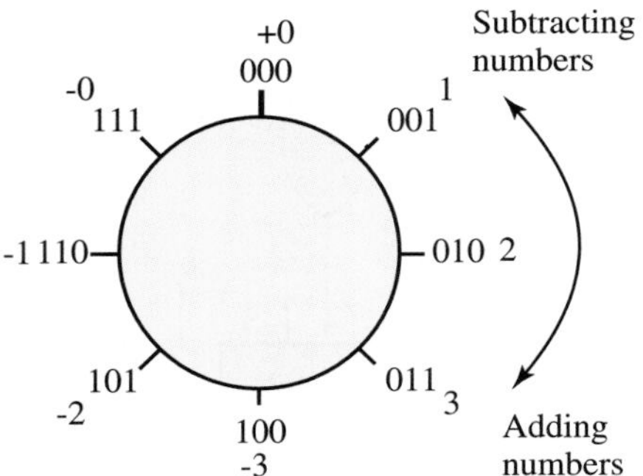

Figure 3-8 Number circle for a three-bit signed one's complement representation.

```
    0 1 0 1 . 1   (+5.5)10
+   1 1 1 0 . 0   (-1.0)10
  ---------------
  1 0 0 1 1 . 1
+ └──────→ 1 . 0
  ---------------
    0 1 0 0 . 1   (+4.5)10
```

Figure 3-9 The end-around carry complicates addition for non integers.

Notice that the distance between −0 and +0 on the number circle is the distance between two integers and is *not* the distance between two successive representable numbers. As an illustration of this point, consider adding $(5.5)_{10}$ and $(-1.0)_{10}$ in one's complement arithmetic, which is shown in Figure 3-9. (Note that we can also treat this as a subtraction problem, in which the subtrahend is negated by complementing all of the bits before adding it to the minuend.) In order to add $(+5.5)_{10}$ and $(-1.0)_{10}$ and obtain the correct result in one's complement, we add the end-around carry into the one's position as shown. This adds complexity to our number circle, because in the gap between +0 and −0, there are valid numbers that represent fractions that are less than 0, yet they appear on the number circle before −0 appears. If the number circle is reordered to avoid this anomaly, then addition must be handled in a more complex manner.

The need to look for two different representations for zero and the potential need to perform another addition for the end-around carry are two important reasons for preferring the two's complement arithmetic to one's complement arithmetic.

3.3 Fixed Point Multiplication and Division

Multiplication and division of fixed point numbers can be accomplished with addition, subtraction, and shift operations. The sections that follow describe methods for performing multiplication and division of fixed point numbers in both unsigned and signed forms using these basic operations. We will first cover unsigned multiplication and division, and then we will cover signed multiplication and division.

3.3.1 *UNSIGNED MULTIPLICATION*

Multiplication of unsigned binary integers is handled in a manner similar to the way it is carried out by hand for decimal numbers. Figure 3-10 illustrates the multiplication process for two unsigned binary integers. Each bit of the multiplier determines whether or not the multiplicand, shifted left according to the position of the multiplier bit, is added into the product. When two unsigned n-bit numbers are multiplied, the result can be as large as $2n$ bits. For the example shown in Figure 3-10, the multiplication of two four-bit operands results in an eight-bit product. When two signed n-bit numbers are multiplied, the result can be as large as only $2(n-1)+1 = (2n-1)$ bits, because this is equivalent to multiplying two $(n-1)$-bit unsigned numbers and then introducing the sign bit.

A hardware implementation of integer multiplication can take a similar form to the manual method. Figure 3-11 shows a layout of a multiplication unit for four-bit numbers, in which there is a four-bit adder, a control unit, three four-bit registers, and a one-bit carry register. In order to multiply two numbers, the multiplicand is placed in the M register, the multiplier is placed in the Q register, and the A and C registers are cleared to zero. During multiplication, the rightmost bit of the multiplier determines whether the multiplicand is added into the product at each step. After the multiplicand is added into the product, the multiplier and the A register are simultaneously shifted to the right. This has the effect of shifting the multiplicand to the left (as for the manual process) and exposing the next bit of the multiplier in position q_0.

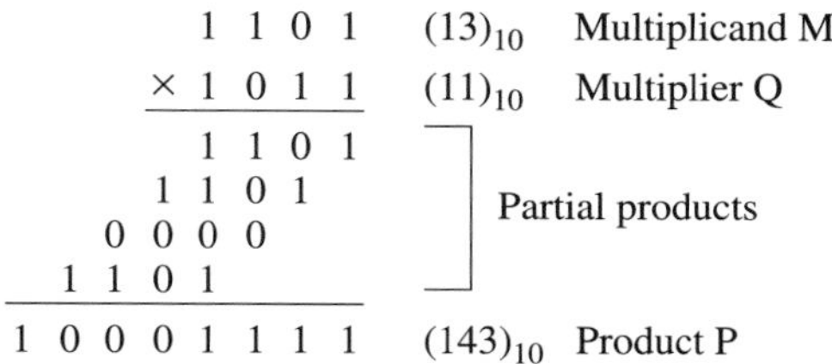

Figure 3-10 Multiplication of two unsigned binary integers.

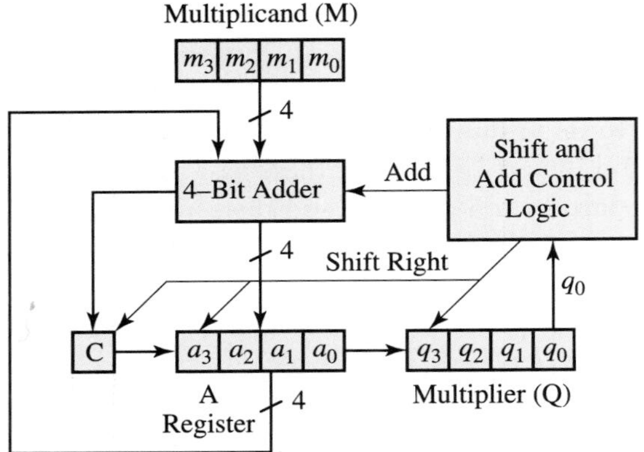

Figure 3-11 A serial multiplier.

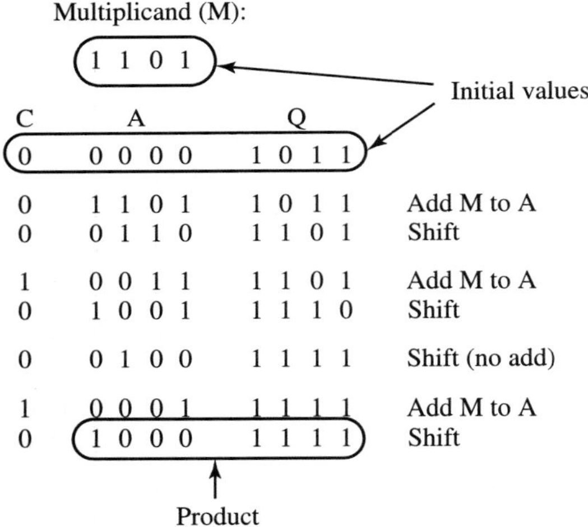

Figure 3-12 An example of multiplication using the serial multiplier.

Figure 3-12 illustrates the multiplication process. Initially, C and A are cleared, and M and Q hold the multiplicand and multiplier, respectively. The rightmost bit of Q is 1, and so the multiplier M is added into the product in the A register. The A and Q registers together make up the eight-bit product, but the A register is where the multiplicand is added. After M is added to A, the A and Q registers are shifted to the right. Since the A and Q registers are linked as a pair to form the eight-bit product, the rightmost bit of A is shifted into the leftmost bit of Q. The rightmost bit of Q is then dropped, C is shifted into the leftmost bit of A, and a 0 is shifted into C.

The process continues for as many steps as there are bits in the multiplier. On the second iteration, the rightmost bit of Q is again 1, and so the multiplicand is added to A and the C/A/Q combination is shifted to the right. On the third iteration, the rightmost bit of Q is 0 so M is not added to A, but the C/A/Q combination is still shifted to the right. Finally, on the fourth iteration, the rightmost bit of Q is again 1, and so M is added to A and the C/A/Q combination is shifted to the right. The product is now contained in the A and Q registers, in which A holds the high-order bits and Q holds the low-order bits.

3.3.2 *UNSIGNED DIVISION*

In longhand binary division, we must successively attempt to subtract the divisor from the dividend, using the fewest number of bits in the dividend as we can. Figure 3-13 illustrates this point by showing that $(11)_2$ does not "fit" in 0 or 01, but *does* fit in 011 as indicated by the pattern 001 that starts the quotient.

Computer-based division of binary integers can be handled in a manner similar to the way that binary integer multiplication is carried out, but with the complication that the only way to tell if the dividend does not "fit" is to do the subtraction and test if the remainder is negative. If the remainder is negative, then the subtraction must be "backed out" by adding the divisor back in, as described later.

In the division algorithm, instead of shifting the product to the right as we did for multiplication, we now shift the quotient to the left, and we subtract instead of adding. When two *n*-bit unsigned numbers are being divided, the result is no larger than *n* bits.

Figure 3-14 shows a layout of a division unit for four-bit numbers in which there is a five-bit adder, a control unit, a four-bit register for the dividend Q, and two five-bit registers for the divisor M and the remainder A. Five-bit registers are used for A and M, instead of 4-bit registers as we might expect, because an extra bit is needed to indicate the sign of the intermediate result. Although this division method is for unsigned numbers, subtraction is used in the process and negative partial results sometimes arise, which extends the range from −16 through +15, thus there is a need for 5 bits to store intermediate results.

```
      0 0 1 0  R1
1 1 ) 0 1 1 1
        1 1
        ---
          0 1
```

Figure 3-13 Example of base 2 division.

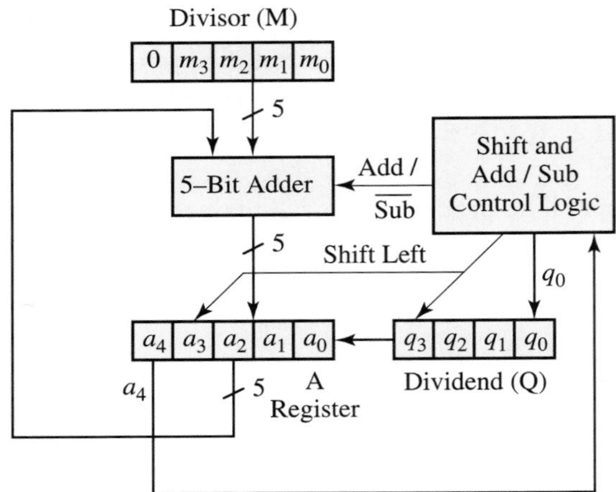

Figure 3-14 A serial divider.

In order to divide two four-bit numbers, the dividend is placed in the Q register, the divisor is placed in the M register, and the A register and the high order bit of M are cleared to zero. The leftmost bit of the A register determines whether the divisor is added back into the dividend at each step. This is necessary in order to restore the dividend when the result of subtracting the divisor is negative, as described previously. This is referred to as **restoring division**, because the dividend is restored to its former value when the remainder is negative. When the result is not negative, then the least significant bit of Q is set to 1, which indicates that the divisor "fits" in the dividend at that point.

Figure 3-15 illustrates the division process. Initially, A and the high order bit of M are cleared, and Q and the low order bits of M are loaded with the dividend and divisor, respectively. The A and Q registers are shifted to the left as a pair and the divisor M is subtracted from A. Since the result is negative, the divisor is added back to restore the dividend, and q_0 is cleared to 0. The process repeats by shifting A and Q to the left, and by subtracting M from A. Again, the result is negative, so the dividend is restored and q_0 is cleared to 0. On the third iteration, A and Q are shifted to the left and M is again subtracted from A, but now the result of the subtraction is not negative, so q_0 is set to 1. The process continues for one final iteration, in which A and Q are shifted to the left and M is subtracted from A, which produces a negative result. The dividend is restored and q_0 is cleared to 0. The quotient is now contained in the Q register and the remainder is contained in the A register.

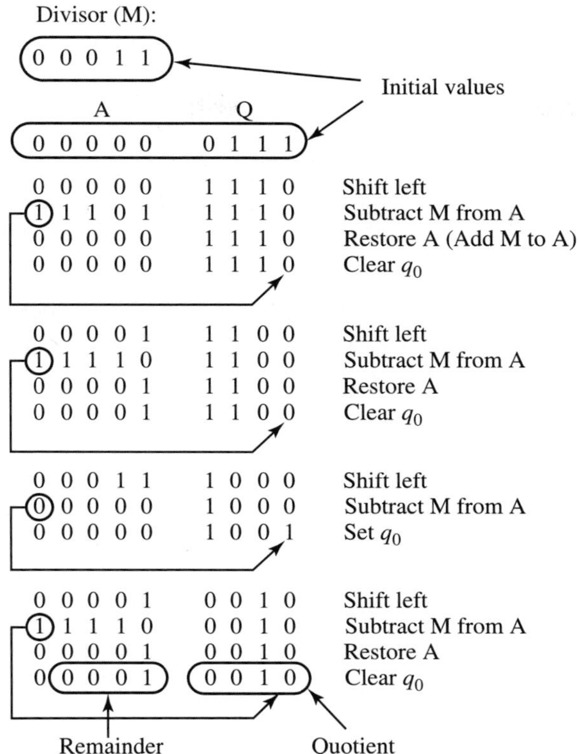

Figure 3-15 An example of division using the serial divider.

3.3.3 *SIGNED MULTIPLICATION AND DIVISION*

If we apply the multiplication and division methods described in the previous sections to signed integers, then we will run into some trouble. Consider multiplying −1 by +1 using four-bit words, as shown in the left side of Figure 3-16. The eight-bit

1 1 1 1	$(-1)_{10}$
× 0 0 0 1	$(+1)_{10}$
1 1 1 1	
0 0 0 0	
0 0 0 0	
0 0 0 0	
0 0 0 0 1 1 1 1	$(+15)_{10}$
(Incorrect; result should be −1)	

1 1 1 1 1 1 1 1	$(-1)_{10}$
× 0 0 0 1	$(+1)_{10}$
1 1 1 1 1 1 1 1	
0 0 0 0 0 0 0	
0 0 0 0 0 0	
0 0 0 0 0	
1 1 1 1 1 1 1 1	$(-1)_{10}$

Figure 3-16 Multiplication of signed integers.

equivalent of +15 is produced instead of −1. What went wrong is that the sign bit did not get extended to the left of the result. This is not a problem for a positive result because the high order bits default to 0, producing the correct sign bit 0.

A solution is shown in the right side of Figure 3-16, in which each partial product is extended to the width of the result, and only the rightmost eight bits of the result are retained. If both operands are negative, then the signs are extended for both operands, again retaining only the rightmost eight bits of the result.

Signed division is more difficult. We will not explore the methods here, but as a general technique, we can convert the operands into their positive forms, perform the division, and then convert the result into its true signed form as a final step.

3.4 Floating Point Arithmetic

Arithmetic operations on floating point numbers can be carried out using the fixed point arithmetic operations described in the previous sections, with attention given to maintaining aspects of the floating point representation. In the sections that follow, we explore floating point arithmetic in base 2 and base 10, keeping the requirements of the floating point representation in mind.

3.4.1 *FLOATING POINT ADDITION AND SUBTRACTION*

Floating point arithmetic differs from integer arithmetic in that exponents must be handled as well as the magnitudes of the operands. As in ordinary base 10 arithmetic using scientific notation, the exponents of the operands must be made equal for addition and subtraction. The fractions are then added or subtracted as appropriate, and the result is normalized.

This process of adjusting the fractional part and also rounding the result can lead to a loss of precision in the result. Consider the unsigned floating point addition $(.101 \times 2^3 + .111 \times 2^4)$ in which the fractions have three significant digits. We start by adjusting the *smaller* exponent to be equal to the *larger* exponent and adjusting the fraction accordingly. Thus we have $.101 \times 2^3 = .010 \times 2^4$, losing $.001 \times 2^3$ of precision in the process. The resulting sum is

$$(.010 + .111) \times 2^4 = 1.001 \times 2^4 = .1001 \times 2^5$$

and rounding to three significant digits, $.100 \times 2^5$, and we have lost another 0.001×2^4 in the rounding process.

Why do floating point numbers have such complicated formats?

We may wonder why floating point numbers have such a complicated structure, with the mantissa being stored in signed magnitude representation, the exponent stored in excess notation, and the sign bit separated from the rest of the magnitude by the intervening exponent field. There is a simple explanation for this structure. Consider the complexity of performing floating point arithmetic in a computer. Before any arithmetic can be done, the number must be unpacked from the form it takes in storage. (See Chapter 2 for a description of the IEEE 754 floating point format.) The exponent and mantissa must be extracted from the packed bit pattern before an arithmetic operation can be performed; after the arithmetic operation(s) are performed, the result must be renormalized and rounded, and then the bit patterns are repacked into the requisite format.

The virtue of a floating point format that contains a sign bit followed by an exponent in excess notation, followed by the magnitude of the mantissa, is that two floating point numbers can be compared for >, <, and = without unpacking. The sign bit is most important in such a comparison, and it appropriately is the MSB in the floating point format. Next most important in comparing two numbers is the exponent, since a change of ± 1 in the exponent changes the value by a factor of 2 (for a base 2 format), whereas a change in even the MSB of the fractional part will change the value of the floating point number by less than that.

In order to account for the sign bit, the signed magnitude fractions are represented as integers and are converted into two's complement form. After the addition or subtraction operation takes place in two's complement, there may be a need to normalize the result and adjust the sign bit. The result is then converted back to signed magnitude form.

3.4.2 *FLOATING POINT MULTIPLICATION AND DIVISION*

Floating point multiplication and division are performed in a manner similar to floating point addition and subtraction, except that the sign, exponent, and fraction of the result can be computed separately. If the operands have the same sign, then the sign of the result is positive. Unlike signs produce a negative result. The exponent of the result before normalization is obtained by adding the exponents of the source operands for multiplication, or by subtracting the divisor exponent from the dividend exponent for division. The fractions are multiplied or divided according to the operation, followed by normalization.

Consider using three-bit fractions in performing the base 2 computation: $(+.101 \times 2^2) \times (-.110 \times 2^{-3})$. The source operand signs differ, which means that the result will have a negative sign. We add exponents for multiplication, and so the exponent of the result is $2 + -3 = -1$. We multiply the fractions, which produces the product .01111. Normalizing the product and retaining only three bits in the fraction produces $-.111 \times 2^{-2}$.

Now consider using three-bit fractions in performing the base 2 computation: $(+.110 \times 2^5) / (+.100 \times 2^4)$. The source operand signs are the same, which means that the result will have a positive sign. We subtract exponents for division, and so the exponent of the result is $5 - 4 = 1$. We divide fractions, which can be done in a number of ways. If we treat the fractions as unsigned integers, then we will have 110/100 = 1 with a remainder of 10. What we really want is a contiguous set of bits representing the fraction instead of a separate result and remainder, and so we can scale the dividend to the left by two positions, producing the result: 11000/100 = 110. We then scale the result to the right by two positions to restore the original scale factor, producing 1.1. Putting it all together, the result of dividing $(+.110 \times 2^5)$ by $(+.100 \times 2^4)$ produces $(+1.10 \times 2^1)$. After normalization, the final result is $(+.110 \times 2^2)$.

3.5 High-Performance Arithmetic

For many applications, the speed of arithmetic operations is the bottleneck to performance. Most supercomputers, such as the Cray, the Tera, and the Intel Hypercube, are considered "super" because they excel at performing fixed and floating point arithmetic. In this section we discuss a number of ways to improve the speed of addition, subtraction, multiplication, and division.

3.5.1 *HIGH PERFORMANCE ADDITION*

The ripple-carry adder that we reviewed in Section 3.2.2 may introduce too much delay into a system. The longest path through the adder is from the inputs of the least significant full adder to the outputs of the most significant full adder. The process of summing the inputs at each bit position is relatively fast (a small two-level circuit suffices), but the carry propagation takes a long time to work its way through the circuit. In fact, the propagation time is proportional to the number of bits in the operands. This is unfortunate, since more significant figures in an addition translate to more time to perform the addition. In this section, we look at a method of speeding the carry propagation in what is known as a **carry-lookahead adder**.

In Appendix B, reduced Boolean expressions for the sum (s_i) and carry outputs (c_{i+1}) of a full adder are created. These expressions are repeated here, with subscripts added to denote the relative position of a full adder in a ripple-carry adder:

$$s_i = \overline{a_i}\overline{b_i}c_i + \overline{a_i}b_i\overline{c_i} + a_i\overline{b_i}\overline{c_i} + a_ib_ic_i$$

$$c_{i+1} = b_ic_i + a_ic_i + a_ib_i$$

We can factor the second equation and obtain

$$c_{i+1} = a_ib_i + (a_i + b_i)c_i$$

which can be rewritten as

$$c_{i+1} = G_i + P_ic_i$$

where $G_i = a_ib_i$ and $P_i = a_i + b_i$.

The G_i and P_i terms are referred to as **generate** and **propagate** functions, respectively, for the effect they have on the carry. When $G_i = 1$, a carry is generated at stage *i*. When $P_i = 1$, then a carry is propagated through stage *i* if either a_i or b_i is a 1. The G_i and P_i terms can be created in one level of logic since they only depend on an AND or an OR of the input variables, respectively.

The carries again take the most time. The carry c_1 out of stage 0 is $G_0 + P_0c_0$, and since $c_0 = 0$ for addition, we can rewrite this as $c_1 = G_0$. The carry c_2 out of stage 1 is $G_1 + P_1c_1$, and since $c_1 = G_0$, we can rewrite this as $c_2 = G_1 + P_1G_0$. The carry c_3 out of stage 2 is $G_2 + P_2c_2$, and since $c_2 = G_1 + P_1G_0$, we can rewrite this as: $c_3 = G_2 + P_2G_1 + P_2P_1G_0$. Continuing one more time for a four-bit adder, the carry out of stage 3 is $G_3 + P_3c_3$, and since $c_3 = G_2 + P_2G_1 + P_2P_1G_0$, we can rewrite this as: $c_4 = G_3 + P_3G_2 + P_3P_2G_1 + P_3P_2P_1G$.

We can now create a four-bit carry-lookahead adder as shown in Figure 3-17. We still have the delay through the full adders as before, but now the carry chain is broken into independent pieces that require one gate delay for G_i and P_i and two more gate delays to generate c_{i+1}. Thus, a depth of three gate delays is added, but the ripple-carry chain is removed. If we assume that each full adder introduces a gate delay of two, then a four-bit carry-lookahead adder will have a maximum gate delay of five, whereas a four-bit ripple-carry adder will have a

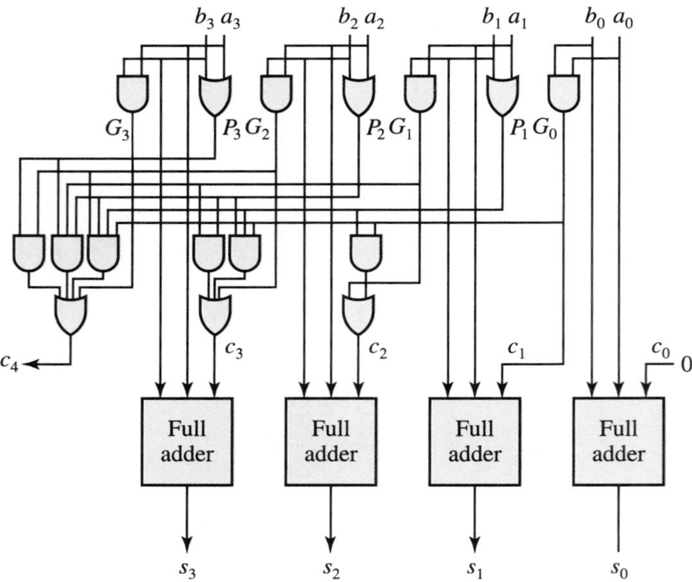

Figure 3-17 Carry-lookahead adder.

maximum gate delay of eight. The difference between the two approaches is more pronounced for wider operands. This process is limited to about eight bits of carry-lookahead, because of gate fan-in limitations discussed in Appendix A. For additions of numbers having more than eight bits, the carry-lookahead circuits can be cascaded to compute the carry in and carry out of each carry-lookahead unit. (See the Example on page 86.)

3.5.2 *HIGH PERFORMANCE MULTIPLICATION*

A number of methods exist for speeding the process of multiplication. Two methods are described in the following sections. The first approach gains performance by skipping over blocks of 1's, which eliminates addition steps. A parallel multiplier is described next, in which a cross product among all pairs of multiplier and multiplicand bits is formed. The result of the cross product is summed by rows to produce the final product.

The Booth Algorithm

The Booth algorithm treats positive and negative numbers uniformly. It operates on the fact that strings of 0's or 1's in the multiplier require no additions—just shifting. Additions or subtractions take place at the boundaries of the strings, where transitions

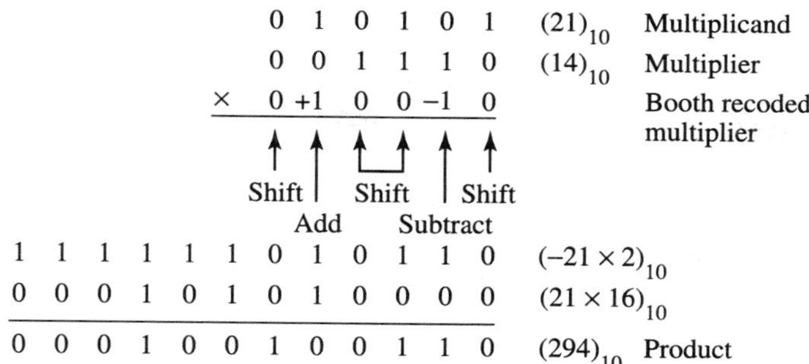

0 1 0 1 0 1 (21)10 Multiplicand
0 0 1 1 1 0 (14)10 Multiplier
× 0 +1 0 0 −1 0 Booth recoded multiplier
Shift Shift Shift
Add Subtract
1 1 1 1 1 1 0 1 0 1 1 0 (−21 × 2)10
0 0 0 1 0 1 0 1 0 0 0 0 (21 × 16)10
0 0 0 1 0 0 1 0 0 1 1 0 (294)10 Product

Figure 3-18 Multiplication of signed integers.

take place from 0 to 1 or from 1 to 0. A string of 1's in the multiplier from bit positions with weights 2^u to 2^v can be treated as $2^{u+1} - 2^v$. For example, if the multiplier is 001110 $(+14)_{10}$, then $u = 3$ and $v = 1$, so $2^4 - 2^1 = 14$.

In a hardware implementation, the multiplier is scanned from right to left. The first transition is observed going from 0 to 1, and so 2^1 is subtracted from the initial value (0). On the next transition, from 1 to 0, 2^4 is added, which results in +14. A 0 is considered to be appended to the right side of the multiplier in order to define the situation in which a 1 is in the rightmost digit of the multiplier.

If the multiplier is recoded according to the Booth algorithm, then fewer steps may be needed in the multiplication process. Consider the multiplication example shown in Figure 3-18. The multiplier $(14)_{10}$ contains three 1's, which means that three addition operations are required for the shift/add multiplication procedure that is described in Section 3.3.1. The Booth recoded multiplier is obtained by scanning the original multiplier from right to left, and placing $a - 1$ in the position where the first 1 in a string is encountered, and placing a +1 in the position where the next 0 is seen. The multiplier 001110 thus becomes 0 +1 0 0 −1 0. The Booth recoded multiplier contains just two nonzero digits: +1 and −1, which means that only one addition operation and one subtraction operation are needed, and so a savings is realized for this example.

A savings is not always realized, however, and in some cases the Booth algorithm may cause more operations to take place than if it is not used at all. Consider the example shown in Figure 3-19, in which the multiplier consists of alternating 1's and 0's. This is the same example shown in Figure 3-18 but with the multiplicand and multiplier swapped. Without Booth recoding of the multiplier, three

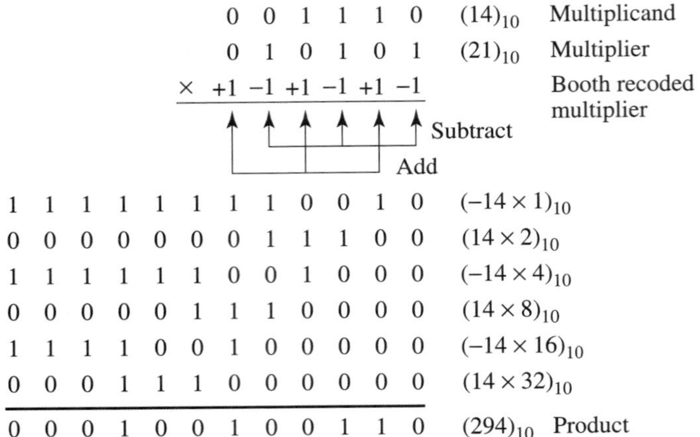

0 0 1 1 1 0 (14)10 Multiplicand
0 1 0 1 0 1 (21)10 Multiplier
× +1 −1 +1 −1 +1 −1 Booth recoded multiplier
Subtract
Add
1 1 1 1 1 1 1 1 0 0 1 0 (−14 × 1)10
0 0 0 0 0 0 0 1 1 1 0 0 (14 × 2)10
1 1 1 1 1 1 0 0 1 0 0 0 (−14 × 4)10
0 0 0 0 0 1 1 1 0 0 0 0 (14 × 8)10
1 1 1 1 0 0 1 0 0 0 0 0 (−14 × 16)10
0 0 0 1 1 1 0 0 0 0 0 0 (14 × 32)10
0 0 0 1 0 0 1 0 0 1 1 0 (294)10 Product

Figure 3-19 A worst case Booth recoded multiplication example.

addition operations are required for the three 1's in the multiplier. The Booth recoded multiplier, however, requires six addition and subtraction operations, which is clearly worse. We improve on this in the next section.

The Modified Booth Algorithm

One solution to this problem is to group the recoded multiplier bits in pairs, known as **bit pair recoding**, which is also known as the **modified Booth algorithm**. Grouping bit pairs from right to left produces three "+1,−1" pairs as shown in Figure 3-20. Since the +1 term is to the left of the −1 term, it has a weight that is twice as large as the weight for the −1 position. Thus, we might think of the pair as having the collective value +2 – 1 = +1.

						0	0	1	1	1	0	$(21)_{10}$	Multiplicand
						0	1	0	1	0	1	$(14)_{10}$	Multiplier
					×	+1	−1	+1	−1	+1	−1		Booth recoded multiplier
						+1		+1		+1			Bit pair recoded multiplier
0	0	0	0	0	0	0	0	1	1	1	0	$(14 \times 1)_{10}$	
0	0	0	0	0	0	1	1	1	0	0	0	$(14 \times 4)_{10}$	
0	0	0	0	1	1	1	0	0	0	0	0	(14×16)	
0	0	0	1	0	0	1	0	0	1	1	0	$(294)_{10}$	Product

Figure 3-20 Multiplication with bit pair recoding of the multiplier.

Booth pair $(i + 1, i)$			Recoded bit pair (i)	Corresponding multiplier bits $(i + 1, i, i - 1)$
0	0	=	0	000 or 111
0	+1	=	+1	001
0	−1	=	−1	110
+1	0	=	+2	011
+1	+1	=	—	
+1	−1	=	+1	010
−1	0	=	−2	100
−1	+1	=	−1	101
−1	−1	=	—	

Figure 3-21 Recoded bit pairs.

In a similar manner, the pair −1,+1 is equivalent to $-2 + 1 = -1$. The pairs +1,+1 and −1,−1 cannot occur. There are a total of seven pairs that can occur, which are shown in Figure 3-21. For each case, the value of the recoded bit pair is multiplied by the multiplicand and is added to the product. In an implementation of bit pair recoding, the Booth recoding and bit pair recoding steps are collapsed into a single step, by observing three multiplier bits at a time, as shown in the corresponding multiplier bit table.

The process of bit pair recoding of a multiplier guarantees that in the worst case, only $w/2$ additions (or subtractions) will take place for a w-bit multiplier.

Array Multipliers

The serial method we used for multiplying two unsigned integers in Section 3.2.1 requires only a small amount of hardware, but the time required to multiply two numbers of length w grows as w^2. We can speed the multiplication process so that it completes in just $2w$ steps by implementing the manual process shown in Figure 3-10 in parallel. The general idea is to form a one-bit product between each multiplier bit and each multiplicand bit, and then sum each row of partial product elements from the top to the bottom in **systolic** (row-by-row) fashion.

The structure of a systolic **array multiplier** is shown in Figure 3-22. A partial product (PP) element is shown at the bottom of the figure. A multiplicand bit (m_i) and a multiplier bit (q_i) are multiplied by the AND gate, which forms a partial product at position (i, j) in the array. This partial product is added with the

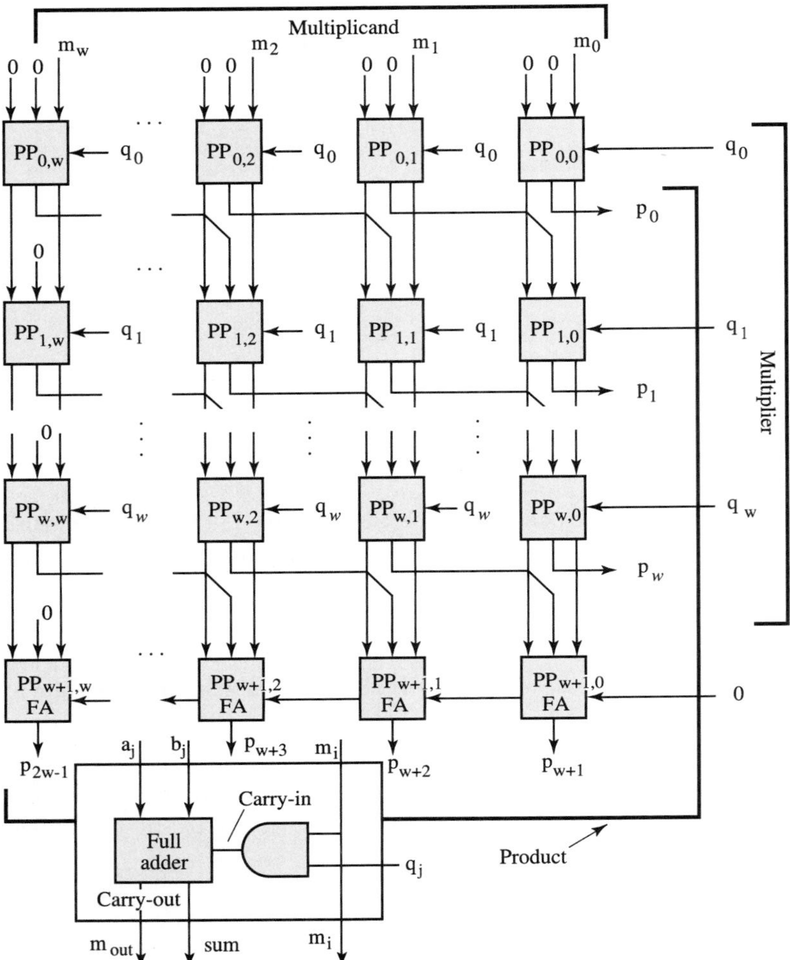

Figure 3-22 Parallel pipelined array multiplier.

partial product from the previous stage (b_j) and any carry that is generated in the previous stage (a_j). The result has a width of $2w$ and appears at the bottom of the array (the high-order w bits) and at the right of the array (the low-order w bits).

3.5.3 *HIGH-PERFORMANCE DIVISION*

We can extend the unsigned integer division technique of Section 3.3.2 to produce a fractional result in computing a/b. The general idea is to scale a and b to look like integers, perform the division process, and then scale the quotient to correspond to the actual result of dividing a by b.

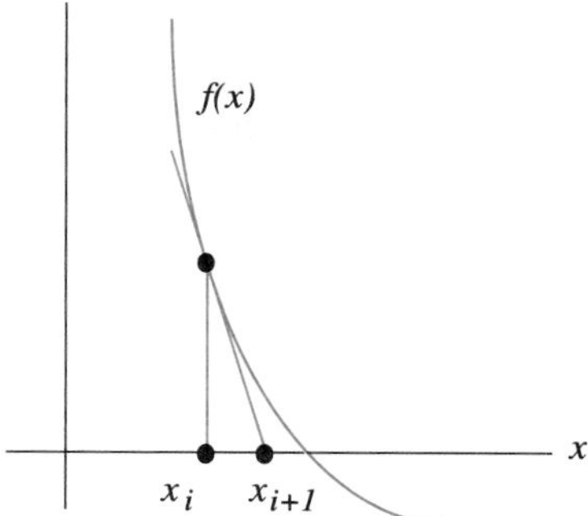

Figure 3-23 Newton's iteration for zero finding. (Adapted from [Goldberg, 1995]).

A faster method of division makes use of a lookup table and iteration. An iterative method of finding a root of a polynomial is called **Newton's iteration**, which is illustrated in Figure 3-23. The goal is to find where the function $f(x)$ crosses the x axis by starting with a guess x_i and then using the error between $f(x_i)$ and zero to refine the guess.

The tangent line at $f(x_i)$ can be represented by the equation

$$y - f(x_i) = f'(x_i)(x - x_i)$$

The tangent line crosses the x axis at

$$x_{i+1} = x_i - \frac{f(x_i)}{f'(x_i)}$$

The process repeats while $f(x_i)$ approaches zero.

The number of bits of precision doubles on each iteration (see [Goldberg, 1995]), and so if we are looking to obtain 32 bits of precision and we start with a single bit of precision, then five iterations are required to reach our target precision. The problem now is to cast division in the form of finding a zero for $f(x_i)$.

Consider the function $1/x - b$, which has a zero at $1/b$. If we start with b, then we can compute $1/b$ by iteratively applying Newton's method. Since $f'(x) = -1/x^2$, we now have

$$x_{i+1} = x_i - \frac{1/x_i - b}{-1/x_i^2} = x_i + x_i - x_i^2 b = x_i(2 - x_i b)$$

B = First three bits of b	Actual base 10 value of 1/B	Corresponding lookup table entry
.100	2	10
.101	1 3/5	01
.110	1 1/3	01
.111	1 1/7	01

Figure 3-24 A three-bit lookup table for computing x_0.

Thus, we only need to perform multiplication and subtraction in order to perform division. Further, if our initial guess for x_0 is good enough, then we may only need to perform the iteration a few times.

Before using this method on an example, we need to consider how we will obtain our initial guess. If we are working with normalized fractions, then it is relatively easy to make use of a lookup table for the first few digits. Consider computing 1/.101101 using a 16-bit normalized base 2 fraction in which the leading 1 is not hidden. The first three bits for any binary fraction will be one of the patterns: .100, .101, .110, or .111. These fractions correspond to the base 10 numbers 1/2, 5/8, 3/4, and 7/8, respectively. The reciprocals of these numbers are 2, 8/5, 4/3, and 8/7, respectively. We can store the binary equivalents in a lookup table, and then retrieve x_0 based on the first three bits of b.

The leading 1 in the fraction does not contribute to the precision, and so the leading three bits of the fraction only provide two bits of precision. Thus, the lookup table only needs two bits for each entry, as shown in Figure 3-24.

Now consider computing 1/.1011011 using this floating point representation. We start by finding x_0 using the table shown in Figure 3-24. The first three bits of the fraction b are 101, which corresponds to $x_0 = 01$. We compute $x_1 = x_0(2 - x_0 b)$ and obtain, in unsigned base 2 arithmetic $x_1 = 01(10 - (01)(.1011011)) = 1.0100101$. Our two bits of precision have now become four bits of precision. For this example, we will retain as much intermediate precision as we can. In general, we only need to retain at most $2p$ bits of intermediate precision for a p-bit result. We iterate again, obtaining eight bits of precision:

$$x_2 = x_1(2 - x_1 b) = 1.0100101(10 - (1.0100101)(.1011011))$$

$$= 1.011001011001001011101$$

We iterate again, obtaining our target 16 bits of precision:

$x_3 = x_2(2 - x_2 b) = (1.0110010110010010111101)(2 -$

$(1.0110010110010010111101)(.1011011)) = 1.011010000001001$

$= (1.40652466)_{10}.$

The precise value is $(1.40659341)_{10}$, but our 16-bit value is as close to the precise value as it can be.

3.5.4 *RESIDUE ARITHMETIC*

Addition, subtraction, and multiplication can all be performed in a single, carryless step using **residue arithmetic**. The residue number system is based on relatively prime integers called **moduli**. The residue of an integer with respect to a particular modulus is the least positive integer remainder of the division of the integer by the modulus. A set of possible moduli is 5, 7, 9, and 4. With these moduli, $5 \times 7 \times 9 \times 4 = 1260$ integers can be uniquely represented. A table showing the representation of the first twenty decimal integers using moduli 5, 7, 9, and 4 is shown in Figure 3-25.

Addition and multiplication in the residue number system result in valid residue numbers, provided the size of the chosen number space is large enough to contain the results. Subtraction requires each residue digit of the subtrahend to be complemented with respect to its modulus before performing addition. Addition

Decimal	Residue 5794	Decimal	Residue 5794
0	0000	10	0312
1	1111	11	1423
2	2222	12	2530
3	3333	13	3641
4	4440	14	4052
5	0551	15	0163
6	1662	16	1270
7	2073	17	2381
8	3180	18	3402
9	4201	19	4513

Figure 3-25 Representation of the first twenty decimal integers in the residue number system for the given moduli.

29 + 27 = 56	
Decimal	Residue 5794
29	4121
27	2603
56	1020

10 × 17 = 170	
Decimal	Residue 5794
10	0312
17	2381
170	0282

Figure 3-26 Examples of addition and multiplication in the residue number system.

and multiplication examples are shown in Figure 3-26. For these examples, the moduli used are 5, 7, 9, and 4. Addition is performed in parallel for each column, with no carry propagation. Multiplication is also performed in parallel for each column, independent of the other columns.

Although residue arithmetic operations can be very fast, there are a number of disadvantages to the system. Division and sign detection are difficult, and a representation for fractions is also difficult. Conversions between the residue number system and weighted number systems are complex and often require involved methods such as the **Chinese remainder theorem**. The conversion problem is important because the residue number system is not very useful without being translated to a weighted number system so that magnitude comparisons can be made. However, for integer applications in which the time spent in addition, subtraction, and multiplication outweighs the time spent in division, conversion, etc., the residue number system may be a practical approach. An important application area is matrix-vector multiplication, which is used extensively in signal processing.

EXAMPLE: WIDE WORD HIGH PERFORMANCE ADDER

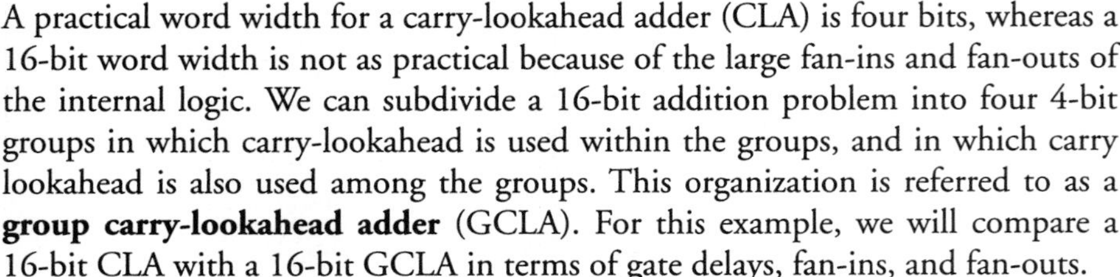

A practical word width for a carry-lookahead adder (CLA) is four bits, whereas a 16-bit word width is not as practical because of the large fan-ins and fan-outs of the internal logic. We can subdivide a 16-bit addition problem into four 4-bit groups in which carry-lookahead is used within the groups, and in which carry lookahead is also used among the groups. This organization is referred to as a **group carry-lookahead adder** (GCLA). For this example, we will compare a 16-bit CLA with a 16-bit GCLA in terms of gate delays, fan-ins, and fan-outs.

Figure 3-27 shows a 16-bit GCLA that is composed of four 4-bit CLAs, with some additional logic that generates the carries between the four-bit groups.

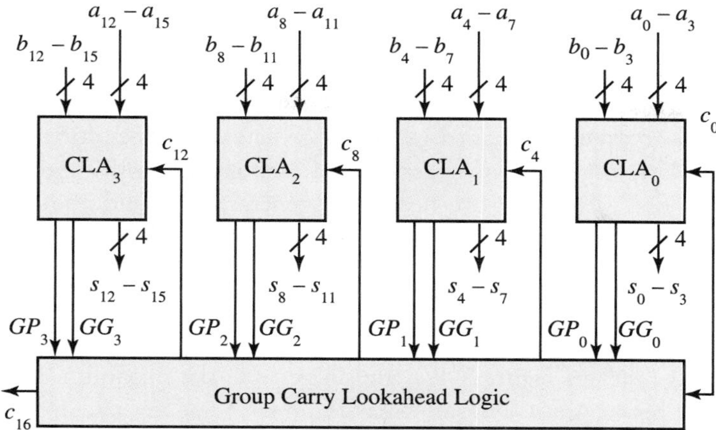

Figure 3-27 A 16-bit group carry-lookahead adder.

Each group behaves as an ordinary CLA, except that the least significant carry into each CLA is treated as a variable instead of as a 0, and **group generate** (*GG*) and **group propagate** (*GP*) signals are generated. A *GG* signal is generated when a carry is generated somewhere within a group and all of the more significant propagate signals are true. This means that a carry into a group will propagate all the way through the group. The corresponding equations for the least significant *GG* and *GP* signals in Figure 3-27 are as follows:

$$GG_0 = G_3 + P_3G_2 + P_3P_2G_1 + P_3P_2P_1G$$
$$GP_0 = P_3P_2P_1G_0$$

The remaining *GG* and *GP* signals are computed similarly.

The carry into each group, except for the carry into CLA_0, is computed from the *GG* and *GP* signals. For example, c_4 is true when GG_0 is true or when GP_0 and c_0 are both true. The corresponding equation is

$$c_4 = GG_0 + GP_0c_0$$

Higher-order carries out of each group are computed in a similar manner:

$$c_8 = GG_1 + GP_1c_4 = GG_1 + GP_1GG_0 + GP_0c_0$$
$$c_{12} = GG_2 + GP_2c_8 = GG_2 + GP_2GG_1 + GP_2GP_1GG_0 + GP_2GP_1GP_0c_0$$
$$c_{16} = GG_3 + GP_3c_{12} = GG_3 + GP_3GG_2 + GP_3GP_2GG_1 + GP_3GP_2GP_1GG_0 + GP_3GP_2GP_1GP_0c_0$$

In terms of gate delays, a 16-bit CLA has a longest path of five gate delays to produce the most significant sum bit, as discussed in Section 3.5.1. Each of the CLAs in the 16-bit GCLA also has at least five gate delays on the longest path. The GG and GP signals are generated in three gate delays, and the carry signals out of each group are generated in two more gate delays, resulting in a total of five gate delays to generate the carry out of each group. In the highest bit position (s_{15}), five gate delays are needed to generate c_{12}, and another five gate delays are needed to generate s_{15}, for a worst-case path of 10 gate delays through the 16-bit GCLA.

With regard to fan-in and fan-out, the maximum fan-in of any gate in a four-bit CLA is four (refer to Figure 3-17), and in general, the maximum fan-in of any gate in an n-bit CLA is n. Thus, the maximum fan-in of any gate in a 16-bit CLA is 16. In comparison, the maximum fan-in for a 16-bit GCLA is five (for generating c_{16}). The fan-outs for both cases are the same as the fan-ins.

In summary, the 16-bit CLA has only half of the depth of the 16-bit GCLA (five gate delays *versus* 10 gate delays). The highest fan-in for a 16-bit CLA is 16, which is more than three times the highest fan-in for a 16-bit GCLA (16 *versus* five). The highest fan-outs are the same as the highest fan-ins for each case. ■

3.6 Case Study: Calculator Arithmetic Using Binary Coded Decimal

Calculator arithmetic has traditionally been done in base 10, rather than in base 2. Calculators need to be small and inexpensive, and for that reason base 10 numbers are represented in binary coded decimal (BCD, see Chapter 2) using 4 bits per BCD digit, instead of using base 2, which would require a somewhat resource-intensive base conversion. A small 4-bit ALU can then do the computations in serial fashion, BCD digit by BCD digit.

3.6.1 *THE HP9100A CALCULATOR*

The popular HP9100A calculator, which came out in the late 1960s, performed the basic arithmetic functions: addition, subtraction, multiplication, and division, as well as square root, e^x, ln x, log x, trigonometric functions, and other functions, all using base 10 arithmetic. The HP9100A is actually a desktop calculator (see Figure 3-28), but was considered small for what it accomplished with the technology of the day. The HP9100 display shows 10 significant digits, but all calculations are performed to 12 significant digits, with the two last significant digits (which are known as **guard digits**) being used for truncation and round off

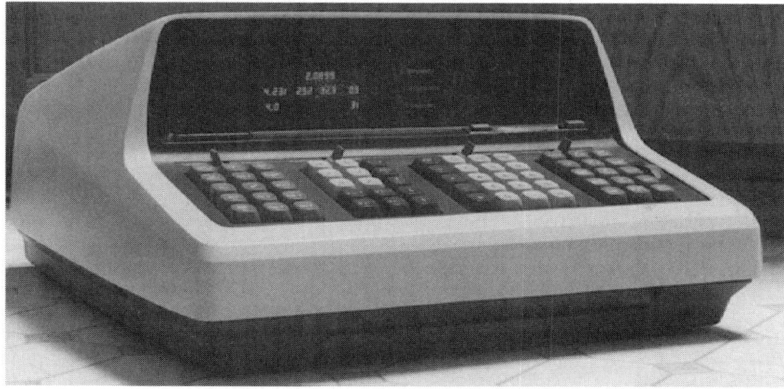

Figure 3-28 HP 9100 series desktop calculator. (Source: The Museum of HP Calculators, http://www.hpmuseum.org.)

errors. Although the HP9100A may seem like a relic today, the arithmetic methods are still relevant.

The next two sections describe general techniques for performing fixed point and floating point BCD addition and subtraction. Other calculator operations described in the remaining sections are performed in a similar manner, making use of the addition and subtraction operations.

3.6.2 *BINARY CODED DECIMAL ADDITION AND SUBTRACTION*

Consider adding $(+255)_{10}$ and $(+63)_{10}$ in BCD representation, as illustrated in Figure 3-29. Each base 10 digit occupies four bit positions, and addition is performed on a BCD digit by BCD digit basis (*not* bit by bit), from right to left, as

	0	1	0	0	← Carries
	0000	0010	0101	0101	$(+255)_{10}$
	$(0)_{10}$	$(2)_{10}$	$(5)_{10}$	$(5)_{10}$	
+	0000	0000	0110	0011	$(+63)_{10}$
	$(0)_{10}$	$(0)_{10}$	$(6)_{10}$	$(3)_{10}$	
	0000	0011	0001	1000	$(+318)_{10}$
	$(0)_{10}$	$(3)_{10}$	$(1)_{10}$	$(8)_{10}$	

Figure 3-29 An addition example using binary coded decimal.

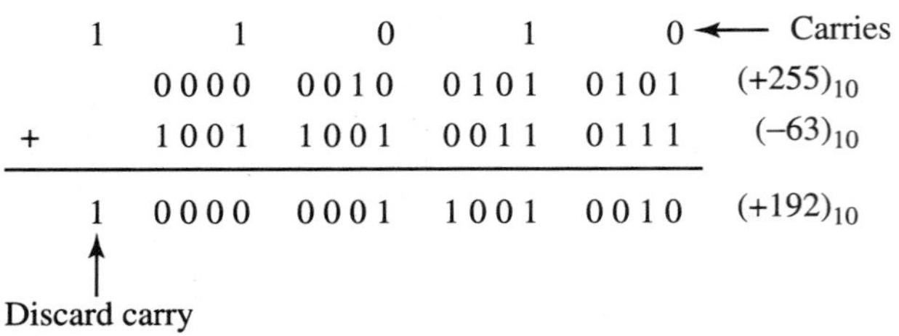

Figure 3-30 BCD addition in ten's complement.

we would normally carry it out by hand using a decimal representation. The result, $(+318)_{10}$, is produced in BCD form as shown.

Subtraction in BCD is handled in a manner similar to the way subtraction is handled in two's complement (adding the negative of the subtrahend) except that ten's complement is used instead of two's complement. Consider performing the subtraction operation $(255 - 63 = 192)_{10}$. We can cast this into the addition problem $(255 + (-63) = 192)_{10}$. We start by forming the nine's complement of 63:

$$\begin{array}{r} 9999 \\ -0063 \\ \hline 9936 \end{array}$$

We then add 1 in order to form the ten's complement:

$$\begin{array}{r} 9936 \\ +0001 \\ \hline 9937 \end{array}$$

The addition operation can now be performed, as shown in Figure 3-30. Notice that the carry-out of the highest digit position is discarded, as in two's complement addition.

Unlike the two's complement representation, we cannot simply look at the leftmost bit to determine the sign. In ten's complement, the number is positive if the leftmost digit is between 0 and 4, inclusive, and is negative otherwise. (The BCD bit patterns for 4 and 5 are 0100 and 0101, respectively, which both have a 0 in the leftmost bit, yet 4 indicates a positive number and 5 indicates a negative number.) If we use an excess 3 encoding for each digit, then the leftmost bit *will* indicate the sign. Figure 3-31 shows the encoding. Notice that six of the bit patterns cannot occur, and so they are marked as **don't cares**, 'd'.

BCD Bit Pattern	Normal BCD value	Excess 3 value	
0 0 0 0	0	d	
0 0 0 1	1	d	
0 0 1 0	2	d	
0 0 1 1	3	0	Positive numbers
0 1 0 0	4	1	Positive numbers
0 1 0 1	5	2	Positive numbers
0 1 1 0	6	3	Positive numbers
0 1 1 1	7	4	Positive numbers
1 0 0 0	8	5	Negative numbers
1 0 0 1	9	6	Negative numbers
1 0 1 0	d	7	Negative numbers
1 0 1 1	d	8	Negative numbers
1 1 0 0	d	9	Negative numbers
1 1 0 1	d	d	
1 1 1 0	d	d	
1 1 1 1	d	d	

Figure 3-31 Excess 3 encoding of BCD digits.

Now consider the design of a BCD full adder. The BCD full adder should sum two BCD digits and a carry-in, and should produce a sum BCD digit and a carry-out, all using excess 3. A design using two's complement full adders is shown in Figure 3-32. The excess 3 BCD digits are added in the upper four two's complement full adders (FAs). Since each operand is represented in excess 3, the result is in excess 6. In order to restore the result to excess 3, we need to subtract 3 from the result. As an alternative, we can add 13 to the result since 16 – 3 = 16 + 13 in a four-bit representation, discarding the carry out of the highest bit position. The latter approach is used in Figure 3-32, in which $13_{10} = 1101_2$ is added to the result. Note that this only works if there is no carry. When there is a carry, then we need to also subtract 10 (or equivalently, add 6) from the result, besides subtracting 3 (or adding 13) to restore the excess 3 representation, and produce a carry out. The approach taken here is to add $3_{10} = 0011_2$ for this situation, which has the same effect as adding (6 + 13) % 16 = 3, as shown in Figure 3-32.[1]

[1]The "%" operator, used in the C programming language, returns the remainder resulting from dividing the two operands.

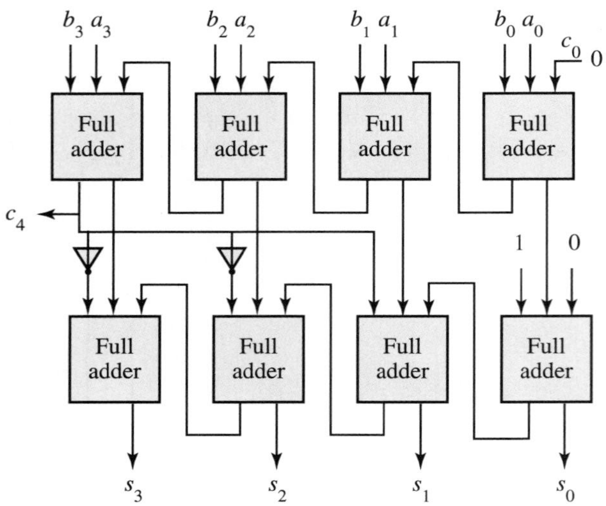

Figure 3-32 A BCD full adder.

Ten's Complement	Signed Magnitude
0 0 2 1	0 0 2 1
+ 9 9 6 6	− 0 0 3 4
9 9 8 7	− 0 0 1 3

Figure 3-33 The computation $(21 - 34 = -13)_{10}$ in ten's complement and signed magnitude.

In order to perform BCD subtraction, we can create a ten's complement subtractor using base 10 full subtractors, as we did for the two's complement subtractor described in Section 3.2.2. Alternatively, we can form the ten's complement negative of the subtrahend, and then apply ordinary BCD addition. Figure 3-33 shows the computation $(21 - 34 = -13)_{10}$ using the latter subtraction method for four-digit numbers. The ten's complement negative of 34 is added to 21, which results in 9987 in ten's complement, which is $(-13)_{10}$ in signed magnitude.

3.6.3 *BCD FLOATING POINT ADDITION AND SUBTRACTION*

Consider a base 10 floating point representation with a two-digit signed magnitude exponent and an eight-digit signed magnitude fraction. On a calculator, a sample entry might look like

$$-.37100000 \times 10^{-12}$$

which is in normalized form.

Now how is the number stored? A calculator user sees signed magnitude for both the exponent and the fraction, but internally, we might use a ten's complement representation for both the exponent and the fraction. For the preceding case, the representation using ten's complement would be 88 for the exponent, and 62900000 for the fraction. Using an excess 3 representation in binary results in an exponent of 1011 1011 and a fraction of 1001 0101 1100 0011 0011 0011 0011 0011. Note that since we are using the leftmost bit for the sign, the exponent range is [−50 to +49] and the fraction range is [−.50000000 to +.49999999].

If we now try to represent +.9 in base 10, then we are again stuck because the leftmost bit of the fraction is used for a sign bit. That is, we cannot use 1100 in the most significant digit of the fraction, because although that is the excess 3 representation of 9, it makes the fraction appear negative. Here is a better solution: Just use ten's complement for base 10 *integer* arithmetic, such as for exponents, and use signed magnitude for fractions.

Here is the summary thus far: We use a ten's complement representation for the exponent since it is an integer, and we use a base 10 signed magnitude representation for the fraction. A separate sign bit is maintained for the fraction, so that each digit can take on any of the 10 values 0 to 9 (except for the first digit, which cannot be a zero) and so we can now represent +.9. We should also represent the exponent in excess 50 to make comparisons easier. The preceding example now looks like this internally, still in excess 3 binary form, with a two-digit excess 50 exponent:

Sign bit:	1
Exponent:	0110 1011
Fraction:	0110 1010 0100 0011 0011 0011 0011 0011 0011

In order to add two numbers in this representation, we just go through the same steps that we did for the base 2 floating point representation described earlier. We start by adjusting the exponent and fraction of the smaller operand until the exponents of both operands are the same. If the difference in exponents is so great that the fraction of the smaller operand is shifted all the way to the right, then the smaller operand is treated as 0. After adjusting the smaller fraction, we convert either or both operands from signed magnitude to ten's complement according to whether we are adding or subtracting and whether the operands are positive or negative. Note that this will work now because we can treat the fractions as integers.

SUMMARY

Computer arithmetic can be carried out as we normally carry out decimal arithmetic by hand, while taking the base into account. A two's complement or a ten's complement representation is normally used for integers, whereas signed magnitude is normally used for fractions due to the difficulty of manipulating positive and negative fractions in a uniform manner.

Performance can be improved by skipping over 1's in the Booth and bit pair recoding techniques. An alternative method of improving performance is to use carryless addition, such as in residue arithmetic. Although carryless addition may be the fastest approach in terms of time complexity and circuit complexity, the more common weighted position codes are normally used in practice in order to simplify comparisons and represent fractions.

FURTHER READING

(Goldberg, 1995) is a concise but thorough source of numerous aspects of computer arithmetic. (Hamacher et al., 1990) provides a classic treatment of integer arithmetic. (Flynn, 1970) gives an early treatment of division by zero finding. (Garner, 1959) gives a complete description of the residue number system, whereas (Koren, 1993) gives a more tutorial treatment of the subject. (Huang and Goodman, 1979) describe how a memory-based residue processor can be constructed. Koren (1993) also provides additional details on cascading carry-lookahead units. (Cochran, 1968) is a good source for the programming of the HP9100A calculator.

Cochran, D. S., "Internal Programming of the 9100A Calculator," *Hewlett-Packard Journal* (Sept. 1968); also see http://www.hpmuseum.org/journals/9100:prg.htm.

Flynn, M. J., "On Division by Functional Iteration," *IEEE Trans. Comp.*, **C-19**, no. 8, pp. 702–706 (Aug. 1970).

Garner, H. L., "The Residue Number System," *IRE Transactions on Electronic Computers*, **8**, pp. 140–147 (Jun. 1959).

Goldberg, D., "Computer Arithmetic," in Patterson, D. A. and J. L. Hennessy, *Computer Architecture: A Quantitative Approach*, 2/e, Morgan Kaufmann (1995).

Hamacher, V. C., Z. G. Vranesic, and S. G. Zaky, *Computer Organization*, 3/e, McGraw-Hill (1990).

Huang, A. and J. W. Goodman, "Number Theoretic Processors, Optical and Electronic," *SPIE Optical Processing Systems*, **185**, pp. 28-35 (1979).

Koren, I., *Computer Arithmetic Algorithms*, Prentice Hall (1993).

PROBLEMS

3.1 Show the results of adding the following pairs of five-bit (i.e., one sign bit and four data bits) two's complement numbers and indicate whether or not overflow occurs for each case

```
  10110      11110      11111
 +10111     +11101     +01111
 ------     ------     ------
```

3.2 One way to determine that overflow has occurred when adding two numbers is to detect that the result of adding two positive numbers is negative, or that the result of adding two negative numbers is positive. The overflow rules are different for subtraction: There is overflow if the result of subtracting a negative number from a positive number is negative or the result of subtracting a positive number from a negative number is positive.

Subtract the numbers shown and determine whether or not an overflow has occurred. Do not form the two's complement of the subtrahend and add: Perform the subtraction bit by bit, showing the borrows generated at each position.

```
  0101
 -0110
 -----
```

3.3 Add the following two's complement and one's complement binary numbers as indicated. For each case, indicate if there is overflow.

```
Two's complement     One's complement
   1011.101             1011.101
  +0111.011            +0111.011
 -----------          -----------
```

3.4 Show the process of serial unsigned multiplication for 1010 (multiplicand) multiplied by 0101 (multiplier). Use the form shown in Figure 3-12.

3.5 Show the process of serial unsigned multiplication for 11.1 (multiplicand) multiplied by 01.1 (multiplier) by treating the operands as integers. The result should be 101.01.

3.6 Show the process of serial unsigned division for 1010 divided by 0101. Use the form shown in Figure 3-15.

3.7 Show the process of serial unsigned division for 1010 divided by 0100, but instead of generating a remainder, compute the fraction by continuing the process. That is, the result should be 10.1_2.

3.8 The equation used in Section 3.5.1 for c_4 in a carry-lookahead adder assumes that c_0 is 0 for addition. If we perform subtraction by using the addition/subtraction unit shown in Figure 3-6, then $c_0 = 1$. Rewrite the equation for c_4 when $c_0 = 1$.

3.9 The 16-bit adder shown here uses a ripple carry among four-bit carry-lookahead adders.

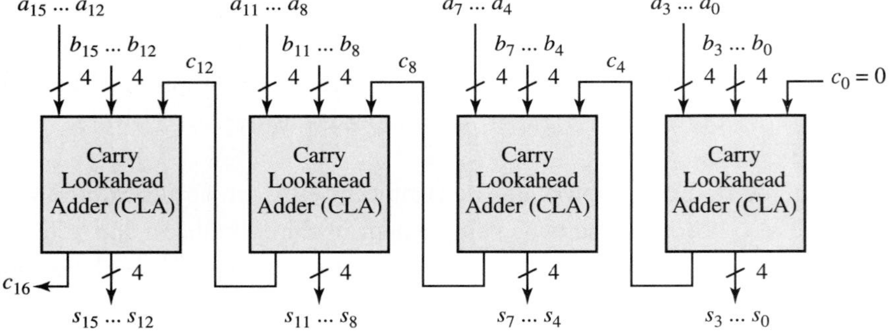

(a) What is the longest gate delay through this adder?

(b) What is the shortest gate delay through this adder, from any input to any output?

(c) What is the gate delay for s_{12}?

3.10 Use the Booth algorithm (not bit pair recoding) to multiply 010011 (multiplicand) by 011011 (multiplier).

3.11 Use bit pair recoding to multiply 010011 (multiplicand) by 011011 (multiplier).

3.12 Compute the maximum gate delay through a 32-bit carry-lookahead adder.

3.13 What is the maximum number of inputs for any logic gate in a 32-bit carry-lookahead adder, using the scheme described in this chapter?

3.14 In a **carry-select adder** a carry is propagated from one adder stage to the next, similar to but not exactly the same as a carry-lookahead adder. As with many other adders, the carry-out of a carry-select adder stage is either 0 or 1. In a carry-select adder, two sums are computed in parallel for each adder stage: One sum assumes a carry-in of 0, and the other sum assumes a carry-in of 1. The actual carry-in selects which of the two sums to use (with a MUX, for example). The basic layout is shown here for an eight-bit carry-select adder:

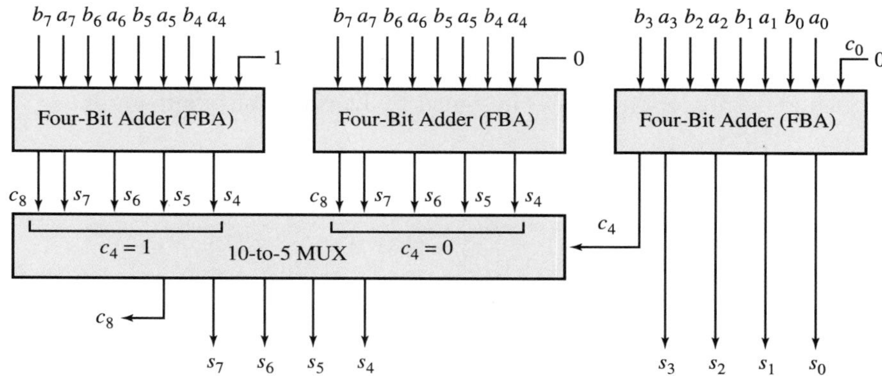

Assume that each four-bit adder (FBA) unit uses carry lookahead internally. Compare the number of gate delays needed to add two eight-bit numbers using FBA units in a carry-select configuration *versus* using FBA units in which the carry is rippled from one FBA to the next.

(a) Draw a diagram of a functionally equivalent eight-bit carry-lookahead configuration using the FBAs shown.

(b) Show the number of gate delays for each adder configuration, by both the eight-bit carry-select adder shown and the adder designed in part (a).

3.15 The path with the maximum gate delay through the array multiplier shown in Figure 3-22 starts in the top right PP element, then travels to the bottom row, then across to the left. The maximum gate delay through a PP element is three. How many gate delays are on the maximum gate delay path through an array multiplier that produces a p-bit result?

3.16 Given multiplication units that each produce a 16-bit unsigned product on two unsigned 8-bit inputs, and 16-bit adders that produce a 16-bit sum and a carry-out on two 16-bit inputs and a carry-in, connect these units so that the overall unit multiplies 16-bit unsigned numbers, producing a 32-bit result.

3.17 Using Newton's iteration for division, we would like to obtain 32 bits of precision. If we use a lookup table that provides eight bits of precision for the initial guess, how many iterations need to be applied?

3.18 Add $(641)_{10}$ to $(259)_{10}$ in unsigned BCD, using as few digits in the result as necessary.

3.19 Add $(123)_{10}$ and $(-178)_{10}$ in signed BCD, using four-digit words.

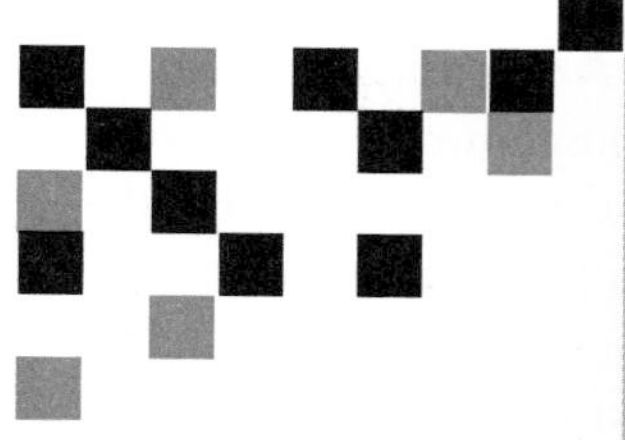

4 THE INSTRUCTION SET ARCHITECTURE

In this chapter, we tackle a central topic in computer architecture: The language understood by the computer's hardware, referred to as its **machine language**. The machine language is usually discussed in terms of its **assembly language**, which is functionally equivalent to the corresponding machine language except that the assembly language uses more intuitive names such as Move, Add, and Jump instead of the actual binary words of the language. (Programmers find constructs such as "Add r0, r1, r2" to be more easily understood and rendered without error than 0110101110101101.)

We begin by describing the **instruction set architecture** (ISA) view of the machine and its operations. The ISA view corresponds to the Assembly Language/machine code level described in Figure 1-4: It is between the high-level language view, where little or none of the machine hardware is visible or of concern, and the control level, where machine instructions are interpreted as register transfer actions, at the functional unit level.

In order to describe the nature of assembly language and assembly language programming, we choose as a model architecture the **ARC** machine, which is a simplification of the commercial SPARC architecture common to Sun computers. (Additional architectural models are covered in *The Computer Architecture Companion* volume. See **`http://www.prenhall.com/murdocca`**.)

We illustrate the utility of the various instruction classes with practical examples of assembly language programming, and we conclude with a case study of the Java bytecodes as an example of a common, portable assembly language that can be implemented using the native language of another machine.

4.1 Hardware Components of the Instruction Set Architecture

The ISA of a computer presents the assembly language programmer with a view of the machine that includes all the programmer-accessible hardware and the instructions that manipulate data within the hardware. In this section, we look at the hardware components as viewed by the assembly language programmer. We begin with a discussion of the system as a whole: The CPU interacting with its internal (main) memory and performing input and output with the outside world.

4.1.1 *THE SYSTEM BUS MODEL REVISITED*

Figure 4-1 revisits the system bus model that was introduced in Chapter 1.

The purpose of the bus is to reduce the number of interconnections between the CPU and its subsystems. Rather than have separate communication paths between memory and each I/O device, the CPU is interconnected with its memory and I/O systems via a shared **system bus**. In more complex systems there may be separate buses between the CPU and memory and CPU and I/O.

Not all of the components are connected to the system bus in the same way. The CPU generates addresses that are placed onto the address bus, and the memory receives addresses from the address bus. The memory never generates addresses, and the CPU never receives addresses, and so there are no corresponding connections in those directions.

In a typical scenario, a user writes a high-level program, which a compiler translates into assembly language. An assembler then translates the assembly language program into machine code, which is stored on a disk. Prior to execution, the machine code program is loaded from the disk into the main memory by an operating system.

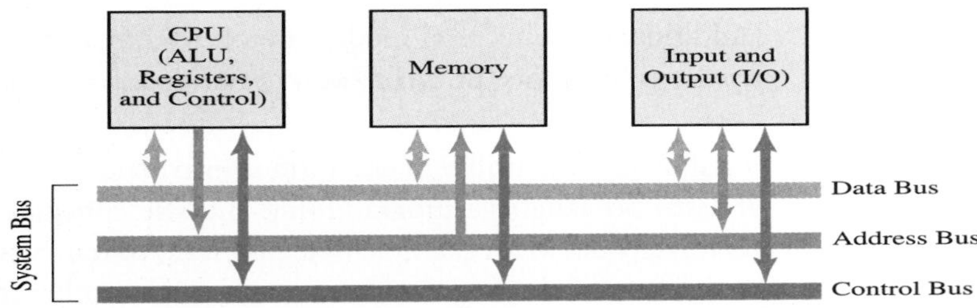

Figure 4-1 The system bus model of a computer system.

During program execution, each instruction is brought into the ALU from the memory, one instruction at a time, along with any data that is needed to execute the instruction. The output of the program is placed on a device such as a video display, or a disk. All of these operations are orchestrated by a control unit, which we will explore in detail in Chapter 6. Communication among the three components (CPU, memory, and I/O) is handled with buses.

An important consideration is that the instructions are executed inside of the ALU, even though all of the instructions and data are initially stored in the memory. This means that instructions and data must be loaded from the memory into the ALU registers, and results must be stored back to the memory from the ALU registers.

4.1.2 *MEMORY*

Computer memory consists of a collection of consecutively numbered (addressed) registers, each one of which normally holds one byte. A **byte** is a collection of eight bits (sometimes referred to by those in the computer communications community as an **octet**). Each register has an address, referred to as a **memory location**. A **nibble**, or **nybble**, as it is sometimes spelled, refers to a collection of four adjacent bits. The meanings of the terms "bit," "byte," and "nibble" are generally agreed upon regardless of the specifics of an architecture, but the meaning of **word** depends upon the particular processor. Typical word sizes are 16, 32, 64, and 128 bits, with the 32-bit word size being the common form for ordinary computers these days, and the 64-bit word growing in popularity. In this text, words will be assumed to be 32 bits wide unless otherwise specified. A comparison of these data types is shown in Figure 4-2.

Bit	0
Nibble	0110
Byte	10110000
16-bit word (halfword)	11001001 01000110
32-bit word	10110100 00110101 10011001 01011000
64-bit word (double)	01011000 01010101 10110000 11110011
	11001110 11101110 01111000 00110101
128-bit word (quad)	01011000 01010101 10110000 11110011
	11001110 11101110 01111000 00110101
	00001011 10100110 11110010 11100110
	10100100 01000100 10100101 01010001

Figure 4-2 Common sizes for data types.

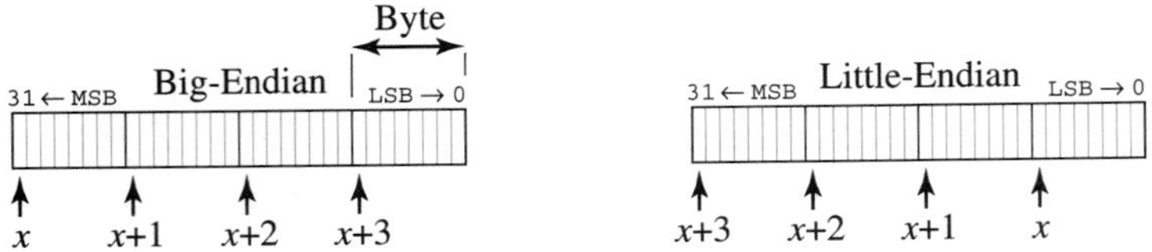

Figure 4-3 Big-endian and little-endian formats.

In a byte-addressable machine, the smallest object that can be referenced in memory is the byte; however, there are usually instructions that read and write multi byte words. Multi byte words are stored as a sequence of bytes, addressed by the byte of the word that has the lowest address. Most machines today have instructions that can access bytes, half-words, words, and double-words.

When multi byte words are used, there are two choices about the order in which the bytes are stored in memory: most significant byte at lowest address, referred to as **big-endian**, or least significant byte stored at lowest address, referred to as **little-endian**. The term "endian" comes from the issue of whether eggs should be broken on the big or little end, which caused a war by bickering politicians in Jonathan Swift's *Gulliver's Travels*. Examples of big- and little-endian formats for a 4-byte, 32-bit word are illustrated in Figure 4-3.

Memory locations are arranged linearly in consecutive order as shown in Figure 4-3. Each of the numbered locations corresponds to a specific stored word (a word is composed of four bytes here). The unique number that identifies each word is referred to as its **address**. Since addresses are counted in sequence beginning with zero, the highest address is one less than the size of the memory. The highest address for a 2^{32} byte memory is $2^{32} - 1$. The lowest address is 0.

The example memory that we will use for the remainder of the chapter is shown in Figure 4-4. This memory has a 32-bit **address space**, which means that a program can access a byte of memory anywhere in the range from 0 to $2^{32} - 1$. The address space for our example architecture is divided into distinct regions, used for the operating system, input and output (I/O), user programs, and the system stack. These regions comprise the **memory map**, as shown in Figure 4-3. The memory map differs from one implementation to another, which is partly why programs compiled for the same type of processor may not be compatible across systems.

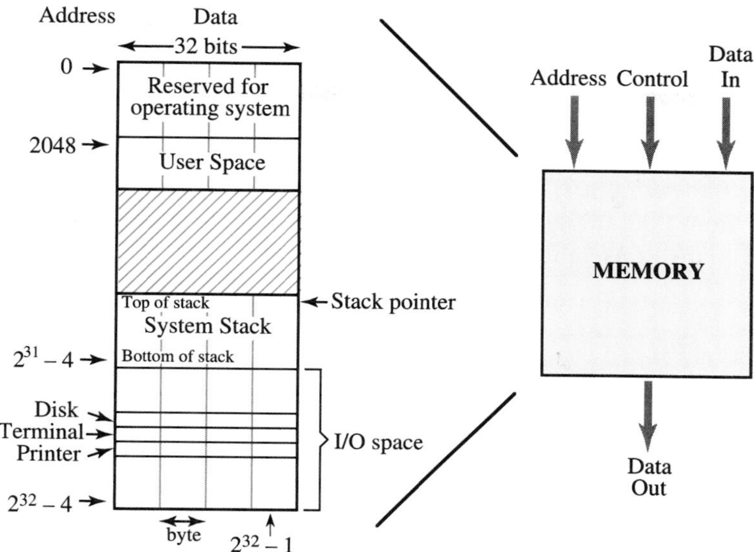

Figure 4-4 A memory map for an example architecture (not drawn to scale).

The lower 2^{11} = 2048 addresses of the memory map are reserved for use by the operating system. The user space is where a user's assembled program is loaded, and it can grow during operation from location 2048 until it meets up with the system stack. The system stack starts at location $2^{31} - 4$ and grows toward lower addresses. The portion of the address space between 2^{31} and $2^{32} - 1$ is reserved for I/O devices. The memory map is thus not entirely composed of real memory, and in fact there may be large gaps where neither real memory nor I/O devices exist. Since I/O devices are treated like memory locations, ordinary memory read and write commands can be used for reading and writing devices. This is referred to as **memory mapped I/O**.

It is important to keep the distinction clear between what is an address and what is data. An address in this example memory is 32 bits wide, and a word is also 32 bits wide, but they are not the same thing. An address is a pointer to a memory location, which holds data.

In this chapter, we assume that the computer's memory is organized in a single address space. The term **address space** refers to the numerical range of memory addresses to which the CPU can refer. In Chapter 7 (Memory), we will see that there are other ways that memory can be organized, but for now, we assume that memory as seen by the CPU has a single range of addresses. What decides the size of that range? It is the size of a memory address that the CPU can place on the address bus during read and write operations. A memory address that is n bits wide can specify one of 2^n items. This memory could be referred to as having an n-bit address space, or equivalently as having a (2^n) byte address space. For example, a machine having a 32-bit address space will have a maximum capacity of 2^{32} (4 GB) of memory. The memory addresses will range from 0 to $2^{32} - 1$, which is 0 to 4,294,967,295 decimal, or in the easier to manipulate hexadecimal format, from 00000000H to FFFFFFFFH. (The 'H' indicates a hexadecimal number in many assembly languages.)

4.1.3 *THE CPU*

Now that we are familiar with the basic components of the system bus and memory, we are ready to explore the internals of the CPU. At a minimum, the CPU consists of a **data section**, which contains registers and an ALU, and a **control section**, which interprets instructions and effects register transfers, as illustrated in Figure 4-5. The data section is also referred to as the **datapath**.

The control unit of a computer is responsible for executing the program instructions, which are stored in the main memory. (Here we will assume that the machine code is interpreted by the control unit one instruction at a time, though in Chapter 9 we shall see that many modern processors can process several instructions simultaneously.) There are two registers that form the interface between the control unit and the data unit, known as the **program counter** (PC)[1] and the **instruction register** (IR). The PC contains the address of the instruction being executed. The instruction that is pointed to by the PC is

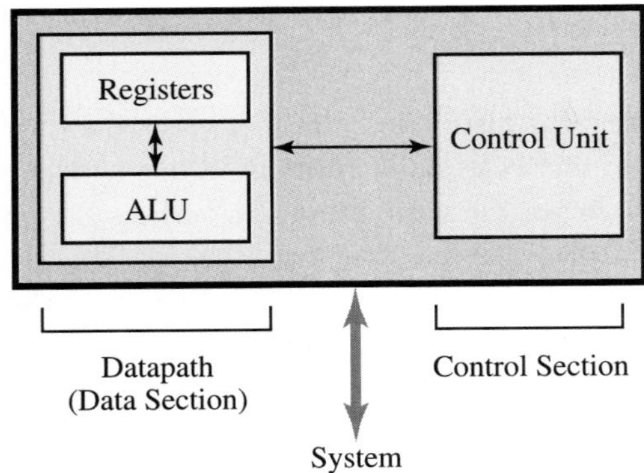

Figure 4-5 High-level view of a CPU.

fetched from the memory and is stored in the IR where it is interpreted. The steps that the control unit carries out in executing a program are as follows:

1) Fetch the next instruction to be executed from memory.

2) Decode the opcode.

3) Read operand(s) from main memory, if any.

4) Execute the instruction and store results.

5) Go to step 1.

This is known as the **fetch-execute cycle**.

The control unit is responsible for coordinating these different units in the execution of a computer program. It can be thought of as a form of a "computer within a computer" in the sense that it makes decisions as to how the rest of the machine behaves. We will treat the control unit in detail in Chapter 6.

The datapath is made up of a collection of registers known as the **register file** and the arithmetic and logic unit (ALU), as shown in Figure 4-6. The figure depicts the datapath of an example processor we will use in the remainder of the chapter.

The register file in the figure can be thought of as a small, fast memory, separate from the system memory, which is used for temporary storage during computation. Typical sizes for a register file range from a few to a few thousand registers. Like the system memory, each register in the register file is assigned an address in sequence starting from zero. These register "addresses" are much smaller than main memory addresses: A register file containing 32 registers would have only a 5-bit address, for example. The major differences between the register file and the system memory is that the register file is contained within the CPU, and is therefore much faster. An instruction that operates on data from the register file can often run ten times faster than the same instruction that operates on data in memory. For this reason, register-intensive programs are faster than the equivalent memory-intensive programs, even if it takes more register operations to do the same tasks that would require fewer operations with the operands located in memory.

---

[1]In Intel processors, the program counter is called the instruction pointer, IP.

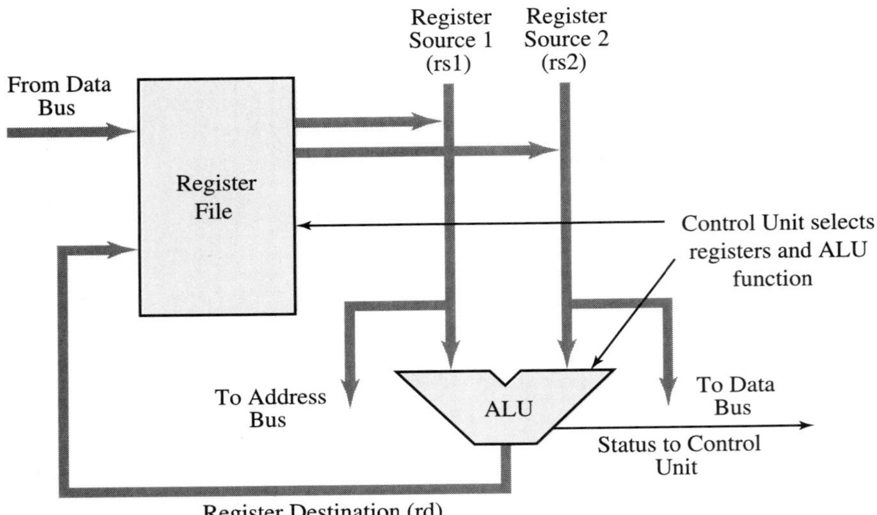

Figure 4-6 An example datapath.

Notice that there are several buses *inside* the datapath of Figure 4-6. Three buses connect the datapath to the system bus. This allows data to be transferred to and from main memory and the register file. Three additional buses connect the register file to the ALU. These buses allow two operands to be fetched from the register file simultaneously, which are operated on by the ALU, with the results returned to the register file.

The ALU implements a variety of binary (two-operand) and unary (one-operand) operations. Examples include add, and, not, or, and multiply. Operations and operands to be used during the operations are selected by the control unit. The two source operands are fetched from the register file onto buses labeled "register source 1 (rs1)" and "register source 2 (rs2)." The output from the ALU is placed on the bus labeled "register destination (rd)," where the results are conveyed back to the register file. In most systems, these connections also include a path to the system bus so that memory and devices can be accessed. This is shown as the three connections labeled "from data bus," "to data bus," and "to address bus."

The Instruction Set

The **instruction set** is the collection of instructions that a processor can execute, and in effect, it defines the processor. The instruction sets for each processor type are completely different one from the other. They differ in the sizes of instructions, the kind of operations they allow, the type of operands they operate on, and the types of results they provide.This incompatibility in instruction sets is in stark contrast to the compatibility of higher-level languages such as C, Pascal, and Ada. Programs written in these higher-level languages can run almost unchanged on many different processors if they are **recompiled** for the target processor.

(One exception to this incompatibility of machine languages are programs compiled into Java bytecodes, which are a machine language for a **virtual machine**. They will run unchanged on any processor that is running the Java Virtual Machine. The Java Virtual Machine, written in the assembly language of the target machine, intercepts each Java byte code and executes it as if it were running on a Java hardware ["real"] machine. See the case study at the end of the chapter for more details.)

Because of this incompatibility among instruction sets, computer systems are often identified by the type of CPU that is incorporated into the computer system. The instruction set determines the programs the system can execute and has a significant impact on performance. Programs compiled for an IBM PC (or compatible) system use the instruction set of an 80x86 CPU, where the "x" is replaced with a digit that corresponds to the version, such as 80586, more commonly referred to as a Pentium processor. These programs will not run on an Apple Macintosh or an IBM RS6000 computer, since the Macintosh and IBM machines execute the instruction set of the Motorola **PowerPC** CPU. This does not mean that all computer systems that use the same CPU can execute the same programs, however. A PowerPC program written for the IBM RS6000 will not execute on the Macintosh without extensive modifications, however, because of differences in operating systems and I/O conventions.

We will cover one instruction set in detail later in the chapter.

Software for Generating Machine Language Programs

A **compiler** is a computer program that transforms programs written in a high-level language such as C, Pascal, or Fortran into machine language. Compilers for the same high-level language generally have the same "front end," the part that recognizes statements in the high-level language. They will have different "back ends," however, one for each target processor. The compiler's back end is responsible for generating machine code for a specific target processor. On the other hand, the same program, compiled by different C compilers for the *same* machine can produce different compiled programs for the same source code, as we will see.

In the process of compiling a program (referred to as the **translation process**), a high-level source program is transformed into **assembly language**, and the assembly language is then translated into machine code for the target machine by an **assembler**. These translations take place at **compile time** and **assembly time**, respectively. The resulting object program can be linked with other object programs at **link time**. The linked program, usually stored on a disk, is loaded into main memory at **load time** and executed by the CPU at **run time**.

Although most code is written in high-level languages, programmers may use assembly language for programs or fragments of programs that are time or space critical. In addition, compilers may not be available for some special-purpose processors, or their compilers may be inadequate to express the special operations which are required. In these cases also, the programmer may need to resort to programming in assembly language.

High-level languages allow us to ignore the target computer architecture during coding. At the machine language level, however, the underlying architecture is the primary consideration. A program written in a high-level language like C, Pascal, or Fortran may look the same and execute correctly after compilation on several different computer systems. The object code that the compiler produces for each machine, however, will be very different for each computer system, even if the systems use the same instruction set, such as programs compiled for the PowerPC but running on a Macintosh *versus* running on an IBM RS6000.

Having discussed the system bus, main memory, and the CPU, we now examine details of a model instruction set, the ARC.

4.2 ARC, a RISC Computer

In the remainder of this chapter, we will study a model architecture that is based on the commercial Scalable Processor Architecture (**SPARC**) processor that was developed at Sun Microsystems in the mid-1980s. The SPARC has become a popular architecture since its introduction, which is partly due to its "open" nature: the full definition of the SPARC architecture is made readily available to the public (SPARC, 1992). In this chapter, we will look at just a subset of the SPARC, which we call "A RISC Computer" (**ARC**). "RISC" is yet another acronym, for **reduced instruction set computer**, which is discussed in Chapter 9. The ARC has most of the important features of the SPARC architecture, but without some of the more complex features that are present in a commercial processor.

4.2.1 *ARC MEMORY*

The ARC is a 32-bit machine with byte-addressable memory: it can manipulate 32-bit data types, but all data is stored in memory as bytes, and the address of a 32-bit word is the address of its byte that has the lowest address. As described earlier in the chapter in the context of Figure 4-4, the ARC has a 32-bit address space, in which our example architecture is divided into distinct regions for use by the operating system code, user program code, the system stack (used to store temporary data), and input and output (I/O). These memory regions are detailed as follows:

- The lowest $2^{11} = 2048$ addresses of the memory map are reserved for use by the operating system.
- The user space is where a user's assembled program is loaded, and it can grow during operation from location 2048 until it meets up with the system stack.
- The system stack starts at location $2^{31} - 4$ and grows toward lower addresses. The reason for this organization of programs growing upward in memory and the system stack growing downward can be seen in Figure 4-4: this organization accommodates both large programs with small stacks and small programs with large stacks.
- The portion of the address space between 2^{31} and $2^{32} - 1$ is reserved for I/O devices—each device has a collection of memory addresses where its data is stored, which is referred to as "memory mapped I/O."

The ARC has several data types (byte, halfword, integer, etc.), but for now we will consider only the 32-bit integer data type. Each integer is stored in memory as a collection of four bytes. ARC is a **big-endian** architecture, so the highest-order byte is stored at the lowest address. The largest possible byte address in the ARC is $2^{32} - 1$, so the address of the highest word in the memory map is three bytes lower than this, or $2^{32} - 4$.

4.2.2 *ARC INSTRUCTION SET*

As we get into details of the ARC instruction set, let us start by making an overview of the CPU:

- The ARC has thirty-two 32-bit general-purpose registers, as well as a PC and an IR.

- There is a **processor status register** (PSR) that contains information about the state of the processor, including information about the results of arithmetic operations. The "arithmetic flags" in the PSR are called the **condition codes**. They specify whether a specified arithmetic operation resulted in a zero value (`z`), a negative value (`n`), a carry-out from the 32-bit ALU (`c`), and an overflow (`v`). The `v` bit is set when the results of the arithmetic operation are too large to be handled by the ALU.

- All instructions are one word (32 bits) in size.

- The ARC is a **load-store** machine: The only allowable memory access operations load a value into one of the registers, or store a value contained in one of the registers into a memory location. All arithmetic operations operate on values that are contained in registers, and the results are placed in a register. There are approximately 200 instructions in the SPARC instruction set, upon which the ARC instruction set is based. A subset of 15 instructions is shown in Figure 4-7. Each instruction is represented by a **mnemonic**, which is a name that represents the instruction.

	Mnemonic	Meaning
Memory	**ld**	Load a register from memory
	st	Store a register into memory
Logic	**sethi**	Load the 22 most significant bits of a register
	andcc	Bitwise logical AND
	orcc	Bitwise logical OR
	orncc	Bitwise logical NOR
	srl	Shift right (logical)
Arithmetic	**addcc**	Add
Control	**call**	Call subroutine
	jmpl	Jump and link (return from subroutine call)
	be	Branch if equal
	bneg	Branch if negative
	bcs	Branch on carry
	bvs	Branch on overflow
	ba	Branch always

Figure 4-7 A subset of the instruction set for the ARC ISA.

Data Movement Instructions

The first two instructions: **ld** (load) and **st** (store) transfer a word between the main memory and one of the ARC registers. These are the only instructions that can access memory in the ARC.

The **sethi** instruction sets the 22 most significant bits (MSBs) of a register with a 22-bit constant contained within the instruction. It is commonly used for constructing an arbitrary 32-bit constant in a register, in conjunction with another instruction that sets the low-order 10 bits of the register.

Arithmetic and Logic Instructions

The **andcc**, **orcc**, and **orncc** instructions perform a bit-by-bit AND, OR, and NOR operation, respectively, on their operands. One of the two source operands must be in a register. The other may either be in a register, or it may be a 13-bit two's complement constant contained in the instruction, which is sign extended to 32 bits when it is used. The result is stored in a register.

For the **andcc** instruction, each bit of the result is set to 1 if the corresponding bits of both operands are 1; otherwise the result bit is set to 0. For the **orcc** instruction, each bit of the register is 1 if either or both of the corresponding source operand bits are 1; otherwise the corresponding result bit is set to 0. The **orncc** operation is the complement of orcc, so each bit of the result is 0 if either or both of the corresponding operand bits are 1, otherwise the result bit is set to 1. The "cc" suffixes specify that after performing the operation, the condition code bits in the PSR are updated to reflect the results of the operation. In particular, the z bit is set if the result register contains all zeros, the n bit is set if the most significant bit of the result register is a 1, and the c and v flags are cleared for these particular instructions. (Why?)

The shift instructions shift the contents of one register into another. The **srl** (shift right *logical*) instruction shifts a register to the right and copies zeros into the leftmost bit(s). The **sra** (shift right *arithmetic*) instruction (not shown) shifts the original register contents to the right, placing a copy of the MSB of the original register into the newly created vacant bit(s) in the left side of the register. This results in sign-extending the number, thus preserving its arithmetic sign.

The **addcc** instruction performs a 32-bit two's complement addition on its operands.

Control Instructions

The **call** and **jmpl** instructions form a pair that are used in calling and returning from a subroutine, respectively. jmpl is also used to transfer control to another part of the program.

The lower five instructions are called **conditional branch** instructions. The **be**, **bneg**, **bcs**, **bvs**, and **ba** instructions cause a branch in the execution of a program. They are called conditional because they test one or more of the condition code bits in the PSR, and branch if the bits indicate the condition is met. They are used in implementing high-level constructs such as goto, if-then-else, and do-while. Detailed descriptions of these instructions and examples of their usages are given in the sections that follow.

4.2.3 *ARC ASSEMBLY LANGUAGE FORMAT*

Each assembly language has its own syntax. We will follow the SPARC assembly language syntax, as shown in Figure 4-8. The format consists of four fields: an optional label field, an opcode field, one or more fields specifying the source and destination operands (if there are operands), and an optional comment field. A label consists of any combination of alphabetic or numeric characters, underscores (_), dollar signs ($), or periods (.), as long as the first character is not a digit. A label must be followed by a colon. The language is sensitive to case, and so a distinction is made between upper- and lower-case letters. The language is "free format" in the sense that any field can begin in any column, but the relative left-to-right ordering must be maintained.

The ARC architecture contains 32 registers labeled %r0 – %r31, which each hold a 32-bit word. There is also a 32-bit processor state register (PSR) that describes the current state of the processor, and a 32-bit **program counter** (PC) that keeps track of the instruction being executed, as illustrated in Figure 4-9. The PSR is labeled %psr and the PC register is labeled %pc. Register %r0 always

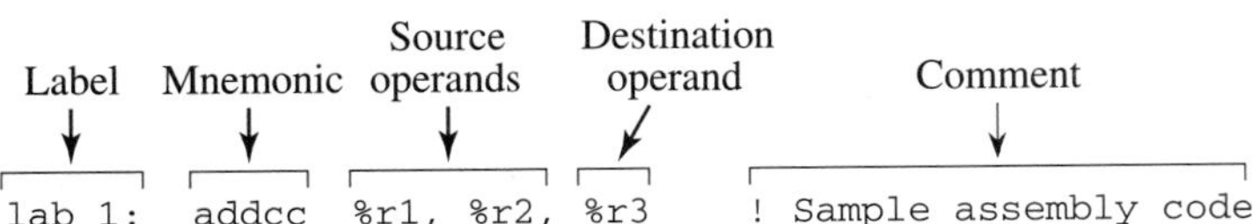

Figure 4-8 Format for a SPARC (as well as ARC) assembly language statement.

Register	Name	Register	Name	Register	Name
Register 00	`%r0 [= 0]`	Register 11	`%r11`	Register 22	`%r22`
Register 01	`%r1`	Register 12	`%r12`	Register 23	`%r23`
Register 02	`%r2`	Register 13	`%r13`	Register 24	`%r24`
Register 03	`%r3`	Register14	`%r14 [%sp]`	Register 25	`%r25`
Register 04	`%r4`	Register 15	`%r15 [link]`	Register 26	`%r26`
Register 05	`%r5`	Register 16	`%r16`	Register 27	`%r27`
Register 06	`%r6`	Register 17	`%r17`	Register 28	`%r28`
Register 07	`%r7`	Register 18	`%r18`	Register 29	`%r29`
Register 08	`%r8`	Register 19	`%r19`	Register 30	`%r30`
Register 09	`%r9`	Register 20	`%r20`	Register 31	`%r31`
Register 10	`%r10`	Register 21	`%r21`		
PSR	`%psr`			PC	`%pc`
←32 bits→				←32 bits→	

Figure 4-9 User-visible registers in the ARC.

contains the value 0, which cannot be changed. Registers `%r14` and `%r15` have additional uses as a **stack pointer** (`%sp`) and a **link register**, respectively, as described later.

Operands in an assembly language statement are separated by commas, and the destination operand always appears in the rightmost position in the operand field. Thus, the example shown in Figure 4-8 specifies adding registers `%r1` and `%r2`, with the result placed in `%r3`. If `%r0` appears in the destination operand field instead of `%r3`, the result is discarded. The default base for a numeric operand is 10, so the assembly language statement

```
addcc %r1, 12, %r3
```

shows an operand of $(12)_{10}$ that will be added to `%r1`, with the result placed in `%r3`. Numbers are interpreted in base 10 unless preceded by "`0x`" or ending in "H," either of which denotes a hexadecimal number. The comment field follows the operand field, begins with an exclamation mark "`!`," and terminates at the end of the line.

4.2.4 *ARC INSTRUCTION FORMATS*

The **instruction format** defines how the various bit fields of an instruction are laid out by the assembler, and how they are interpreted by the ARC control unit. The ARC architecture has just a few instruction formats. The five formats are:

SETHI, **Branch**, **Call**, **Arithmetic**, and **Memory**, as shown in Figure 4-10. Each instruction has a mnemonic form such as "ld," and an opcode. A particular instruction format may have more than one opcode field, which collectively identify an instruction in one of its various forms. (Note that these four instruction formats do not directly correspond to the four instruction classifications shown in Figure 4-7.)

The leftmost two bits of each instruction form the op (opcode) field, which identifies the format. The SETHI and Branch formats both contain 00 in the op field, and so they can be considered together as the SETHI/Branch format. The actual SETHI or Branch format is determined by the bit pattern in the op2 opcode field (010 = Branch; 100 = SETHI). Bit 29 in the Branch format always contains a zero. The five-bit rd field identifies the target register for the SETHI operation.

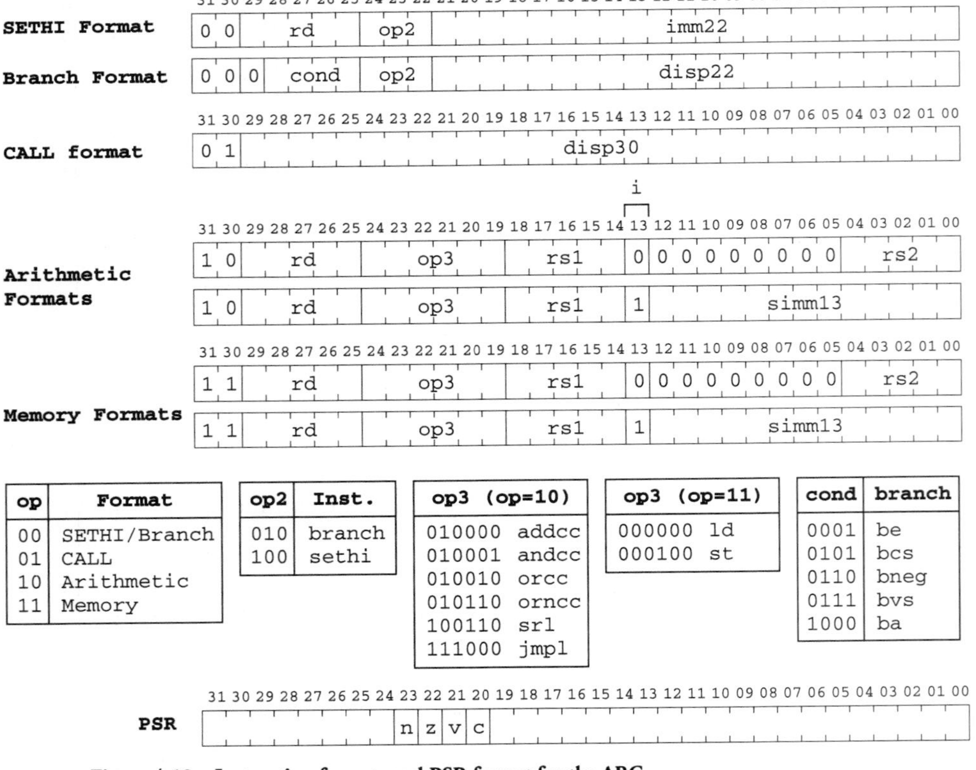

op	Format
00	SETHI/Branch
01	CALL
10	Arithmetic
11	Memory

op2	Inst.
010	branch
100	sethi

op3 (op=10)	
010000	addcc
010001	andcc
010010	orcc
010110	orncc
100110	srl
111000	jmpl

op3 (op=11)	
000000	ld
000100	st

cond	branch
0001	be
0101	bcs
0110	bneg
0111	bvs
1000	ba

Figure 4-10 Instruction formats and PSR format for the ARC.

The `cond` field identifies the type of branch, based on the condition code bits (`n`, `z`, `v`, and `c`) in the PSR, as indicated at the bottom of Figure 4-10. The result of executing an instruction in which the mnemonic ends with "`cc`" sets the condition code bits such that `n=1` if the result of the operation is negative; `z=1` if the result is zero; `v=1` if the operation causes an overflow; and `c=1` if the operation produces a carry. The instructions that do not end in "`cc`" do not affect the condition codes. The `imm22` and `disp22` fields each hold a 22-bit constant that is used as the operand for the SETHI format (for `imm22`) or for calculating a displacement for a branch address (for `disp22`).

The CALL format contains only two fields: the `op` field, which contains the bit pattern `01`, and the `disp30` field, which contains a 30-bit displacement that is used in calculating the address of the called routine.

The Arithmetic (`op = 10`) and Memory (`op = 11`) formats both make use of `rd` fields to identify either a source register for `st`, or a destination register for the remaining instructions. The `rs1` field identifies the first source register, and the `rs2` field identifies the second source register. The `op3` opcode field identifies the instruction according to the `op3` tables shown in Figure 4-10.

The `simm13` field is a 13-bit immediate value that is sign extended to 32 bits for the second source when the `i` (immediate) field is 1. The meaning of "sign extended" is that the leftmost bit of the `simm13` field (the sign bit) is copied to the left into the remaining bits that make up a 32-bit integer, before adding it to `rs1` in this case. This ensures that a two's complement negative number remains negative (and a two's complement positive number remains positive). For instance, $(-13)_{10} = (1111111110011)_2$, and after sign extension to a 32-bit integer, we have $(11111111111111111111111111110011)_2$, which is still equivalent to $(-13)_{10}$.

The Arithmetic instructions need two source operands and a destination operand, for a total of three operands. The Memory instructions only need two operands: one for the address and one for the data. The remaining source operand is also used for the address, however. The operands in the `rs1` and `rs2` fields are added to obtain the address when `i = 0`. When `i = 1`, then the `rs1` field and the `simm13` field are added to obtain the address. For the first few examples we will encounter, `%r0` will be used for `rs2` and so only the remaining source operand will be specified.

4.2.5 *ARC DATA FORMATS*

The ARC supports 12 different data formats, as illustrated in Figure 4-11. The data formats are grouped into three types: signed integer, unsigned integer, and floating point. Within these types, allowable format widths are byte (8 bits), half-word (16 bits), word/singleword (32 bits), **tagged** word (32 bits, in which the two least significant bits form a **tag** and the most significant 30 bits form the value), **doubleword** (64 bits), and **quadword** (128 bits).

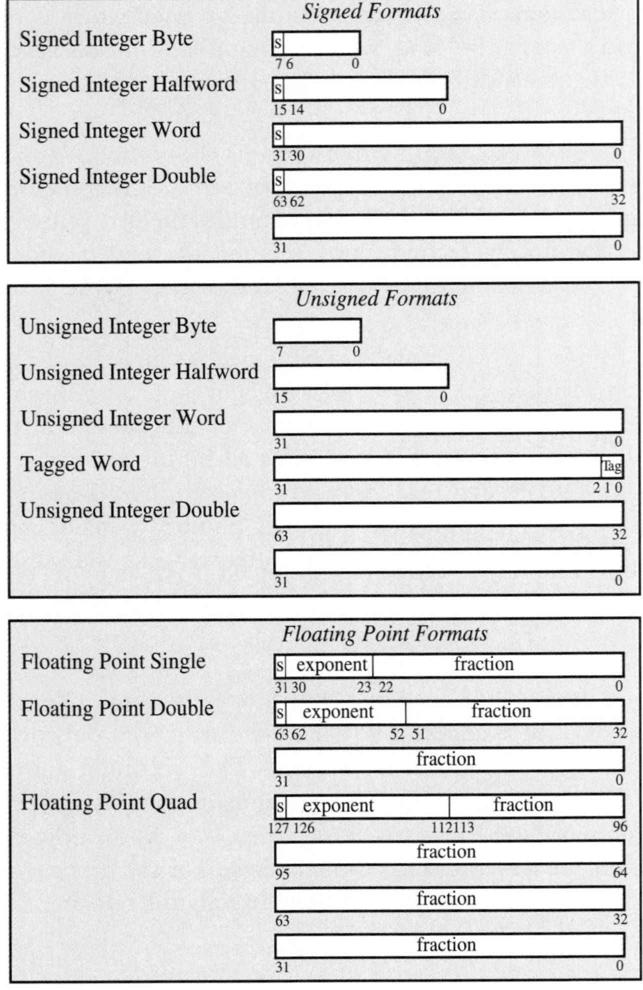

Figure 4-11 ARC data formats.

In reality, the ARC does not differentiate between unsigned and signed integers. Both are stored and manipulated as two's complement integers. It is their interpretation that varies. In particular, one subset of the branch instructions assumes that the value(s) being compared are signed integers, while the other subset assumes they are unsigned. Likewise, the `c` bit indicates unsigned integer overflow, and the `v` bit, signed overflow.

The tagged word uses the two least significant bits to indicate **overflow**, in which an attempt is made to store a value that is larger than 30 bits into the allocated 30 bits of the 32-bit word. Tagged arithmetic operations are used in languages with dynamically typed data, such as Lisp and Smalltalk. In its generic form, a 1 in either bit of the tag field indicates an overflow situation for that word. The tags can be used to ensure proper alignment conditions (that words begin on four-byte boundaries, quadwords begin on eight-byte boundaries, etc.), particularly for pointers.

The floating point formats conform to the IEEE 754-1985 standard (see Chapter 2). There are special instructions that invoke floating point formats not described here and that can be found in (SPARC, 1992).

4.2.6 *ARC INSTRUCTION DESCRIPTIONS*

Now that we know the instruction formats, we can create detailed descriptions of the 15 instructions listed in Figure 4-7, which are given in this section. The translation to object code is provided only as a reference and is described in detail in the next chapter. In the descriptions, a reference to the *contents* of a memory location (for `ld` and `st`) is indicated by square brackets, as in "`ld [x], %r1`," which copies the contents of location `x` into `%r1`. A reference to the *address* of a memory location is specified directly, without brackets, as in "`call sub_r`," which makes a call to subroutine `sub_r`. Only `ld` and `st` can access memory; therefore only `ld` and `st` use brackets. Registers are always referred to in terms of their contents, and never in terms of an address, and so there is no need to enclose references to registers in brackets.

Instruction: `ld`

Description: Load a register from main memory. The memory address must be aligned on a word boundary (that is, the address must be evenly divisible by 4). The address is computed by adding the contents of the register in the `rs1` field to either the contents of the register in the `rs2` field or the value in the `simm13` field, as appropriate for the context.

Example usage: `ld [x], %r1`

or `ld [x], %r0, %r1`

or `ld %r0+x, %r1`

Meaning: Copy the contents of memory location `x` into register `%r1`.
Object code: `11000010000000000010100000010000     (x = 2064)`

Instruction: `st`
Description: Store a register into main memory. The memory address must be aligned on a word boundary. The address is computed by adding the contents of the register in the `rs1` field to either the contents of the register in the `rs2` field or the value in the `simm13` field, as appropriate for the context. The `rd` field of this instruction is actually used for the source register.
Example usage: `st %r1, [x]`
Meaning: Copy the contents of register `%r1` into memory location `x`.
Object code: `11000010001000000010100000010000     (x = 2064)`

Instruction: `sethi`
Description: Set the high 22 bits and zero the low 10 bits of a register. If the operand is 0 and the register is `%r0`, then the instruction behaves as a **no-op (NOP)**, which means that no operation takes place.
Example usage: `sethi 0x304F15, %r1`
Meaning: Set the high 22 bits of `%r1` to $(304F15)_{16}$, and set the low 10 bits to zero.
Object code: `00000011001100000100111100010101`

Instruction: `andcc`
Description: Bitwise AND the source operands into the destination operand. The condition codes are set according to the result.
Example usage: `andcc %r1, %r2, %r3`
Meaning: Logically AND `%r1` and `%r2` and place the result in `%r3`.
Object code: `10000110100010000100000000000010`

Instruction: `orcc`
Description: Bitwise OR the source operands into the destination operand. The condition codes are set according to the result.
Example usage: `orcc %r1, 1, %r1`
Meaning: Set the least significant bit of `%r1` to 1.
Object code: `10000010100100000110000000000001`

Instruction: `orncc`
Description: Bitwise NOR the source operands into the destination operand. The condition codes are set according to the result.
Example usage: `orncc %r1, %r0, %r1`
Meaning: Complement `%r1`.
Object code: `10000010101100000100000000000000`

Instruction: `srl`

Description: Shift a register to the right by 0 to 31 bits. The vacant bit positions in the left side of the shifted register are filled with 0's.

Example usage: `srl %r1, 3, %r2`

Meaning: Shift `%r1` right by three bits and store in `%r2`. Zeros are copied into the three most significant bits of `%r2`.

Object code: `10000101001100000110000000000011`

Instruction: `addcc`

Description: Add the source operands into the destination operand using two's complement arithmetic. The condition codes are set according to the result.

Example usage: `addcc %r1, 5, %r1`

Meaning: Add 5 to `%r1`.

Object code: `10000010100000000110000000000101`

Instruction: `call`

Description: Call a subroutine and store the address of the current instruction (where the call itself is stored) in `%r15`, which effects a "call and link" operation. In the assembled code, the `disp30` field in the CALL format will contain a 30-bit displacement from the address of the `call` instruction. The address of the next instruction to be executed is computed by adding 4 × `disp30` (which shifts `disp30` to the high 30 bits of the 32-bit address) to the address of the current instruction. Note that `disp30` can be negative.

Example usage: `call sub_r`

Meaning: Call a subroutine that begins at location `sub_r`. For the object code shown, `sub_r` is 25 words (100 bytes) farther in memory than the call instruction.

Object code: `01000000000000000000000000011001`

Instruction: `jmpl`

Description: Jump and link (return from subroutine). Jump to a new address and store the address of the current instruction (where the `jmpl` instruction is located) in the destination register.

Example usage: `jmpl %r15 + 4, %r0`

Meaning: Return from subroutine. The value of the PC for the call instruction was previously saved in `%r15`, and so the return address should be computed for the instruction that follows the call, at `%r15 + 4`. The current address is discarded in `%r0`.

Object code: `10000001110000011111000000000100`

Instruction: `be`

Description: If the `z` condition code is 1, then branch to the address computed by adding 4 × `disp22` in the Branch instruction format to the address of the current instruction. If the `z` condition code is 0, then control is transferred to the instruction that follows `be`.

Example usage: `be label`

Meaning: Branch to `label` if the `z` condition code is 1. For the object code shown, `label` is five words (20 bytes) farther in memory than the `be` instruction.

Object code: `00000010100000000000000000000101`

Instruction: `bneg`

Description: If the `n` condition code is 1, then branch to the address computed by adding 4 × `disp22` in the Branch instruction format to the address of the current instruction. If the `n` condition code is 0, then control is transferred to the instruction that follows `bneg`.

Example usage: `bneg label`

Meaning: Branch to `label` if the `n` condition code is 1. For the object code shown, `label` is five words farther in memory than the `bneg` instruction.

Object code: `00001100100000000000000000000101`

Instruction: `bcs`

Description: If the `c` condition code is 1, then branch to the address computed by adding 4 × `disp22` in the Branch instruction format to the address of the current instruction. If the `c` condition code is 0, then control is transferred to the instruction that follows `bcs`.

Example usage: `bcs label`

Meaning: Branch to `label` if the `c` condition code is 1. For the object code shown, `label` is five words farther in memory than the `bcs` instruction.

Object code: `00001010100000000000000000000101`

Instruction: `bvs`

Description: If the `v` condition code is 1, then branch to the address computed by adding 4 × `disp22` in the Branch instruction format to the address of the current instruction. If the `v` condition code is 0, then control is transferred to the instruction that follows `bvs`.

Example usage: `bvs label`

Meaning: Branch to `label` if the `v` condition code is 1. For the object code shown, `label` is five words farther in memory than the `bvs` instruction.

Object code: `00001110100000000000000000000101`

Instruction: `ba`

Description: Branch to the address computed by adding 4 × `disp22` in the Branch instruction format to the address of the current instruction.

Example usage: `ba label`

Meaning: Branch to `label` regardless of the settings of the condition codes. For the object code shown, `label` is five words earlier in memory than the `ba` instruction.

Object code: `00010000101111111111111111111011`

4.3 Pseudo-Ops

In addition to the ARC instructions that are supported by the architecture, there are also **pseudo-operations** (pseudo-ops) that are not opcodes at all, but rather instructions to the assembler to perform some action at assembly time. A list of pseudo-ops and examples of their usages are shown in Figure 4-12. Note that unlike processor opcodes, which are specific to a given machine, the kind and nature of the pseudo-ops are specific to a given *assembler*, because they are executed by the assembler itself.

The `.equ` pseudo-op instructs the assembler to *equate* a value or a character string with a symbol, so that the symbol can be used throughout a program as if the value or string is written in its place. The `.begin` and `.end` pseudo-ops tell the assembler when to start and stop assembling. Any statements that appear before `.begin` or after `.end` are ignored. A single program may have more than one `.begin`/`.end` pair, but there must be a `.end` for every `.begin`, and there must be at least one `.begin`. The use of `.begin` and `.end` is helpful in making portions of the program invisible to the assembler during debugging.

The `.org` (origin) pseudo-op causes the next instruction to be assembled with the assumption it will be placed in the specified memory location at run-time (location 2048 in Figure 4-12). The `.dwb` (define word block) pseudo-op reserves a block of four-byte words, typically for an array. The **location counter** (which keeps track of which instruction is being assembled by the assembler) is moved ahead of the block according to the number of words specified by the argument to `.dwb` multiplied by 4.

Pseudo-Op	Usage	Meaning
`.equ`	`X .equ #10`	Treat symbol `X` as $(10)_{16}$
`.begin`	`.begin`	Start assembling
`.end`	`.end`	Stop assembling
`.org`	`.org 2048`	Change location counter to 2048
`.dwb`	`.dwb 25`	Reserve a block of 25 words
`.global`	`.global Y`	`Y` is used in another module
`.extern`	`.extern Z`	`Z` is defined in another module
`.macro`	`.macro M a, b, ...`	Define macro `M` with formal parameters `a, b, ...`
`.endmacro`	`.endmacro`	End of macro definition
`.if`	`.if <cond>`	Assemble if `<cond>` is true
`.endif`	`.endif`	End of `.if` construct

Figure 4-12 Pseudo-ops for the ARC assembly language.

The `.global` and `.extern` pseudo-ops deal with names of variables and addresses that are defined in one assembly code module and are used in another. The `.global` pseudo-op makes a label available for use in other modules. The `.extern` pseudo-op identifies a label that is used in the local module and is defined in another module (which should be marked with a `.global` in that module). We will see how `.global` and `.extern` are used when linking and loading are covered in the next chapter. The `.macro`, `.endmacro`, `.if`, and `.endif` pseudo-ops are also covered in the next chapter.

4.4 Examples of Assembly Language Programs

The process of writing an assembly language program is similar to the process of writing a high-level program, except that many of the details that are abstracted away in high-level programs are made explicit in assembly language programs. In this section, we take a look at two examples of ARC assembly language programs.

Program: Add Two Integers

Consider writing an ARC assembly language program that adds the integers 15 and 9. One possible coding is shown in Figure 4-13. The program begins and ends with a `.begin`/`.end` pair. The `.org` pseudo-op instructs the assembler to begin assembling so that the assembled code is loaded into memory starting at location 2048. The operands 15 and 9 are stored in variables `x` and `y`, respectively. We can only add numbers that are stored in registers in the ARC (because only `ld` and `st` can access main memory), and so the program begins by loading registers `%r1` and `%r2` with `x` and `y`. The `addcc` instruction adds `%r1` and `%r2` and places the result in `%r3`. The `st` instruction then stores `%r3` in memory location `z`. The `jmpl` instruction with operands `%r15 + 4, %r0` causes a

```
! This programs adds two numbers
        .begin
        .org 2048
prog1:  ld      [x], %r1          ! Load x into %r1
        ld      [y], %r2          ! Load y into %r2
        addcc   %r1, %r2, %r3     ! %r3 ← %r1 + %r2
        st      %r3, [z]          ! Store %r3 into z
        jmpl    %r15 + 4, %r0     ! Return
x:      15
y:      9
z:      0
        .end
```

Figure 4-13 An ARC assembly language program adds two integers.

return to the next instruction in the calling routine, which is the operating system if this is the highest level of a user's program, as we can assume it is here. The variables `x`, `y`, and `z` follow the program.

In practice, the SPARC code equivalent to the ARC code shown in Figure 4-13 is not entirely correct. The `ld`, `st`, and `jmpl` instructions all take at least two instruction cycles to complete, and since SPARC begins a new instruction at each clock tick, these instructions need to be followed by an instruction that does not rely on their results. This property of launching a new instruction before the previous one has completed is called **pipelining** and is covered in more detail in Chapter 9.

Program: Sum an Array of Integers

Now consider a more complex program that sums an array of integers. One possible coding is shown in Figure 4-14. As in the previous example, the program begins and ends with a `.begin`/`.end` pair. The `.org` pseudo-op instructs the

```
! This program sums LENGTH numbers
! Register usage:       %r1 - Length of array a
!                       %r2 - Starting address of array a
!                       %r3 - The partial sum
!                       %r4 - Pointer into array a
!                       %r5 - Holds an element of a
            .begin                 ! Start assembling
            .org   2048            ! Start program at 2048
a_start     .equ   3000            ! Address of array a
            ld     [length], %r1   ! %r1 ← length of array a
            ld     [address],%r2   ! %r2 ← address of a
            andcc  %r3, %r0, %r3   ! %r3 ← 0
loop:       andcc  %r1, %r1, %r0   ! Test # remaining elements
            be     done           ! Finished when length=0
            addcc  %r1, -4, %r1    ! Decrement array length
            addcc  %r1, %r2, %r4   ! Address of next element
            ld     %r4, %r5        ! %r5 ← Memory[%r4]
            addcc  %r3, %r5, %r3   ! Sum new element into r3
            ba     loop            ! Repeat loop.

done:       jmpl   %r15 + 4, %r0   ! Return to calling routine

length:            20              ! 5 numbers (20 bytes) in a
address:           a_start
            .org   a_start         ! Start of array a
a:                  25             ! length/4 values follow
                   -10
                    33
                    -5
                     7
            .end                         ! Stop assembling
```

Figure 4-14 An ARC program sums five integers.

assembler to begin assembling so that the assembled code is loaded into memory starting at location 2048. A pseudo-operand is created for the symbol a_start, which is assigned a value of 3000.

The program begins by loading the length of array a, which is given in bytes, into %r1. The program then loads the starting address of array a into %r2, and clears %r3, which will hold the partial sum. Register %r3 is cleared by ANDing it with %r0, which always holds the value 0. Register %r0 can be ANDed with any register for that matter, and the result will still be zero.

The label loop begins a loop that adds successive elements of array a into the partial sum (%r3) on each iteration. The loop starts by checking if the number of remaining array elements to sum (%r1) is zero. It does this by ANDing %r1 with itself, which has the side effect of setting the condition codes. We are interested in the z flag, which will be set to 1 if %r1 = 0. The remaining flags (n, v, and c) are set accordingly. The value of z is tested by making use of the be instruction. If there are no remaining array elements to sum, then the program branches to done, which returns to the calling routine (which might be the operating system, if this is the top level of a user program).

If the loop is not exited after the test for %r1 = 0, then %r1 is decremented by the width of a word in bytes (4) by adding –4. The starting address of array a (which is stored in %r2) and the index into a (%r1) are added into %r4, which then points to a new element of a. The element pointed to by %r4 is then loaded into %r5, which is added into the partial sum (%r3). The top of the loop is then revisited as a result of the "ba loop" statement. The variable length is stored after the instructions. The five elements of array a are placed in an area of memory according to the argument to the .org pseudo-op (location 3000).

Notice that there are three instructions for computing the address of the next array element, given the address of the top element in %r2 and the length of the array in bytes in %r1:

```
addcc %r1, -4, %r1     ! Point to next element to be added
addcc %r1, %r2, %r4    ! Add it to the base of the array
ld %r4, %r5            ! Load the next element into %r5.
```

This technique of computing the address of a data value as the sum of a base plus an index is so frequently used that the ARC and most other assembly languages have special "addressing modes" to accomplish it. In the case of ARC, the ld instruction address is computed as the sum of two registers or a register plus a 13-bit constant. Recall that register `%r0` always contains the value zero, so by specifying `%r0`, which is being done implicitly in the `ld` line, we are wasting an opportunity to have the `ld` instruction itself perform the address calculation. A single register can hold the operand address, and we can accomplish in two instructions what takes three instructions in the example:

```
addcc %r1, -4, %r1     ! Point to next element to be added
ld %r1 + %r2, %r5      ! Load the next element into %r5.
```

Notice that we also save a register, `%r4`, which was used as a temporary place holder for the address.

4.4.1 *VARIATIONS IN MACHINE ARCHITECTURES AND ADDRESSING*

The ARC is typical of a load/store computer. Programs written for load/store machines generally execute faster, in part due to reducing CPU-memory traffic by loading operands into the CPU only once, and storing results only when the computation is complete. The increase in program memory size is usually considered to be a worthwhile price to pay.

Such was not the case when memories were orders of magnitude more expensive and CPUs were orders of magnitude smaller, as was the situation earlier in the computer age. Under those earlier conditions, for CPUs that had perhaps only a single register to hold arithmetic values, intermediate results had to be stored in memory. Machines had **three-address**, **two-address**, and **one-address** arithmetic instructions. By this we mean that an instruction could do arithmetic with three, two, or one of its operands or results in memory, as opposed to the ARC, where all arithmetic and logic operands *must* be in registers.

Let us consider how the C expression A = B×C+D might be evaluated by each of the three- two- and one-address instruction types. In the following examples, when referring to a variable "A," this actually means "the operand whose address is A." In order to calculate some performance statistics for the program fragments, we will make the following assumptions:

- Addresses and data words are 16-bits, or 2 bytes in size—a not uncommon size in earlier machines.

- Opcodes are 8 bits in size.

We will compute both program size and program memory traffic , in bytes, with these assumptions.

Memory traffic has two components: the instruction itself, which must be fetched from memory to the CPU in order to be executed, and the data values—operands must be moved into the CPU in order to be operated upon, and results must be moved back to memory when the computation is complete. Observing these computations will allow us to visualize some of the trade-offs between program size and memory traffic that the various instruction classes offer. The reader should note that opcodes such as `mult` and `add` are generic; they are not ARC instructions.

Three-Address Instructions

In a three-address instruction, the expression A = B×C+D might be coded as

```
mult  B, C, A      ! A←B×C
add   D, A, A      ! A←A+D
```

which means multiply B by C and store the result at A. (At this point in the program, A is being used as a storage location for temporary results.) Then add D to A and store the result at address A. Each instruction is 1 + 2 + 2 + 2 = 7 bytes in size. Thus the program size is 7 + 7 or 14 bytes. Memory traffic for each instruction is computed as the sum of instruction fetch, 7 bytes, plus data traffic, 2 + 2 + 2 = 6 bytes for a total of 13 bytes. Thus the total program memory traffic is (7 + 6) + (7 + 6) or 26 bytes.

Two-Address Instructions

In a two-address instruction, one of the operands is overwritten by the result. Here, the code for the expression A = B×C+D is

```
load  B, A         ! A←B
mult  C, A         ! A←A×C
add   D, A         ! A←A+D
```

Each of the three instructions is now 1 + 2 + 2 = 5 bytes in size, so the program size is now 3 × 5 = 15 bytes. In computing memory traffic we should note that each of the three instruction fetches will result in 5 bytes of traffic, as described above. However the data traffic of the first instruction will be 2 words, or 4 bytes, whereas the data traffic of the last two instructions will be 3 words, or 6 bytes. This is because for the last two instructions both operands must be loaded into the CPU, requiring 2 words, or 4 bytes, and the result must be stored in memory, requiring 1 word or 2 bytes. Thus the total memory traffic for the three instructions will be (5 + 4) + (5 + 6) + (5 + 6) = 31 bytes.

One-Address, or Accumulator Instructions

A one-address instruction employs a single programmer-accessible arithmetic register in the CPU, known as the **accumulator**. The accumulator typically holds one arithmetic operand and also serves as the target for the result of an arithmetic operation. The one-address format is not in common use these days but was more common in the early days of computing, when registers were more expensive and frequently served multiple purposes. It serves as temporary storage for one of the operands and also for the result. The code for the expression A = B×C+D is now

```
load  B          ! Acc←B
mult  C          ! Acc←Acc×C
add   D          ! Acc←Acc+D
store A          ! A←Acc
```

The `load` instruction loads B into the accumulator, `mult` multiplies C by the accumulator and stores the result in the accumulator, and `add` does the corresponding addition. The `store` instruction stores the accumulator in A. Each instruction is now 1 + 2 = 3 bytes in size, so total program size 3 × 4 = 12 bytes. Notice that each instruction results on only one word, or 2 bytes being fetched or stored. Thus memory traffic for each instruction is (3 + 2) = 5 bytes, so total memory traffic for the program is 4 × 5 = 20 bytes.

Note that the one-address machine has the smallest program size and the smallest instruction traffic of all the machine classes. This explains the popularity of accumulator machines in the earliest computers, when registers and memory cost hundreds of dollars per bit.

Special-Purpose Registers

In addition to the general-purpose registers and the accumulator described previously, most modern architectures include other registers that are dedicated to specific purposes. Examples include the following:

- Memory index registers: The Intel 80x86 source index (SI) and destination index (DI) registers. These are used to point to the beginning or end of an array in memory. Special "string" instructions transfer a byte or a word from the starting memory location pointed to by SI to the ending memory location pointed to by DI, and then increment or decrement these registers to point to the next byte or word.

- Floating point registers: Many current-generation processors have special registers and instructions that handle floating point numbers.

- Registers to support time , and timing operations: The PowerPC 601 processor has real-time clock registers that provide a high-resolution measure of real time for indicating the date and the time of day. They provide a range of approximately 135 years, with a resolution of 128 ns.

- Registers in support of the operating system: Most modern processors have registers to support the memory system.

- Registers that can be accessed only by "privileged instructions," or when in "Supervisor mode." In order to prevent accidental or malicious damage to the system, many processors have special instructions and registers that are unavailable to the ordinary user and application program. These instructions and registers are used only by the operating system.

4.4.2 *PERFORMANCE OF INSTRUCTION SET ARCHITECTURES*

While the program size and memory usage statistics calculated previously are observed out of context from the larger programs in which they would be contained, they do show that having even one temporary storage register in the CPU can have a significant effect on program performance. In fact, the Intel Pentium processor, considered among the faster of the general-purpose CPUs, has only a single accumulator, though it has a number of special-purpose registers that support it. There are many other factors that affect real-world performance of an instruction set, such as the time an instruction takes to perform its function and the speed at which the processor can run.

4.5 Accessing Data in Memory—Addressing Modes

Up to this point, we have seen four ways of computing the address of a value in memory: (1) a constant value, known at assembly time, (2) the contents of a register, (3) the sum of two registers, and (4) the sum of a register and a constant.

Table 4-1 gives names to these addressing modes and shows a few others as well. Notice that the syntax of the table differs from that of the ARC. This is a com-

Addressing Mode	Syntax	Meaning
Immediate	#K	K
Direct	K	M[K]
Indirect	(K)	M[M[K]]
Register Indirect	(Rn)	M[Rn]
Register indexed	(Rm + Rn)	M[Rm + Rn]
Register based	(Rm + X)	M[Rm + X]
Register based indexed	(Rm + Rn + X)	M[Rm + Rn + X]

Table 4-1 Addressing Modes

mon, unfortunate feature of assembly languages: Each one differs from the rest in its syntax conventions. The notation M[x] in the Meaning column assumes memory is an array, M, whose byte index is given by the address computation in brackets. There may seem to be a bewildering assortment of addressing modes, but each has its usage:

- Immediate addressing allows a reference to a constant that is known at assembly time.
- Direct addressing is used to access data items whose address is known at assembly time.
- Indirect addressing is used to access a pointer variable whose address is known at compile time. This addressing mode is seldom supported in modern processors because it requires two memory references to access the operand, making it a complicated instruction. Programmers who wish to access data in this form must use two instructions, one to access the pointer and another to access the value to which it refers. This has the beneficial side effect of exposing the complexity of the addressing mode, perhaps discouraging its use.
- Register indirect addressing is used when the address of the operand is not known until run time. Stack operands fit this description and are accessed by register indirect addressing, often in the form of push and pop instructions that also decrement and increment the register, respectively.

- Register indexed, register based, and register-based indexed addressing are used to access components of arrays such as the one in Figure 4-14, and components buried beneath the top of the stack, in a data structure known as the **stack frame**, which is discussed in the next section.

4.6 Subroutine Linkage and Stacks

A **subroutine**, sometimes called a **function** or **procedure**, is a sequence of instructions that is invoked in a manner that makes it appear to be a single instruction in a high-level view. When a program calls a subroutine, control is passed from the program to the subroutine, which executes a sequence of instructions and then returns to the location just past where it was called. There are a number of methods for passing arguments to and from the called routine, referred to as **calling conventions**. The process of passing arguments between routines is referred to as **subroutine linkage**.

One calling convention simply places the arguments in registers. The code in Figure 4-15 shows a program that loads two arguments into %r1 and %r2, calls subroutine add_1, and then retrieves the result from %r3. Subroutine add_1 takes its operands from %r1 and %r2 and places the result in %r3 before returning via the jmpl instruction. This method is fast and simple, but it will not work if the number of arguments that are passed between the routines exceeds the number of free registers, or if subroutine calls are deeply nested.

A second calling convention creates a **data link area**. The address of the data link area is passed in a predetermined register to the called routine. Figure 4-16 shows an example of this method of subroutine linkage. The .dwb pseudo-op in the calling routine sets up a data link area that is three words long, at addresses x,

```
! Calling routine                ! Called routine
                                 ! %r3 ← %r1 + %r2
      .
      .
      .
      ld     [x], %r1
      ld     [y], %r2            add_1:  addcc   %r1, %r2, %r3
      call   add_1                       jmpl    %r15 + 4, %r0
      st     %r3, [z]
      .
      .
      .
x:    53
y:    10
z:     0
```

Figure 4-15 Subroutine linkage using registers.

```
! Calling routine                   ! Called routine
                                    ! x[2] ← x[0] + x[1]
    .
    .
    .
    st      %r1, [x]                add_2:  ld      %r5, %r8
    st      %r2, [x+4]                      ld      %r5 + 4, %r9
    sethi   x, %r5                          addcc   %r8, %r9, %r10
    srl     %r5, 10, %r5                    st      %r10, %r5 + 8
    call    add_2                           jmpl    %r15 + 4, %r0
    ld      [x+8], %r3
    .
    .
    .
! Data link area
x:  .dwb    3
```

Figure 4-16 Subroutine linkage using a data link area.

x+4, and x+8. The calling routine loads its two arguments into x and x+4, calls subroutine add_2, and then retrieves the result passed back from add_2 from memory location x+8. The address of data link area x is passed to add_2 in register %r5.

Note that sethi must have a constant for its source operand, and so the assembler recognizes the sethi construct shown for the calling routine and replaces x with its address. The srl that follows the sethi moves the address x into the least significant 22 bits of %r5, since sethi places its operand into the leftmost 22 bits of the target register. An alternative approach to loading the address of x into %r5 would be to use a storage location for the address of x, and then simply apply the ld instruction to load the address into %r5. While the latter approach is simpler, the sethi/srl approach is faster because it does not involve a time-consuming access to the memory.

Subroutine add_2 reads its two operands from the data link area at locations %r5 and %r5 + 4, and places its result in the data link area at location %r5 + 8 before returning. By using a data link area, arbitrarily large blocks of data can be passed between routines without copying more than a single register during subroutine linkage. Recursion can create a burdensome bookkeeping overhead, however, since a routine that calls itself will need several data link areas. Data link areas have the advantage that their size can be unlimited, but also have the disadvantage that the size of the data link area must be known at assembly time.

A third calling convention uses a stack. The general idea is that the calling routine pushes all of its arguments (or pointers to arguments, if the data objects are large) onto a last-in-first-out stack. The called routine then pops the passed arguments

Calling routine	Called routine

`! Calling routine`
`    .`
`    .`
`%sp .equ   %r14`
`    addcc %sp, -4, %sp`
`    st    %r1, %sp`
`    addcc %sp, -4, %sp`
`    st    %r2, %sp`
`    call  add_3`
`    ld    %sp, %r3`
`    addcc %sp, 4, %sp`
`    .`
`    .`
	`! Called routine`
	`! Arguments are on stack.`
	`! %sp[0] ← %sp[0] + %sp[4]`
	`   %sp  .equ   %r14`
	`add_3: ld     %sp, %r8`
	`       addcc  %sp, 4, %sp`
	`       ld     %sp, %r9`
	`       addcc  %r8, %r9, %r10`
	`       st     %r10, %sp`
	`       jmpl   %r15 + 4, %r0`

Figure 4-17 Subroutine linkage using a stack.

from the stack, and pushes any return values onto the stack. The calling routine then retrieves the return value(s) from the stack and continues execution. A register in the CPU, known as the **stack pointer**, contains the address of the top of the stack. Many machines have `push` and `pop` instructions that automatically decrement and increment the stack pointer as data items are pushed and popped.

An advantage of using a stack is that its size grows and shrinks as needed. This supports arbitrarily deep nesting of procedure calls without having to declare the size of the stack at assembly time. An example of passing arguments using a stack is shown in Figure 4-17. Register `%r14` serves as the stack pointer (`%sp`), which is initialized by the operating system prior to execution of the calling routine. The calling routine places its arguments (`%r1` and `%r2`) onto the stack by decrementing the stack pointer (which moves `%sp` to the next free word above the stack) and by storing each argument on the new top of the stack. Subroutine `add_3` is called, which pops its arguments from the stack, performs an addition operation, and then stores its return value on the top of the stack before returning. The calling routine then retrieves its argument from the top of the stack and continues execution.

For each of the calling conventions, the `call` instruction is used, which saves the current PC in `%r15`. When a subroutine finishes execution, it needs to return to the instruction that *follows* the call, which is one word (four bytes) past the saved PC. Thus, the statement "`jmpl %r15 + 4, %r0`" completes the return. If the called routine calls *another* routine, however, then the value of the PC that was originally saved in `%r15` will be overwritten by the nested call, which means that a correct return to the original calling routine through `%r15` will no longer be possible. In order to allow nested calls and returns, the current value of `%r15`

```
/* C program showing nested subroutine calls */
main()
{
    int w, z;            /* Local variables */
    w = func_1(1,2);     /* Call subroutine func_1 */
    z = func_2(10);      /* Call subroutine func_2 */
}                        /* End of main routine */

int func_1(x,y)          /* Compute x * x + y */
int x, y;           /* Parameters passed to func_1 */
{
    int i, j;            /* Local variables */
    i = x * x;
    j = i + y;
    return(j);      /* Return j to calling routine */
}

int func_2(a)            /* Compute a * a + a + 5 */
int a;                   /* Parameter passed to func_2 */
{
    int m, n;            /* Local variables */
    n = a + 5;
    m = func_1(a,n);
    return(m);           /* Return m to calling routine */
}
```

Figure 4-18 A C program illustrating nested function calls.

(which is called the **link register**) should be saved on the stack, along with any other registers that need to be restored after the return.

If a register-based calling convention is used, then the link register should be saved in one of the unused registers before a nested call is made. If a data link area is used, then there should be space reserved within it for the link register. If a stack scheme is used, then the link register should be saved on the stack. For each of the calling conventions, the link register and the local variables in the called routines should be saved before a nested call is made: otherwise, a nested call to the same routine will cause the local variables to be overwritten.

There are many variations to the basic calling conventions, but the stack-oriented approach to subroutine linkage is probably the most popular. When a stack-based calling convention is used that handles nested subroutine calls, a **stack frame** is built that contains arguments that are passed to a called routine, the return address for the calling routine, and any local variables. A sample high-level program is shown in Figure 4-18 that illustrates nested function

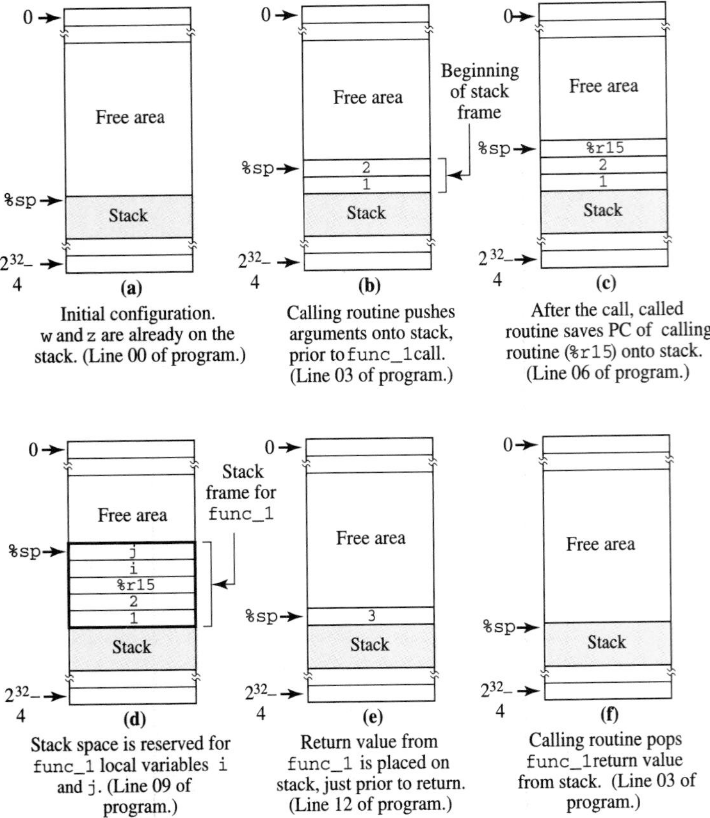

Figure 4-19 (a–f) Stack behavior during execution of the program shown in Figure 4-18.

calls. The operation that the program performs is not important, nor is the fact that the C programming language is used, but what is important is how the subroutine calls are implemented.

The behavior of the stack for this program is shown in Figure 4-19. The main program calls `func_1` with arguments 1 and 2, and then calls `func_2` with argument 10 before finishing execution. Function `func_1` has two local variables `i` and `j` that are used in computing the return value `j`. Function `func_2` has two local variables `m` and `n` that are used in creating the arguments to pass through to `func_1` before returning `m`.

The stack pointer (`%r14` by convention, which will be referred to as `%sp`) is initialized before the program starts executing, usually by the operating system. The

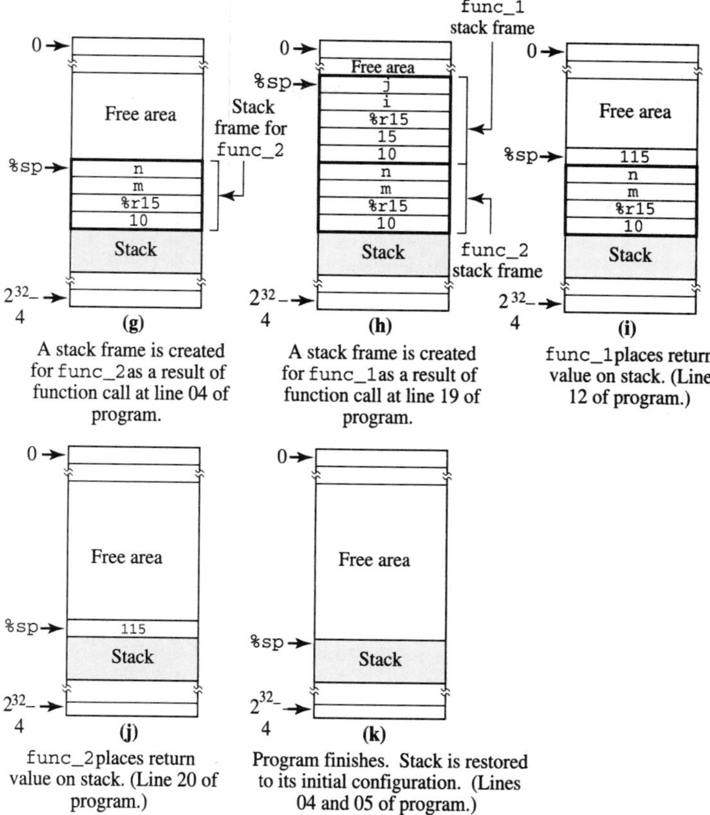

Figure 4-19 (g–k).

compiler is responsible for implementing the calling convention, and so the compiler produces code for pushing parameters and the return address onto the stack, reserving room on the stack for local variables, and then reversing the process as routines return from their calls. The stack behavior shown in Figure 4-19 is thus produced as the result of executing compiler generated code, but the code may just as well have been written directly in assembly language.

As the main program begins execution, the stack pointer points to the top element of the system stack (Figure 4-19a). When the main routine calls `func_1` at line `03` of the program shown in Figure 4-18 with arguments 1 and 2, the arguments are pushed onto the stack, as shown in Figure 4-19b. Control is then transferred to `func_1` through a `call` instruction (not shown), and `func_1` then saves the return address, which is in `%r15` as a result of the `call` instruction, onto the stack (Figure 4-19c). Stack space is reserved for local variables `i` and `j` of `func_1` (Figure 4-19d). At this point, we have a complete stack frame for the `func_1` call as shown in Figure 4-19d, which is composed of the arguments passed to `func_1`, the return address to the main routine, and the local variables for `func_1`.

Just prior to `func_1` returning to the calling routine, it releases the stack space for its local variables, retrieves the return address from the stack, releases the stack space for the arguments passed to it, and then pushes its return value onto the stack, as shown in Figure 4-19e. Control is then returned to the calling routine through a `jmpl` instruction, and the calling routine is then responsible for retrieving the returned value from the stack and decrementing the stack pointer to its position from before the call, as shown in Figure 4-19f. Routine `func_2` is then executed, and the process of building a stack frame starts all over again, as shown in Figure 4-19g. Since `func_2` makes a call to `func_1` before it returns, there will be stack frames for both `func_2` and `func_1` on the stack at the same time, as shown in Figure 4-19h. The process then unwinds as before, finally resulting in the stack pointer at its original position, as shown in Figure 4-19i–k.

4.7 Input and Output in Assembly Language

Finally, we come to ways in which an assembly language program can communicate with the outside world: input and output (I/O) activities. One way that communication between I/O devices and the rest of the machine can be handled is with special instructions, and with a special I/O bus reserved for this purpose. An alternative method for interacting with I/O devices is through the use of memory mapped I/O, in which devices occupy sections of the address space where no ordinary memory exists. Devices are accessed as if they are memory locations, and so there is no need for handling devices with new instructions.

As an example of memory mapped I/O, consider again the memory map for the ARC, which is illustrated in Figure 4-20. We see a few new regions of memory, for two add-in video memory modules and for a **touchscreen**. A touchscreen comes in two forms, photonic and electrical. An illustration of the photonic version is shown in Figure 4-21. A matrix of beams covers the screen in the horizontal and vertical dimensions. If the beams are interrupted (by a finger, for example) then the position is determined by the interrupted beams. (In an alternative version of the touchscreen, the display is covered with a touch sensitive surface. The user must make contact with the screen in order to register a selection.)

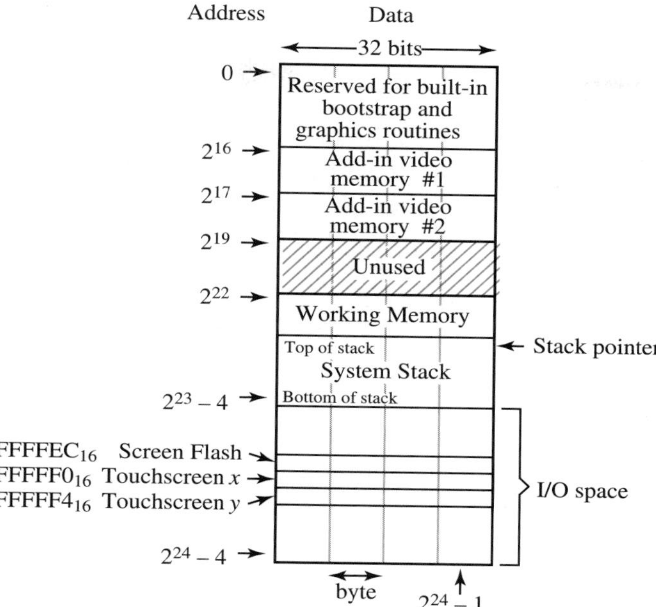

Figure 4-20 Memory map for the ARC, showing memory mapping.

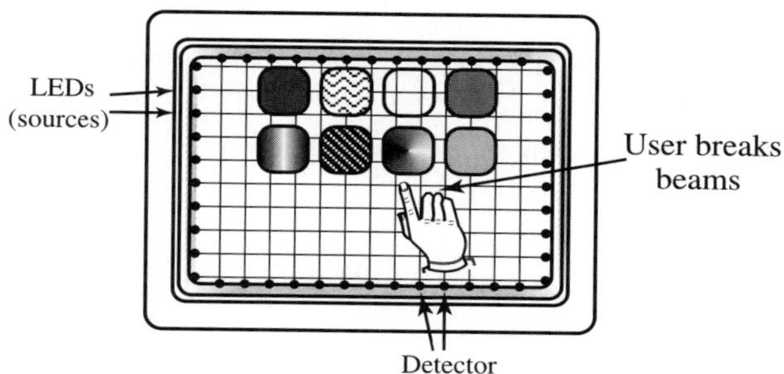

Figure 4-21 A user selecting an object on a touchscreen.

The only real memory occupies the address space between 2^{22} and $2^{23} - 1$. (Remember: $2^{23} - 4$ is the address of the leftmost byte of the highest word in the big-endian format.) The rest of the address space is occupied by other components. The address space between 0 and $2^{16} - 1$ (inclusive) contains built-in programs for the power-on bootstrap operation and basic graphics routines. The address space between 2^{16} and $2^{19} - 1$ is used for two add-in video memory modules, which we will study in Problem 4.3. Note that valid information is

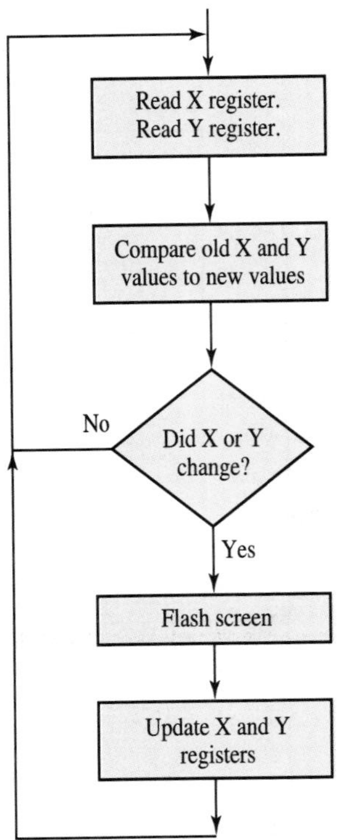

Figure 4-22 Flowchart illustrating the control structure of a program that tracks a touchscreen.

available only when the add-in memory modules are physically inserted into the machine.

Finally, the address space between 2^{23} and $2^{24} - 1$ is used for I/O devices. For this system, the X and Y coordinates that mark the position where a user has made a selection are automatically updated in registers that are placed in the memory map. The registers are accessed by simply reading from the memory locations where these registers are located. The "screen flash" location causes the screen to flash whenever it is written.

Suppose that we would like to write a simple program that flashes the screen whenever the user changes position. The flowchart in Figure 4-22 illustrates how this might be done. The X and Y registers are first read and are then compared with the previous X and Y values. If either position has changed, then the screen is flashed and the previous X and Y values are updated and the process repeats. If neither position has changed, then the process simply repeats. This is an example of the programmed I/O method of accessing a device. (See Problem 4.3 at the end of the chapter for a more detailed description.)

4.8 Case Study: The Java Virtual Machine ISA

Java is a high-level programming language developed by Sun Microsystems that has taken a prominent position in the programming community. A key aspect of Java is that Java binary codes are platform-independent, which means that the same compiled code can run without modification on any computer that supports the **Java Virtual Machine** (JVM). The JVM is how Java achieves its platform-independence: A standard specification of the JVM is implemented in the native instruction sets of many underlying machines, and compiled Java codes can then run in any JVM environment.

Programs that are written in fully compiled languages like C, C++, and Fortran are compiled into the native code of the target architecture and are generally not portable across platforms unless the source code is recompiled for the target machine. Interpreted languages, like Perl, Tcl, AppleScript, and shell script, are largely platform independent but can execute 100 to 200 times slower than a fully compiled language. Java programs are compiled into an intermediate form known as **bytecodes**, which execute on the order of 10 times more slowly than fully compiled languages, but the cross-platform compatibility and other language features make Java a favorable programming language for many applications.

A high-level view of the JVM architecture is shown in Figure 4-23. The JVM is a stack-based machine, which means that the operands are pushed and popped from a stack, instead of being transferred among general-purpose registers. There are, however, a number of special-purpose registers, and also a number of local variables that serve the function of general-purpose registers in a "real" (non-virtual) architecture. The Java Execution Engine takes compiled Java bytecodes as its input and interprets the bytecodes in a software implementation of the JVM, or executes the bytecodes directly in a hardware implementation of the JVM.

Figure 4-24 shows a Java implementation of the SPARC program we studied in Figure 4-13. The figure shows both the Java source program and the bytecodes into which it was compiled. The bytecode file is known as a Java **class file** (which is what a compiled Java program is called).

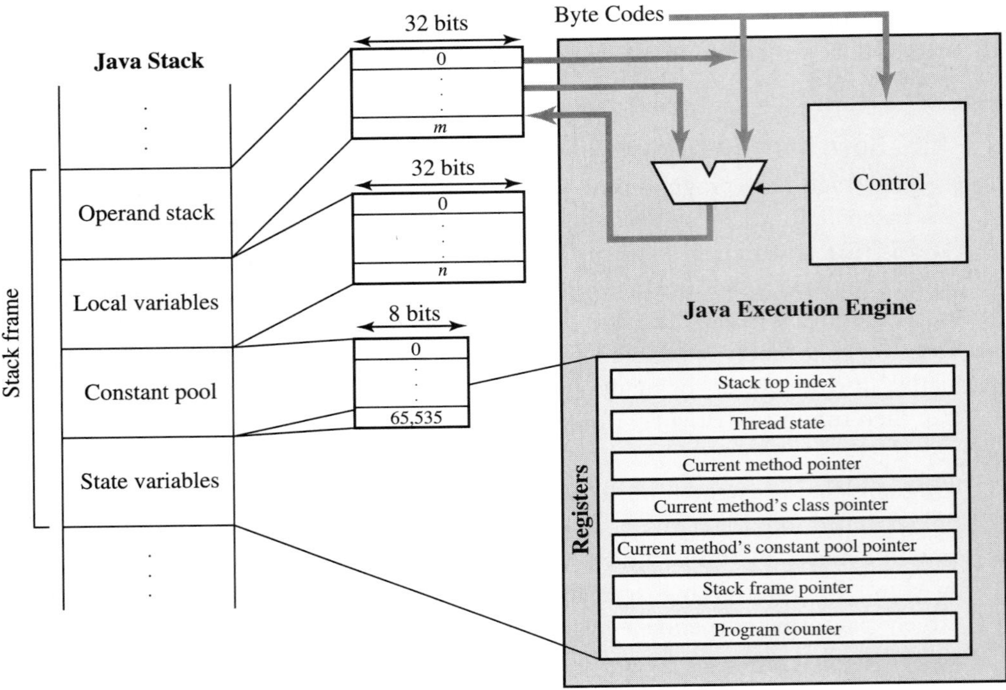

Figure 4-23 Architecture of the Java virtual machine.

Only a small number of bytes in a class file actually contain instructions; the rest is overhead that the file must contain in order to run on the JVM. In Figure 4-25 we have "disassembled" the bytecodes back to their higher-level format. The bytecode locations are given in hexadecimal, starting at location `0x00`. The first 4 bytes contain the magic number `0xcafebabe`, which identifies the program as a compiled Java class file. The major version and minor version numbers refer to the Java runtime system for which the program is compiled. The number of entries in the **constant pool** follows, which is actually 17 in this example: The first entry (constant pool location 0) is always reserved for the JVM and is not included in the class file, although indexing into the constant pool starts at location 0 as if it is explicitly represented. The constant pool contains the names of **methods** (functions), attributes, and other information used by the run-time system.

The remainder of the file is mostly composed of the constant pool and executable Java instructions. We will not cover all details of the Java class file here. The reader is referred to (Meyer & Downing, 1997) for a full description of the Java class file format.

```
// This is file add.java

public class add {
    public static void main(String args[]) {
        int x=15, y=9, z=0;
        z = x + y;
        }
    }
```

```
0000 cafe babe 0003 002d 0012 0700 0e07 0010   ................
0010 0a00 0200 040c 0007 0005 0100 0328 2956   .............()V
0020 0100 1628 5b4c 6a61 7661 2f6c 616e 672f   ...([Ljava/lang/
0030 5374 7269 6e67 3b29 5601 0006 3c69 6e69   String;)V...<ini
0040 743e 0100 0443 6f64 6501 000d 436f 6e73   t>...Code...Cons
0050 7461 6e74 5661 6c75 6501 000a 4578 6365   tantValue...Exce
0060 7074 696f 6e73 0100 0f4c 696e 654e 756d   ptions...LineNum
0070 6265 7254 6162 6c65 0100 0e4c 6f63 616c   berTable...Local
0080 5661 7269 6162 6c65 7301 000a 536f 7572   Variables...Sour
0090 6365 4669 6c65 0100 0361 6464 0100 0861   ceFile...add...a
00a0 6464 2e6a 6176 6101 0010 6a61 7661 2f6c   dd.java...java/l
00b0 616e 672f 4f62 6a65 6374 0100 046d 6169   ang/Object...mai
00c0 6e00 2100 0100 0200 0000 0000 0200 0900   n...............
00d0 1100 0600 0100 0800 0000 2d00 0200 0400   ................
00e0 0000 0d10 0f3c 1009 3d03 3e1b 1c60 3eb1   ................
00f0 0000 0001 000b 0000 000e 0003 0000 0004   ................
0100 0008 0006 000c 0002 0001 0007 0005 0001   ................
0110 0008 0000 001d 0001 0001 0000 0005 2ab7   ................
0120 0003 b100 0000 0100 0b00 0000 0600 0100   ................
0130 0000 0100 0100 0d00 0000 0200 0f00        ..............
```

Figure 4-24 Java program and compiled class file.

The actual code that corresponds to the Java source program, which simply adds the constants 15 and 9 and returns the result (24) to the calling routine on the stack, appears in locations `0x00e3–0x00ef`. You should be aware, as you follow the example, that variables x, y, and z in Figure 4-24 are defined as ints, and Java ints are 32 bits in size. Figure 4-26 shows how that portion of the bytecode is interpreted. The program converts the constants 15 and 9 into 32-bit words by sign extension and pushes the words onto the stack, using local variables 0 and 1 as intermediaries. In a bit of unnecessary gymnastics, the program pops these two values from the stack into two local variables, and then immediately pushes them back onto the stack! It then invokes the `iadd` instruction, which pops the top two stack elements, adds them, and places the result on the top of the stack. The program then returns.

These unnecessary stack operations represent some of the reasons why the JVM runs 10 times slower than native code. The program pushes the arguments, then pops them into local variables 1 and 2, and then pushes them back onto the Java stack before adding them. This transfer would be viewed as redundant by native code compilers for other languages and would be eliminated. Given this example

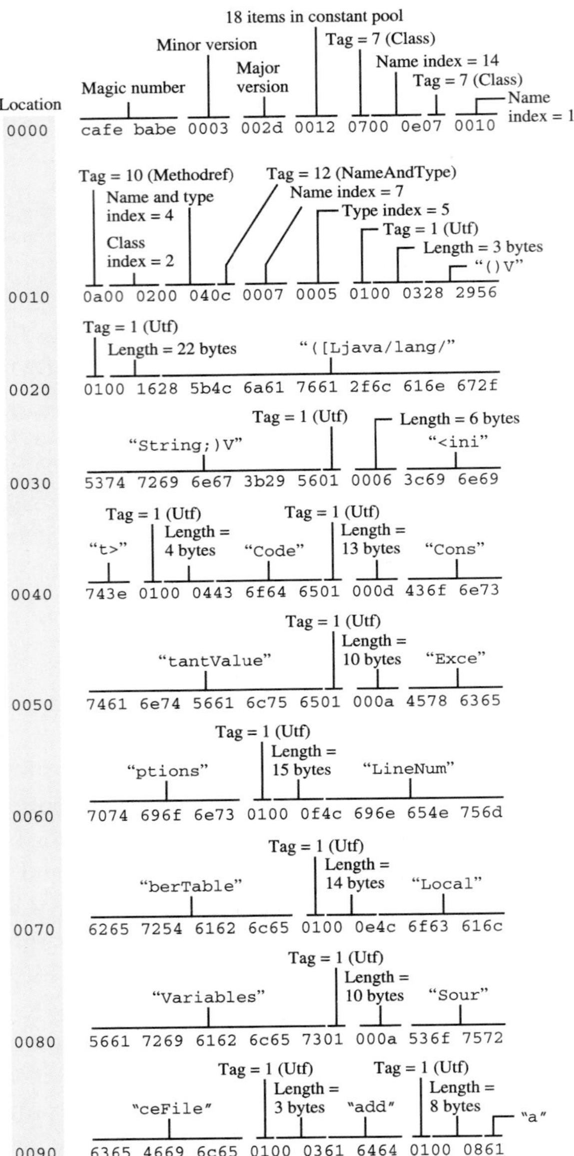

Figure 4-25 A Java class file.

alone, there is probably considerable room for speed improvements from the 10 times slower execution time of today's JVMs. Other improvements may also come in the form of **just-in-time** (JIT) compilers. Rather than interpreting the JVM bytecodes one by one into the target machine code each time they are

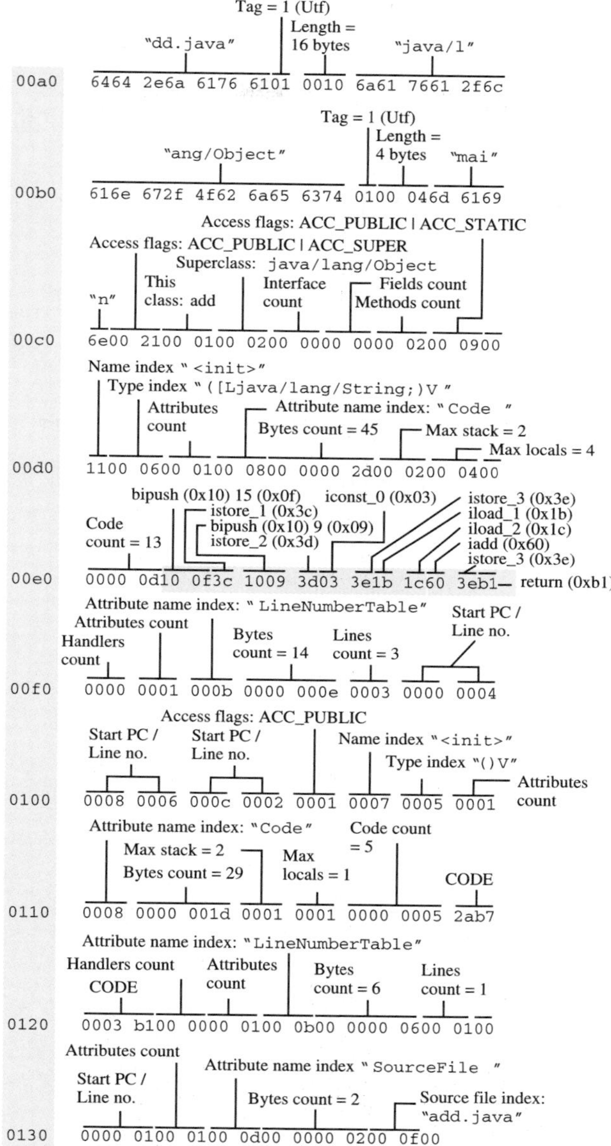

Figure 4-25 A Java class file (Continued).

encountered, JIT compilers take advantage of the fact that most programs spend most of their time in loops and other iterative routines. As the JIT encounters each line of code for the first time, it compiles it into native code and stores it

Location	Code	Mnemonic	Meaning
0x00e3	0x10	bipush	Push next word onto stack
0x00e4	0x0f	15	Argument to bipush
0x00e5	0x3c	istore_1	Pop stack to local variable 1
0x00e6	0x10	bipush	Push next word onto stack
0x00e7	0x09	9	Argument to bipush
0x00e8	0x3d	istore_2	Pop stack to local variable 2
0x00e9	0x03	iconst_0	Push constant word 0 onto stack
0x00ea	0x3e	istore_3	Pop stack to local variable 3
0x00eb	0x1b	iload_1	Push local variable 1 onto stack
0x00ec	0x1c	iload_2	Push local variable 2 onto stack
0x00ed	0x60	iadd	Add top two stack elements
0x00ee	0x3e	istore_3	Pop stack to local variable 3
0x00ef	0xb1	return	Return

Figure 4-26 Disassembled version of the code that implement the Java program in Figure 4-24.

away in memory for possible later use. The next time that code is executed, it is the native, compiled form that is executed rather than the bytecodes.

■ SUMMARY

In this chapter, we introduced the ARC ISA and studied some general properties of ISAs. In the design of an instruction set, a balance must be struck between system performance and the characteristics of the technology in which the processor is implemented. Interaction between the CPU and the memory is a key consideration.

When a memory access is made, the way in which the address is calculated is called the memory addressing mode. We examined the sequence of computations that can be combined to make up an addressing mode. We also looked at some specific cases that are commonly identified by name.

We also looked at several parts of a computer system that play a role in the execution of a program. We learned that programs are made up of sequences of instructions, which are taken from the instruction set of the CPU. In the next chapter, we will study how these sequences of instructions are translated into object code.

■ FURTHER READING

The material in this chapter is for the most part a collection of the historical experience gained in fifty years of stored program computer designs. Although each generation of computer systems is typically identified by a specific hardware technology, there have also been historically important instruction set architectures. In the first-generation systems of the 1950s, such as von Neuman's EDVAC, Eckert and Mauchly's UNIVAC, and the IBM 701, programming was performed by hand in machine language. Although simple, these instruction set architectures defined the fundamental concepts surrounding opcodes and operands.

The concept of an instruction set architecture as an identifiable entity can be traced to the designers of the IBM S/360 in the 1960s. The VAX architecture for Digital Equipment Corporation can also trace its roots to this period, when the minicomputers, the PDP-4 and PDP-8, were being developed. Both the 360 and VAX are two-address architectures. Significant one-address architectures include the Intel 8080, which is the predecessor to the modern 80x86, and its contemporary at that time, the Zilog Z-80. As a zero-address architecture, the Burroughs B5000 is also of historical significance.

There are a host of references that cover the various machine languages in existence, too many to enumerate here, and so we mention only a few of the more celebrated cases. The machine languages of Babbage's machines are covered in (Bromley, 1987). The machine language of the early Institute for Advanced Study (IAS) computer is covered in (Stallings, 1996). The IBM 360 machine language is covered in (Struble, 1975). The machine language of the 68000 can be found in (Gill *et al.*, 1987) and the machine language of the SPARC can be found in (SPARC, 1992). A full description of the JVM and the Java class file format can be found in (Meyer & Downing, 1997.)

Bromley, A. G., "The Evolution of Babbage's Calculating Engines," *Annals of the History of Computing*, **9**, pp. 113–138 (1987).

Gill, A., E. Corwin, and A. Logar, *Assembly Language Programming for the 68000*, Prentice-Hall (1987).

Meyer, J. and T. Downing, *Java Virtual Machine*, O'Reilly & Associates (1997).

SPARC International, Inc., *The SPARC Architecture Manual: Version 8*, Prentice Hall (1992).

Stallings, W., *Computer Organization and Architecture*, 4/e, Prentice Hall (1996).

Struble, G. W., *Assembler Language Programming: The IBM System/360 and 370*, 2/e, Addison-Wesley (1975).

PROBLEMS

4.1 A memory has 2^{24} addressable locations. What is the smallest width in bits that the address can be while still being able to address all 2^{24} locations?

4.2 What are the lowest and highest addresses in a 2^{20} byte memory, in which a four-byte word is the smallest addressable unit?

4.3 The memory map for the ARC is shown in Figure 4-20.

(a) How much memory (in bytes) is available for each of the add-in video memory modules? (Give your answer as powers of two or sums of powers of two, e.g., 2^{10}.)

(b) When a finger is drawn across the touchscreen, the horizontal (x) and vertical (y) positions of the joystick are updated in registers that are accessed at locations $(\texttt{FFFFF0})_{16}$ and $(\texttt{FFFFF4})_{16}$, respectively. When the number '1' is written to the register at memory location $(\texttt{FFFFEC})_{16}$ the screen flashes, and then location $(\texttt{FFFFEC})_{16}$ is automatically cleared to zero by the hardware (the software does not have to clear it). Write an ARC program that flashes the screen every time the user's position changes. Use the skeleton program shown.

```
       .begin
       ld     [x], %r7      ! %r7 and %r8 now point to the
       ld     [y], %r8      ! touchscreen x and y locations
       ld     [flash], %r9    ! %r9 points to flash location
loop:ld       %r7, %r1        ! Load current touchscreen
       ld     %r8, %r2        ! position in %r1=x and %r2=y
       ld     [old_x], %r3    ! Load old touchscreen
       ld     [old_y], %r4    ! position in %r3=x and %r4=y
       orncc %r3, %r0, %r3    ! Form 1's complement of old_x
       addcc %r3, 1, %r3      ! Form 2's complement of old_x
       addcc %r1, %r3, %r3    ! %r3 <- x - old_x
       be     x_not_moved     ! Branch if x did not change
       ba     moved      ! x changed, so no need to check y
x_not_moved:    ! Your code starts here, about four lines.

            <— YOUR CODE GOES HERE

   ! This portion of the code is entered only if
   ! touchscreen cursor is moved.
   ! Flash screen; store new x, y values; repeat.
```

```
moved:orcc  %r0, 1, %r5     ! Place 1 in %r5
      st    %r5, %r9        ! Store 1 in flash register
      st    %r1, [old_x]    ! Update old joystick position
      st    %r2, [old_y]    !   with current position
      ba    loop            ! Repeat
flash:    #FFFFEC           ! Location of flash register
x:        #FFFFF0    ! Location of touchscreen x register
y:        #FFFFF4    ! Location of touchscreen y register
old_x:    0               ! Previous x position
old_y:    0               ! Previous y position
      .end
```

4.4 Write an ARC subroutine that performs a swap operation on the 32-bit operands `x = 25` and `y = 50`, which are stored in memory. Use as few registers as you can.

4.5 A section of ARC assembly code is shown here. What does it do? Express your answer in terms of the actions it goes through. Does it add up numbers or clear something out? Does it simulate a **for** loop, a **while** loop, or something else? Assume that `a` and `b` are memory locations that are defined elsewhere in the code.

```
Y:    ld     [k], %r1
      addcc  %r1, -4, %r1
      st     %r1, [k]
      bneg   X
      ld     [a], %r1, %r2
      ld     [b], %r1, %r3
      addcc  %r2, %r3, %r4
      st     %r4, %r1, [c]
      ba     Y
X:    jmpl   %r15 + 4, %r0
k:    40
```

4.6 A pocket pager contains a small processor with 2^7 8-bit words of memory. The ISA has four registers: R0, R1, R2, and R3. The instruction set is shown in Figure 4-27, as well as the bit patterns that correspond to each register, the instruction format, and the **modes**, which determine if the operand is a register (mode bit = 0) or the operand is a memory location (mode bit = 1). Either or both of the operands can be registers, but both operands cannot be memory locations. If the source or destination is a memory location, then the cor-

INSTRUCTION FORMAT

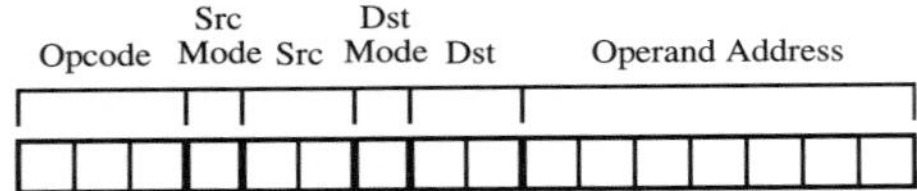

MODE BIT PATTERNS

Mode	Bit Pattern
Register	0
Direct	1

REGISTER BIT PATTERNS

Register	Bit Pattern
R0	00
R1	01
R2	10
R3	11

INSTRUCTION SET

Mnemonic	Opcode	Meaning
LOAD	000	Dst←Src or Memory
STORE	001	Dst or Memory←Src
ADD	010	Dst←Src + Dst
AND	011	Dst←AND(Src, Dst)
BZERO	100	Branch if Src = 0
JUMP	101	Unconditional jump
COMP	110	Dst←Complement of Src
RSHIFT	111	Dst←Src shifted right 1 bit

Note: Dst = Destination register
Src = Source register

Figure 4-27 A pocket pager ISA.

responding source or destination field in the instruction is not used since the address field is used instead.

(a) Write a program using object code (not assembly code) that swaps the contents of registers R0 and R1. You are free to use the other registers as necessary, but do not use memory. Use no more than four lines of code (fewer lines are possible). Place 0's in any positions where the value does not matter.

(b) Write a program using object code that swaps the contents of memory locations 12 and 13. As in part (a), you are free to use the other registers as necessary, but do not use other memory locations. Place 0's in any positions where the value does not matter.

4.7 An ARC program calls the subroutine `foo`, passing it three arguments, `a`, `b`, and `c`. The subroutine has two local variables, `m` and `n`. Show the position of the stack pointer and the contents of the relevant stack elements for a stack based calling convention at the points in the program shown. Note that subroutine `foo` does not return anything.

(1) just before executing the `call` at label `x`

(2) when the stack frame for foo is completed

(3) just before executing the ld at label z (i.e., when the calling routine resumes)

Use the stack notation shown in Figure 4-19.

```
   ! Push the arguments a, b, and c
x:       call  foo
z:       ld    %r1, %r2
               .
               .
               .
foo:! Subroutine starts here
               .
               .
               .
y:       jmpl  %r15 + 4, %r0
```

4.8 Why does sethi only load the high 22 bits of a register? It would be more useful if sethi loaded all 32 bits of a register. What is the problem with having sethi load all 32 bits?

4.9 Which of the three subroutine linkage conventions covered in this chapter (registers, data link area, stack) is used in Figure 4-14?

4.10 A program compiled for a SPARC ISA writes the 32-bit unsigned integer 0xABCDEF01 to a file and reads it back correctly. The same program compiled for a Pentium ISA also works correctly. However, when the file is transferred between machines, the program incorrectly reads the integer from the file as 0x01EFCDAB. What is going wrong?

4.11 Refer to Figure 4-25. Show the Java assembly language instructions for the code shown in locations 0x011e–0x0122. Use the syntax format shown in locations 0x00e3–0x0ef of that same figure.

You will need to make use of the following Java instructions:

invokespecial n (opcode 0xb7)—Invoke a method with index n into the constant pool. Note that n is a 16-bit (two-byte) index that follows the invokespecial opcode.

`aload_0` (opcode `0x2a`)—Push local variable 0 onto the stack.

4.12 Is the JVM a little-endian or big-endian machine? Hint: Examine the first line of the bytecode program in Figure 4-24.

4.13 Write an ARC program that implements the bytecode program shown in Figure 4-26. Assume that, analogous to the code in the figure, the arguments are passed on a stack, and that the return value is placed on the top of the stack.

4.14 Assume that a JVM is implemented in hardware, so that it executes the Java byte codes directly in 32-bit hardware.XXX

(a) How much memory traffic in bytes will be generated when the program of Figure 4-26 executes?

(b) Do Problem 4-13, and compute the memory traffic your program generates. Then compare that traffic with the amount generated by the program discussed in part a) of this problem. If most of the execution time of a program is due to its memory accesses, how much faster will your program be compared to the program in Figure 4-26?

4.15 Can a Java bytecode program ever run as fast as a program written in the native language of the processor? Defend your answer in one or two paragraphs.

4.16 (a) Write three-address, two-address, and one-address programs to compute the function A = (B–C)*(D–E). Assume 8-bit opcodes, 16-bit operands and addresses, and that data is moved to and from memory in 16-bit chunks. (Also assume that the opcode must be transferred from memory by itself.) Your code should not overwrite any of the operands. Use any temporary registers needed.

(b) Compute the size of your program in bytes.

(c) Compute the memory traffic your program will generate at execution time, including instruction fetches.

4.17 Repeat Problem 4.16, using ARC assembly language. Note that the subtract mnemonic is `subcc` and that the multiplication mnemonic is `smul`.

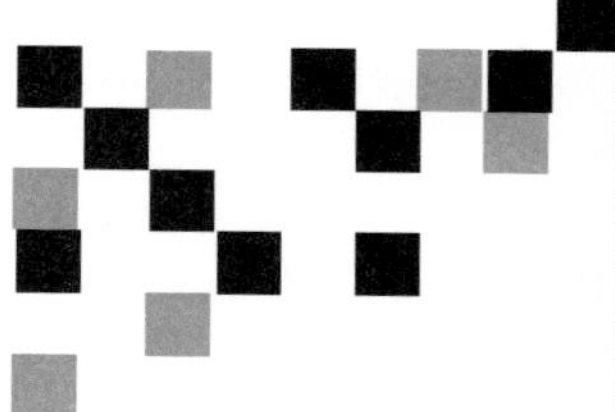

5

LANGUAGES AND THE MACHINE

In the last chapter, we looked at the relationship between the ISA, the assembly language, and machine language. We also saw in some detail how instructions effected register transfers and the movement of data between memory and the CPU, but we touched only briefly on the actual process of assembly and program linking and loading. In this chapter, we widen our view of the relationships between computer languages and the machine.

We begin by discussing **compilation**, the process of translating a program written in a high-level language into a functionally equivalent program in assembly language. Following that, we discuss the process of **assembly**, the translation of an assembly language program into a functionally equivalent machine language program. We then discuss **linking**, the process of linking separately assembled modules into a single program, and **loading**, the process of moving programs into memory and preparing them for execution. Following that, we discuss the use of assembly language **macros**, which can be thought of as akin to assembly-time procedures, with the exception that they are placed inline, or expanded, in the assembly language program at every location where they are invoked.

5.1 The Compilation Process

As we will see later in the chapter, the process of assembling an assembly language program into machine code is rather straightforward, because there is a one-to-one mapping between assembly language statements and the equivalent machine binary codes. High-level languages, on the other hand, present a much more complex problem.

5.1.1 *THE STEPS OF COMPILATION*

Consider a simple assignment statement

```
A = B + 4;
```

The compiler is faced with a number of fairly complex tasks in converting this statement into one or more assembly language statements:

- Reducing the program text to the basic symbols of the language, for example, into identifiers such as `A` and `B`, denotations such as the constant value `4`, and program delimiters such as = and +. This portion of compilation is referred to as **lexical analysis**.

- Parsing the symbols to recognize the underlying program structure. In the preceding sample statement, for example, the **parser** must recognize the statement as being an assignment statement of the form

  Identifier "=" Expression

  where Expression is further parsed into the form

  Identifier "+" Constant

  Parsing is sometimes called **syntactic analysis**.

- Name analysis: Associating the names A and B with particular program variables, and further associating them with particular memory locations where the variables will be located at run time.

- Type analysis: Determining the type of all data items. In the preceding case, the variables `A` and `B` and constant `4` would be recognized as being of type `int` in some languages. Name and type analysis are sometimes referred to together as **semantic analysis**: Determining the underlying meaning of program components.

- **Action mapping** and **code generation**: Associating program statements with their appropriate assembly language sequence. In the preceding statement, the assembly language sequence might be as follows:

```
                   !Simple assignment statement
ld [B], %r0, %r1   !get variable B into a register
add %r1, 4, %r2    !compute the value of the expr.
st %r2, %r0, [A]   !make the assignment
```

- There are additional steps that the compiler must take, such as allocating variables to registers, tracking register usage, and, should the programmer desire it, optimizing the program.

5.1.2 *THE COMPILER MAPPING SPECIFICATION*

When the compiler itself is being created, information about the particular ISA must be embedded into it. (Note that the ISA on which the compiler executes does not need to be the same as the ISA code that the compiler generates, a process known as **cross compilation**.) This embedding is sometimes called the **mapping specification** for the compiler. For example, the compiler writer must decide how to map variables and constants of various types into the machine's resources. This may be a function of both the machine and the high-level language. In the C language, for example, integers (ints) can be 16, 32, or some other number of bits in size, while Java specifies that all ints be 32 bits in size. The example in the previous section, if considered for the C language, maps integers to ARC 32-bit words.

The compiler writer must also take into account the features and limitations of the machine when mapping high-level language constructs to assembly language statements or statement sequences. For example, the ARC instruction set requires that all arithmetic operands must be either immediate constants or register variables. Therefore the compiler must generate code to get all variables into registers before any arithmetic instructions can be executed. This is the reason for the instruction

```
ld [B], %r1
```

in the preceding example.

In this text, we concentrate on the mapping of common high-level language constructs to their equivalent assembly language constructs, leaving the details of lexical and syntactic and semantic analysis to compiler texts. (Several compiler texts are described in the Further Reading section at the end of this chapter for the interested reader.)

5.1.3 *HOW THE COMPILER MAPS THE THREE INSTRUCTION CLASSES INTO ASSEMBLY CODE*

Let us consider in detail the mapping of the three instruction classes—data movement, arithmetic, and control flow—from high-level language into assembly language. In the discussion and examples that follow we will use C as the example language. We choose C because of its popularity and because its syntax and semantics, while certainly high level, are still fairly close to assembly language concepts. The reader who is unfamiliar with C should not be distracted by this choice; the syntax and semantics of C are easy to understand and carry over to other high-level languages.

Variable Storage in Memory

In the preceding example, and in most of the programming examples in this text, it has been assumed that variables can be accessed directly by their name, which is mapped to a memory location that is known at the time the program is assembled, sometimes called "assembly time." In the preceding example, `A = B + 4`, it is assumed that the variables `A` and `B` have addresses that are known when the statement is compiled. In fact, only **global variables**, known as **static variables** in C, have addresses that are known at compile time. Variables declared inside of functions or inside of blocks that are not explicitly declared as static or global only come into existence when the function or block is entered, and they disappear when the function or block is exited for the last time. These variables are called **local**, or in C, **automatic variables**. In most programs, local variables are actually much more common than global variables.

Given this ephemeral nature of local variables, a natural way of implementing them is on a last-in-first-out stack as described in Chapter 4. Variables that are stored on the stack come into existence when the stack frame is created and the function is called, and they disappear when the function is exited for the last time. While the previous chapter employed the stack pointer, `%sp`, to access the stack frame, it is also common to copy the contents of `%sp` into another register called the frame pointer `%fp` (also known as the base pointer) upon entry into the function, and then to use `%fp` to access variables on the stack frame for the duration of the function's life. This is because temporary variables may be continually pushed and popped onto and off of the stack during the lifetime of the function, resulting in a changing offset between `%sp` and the items on the stack frame. Using `%fp` means that the compiler can define a constant offset between `%fp` and a value stored on the stack that will remain fixed for the life of the frame. **Based addressing** is used to access stack variables. For example, an ARC variable located on the stack at a location 12 bytes below `%fp` can be loaded into register `%r1` by the instruction

```
ld %fp, -12, %r1
```

or, to use the more common notation,

```
ld [%fp - 12], %r1
```

The use of based addressing thus allows the address arithmetic, "add the contents of `%fp` to `-12`" to be performed in a single instruction. Based addressing is so common that all popular instruction sets contain that addressing mode. Some instruction sets contain even more complicated addressing modes to assist in accessing complex data structures that are stored in the stack frame.

To emphasize the point, variables that are stored on the stack have memory addresses that are not known until run time. Their compile-time addresses are known as offsets from `%fp`. It is only at function entry time that the actual memory address of the value is known. Thus even though stack variable addresses such as `[%fp - 12]` are much more common than global variable addresses such as `A`, we will assume global variables are used in the following discussion because of the greater ease in understanding the relationship between the high-level language variable name and the address as specified in assembly language. With that provision, let us now proceed to discuss three classes of program statements: Data movement, arithmetic, and control flow.

5.1.4 *DATA MOVEMENT*

In addition to simple scalar variables, most programming languages provide various kinds of more complex data structures, including fixed record structures such as the C `struct` data type, which is similar to the Pascal **record**, and the array data type common to most programming languages.

Structures

An example of a C `struct` is the representation of a point in three-dimensional space having integer coordinates *x*, *y*, and *z*. In C, this structure could be declared as

```
struct point {
   int x;
   int y;
   int z;
}
```

An instance of this `struct` would be defined by the C statement

```
struct point pt;
```

Having defined point `pt`, the programmer can now refer to the individual components of `pt` by notation such as `pt.x`, which refers to the `x` component of struct pt. The compiler would lay out this structure in memory as three consecutive memory locations.

The memory address of the entire structure is taken to be the lowest, or base address of the structure, so the x component would be located at address pt, the y component at address pt + 4, and the z component at address pt + 8. Thus the y component of pt would be loaded into register %r1 by the instruction

```
ld [pt + 4], %r1      !%r1 ← y
```

Arrays

Most programming languages also allow the declaration of arrays of objects, that is, collections of identical components that can be referred to either individually or collectively. In C, an array of ten integers can be defined with

```
int A[10];
```

This definition would result in a collection of ten integers, indexed from 0 to 9.

The components of a struct must be explicitly named at programming time, for example, pt.z. References such as pt.i, where i is a variable whose name is not determined until run time are not allowed. With arrays, on the other hand, the array index can be computed at run time. For example, the programmer may specify array element A[i], where i is a variable whose value is computed at run time and that may assume any integer value from 0 through 9. Whereas in C the index of the first element in the array always has an index of 0, other programming languages allow more flexibility. In Pascal, for example, array declarations such as

```
A: array [-10..10] of integer
```

are permitted. This declaration would result in an array of 21 integers with indices running from –10 to +10.

Accessing array elements presents a more complicated issue because of this need to compute the index at run time, and the possibility that indices may not begin with 0. The general expression for computing the machine address of an array element at run time is given by

$$\text{ElementAddress} = \text{BASE} + (\text{INDEX} - \text{START})*\text{SIZE}$$

where BASE is the starting address of the array, INDEX is the index of the desired element, START is the starting index of the array, and SIZE is the size of an individual element in bytes. Thus, element 5 in the Pascal array declared previously would have an address of A + (5 – (–10))*4 = A + 60. In ARC assembly language, assuming BASE in `%r2`, INDEX in `%r3`, START in `%r4`, and assuming SIZE = 4, the code to load an array value into memory would be given by

```
sub %r3, %r4, %r6       !%r6 ← INDEX - START
sll %r6, 2, %r6         !%r6 ← %r6 * 4
ld [A + %r6], %r1       !%r1 ← array value
```

(`sll` is "shift left logical," which shifts `%r6` 2 bits to the left is this example, bringing in two 0's on the right). Note that it costs three instructions to access an array element, and more if SIZE is not a power of 2. Also note that in the C programming language, which specifies that START = 0, one machine instruction is saved for each array access. This may result in a considerable savings in scientific and engineering calculations, where heavy array references are common.

5.1.5 *ARITHMETIC INSTRUCTIONS*

Arithmetic instructions are mapped pretty much as expected from their usage. There is a possible complication in load/store machines such as ARC and commercial RISC machines, however. Regardless of how many registers with which a machine is endowed, there is always the possibility that the compiler will encounter an arithmetic instruction that requires more registers than are available. In this case the compiler must temporarily store variables on the stack, a so-called "register spill." Compilers use sophisticated techniques to decide which registers are available, using a graph-theoretic technique known as register coloring, and to decide when the value in a register is no longer needed to store a particular value, which is known as "live-dead analysis."

5.1.6 *PROGRAM CONTROL FLOW*

Most ISAs use unconditional and conditional branches and the CPU's arithmetic flags to implement program control flow structures. In this section, we consider the mapping of the most common control flow statements.

The `goto` *Statement*

The most trivial control flow statement is the `goto` statement, `goto Label`, which is simply implemented by the `ba` (branch always) unconditional branch:

```
ba Label
```

The `if-else` *Statement*

The C `if-else` statement has the syntax

```
if (expr) stmt1 else stmt2;
```

which has the meaning, "If `expr` yields a value of true, execute `stmt1`, otherwise execute `stmt2`." Thus the compiler must evaluate the truth of `expr`, and execute one or the other of the two statements depending upon the truth or falsity of the expression. Assume for brevity in the following example that `expr` is (`%r1 == %r2`), and introducing the `bne`, branch if not equal instruction, then the code to implement the `if-else` statement is

```
       subcc %r1, %r2, %r0  ! set flags, discard rslt
       bne Over
       !stmt1 code
       ba End               ! exit if-else
Over:  !stmt2 code
End:   ! ...
```

Note that the sign of the conditional branch, `bne`, branch if *not equal*, is the inverse of the expression (`%r1 == %r2`), *equals*. This is because the code falls through to the `stmt1` code if the condition is met, and must branch around this code if the condition is not met.

The `while` *Statement*

The C `while` statement has the syntax

```
while (expr) stmt;
```

The statement means, "Evaluate `expr`. If it is true, execute `stmt`, and repeat this process until `expr` evaluates to false." The assembly language mapping of this statement has the interesting feature that the most efficient mapping has the expression evaluation code following the statement code. Consider the C while statement:

```
while (%r1 == %r2) %r3 = %r3 + 1;
```

where again we use register variables to simplify the code. This statement is efficiently implemented as

```
        ba Test
True:   add %r3, 1, %r3
Test:   subcc %r1, %r2, %r0
        be True
```

The reader can verify that placing the expression evaluation code below the statement code is more efficient than having the expression evaluation code above the statement code.

The `do-while` *statement*

C also has a `do-while` statement with the syntax

```
do stmt while (expr);
```

This statement works like the preceding `while` statement except that `stmt` is always executed once prior to testing `expr`. It is implemented exactly like the preceding `while` statement except that the first `ba` instruction is eliminated.

The `for` *Statement*

The C `for` statement has the syntax

```
for (expr1; expr2; expr3) stmt;
```

The C language definition says that this statement is equivalent to

```
expr1;
while (expr2) {
   stmt
   expr3;
}
```

Thus, it is implemented exactly like the preceding `while` statements, with the addition of code for `expr1` and `expr3`.

5.2 The Assembly Process

The process of translating an assembly language program into a machine language program is referred to as the **assembly process**. The assembly process is straightforward and rather simple, since there is a straightforward one-to-one mapping of assembly language statements to their machine language counterparts. This is in opposition to compilation, for example, in which a given high-level language statement may be translated into a number of computationally equivalent machine language statements.

While assembly is a straightforward process, it is tedious and error-prone if done by hand. In fact, the assembler was one of the first software tools developed after the invention of the digital electronic computer.

Commercial assemblers provide at least the following capabilities:

- Allow the programmer to specify the run-time location of data values and programs. (Most often, however, the programmer would not specify an absolute starting location for a program, because the program will be moved around, or relocated, by the linker and perhaps the loader, as discussed later.)
- Provide a means for the programmer to initialize data values in memory prior to program execution.
- Provide assembly language mnemonics for all machine instructions and addressing modes, and translate valid assembly language statements into their equivalent machine language binary values.
- Permit the use of symbolic labels to represent addresses and constants.
- Provide a means for the programmer to specify the starting address of the program, if there is one. (There would not be a starting address if the module being assembled is a procedure or function, for example.)
- Provide a degree of assemble-time arithmetic.
- Include a mechanism that allows variables to be defined in one assembly language program and used in another, separately assembled program.
- Provide for the expansion of **macro routines**, that is, routines that can be defined once and then instantiated as many times as needed.

```
! This program adds two numbers
        .begin
        .org 2048
main:   ld      [x], %r1          ! Load x into %r1
        ld      [y], %r2          ! Load y into %r2
        addcc   %r1, %r2, %r3     ! %r3 ← %r1 + %r2
        st      %r3, [z]          ! Store %r3 into z
        jmpl    %r15 + 4, %r0     ! Return
x:      15
y:      9
z:      0
        .end
```

Figure 5-1 A simple ARC program that adds two numbers

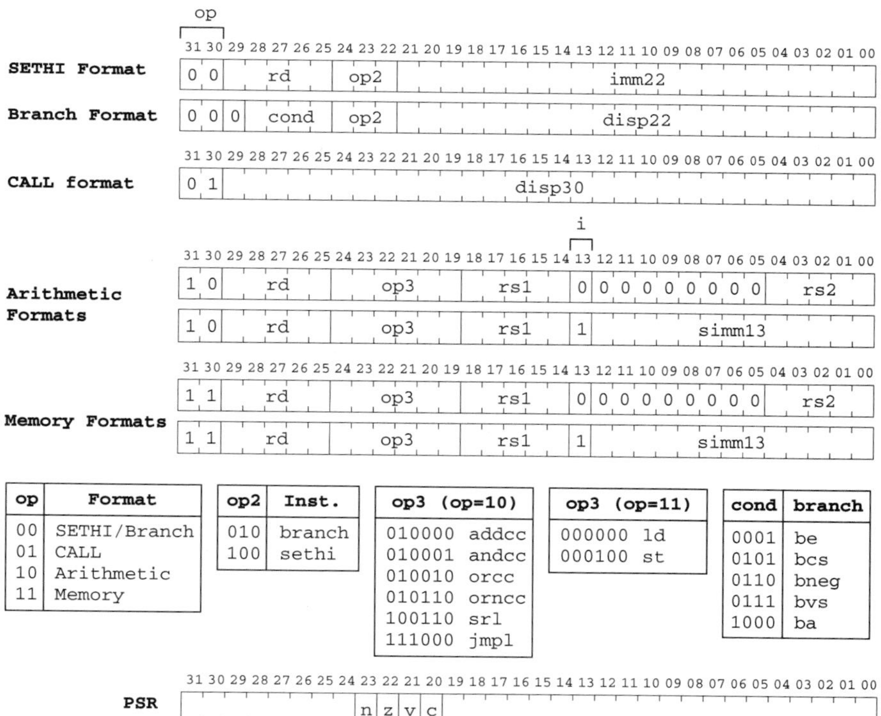

Figure 5-2 Instruction formats and PSR format for the ARC.

We shall illustrate how the assembly process proceeds by "hand assembling" a simple program from ARC assembly language to ARC machine language. The program we will assemble is similar to Figure 4-13, reproduced for convenience as Figure 5-1. In assembling this program, we use the ARC encoding formats shown in Figure 4-10, reproduced here as Figure 5-2. The figure shows the encoding of ARC machine language. That is, it specifies the target binary machine language of the ARC computer that the assembler must generate from the assembly language text.

5.2.1 *ASSEMBLY AND TWO PASS ASSEMBLERS*

Most assemblers pass over the assembly language text twice and are referred to as "two-pass assemblers." The first pass is dedicated to determining the addresses of all data items and machine instructions and selecting which machine instruction should be produced for each assembly language instruction (but not yet generating machine code).

The addresses of data items and instructions are determined by employing an assemble-time analog to the program counter, referred to as the **location counter.** The location counter keeps track of the address of the current instruction or data item as assembly proceeds. It is generally initialized to 0 at the start of the first pass and is incremented by the size of each instruction. The `.org` pseudo-operation causes the location counter to be set to the value specified by the `.org` statement. For example, if the assembler encounters the statement

```
.org 1000
```

it would set the location counter to 1000, and the next instruction or data item would be assembled at that address. During this pass, the assembler also performs any assembly-time arithmetic operations and inserts the definitions of all labels and constant values into a table, referred to as the **symbol table**.

The primary reason for requiring a second pass is to allow symbols to be used in the program before they are defined, which is known as **forward referencing**. After the first pass, the assembler will have identified and entered all symbols into its symbol table, and during a second pass generates the machine code, inserting the values of symbols, which are then known.

Let us now hand assemble the program shown in Figure 5-1 into machine code. When the assembler encounters the first instruction,

```
ld    [x], %r1
```

it uses a pattern-matching process to recognize that it is a load instruction. Further pattern matching deduces that it is of the form "load *from* a memory address specified as a constant value (x in this case) plus the contents of a register (`%r0` in this case) *into* a register (`%r1` in this case)." This corresponds to the second Memory format shown in Figure 5-2. Examining the second Memory format, we find that the `op` field for this instruction (`ld`) is `11`. The destination of this `ld` instruction goes in the `rd` field, which is `00001` for `%r1` in this case. The `op3` field is `000000` for `ld`, as shown in the `op3` box below the Memory formats. The `rs1` field identifies the register, `%r0` in this case, that is added to the `simm13` field to form the source operand address. The `i` bit comes next. Notice that the `i` bit is used to distinguish between the first Memory format (`i=0`) and the second (`i=0`). Therefore, the `i` bit is set to 1. The `simm13` field specifies the address of the label `x`, which appears five words after the first instruction. Since the first instruction occurs at location 2048, and since each word is composed of four bytes, the address of `x` is 5 × 4 = 20 bytes after the beginning of the program. The address of `x` is then 2048 + 20 = 2068, which is represented by the bit pattern 0100000010100. This pattern fits into the signed 13-bit `simm13` field.

The first line is thus assembled into the following bit pattern

```
11 00001 000000 00000 1 0100000010100
op   rd    op3   rs1  i     simm13
```

The next instruction is similar in form, and the corresponding bit pattern is

```
11 00010 000000 00000 1 0100000011000
op   rd    op3   rs1  i     simm13
```

The assembly process continues until all eight lines are assembled, as shown:

```
ld [x], %r1         1100 0010 0000 0000 0010 1000 0001 0100
ld [y], %r2         1100 0100 0000 0000 0010 1000 0001 1000
addcc %r1,%r2,%r3   1000 0110 1000 0000 0100 0000 0000 0010
st %r3, [z]         1100 0110 0010 0000 0010 1000 0001 1100
jmpl %r15+4, %r0    1000 0001 1100 0011 1110 0000 0000 0100
15                  0000 0000 0000 0000 0000 0000 0000 1111
9                   0000 0000 0000 0000 0000 0000 0000 1001
0                   0000 0000 0000 0000 0000 0000 0000 0000
```

As a general approach, the assembly process is carried out by reading assembly language statements sequentially, from first to last, and generating machine code for each statement. And as mentioned earlier, a difficulty with this approach is caused by forward referencing. Consider the program fragment shown in Figure 5-3. When the assembler sees the `call` statement, it does not yet know the location of `sub_r` since the `sub_r` label has not yet been seen. Thus, the reference is entered into the symbol table and marked as unresolved. The reference is resolved when the

```
              .
              .
              .
              call sub_r    ! Subroutine is invoked here
              .
              .
              .
sub_r:        st   %r1, [w] ! Subroutine is defined here
              .
              .
              .
```

Figure 5-3 An example of forward referencing.

definition of `sub_r` is found later in the program. The process of building a symbol table is described later.

5.2.2 *ASSEMBLY AND THE SYMBOL TABLE*

In the first pass of the two-pass assembly process, a **symbol table** is created. A symbol is either a label or a symbolic name that refers to a value used during the assembly process. The symbol table is generated in the first pass of assembly.

As an example of how a two-pass assembler operates, consider assembling the code in Figure 4-14. Starting from the `.begin` statement, the assembler encounters the statement

```
.org 2048
```

This causes the assembler to set the location counter to 2048, and assembly proceeds from that address. The first statement encountered is

```
a_start  .equu  3000
```

An entry is created in the symbol table for `a_start`, which is given the value 3000. (Note that `.equ` statements do not generate any code, and thus are not assigned addresses during assembly.)

Assembly proceeds as the assembler encounters the first machine instruction,

```
ld  [length],  %r1
```

This instruction is assembled at the address specified by the location counter, 2048. The location counter is then incremented by the size of the instruction, 4 bytes, to 2052. Notice that when the symbol `length` is encountered the assembler has not

Symbol	Value
a_start	3000
length	—

(a)

Symbol	Value
a_start	3000
length	2092
address	2096
loop	2060
done	2088
a	3000

(b)

Figure 5-4 Symbol table for the ARC program shown in Figure 4-14, (a) after symbols a_start and length are seen; and (b) after completion.

seen any definition for it. An entry is created in the symbol table for `length`, but it is initially assigned the value "undefined," as shown by the "—" in Figure 5-4a.

The assembler then encounters the second instruction

```
ld [address], %r2
```

It assembles this instruction at address 2052 and enters the symbol `address` into the symbol table, again setting its value to "undefined," since its definition has not been seen. It then increments the location counter by 4 to 2056. The `andcc` instruction is assembled at address 2056, and the location counter is incremented by the size of the instruction, again 4 bytes, to 2060. The next symbol that is seen is `loop`, which is entered into the symbol table with a value of 2060, the value of the location counter. The next symbol that is encountered that is not in the symbol table is `done`, which is also entered into the symbol table without a value since it likewise has not been defined.

The first pass of assembly continues, and the unresolved symbols `length`, `address`, and `done` are assigned the values 2092, 2096, and 2088, respectively, as they are encountered. The label `a` is encountered and is entered into the table with a value of 3000. The label `done` appears at location 2088 because there are 10 instructions (40 bytes) between the beginning of the program and `done`. Addresses for the remaining labels are computed in a similar manner. If any labels are still undefined at the end of the first pass, then an error exists in the program and the assembler will flag the undefined symbols and terminate.

After the symbol table is created, the second pass of assembly begins. The program is read a second time, starting from the `.begin` statement, but now object

Location counter		Instruction	Object code
		`.begin`	
		`.org 2048`	
	`a_start`	`.equ 3000`	
`2048`		`ld [length],%r1`	11000010 00000000 00101000 00101100
`2052`		`ld [address],%r2`	11000100 00000000 00101000 00110000
`2056`		`andcc %r3,%r0,%r3`	10000110 10001000 11000000 00000000
`2060`	`loop:`	`andcc %r1,%r1,%r0`	10000000 10001000 01000000 00000001
`2064`		`be done`	00000010 10000000 00000000 00000110
`2068`		`addcc %r1,-4,%r1`	10000010 10000000 01111111 11111100
`2072`		`addcc %r1,%r2,%r4`	10001000 10000000 01000000 00000010
`2076`		`ld %r4,%r5`	11001010 00000001 00000000 00000000
`2080`		`ba loop`	00010000 10111111 11111111 11111011
`2084`		`addcc %r3,%r5,%r3`	10000110 10000000 11000000 00000101
`2088`	`done:`	`jmpl %r15+4,%r0`	10000001 11000011 11100000 00000100
`2092`	`length:`	`20`	00000000 00000000 00000000 00010100
`2096`	`address:`	`a_start`	00000000 00000000 00001011 10111000
		`.org a_start`	
`3000`	`a:`	`25`	00000000 00000000 00000000 00011001
`3004`		`-10`	11111111 11111111 11111111 11110110
`3008`		`33`	00000000 00000000 00000000 00100001
`3012`		`-5`	11111111 11111111 11111111 11111011
`3016`		`7`	00000000 00000000 00000000 00000111
		`.end`	

Figure 5-5 Output from the second pass of the assembler for the ARC program shown in Figure 4-14.

code is generated. The first statement that is encountered that causes code to be generated is `ld` at location 2048. The symbol table shows that the address portion of the `ld` instruction is $(2092)_{10}$ for the address of `length`, and so one word of code is generated using the Memory format, as shown in Figure 5-5. The second pass continues in this manner until all of the code is translated. The assembled program is shown in Figure 5-5. Notice that the displacements for branch addresses are given in words, rather than in bytes, because the branch instructions multiply the displacements by four.

5.2.3 *FINAL TASKS OF THE ASSEMBLER*

After assembly is complete the assembler must add additional information to the assembled module for the linker and loader:

The module name and size. If the execution model involves memory segments for code, data, stack, etc. then the sizes and identities of the various segments must be specified.

- The address of the start symbol, if one is defined in the module. Most assemblers and high-level languages provide for a special reserved label that the programmer can use to indicate where the program should start execution. For example, C specifies that execution will start at the function named `main()`. In Figure 5-1 the label "main" is a signal to the assembler that execution should start at that location.

- Information about global and external symbols. The linker will need to know the addresses of any global symbols defined in the module and exported by it, and it will likewise need to know which symbols remain undefined in the module because they are defined as global in another module.

- Information about any library routines that are referenced by the module. Some libraries contain commonly used functionality such as math or other specialized functions. We will have more to say about library usage in later sections.

- The values of any constants that are to be loaded into memory. Some loaders expect data initialization to be specified separately from the binary code.

- Relocation information. When the linker is invoked most of the modules that are to be linked will need to be relocated as the modules are concatenated. The whole issue of module relocation is complicated because some address references can be relocated and others cannot. We discuss relocation later, but here we note that the assembler specifies which addresses can be relocated and which others cannot.

5.2.4 *LOCATION OF PROGRAMS IN MEMORY*

Up until now we have assumed that programs are located in memory at an address that is specified by a `.org` pseudo operation. This may indeed be the case in systems programming, where the programmer has a reason for wanting a program to be located at a specific memory location, but typically the programmer does not care where the program is located in memory. Furthermore, when separately assembled or compiled programs are linked together, it is difficult or impossible for the programmer to know exactly where each module will be located after linking, as they are concatenated one after the other. For this reason most addresses are specified as being **relocatable** in memory, except perhaps for addresses such as I/O addresses, which may be fixed at an absolute memory location.

In the next section we discuss relocation in more detail; here we merely note that it is the assembler's responsibility to mark symbols as being relocatable. Whether a given symbol is relocatable or not depends upon both the assembly language and the operating system's conventions. In any case, this relocation information is included in the assembled module for use by the linker and/or loader in a **relocation dictionary**. Symbols that are relocatable are often marked with an "R" after their value in the assembler's listing file.

5.3 Linking and Loading

Most applications of any size will have a number of separately compiled or assembled modules. These modules may be generated by different programming languages or they may be present in a library provided as part of the programming language environment or operating system. Each module must provide the information described previously, so that they can be linked together for loading and execution.

A **linkage editor**, or **linker**, is a software program that combines separately assembled programs (called **object modules**) into a single program, which is called a **load module**. The linker resolves all global-external references and relocates addresses in the separate modules. The load module can then be loaded into memory by a **loader**, which may also need to modify addresses if the program is loaded at a location that differs from the loading origin used by the linker.

A relatively new technique called **dynamic link libraries** (**DLLs**), popularized by Microsoft in the Windows operating system and present in similar forms in other operating systems, postpones the linking of some components until they are actually needed at run time. We will have more to say about dynamic linking later in this section.

5.3.1 *LINKING*

In combining the separately compiled or assembled modules into a load module, the linker must

- Resolve address references that are external to modules as it links them.
- Relocate each module by combining them end-to-end as appropriate. During this relocation process many of the addresses in the module must be changed to reflect their new location.
- Specify the starting symbol of the load module.
- If the memory model includes more than one memory segment, the linker must specify the identities and contents of the various segments.

Resolving External References

In resolving address references the linker needs to distinguish local symbol names (used within a single source module) from global symbol names (used in more than one module). This is accomplished by making use of the `.global` and `.extern` pseudo-ops during assembly. The `.global` pseudo-op instructs the assembler to mark a symbol as being available to other object modules during the linking phase. The `.extern` pseudo-op identifies a label that is used in one module but is defined in another. A `.global` is thus used in the module where a symbol is defined (such as where a subroutine is located) and a `.extern` is used in every other module that refers to it. Note that only address labels can be global or external: It would be meaningless to mark a `.equ` symbol as global or external, since `.equ` is a pseudo-op that is used during the assembly process only, and the assembly process is completed by the time that the linking process begins.

All labels referred to in one program by another, such as subroutine names, will have a line of the form shown in the source module:

```
    .global symbol1, symbol2, ...
```

All other labels are local, which means the same label can be used in more than one source module without risking confusion since local labels are not used after the assembly process finishes. A module that refers to symbols defined in another module should declare those symbols using the form

```
    .extern symbol1, symbol2, ...
```

As an example of how `.global` and `.extern` are used, consider the two assembly code source modules shown in Figure 5-6. Each module is separately assembled into an object module, each with its own symbol table, as shown in Figure 5-7. The symbol tables have an additional field that indicates if a symbol is global or external. Program `main` begins at location 2048, and each instruction is four bytes long, so `x` and `y` are at locations 2064 and 2068, respectively. The symbol `sub` is marked as external as a result of the `.extern` pseudo-op. As part of the assembly process the assembler includes header information in the module about symbols that are global and external so they can be resolved at link time.

``
! Main program
      .begin
      .org 2048
      .extern sub
main: ld   [x], %r2
      ld   [y], %r3
      call sub
      jmpl %r15 + 4,%r0
   x: 105
   y: 92
      .end
``
	``
	! Subroutine library
	      .begin
	ONE .equu 1
	      .org 2048
	      .global sub
	sub: orncc %r3, %r0, %r3
	     addcc %r3, ONE, %r3
	     jmpl %r15 + 4, %r0
	     .end
	``

```
! Main program
      .begin
      .org  2048
      .extern sub
main: ld    [x], %r2
      ld    [y], %r3
      call  sub
      jmpl  %r15 + 4,%r0
   x: 105
   y:  92
      .end
```

```
! Subroutine library
      .begin
ONE   .equ     1
      .org   2048
      .global sub
sub:  orncc %r3, %r0, %r3
      addcc %r3, ONE, %r3
      jmpl  %r15 + 4, %r0
      .end
```

Figure 5-6 A program calls a subroutine that subtracts two integers.

Symbol	Value	Global/ External	Reloc- atable
sub	–	External	–
main	2048	No	Yes
x	2064	No	Yes
y	2068	No	Yes

Main Program

Symbol	Value	Global/ External	Reloc- atable
ONE	1	No	No
sub	2048	Global	Yes

Subroutine Library

Figure 5-7 Symbol tables for the assembly code source modules shown in Figure 5-6.

Relocation

Notice in Figure 5-6 that the two programs, main and sub, both have the same starting address, 2048. Obviously, they cannot both occupy that same memory address. If the two modules are assembled separately, there is no way for an assembler to know about the conflicting starting addresses during the assembly phase. In order to resolve this problem, the assembler marks symbols that may have their address changed during linking as **relocatable**, as shown in the relocatable fields of the symbol tables shown in Figure 5-7. The idea is that a program that is assembled at a starting address of 2048 can be loaded at address 3000 instead, for instance, as long as all references to relocatable addresses within the program are increased by 3000 – 2048 = 952. Relocation is performed by the linker so that relocatable addresses are changed by the same amount that the loading origin is changed, but absolute, or non-relocatable addresses (such as the highest possible stack address, which is $2^{31} - 4$ for 32-bit words) stay the same regardless of the loading origin.

The assembler is responsible for determining which labels are relocatable when it builds the symbol table. It has no meaning to call an external label relocatable, since the label is defined in another module, so `sub` has no relocatable entry in the symbol table in Figure 5-7 for program `main`, but it is marked as relocatable in the subroutine library. The assembler must also identify code in the object module that needs to be modified as a result of relocation. Absolute numbers, such as constants (marked by `.equ`, or that appear in memory locations, such as the contents of `x` and `y`, which are 105 and 92, respectively) are not relocatable. Memory locations that are positioned relative to a `.org` statement, such as `x` and `y` (not the contents of `x` and `y`!), are generally relocatable. References to fixed locations, such as a permanently resident graphics routine that may be hardwired into the machine, are not relocatable. All of the information needed to relocate a module is stored in the relocation dictionary contained in the assembled file and is therefore available to the linker.

5.3.2 *LOADING*

The **loader** is a software program that places the load module into main memory. Conceptually the tasks of the loader are not difficult. It must load the various memory segments with the appropriate values and initialize certain registers, such as the stack pointer `%sp` and the program counter `%pc`, to their initial values.

If there is only one load module executing at any time, then this model works well. In modern operating systems, however, several programs are resident in memory at any time, and there is no way that the assembler or linker can know at which address they will reside. The loader must relocate these modules at load time by adding an offset to all of the relocatable code in a module. This kind of loader is known as a **relocating loader**. The relocating loader does not simply repeat the job of the linker: The linker has to combine several object modules into a single load module, whereas the loader simply modifies relocatable addresses within a single load module so that several programs can reside in memory simultaneously. A **linking loader** performs both the linking process and the loading process: It resolves external references, relocates object modules, and loads them into memory.

The linked executable file contains header information describing where it should be loaded, starting addresses, and possibly relocation information, and entry points for any routines that should be made available externally.

An alternative approach that relies on memory management accomplishes relocation by loading a segment base register with the appropriate base to locate the code (or data) at the appropriate place in physical memory. The **memory management unit (MMU)** adds the contents of this base register to all memory references. As a result, each program can begin execution at address 0 and rely on the MMU to relocate all memory references transparently.

Dynamic Link Libraries

Returning to dynamic link libraries, the concept has a number of attractive features. Commonly used routines such as memory management or graphics packages need be present at only one place, the DLL library. This results in smaller program sizes because each program does not need to have its own copy of the DLL code, as would otherwise be needed. All programs share the exact same code, even while simultaneously executing.

Furthermore, the DLL can be upgraded with bug fixes or feature enhancements in just one place, and programs that use it need not be recompiled or relinked in a separate step. These same features can also become disadvantages, however, because program behavior may change in unintended ways (such as running out of memory as a result of a larger DLL). The DLL library must be present at all times and must contain the version expected by each program. Many Windows users have seen the cryptic message, "A file is missing from the dynamic link library." Complicating the issue in the Windows implementation, there are a number of locations in the file system where DLLs are placed. The more sophisticated user may have little difficulty resolving these problems, but the naive user may be baffled.

A PROGRAMMING EXAMPLE

Consider the problem of adding two 64-bit numbers using the ARC assembly language. We can store the 64-bit numbers in successive words in memory and then separately add the low- and high-order words. If a carry is generated from adding the low-order words, then the carry is added into the high-order word of the result. (See Problem 5.3 for the generation of the symbol table, and Problem 5.4 for the translation of the assembly code in this example to machine code.)

Figure 5-8 shows one possible coding. The 64-bit operands `A` and `B` are stored in memory in a big-endian format, in which the most significant 32 bits are stored in lower memory addresses than the least significant 32 bits. The program begins by loading the high- and low-order words of `A` into `%r1` and `%r2`, respectively, and then loading the high- and low-order words of `B` into `%r3` and `%r4`, respectively. Subroutine `add_64` is called, which adds `A` and `B` and places the

```
! Perform a 64-bit addition: C ← A + B
! Register usage: %r1 - Most significant 32 bits of A
!                 %r2 - Least significant 32 bits of A
!                 %r3 - Most significant 32 bits of B
!                 %r4 - Least significant 32 bits of B
!                 %r5 - Most significant 32 bits of C
!                 %r6 - Least significant 32 bits of C
!                 %r7 - Used for restoring carry bit
           .begin                    ! Start assembling
           .org   2048               ! Start program at 2048
main:      ld     [A], %r1           ! Get high word of A
           ld     [A+4], %r2         ! Get low word of A
           ld     [B], %r3           ! Get high word of B
           ld     [B+4], %r4         ! Get low word of B
           call   add_64             ! Perform 64-bit addition
           st     %r5, [C]           ! Store high word of C
           st     %r6, [C+4]         ! Store low word of C
                  .
                  .
                  .
           .org   3072               ! Start add_64 at 3072
add_64:    addcc  %r2, %r4, %r6      ! Add low order words
           bcs    lo_carry           ! Branch if carry set
           addcc  %r1, %r3, %r5      ! Add high order words
           jmpl   %r15 + 4, %r0      ! Return to calling routine
lo_carry:  addcc  %r1, %r3, %r5      ! Add high order words
           bcs    hi_carry           ! Branch if carry set
           addcc  %r5, 1, %r5        ! Add in carry
           jmpl   %r15, 4, %r0       ! Return to calling routine
hi_carry:  addcc  %r5, 1, %r5        ! Add in carry
           sethi  #3FFFFF, %r7       ! Set up %r7 for carry
           addcc  %r7, %r7, %r0      ! Generate a carry
           jmpl   %r15 + 4, %r0      ! Return to calling routine
A:                        0          ! High 32 bits of 25
                         25          ! Low 32 bits of 25
B:                #FFFFFFFF          ! High 32 bits of -1
                  #FFFFFFFF          ! Low 32 bits of -1
C:                        0          ! High 32 bits of result
                          0          ! Low 32 bits of result
           .end                      ! Stop assembling
```

Figure 5-8 An ARC program adds two 64-bit integers.

high-order word of the result in `%r5` and the low-order word of the result in `%r6`. The 64-bit result is then stored in `C`, and the program returns.

Subroutine `add_64` starts by adding the low-order words. If a carry is not generated, then the high-order words are added and the subroutine finishes. If a carry is generated from adding the low-order words, then it must be added into the high-order word of the result. If a carry is not generated when the high-order words are added, then the carry from the low-order word of the result is simply added into the high-order word of the result and the subroutine finishes. If, however, a carry is generated when the high-order words are added, then when the carry from the low-order word is added into the high-order word, the final state of the condition codes will show that there is no carry-out of the high-order word, which is incorrect. The condition code for the carry is restored by placing a large number in `%r7` and then adding it to itself. The condition codes for `n`, `z`, and `v` may not have correct values at this point, however. A complete solution is not detailed here, but in short, the remaining condition codes can be set to their proper values by repeating the `addcc` just prior to the `%r7` operation, taking into account the fact that the `c` condition code must still be preserved. ■

5.4 Macros

If a stack based calling convention is used, then a number of registers may frequently need to be pushed and popped from the stack during calls and returns. In order to push ARC register `%r15` onto the stack, we need first to decrement the stack pointer (which is in `%r14`) and then copy `%r15` to the memory location pointed to by `%r14`, as shown in the following code

```
addcc %r14, -4, %r14 ! Decrement stack pointer
st    %r15, %r14     ! Push %r15 onto stack
```

A more compact notation for accomplishing this might be

```
push  %r15           ! Push %r15 onto stack
```

The compact form assigns a new label (`push`) to the sequence of statements that actually carry out the command. The `push` label is referred to as a **macro**, and the process of translating a macro into its assembly language equivalent is referred to as **macro expansion**.

A macro can be created through the use of a **macro definition**, as shown for `push` in Figure 5-9. The macro begins with a `.macro` pseudo-op, and termi-

```
! Macro definition for 'push'
.macro    push arg1         ! Start macro definition
addcc     %r14, -4, %r14    ! Decrement stack pointer
st        arg1, %r14        ! Push arg1 onto stack
.endmacro                   ! End macro definition
```

Figure 5-9 A macro definition for `push`.

nates with a `.endmacro` pseudo-op. On the `.macro` line, the first symbol is the name of the macro (`push` here), and the remaining symbols are command line arguments that are used within the macro. There is only one argument for macro `push`, which is `arg1`. This corresponds to `%r15` in the statement "`push %r15`," or to `%r1` in the statement "`push %r1`," etc. The argument (`%r15` or `%r1`) for each case is said to be "bound" to `arg1` during the assembly process.

Additional *formal* parameters can be used, separated by commas as in

```
.macro name arg1, arg2, arg3, ...
```

and the macro is then invoked with the same number of *actual* parameters:

```
name %r1, %r2, %r3, ...
```

The body of the macro follows the `.macro` pseudo-op. Any commands can follow, including other macros, or even calls to the same macro, which allows for a recursive expansion at assembly time. The parameters that appear in the `.macro` line can replace any text within the macro body, and so they can be used for labels, instructions, or operands.

It should be noted that during macro expansion formal parameters are replaced by actual parameters using a simple textual substitution. Thus, one can invoke the `push` macro with either memory or register arguments:

```
push %r1
```

or

```
push foo
```

The programmer needs to be aware of this feature of macro expansion when the macro is defined, lest the expanded macro contain illegal statements.

Additional pseudo-ops are needed for recursive macro expansion. The `.if` and `.endif` pseudo-ops open and close a conditional assembly section, respectively. If the argument to `.if` is true (at macro expansion time), then the code that follows, up to the corresponding `.endif`, is assembled. If the argument to `.if` is false, then the code between `.if` and `.endif` is ignored by the assembler. The conditional operator for the `.if` pseudo-op can be any member of the set $\{<, =, >, \geq, \neq, \text{or} \leq\}$.

```
! A recursive macro definition
.macro  recurs_add X           ! Start macro definition
.if     X > 2                  ! Assemble code if X > 2
        recurs_add   X - 1     ! Recursive call
.endif                         ! End .if construct
        addcc  %r1, %rX, %r1 ! Add argument into %r1
.endmacro                      ! End macro definition

recurs_add     4               ! Invoke the macro
        Expands to:
addcc   %r1, %r2, %r1
addcc   %r1, %r3, %r1
addcc   %r1, %r4, %r1
```

Figure 5-10 A recursive macro definition, and the corresponding macro expansion.

Figure 5-10 shows a recursive macro definition and its expansion during the assembly process. The expanded code sums the contents of registers `%r1` through `%rX` and places the result in `%r1`. The argument `X` is tested in the `.if` line. If `X` is greater than 2, then the macro is called again, but with the argument `X - 1`. If the macro `recurs_add` is invoked with an argument of `4`, then three lines of code are generated, as shown in the bottom of the figure. The first time that `recurs_add` is invoked, `X` has a value of `4`. The macro is invoked again with `X = 3` and `X = 2`, at which point the first `addcc` statement is generated. The second and third `addcc` statements are then generated as the recursion unwinds.

As mentioned earlier, for an assembler that supports macros, there must be a macro expansion phase that takes place prior to the two-pass assembly process. Macro expansion is normally performed by a **macro preprocessor** before the program is assembled. The macro expansion process may be invisible to a programmer, however, since it may be invoked by the assembler itself. Macro expansion typically requires two passes, in which the first pass records macro definitions and the second pass generates assembly language statements. The second pass of macro expansion can be very involved, however, if recursive macro definitions are supported. A more detailed description of macro expansion can be found in (Donovan, 1972).

5.5 Case Study: Extensions to the Instruction Set—The Intel MMX™ and Motorola AltiVec™ SIMD Instructions

As integrated circuit technology provides ever-increasing capacity within the processor, processor vendors search for new ways to use that capacity. One way that both Intel and Motorola capitalized on the additional capacity was to extend their ISAs with new registers and instructions that are specialized for processing streams or blocks of data. Intel provides the MMX extension to its Pentium processors and Motorola provides the AltiVec extension to its PowerPC processors. In this section we will discuss why the extensions are useful and how the two companies implemented them.

5.5.1 *BACKGROUND*

The processing of graphics, audio, and communication streams requires that the same repetitive operations be performed on large blocks of data. For example, a graphic image may be several megabytes in size, with repetitive operations required on the entire image for filtering, image enhancement, or other processing. So-called streaming audio (audio that is transmitted over a network in real time) may require continuous operation on the stream as it arrives. Likewise, 3-D image generation, virtual reality environments, and even computer games require extraordinary amounts of processing power. In the past the solution adopted by many computer system manufacturers was to include special-purpose processors explicitly for handling these kinds of operations.

Although Intel and Motorola took slightly different approaches, the results are quite similar. Both instruction sets are extended with **SIMD** (single instruction stream/multiple data stream) instructions and data types. The SIMD approach applies the same instruction to a **vector** of data items simultaneously. The term "vector" refers to a collection of data items, usually bytes or words.

Vector processors and processor extensions are by no means a new concept. The earliest CRAY and IBM 370 series computers had vector operations or extensions. In fact, these machines had much more powerful vector processing capabilities than these first microprocessor-based offerings from Intel and Motorola. Nevertheless, the Intel and Motorola extensions provide a considerable speedup in the localized, recurring operations for which they were designed. These extensions are covered in more detail in the following discussions, but Figure 5-11 gives an introduction to the process. The figure shows the Intel PADDB (Packed Add Bytes) instruction, which performs 8-bit addition on the vector of eight

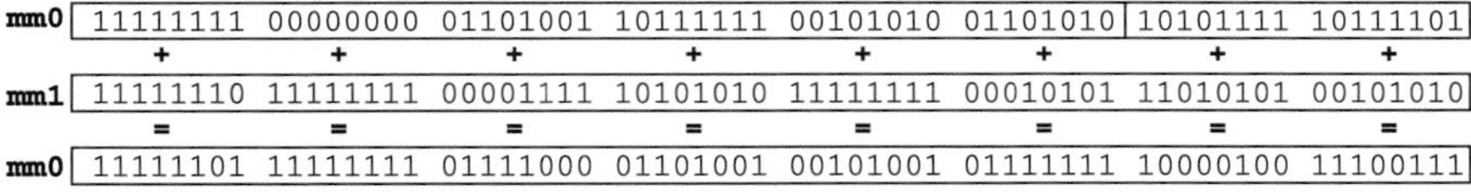

Figure 5-11 The vector addition of eight bytes by the Intel PADDB mm0, mm1 instruction.

bytes in register MM0 with the vector of eight bytes in register MM1, storing the results in register MM0.

5.5.2 *THE BASE ARCHITECTURES*

Before we cover the SIMD extensions to the two processors, we will take a look at the base architectures of the two machines. Surprisingly, the two processors could hardly be more different in their ISAs.

The Intel Pentium

Aside from special-purpose registers that are used in operating system–related matters, the Pentium ISA contains eight 32-bit integer registers, with each register having its own "personality." For example, the Pentium ISA contains a single accumulator (EAX), which holds arithmetic operands and results. The processor also includes eight 80-bit floating point registers, which, as we will see, also serve as vector registers for the MMX instructions. The Pentium instruction set would be characterized as **CISC** (complicated instruction set computer). We will discuss CISC versus RISC (reduced instruction set computer) in more detail in Chapter 10, but for now, suffice it to say that the Pentium instructions vary in size from a single byte to 9 bytes in length, and many Pentium instructions accomplish very complicated actions. The Pentium has many addressing modes, and most of its arithmetic instructions allow one operand or the result to be in either memory or a register. Much of the Intel ISA was shaped by the decision to make it binary compatible with the earliest member of the family, the 8086/8088, introduced in 1978. (The 8086 ISA was itself shaped by Intel's decision to make it assembly language compatible with the venerable 8-bit 8080, introduced in 1973.)

The Motorola PowerPC

The PowerPC, in contrast, was developed by a consortium of IBM, Motorola and Apple, "from the ground up," forsaking backward compatibility for the ability to incorporate the latest in RISC technology. The result was an ISA with fewer, simpler instructions, all instructions exactly one 32-bit word wide, thirty-two 32-bit general-purpose integer registers, and thirty-two 64-bit floating point registers. The ISA employs the "load/store" approach to memory access: Memory operands have to be loaded into registers by load and store instructions before they can be used. All other instructions must access their operands and results in registers.

As we shall see, the primary influence that the core ISAs just described have on the vector operations is in the way they access memory.

5.5.3 *VECTOR REGISTERS*

Both architectures provide an additional set of dedicated registers in which vector operands and results are stored. Figure 5-12 shows the vector register sets for the two processors. Intel, perhaps for reasons of space, "aliases" its floating point registers as MMX registers. This means that the Pentium's eight 64-bit floating point registers also do double duty as MMX registers. This approach has the disadvantage that the registers can be used for only one kind of operation at a time. The register set must be "flushed" with a special instruction, EMMS (Empty MMX State) after executing MMX instructions and before executing floating point instructions.

Motorola, perhaps because its PowerPC processor occupies less silicon, implemented thirty-two128-bit vector registers as a new set, separate and distinct from its floating point registers.

Vector Operands

Both Intel and Motorola's vector operations can operate on 8-, 16-, 32-, 64-, and, in Motorola's case, 128-bit integers. Unlike Intel, which supports only integer vectors, Motorola also supports 32-bit floating point numbers and operations. Both of their vector registers can be filled, or packed, with 8-, 16-, 32-, 64-, and in the Motorola case, 128-bit data values. For byte operands, this results

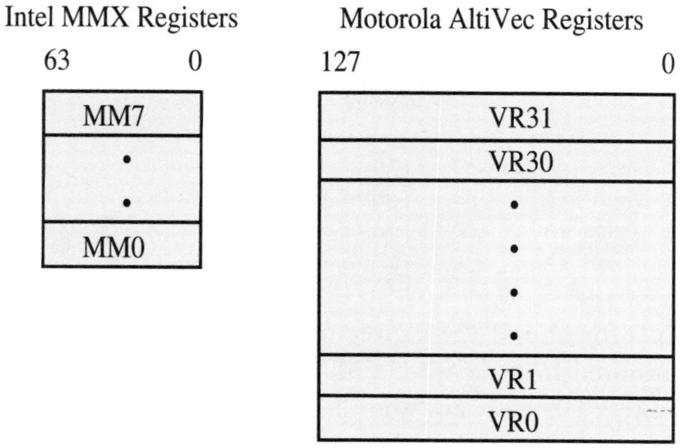

Figure 5-12 Intel and Motorola vector registers.

in 8- or 16-way parallelism, as 8 or 16 bytes are operated on simultaneously. This is how the SIMD nature of the vector operation is expressed: The same operation is performed on all the objects in a given vector register.

Loading to and Storing From the Vector Registers

Intel continues its CISC approach in the way it loads operands into its vector registers. There are two instructions for loading and storing values to and from the vector registers, MOVD and MOVQ, which move 32-bit doublewords and 64-bit quadwords, respectively. (The Intel word is 16 bits in size.) The syntax is

```
MOVD    mm, mm/m32      ;move doubleword to a vector reg.
MOVD    mm/m32, mm      ;move doubleword from a vector reg.
MOVQ    mm, mm/m64      ;move quadword to a vector reg.
MOVQ    mm/m64, mm      ;move quadword from a vector reg.
```

- ***mm*** stands for one of the 8 MM vector registers;
- ***mm/mm32*** stands for either one of the integer registers, an MM register, or a memory location;
- ***mm/m64*** stands for either an MM register or a memory location.

In addition, in the Intel vector arithmetic operations one of the operands can be in memory, as we will see.

Motorola likewise remained true to its professed RISC philosophy in its load and store operations. The only way to access an operand in memory is through the vector load and store operations. There is no way to move an operand between any of the other internal registers and the vector registers. All operands must be loaded from memory and stored to memory. Typical load opcodes are

```
lvebx   vD, rA|0, rB   ;load byte to vector reg vD, indexed.
lvehx   vD, rA|0, rB   ;move halfword to vector reg vD indexed.
lvewx   vD, rA|0, rB   ;move word to vector reg vD indexed.
lvx     vD, rA|0, rB   ;move doubleword to vector reg vD.
```

where vD stands for one of the 32 vector registers. The memory address of the operand is computed from (`rA`|0 + `rB`), where `rA` and `rB` represent any two of the integer registers `r0–r32`, and the "|0" symbol means that the value zero may be substituted for rA. The byte, half-word, word, or doubleword is fetched from that address. (PowerPC words are 32 bits in size.)

The term "indexed" in the preceding list refers to the location where the byte, halfword, or word will be stored in the vector register. The least significant bits of the memory address specify the index into the vector register. For example, LSBs 011 would specify that the byte should be loaded into the third byte of the register. Other bytes in the vector register are undefined.

The store operations work exactly like the load instructions except that the value from one of the vector registers is stored in memory.

5.5.4 *VECTOR ARITHMETIC OPERATIONS*

The vector arithmetic operations form the heart of the SIMD process. We will see that there is a new form of arithmetic, **saturation arithmetic**, and several new and exotic operations.

Saturation Arithmetic

Both vector processors provide the option of doing **saturation arithmetic** instead of the more familiar modulo wraparound kind discussed in Chapters 2 and 3. Saturation arithmetic works just like two's complement arithmetic as long as the results do not overflow or underflow. When results do overflow or underflow, in saturation arithmetic the result is held at the maximum or minimum allowable value, respectively, rather than being allowed to wrap around. For example, two's complement bytes are saturated at the high end at +127 and at the low end at −128. Unsigned bytes are saturated at 255 and 0. If an arithmetic result overflows or underflows these bounds, the result is clipped, or "saturated," at the boundary.

The need for saturation arithmetic is encountered in the processing of color information. If color is represented by a byte in which 0 represents black and 255 represents white, then saturation allows the color to remain pure black or pure white after an operation rather than inverting upon overflow or underflow.

Instruction Formats

As the two architectures have different approaches to addressing modes, so their SIMD instruction formats also differ. Intel continues using two-address instructions, where the first source operand can be in an MM register, an integer register, or memory, and the second operand and destination is an MM register:

```
OP mm, mm32or64          ;mm ← mm OP mm/mm32/64
```

Motorola requires all operands to be in vector registers and employs three operand instructions:

```
OP Vd, Va, Vb [,Vc]    ; Vd ← Va OP Vb [OP Vc]
```

This approach has the advantage that no vector register need be overwritten. In addition, some instructions can employ a third operand, `Vc`.

Arithmetic Operations

Perhaps not too surprisingly, the MMX and AltiVec instructions are quite similar. Both provide operations on 8-, 16-, 32-, 64-, and, in the AltiVec case, 128-bit operands. InTable 5-1 we see examples of the variety of operations provided by the

Operation	Operands (bits)	Arithmetic
Integer Add, Subtract, signed and unsigned(B)	8, 16, 32, 64, 128	Modulo, Saturated
Integer Add, Subtract, store carry-out in vector register(M)	32	Modulo
Integer Multiply, store high- or low order half (I)	16←16×16	—
Integer multiply add: Vd = Va *Vb + Vc (B)	16←8×8 32←16×16	Modulo, Saturated
Shift Left, Right, Arithmetic Right(B)	8, 16, 32, 64(I)	—
Rotate Left, Right (M)	8, 16, 32	—
AND, AND NOT, OR, NOR, XOR(B)	64(I), 128(M)	—
Integer Multiply every other operand, store entire result, signed and unsigned(M)	16←8×8 32←16×16	Modulo, Saturated
Maximum, minimum. Vd←Max,Min(Va, Vb) (M)	8, 16, 32	Signed, Unsigned
Vector sum across word. Add objects in vector, add this sum to object in second vector, place result in third vector register.(M)	Various	Modulo, Saturated
Vector floating point operations, add, subtract, multiply-add, *etc.* (M)	32	IEEE Floating Point

Table 5-1 MMX and AltiVec arithmetic instructions.

two technologies. The primary driving forces for providing these particular operations is a combination of wanting to provide potential users of the technology with operations that they will find needed and useful in their particular application, the amount of silicon available for the extension, and the base ISA.

5.5.5 *VECTOR COMPARE OPERATIONS*

The ordinary paradigm for conditional operations—compare and branch on condition—will not work for vector operations, because each operand undergoing the comparison can yield different results. For example, comparing two word vectors for equality could yield TRUE, FALSE, FALSE, TRUE. There is no good way to employ branches to select different code blocks depending upon the truth or falsity of the comparisons. As a result, vector comparisons in both MMX and AltiVec technologies result in the explicit generation of TRUE or FALSE. In both cases, TRUE is represented by all 1's, and FALSE by all 0's in the destination operand. For example, byte comparisons yield FFH or 00H, 16-bit comparisons yield FFFFH or 0000H, and so on for other operands. These values, all 1's or all 0's, can then be used as masks to update values.

Example: Comparing Two Byte Vectors for Equality

Consider comparing two MMX byte vectors for equality. Figure 5-13 shows the results of the comparison: Strings of 1's where the comparison succeeded, and 0's where it failed. This comparison can be used in subsequent operations. Consider the high-level language conditional statement:

```
if (mm0 == mm1) mm2 = mm2 else mm2 = 0;
```

The comparison in Figure 5-13 yields the mask that can be used to control the byte-wise assignment. Register mm2 is ANDed with the mask in mm0 and the result stored in mm2, as shown in Figure 5-14. By using various combinations of comparison operations and masks, a full range of conditional operations can be implemented.

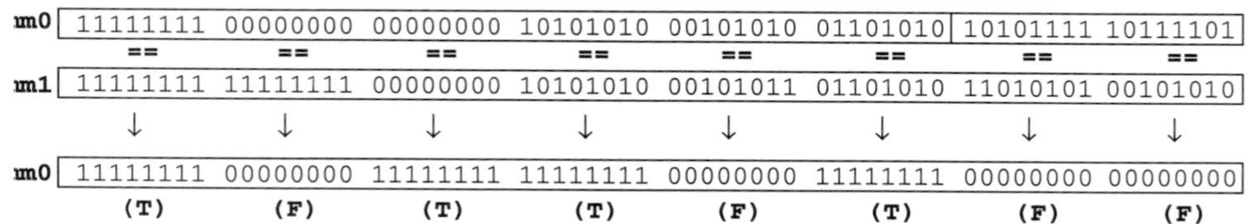

Figure 5-13 Comparing two MMX byte vectors for equality.

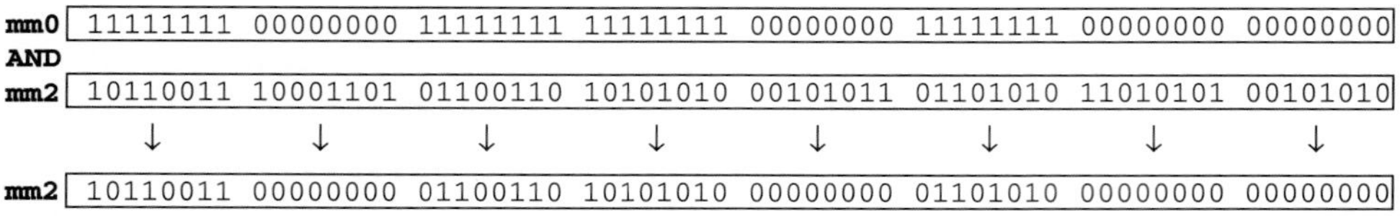

mm0	11111111	00000000	11111111	11111111	00000000	11111111	00000000	00000000
AND								
mm2	10110011	10001101	01100110	10101010	00101011	01101010	11010101	00101010
	↓	↓	↓	↓	↓	↓	↓	↓
mm2	10110011	00000000	01100110	10101010	00000000	01101010	00000000	00000000

Figure 5-14 Conditional assignment of an MMX byte vector.

Vector Permutation Operations

The AltiVec ISA also includes a useful instruction that allows the contents of one vector to be permuted, or rearranged, in an arbitrary fashion, and the permuted result stored in another vector register.

5.5.6 *CASE STUDY SUMMARY*

The SIMD extensions to the Pentium and PowerPC processors provide powerful operations that can be used for block data processing. At present there are no common compiler extensions for these instructions. As a result, programmers who want to use these extensions must be willing to program in assembly language.

An additional problem is that not all Pentium or PowerPC processors contain the extensions, only specialized versions. While the programmer can test for the presence of the extensions, in their absence the programmer must write a "manual" version of the algorithm. This means providing two sets of code, one that utilizes the extensions and one that utilizes the base ISA.

■ SUMMARY

A high-level programming language like C or Pascal allows the low-level architecture of a computer to be treated as an abstraction. An assembly language program, on the other hand, takes a form that is very dependent on the underlying architecture. The instruction set architecture (ISA) is made visible to the programmer, who is responsible for handling register usage and subroutine linkage. Some of the complexity of assembly language programming is managed through the use of macros, which differ from subroutines or functions, in that macros generate inline code at assembly time, whereas subroutines are executed at run time.

A linker combines separately assembled modules into a single load module, which typically involves relocating code. A loader places the load module in memory and starts the execution of the program. The loader may also need to perform relocation if two or more load modules overlap in memory.

In practice the details of assembly, linking and loading are highly system dependent and language dependent. Some simple assemblers merely produce executable binary files, but more commonly an assembler will produce additional information so that modules can be linked by a linker. Some systems provide linking loaders that combine the linking task with the loading task. Others separate linking from loading. Some loaders can only load a program at the address specified in the binary file, while more commonly, relocating loaders can relocate programs to a load-time-specified address. The file formats that support these processes are also operating system dependent.

Before compilers were developed, programs were written directly in assembly language. Nowadays, assembly language is not normally used directly since compilers for high-level languages are so prevalent and also produce efficient code, but assembly language is still important for understanding aspects of computer architecture, such as how to link programs that are compiled for different calling conventions, and for exploiting extensions to architectures such as MMX and AltiVec.

■ FURTHER READING

Compilers and compilation are treated by (Aho et al., 1985) and (Waite and Carter, 1993). There are a great many references on assembly language programming. (Donovan, 1972) is a classic reference on assemblers, linkers, and loaders. (Gill et al., 1987) covers the 68000. (Goodman and Miller, 1993) serves as a good instructional text, with examples taken from the MIPS architecture. The appendix in (Patterson and Hennessy, 1998) also covers the MIPS architecture. (SPARC, 1992) deals specifically with the definition of the SPARC and SPARC assembly language.

Aho, A. V., R. Sethi, and J. D. Ullman, *Compilers*, Addison-Wesley (1985).

Donovan, J. J., *Systems Programming*, McGraw-Hill (1972).

Gill, A., E. Corwin, and A. Logar, *Assembly Language Programming for the 68000*, Prentice Hall (1987).

Goodman, J. and K. Miller, *A Programmer's View of Computer Architecture*, Saunders College Publishing (1993).

Patterson, D. A. and J. L. Hennessy, *Computer Organization and Design: The Hardware/Software Interface*, 2/e, Morgan Kaufmann (1998).

SPARC International, Inc., *The SPARC Architecture Manual: Version 8*, Prentice Hall (1992).

Waite, W. M. and L. R. Carter, *An Introduction to Compiler Construction*, HarperCollins (1993).

■ PROBLEMS

5.1 Create a symbol table for the following ARC segment shown using a form similar to Figure 5-7. Use "U" for any symbols that are undefined.

```
x           .equ    4000
            .org    2048
            ba      main
            .org    2072
main:       sethi   x, %r2
            srl     %r2, 10, %r2
lab_4:      st      %r2, [k]
            addcc   %r1, -1, %r1
foo:        st      %r1, [k]
            andcc   %r1, %r1, %r0
            beq     lab_5
            jmpl    %r15 + 4, %r0
cons:       .dwb    3
```

5.2 Translate the following ARC code into object code. Assume that x is at location $(4096)_{10}$.

```
k           .equ    1024
                .
                .
                .
            addcc   %r4 + k, %r4
            ld      %r14, %r5
            addcc   %r14, -1, %r14
            st      %r5, [x]
                .
                .
                .
```

5.3 Create a symbol table for the program shown in Figure 5-8, using a form similar to Figure 5-7.

5.4 Translate subroutine `add_64` shown in Figure 5-8, including variables *A*, `B`, and `C`, into object code.

5.5 A **disassembler** is a software program that reads an object module and re-creates the source assembly language module. Given the following object code, disassemble the code into ARC assembly language statements. Since there is not enough information in the object code to determine symbol names, choose symbols as you need them from the alphabet, consecutively, from "a" to "z."

```
10000010 10000000 01100000 00000001
10000000 10010001 01000000 00000110
00000010 10000000 00000000 00000011
10001101 00110001 10100000 00001010
00010000 10111111 11111111 11111100
10000001 11000011 11100000 00000100
```

5.6 Given the following two macros `push` and `pop`, unnecessary instructions can be inserted into a program if a `push` immediately follows a `pop`. Expand the macro definitions shown and identify the unnecessary instructions.

```
    .begin
    .macro     push   arg1
    addcc      %r14, -4, %r14
    st     arg1, %r14
    .endmacro
    .macro     pop    arg1
    ld     %r14, arg1
    addcc  %r14, 4, %r14
    .endmacro
! Start of program
    .org   2048
    pop    %r1
    push   %r2
         .
         .
         .
    .end
```

5.7 Write a macro called `return` that performs the function of the `jmpl` statement as it is used in Figure 5-5.

5.8 In Figure 4-16, the operand `x` for `sethi` is filled in by the assembler, but the statement will not work as intended if $x \geq 2^{22}$ because there are only 22 bits in the `imm22` field of the sethi format. In order to place an arbitrary 32-bit address into `%r5` at run time, we can use `sethi` for the upper 22 bits, and then use `addcc` for the lower 10 bits. For this we add two new pseudo-ops, `.high22` and `.low10`, which construct the bit patterns for the high 22 bits and the low 10 bits of the address, respectively. The construct

```
sethi .high22(#FFFFFFFF), %r1
```

expands to

```
sethi #3FFFFF, %r1
```

and the construct

```
addcc %r1, .low10(#FFFFFFFF), %r1
```

expands to

```
addcc %r1, #3FF, %r1.
```

Rewrite the calling routine in Figure 4-16 using `.high22` and `.low10` so that it works correctly regardless of where `x` is placed in memory.

5.9 Assume that you have the subroutine `add_64` shown in Figure 5-8 available to you. Write an ARC routine called `add_128` that adds two 64-bit numbers, making use of `add_64`. The two 128-bit operands are stored in memory locations that begin at `x` and `y`, and the result is stored in the memory location that begins at `z`.

5.10 Write a macro called `subcc` that has a usage similar to `addcc`, and that subtracts its second source operand from the first.

5.11 Does ordinary, nonrecursive macro expansion happen at assembly time or at execution time? Does recursive macro expansion happen at assembly time or at execution time?

5.12 An assembly language programmer proposes to increase the capability of the `push` macro defined in Figure 5-9 by providing a second argument, arg2. The second argument would replace the `addcc %r14, -4, %r14` with `addcc arg2, -4, arg2`. Explain what the programmer is trying to accomplish and what dangers lurk in this approach.

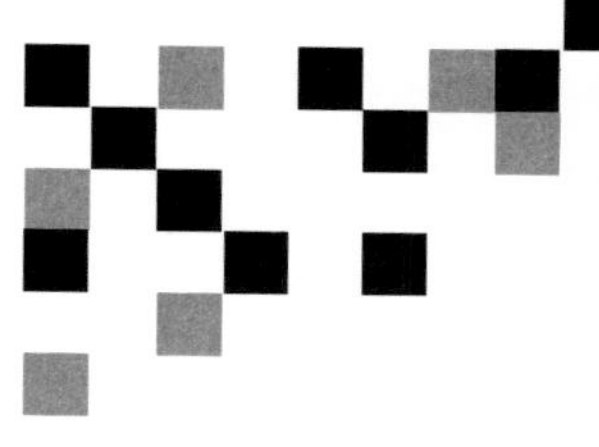

6

DATAPATH AND CONTROL

In the previous chapters, we examined the computer at the Application level, the High Level Language level, and the Assembly Language level (as shown in Figure 1-4). In Chapter 4, we introduced the concept of an ISA: an instruction set that effects operations on registers and memory. In this chapter, we explore the part of the machine that is responsible for implementing these operations: the control unit of the CPU. In this context, we view the machine at the **microarchitecture** level (the Microprogrammed/Hardwired Control level in Figure 1-4). The microarchitecture consists of the control unit and the programmer-visible registers, functional units such as the ALU, and any additional registers that may be required by the control unit.

A given ISA may be implemented with different microarchitectures. For example, the Intel Pentium ISA has been implemented in different ways, all of which support the same ISA. Not only Intel, but a number of competitors, such as AMD and Cyrix, have implemented Pentium ISAs. A certain microarchitecture might stress high instruction execution speed, while another stresses low power consumption, and another low processor cost. Being able to modify the microarchitecture while keeping the ISA unchanged means that processor vendors can take advantage of new IC and memory technology while affording users upward compatibility for their software investment. Programs run unchanged on different processors as long as the processors implement the same ISA, regardless of the underlying microarchitectures.

In this chapter, we examine two polarizingly different microarchitecture approaches: microprogrammed control units and hardwired control units, and we examine them by showing how a subset of the ARC processor can be implemented using these two design techniques.

6.1 Basics of the Microarchitecture

The functionality of the microarchitecture centers around the fetch-execute cycle, which is in some sense the "heart" of the machine. As discussed in Chapter 4, the steps involved in the fetch-execute cycle are as follows:

1. Fetch the next instruction to be executed from memory.
2. Decode the opcode.
3. Read operand(s) from main memory or registers, if any.
4. Execute the instruction and store results.
5. Go to Step 1.

It is the microarchitecture that is responsible for making these five steps happen. The microarchitecture fetches the next instruction to be executed, determines which instruction it is, fetches the operands, executes the instruction, stores the results, and then repeats.

The microarchitecture consists of a **data section**, which contains registers and an ALU, and a **control section**, as illustrated in Figure 6-1. The data section is also referred to as the **datapath**. Microprogrammed control uses a special purpose **microprogram**, not visible to the user, to implement operations on the registers and on other parts of the machine. Often, the microprogram contains many program steps that collectively implement a single (macro)instruction. **Hardwired**

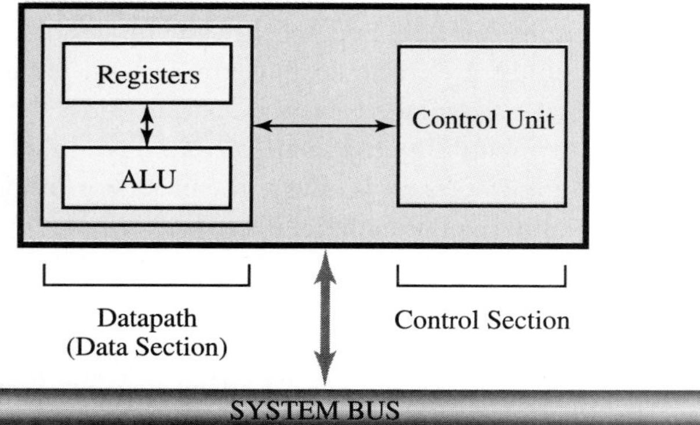

Figure 6-1 High-level view of a microarchitecture.

control units adopt the view that the steps to be taken to implement an operation comprise states in a finite state machine, and the design proceeds using conventional digital design methods (such as the methods covered in Appendix A). In either case, the datapath remains largely unchanged, although there may be minor differences to support the differing forms of control. In designing the ARC control unit, the microprogrammed approach will be explored first, and then the hardwired approach, and for both cases the datapath will remain unchanged.

6.2 A Microarchitecture for the ARC

In this section, we consider a microprogrammed approach for designing the ARC control unit. We begin by describing the datapath and its associated control signals.

The instruction set and instruction format for the ARC subset is repeated from Chapter 4 in Figure 6-2. There are 15 instructions that are grouped into four formats according to the leftmost two bits of the coded instruction. The Processor Status Register `%psr` is also shown.

6.2.1 *THE DATAPATH*

A datapath for the ARC is illustrated in Figure 6-3. The datapath contains 32 user-visible data registers (`%r0–%r31`), the program counter (`%pc`), the instruction register (`%ir`), the ALU, four temporary registers not visible at the ISA level (`%temp0–%temp3`), and the connections among these components. The number adjacent to a diagonal slash on some of the lines is a simplification that indicates the number of separate wires that are represented by the corresponding single line.

Registers `%r0–%r31` are directly accessible by a user. Register `%r0` always contains the value 0 and cannot be changed. The `%pc` register is the program counter, which points to the instruction to be read from the main memory. The user has direct access to `%pc` only through the `call` and `jmpl` instructions. The temporary registers are used in interpreting the ARC instruction set and are not visible to the user. The `%ir` register holds the current instruction that is being executed. It is not visible to the user.

The ALU

The ALU performs one of 16 operations on the A and B buses according to the table shown in Figure 6-4. For every ALU operation, the 32-bit result is placed

Mnemonic	Meaning
ld	Load a register from memory
st	Store a register into memory
sethi	Load the 22 most significant bits of a register
andcc	Bitwise logical AND
orcc	Bitwise logical OR
orncc	Bitwise logical NOR
srl	Shift right (logical)
addcc	Add
call	Call subroutine
jmpl	Jump and link (return from subroutine call)
be	Branch if equal
bneg	Branch if negative
bcs	Branch on carry
bvs	Branch on overflow
ba	Branch always

```
                 op
                 31 30 29 28 27 26 25 24 23 22 21 20 19 18 17 16 15 14 13 12 11 10 09 08 07 06 05 04 03 02 01 00
SETHI Format     | 0 0 |  rd  | op2 |                          imm22                          |
Branch Format    | 0 0 0 | cond | op2 |                        disp22                         |

                 31 30 29 28 27 26 25 24 23 22 21 20 19 18 17 16 15 14 13 12 11 10 09 08 07 06 05 04 03 02 01 00
CALL format      | 0 1 |                               disp30                               |

                                                                       i
                 31 30 29 28 27 26 25 24 23 22 21 20 19 18 17 16 15 14 13 12 11 10 09 08 07 06 05 04 03 02 01 00
Arithmetic       | 1 0 |  rd  |  op3  |  rs1  | 0 | 0 0 0 0 0 0 0 0 |  rs2  |
Formats          | 1 0 |  rd  |  op3  |  rs1  | 1 |        simm13        |

                 31 30 29 28 27 26 25 24 23 22 21 20 19 18 17 16 15 14 13 12 11 10 09 08 07 06 05 04 03 02 01 00
                 | 1 1 |  rd  |  op3  |  rs1  | 0 | 0 0 0 0 0 0 0 0 |  rs2  |
Memory Formats   | 1 1 |  rd  |  op3  |  rs1  | 1 |        simm13        |
```

op	Format
00	SETHI/Branch
01	CALL
10	Arithmetic
11	Memory

op2	Inst.
010	branch
100	sethi

op3 (op=10)	
010000	addcc
010001	andcc
010010	orcc
010110	orncc
100110	srl
111000	jmpl

op3 (op=11)	
000000	ld
000100	st

cond	branch
0001	be
0101	bcs
0110	bneg
0111	bvs
1000	ba

```
      31 30 29 28 27 26 25 24 23 22 21 20 19 18 17 16 15 14 13 12 11 10 09 08 07 06 05 04 03 02 01 00
PSR   |                 | n | z | v | c |                                                          |
```

Figure 6-2 Instruction subset and instruction formats for the ARC.

on the C bus, unless it is blocked by the C bus MUX when a word of memory is placed onto the C bus instead.

The ANDCC and AND operations perform a bit-by-bit logical AND of corresponding bits on the A and B buses. Note that only operations that end with "CC" affect the condition codes, and so ANDCC affects the condition codes whereas AND does not. (There are times when we wish to execute arithmetic and

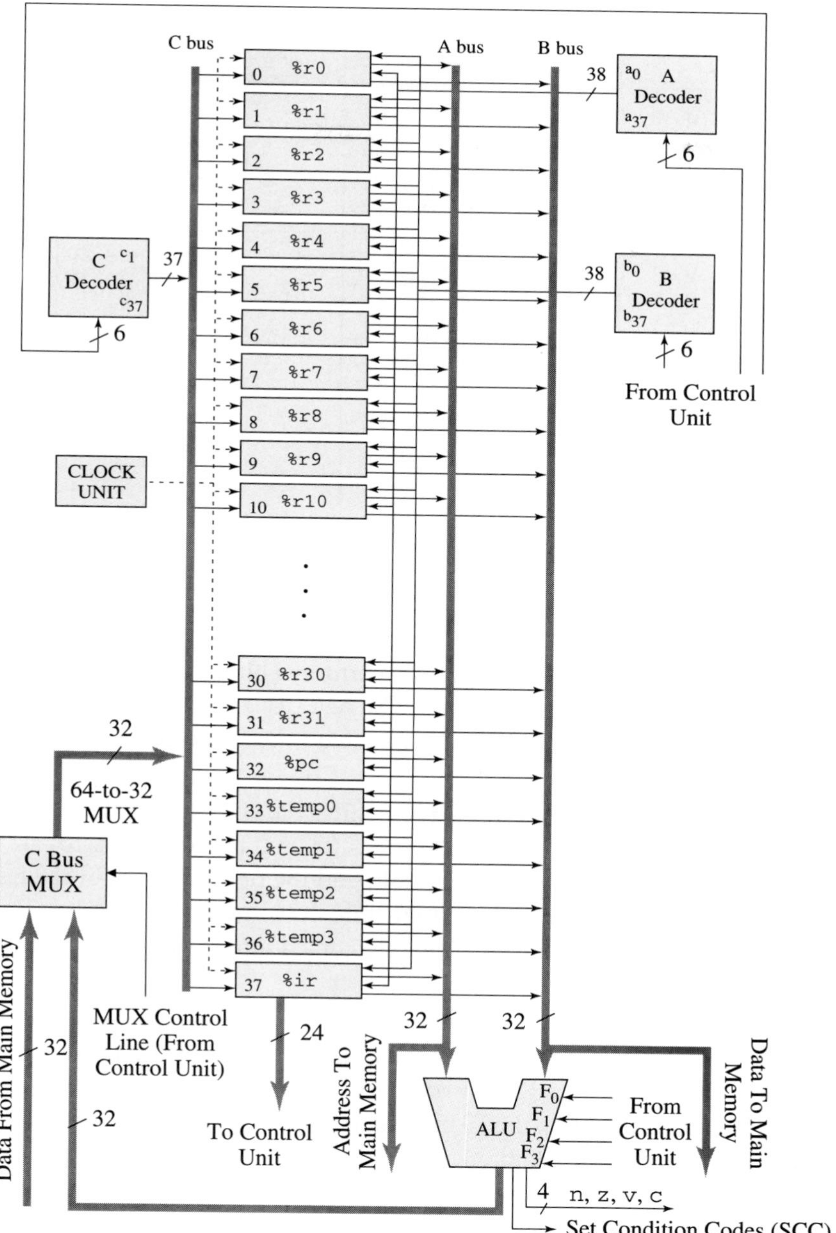

Figure 6-3 The datapath of the ARC.

logic instructions without disturbing the condition codes.) The ORCC and OR operations perform a bit-by-bit logical OR of corresponding bits on the A and B

F_3 F_2 F_1 F_0	Operation	Changes Condition Codes
0 0 0 0	ANDCC (A, B)	yes
0 0 0 1	ORCC (A, B)	yes
0 0 1 0	NORCC (A, B)	yes
0 0 1 1	ADDCC (A, B)	yes
0 1 0 0	SRL (A, B)	no
0 1 0 1	AND (A, B)	no
0 1 1 0	OR (A, B)	no
0 1 1 1	NOR (A, B)	no
1 0 0 0	ADD (A, B)	no
1 0 0 1	LSHIFT2 (A)	no
1 0 1 0	LSHIFT10 (A)	no
1 0 1 1	SIMM13 (A)	no
1 1 0 0	SEXT13 (A)	no
1 1 0 1	INC (A)	no
1 1 1 0	INCPC (A)	no
1 1 1 1	RSHIFT5 (A)	no

Figure 6-4 ARC ALU operations.

buses. The NORCC and NOR operations perform a bit-by-bit logical NOR of corresponding bits on the A and B buses. The ADDCC and ADD operations carry out addition using two's complement arithmetic on the A and B buses.

The SRL (shift right logical) operation shifts the contents of the A bus to the right by the amount specified on the B bus (from 0 to 31 bits). Zeros are copied into the leftmost bits of the shifted result, and the rightmost bits of the result are discarded. LSHIFT2 and LSHIFT10 shift the contents of the A bus to the left by two and 10 bits, respectively. Zeros are copied into the rightmost bits.

SIMM13 retrieves the least significant 13 bits of the A bus and places zeros in the 19 most significant bits. SEXT13 performs a sign extension of the 13 least significant bits on the A bus to form a 32-bit word. That is, if the leftmost bit of the 13 bit group is 1, then 1's are copied into the 19 most significant bits of the result; otherwise 0's are copied into the 19 most significant bits of the result. The INC operation increments the value on the A bus by 1, and the INCPC operation increments the value on the A bus by four, which is used in incrementing the PC register by one word (four bytes). INCPC can be used on any register placed on the A bus.

The RSHIFT5 operation shifts the operand on the A bus to the right by 5 bits, copying the leftmost bit (the sign bit) into the 5 new bits on the left. This has the effect of performing a 5-bit sign extension. When applied three times in succession to a 32-bit instruction, this operation also has the effect of placing the leftmost bit of the COND field in the Branch format (refer to Figure 6-2) into the position of bit 13. This operation is useful in decoding the Branch instructions, as we will see later in the chapter. The sign extension for this case is inconsequential.

Every arithmetic and logic operation can be implemented with just these ALU operations. As an example, a subtraction operation can be implemented by forming the two's complement negative of the subtrahend (making use of the `NOR` operation and adding 1 to it with `INC`) and then performing addition on the operands. A shift to the left by one bit can be performed by adding a number to itself. A "do-nothing" operation, which is frequently needed for simply passing data through the ALU without changing it, can be implemented by logically ANDing an operand with itself and discarding the result in `%r0`. A logical XOR can be implemented with the AND, OR, and NOR operations, making use of DeMorgan's theorem (see Problem 6.5).

The ALU generates the `c`, `n`, `z`, and `v` condition codes, which are true for a carry, negative, zero, or overflow result, respectively. The condition codes are changed only for the operations indicated in Figure 6-4. A signal (SCC) is also generated that tells the `%psr` register when to update the condition codes.

The ALU can be implemented in a number of ways. For the sake of simplicity, let us consider using a **lookup table** (LUT) approach. The ALU has two 32-bit data inputs *A* and *B*, a 32-bit data output *C*, a four-bit control input *F*, a four-bit condition code output (*N, V, C, Z*), and a signal (SCC) that sets the flags in the `%psr` register. We can decompose the ALU into a cascade of 32 LUTs that implement the arithmetic and logic functions, followed by a **barrel shifter** that implements the shifts. A block diagram is shown in Figure 6-5.

The barrel shifter shifts the input word by an arbitrary amount (from 0 to 31 bits) according to the settings of the control inputs. The barrel shifter performs shifts in levels, in which a different bit of the Shift Amount (SA) input is observed at each level. A partial gate-level layout for the barrel shifter is shown in Figure 6-6. Starting at the bottom of the circuit, we can see that the outputs of the bottom stage will be the same as the inputs to that stage if the SA_0 bit is 0. If the SA_0 bit is 1, then each output position will take on the value of its immediate left or right neighbor, according to the direction of the shift, which is indicated by the Shift Right input. At the next higher level, the method is applied again, except that the SA_1 bit is observed and the amount of the shift is doubled.

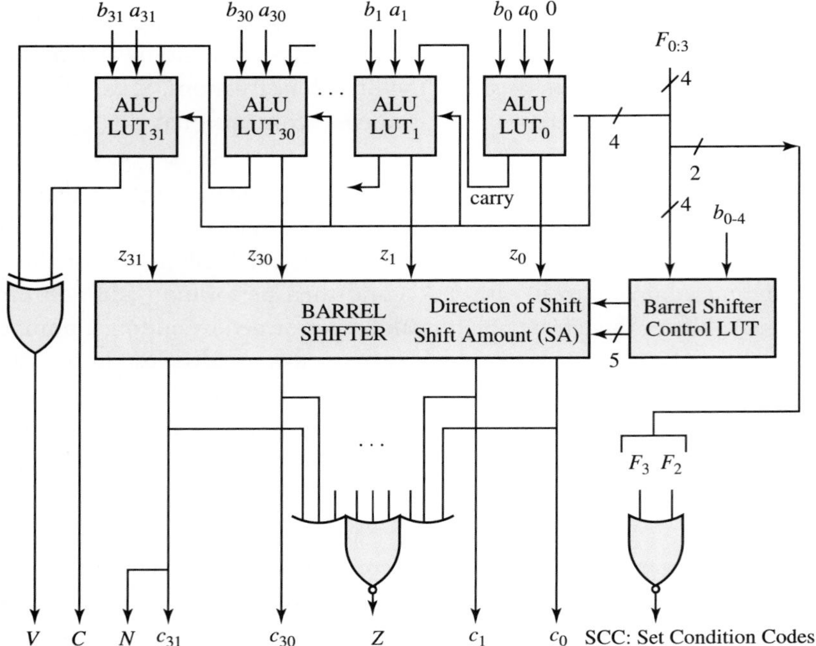

Figure 6-5 Block diagram of the 32-bit ALU.

The process continues until bit SA_4 is observed at the highest level. Zeros are copied into positions that have no corresponding inputs. With this structure, an arbitrary shift from 0 to 31 bits to the left or the right can be implemented.

Each of the 32 ALU LUTs is implemented almost identically, using the same lookup table entries, except for changes in certain positions such as for the `INC` and `INCPC` operations (see Figure 6-7). The first few entries for each LUT are shown in Figure 6-7. The barrel shifter control LUT is constructed in a similar manner, but with different LUT entries.

The condition code bits `n`, `z`, `v`, and `c` are implemented directly. The `n` and `c` bits are taken directly from the c_{31} output of the barrel shifter and the carry-out position of ALU LUT$_{31}$, respectively. The `z` bit is computed as the NOR over the barrel shifter outputs. The `z` bit is 1 only if all of the barrel shifter outputs are 0. The `v` (overflow) bit is set if the carry into the most significant position is different from the carry-out of the most significant position, which is implemented with an XOR gate.

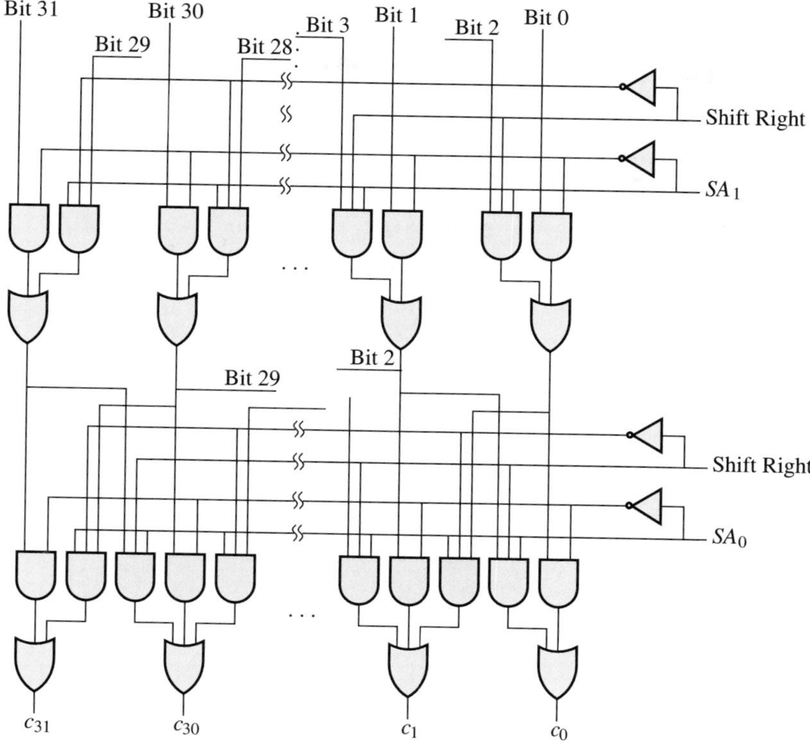

Figure 6-6 Gate-level layout of barrel shifter.

Only the operations that end in "CC" should set the condition codes, and so a signal is generated that informs the condition codes to change, as indicated by the label "SCC: Set Condition Codes." This signal is true when both F_3 and F_2 are false.

The Registers

All of the registers are composed of *falling-edge-triggered* D flip-flops (see Appendix A). This means that the outputs of the flip-flops do not change until the clock makes a transition from high to low (the *falling edge* of the clock). The registers all take a similar form, and so we will only look at the design of register `%r1`. All of the datapath registers are 32 bits wide, and so 32 flip-flops are used for the design of `%r1`, which is illustrated in Figure 6-8.

The CLK input to register `%r1` is ANDed with the select line (c_1) from the C decoder. This ensures that `%r1` only changes when the control section instructs it

	F_3	F_2	F_1	F_0	*Carry In*	a_i	b_i	z_i	*Carry Out*
ANDCC	0	0	0	0	0	0	0	0	0
	0	0	0	0	0	0	1	0	0
	0	0	0	0	0	1	0	0	0
	0	0	0	0	0	1	1	1	0
	0	0	0	0	1	0	0	0	0
	0	0	0	0	1	0	1	0	0
	0	0	0	0	1	1	0	0	0
	0	0	0	0	1	1	1	1	0
ORCC	0	0	0	1	0	0	0	0	0
	0	0	0	1	0	0	1	1	0
	0	0	0	1	0	1	0	1	0
	0	0	0	1	0	1	1	1	0
	0	0	0	1	1	0	0	0	0
	0	0	0	1	1	0	1	1	0
					.				.
					.				.
					.				.

Figure 6-7 Truth table for most of the ALU LUTs.

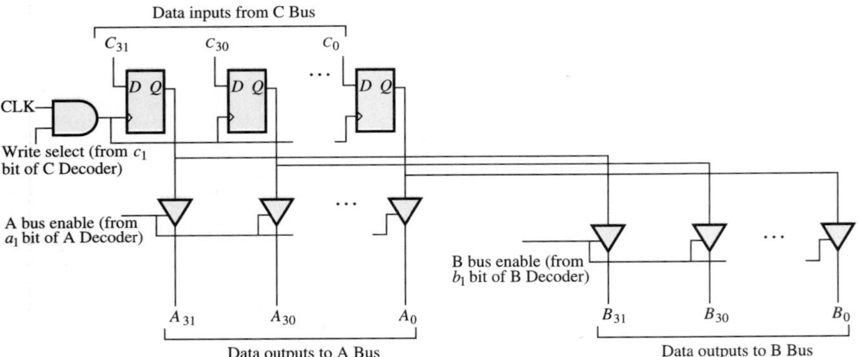

Figure 6-8 Design of register `%r1`.

to change. The data inputs to `%r1` are taken directly from the corresponding lines of the C bus. The outputs are written to the corresponding lines of the A and B buses through tri state buffers, which are "electrically disconnected" unless their enable inputs are set to 1. The outputs of the buffers are enabled onto the A and B buses by the a_1 and b_1 outputs of the A and B decoders, respectively. If neither a_1 nor b_1 are high (meaning they are equal to 1), then the outputs of `%r1` are electrically disconnected from both the A and B buses since the tri-state buffers are disabled.

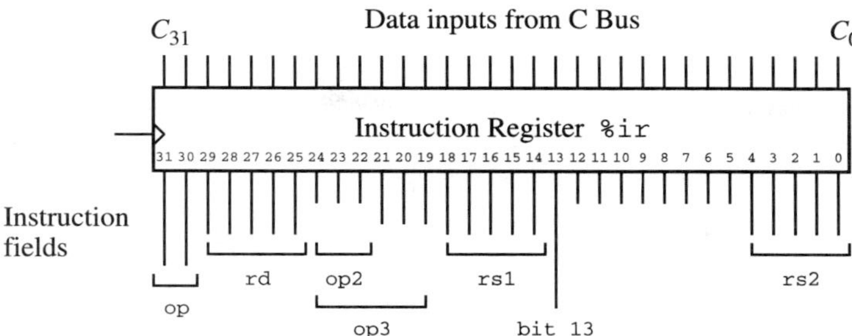

Figure 6-9 Outputs to control unit from register `%ir`**.**

The remaining registers take a similar form, with a few exceptions. Register `%r0` always contains a 0, which cannot be changed. Register `%r0` thus has no inputs from the C bus nor any inputs from the C decoder and does not need flip-flops (see Problem 6.11). The `%ir` register has additional outputs that correspond to the `rd`, `rs1`, `rs2`, `op`, `op2`, `op3`, and bit 13 fields of an instruction, as illustrated in Figure 6-9. These outputs are used by the control section in interpreting an instruction, as we will see in Section 6.2.4. The program counter can only contain values that are evenly divisible by 4, and so the rightmost two bits in `%pc` can be hardwired to 0.

The A, B, and C decoders shown in Figure 6-3 simplify register selection. The six-bit inputs to the decoders select a single register for each of the A, B, and C buses. There are $2^6 = 64$ possible outputs from the decoders, but there are only 38 data registers. The index shown to the left of each register (in base 10) in Figure 6-3 indicates the value that must be applied to a decoder input to select the corresponding register. The 0 output of the C decoder is not used because `%r0` cannot be written. Indices that are greater than 37 do not correspond to any registers and are free to be used when no registers are to be connected to a bus.

6.2.2 *THE CONTROL SECTION*

The entire microprogrammed ARC microarchitecture is shown in Figure 6-10. The figure shows the datapath, the control unit, and the connections between them. At the heart of the control unit is a 2048-word × 41-bit read-only memory (ROM) that contains values for all of the lines that must be controlled to implement each user-level instruction. The ROM is referred to as a **control store** in this context. Each 41-bit word is called a **microinstruction**. The control unit is responsible for fetching microinstructions and executing them, much in the same way as

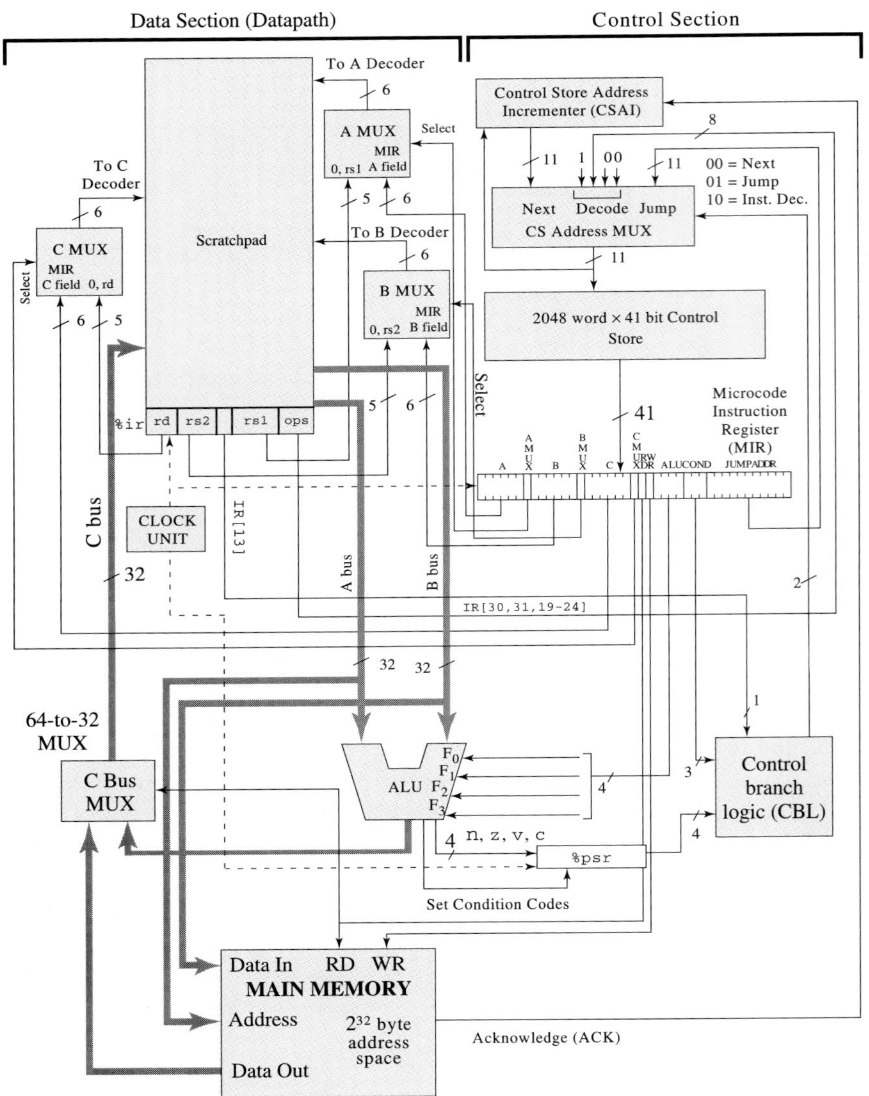

Figure 6-10 The microarchitecture of the ARC.

user-level ARC macroinstructions are fetched and executed. This microinstruction execution is controlled by the microprogram instruction register (MIR), the processor status register (`%psr`), and a mechanism for determining the next microinstruction to be executed: the Control Branch Logic (CBL) unit and the Control Store (CS) Address MUX. A separate PC for the microprogram is not needed to

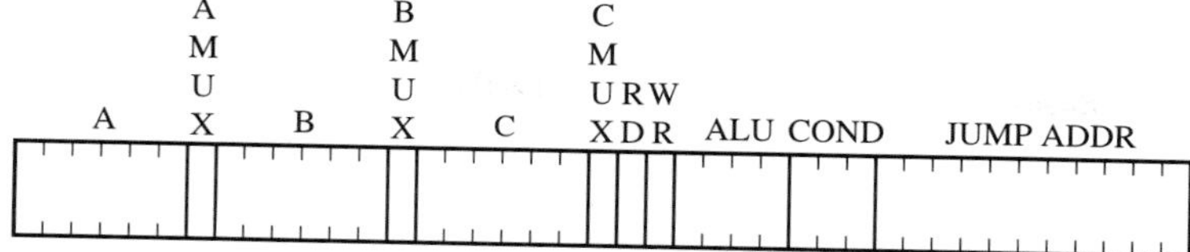

Figure 6-11 The microword format.

store the address of the next microinstruction, because it is recomputed on every clock cycle and therefore does not need to be stored for future cycles.

When the microarchitecture begins operation (at power-on time, for example), a reset circuit (not shown) places the microword at location 0 in the control store into the MIR and executes it. From that point onward, a microword is selected for execution from either the Next, the Decode, or the Jump inputs to the CS Address MUX, according to the settings in the COND field of the MIR and the output of the CBL logic. After each microword is placed in the MIR, the datapath performs operations according to the settings in the individual fields of the MIR. This process is detailed in the following discussion.

A microword contains 41 bits that comprise 11 fields as shown in Figure 6-11. Starting from the left, the A field determines which of the registers in the datapath are to be placed on the A bus. The bit patterns for the registers correspond to the binary representations of the base 10 register indices shown in Figure 6-3 (000000–100101). The AMUX field selects whether the A decoder takes its input from the A field of the MIR (AMUX = 0) or from the `rs1` field of `%ir` (AMUX = 1).

In a similar manner, the B field determines which of the registers in the datapath are to be placed on the B bus. The BMUX field selects whether the B decoder takes its input from the B field of the MIR (BMUX = 0) or from the `rs2` field of `%ir` (BMUX = 1). The C field determines which of the registers in the datapath is to be written from the C bus. The CMUX field selects whether the C decoder takes its input from the C field of the MIR (CMUX = 0) or from the `rd` field of `%ir` (CMUX = 1). Since `%r0` cannot be changed, the bit pattern 000000 can be used in the C field when none of these registers are to be changed.

The RD and WR lines determine whether the memory will be read or written, respectively. A read takes place if RD = 1, and a write takes place if WR = 1. Both the RD and WR fields cannot be set to 1 at the same time, but both fields can be 0 if nei-

C_2	C_1	C_0	Operation
0	0	0	Use NEXT ADDR
0	0	1	Use JUMP ADDR if `n` = 1
0	1	0	Use JUMP ADDR if `z` = 1
0	1	1	Use JUMP ADDR if `v` = 1
1	0	0	Use JUMP ADDR if `c` = 1
1	0	1	Use JUMP ADDR if `IR[13]` = 1
1	1	0	Use JUMP ADDR
1	1	1	DECODE

Figure 6-12 Settings for the COND field of the microword.

ther a read nor a write operation is to take place. For both RD and WR, the address for the memory is taken directly from the A bus. The data input to the memory is taken from the B bus, and the data output from the memory is placed on the C bus. The RD line controls the 64-to-32 C bus MUX, which determines whether the C bus is loaded from the memory (RD = 1) or from the ALU (RD = 0).

The ALU field determines which of the ALU operations is performed according to the settings shown in Figure 6-4. All 16 possible ALU field bit patterns correspond to valid ALU operations. This means that there is no way to "turn the ALU off" when it is not needed, such as during a read or write to memory. For this situation, an ALU operation should be selected that has no unwanted side effects. For example, `ANDCC` changes the condition codes and would not be appropriate, whereas the `AND` operation does not affect the condition codes and would therefore be appropriate.

The COND (conditional jump) field instructs the **microcontroller** to take the next microword from either the next control store location, or from the location in the JUMP ADDR field of the MIR, or from the opcode bits of the instruction in `%ir`. The COND field is interpreted according to the table shown in Figure 6-12. If the COND field is 000, then no jump is taken, and the Next input to the CS address MUX is used. The Next input to the CS address MUX is computed by the control store address incrementer (CSAI) shown in Figure 6-10, which increments the current output of the CS address MUX by 1. If the COND field is 001, 010, 011, 100, or 101, then a conditional jump is taken to the control store location in the JUMP ADDR field, according to the value of the `n`, `z`, `v`, or `c` flags, or bit 13 of `%ir`, respectively. The syntax "`IR[13]`" means "bit 13 of the instruction register `%ir`." If the COND field is 110, then an unconditional jump is taken.

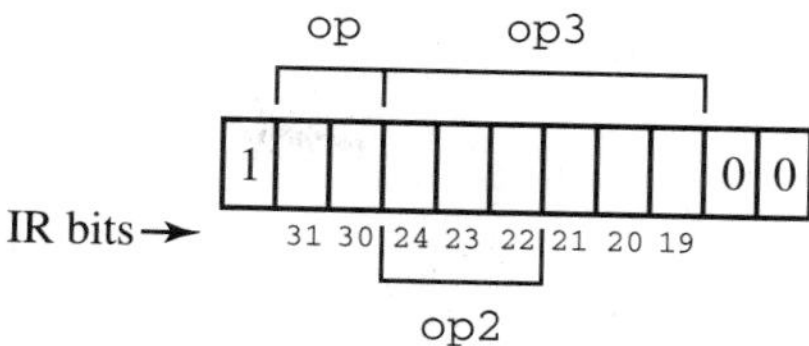

Figure 6-13 DECODE format for a microinstruction address.

The bit pattern 111 is used in the COND field when an instruction is being decoded. When the COND field is 111, then the next control store location that is copied into the MIR is taken from neither the Next input to the CS address MUX nor the Jump input, but is taken from a combination of 11 bits created by appending 1 to the left of bits 30 and 31 of `%ir` and appending 00 to the right of bits 19-24 of `%ir`. This DECODE address format is shown in Figure 6-13. The purpose of using this addressing scheme is to allow an instruction to be decoded in a single step, by branching to a different location according to the settings in the `op`, `op2`, and `op3` fields of an instruction.

Finally, the JUMP ADDR field appears in the rightmost 11 bits of the microword format. There are 2^{11} microwords in the control store, and so 11 bits are needed in the JUMP ADDR field in order to jump to any microstore location.

6.2.3 *TIMING*

The microarchitecture operates on a two-phase clock cycle, in which the master sections of all of the registers change on the rising edge of the clock and the slave sections change on the falling edge of the clock, as shown in Figure 6-14. All of

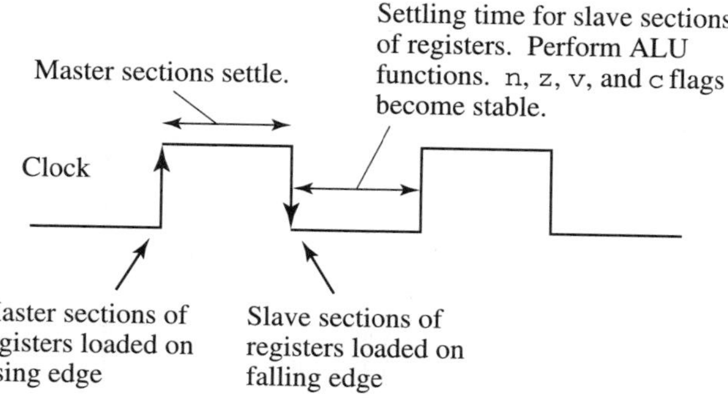

Figure 6-14 Timing relationships for the registers.

the registers use falling-edge-triggered master/slave D flip-flops except for `%r0`, which does not need flip-flops. On the falling edge of the clock, data stored in the master sections of the registers are clocked into the slave sections. This makes the data available for operations involving the ALU. While the clock is low, the ALU, CBL, and MUX functions are performed, which settle in time for the rising edge of the clock. On the rising edge of the clock, the new values of the registers are written into the master sections. The registers settle while the clock is high, and the process then repeats.

6.2.4 *DEVELOPING THE MICROPROGRAM*

In a microprogrammed architecture, instructions are interpreted by the microprogram in the control store. The microprogram is often referred to as **firmware** because it bridges the gap between the hardware and the software. The microarchitecture shown in Figure 6-10 needs firmware in order to execute ARC instructions, and one possible coding is described in this section.

A portion of a microprogram that implements the fetch-execute cycle for the ARC is shown in Figure 6-15. In the control store, each microstatement is stored in coded form (1's and 0's) in a single microword. For simplicity, the **microassembly language** shown in Figure 6-15 is loosely defined here, and we will leave out labels, pseudo-ops, etc., that we would normally associate with a full-featured assembly language. Translation to the 41-bit format used in the microstore is not difficult to perform by hand for a small microprogram and is frequently performed manually in practice (as we will do here) rather than creating a suite of software tools for such a small program.

Although our microassembly language is indeed an assembly language, it is not the same kind of assembly language as the ARC that we studied in Chapter 4. The ARC assembly language is visible to the user and is used for coding general-purpose programs. Our microassembly language is used for coding firmware and is not visible to the user. The sole purpose of the firmware is to interpret a user-visible instruction set. A change to the instruction set involves changes to the firmware, whereas a change in user-level software has no influence on the firmware.

Each statement in the microprogram shown in Figure 6-15 is preceded by a decimal number that indicates the address of the corresponding microword in the 2048-word control store. The address is followed by a colon. The operation statements follow the address and are terminated by semicolons. An optional comment follows the operation field and begins with a slash '`/`.' The comment terminates at

```
Address  Operation Statements                         Comment

   0: R[ir] ← AND(R[pc],R[pc]); READ;            / Read an ARC instruction from main memory
   1: DECODE;                                    / 256-way jump according to opcode
      / sethi
1152: R[rd] ← LSHIFT10(ir); GOTO 2047;           / Copy imm22 field to target register
      / call
1280: R[15] ← AND(R[pc],R[pc]);                  / Save %pc in %r15
1281: R[temp0] ← ADD(R[ir],R[ir]);               / Shift disp30 field left
1282: R[temp0] ← ADD(R[temp0],R[temp0]);         / Shift again
1283: R[pc] ← ADD(R[pc],R[temp0]);               / Jump to subroutine
      GOTO 0;
      / addcc
1600: IF R[IR[13]] THEN GOTO 1602;               / Is second source operand immediate?
1601: R[rd] ← ADDCC(R[rs1],R[rs2]);              / Perform ADDCC on register sources
      GOTO 2047;
1602: R[temp0] ← SEXT13(R[ir]);                  / Get sign extended simm13 field
1603: R[rd] ← ADDCC(R[rs1],R[temp0]);            / Perform ADDCC on register/simm13
      GOTO 2047;                                 / sources
      / andcc
1604: IF R[IR[13]] THEN GOTO 1606;               / Is second source operand immediate?
1605: R[rd] ← ANDCC(R[rs1],R[rs2]);              / Perform ANDCC on register sources
      GOTO 2047;
1606: R[temp0] ← SIMM13(R[ir]);                  / Get simm13 field
1607: R[rd] ← ANDCC(R[rs1],R[temp0]);            / Perform ANDCC on register/simm13
      GOTO 2047;                                 /   sources
      / orcc
1608: IF R[IR[13]] THEN GOTO 1610;               / Is second source operand immediate?
1609: R[rd] ← ORCC(R[rs1],R[rs2]);               / Perform ORCC on register sources
      GOTO 2047;
1610: R[temp0] ← SIMM13(R[ir]);                  / Get simm13 field
1611: R[rd] ← ORCC(R[rs1],R[temp0]);             / Perform ORCC on register/simm13 sources
      GOTO 2047;
      / orncc
1624: IF R[IR[13]] THEN GOTO 1626;               / Is second source operand immediate?
1625: R[rd] ← NORCC(R[rs1],R[rs2]);              / Perform ORNCC on register sources
      GOTO 2047;
1626: R[temp0] ← SIMM13(R[ir]);                  / Get simm13 field
1627: R[rd] ← NORCC(R[rs1],R[temp0]);            / Perform NORCC on register/simm13
      GOTO 2047;                                 /   sources
      / srl
1688: IF R[IR[13]] THEN GOTO 1690;               / Is second source operand immediate?
1689: R[rd] ← SRL(R[rs1],R[rs2]);                / Perform SRL on register sources
      GOTO 2047;
1690: R[temp0] ← SIMM13(R[ir]);                  / Get simm13 field
1691: R[rd] ← SRL(R[rs1],R[temp0]);              / Perform SRL on register/simm13 sources
      GOTO 2047;
      / jmpl
1760: IF R[IR[13]] THEN GOTO 1762;               / Is second source operand immediate?
1761: R[pc] ← ADD(R[rs1],R[rs2]);                / Perform ADD on register sources
      GOTO 0;
```

Figure 6-15 Partial microprogram for the ARC. Microwords are shown in logical sequence (not numerical sequence).

the end of the line. More than one operation is allowed per line, as long as all of the operations can be performed in a single instruction cycle. The ALU operations come from Figure 6-4, and there are a few others, as we will see. Note that the 65 statements are shown in logical sequence, rather than in numerical sequence.

Before the microprogram begins execution, the PC is set up with the starting address of a program that has been loaded into the main memory. This may hap-

```
1762: R[temp0] ← SEXT13(R[ir]);                 / Get sign extended simm13 field
1763: R[pc] ← ADD(R[rs1],R[temp0]);             / Perform ADD on register/simm13 sources
      GOTO 0;
      / ld
1792: R[temp0] ← ADD(R[rs1],R[rs2]);            / Compute source address
      IF R[IR[13]] THEN GOTO 1794;
1793: R[rd] ← AND(R[temp0],R[temp0]);           / Place source address on A bus
      READ; GOTO 2047;
1794: R[temp0] ← SEXT13(R[ir]);                 / Get simm13 field for source address
1795: R[temp0] ← ADD(R[rs1],R[temp0]);          / Compute source address
      GOTO 1793;
      / st
1808: R[temp0] ← ADD(R[rs1],R[rs2]);            / Compute destination address
      IF R[IR[13]] THEN GOTO 1810;
1809: R[ir] ← RSHIFT5(R[ir]); GOTO 40;          / Move rd field into position of rs2 field
  40: R[ir] ← RSHIFT5(R[ir]);                   / by shifting to the right by 25 bits.
  41: R[ir] ← RSHIFT5(R[ir]);
  42: R[ir] ← RSHIFT5(R[ir]);
  43: R[ir] ← RSHIFT5(R[ir]);
  44: R[0] ← AND(R[temp0], R[rs2]);             / Place destination address on A bus and
      WRITE; GOTO 2047;                         /   place operand on B bus
1810: R[temp0] ← SEXT13(R[ir]);                 / Get simm13 field for destination address
1811: R[temp0] ← ADD(R[rs1],R[temp0]);          / Compute destination address
      GOTO 1809;
      / Branch instructions: ba, be, bcs, bvs, bneg
1088: GOTO 2;                                   / Decoding tree for branches
   2: R[temp0] ← LSHIFT10(R[ir]);               / Sign extend the 22 LSB's of %temp0
   3: R[temp0] ← RSHIFT5(R[temp0]);             / by shifting left 10 bits, then right 10
   4: R[temp0] ← RSHIFT5(R[temp0]);             / bits. RSHIFT5 does sign extension.
   5: R[ir] ← RSHIFT5(R[ir]);                   / Move COND field to IR[13] by
   6: R[ir] ← RSHIFT5(R[ir]);                   / applying RSHIFT5 three times. (The
   7: R[ir] ← RSHIFT5(R[ir]);                   / sign extension is inconsequential.)
   8: IF R[IR[13]] THEN GOTO 12;                / Is it ba?
      R[ir] ← ADD(R[ir],R[ir]);
   9: IF R[IR[13]] THEN GOTO 13;                / Is it not be?
      R[ir] ← ADD(R[ir],R[ir]);
  10: IF Z THEN GOTO 12;                        / Execute be
      R[ir] ← ADD(R[ir],R[ir]);
  11: GOTO 2047;                                / Branch for be not taken
  12: R[pc] ← ADD(R[pc],R[temp0]);              / Branch is taken
      GOTO 0;
  13: IF R[IR[13]] THEN GOTO 16;                / Is it bcs?
      R[ir] ← ADD(R[ir],R[ir]);
  14: IF C THEN GOTO 12;                        / Execute bcs
  15: GOTO 2047;                                / Branch for bcs not taken
  16: IF R[IR[13]] THEN GOTO 19;                / Is it bvs?
  17: IF N THEN GOTO 12;                        / Execute bneg
  18: GOTO 2047;                                / Branch for bneg not taken
  19: IF V THEN GOTO 12;                        / Execute bvs
  20: GOTO 2047;                                / Branch for bvs not taken
2047: R[pc] ← INCPC(R[pc]); GOTO 0;             / Increment %pc and start over
```

Figure 6-15 (continued).

pen as the result of an initialization sequence when the computer is powered on or by the operating system during the normal course of operation.

The first task in the execution of a user-level program is to bring the instruction pointed to by the PC from the main memory into the IR. Recall from Figure 6-10 that the address lines to main memory are taken from the A bus. In line 0, the PC is loaded onto the A bus, and a Read operation is initiated to memory. The notation "`R[x]`" means "register `x`," in which `x` is replaced with one of the registers in the datapath, and so "`R[1]`" means "register `%r1`," "`R[ir]`" means "register `%ir`," and "`R[rs1]`" means the register that appears in the 5-bit `rs1` field of an instruction (refer to Figure 6-2).

The expression "`AND(R[pc],R[pc])`" simply performs a logical AND of `%pc` with itself in a literal interpretation. This operation is not very useful in a logical sense, but what we are interested in are the side effects. In order to place `%pc` onto the A bus, we have to choose an ALU operation that uses the A bus but does not affect the condition codes. There is a host of alternative choices that can be used, and the AND approach is arbitrarily chosen here. Note that the result of the AND operation is discarded because the C bus MUX in Figure 6-10 only allows the data output from main memory onto the C bus during a read operation.

A read operation normally takes more time to complete than the time required for one microinstruction to execute. The access time of main memory can vary depending on the memory organization, as we will see in Chapter 7. In order to account for variations in the access times of memory, the control store address incrementer (CSAI) does not increment the address until an acknowledge (ACK) signal is sent, which indicates that the memory has completed its operation.

Flow of control within the microprogram defaults to the next higher numbered statement unless a GOTO operation or a DECODE operation is encountered, and so microword 1 (line 1) is read into the MIR on the next cycle. Notice that some of the microcode statements in Figure 6-15 take up more than one line on the page, but are part of a single microinstruction. See, for example, lines 1283 and 1601.

Now that the instruction is in the IR as a result of the read operation in line 0, the next step is to decode the opcode fields. This is performed by taking a 256-way branch into the microcode, as indicated by the `DECODE` keyword in line 1 of the microprogram. The 11-bit pattern for the branch is constructed by appending a 1 to the left of bits 30 and 31 of the IR, followed by bits 19-24 of the IR, followed by the pattern 00. After the opcode fields are decoded, execution of the microcode continues according to which of the 15 ARC instructions is being interpreted.

As an example of how the decode operation works, consider the `addcc` instruction. According to the Arithmetic instruction format in Figure 6-2, the `op` field is 10 and the `op3` field is 010000. If we append a 1 to the left of the `op` bit pattern, followed by the `op3` bit pattern, followed by 00, the `DECODE` address is $11001000000 = (1600)_{10}$. This means that the microinstructions that interpret the `addcc` instruction begin at control store location 1600.

A number of DECODE addresses should never arise in practice. There is no Arithmetic instruction that corresponds to the invalid op3 field 111111, but if this situation does arise, possibly due to an errant program, then a microstore routine should be placed at the corresponding DECODE address 11011111100 = $(1788)_{10}$ in order to deal with the illegal instruction. These locations are left blank in the microprogram shown in Figure 6-15.

Instructions in the SETHI/Branch and Call formats do not have op3 fields. The SETHI/Branch formats have op and op2 fields, and the Call format has only the op field. In order to maintain a simple decoding mechanism, we can create duplicate entries in the control store. Consider the SETHI format. If we follow the rule for constructing the DECODE address, then the DECODE address will have a 1 in the leftmost position, followed by 00 for the op field, followed by 100, which identifies SETHI in bit positions 19–21, followed by the bits in positions 22–24 of the IR, followed by 00, resulting in the bit pattern 100100xxx00 where xxx can take on any value, depending on the imm22 field. There are eight possible bit patterns for the xxx bits, and so we need to have duplicate SETHI codes at locations 100100**000**00, 100100**001**00, 100100**010**00, 100100**011**00, 100100**100**00, 100100**101**00, 100100**110**00, and 100100**111**00. DECODE addresses for the Branch and CALL formats are constructed in duplicate locations in a similar manner. Only the lowest addressed version of each set of duplicate codes is shown in Figure 6-15.

Although this method of decoding is fast and simple, a large amount of control store memory is wasted. An alternative approach that wastes much less space is to modify the decoder for the control store so that all possible branch patterns for SETHI point to the same location, and the same for the Branch and Call format instructions. For our microarchitecture, we will stay with the simpler approach and pay the price of having a large control store.

Consider now how the ld instruction is interpreted. The microprogram begins at location 0 and at this point does not know that ld is the instruction that the PC points to in main memory. Line 0 of the microprogram begins the Read operation as indicated by the READ keyword, which brings an instruction into the IR from the main memory address pointed to by the PC. For this case, let us assume that the IR now contains the 32-bit pattern

11	00010	000000	00101	1	0000001010000
op	rd	op3	rs1	i	simm13

which is a translation of the ARC assembly code: `ld %r5 + 80, %r2`. Line 1 then performs a branch to control store address $(11100000000)_2 = (1792)_{10}$.

At line 1792, execution of the `ld` instruction begins. In line 1792, the immediate bit `i` is tested. For this example, `i = 1`, and so control is transferred to microword 1794. If instead we had `i = 0`, then control would pass to the next higher numbered microword, which is 1793 for this case. Line 1792 adds the registers in the `rs1` and `rs2` fields of the instruction, in anticipation of a nonimmediate form of `ld`, but this only makes sense if `i = 0`, which it is not for this example. The result that is stored in `%temp0` is thus discarded when control is transferred to microword 1794, but this introduces no time penalty and does not produce any unwanted side effects (ADD does not change the condition codes).

In microword 1794, the `simm13` field is extracted (using sign extension, as indicated by the SEXT13 operation), which is added with the register in the `rs1` field in microword 1795. Control is then passed to microword 1793, which is where the `READ` operation takes place. Control passes to line 2047, where the PC is incremented in anticipation of reading the next instruction from main memory. Since instructions are four bytes long and must be aligned on word boundaries in memory, the PC is incremented by four. Control then returns to line 0, where the process repeats. A total of seven microinstructions are thus executed in interpreting the `ld` instruction. These microinstructions are repeated as follows:

```
   0: R[ir] ← AND(R[pc],R[pc]); READ;        / Read an ARC instruction from main memory.
   1: DECODE;                                / 256-way jump according to opcode
1792: R[temp0] ← ADD(R[rs1],R[rs2]);         / Compute source address
      IF IR[13] THEN GOTO 1794;
1794: R[temp0] ← SEXT13(R[ir]);              / Get simm13 field for source address
1795: R[temp0] ← ADD(R[rs1],R[temp0]);        Compute source address
      GOTO 1793;
1793: R[rd] ← AND(R[temp0],R[temp0]);        / Place source address on A bus
      READ; GOTO 2047;
2047: R[pc] ← INCPC(R[pc]); GOTO 0;          / Increment %pc and start over
```

The remaining instructions, except for branches, are interpreted similar to the way `ld` is interpreted. Additional decoding is needed for the branch instructions because the type of branch is determined by the COND field of the branch format (bits 25–28), which is not used during a `DECODE` operation. The approach used here is to shift the COND bits into `IR[13]` one bit at a time, and then jump to different locations in the microcode depending on the COND bit pattern.

For branch instructions, the DECODE operation on line 1 of the microprogram transfers control to location 1088. We need more space for the branch instructions than the four-word per instruction allocation, so line 1088 transfers control to line 2 which is the starting address of a large section of available control store memory.

Lines 2–4 extract the 22-bit displacement for the branch by zeroing the high-order 10 bits and storing the result in %temp0. This is accomplished by shifting %ir to the left by 10 bits and storing it in %temp0, and then shifting the result back to the right by 10 bits. (Notice that sign extension is performed on the displacement, which may be negative. RSHIFT5 implements sign extension.) Lines 5–7 shift %ir to the right by 15 bits so that the most significant COND bit (IR[28]) lines up in position IR[13], which allows the Jump on IR[13]=1 operation to test each bit. Alternatively, we could shift the COND field to IR[31] one bit at a time and use the Jump on n condition to test each bit. (Note that there is a subtle error in how the PC is updated in line 12. See Problem 6.21 for an explanation.)

Line 8 starts the branch decoding process, which is summarized in Figure 6-16. If IR[28], which is now in IR[13], is set to 1, then the instruction is ba, which is executed in line 12. Notice that control returns to line 0, rather than to line 2047, so that the PC does not get changed twice for the same instruction.

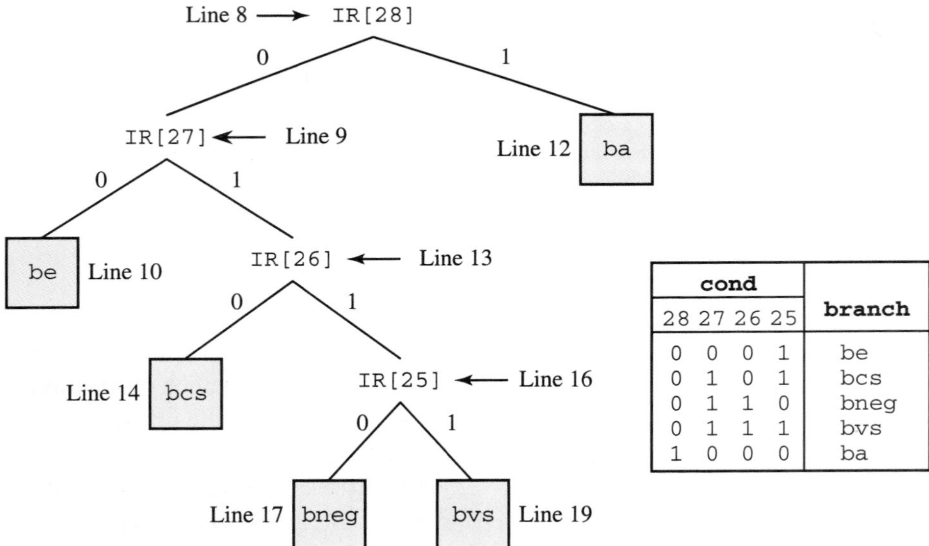

cond				branch
28	27	26	25	
0	0	0	1	be
0	1	0	1	bcs
0	1	1	0	bneg
0	1	1	1	bvs
1	0	0	0	ba

Figure 6-16 Decoding tree for branch instructions, showing corresponding microprogram lines.

If `IR[28]` is zero, then `%ir` is shifted to the left by one bit by adding it to itself, so that `IR[27]` lines up in position `IR[13]`. Bit `IR[27]` is tested in line 9. If `IR[27]` is zero, then the `be` instruction is executed in line 10; otherwise `%ir` is shifted to the left and `IR[26]` is then tested in line 13. The remaining branch instructions are interpreted in a similar manner.

Microassembly Language Translation

A microassembly language microprogram must be translated into binary object code before it is stored in the control store, just as an assembly language program must be translated into a binary object form before it is stored in main memory. Each line in the ARC microprogram corresponds to exactly one word in the control store, and there are no unnumbered forward references in the microprogram, so we can assemble the ARC microprogram one line at a time in a single pass. Consider assembling line 0 of the microprogram shown in Figure 6-15:

```
0: R[ir] ← AND(R[pc],R[pc]); READ;
```

We can fill in the fields of the 41-bit microword as follows:

A	AMUX	B	BMUX	C	CMUX	RD	WR	ALU	COND	JUMP ADDR
1 0 0 0 0 0	0	1 0 0 0 0 0	0	1 0 0 1 0 1	0	1	0	0 1 0 1	0 0 0	0 0 0 0 0 0 0 0 0 0 0

The PC is enabled onto both the A and B buses for the AND operation, which transfers a word through the ALU without changing it. The A and B fields have the bit pattern for the PC ($32_{10} = 100000_2$). The AMUX and BMUX fields both contain 0's, since the inputs to these MUXes are taken from the MIR. The target of the Read operation is the IR, which has a corresponding bit pattern of ($37_{10} = 100101_2$) for the C field. The CMUX field contains a 0 because the input to the CMUX is taken from the MIR. A read operation to memory takes place, and so the RD field contains a 1 and the WR field contains a 0. The ALU field contains 0101, which corresponds to the `AND` operation. Note that the condition codes are not affected, which would happen if `ANDCC` is used instead. The COND field contains 000 since control passes to the next microword, and so the bit pattern in the JUMP ADDR field does not matter. Zeros are arbitrarily placed in the JUMP ADDR field.

The second microword implements the 256-way branch. For this case, all that matters is that the bit pattern 111 appears in the COND field for the DECODE operation and that no registers, memory, or condition codes are disturbed. The corresponding bit pattern is then

A	AMUX	B	BMUX	C	CMUX	RD	WR	ALU	COND	JUMP ADDR
000000	0	000000	0	000000	0	0	0	0101	111	00000000000

A number of different bit patterns would also work for line 1. For example, any bit patterns can appear in the A, B, or JUMP ADDR fields when a `DECODE` operation takes place. The use of the zero bit patterns is an arbitrary choice. The ALU field is 0101, which is for `AND`, which does not affect the condition codes. Any other ALU operation that does not affect the condition codes can also be used.

The remainder of the microprogram is translated in a similar manner. The translated microprogram is shown in Figure 6-17, except for gaps where duplicate branch code would appear or where "illegal instruction" code would appear.

EXAMPLE

Consider adding an instruction called `subcc` to the microcoded implementation of the ARC instruction set, which subtracts its second source operand from the first, using two's complement arithmetic. The new instruction uses the Arithmetic format and an `op3` field of 001100.

We need to modify the microprogram to add this new instruction. We start by computing the starting location of `subcc` in the control store, by appending a '1' to the left of the `op` field, which is 10, followed by the `op3` field, which is 001100, followed by 00. This results in the bit pattern 11000110000, which corresponds to control store location $(1584)_{10}$. We can then create microassembly code that is similar to the `addcc` microassembly code at location 1600, except that the two's complement negative of the subtrahend (the second source operand) is formed before performing the addition. The subtrahend is complemented by making use of the `NOR` operation, and 1 is added to it by using the

Microstore Address	A	AMUX	B	BMUX	C	CMUX	RD	WR	ALU	COND	JUMP ADDR
0	100000	0	100000	0	100101	0	1	0	0101	000	00000000000
1	000000	0	000000	0	000000	0	0	0	0101	111	00000000000
1152	100101	0	000000	0	000000	1	0	0	1010	110	11111111111
1280	100000	0	100000	0	001111	0	0	0	0101	000	00000000000
1281	100101	0	100101	0	100001	0	0	0	1000	000	00000000000
1282	100001	0	100001	0	100001	0	0	0	1000	000	00000000000
1283	100000	0	100001	0	100000	0	0	0	1000	110	00000000000
1600	000000	0	000000	0	000000	0	0	0	0101	101	11001000010
1601	000000	1	000000	1	000000	1	0	0	0011	110	11111111111
1602	100101	0	000000	0	100001	0	0	0	1100	000	00000000000
1603	000000	1	100001	0	000000	1	0	0	0011	110	11111111111
1604	000000	0	000000	0	000000	0	0	0	0101	101	11001000110
1605	000000	1	000000	1	000000	1	0	0	0000	110	11111111111
1606	100101	0	000000	0	100001	0	0	0	1011	000	00000000000
1607	000000	1	100001	0	000000	1	0	0	0000	110	11111111111
1608	000000	0	000000	0	000000	0	0	0	0101	101	11001001010
1609	000000	1	000000	1	000000	1	0	0	0001	110	11111111111
1610	100101	0	000000	0	100001	0	0	0	1011	000	00000000000
1611	000000	1	100001	0	000000	1	0	0	0001	110	11111111111
1624	000000	0	000000	0	000000	0	0	0	0101	101	11001011010
1625	000000	1	000000	1	000000	1	0	0	0010	110	11111111111
1626	100101	0	000000	0	100001	0	0	0	1011	000	00000000000
1627	000000	1	100001	0	000000	1	0	0	0010	110	11111111111
1688	000000	0	000000	0	000000	0	0	0	0101	000	11010011010
1689	000000	1	000000	1	000000	1	0	0	0100	110	11111111111
1690	100101	0	000000	0	100001	0	0	0	1011	000	00000000000
1691	000000	1	100001	0	000000	1	0	0	0100	110	11111111111
1760	000000	0	000000	0	000000	0	0	0	0101	101	11011100010
1761	000000	1	000000	1	100000	0	0	0	1000	110	00000000000
1762	100101	0	000000	0	100001	0	0	0	1100	000	00000000000
1763	000000	1	100001	0	100000	0	0	0	1000	110	00000000000
1792	000000	1	000000	1	100001	0	0	0	1000	101	11100000010

Figure 6-17 Assembled microprogram for the ARC instruction subset.

`INC` operation. The subtraction is then completed by using the code for `addcc`. A microassembly coding for `subcc` is as follows:

```
1584: R[temp0] ← SEXT13(R[ir]);              / Extract rs2 operand
      IF IR[13] THEN GOTO 1586;              / Is second source immediate?
1585: R[temp0] ← R[rs2];                     / Extract sign extended immediate operand
1586: R[temp0] ← NOR(R[temp0], R[0]);        / Form one's complement of subtrahend
1587: R[temp0] ← INC(R[temp0]); GOTO 1603;   / Form two's complement of subtrahend
```

	A	AMUX	B	BMUX	C	CMUX	RD	WR	ALU	COND	JUMP ADDR
1793	100001	0	100001	0	000000	1	1	0	0101	110	11111111111
1794	100101	0	000000	0	100001	0	0	0	1100	000	00000000000
1795	000000	1	100001	0	100001	0	0	0	1000	110	11100000001
1808	000000	1	000000	1	100001	0	0	0	1000	101	11100010010
1809	100101	0	000000	0	100101	0	0	0	1111	110	00000101000
40	100101	0	000000	0	100101	0	0	0	1111	000	00000000000
41	100101	0	000000	0	100101	0	0	0	1111	000	00000000000
42	100101	0	000000	0	100101	0	0	0	1111	000	00000000000
43	100101	0	000000	0	100101	0	0	0	1111	000	00000000000
44	100001	0	000000	1	000000	0	0	1	0101	110	11111111111
1810	100101	0	000000	0	100001	0	0	0	1100	000	00000000000
1811	000000	1	100001	0	100001	0	0	0	1000	110	11100010001
1088	000000	0	000000	0	000000	0	0	0	0101	110	00000000010
2	100101	0	000000	0	100001	0	0	0	1010	000	00000000000
3	100001	0	000000	0	100001	0	0	0	1111	000	00000000000
4	100001	0	000000	0	100001	0	0	0	1111	000	00000000000
5	100101	0	000000	0	100101	0	0	0	1111	000	00000000000
6	100101	0	000000	0	100101	0	0	0	1111	000	00000000000
7	100101	0	000000	0	100101	0	0	0	1111	000	00000000000
8	100101	0	100100	0	100101	0	0	0	1000	101	00000001100
9	100101	0	100100	0	100101	0	0	0	1000	101	00000001101
10	100101	0	100100	0	100101	0	0	0	1000	010	00000001100
11	000000	0	000000	0	000000	0	0	0	0101	110	11111111111
12	100000	0	100001	0	100000	0	0	0	1000	110	00000000000
13	100101	0	100101	0	100101	0	0	0	1000	101	00000010000
14	000000	0	000000	0	000000	0	0	0	0101	100	00000001100
15	000000	0	000000	0	000000	0	0	0	0101	110	11111111111
16	000000	0	000000	0	000000	0	0	0	0101	101	00000010011
17	000000	0	000000	0	000000	0	0	0	0101	001	00000001100
18	000000	0	000000	0	000000	0	0	0	0101	110	11111111111
19	000000	0	000000	0	000000	0	0	0	0101	011	00000001100
20	000000	0	000000	0	000000	0	0	0	0101	110	11111111111
2047	100000	0	000000	0	100000	0	0	0	1110	110	00000000000

Figure 6-17 (continued).

The corresponding microcode for one possible translation is then

	A	AMUX	B	BMUX	C	CMUX	RD	WR	ALU	COND	JUMP ADDR
1584	100101	0	000000	0	100001	0	0	0	1100	101	11000110010
1585	000000	0	000000	1	100001	0	0	0	1000	000	00000000000
1586	100001	0	000000	0	100001	0	0	0	0111	000	00000000000
1587	100001	0	000000	0	100001	0	0	0	1101	110	11001000011

■

6.2.5 *TRAPS AND INTERRUPTS*

A **trap** is an automatic procedure call initiated by the hardware after an exceptional condition caused by an executing program, such as an illegal instruction, overflow, underflow, dividing by zero, etc. When a trap occurs, control is transferred to a "trap handler," which is a routine that is part of the operating system. The handler might do something like print a message and terminate the offending program.

One way to handle traps is to modify the microcode, possibly to check the status bits. For instance, we can check the v bit to see if an overflow has occurred. The microcode can then load an address into the PC (if a trap occurs) for the starting location of the trap handler.

Normally, there is a fixed section of memory for trap handler starting addresses where only a single word is allocated for each handler. This section of memory forms a **branch table** that transfers control to the handlers, as illustrated in Figure 6-18. The reason for using a branch table is that the absolute addresses for each type of trap can be embedded in the microcode this way, while the targets of the jumps can be changed at the user level to handle traps differently.

A historically common trap is for floating point instructions, which may be **emulated** by the operating system if they are not implemented directly in hardware. Floating point instructions have their own opcodes, but if they are not implemented by the hardware (that is, the microcode does not know about them) then they will generate an illegal instruction trap when an attempt is made to execute them. When an illegal instruction occurs, control is passed to the illegal instruction handler, which checks to see if the trap is caused by a floating point instruction and then passes control to a floating point emulation routine as

Address	Contents	Trap Handler
	⋮	
60	JUMP TO 2000	Illegal instruction
64	JUMP TO 3000	Overflow
68	JUMP TO 3600	Underflow
72	JUMP TO 5224	Zerodivide
76	JUMP TO 4180	Disk
80	JUMP TO 5364	Printer
84	JUMP TO 5908	TTY
88	JUMP TO 6048	Timer
	⋮	

Figure 6-18 A branch table for trap handlers and interrupt service routines.

appropriate for the cause of the trap. Although floating point units are normally integrated into CPU chips these days, this method is still used when extending the instruction set for other instructions, such as graphics extensions to the ISA.

Interrupts are similar to traps but are initiated after a hardware **exception** such as a user hitting a key on a keyboard, an incoming telephone call for a modem, a power fluctuation, an unsafe operating temperature, etc. Traps are *synchronous* with a running program, whereas interrupts are *asynchronous*. Thus, a trap will always happen at the same place in the same program running with the same data set, whereas the timing of interrupts is largely unpredictable.

When a key is pressed on an interrupt based keyboard, the keyboard circuitry asserts an interrupt line on the bus, and the CPU then asserts an acknowledge line as soon as it is ready (this is where **bus arbitration** comes in, which is covered in Chapter 8, if more than one device wants to interrupt at the same time). The keyboard circuitry then places an **interrupt vector** onto the data bus, thus identifying itself to the CPU as the keyboard interrupt. The CPU then pushes the program counter and processor status register (where the flags are stored) onto the stack. The interrupt vector is used to index into the branch table, which lists the starting addresses of the interrupt service routines.

When a trap handler or an interrupt service routine begins execution, it saves the registers that it plans to modify on the stack, performs its task, restores the registers, and then returns from the interrupt. The process of returning from a trap is different from returning from a subroutine, since the process of entering a trap is different from a subroutine call (because the `%psr` register is also saved and restored). For the ARC, the `rett` instruction (see Chapter 8) is used for returning from a trap or interrupt. Interrupts can interrupt other interrupts, and so the first thing that an interrupt service routine might do is to raise its priority (using a special **supervisor mode** instruction) so that no interrupts of lower priority are accepted.

6.2.6 *NANOPROGRAMMING*

If the microstore is wide and has lots of the same words, then we can save microstore memory by placing one copy of each unique microword in a **nanostore**, and then use the microstore to index into the nanostore. For instance, in the microprogram shown in Figure 6-15, lines 1281 and 1282 are the same. Lines 3, 4, and 40-44 are the same, and there are a number of other microinstructions that recur, especially for the duplicated branch microcode and the duplicated illegal instruction microcode.

Figure 6-19a illustrates the space requirement for the original microstore ROM. There are n=2048 words that are each 41 bits wide, giving an area complexity of

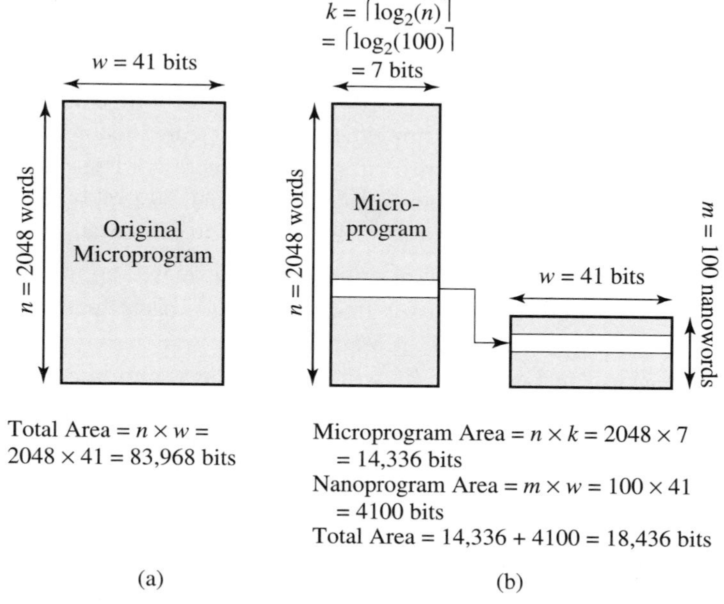

Figure 6-19 (a) Microprogramming versus (b) nanoprogramming.

$2048 \times 41 = 83{,}968$ bits. Suppose now that there are 100 unique microwords in the ROM (the microprogram in Figure 6-15 is only partially complete so we cannot measure the number of unique microwords directly). Figure 6-19b illustrates a configuration that uses a nanostore, in which an area savings can be realized if there are a number of bit patterns that recur in the original microcode sequence. The unique microwords (100 for this case) form a nanoprogram, which is stored in a ROM that is 100 words deep by 41 bits wide.

The microprogram now indexes into the nanostore. The microprogram has the same number of microwords regardless of whether or not a nanostore is used, but when a nanostore is used, *pointers* into the nanostore are stored in the microstore rather than the wider 41-bit words. For this case, the microstore is now 2048 words deep by $\lceil \log_2(100) \rceil = 7$ bits wide. The area complexity using a nanostore is then $100 \times 41 + 2048 \times 7 = 18{,}436$ bits, which is a considerable savings in area over the original microcoded approach.

For small m and large n, where m is the length of the nanoprogram, we can realize a large savings in memory. This frees up area that can be applied in some other way, possibly to improve performance. However, instead of accessing only the microstore, we must now access the microstore first, followed by an access to the nanostore. The machine will thus run more slowly but will fit into a smaller area.

6.3 Hardwired Control

An alternative approach to a microprogrammed control unit is to use a **hardwired** approach, in which a direct implementation is created using flip-flops and logic gates, instead of using a control store and a microword selection mechanism. States in a finite state machine replace steps in the microprogram.

In order to manage the complexity of design for a hardwired approach, a **hardware description language** (HDL) is frequently used to represent the control structure. One example of an HDL is **VHDL**, which is an acronym for **VHSIC Hardware Description Language** (in which VHSIC is yet another acronym for **Very High Speed Integrated Circuit**). VHDL is used for describing an architecture at a very high level and can be compiled into hardware designs through a process known as **silicon compilation**. For the hardwired control unit we will design here, a lower-level HDL that is sometimes referred to as a **register transfer language** (RTL) is more appropriate.

We will define a simple HDL/RTL in this section that loosely resembles Hill and Peterson's **A Hardware Programming Language** (AHPL) (Hill and Peterson,

```
           ┌ MODULE: MOD_4_COUNTER.
Preamble  <  INPUTS: x.
           │ OUTPUTS: Z[2].
           └ MEMORY:

           ┌ 0: Z ← 0,0;
           │    GOTO {0 CONDITIONED ON x,
           │          1 CONDITIONED ON x̄}.
           │ 1: Z ← 0,1;
           │    GOTO {0 CONDITIONED ON x,
Statements <          2 CONDITIONED ON x̄}.
           │ 2: Z ← 1,0;
           │    GOTO {0 CONDITIONED ON x,
           │          3 CONDITIONED ON x̄}.
           │ 3: Z ← 1,1;
           └    GOTO 0.

Epilogue   ┌ END SEQUENCE.
           └ END MOD_4_COUNTER.
```

Figure 6-20 HDL sequence for a resettable modulo 4 counter.

1987). The general idea is to express a control sequence as a series of numbered statements, which can then be directly translated into a hardware design. Each statement consists of a data portion and a transfer portion, as follows:

```
5: A ← ADD(B,C);                       ! Data portion
   GOTO {10 CONDITIONED ON IR[12]}.    ! Control portion
```

The statement is labeled "5," which means that it is preceded by statement 4 and is succeeded by statement 6, unless an out-of-sequence transfer of control takes place. The left arrow (←) indicates a data transfer, to register A for this case. The "`ADD(B,C)`" construct indicates that registers B and C are sent to a combinational logic unit (CLU) that performs the addition. Comments begin with an exclamation mark (`!`) and terminate at the end of the line. The `GOTO` construct indicates a transfer of control. For this case, control is transferred to statement 10 if bit 12 of register IR is true; otherwise control is transferred to the next higher numbered statement (6 for this case).

Figure 6-20 shows an HDL description of a modulo 4 counter. The counter produces the output sequence 00, 01, 10, 11 and then repeats as long as the input line x is 0. If the input line is set to 1, then the counter returns to state 0 at the end of the next clock cycle. The comma is the catenation operator, and so the statement "`Z ← 0,0;`" assigns the two-bit pattern `00` to the two-bit output `Z`.

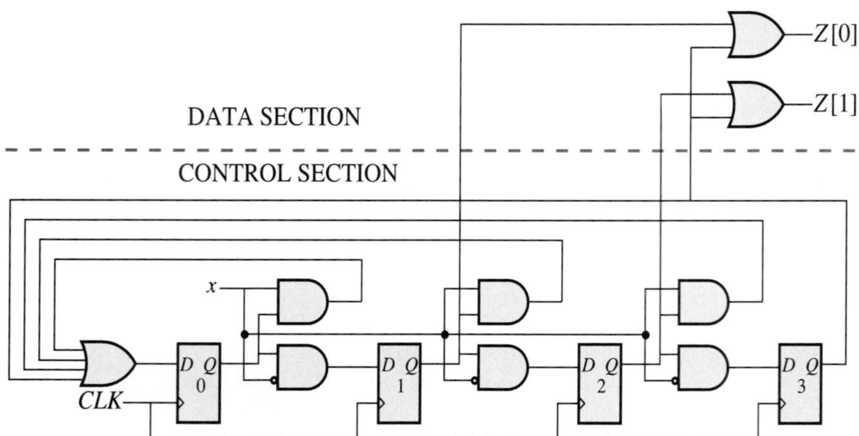

Figure 6-21 Logic design for a modulo 4 counter described in HDL.

The HDL sequence is composed of three sections: the *preamble*, the *numbered statements*, and the *epilogue*. The preamble names the module with the "`MODULE`" keyword and declares the inputs with the "`INPUTS`" keyword, the outputs with the "`OUTPUTS`" keyword, and the arity (number of signals) of both, as well as any additional storage with the "`MEMORY`" keyword (none for this example). The numbered statements follow the preamble. The epilogue closes the sequence with the key phrase "`END SEQUENCE`." The key phrase "`END MOD_4_COUNTER`" closes the description of the module. Anything that appears between "`END SEQUENCE`" and "`END MOD_4_COUNTER`" occurs *continuously*, independent of the statement number. There are no such statements for this case.

In translating an HDL description into a design, the process can be decomposed into separate parts for the control section and the data section. The control section deals with how transitions are made from one statement to another. The data section deals with producing outputs and changing the values of any memory elements.

We consider the control section first. There are four numbered statements, and so we will use four flip-flops, one for each statement, as illustrated in Figure 6-21. This is referred to as a **one-hot encoding** approach, because exactly one flip-flop holds a true value at any time. Although four states can be encoded using only two flip-flops, studies have shown that the one-hot encoding approach results in approximately the same circuit area when compared with a more densely encoded approach. More important, the transfers from one state to the next are generally simpler and can be implemented with shallow combinational logic circuits, which means that the clock rate can be faster for the one-hot encoding approach than for the densely encoded approach.

In designing the control section, we first draw the flip-flops, apply labels as appropriate, and connect the clock inputs. The next step is simply to scan the numbered statements in order and add logic as appropriate for the transitions. From statement 0, there are two possible transitions to statements 0 or 1, conditioned on x or its complement, respectively. The output of flip-flop 0 is thus connected to the inputs of flip-flops 0 and 1, through AND gates that take the value of the x input into account. Note that the AND gate into flip-flop 1 has a circle at one of its inputs, which is a simplified notation that means x is complemented by an inverter before entering the AND gate.

A similar arrangement of logic gates is applied for statements 1 and 2, and no logic is needed at the output of flip-flop 3 because statement 3 returns to statement 1 unconditionally. The control section is now complete and can execute correctly on its own. No outputs are produced, however, until the data section is implemented.

We now consider the design of the data section, which is trivial for this case. Both bits of the output Z change in every statement, and so there is no need to condition the generation of an output on the state. We only need to produce the correct output values for each of the statements. The least significant bit of Z is true in statements 1 and 3, and so the outputs of the corresponding control flip-flops are ORed to produce $Z[0]$. The most significant bit of Z is true in statements 2 and 3, and so the outputs of the corresponding control flip-flops are ORed to produce $Z[1]$. The entire circuit for the mod 4 counter is now complete, as shown in Figure 6-21.

We can now use our HDL in describing the control section of the ARC microarchitecture. There is no need to design the data section, since we have already defined its form in Figure 6-10. The data section is the same for both the microcoded and hardwired approaches. As for the microcoded approach, the operations that take place for a hardwired approach are as follows:

1. Fetch the next instruction to be executed from memory.

2. Decode the opcode.

3. Read operand(s) from main memory or registers, if any.

4. Execute the instruction and store results.

5. Go to Step 1.

The microcode of Figure 6-15 can serve as a guide for what needs to be done. The first step is to fetch the next user-level instruction from main memory. The following HDL line describes this operation:

```
0: ir ← AND(pc, pc); Read = 1
```

The structure of this statement is very similar to the first line of the microprogram, which may not be surprising since the same operations must be carried out on the same datapath.

Now that the instruction has been fetched, the next operation is to decode the opcode. This is where the power of a hardwired approach comes into play. Since every instruction has an `op` field, we can decode that field first, and then decode the `op2`, `op3`, and `cond` fields as appropriate for the instruction.

The next line of the control sequence decodes the `op` field:

1: GOTO {2 CONDITIONED ON $\overline{\texttt{IR[31]}}\times\overline{\texttt{IR[30]}}$, ! Branch/Sethi format: op=00
4 CONDITIONED ON $\overline{\texttt{IR[31]}}\times\texttt{IR[30]}$, ! Call format: op=01
8 CONDITIONED ON $\texttt{IR[31]}\times\overline{\texttt{IR[30]}}$, ! Arithmetic format: op=10
10 CONDITIONED ON $\texttt{IR[31]}\times\texttt{IR[30]}$}. ! Memory format: op=11

The product symbol "×" indicates a logical AND operation. Control is thus transferred to one of the four numbered statements 2, 4, 8, or 10 depending on the bit pattern in the `op` field.

Figure 6-22 shows a complete HDL description of the control section. We may have to do additional decoding depending on the value of the `op` field. At line 4, which is for the Call format, no additional decoding is necessary. The `call` instruction is then implemented in statements 4-7, which are similar to the microcoded version.

In statement 2, additional decoding is performed on the `op2` field, which is checked to determine if the instruction is `sethi` or a branch. Since there are

```
MODULE: ARC_CONTROL_UNIT.
INPUTS:
OUTPUTS: C, N, V, Z.  ! These are set by the ALU
MEMORY: R[16][32], pc[32], ir[32], temp0[32], temp1[32], temp2[32],
        temp3[32].

0: ir ← AND(pc, pc); Read ← 1;          ! Instruction fetch
    ! Decode op field
1: GOTO {2 CONDITIONED ON ir[31]×ir[30],   ! Branch/sethi format: op=00
         4 CONDITIONED ON ir[31]×ir[30],   ! Call format: op=01
         8 CONDITIONED ON ir[31]×ir[30],   ! Arithmetic format: op=10
        10 CONDITIONED ON ir[31]×ir[30]}.  ! Memory format: op=11
    ! Decode op2 field
2: GOTO 19 CONDITIONED ON ir[24].          ! Goto 19 if Branch format
3: R[rd] ← ir[imm22];                      ! sethi
   GOTO 20.
4: R[15] ← AND(pc, pc).                    ! call: save pc in register 15
5: temp0 ← ADD(ir, ir).                    ! Shift disp30 field left
6: temp0 ← ADD(ir, ir).                    ! Shift again
7: pc ← ADD(pc, temp0); GOTO 0.            ! Jump to subroutine
    ! Get second source operand into temp0 for Arithmetic format
8: temp0  ← { SEXT13(ir) CONDITIONED ON ir[13]×NOR(ir[19:22]),    ! addcc
  R[rs2] CONDITIONED ON ir[13]×NOR(ir[19:22]),                    ! addcc
  SIMM13(ir) CONDITIONED ON ir[13]×OR(ir[19:22]),   ! Remaining
  R[rs2] CONDITIONED ON ir[13]×OR(ir[19:22])}.  ! Arithmetic instructions
    ! Decode op3 field for Arithmetic format
9: R[rd] ← {
    ADDCC(R[rs1], temp0) CONDITIONED ON XNOR(IR[19:24], 010000),  ! addcc
    ANDCC(R[rs1], temp0) CONDITIONED ON XNOR(IR[19:24], 010001),  ! andcc
    ORCC(R[rs1], temp0) CONDITIONED ON XNOR(IR[19:24], 010010),   ! orcc
    NORCC(R[rs1], temp0) CONDITIONED ON XNOR(IR[19:24], 010110),  ! orncc
    SRL(R[rs1], temp0) CONDITIONED ON XNOR(IR[19:24], 100110),    ! srl
    ADD(R[rs1], temp0) CONDITIONED ON XNOR(IR[19:24], 111000)};   ! jmpl
    GOTO 20.
    ! Get second source operand into temp0 for Memory format
10: temp0  ← {SEXT13(ir) CONDITIONED ON ir[13],
              R[rs2] CONDITIONED ON ir[13]}.
11: temp0  ← ADD(R[rs1], temp0).
    ! Decode op3 field for Memory format
    GOTO {12 CONDITIONED ON ir[21],                                ! ld
          13 CONDITIONED ON ir[21]}.                               ! st
12: R[rd] ← AND(temp0, temp0); Read ← 1; GOTO 20.
13: ir  ← RSHIFT5(ir).
```

Figure 6-22 HDL description of the ARC control unit.

only two possibilities, only one bit of `op2` needs to be checked in line 2. Line 3 then implements `sethi` and line 19 implements the branch instructions.

Line 8 begins the Arithmetic format section of the code. Line 8 gets the second source operand, which can be either immediate or direct and can be sign extended to 32 bits (for `addcc`) or not sign extended. Line 9 implements the Arithmetic format instructions, conditioned on the `op3` field. The XNOR function returns true if its arguments are equal; otherwise it returns false, which is useful in making comparisons.

```
14: ir  ← RSHIFT5(ir).
15: ir  ← RSHIFT5(ir).
16: ir  ← RSHIFT5(ir).
17: ir  ← RSHIFT5(ir).
18: r0  ← AND(temp0, R[rs2]); Write  ← 1; GOTO 20.
19: pc  ← {  ! Branch instructions
    ADD(pc, temp0) CONDITIONED ON ir[28] + ir[28]×ir[27]×Z +
        ir[28]×ir[27]×ir[26]×C + ir[28]×ir[27]×ir[26]×ir[25]×N +
        ir[28]×ir[27]×ir[26]×ir[25]×V,
    INCPC(pc) CONDITIONED ON ir[28]×ir[27]×Z +
        ir[28]×ir[27]×ir[26]×C + ir[28]×ir[27]×ir[26]×ir[25]×N +
        ir[28]×ir[27]×ir[26]×ir[25]×V};
    GOTO 0.
20: pc ← INCPC(pc); GOTO 0.
END SEQUENCE.
END ARC_CONTROL_UNIT.
```

Figure 6-22 **(Continued).**

Line 10 begins the Memory format section of the code. Line 10 gets the second source operand, which can either be a register or an immediate operand. Line 11 decodes the `op3` field. Since the only Memory format instructions are `ld` and `st`, only a single bit (`IR[21]`) needs to be observed in the `op3` field. Line 12 then implements the `ld` instruction, and lines 13-18 implement the `st` instruction. Finally, line 20 increments the program counter and transfers control back to the first statement.

Now that the control sequence is defined, the next step is to design the logic for the control section. Since there are 21 statements, there are 21 flip-flops in the control section, as shown in Figure 6-23. A control signal (CS_i) is produced for each of the 21 states, which is used in the data section of the hardwired controller.

In Figure 6-24, the data section of the hardwired controller generates the signals that control the datapath. There are 27 OR gates that correspond to the 27 signals that control the datapath. (Refer to Figure 6-10. Count the 27 signals that originate in the control section that terminate in the datapath.) The AMUX signal is set to 1 only in lines 9 and 11, which correspond to operations that place `rs1` onto the A bus. Signals CS_9 and CS_{11} CS_{11} are thus logically OR'd to produce AMUX. Likewise, `rd` is placed on the C bus in lines 3, 9, and 12, and so CS_3, CS_9, and CS_{12} are logically OR'd to produce CMUX.

The BMUX signal is more complex. `rs2` is placed on the B bus in lines 8, 10, and 18, and so CS_8, CS_{10}, and CS_{18} are used to generate BMUX as shown. However, in line 8, BMUX is set (indicating `rs2` is placed on the B bus) only if `IR[13] = 0` and `IR[19:22]` are all 0 (for the rightmost 4 bits of the 6-bit `op3` pattern for `addcc`: 010000). The corresponding logic is shown for this case.

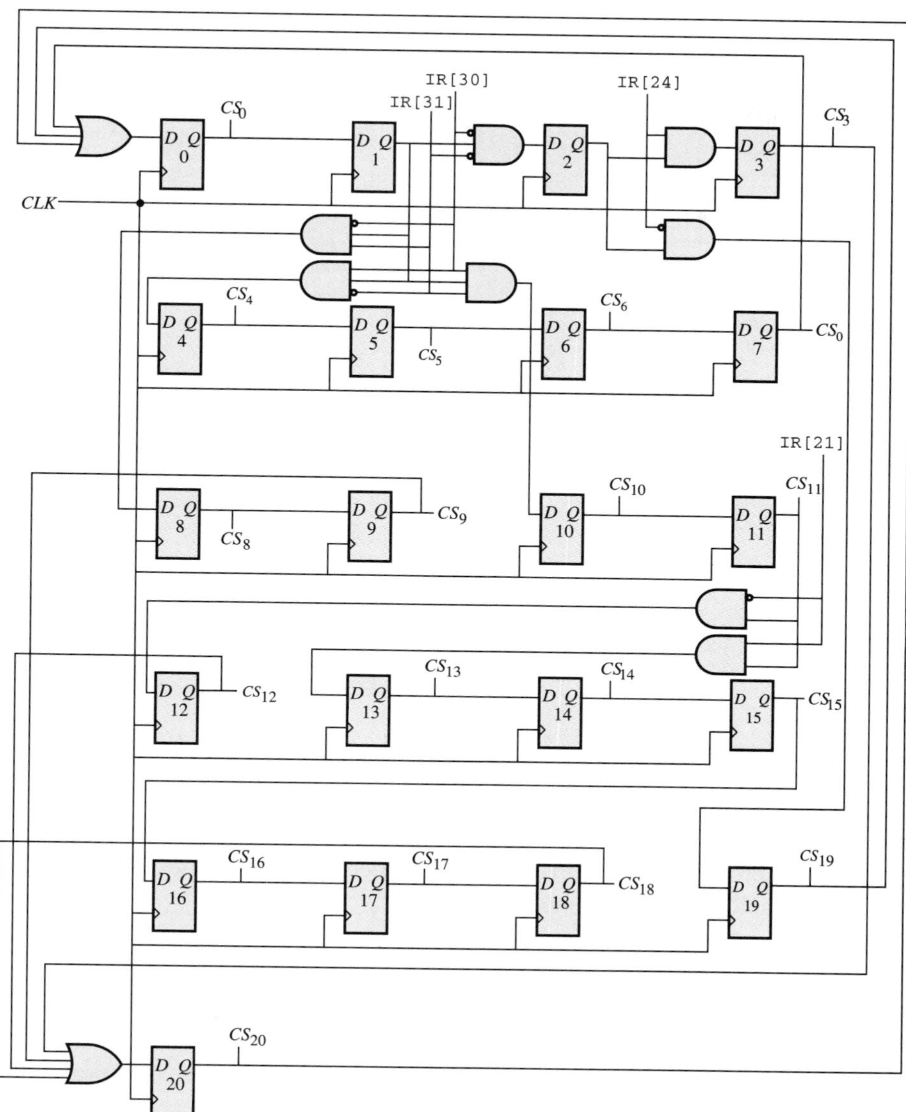

Figure 6-23 The hardwired control section of the ARC: generation of the control signals.

Likewise, in line 10, BMUX is set to 1 only when `IR[13] = 0`. Again, the corresponding logic is shown.

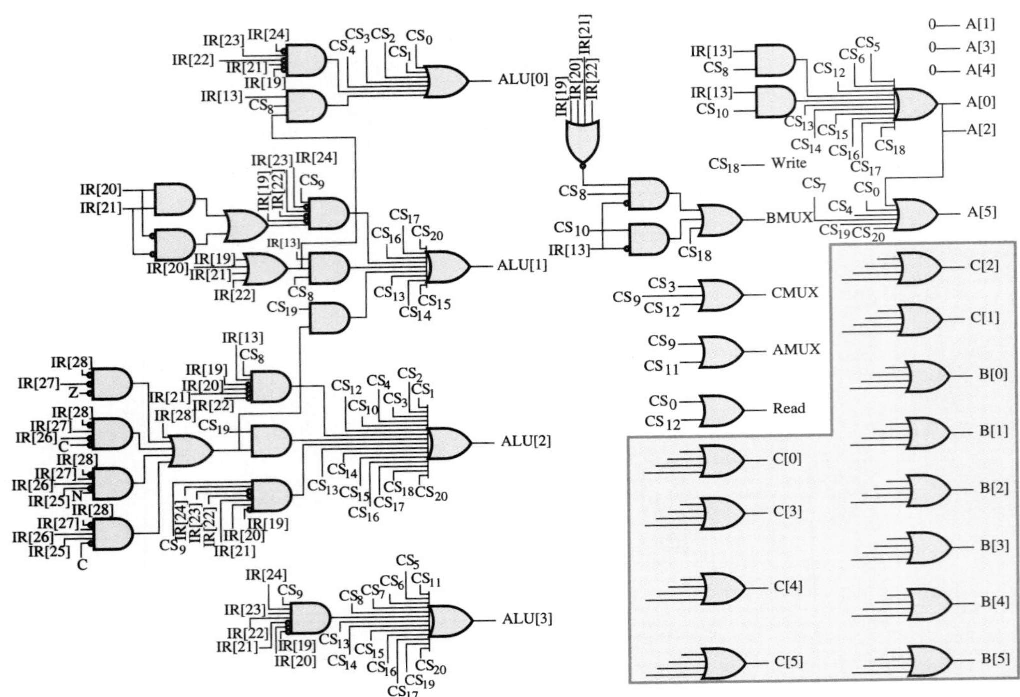

Figure 6-24 The hardwired control section of the ARC: signals from the data section of the control unit to the datapath. (Shaded areas are not detailed.)

The Read signal is set in lines 10 and 12, and so CS_0 and CS_{12} are logically OR'd to produce Read. The Write signal is generated only in line 18, and thus needs no logic other than the signal CS_{18}.

There are four signals that control the ALU: ALU[0], ALU[1], ALU[2], and ALU[3], which correspond to F_0, F_1, F_2, and F_3, respectively, in the ALU operation table shown in Figure 6-4. These four signals need values in each of the 20 HDL lines. In line 0, the ALU operation is AND, which corresponds to ALU[3:0] = 0101. Line 1 has no ALU operation specified, and so we can arbitrarily choose an ALU operation that has no side effects, like AND (0101). Continuing in this way, taking `CONDITIONED ON` statements into account, produces the logic for ALU[3:0] as shown in the figure.

The control signals are sent to the datapath, similar to the way that the MIR controls the datapath in the microprogrammed approach of Figure 6-10. The hardwired and microcontrolled approaches can thus be considered interchangeable, except with varying costs. There are only 21 flip-flops in the hardwired approach, but there are 2048 × 41 = 83,968 flip-flops in the microprogrammed approach (although in actuality, a ROM would be used, which consumes less space because smaller storage elements than flip/flops can be used). The amount of additional combinational logic is comparable. The hardwired approach is faster in executing ARC instructions, especially in decoding the Branch format instructions, but is more difficult to change once it is committed to fabrication.

EXAMPLE

Consider adding the same `subcc` instruction from the previous EXAMPLE to the hardwired implementation of the ARC instruction set. As before, the `subcc` instruction uses the Arithmetic format and an `op3` field of 001100.

Only line 9 of the HDL code needs to be changed, by inserting the expression

```
ADDCC (R[rs1], INC_1(temp0)) CONDITIONED ON XNOR(IR[19:24], 001100), ! subcc
```

before the line for `addcc`.

The corresponding signals that need to be modified are `ALU[3:0]`. The `INC_1` construct in the preceding line indicates that an adder CLU, which would be defined in another HDL module, should be created (in a hardwired control unit, there is a lot of flexibility in what can be done). ■

6.4 Case Study: The VHDL Hardware Description Language

In this section we present a brief overview of VHDL (VHSIC Hardware Description Language, in which VHSIC is yet another acronym for Very High Speed Integrated Circuit). Hardware description languages (HDLs), like VHDL and AHPL, are languages used for describing computer hardware, focusing primarily on logic devices and IC design. In the case of VHDL, however, designs can be specified at many different levels. For example, the control unit implemented in this chapter could be specified in VHDL.

We first cover the background that led to the development of VHDL and then describe some of its properties. We then take a look at a VHDL specification of the majority function.

6.4.1 *BACKGROUND*

VHDL was the result of a collaboration between the Department of Defense (DOD) and many U.S. industries. DOD, primarily through its Defense Advanced Research Products Agency (DARPA), realized in the late 1970s that IC design and fabrication was becoming so complex that a set of integrated design tools was needed for both design and simulation. It was felt that the tools should allow the user to specify a circuit or system from the highest, or behavioral level down to the lowest levels of actual IC layout and design, and furthermore, all of these specifications should be verifiable by simulators and other rule checkers.

The first preliminary requirements definition for the language was issued by DOD in 1981, as a recognition of the need for a more consistent approach to computer hardware design. The contract for the first version of the language was won by a consortium of IBM, Texas Instruments, and Intermetrics, a software engineering firm specializing in programming language design and implementation.

The consortium released a preliminary version for testing and comment in 1985. An updated version was submitted to the IEEE for standardization in 1986, the result being named IEEE 1076-1987. In 1993, a newer version, IEEE 1076-1993, was approved that addressed a number of minor problems and added several new features.

By almost any measure VHDL is a success, with many users both inside and outside the defense contractor community. DOD now requires that all application-specific integrated circuits (ASICs) be accompanied by their VHDL model for checking and simulation. Almost all CAD vendors now support VHDL in their toolsets.

6.4.2 *WHAT IS VHDL?*

In its most basic terms VHDL is a hardware description language that can be used to describe and model digital systems. VHDL has an inherent sense of time and can manage the progression of events through time. Unlike most procedural languages that are in common use, VHDL supports **concurrent execution** and is **event driven**.

Concurrent Execution

Concurrent execution means that unless special efforts are taken to specify sequential execution, all of the statements in a VHDL specification are executed in parallel. This is the way it should be, since when power is applied to a digital system the system runs "in parallel." That is, current flows through circuits according to the rules of physics and logic, without any inherent sense of "which came first."

Event-Driven Systems

VHDL deals with signals propagating through digital systems, and therefore logically and naturally supports the concept of changes in state as a function of time. Having a sense of time, it supports concepts such as "after," "until," and "wait." As an event-driven system, it begins execution by executing any initialization code and then records all changes in signal values, from 0→1 and 1→0, occurring at the inputs and outputs of components. It records these changes, or events, in a time-ordered queue, known as the event queue. It examines these events, and if an event has an effect upon some component, that effect is evaluated. If the effect causes further events to take place, the simulator likewise places these new events in the event queue, and the process continues until and unless there are no further events to process.

Levels of Abstraction and Hierarchical Decomposition

As mentioned previously, VHDL specifications can be written at almost any level of abstraction from the purely algorithmic level, where behavior is specified by formal algorithms, to the logic level, where behavior is specified by Boolean expressions.

Furthermore, a VHDL specification may be composed of a hierarchy of components—that is, components may contain components, which may themselves contain components. This models the physical world, where, for example, a motherboard may contain IC chips, which are composed of modules, which are in turn composed of submodules, all the way down to individual logic gates, and finally transistors.

6.4.3 *A VHDL SPECIFICATION OF THE MAJORITY FUNCTION*

Let us explore how VHDL can be used to implement a small digital component by examining several implementations of the **majority function**, which produces a 1 at its output when more than half of its inputs are 1, otherwise it produces a 0 at its output. This is a useful function for fault tolerance, in which multiple systems that perform the same operations on the same data set "vote," and if one of the systems deviates from the others, its output is effectively

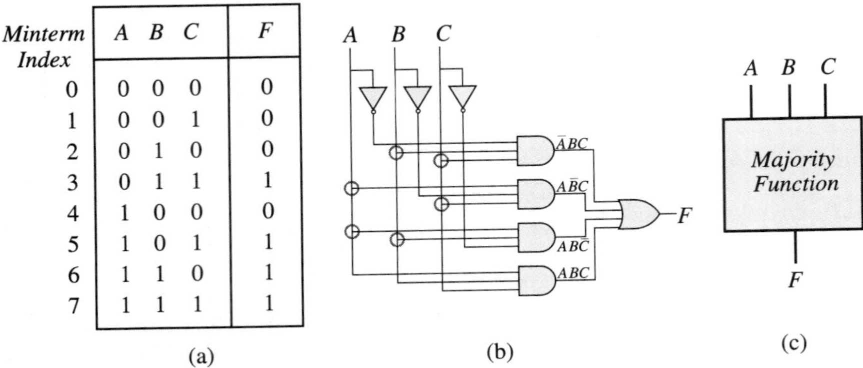

Minterm Index	A	B	C	F
0	0	0	0	0
1	0	0	1	0
2	0	1	0	0
3	0	1	1	1
4	1	0	0	0
5	1	0	1	1
6	1	1	0	1
7	1	1	1	1

Figure 6-25 The majority function: (a) truth table, (b) AND-OR implementation, (c) black box representation.

ignored. The majority function is discussed in detail in Appendix A. Its truth table is shown in Figures A-15 and A-16, reproduced here as Figure 6-25.

In VHDL the specification of any component such as the majority function is split into two parts, an **entity** part and an **architecture** part. These correspond roughly to the syntactic and semantic parts of a language specification: The entity part describes the interface of the component without saying anything about its internal structure. The architecture part describes the internal behavior of the component. Here is an entity specification for the three-input majority function:

```
-- Interface
entity MAJORITY is
   port
      (A_IN, B_IN, C_IN : in BIT
       F_OUT            : out BIT);
end MAJORITY;
```

Keywords are shown in bold, and comments begin with "`--`" and end at the end of the line. Statements are separated by semicolons, "`;`".

The **`entity`** specification describes just the "black box" input and output signals in Figure 6-25c. The **`port`** declaration describes the kind of signals going into and out of the entity. Port modes include **`in`** for signals that flow into the entity, **`out`** for signals that flow out of the entity, and **`inout`** for bidirectional signals. There are also several other special-purpose port modes.

With the interface to the majority component specified we can now model the internal functioning of the component, using the **architecture** specification:

Behavioral Model for the Majority Component

```
-- Body
architecture LOGIC_SPEC of MAJORITY is
begin
-- compute the output using a Boolean expression
F_OUT     <= (not A_IN and B_IN and C_IN) or
             (A_IN and not B_IN and C_IN) or
             (A_IN and B_IN and not C_IN) or
             (A_IN and B_IN and C_IN) after 4 ns;
end LOGIC_SPEC;
```

This model describes the relationship between the entity declaration of MAJORITY and the architecture of MAJORITY. The names A_IN, B_IN, C_IN, and F_OUT in the architecture model must match the names used in the entity declaration.

This kind of architectural specification is referred to as a behavioral one, since it defines the input/output function by specifying an explicit transfer function. That function is a Boolean expression that implements the Boolean function shown in Figures 6-25a and b. Notice, however, that even at this level of specification we can include a time delay between inputs and outputs, using the **after** keyword. In this case, the event computing the value of F_OUT will be triggered 4 ns after a change in any of the input values.

It is also possible to specify the architecture at a level closer to the hardware by specifying logic gates instead of logic equations. This is referred to as a structural model. The following is an example of such a specification.

Structural Model for the Majority Component

In generating a structural model for the MAJORITY entity we will follow the gate design given in Figure 6-25b. We begin the model by describing a collection of logic operators, in a special construct of VHDL known as a **package**. The package is assumed to be stored in a working library called WORK. Following the package specification we repeat the **entity** declaration and then, using the package and entity declarations, we specify the internal workings of the majority component by specifying the architecture at a structural level:

```
-- Package declaration, in library WORK
package LOGIC_GATES is
component AND3
   port (A, B, C : in BIT; X : out BIT);
end component;
component OR4
   port (A, B, C, D : in BIT; X : out BIT);
end component;
component NOT1
   port (A : in BIT; X : out BIT);
end component;

-- Interface
entity MAJORITY is
   port
      (A_IN, B_IN, C_IN     : in BIT
       F_OUT                : out BIT);
end MAJORITY;

-- Body
-- Uses components declared in package LOGIC_GATES
-- in the WORK library
-- import all the components in WORK.LOGIC_GATES
use WORK.LOGIC_GATES.all
architecture LOGIC_SPEC of MAJORITY is
-- declare signals used internally in MAJORITY
signal A_BAR, B_BAR, C_BAR, I1, I2, I3, I4: BIT;
begin
-- connect the logic gates
NOT_1 : NOT1 port map (A_IN, A_BAR);
NOT_2 : NOT1 port map (B_IN, B_BAR);
NOT_3 : NOT1 port map (C_IN, C_BAR);
AND_1 : AND3 port map (A_BAR, B_IN, C_IN, I1);
AND_2 : AND3 port map (A_IN, B_BAR, C_IN, I2);
AND_3 : AND3 port map (A_IN, B_IN, C_BAR, I3);
AND_4 : AND3 port map (A_IN, B_IN, C_IN, I4);
OR_1 : OR3 port map (I1, I2, I3, I4, F_OUT);
end LOGIC_SPEC;
```

The **package** declaration supplies three gates: a three-input AND gate, AND3; a four-input OR gate, OR4; and a NOT gate, NOT1. The architectures of these gates are assumed to be declared elsewhere in the package. The **entity** declaration is unchanged, as we would expect, since it specifies MAJORITY as a "black box."

The body specification begins with a **use** clause, which imports **all** of the declarations in the LOGIC_GATES package within the WORK library. The **signal** declaration declares seven BIT signals that will be used internally. These signals are used to interconnect the components within the architecture.

The instantiations of the three NOT gates follow, NOT_1, NOT_2, and NOT_3, all of which are NOT1 gates, and the mapping of their input and output signals is specified, following the **port map** keywords. Signals at the inputs and outputs of the logic gates are mapped according to the order in which they were declared within the package.

The rest of the body specification connects the NOT gates, the AND gates, and the OR gate, as shown in Figure 6-25b.

Notice that this form of architecture specification separates the design and implementation of the logic gates from the design of the MAJORITY entity. It would be possible to have several different implementations of the logic gates in different packages and to use any one of them by merely changing the **uses** clause.

6.4.4 *NINE-VALUE LOGIC SYSTEM*

This brief treatment of VHDL only gives a small taste of the scope and power of the language. The full language contains capabilities to specify clock signals and various timing mechanisms, sequential processes, and several different kinds of signals. There is an IEEE standard nine-value logic system, known as STD_ULOGIC, IEEE 1164-1993. It has the following logic values:

```
type STD_ULOGIC is (
    'U',      -- Uninitialized
    'X',      -- Forcing unknown
    '0',      -- Forcing 0
    '1',      -- Forcing 1
    'Z',      -- High impedance
    'W',      -- Weak unknown
    'L',      -- Weak 0
    'H',      -- Weak 1
    '-',      -- Don't care
    );
```

Without getting into too much detail, these values allow the user to detect logic flaws within a design and to follow the propagation of uninitialized or weak signals through the design.

■ SUMMARY

A microarchitecture consists of a datapath and a control section. The datapath contains data registers, an ALU, and the connections among them. The control section contains registers for microinstructions (for a microprogramming approach) and for condition codes, and a controller. The controller can be microprogrammed or hardwired. A microprogrammed controller interprets microinstructions by executing a microprogram that is stored in a control store. A hardwired controller is organized as a collection of flip-flops, which maintain state information, and combinational logic, which implements transitions among the states.

The hardwired approach is fast and consumes a small amount of hardware in comparison with the microprogrammed approach. The microprogrammed approach is flexible and simplifies the process of modifying the instruction set. The control store consumes a significant amount of hardware, which can be reduced to a degree through the use of nanoprogramming. Nanoprogramming adds delay to the microinstruction execution time. The choice of microprogrammed or hardwired control thus involves trade-offs: The microprogrammed approach is large and slow but is flexible and lends itself to simple implementations, whereas the hardwired approach is small and fast but is difficult to modify and typically results in more complicated implementations.

■ FURTHER READING

(Wilkes et al., 1958) is a classic reference on microprogramming. (Mudge, 1978) covers microprogramming on the DEC PDP 11/60. (Tanenbaum, 1990) and (Mano, 1991) provide instructional examples of microprogrammed architectures. (Hill and Peterson, 1987) gives a tutorial treatment of the AHPL hardware description language and hardwired control in general. (Lipsett et al., 1989) and (Navabi, 1993) describe the commercial VHDL hardware description language and provide examples of its use. (Gajski, 1988) covers various aspects of silicon compilation.

Gajski, D., *Silicon Compilation*, Addison Wesley (1988).

Hill, F. J. and G. R. Peterson, *Digital Systems: Hardware Organization and Design*, 3/e, John Wiley & Sons (1987).

Lipsett, R., C. Schaefer, and C. Ussery, *VHDL: Hardware Description and Design*, Kluwer Academic Publishers (1989).

Mano, M., *Digital Design*, 2/e, Prentice Hall (1991).

Mudge, J. Craig, *Design Decisions for the PDP11/60 Mid-Range Minicomputer*, in *Computer Engineering, A DEC View of Hardware Systems Design*, Digital Press (1978).

Navabi, Z., *VHDL: Analysis and Modeling of Digital Systems*, McGraw-Hill (1993).

Tanenbaum, A., *Structured Computer Organization*, 3/e, Prentice Hall (1990).

Wilkes, M. V., W. Redwick, and D. Wheeler, "The Design of a Control Unit of an Electronic Digital Computer," *Proc. IRE*, **105**, p. 21 (1958).

PROBLEMS

6.1 Design a 1-bit arithmetic logic unit (ALU) using the circuit shown in Figure 6-26 that performs bitwise addition, AND, OR, and NOT on the 1-bit inputs A and B. A 1-bit output Z is produced for each operation, and a carry is also produced for the case of addition. The carry is zero for AND, OR, and NOT. Design the 1-bit ALU using the components shown in the diagram. Just draw the connections among the components. Do not add any logic gates, MUXes, or anything else. *Note*: The full adder takes two one-bit inputs (X and Y) and a carry in, and produces a sum and a carry out.

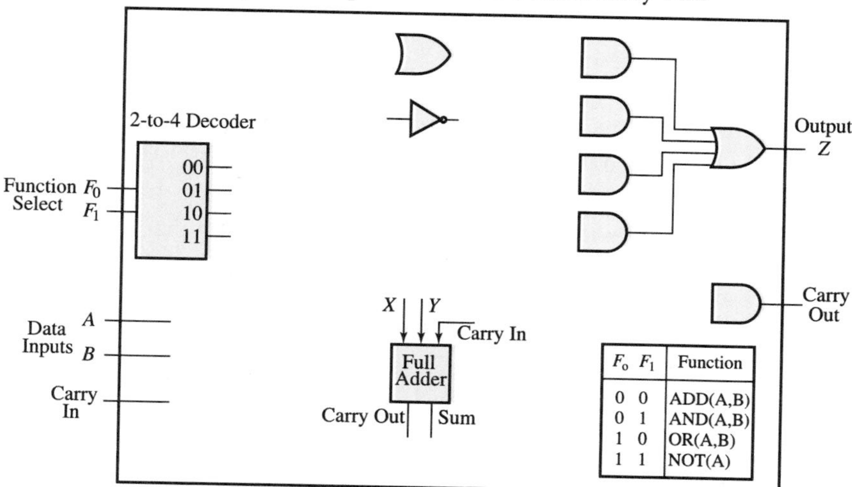

F_0 F_1	Function
0 0	ADD(A,B)
0 1	AND(A,B)
1 0	OR(A,B)
1 1	NOT(A)

Figure 6-26 **A one-bit ALU.**

6.2 Design an ALU that takes two 8-bit operands X and Y and produces an 8-bit output Z. There is also a 2-bit control input C in which 00 selects logical AND, 01 selects OR, 10 selects NOR, and 11 selects XOR. In designing your ALU, follow this procedure: (1) draw a block diagram of eight 1-bit ALUs that each accept a single bit from X and Y and both control bits and produce the corresponding single-bit output for Z; (2) create a truth table that describes a 1-bit ALU; (3) design one of the 1-bit ALUs using an 8-to-1 MUX.

6.3 Design a control unit for a simple hand-held video game in which a character on the display catches objects. Treat this as an FSM problem, in which you only show the state transition diagram. Do not show a circuit. The input to the control unit is a two-bit vector in which 00 means "Move Left," 01 means "Move Right," 10 means "Do Not Move," and 11 means "Halt." The output Z is 11 if the machine is halted, and is 00, 01, or 10 otherwise, corresponding to the input patterns. Once the machine is halted, it must remain in the halted state indefinitely.

6.4 In Figure 6-3, there is no line from the output of the C decoder to `%r0`. Why is this the case?

6.5 Refer to Figure 6-27. Registers 0, 1, and 2 are general-purpose registers. Register 3 is initialized to the value +1, which can be changed by the microcode, but you must make certain that it does not get changed.

(a) Write a control sequence that forms the two's complement difference of the contents of registers 0 and 1, leaving the result in register 0. Symbolically, this might be written as r0 ← r0–r1. Do not change any registers except r0 and r1 (if needed). Fill in the following table with 0's or 1's (use 0's when the choice of 0 or 1 does not matter) as appropriate. Assume that when no registers are selected for the A bus or the B bus, the bus takes on a value of 0.

Write Enables				A-bus enables				B-bus enables						
0	1	2	3	0	1	2	3	0	1	2	3	F_0	F_1	Time
														0
														1
														2

(b) Write a control sequence that forms the exclusive-OR of the contents of

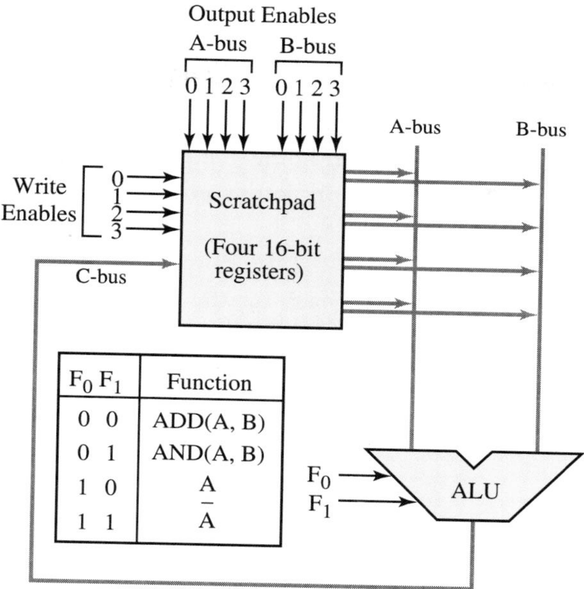

Figure 6-27 A small microarchitecture.

registers 0 and 1, leaving the result in register 0. Symbolically, this might be written as: r0 ← XOR(r0, r1). Use the same style of solution as for part (a).

6.6 Write the binary form for the microinstructions shown. Use the style shown in Figure 6-17. Use the value 0 for any fields that are not needed.

```
60: R[temp0] ← NOR(R[0],R[temp0]); IF Z THEN GOTO 64;
61: R[rd] ← INC(R[rs1]);
```

6.7 Three binary words are shown below, each of which can be interpreted as a microinstruction. Write the mnemonic version of the binary words using the microassembly language introduced in this chapter.

A	AMUX	B	BMUX	C	CMUX	RD	WR	ALU	COND	JUMP ADDR
1 0 0 1 0 1	0	0 0 0 0 0 0	0	1 0 0 0 0 1	0	0	0	1 1 0 0	0 0 0	0 0 0 0 0 0 0 0 0 0 0
0 0 0 0 0 0	1	1 0 0 0 0 1	0	1 0 0 0 0 1	0	0	0	1 0 0 0	1 1 0	1 1 1 0 0 0 0 0 0 0 1
0 0 0 0 0 0	1	0 0 0 0 0 0	1	1 0 0 0 0 1	0	0	0	1 0 0 0	1 0 1	1 1 1 0 0 0 1 0 0 1 0

6.8 Rewrite the microcode for the `call` instruction starting at line 1280 so that only three lines of microcode are used instead of four. Use the LSHIFT2 operation once instead of using ADD twice.

6.9 (a) How many microinstructions are executed in interpreting the `subcc` instruction that was introduced in the first Example in this chapter? Write the numbers of the microinstructions in the order they are executed, starting with microinstruction 0.

(b) Using the hardwired approach for the ARC microcontroller, how many states are visited in interpreting the `addcc` instruction? Write the states in the order they are executed, starting with state 0.

6.10 (a) List the microinstructions that are executed in interpreting the `ba` instruction.

(b) List the states (Figure 6-22) that are visited in interpreting the `ba` instruction.

6.11 Register `%r0` can be designed using only tri-state buffers. Show this design.

6.12 What bit pattern should be placed in the C field of a microword if none of the registers are to be changed?

6.13 A control unit for a machine tool is shown in Figure 6-28. You are to create the microcode for this machine. The behavior of the machine is as follows: If the Halt input *A* is ever set to 1, then the output of the machine stays halted forever and outputs a perpetual 1 on the *X* line, and 0 on the *V* and *W* lines. A waiting light (output *V*) is enabled (set to 1) when no inputs are enabled. That is, *V* is lit when the *A*, *B*, and *C* inputs are 0, and the machine is not halted. A bell is sounded (*W* = 1) on every input event (*B* = 1 and/or C = 1) except when the machine is halted. Input *D* and output *S* can be used for state information for your microcode. Use 0's for any fields that do not matter. *Hint*: Fill in the lower half of the table first.

6.14 For this problem, you are to extend the ARC instruction set to include a new instruction by modifying the microprogram. The new ARC instruction to be microcoded is

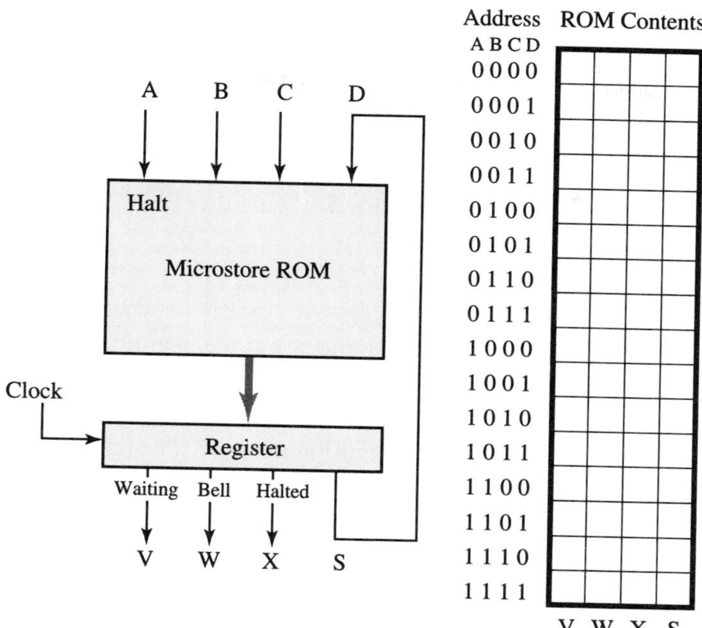

Figure 6-28 Control unit for a machine tool.

`xorcc`—Perform an exclusive OR on the operands, and set the condition codes accordingly. This is an Arithmetic format instruction. The `op3` field is 010011.

Show the new microinstructions that will be added for `xorcc`.

6.15 Show a design for a four-word register stack, using 32-bit registers of the following form:

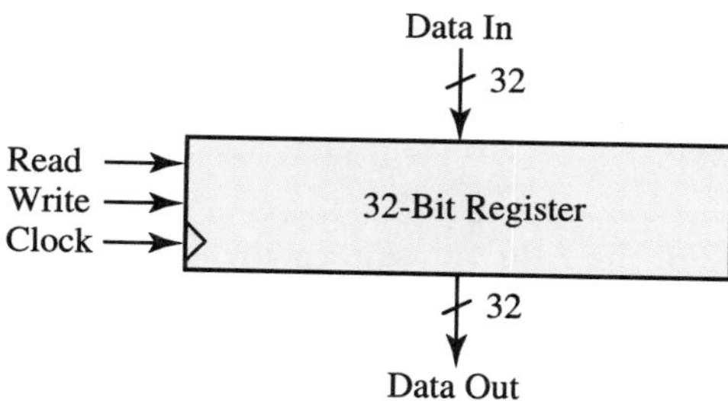

Four registers are stacked so that the output of the top register is the input to the second register, which outputs to the input of the third, which outputs to the input of the fourth. The input to the stack goes into the top register, and the output of the stack is taken from the output of the top register (*not* the bottom register). There are two additional control lines, `push` and `pop`, which cause data to be pushed onto the stack or popped off the stack, respectively, when the corresponding line is 1. If neither line is 1, or if both lines are 1, then the stack is unchanged.

6.16 In line 1792 of the ARC microprogram, the conditional `GOTO` appears at the end of the line, but in line 8 it appears at the beginning. Does the position of the `GOTO` within a microassembly line matter?

6.17 A microarchitecture is shown in Figure 6-29. The datapath has four registers and an ALU. The control section is a finite state machine, in which there is a RAM and a register. For this microarchitecture, a compiler translates a high-level program directly into microcode; there is no intermediate assembly language form, and so there are no instruction fetch or decode cycles.

You are to write the microcode that implements the instructions listed at the end of this problem. The microcode should be stored in locations 0, 1, 2, and 3 of the RAM. Although there are no lines that show it, assume that the n and z bits are both 0 when $C_0C_1 = 00$. That is, A_{23} and A_{22} are both 0 when there is no possible jump. *Note*: Each bit of the A, B, and C fields corresponds directly to a register. Thus, the pattern 1000 selects register R3, *not* register 8, which does not exist. There are some complexities with respect to how branches are made in this microarchitecture, but you do not need to be concerned with how this is done in order to generate the microcode.

`0: R1 ← ADD(R2, R3)`
`1: Jump if negative to` $(15)_{10}$
`2: R3 ← AND(R1, R2)`
`3: Jump to` $(20)_{10}$

6.18 In line 2047 of the ARC microprogram shown in Figure 6-15, would the program behave differently if the "`GOTO 0`" portion of the instruction is deleted?

6.19 In **horizontal microprogramming** the microwords are wide, whereas in

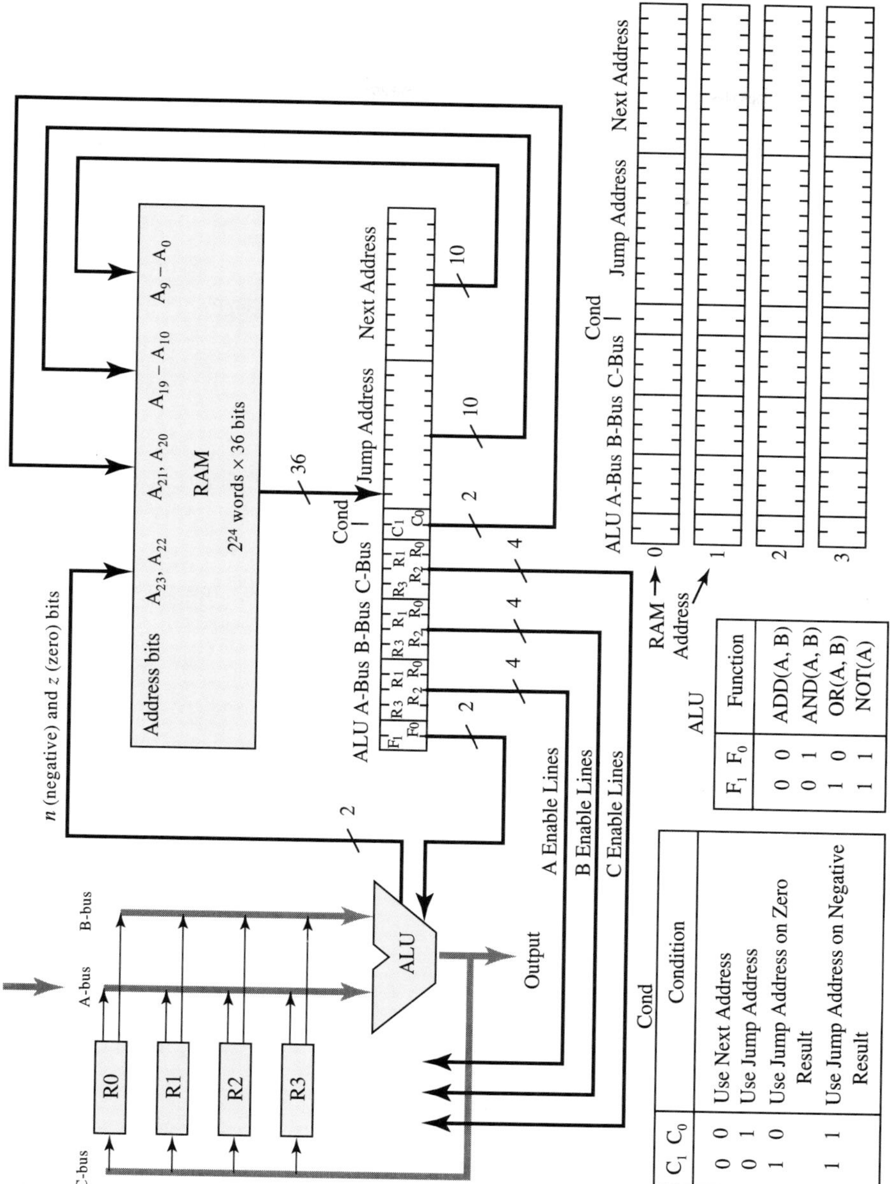

Figure 6-29 An example microarchitecture.

vertical microprogramming the words are narrow. In general, horizontal microwords can be executed quickly but require more space than vertical microwords, which take more time to execute. If we make the microword format shown in Figure 6-11 more horizontal by expanding the A, B, and C fields to contain a single bit for each of the 38 registers instead of a coded six-bit version, then we can eliminate the A, B, and C decoders shown in Figure 6-3. This allows the clock frequency to be increased but also increases the space for the microstore.

(a) How wide will the new horizontal microword be?

(b) By what percentage will the microstore increase in size?

6.20 Refer to Figure 6-7. Show the ALU LUT_0 and ALU LUT_x ($x > 0$) entries for the INC(A) operation.

6.21 On some architectures, there is special hardware that updates the PC, while taking into account the fact that the rightmost two bits are always 0. There is no special hardware presented in this chapter for updating the PC, and the branch microcode in lines 2–20 of Figure 6-15 has an error in how the PC is updated on line 12 because branch displacements are given in terms of words. Identify the error and explain how to fix it.

7 MEMORY

In the past few decades, CPU processing speed as measured by the number of instructions executed per second has doubled every 18 months, for the same price. Computer memory has experienced a similar increase along a different dimension, quadrupling in size every 36 months, for the same price. Memory speed, however, has only increased at a rate of less than 10% per year. Thus, while processing speed increases at the same rate that memory size increases, the gap between the speed of the processor and the speed of memory also increases.

As the gap between processor and memory speeds grows, architectural solutions help bridge the gap. A typical computer contains several types of memory, ranging from fast, expensive internal registers (see Appendix A) to slow, inexpensive removable disks. The interplay between these different types of memory is exploited so that a computer behaves as if it has a single, large, fast memory, when in fact it contains a range of memory types that operate in a highly coordinated fashion. We begin the chapter with a high-level discussion of how these different memories are organized, in what is referred to as the **memory hierarchy**.

7.1 The Memory Hierarchy

Memory in a conventional digital computer is organized in a hierarchy as illustrated in Figure 7-1. At the top of the hierarchy are registers that are matched in speed to the CPU but tend to be large and consume a significant amount of power. There are normally only a small number of registers in a processor, on the order of a few hundred or less. At the bottom of the hierarchy are secondary and off-line storage memories such as hard magnetic disks and magnetic tapes, in which the cost per stored bit is small in terms of money and electrical power, but the access time is very long when compared with registers. Between the registers and secondary storage are a number of other forms of memory that bridge the gap between the two.

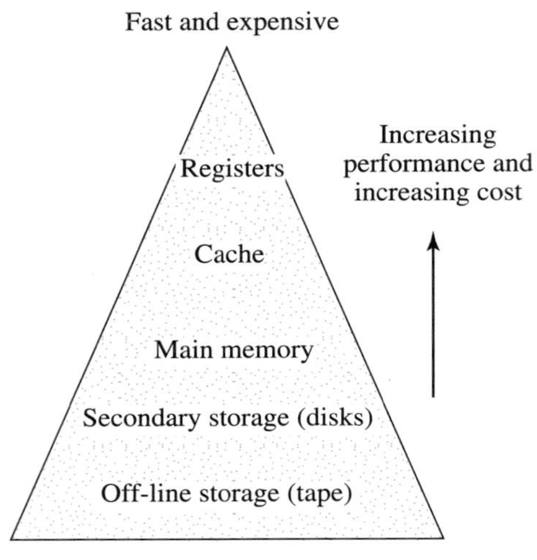

Figure 7-1 The memory hierarchy.

Memory Type	Access Time	Cost /MB	Typical Amount Used	Typical Cost
Registers	1ns	High	1KB	–
Cache	5-20 ns	$100	1MB	$100
Main memory	60-80ns	$1.10	64 MB	$70
Disk memory	10 ms	$0.05	4 GB	$200

Table 7-1 Properties of the memory hierarchy

As we move up through the hierarchy, greater performance is realized, at a greater cost. Table 7-1 shows some of the properties of the components of the memory hierarchy in the late 1990s. Notice that typical cost, arrived at by multiplying cost/MB × typical amount used (in which "MB" is a unit of megabytes), is approximately the same for each member of the hierarchy. Notice also that access times vary by approximately factors of 10 except for disks, which have access times 100,000 times slower than main memory. This large mismatch has an important influence on how the operating system handles the movement of blocks of data between disks and main memory, as we will see later in the chapter.

7.2 Random Access Memory

In this section, we look at the structure and function of **random access memory** (RAM). In this context the term "random" means that any memory location can be accessed in the same amount of time, regardless of its position in the memory.

Figure 7-2 shows the functional behavior of a RAM cell used in a typical computer. The figure represents the memory element as a D flip-flop, with additional controls to allow the cell to be selected, read, and written. There is a (bidirectional) data line for data input and output. We will use cells similar to the one shown in the figure when we discuss RAM chips. Note that this illustration does not necessarily represent the actual physical implementation, but only its functional behavior. There are many ways to implement a memory cell.

RAM chips that are based upon flip-flops, as in Figure 7-2, are referred to as **static** RAM (SRAM) chips because the contents of each location persist as long as power is applied to the chips. **Dynamic RAM** chips, referred to as **DRAMs**, employ a **capacitor**, which stores a minute amount of electric charge, in which the charge level represents a 1 or a 0. Capacitors are much smaller than flip-flops, and so a capacitor based DRAM can hold much more information in the same area than an SRAM. Since the charges on the capacitors dissipate with time, the charge in the capacitor storage cells in DRAMs must be restored, or **refreshed**, frequently.

DRAMs are susceptible to premature discharging as a result of interactions with naturally occurring gamma rays. This is a statistically rare event, and a system may run for days before an error occurs. For this reason, early personal comput-

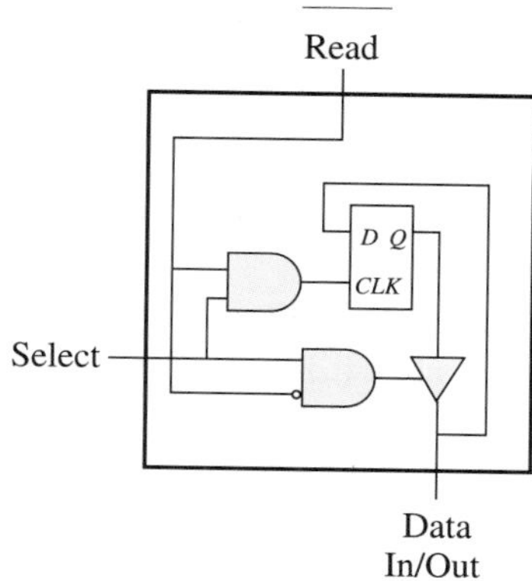

Figure 7-2 Functional behavior of a RAM cell.

ers (PCs) did not use error detection circuitry, since PCs would be turned off at the end of the day, and so undetected errors would not accumulate. This helped to keep the prices of PCs competitive. With the drastic reduction in DRAM prices and the increased uptimes of PCs operating as automated teller machines (ATMs) and network file servers (NFSs), error detection circuitry is now commonplace in PCs.

In the next section we explore how RAM cells are organized into chips.

7.3 Chip Organization

A simplified pinout of a RAM chip is shown in Figure 7-3. An m-bit address, having lines numbered from 0 to $m-1$ is applied to pins A_0–A_{m-1}, while asserting $\overline{CS}$ (Chip Select), and either $\overline{WR}$ (for writing data to the chip) or WR (for reading data from the chip). The overbars on CS and WR indicate that the chip is selected when $CS = 0$ and that a write operation will occur when $WR = 0$. When reading data from the chip, after a time period T_{AA} (the time delay from when the address lines are made valid to the time the data is available at the output), the w-bit data word appears on the data lines D_0–D_{w-1}. When writing data to a chip, the data lines must also be held valid for a time period T_{AA}. Notice that the data lines are bidirectional in Figure 7-3, which is normally the case.

The address lines A_0–A_{m-1} in the RAM chip shown in Figure 7-3 contain an address, which is decoded from an m-bit address into one of 2^m locations within the chip, each of which has a w-bit word associated with it. The chip thus contains $2^m \times w$ bits.

Now consider the problem of creating a RAM that stores 4 four-bit words. A RAM can be thought of as a collection of registers. We can use four-bit registers to store the words and then introduce an addressing mechanism that allows one of the words to be selected for reading or for writing. Figure 7-4 shows a design

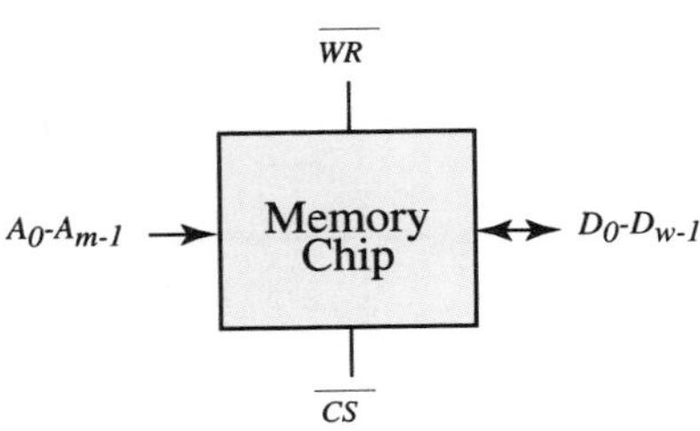

Figure 7-3 Simplified RAM chip pinout.

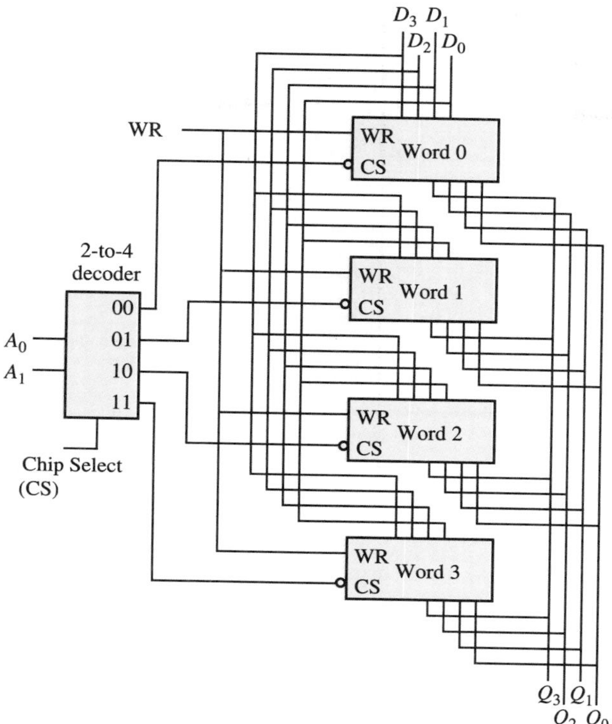

Figure 7-4 A four-word memory with four bits per word in a 2D organization.

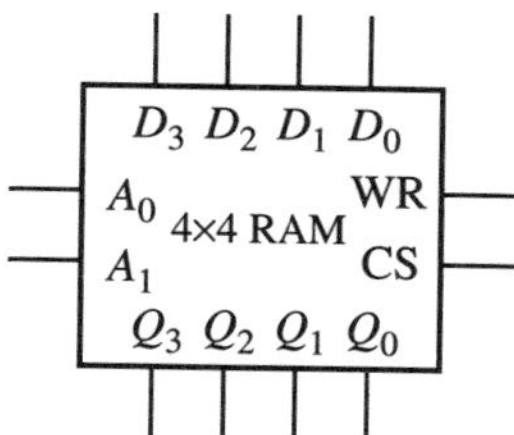

Figure 7-5 A simplified version of the four-word by four-bit RAM.

for the memory. Two address lines A_0 and A_1 select a word for reading or writing via the 2-to-4 decoder. The outputs of the registers can be safely tied together without risking an electrical short because the 2-to-4 decoder ensures that at most one register is enabled at a time, and the disabled registers are electrically disconnected through the use of tri-state buffers. The Chip Select line in the decoder is not necessary but will be used later in constructing larger RAMs. A simplified drawing of the RAM is shown in Figure 7-5.

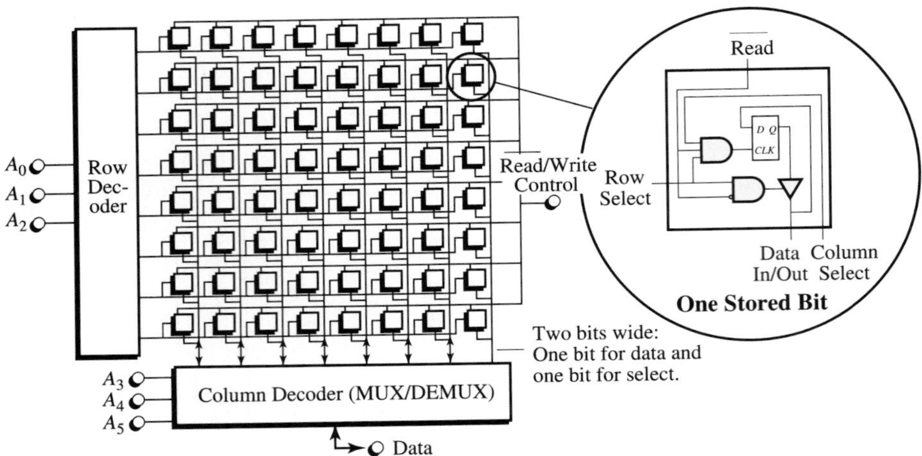

Figure 7-6 2-1/2D organization of a 64-word by one-bit RAM.

There are two common ways to organize the generalized RAM shown in Figure 7-3. In the smallest RAM chips it is practical to use a single decoder to select one out of 2^m words, each of which is w bits wide. However, this organization is not economical in ordinary RAM chips. Consider that a 64M×1 chip has 26 address lines (64M = 2^{26}). This means that a conventional decoder would need 2^{26} 26-input AND gates, which manifests itself as a large cost in terms of chip area—and this is just for the decode.

Since most ICs are roughly square, an alternate decoding structure that significantly reduces the decoder complexity decodes the rows separately from the columns. This is referred to as a 2-1/2D organization. The 2-1/2D organization is by far the most prevalent organization for RAM ICs. Figure 7-6 shows a 2^6-word × 1-bit RAM with a 2-1/2D organization. The six address lines are evenly split between a row decoder and a column decoder (the column decoder is actually a MUX/DEMUX combination). A single bidirectional data line is used for input and output.

During a read operation, an entire row is selected and fed into the column MUX, which selects a single bit for output. During a write operation, the single bit to be written is distributed by the DEMUX to the target column, while the row decoder selects the proper row to be written.

In practice, to reduce pin count, there are generally only $m/2$ address pins on the chip, and the row and column addresses are time-multiplexed on these $m/2$ address lines. First, the $m/2$-bit row address is applied along with a row address strobe, $\overline{RAS}$, signal. The row address is latched and decoded by the chip. Then the $m/2$-bit column address is applied, along with a column address strobe, $\overline{CAS}$. There may be additional pins to control the chip refresh and other memory functions.

Even with this 2-1/2D organization and splitting the address into row and column components, there is still a great fan-in/fan-out demand on the decoder logic gates, and the (still) large number of address pins forces memory chips into large footprints on printed circuit boards (PCBs). In order to reduce the fan-in/fan-out constraints, **tree decoders** may be used, which are discussed in Section 7.8.1. A newer memory architecture that serializes the address lines onto a single input pin is discussed in Section 7.9.

Although DRAMs are very economical, SRAMs offer greater speed. The refresh cycles, error detection circuitry, and the low operating powers of DRAMs create a speed difference that is roughly 1/4 of SRAM speed, but SRAMs also incur a significant cost.

The performance of both types of memory (SRAM and DRAM) can be improved. Normally a number of words constituting a **block** will be accessed in succession. In this situation, memory accesses can be **interleaved** so that while one memory is accessing address A_m, other memories are accessing A_{m+1}, A_{m+2}, A_{m+3} etc. In this way the access time for each word can appear to be many times faster.

7.3.1 *CONSTRUCTING LARGE RAMS FROM SMALL RAMS*

We can construct larger RAM modules from smaller RAM modules. Both the word size and the number of words per module can be increased. For example, eight 16M × 1-bit RAM modules can be combined to make a 16M × 8-bit RAM module, and 32 16M × 1-bit RAM modules can be combined to make a 64M × 8-bit RAM module.

As a simple example, consider using the 4-word × 4-bit RAM chip shown in Figure 7-5, as a building block to first make a 4-word × 8-bit module, and then an 8-word × 4-bit module. We would like to increase the width of the 4-bit words and also increase the number of words. Consider first the problem of increasing the word width from four bits to eight. We can accomplish this by simply using two chips, tying their $\overline{CS}$ lines together so they are both selected together, and juxtaposing their data lines, as shown in Figure 7-7.

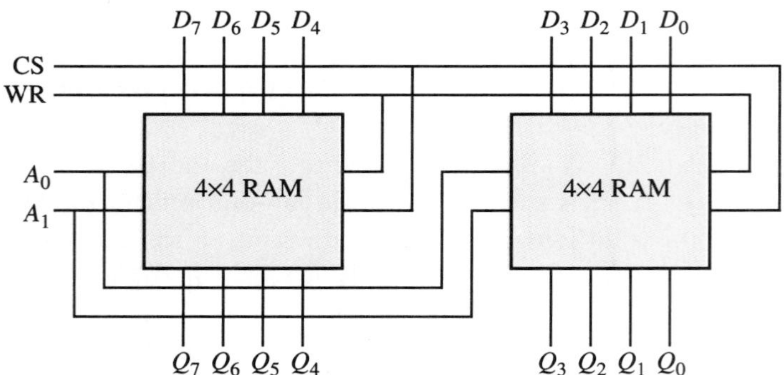

Figure 7-7 Two four-word by four-bit RAMs are used in creating a four-word by eight-bit RAM.

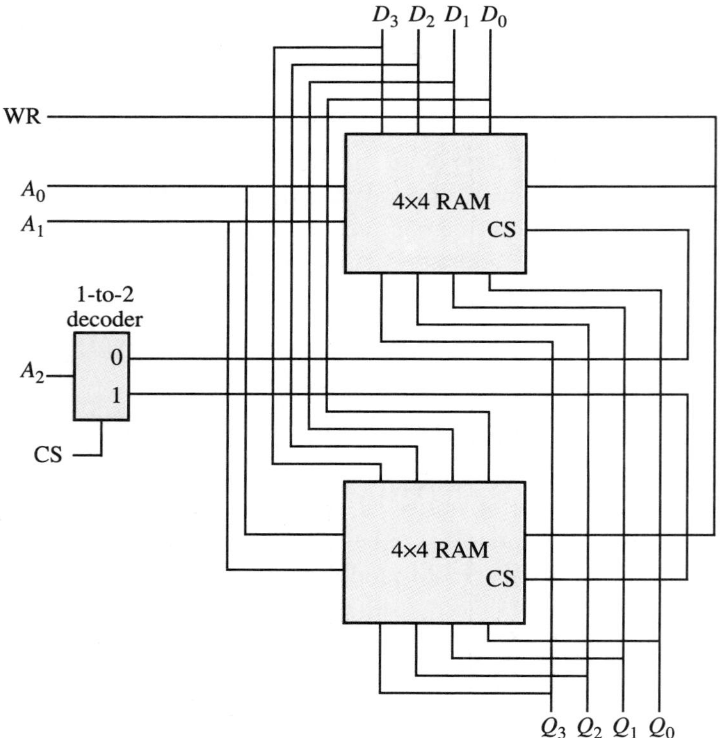

Figure 7-8 Two four-word by four-bit RAMs are used in creating an

Consider now the problem of increasing the number of words from four to eight. Figure 7-8 shows a configuration that accomplishes this. The eight words are distributed over the two four-word RAMs. Address line A_2 is needed because there are now eight words to be addressed. A decoder for A_2 enables either the upper or lower memory module by using the $\overline{CS}$ lines, and then the remaining address lines (A_0 and A_1) are decoded within the enabled module. A combination of these two approaches can be used to scale both the word size and number of words to arbitrary sizes.

7.4 Commercial Memory Modules

Commercially available memory chips are commonly organized into standard configurations. Figure 7-9 (Texas Instruments, 1991) shows an organization of eight 2^{20}-bit chips on a single-in-line memory module (SIMM) that form a $2^{20} \times 8$ (1 MB) module. The electrical contacts (numbered 1–30) all lie in a single line. For 2^{20} memory locations we need 20 address lines, but only 10 address lines ($A0$–$A9$) are provided. The 10-bit addresses for the row and column are loaded separately, and the Column Address Strobe and Row Address Strobe signals are applied after the corresponding portion of the address is made available. Although this organization appears to double the time it takes to access any particular memory location, on average the access time is much better since only the row or column address needs to be updated.

PIN NOMENCLATURE	
A0-A9	Address Inputs
$\overline{\text{CAS}}$	Column-Address Strobe
DQ1-DQ8	Data In/Data Out
NC	No Connection
$\overline{\text{RAS}}$	Row-Address Strobe
V_{cc}	5-V Supply
V_{SS}	Ground
$\overline{\text{W}}$	Write Enable

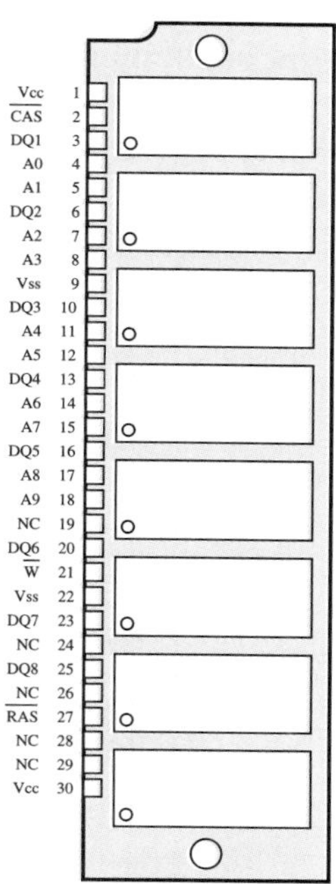

Figure 7-9 Single-in-line memory module (Adapted from Texas Instruments, 1991).

The eight data bits on lines *DQ*1–*DQ*8 form a byte that is read or written in parallel. In order to form a 32-bit word, four SIMM modules are needed. As with the other "active low" signals, the Write Enable line has a bar over the corresponding symbol ($\overline{W}$), which means that a write takes place when a 0 is placed on this line. A read takes place otherwise. The $\overline{RAS}$ line also causes a refresh operation, which must be performed at least every 8 ms to restore the charges on the capacitors.

7.5 Read-Only Memory

When a computer program is loaded into the memory, it remains in the memory until it is overwritten or until the power is turned off. For some applications, the program never changes, and so it is hardwired into a **read-only memory** (ROM). ROMs are used to store programs in videogames, calculators, microwave ovens, and automobile fuel injection controllers, among many other applications.

The ROM is a simple device. All that is needed is a decoder, some output lines, and a few logic gates. There is no need for flip-flops or capacitors. Figure 7-10 shows a four-word ROM that stores four 4-bit words (0101, 1011, 1110, and 0000). Each address input (00, 01, 10, or 11) corresponds to a different stored word.

For high-volume applications, ROMs are factory programmed. As an alternative, for low-volume or prototyping applications, programmable ROMs (PROMs) are often used, which allow their contents to be written by a user with a relatively inexpensive device called a **PROM burner**. Unfortunately for the early videogame industry, these PROM burners are also capable of reading the contents of a PROM, which can then be duplicated onto another PROM, or worse still, the

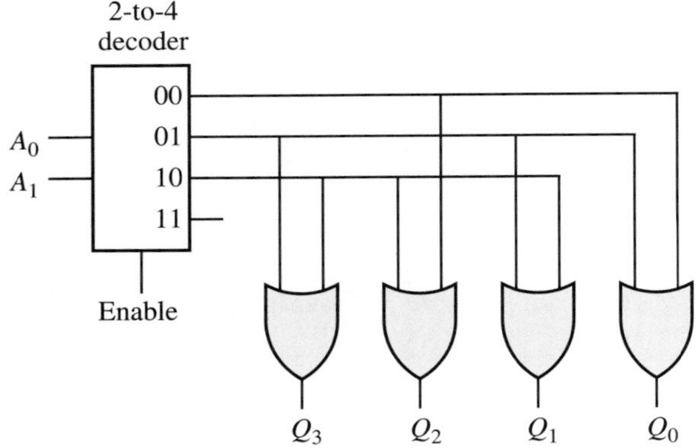

Location	Stored word
00	0101
01	1011
10	1110
11	0000

Figure 7-10 A ROM stores 4 four-bit words.

contents can be deciphered through reverse engineering and then modified and written to a new, contraband game cartridge.

Although the PROM allows the designer to delay decisions about what information is stored, it can only be written once, or can be rewritten only if the existing pattern is a subset of the new pattern. Erasable PROMs (EPROMs) can be written several times, after being erased with ultraviolet light (for UVPROMs) through a window that is mounted on the integrated circuit package. Electrically erasable PROMs (EEPROMs) allow their contents to be rewritten electrically. Newer **flash** memories can be electrically rewritten tens of thousands of times and are used extensively in digital video cameras and for control programs in set-top cable television decoders and other devices.

PROMs will be used later in the text for control units and for **arithmetic logic units** (ALUs). As an example of this type of application, consider creating an ALU that performs the four functions Add, Subtract, Multiply, and Divide on eight-bit operands. We can generate a truth table that enumerates all 2^{16} possible combinations of operands and all 2^2 combinations of functions and send the truth table to a PROM burner, which loads it into the PROM.

This brute force **lookup table** (LUT) approach is not as impractical as it may seem and is actually used in a number of situations. The PROM does not have to be very big: There are $2^8 \times 2^8$ combinations of the two input operands, and there are 2^2 functions, so we need a total of $2^8 \times 2^8 \times 2^2 = 2^{18}$ words in the PROM, which is small by current standards. The configuration for the PROM ALU is shown in Figure 7-11. The address lines are used for the operands and for the function select inputs, and the outputs are produced by simply recalling the pre-

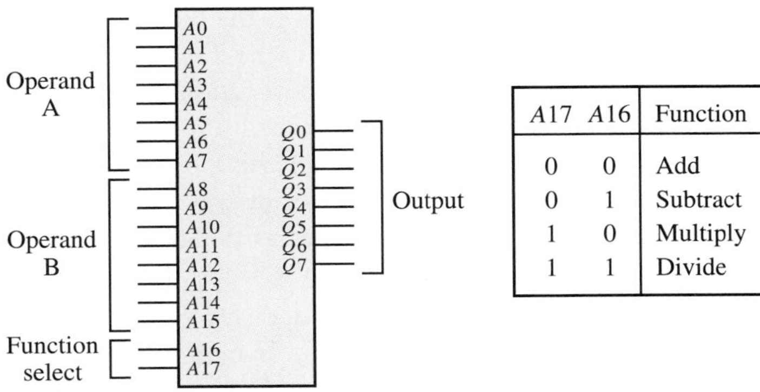

A17	A16	Function
0	0	Add
0	1	Subtract
1	0	Multiply
1	1	Divide

Figure 7-11 A lookup table (LUT) implements an eight-bit ALU.

computed word stored at the addressed location. This approach is typically faster than using a hardware implementation for the functions, but it is not extensible to large word widths without applying some form of decomposition. 32-bit operands are standard on computers today, and a corresponding PROM ALU would require $2^{32} \times 2^{32} \times 2^2 = 2^{66}$ words, which is prohibitively large.

7.6 Cache Memory

When a program executes on a computer, most of the memory references are made to a small number of locations. Typically, 90% of the execution time of a program is spent in just 10% of the code. This property is known as the **locality principle**. When a program references a memory location, it is likely to reference that same memory location again soon, which is known as **temporal locality**. Similarly, there is **spatial locality**, in which a memory location that is near a recently referenced location is more likely to be referenced than a memory location that is farther away. Temporal locality arises because programs spend much of their time in iteration or in recursion, and thus the same section of code is visited a disproportionately large number of times. Spatial locality arises because data tends to be stored in contiguous locations. Although 10% of the code accounts for the bulk of memory references, accesses within the 10% tend to be clustered. Thus, for a given interval of time, most of memory accesses come from an even smaller set of locations than 10% of a program's size.

Memory access is generally slow when compared with the speed of the central processing unit (CPU), and so the memory poses a significant bottleneck in computer performance. Since most memory references come from a small set of locations, the locality principle can be exploited in order to improve performance. A small but fast **cache memory**, in which the contents of the most commonly accessed locations are maintained, can be placed between the main memory and the CPU. When a program executes, the cache memory is searched first, and the referenced word is accessed in the cache if the word is present. If the referenced word is not in the cache, then a free location is created in the cache and the referenced word is brought into the cache from the main memory. The word is then accessed in the cache. Although this process takes longer than accessing main memory directly, the overall performance can be improved if a high proportion of memory accesses are satisfied by the cache.

Modern memory systems may have several levels of cache, referred to as Level 1 (L1), Level 2 (L2), and even, in some cases, Level 3 (L3). In most instances the L1 cache is implemented right on the CPU chip. Both the Intel Pentium and the IBM-Motorola PowerPC G3 processors have 32 Kbytes of L1 cache on the CPU chip.

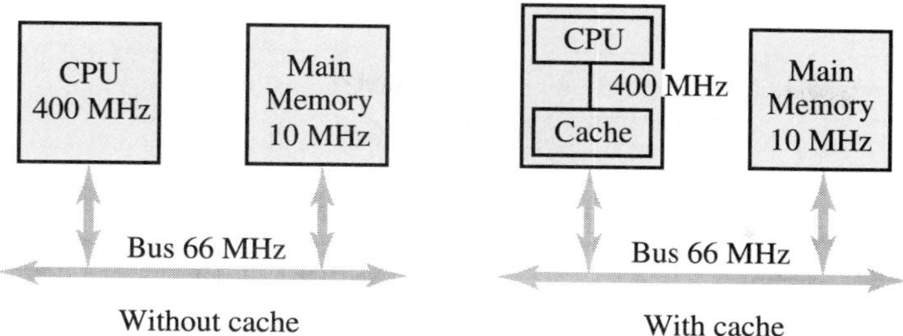

Figure 7-12 Placement of cache in a computer system.

A cache memory is faster than main memory for a number of reasons. Faster electronics can be used, which also results in a greater expense in terms of money, size, and power requirements. Since the cache is small, this increase in cost is relatively small. A cache memory has fewer locations than a main memory, and as a result it has a shallow decoding tree, which reduces the access time. The cache is placed both physically closer and logically closer to the CPU than the main memory, and this placement avoids communication delays over a **shared bus**.

A typical situation is shown in Figure 7-12. A simple computer without a cache memory is shown in the left side of the figure. This cacheless computer contains a CPU that has a clock speed of 400 MHz but communicates over a 66-MHz bus to a main memory that supports a lower clock speed of 10 MHz. A few bus cycles are normally needed to synchronize the CPU with the bus, and thus the difference in speed between main memory and the CPU can be as large as a factor of 10 or more. A cache memory can be positioned closer to the CPU as shown in the right side of Figure 7-12, so that the CPU sees fast accesses over a 400-MHz direct path to the cache.

7.6.1 *ASSOCIATIVE MAPPED CACHE*

A number of hardware schemes have been developed for translating main memory addresses to cache memory addresses. The user does not need to know about the address translation, which has the advantage that cache memory enhancements can be introduced into a computer without a corresponding need for modifying application software.

The choice of cache mapping scheme affects cost and performance, and there is no single best method that is appropriate for all situations. In this section, an **associative** mapping scheme is studied. Figure 7-13 shows an associative map-

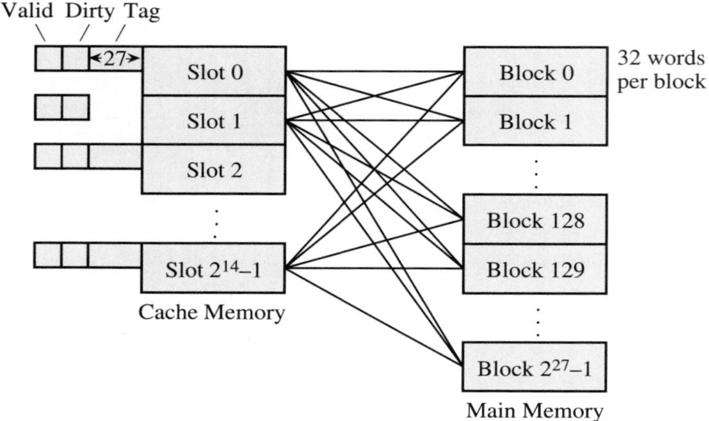

Figure 7-13 An associative mapping scheme for a cache memory.

ping scheme for a 2^{32}-word memory space that is divided into 2^{27} **blocks** of 2^5 = 32 words per block. The main memory is not physically partitioned in this way, but this is the view of main memory that the cache sees. Cache blocks, or **cache lines**, as they are also known, typically range in size from 8 to 64 bytes. Data is moved in and out of the cache a line at a time using memory interleaving (discussed earlier).

The cache for this example consists of 2^{14} **slots** into which main memory blocks are placed. There are more main memory blocks than there are cache slots, and any one of the 2^{27} main memory blocks can be mapped into each cache slot (with only one block placed in a slot at a time). To keep track of which one of the 2^{27} possible blocks is in each slot, a 27-bit **tag** field is added to each slot that holds an identifier in the range from 0 to $2^{27} - 1$. The tag field is the most significant 27 bits of the 32-bit memory address presented to the cache. All the tags are stored in a special tag memory where they can be searched in parallel. Whenever a new block is stored in the cache, its tag is stored in the corresponding tag memory location.

When a program is first loaded into main memory, the cache is cleared, and so while a program is executing, a **valid** bit is needed to indicate whether or not the slot holds a block that belongs to the program being executed. There is also a **dirty** bit that keeps track of whether or not a block has been modified while it is in the cache. A slot that is modified must be written back to the main memory before the slot is reused for another block.

A referenced location that is found in the cache results in a **hit**; otherwise, the result is a **miss**. When a program is initially loaded into memory, the valid bits are all set to 0. The first instruction that is executed in the program will therefore cause a miss, since none of the program is in the cache at this point. The block that causes the miss is located in the main memory and is loaded into the cache.

In an associative mapped cache, each main memory block can be mapped to any slot. The mapping from main memory blocks to cache slots is performed by partitioning an address into fields for the tag and the word (also known as the "byte" field) as follows:

Tag	Word
27 bits	5 bits

When a reference is made to a main memory address, the cache hardware intercepts the reference and searches the cache tag memory to see if the requested block is in the cache. For each slot, if the valid bit is 1, then the tag field of the referenced address is compared with the tag field of the slot. All of the tags are searched in parallel, using an **associative memory** (which is something different from an associative mapping scheme. See Section 7.8.3 for more on associative memories.) If any tag in the cache tag memory matches the tag field of the memory reference, then the word is taken from the position in the slot specified by the word field. If the referenced word is not found in the cache, then the main memory block that contains the word is brought into the cache and the referenced word is then taken from the cache. The tag, valid, and dirty fields are updated, and the program resumes execution.

Consider how an access to memory location $(A035F014)_{16}$ is mapped to the cache. The leftmost 27 bits of the address form the tag field, and the remaining five bits form the word field, as follows:

Tag	Word
1 0 1 0 0 0 0 0 0 0 1 1 0 1 0 1 1 1 1 1 0 0 0 0 0 0 0	1 0 1 0 0

If the addressed word is in the cache, it will be found in word $(14)_{16}$ of a slot that has a tag of $(501AF80)_{16}$, which is made up of the 27 most significant bits of the address. If the addressed word is not in the cache, then the block corresponding to the tag field $(501AF80)_{16}$ will be brought into an available slot in the cache from the main memory, and the memory reference that caused the "cache miss" will then be satisfied from the cache.

Although this mapping scheme is powerful enough to satisfy a wide range of memory access situations, there are two implementation problems that limit performance. First, the process of deciding which slot should be freed when a new block is brought into the cache can be complex. This process requires a significant amount of hardware and introduces delays in memory accesses. A second problem is that when the cache is searched, the tag field of the referenced address must be compared with all 2^{14} tag fields in the cache. (Alternative methods that limit the number of comparisons are described in Sections 7.6.2 and 7.6.3.)

Replacement Policies in Associative Mapped Caches

When a new block needs to be placed in an associative mapped cache, an available slot must be identified. If there are unused slots, such as when a program begins execution, then the first slot with a valid bit of 0 can simply be used. When all of the valid bits for all cache slots are 1, however, then one of the active slots must be freed for the new block. Four replacement policies that are commonly used are **least recently used** (LRU), **first-in first-out** (FIFO), **least frequently used** (LFU), and **random**. A fifth policy that is used for analysis purposes only is **optimal.**

For the LRU policy, a time stamp is added to each slot, which is updated when any slot is accessed. When a slot must be freed for a new block, the contents of the least recently used slot, as identified by the age of the corresponding time stamp, are discarded and the new block is written to that slot. The LFU policy works similarly, except that only one slot is updated at a time by incrementing a frequency counter that is attached to each slot. When a slot is needed for a new block, the least frequently used slot is freed. The FIFO policy replaces slots in round-robin fashion, one after the next in the order of their physical locations in the cache. The random replacement policy simply chooses a slot at random.

The optimal replacement policy is not practical but is used for comparison purposes to determine how effective other replacement policies are to the best possible. That is, the optimal replacement policy is determined only after a program has already executed, and so it is of little help to a running program.

Studies have shown that the LFU policy is only slightly better than the random policy. The LRU policy can be implemented efficiently and is sometimes preferred over the others for that reason. A simple implementation of the LRU policy is covered in Section 7.6.7.

Advantages and Disadvantages of the Associative Mapped Cache

The associative mapped cache has the advantage that any main memory block can be placed into any cache slot. This means that regardless of how irregular the data and program references are, if a slot is available for the block, it can be stored in the cache. This results in considerable hardware overhead needed for cache bookkeeping. Each slot must have a 27-bit tag that identifies its location in main memory, and each tag must be searched in parallel. This means that in the preceding example the tag memory must be 27×2^{14} bits in size, and as described previously, there must be a mechanism for searching the tag memory in parallel. Memories that can be searched for their contents, in parallel, are referred to as **associative**, or **content-addressable**, memories. We will discuss this kind of memory later in the chapter.

By restricting where each main memory block can be placed in the cache, we can eliminate the need for an associative memory. This kind of cache is referred to as a **direct mapped cache**, which is discussed in the next section.

7.6.2 *DIRECT MAPPED CACHE*

Figure 7-14 shows a direct mapping scheme for a 2^{32} word memory. As before, the memory is divided into 2^{27} blocks of $2^5 = 32$ words per block, and the cache consists of 2^{14} slots. There are more main memory blocks than there are cache slots, and a total of $2^{27}/2^{14} = 2^{13}$ main memory blocks can be mapped onto each cache slot. In order to keep track of which of the 2^{13} possible blocks is in each

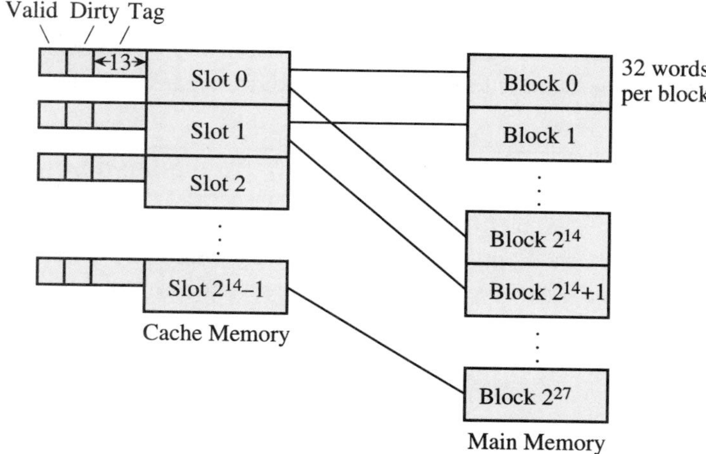

Figure 7-14 A direct mapping scheme for cache memory.

slot, a 13-bit tag field is added to each slot that holds an identifier in the range from 0 to $2^{13}-1$.

This scheme is called "direct mapping" because each cache slot corresponds to an explicit set of main memory blocks. For a direct mapped cache, each main memory block can be mapped to only one slot, but each slot can receive more than one block. The mapping from main memory blocks to cache slots is performed by partitioning an address into fields for the tag, the slot, and the word, as follows:

Tag	Slot	Word
13 bits	14 bits	5 bits

The 32-bit main memory address is partitioned into a 13-bit tag field, followed by a 14-bit slot field, followed by a 5-bit word field. When a reference is made to a main memory address, the slot field identifies in which of the 2^{14} slots the block will be found if it is in the cache. If the valid bit is 1, then the tag field of the referenced address is compared with the tag field of the slot. If the tag fields are the same, then the word is taken from the position in the slot specified by the word field. If the valid bit is 1 but the tag fields are not the same, then the slot is written back to main memory if the dirty bit is set, and the corresponding main memory block is then read into the slot. For a program that has just started execution, the valid bit will be 0, and so the block is simply written to the slot. The valid bit for the block is then set to 1, and the program resumes execution.

Consider how an access to memory location $(A035F014)_{16}$ is mapped to the cache. The bit pattern is partitioned according to the word format shown previously. The leftmost 13 bits form the tag field, the next 14 bits form the slot field, and the remaining five bits form the word field, as follows:

Tag	Slot	Word
1 0 1 0 0 0 0 0 0 0 1 1 0	1 0 1 1 1 1 1 0 0 0 0 0 0 0	1 0 1 0 0

If the addressed word is in the cache, it will be found in word $(14)_{16}$ of slot $(2F80)_{16}$, which will have a tag of $(1406)_{16}$.

Advantages and Disadvantages of the Direct Mapped Cache

The direct mapped cache is a relatively simple scheme to implement. The tag memory in the preceding example is only 13×2^{14} bits in size, less than half of the associative mapped cache. Furthermore, there is no need for an associative search, since the slot field of the main memory address from the CPU is used to "direct" the comparison to the single slot where the block will be if it is indeed in the cache.

This simplicity comes at a cost. Consider what happens when a program references locations that are 2^{19} words apart, which is the size of the cache. This pattern can arise naturally if a matrix is stored in memory by rows and is accessed by columns. Every memory reference will result in a miss, which will cause an entire block to be read into the cache even though only a single word is used. Worse still, only a small fraction of the available cache memory will actually be used.

Now it may seem that any programmer who writes a program this way deserves the resulting poor performance, but in fact, fast matrix calculations use power-of-two dimensions (which allows shift operations to replace costly multiplications and divisions for array indexing), and so the worst-case scenario of accessing memory locations that are 2^{19} addresses apart is not all that unlikely. To avoid this situation without paying the high implementation price of a fully associative cache memory, the **set associative mapping** scheme can be used, which combines aspects of both direct mapping and associative mapping. Set associative mapping, which is also known as **set direct mapping**, is described in the next section.

7.6.3 *SET ASSOCIATIVE MAPPED CACHE*

The set associative mapping scheme combines the simplicity of direct mapping with the flexibility of associative mapping. Set associative mapping is more practical than fully associative mapping because the associative portion is limited to just a few slots that make up a set, as illustrated in Figure 7-15. For this example, two blocks make up a set, and so it is a **two-way** set associative cache. If there are four blocks per set, then it is a four-way set associative cache.

Since there are 2^{14} slots in the cache, there are $2^{14}/2 = 2^{13}$ sets. When an address is mapped to a set, the direct mapping scheme is used, and then associative mapping is used within a set. The format for an address has 13 bits in the set field, which identifies the set in which the addressed word will be found if it is in the cache. There are five bits for the word field as before and there is a 14-bit tag field that together make up the remaining 32 bits of the address, as follows:

Tag	Set	Word
14 bits	13 bits	5 bits

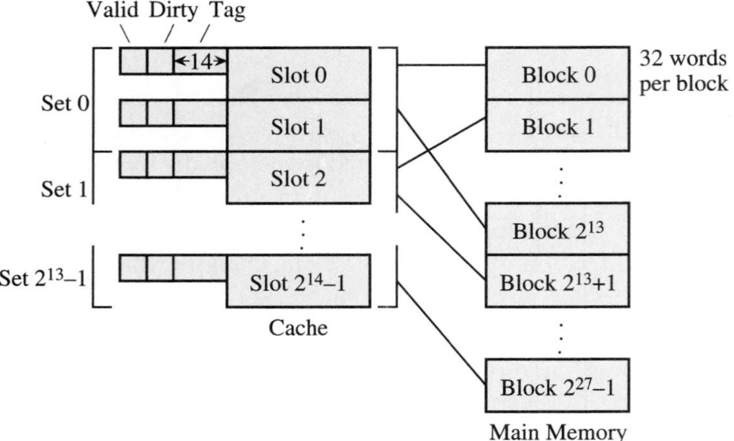

Figure 7-15 A set associative mapping scheme for a cache memory.

As an example of how the set associative cache views a main memory address, consider again the address $(A035F014)_{16}$. The leftmost 14 bits form the tag field, followed by 13 bits for the set field, followed by 5 bits for the word field, as follows:

Tag	Set	Word
1 0 1 0 0 0 0 0 0 0 1 1 0 1	0 1 1 1 1 1 0 0 0 0 0 0 0	1 0 1 0 0

As before, the partitioning of the address field is known only to the cache, and the rest of the computer is oblivious to any address translation.

Advantages and Disadvantages of the Set Associative Mapped Cache

In the preceding example, the tag memory increases only slightly from the direct mapping example, to 13×2^{14} bits, and only two tags need to be searched for each memory reference. The set associative cache is almost universally used in today's microprocessors.

7.6.4 *CACHE PERFORMANCE*

Notice that we can readily replace the cache direct mapping hardware with associative or set associative mapping hardware, without making any other changes to the computer or the software. Only the run-time performance will change between methods.

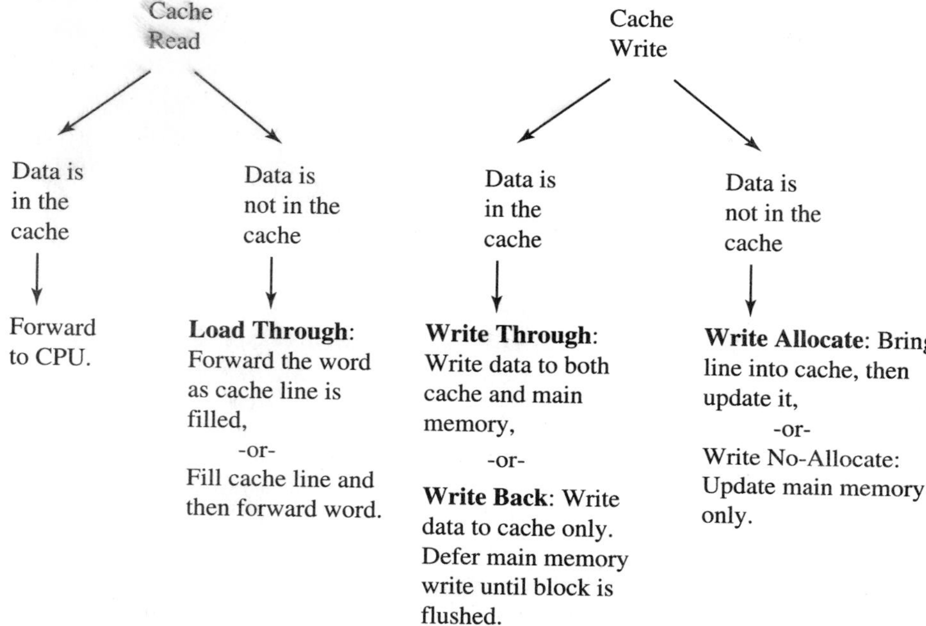

Figure 7-16 Cache read and write policies.

Run-time performance is the purpose behind using a cache memory, and there are a number of issues that need to be addressed as to what triggers a word or block to be moved between the cache and the main memory. Cache read and write policies are summarized in Figure 7-16. The policies depend upon whether or not the requested word is in the cache. If a cache read operation is taking place, and the referenced data is in the cache, then there is a "cache hit" and the referenced data is immediately forwarded to the CPU. When a cache miss occurs, then the entire block that contains the referenced word is read into the cache.

In some cache organizations, the word that causes the miss is immediately forwarded to the CPU as soon as it is read into the cache, rather than waiting for the remainder of the cache slot to be filled, which is known as a **load-through** operation. For a noninterleaved main memory, if the word occurs in the last position of the block, then no performance gain is realized since the entire slot is brought in before load-through can take place. For an interleaved main memory, the order of accesses can be organized so that a load-through operation will always result in a performance gain.

For write operations, if the word is in the cache, then there may be *two* copies of the word, one in the cache and one in main memory. If both are updated simultaneously, this is referred to as **write-through**. If the write is deferred until the cache line is flushed from the cache, this is referred to as **write-back**. Even if the data item is not in the cache when the write occurs, there is the choice of bringing the block containing the word into the cache and then updating it, known as **write-allocate**, or to update it in main memory without involving the cache, known as **write-no-allocate**.

Some computers have separate caches for instructions and data, which is a variation of a configuration known as the **Harvard architecture** (also known as a **split cache**), in which instructions and data are stored in separate sections of memory. Since instruction slots can never be dirty (unless we write self-modifying code, which is rare these days), an instruction cache is simpler than a data cache. In support of this configuration, observations have shown that most of the memory traffic moves away from main memory rather than toward it. Statistically, there is only one write to memory for every four read operations from memory. One reason for this is that instructions in an executing program are only read from the main memory and are never written to the memory except by the system loader. Another reason is that operations on data typically involve reading two operands and storing a single result, which means there are two read operations for every write operation. A cache that only handles reads, while sending writes directly to main memory can thus also be effective, although not necessarily as effective as a fully functional cache.

As to which cache read and write policies are best, there is no simple answer. The organization of a cache is optimized for each computer architecture and the mix of programs that the computer executes. Cache organization and cache sizes are normally determined by the results of simulation runs that expose the nature of memory traffic.

7.6.5 *HIT RATIOS AND EFFECTIVE ACCESS TIMES*

Two measures that characterize the performance of a cache memory are the **hit ratio** and the **effective access time**. The hit ratio is computed by dividing the number of times referenced words are found in the cache by the total number of memory references. The effective access time is computed by dividing the total time spent accessing memory (summing the main memory and cache access times) by the total number of memory references. The corresponding equations are as follows:

$$\text{Hit ratio} = \frac{\text{No. times referenced words are in cache}}{\text{Total number of memory accesses}}$$

$$\text{Eff. access time} = \frac{(\#\ \text{hits})(\text{Time per hit}) + (\#\ \text{misses})(\text{Time per miss})}{\text{Total number of memory access}}$$

Consider computing the hit ratio and the effective access time for a program running on a computer that has a direct mapped cache with four 16-word slots. The layout of the cache and the main memory are shown in Figure 7-17. The cache access time is 80 ns, and the time for transferring a main memory block to the cache is 2500 ns. Assume that load-through is used in this architecture and that the cache is initially empty. A sample program executes from memory locations 48–95, and then loops 10 times from 15–31 before halting.

We record the events as the program executes as shown in Figure 7-18. Since the memory is initially empty, the first instruction that executes causes a miss. A miss thus occurs at location 48, which causes main memory block #3 to be read into cache slot #3. This first memory access takes 2500 ns to complete. Load-through is used for this example, and so the word that causes the miss at location 48 is passed directly to the CPU while the rest of the block is loaded into the cache slot. The next event consists of 15 hits for locations 49 through 63. The events that follow are recorded in a similar manner, and the result is a total of 213 hits and five misses. The total number of accesses is 213 + 5 = 218. The hit ratio and effective access time are computed as follows:

$$\text{Hit ratio} = \frac{213}{218} = 97.7\%$$

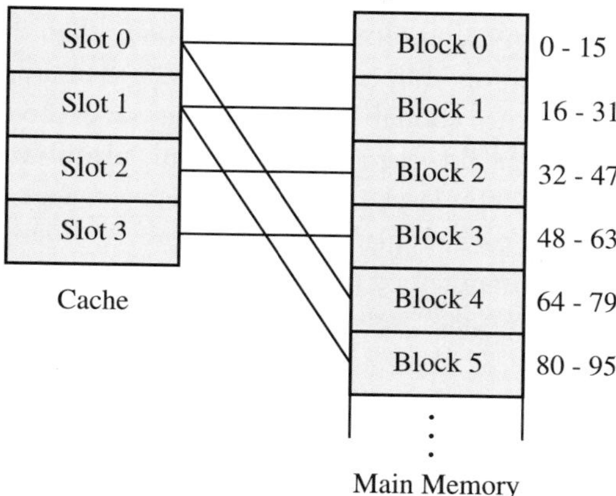

Figure 7-17 An example of a direct mapped cache memory.

Event	Location	Time	Comment
1 miss	48	2500ns	Memory block 3 to cache slot 3
15 hits	49-63	80ns×15=1200ns	
1 miss	64	2500ns	Memory block 4 to cache slot 0
15 hits	65-79	80ns×15=1200ns	
1 miss	80	2500ns	Memory block 5 to cache slot 1
15 hits	81-95	80ns×15=1200ns	
1 miss	15	2500ns	Memory block 0 to cache slot 0
1 miss	16	2500ns	Memory block 1 to cache slot 1
15 hits	17-31	80ns×15=1200ns	
9 hits	15	80ns×9=720ns	Last nine iterations of loop
144 hits	16-31	80ns×144=12,240ns	Last nine iterations of loop
Total hits = 213	Total misses = 5		

Figure 7-18 A table of events for a program executing on an architecture with a small direct mapped cache memory.

$$\text{Effective access time} = \frac{(213)(80 \text{ ns}) + (5)(2500 \text{ ns})}{218} = 136 \text{ ns}$$

Although the hit ratio is 97.6%, the effective access time for this example is almost 75% longer than the cache access time. This is due to the large amount of time spent in accessing a block from main memory.

7.6.6 *MULTILEVEL CACHES*

As the sizes of silicon ICs have increased, and the packing density of components on ICs has increased, it has become possible to include cache memory on the same IC as the processor. Since the on-chip processing speed is faster than the speed of communication between chips, an on-chip cache can be faster than an off-chip cache. Current technology is not dense enough to allow the entire cache to be placed on the same chip as the processor, however. For this reason, **multilevel caches** have been developed, in which the fastest level of the cache, L1, is on the same chip as the processor, and the remaining cache is placed off of the processor chip. Data and instruction caches are separately maintained in the L1 cache. The L2 cache is **unified**, which means that the same cache holds both data and instructions.

In order to compute the hit ratio and effective access time for a multilevel cache, the hits and misses must be recorded among both caches. Equations that represent the overall hit ratio and the overall effective access time for a two-level cache are shown next. H_1 is the hit ratio for the on-chip cache, H_2 is the hit ratio for the off-chip cache, and T_{EFF} is the overall effective access time. The method can be extended to any number of levels.

$$H_1 = \frac{\text{No. times accessed word is in on-chip cache}}{\text{Total number of memory accesses}}$$

$$H_2 = \frac{\text{No. times accessed word is in off-chip cache}}{\text{No. times accessed word is not in on-chip cache}}$$

$$T_{EFF} = (\text{No. on-chip cache hits})(\text{On-chip cache hit time}) + (\text{No. off-chip cache hits})(\text{Off-chip cache hit time}) + (\text{No. off-chip cache misses})(\text{Off-chip cache miss time}) / \text{Total number of memory accesses}$$

7.6.7 *CACHE MANAGEMENT*

Management of a cache memory presents a complex problem to the system programmer. If a given memory location represents an I/O port, as it may in memory-mapped systems, then it probably should not appear in the cache at all. If it is cached, the value in the I/O port may change, and this change will not be reflected in the value of the data stored in the cache. This is known as "stale" data: The copy that is in the cache is "stale" compared with the value in main memory. Likewise, in **shared memory multiprocessor** environments (see Chapter 10), where more than one processor may access the same main memory, either the cached value or the value in main memory may become stale due to the activity of one or more of the CPUs. At a minimum, the cache in a multiprocessor environment should implement a write-through policy for those cache lines that map to shared memory locations.

For these reasons, and others, most modern processor architectures allow the system programmer to have some measure of control over the cache. For example, the Motorola PPC 601 processor's cache, which normally enforces a write-back policy, can be set to a write-through policy on a per-line basis. Other instructions allow individual lines to be specified as noncacheable, or to be marked as invalid, loaded, or flushed.

Internal to the cache, replacement policies (for associative and set associative caches) need to be implemented efficiently. An efficient implementation of the LRU replacement policy can be achieved with the **Neat Little LRU Algorithm** (origin unknown). Continuing with the cache example used in Section 7.6.5, we construct a matrix in which there is a row and a column for every slot in the cache, as shown in Figure 7-19. Initially, all of the cells are set to 0. Each time

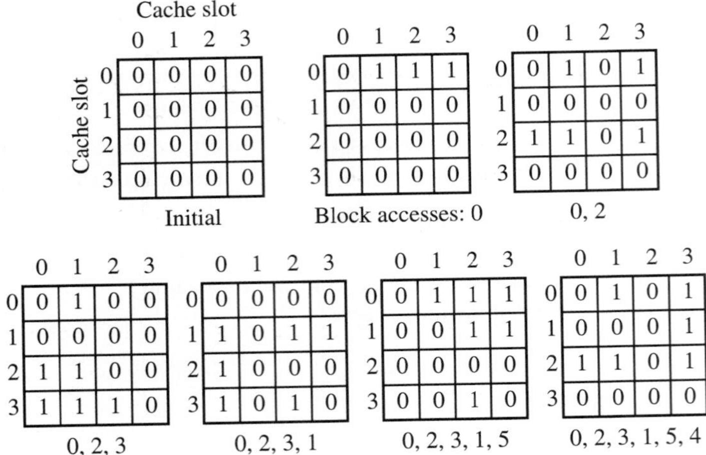

Figure 7-19 A sequence is shown for the Neat Little LRU Algorithm for a cache with four slots. Main memory blocks are accessed in the sequence 0, 2, 3, 1, 5, 4.

that a slot is accessed, 1's are written into each cell in the row of the table that corresponds to that slot. Zeros are then written into each cell in the column that corresponds to that slot. Whenever a slot is needed, the row that contains all 0's is the oldest and is used next. At the beginning of the process, more than one row will contain all 0's, and so a tie-breaking mechanism is needed. The first row with all 0's is one method that will work, which we use here.

The example shown in Figure 7-19 shows the configuration of the matrix as blocks are accessed in the order 0, 2, 3, 1, 5, 4. Initially, the matrix is filled with 0's. After a reference is made to block 0, the row corresponding to block 0 is filled with 1's and the column corresponding to block 0 is filled with 0's. For this example, block 0 happens to be placed in slot 0, but for other situations, block 0 can be placed in any slot. The process continues until all cache slots are in use at the end of the sequence 0, 2, 3, 1. In order to bring the next block (5) into the cache, a slot must be freed. The row for slot 0 contains 0's, and so it is the least recently used slot. Block 5 is then brought into slot 0. Similarly, when block 4 is brought into the cache, slot 2 is overwritten.

7.7 Virtual Memory

Despite the enormous advancements in creating ever larger memories in smaller areas, computer memory is still like closet space, in the sense that we can never have enough of it. An economical method of extending the apparent size of the main memory is to augment it with disk space, which is one aspect of **virtual memory** that we cover in this section. Disk storage appears near the bottom of the memory hierarchy, with a lower cost per bit than main memory, and so it is reasonable to use disk storage to hold the portions of a program or data sets that do not entirely fit into the main memory. In a different aspect of virtual memory, complex address mapping schemes are supported, which give greater flexibility in how the memory is used. We explore these aspects of virtual memory next.

7.7.1 *OVERLAYS*

An early approach of using disk storage to augment the main memory made use of **overlays**, in which an executing program overwrites its own code with other code as needed. In this scenario, the programmer has the responsibility of managing memory usage. Figure 7-20 shows an example in which a program contains a main routine and three subroutines *A*, *B*, and *C*. The physical memory is smaller than the size of the program but is larger than any single routine. A strategy for managing memory using overlays is to modify the program so that it keeps track of which subroutines are in memory and reads in subroutine code as needed. Typically, the main routine serves as the **driver** and manages the bulk of the bookkeeping. The driver stays in memory while other routines are brought in and out.

Figure 7-20 shows a **partition graph** that is created for the example program. The partition graph identifies which routines can overlay others based on which subroutines call others. For this example, the main routine is always present, and

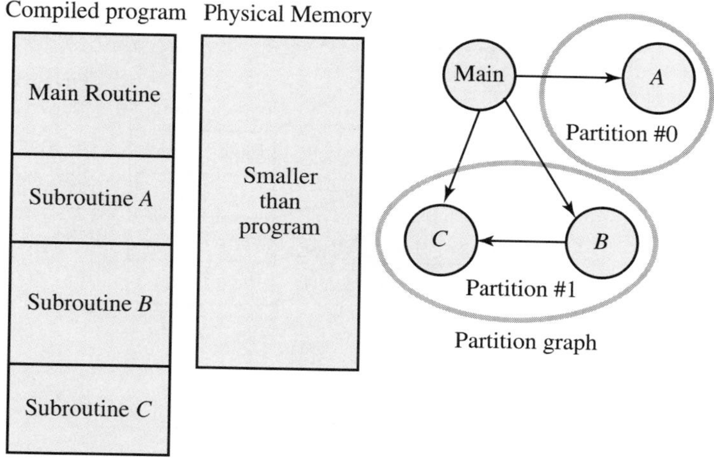

Figure 7-20 A partition graph for a program with a main routine and three subroutines.

supervises which subset of subroutines are in memory. Subroutines *B* and *C* are kept in the same partition in this example because *B* calls *C*, but subroutine *A* is in its own partition because only the main routine calls *A*. Partition #0 can thus overlay partition #1, and partition #1 can overlay partition #0.

Although this method will work well in a variety of situations, a cleaner solution might be to let an operating system manage the overlays. When more than one program is loaded into memory, however, then the routines that manage the overlays cannot operate without interacting with the operating system in order to find out which portions of memory are available. This scenario introduces a great deal of complexity into managing the overlay process since there is a heavy interaction between the operating system and each program. An alternative method that can be managed by the operating system alone is called **paging**, which is described in the next section.

7.7.2 *PAGING*

Paging is a form of automatic overlaying that is managed by the operating system. The address space is partitioned into equal sized blocks, called **pages**. Pages are normally an integral power of two in size such as 2^{10} = 1024 bytes. Paging makes the physical memory appear larger than it truly is by mapping the physical memory address space to some portion of the virtual memory address space, which is normally stored on a disk. An illustration of a virtual memory mapping scheme is shown in Figure 7-21. Eight virtual pages are mapped to four physical **page frames**.

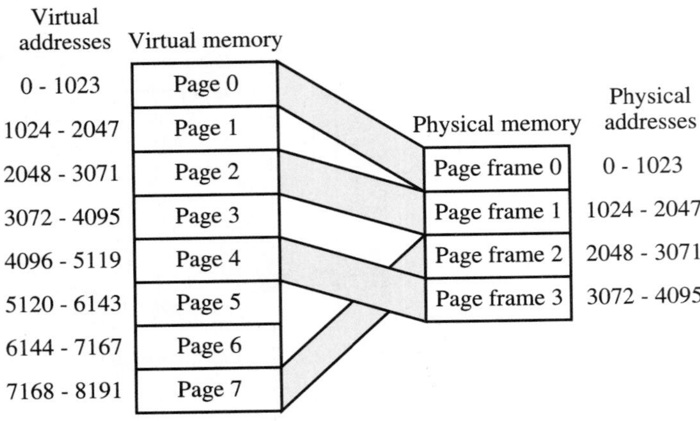

Figure 7-21 A mapping between a virtual and a physical memory.

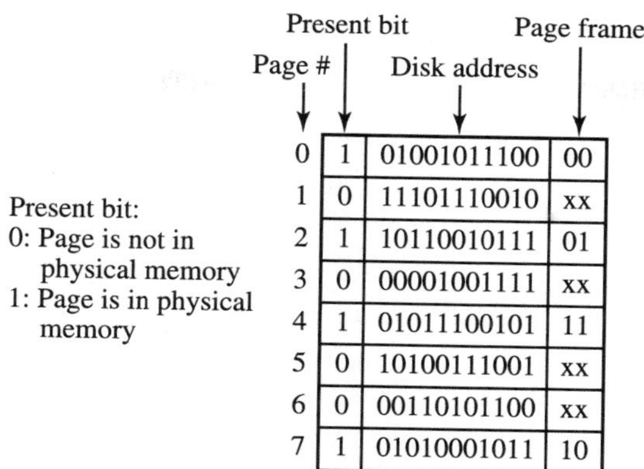

Present bit
Page frame
Page #
Disk address
Present bit:
0: Page is not in physical memory
1: Page is in physical memory
0 1 01001011100 00
1 0 11101110010 xx
2 1 10110010111 01
3 0 00001001111 xx
4 1 01011100101 11
5 0 10100111001 xx
6 0 00110101100 xx
7 1 01010001011 10

Figure 7-22 A page table for a virtual memory.

An implementation of virtual memory must handle references that are made outside of the portion of virtual space that is mapped to physical space. The following sequence of events is typical when a referenced virtual location is not in physical memory, which is referred to as a **page fault:**

1. A page frame is identified to be overwritten. The contents of the page frame are written to secondary memory if changes were made to it, so that the changes are recorded before the page frame is overwritten.

2. The virtual page that we want to access is located in secondary memory and is written into physical memory, in the page frame located in (1).

3. The page table (see Figure 7-22) is updated to map the new section of virtual memory onto the physical memory.

4. Execution continues.

For the virtual memory shown in Figure 7-21, there are $2^{13} = 8192$ virtual locations and so an executing program must generate 13-bit addresses, which are interpreted as a 3-bit page number and a 10-bit offset within the page. Given the 3-bit page number, we need to find out where the page is: It is either in one of the four page frames, or it is in secondary memory. In order to keep track of which pages are in physical memory, a **page table** is maintained, as illustrated in Figure 7-22, which corresponds to the mapping shown in Figure 7-21.

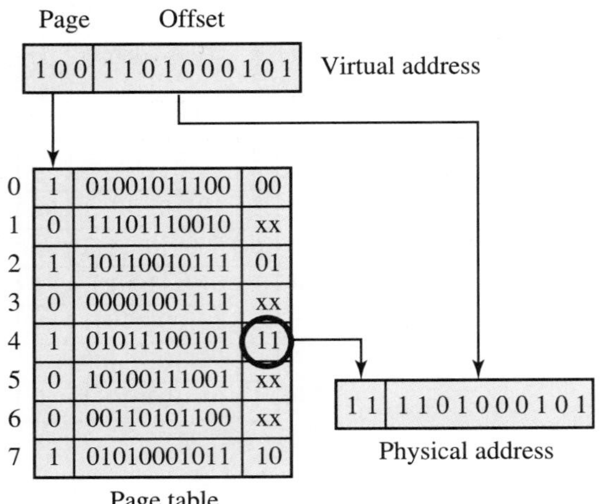

Figure 7-23 A virtual address is translated into a physical address.

The page table has as many entries as there are virtual pages. The present bit indicates whether or not the corresponding page is in physical memory. The disk address field is a pointer to the location that the corresponding page can be found on a disk unit. The operating system normally manages the disk accesses, and so the page table only needs to maintain the disk addresses that the operating system assigns to blocks when the system starts up. The disk addresses normally do not change during the course of computation. The page frame field indicates which physical page frame holds a virtual page, if the page is in physical memory. For pages that are not in physical memory, the page frame fields are invalid, and so they are marked with "xx" in Figure 7-22.

In order to translate a virtual address to a physical address, we take two page frame bits from the page table and append them to the left of the 10-bit offset, which produces the physical address for the referenced word. Consider the situation shown in Figure 7-23, in which a reference is made to virtual address 1001101000101. The three leftmost bits of the virtual address (100) identify the page. The bit pattern that appears in the page frame field (11) is appended to the left of the 10-bit offset (1101000101), and the resulting address (111101000101) indicates which physical memory address holds the referenced word.

It may take a relatively long period of time for a program to be loaded into memory. The entire program may never be executed, and so the time required to load the program from a disk into the memory can be reduced by loading only the

After fault on page #1

0	0	01001011100	xx
1	1	11101110010	00
2	0	10110010111	xx
3	0	00001001111	xx
4	0	01011100101	xx
5	0	10100111001	xx
6	0	00110101100	xx
7	0	01010001011	xx

After fault on page #2

0	0	01001011100	xx
1	1	11101110010	00
2	1	10110010111	01
3	0	00001001111	xx
4	0	01011100101	xx
5	0	10100111001	xx
6	0	00110101100	xx
7	0	01010001011	xx

After fault on page #3

0	0	01001011100	xx
1	1	11101110010	00
2	1	10110010111	01
3	1	00001001111	10
4	0	01011100101	xx
5	0	10100111001	xx
6	0	00110101100	xx
7	0	01010001011	xx

Final

0	0	01001011100	xx
1	0	11101110010	xx
2	1	10110010111	01
3	1	00001001111	10
4	1	01011100101	11
5	1	10100111001	00
6	0	00110101100	xx
7	0	01010001011	xx

Figure 7-24 The configuration of a page table changes as a program executes. Initially, the page table is empty. In the final configuration, four pages are in physical memory.

portion of the program that is needed for a given interval of time. The **demand paging** scheme does not load a page into memory until there is a page fault. After a program has been running for a while, only the pages being used will be in physical memory (this is referred to as the **working set**), so demand paging does not have a significant impact on long running programs.

Consider again the memory mapping shown in Figure 7-21. The size of the virtual address space is 2^{13} words, and the physical address space is 2^{12} words. There are eight pages that each contain 2^{10} words. Assume that the memory is initially empty and that demand paging is used for a program that executes from memory locations 1030 to 5300. The execution sequence will make accesses to pages 1, 2, 3, 4, and 5, in that order. The page replacement policy is FIFO. Figure 7-24 shows the configuration of the page table as execution proceeds. The first access to memory will cause a page fault on virtual address 1030, which is in page #1. The page is brought into physical memory, and the valid bit and page frame field are updated in the page table. Execution continues, until page #5 must be brought in, which forces out page #1 due to the FIFO page replacement policy. The final configuration of the page table in Figure 7-24 is shown after location 5300 is accessed.

7.7.3 *SEGMENTATION*

Virtual memory as we have discussed it up to this point is one dimensional in the sense that addresses grow either up or down. **Segmentation** divides the address space into **segments**, which may be of arbitrary size. Each segment is its own one-dimensional address space. This allows tables, stacks, and other data structures to be maintained as logical entities that grow without bumping into each other. Segmentation allows for **protection**, so that a segment may be specified as "read only" to prevent changes, or "execute only" to prevent unauthorized copying. This also protects users from trying to write data into instruction areas.

When segmentation is used with virtual memory, the size of each segment's address space can be very large, and so the physical memory devoted to each segment is not committed until needed.

Figure 7-25 illustrates a segmented memory. The executable code for a word processing program is loaded into segment #0. This segment is marked as "execute only" and is thus protected from writing. Segment #1 is used for the data space for user #0 and is marked as "read/write" for user #0, so that no other user can have access to this area. Segment #2 is used for the data space for user #1 and is marked as "read/write" for user #1. The same word processor can be used by both user #0 and user #1, in which case the code in segment #0 is shared, but each user has a separate data segment.

Segmentation is not the same thing as paging. With paging, the user does not see the automatic overlaying. With segmentation, the user is aware of where segment boundaries are. The operating system manages protection and mapping, and so an ordinary user does not normally need to deal with bookkeeping, but a more sophis-

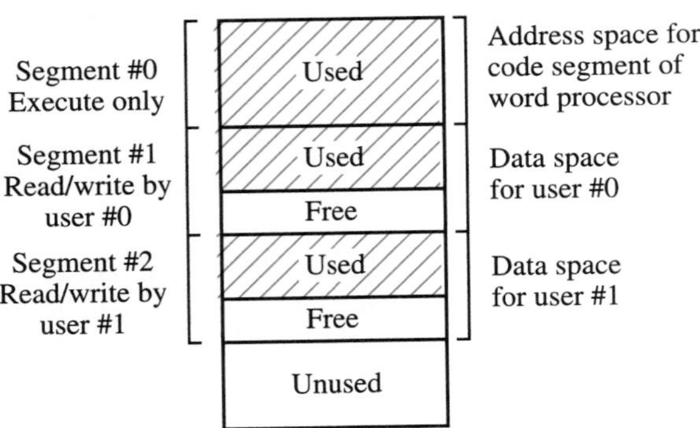

Figure 7-25 A segmented memory allows two users to share the same word processor.

ticated user such as a computer programmer may see the segmentation frequently when array pointers are pushed past segment boundaries in errant programs.

In order to specify an address in a segmented memory, the user's program must specify a segment number and an address within the segment. The operating system then translates the user's segmented address to a physical address.

7.7.4 *FRAGMENTATION*

When a computer is booted up, it goes through an initialization sequence that loads the operating system into memory. A portion of the address space may be reserved for I/O devices, and the remainder of the address space is then available for use by the operating system. This remaining portion of the address space may be only partially filled with physical memory: The rest comprises a dead zone, which must never be accessed since there is no hardware that responds to the dead zone addresses.

Figure 7-26a shows the state of a memory just after the initialization sequence. The "free area" is a section of memory that is available to the operating system for loading and executing programs. During the course of operation, programs of various sizes will be loaded into memory and executed. When a program finishes execution, the memory space that is assigned to that program is released to the operating system. As programs are loaded and executed, the free area becomes

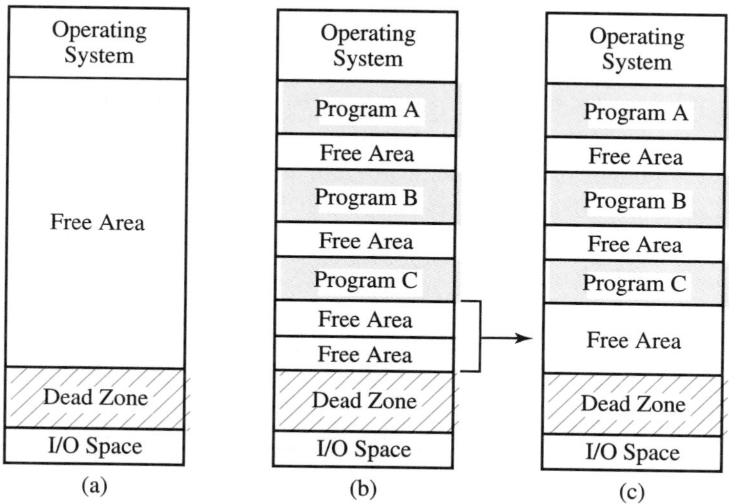

Figure 7-26 (a) Free area of memory after initialization; (b) after fragmentation; (c) after coalescing.

subdivided into a collection of small areas, none of which may be large enough to hold a program that would fit unless some or all of the free areas are combined into a single large area. This is a problem known as **fragmentation** and is encountered with segmentation, because the segments must ultimately be mapped within a single linear address space.

Figure 7-26b illustrates the fragmentation problem. When the operating system needs to find a free area that is large enough to hold a program, it will rarely find an exact match. The free area will generally be larger than the program, which has the effect of subdividing the free areas more finely as programs are mismatched with free areas. One method of assigning programs to free areas is called **first fit**, in which the free areas are scanned until a large enough area is found that will satisfy the program. Another method is called **best fit**, in which the free area is used that wastes the least amount of space. While best fit makes better use of memory than first fit, it requires more time because all of the free areas must be scanned.

Regardless of which algorithm is used, the process of assigning programs or data to free areas tends to produce smaller free areas (Knuth, 1974). This makes it more difficult to find a single contiguous free area that is large enough to satisfy the needs of the operating system. An approach that helps to solve this problem coalesces adjacent free areas into a single larger free area. In Figure 7-26b, the two adjacent free areas are combined into a single free area, as illustrated in Figure 7-26c.

7.7.5 *VIRTUAL MEMORY VERSUS CACHE MEMORY*

Virtual memory is divided into pages, which are relatively large when compared with cache memory blocks, which tend to be only a few words in size. Copies of the most heavily used blocks are kept in cache memory as well as in main memory, and also in the virtual memory image that is stored on a hard disk. When a memory reference is made on a computer that contains both cache and virtual memories, the cache hardware sees the reference first and satisfies the reference if the word is in the cache. If the referenced word is not in the cache, then the block that contains the word is read into the cache from the main memory, and the referenced word is then taken from the cache. If the page that contains the word is not in the main memory, then the page is brought into the main memory from a disk unit, and the block is then loaded into the cache so that the reference can be satisfied.

The use of virtual memory causes some intricate interactions with the cache. For example, since more than one program may be using the cache and the virtual memory, the timing statistics for two runs of a program executing on the same set of data may be different. Also, when a dirty block needs to be written back to main memory, it is possible that the page frame that contains the corresponding virtual page has been overwritten. This causes the page to be loaded back to main memory from secondary memory in order to flush the dirty block from the cache memory to the main memory.

7.7.6 *THE TRANSLATION LOOKASIDE BUFFER*

The virtual memory mechanism, while being an elegant solution to the problem of accessing large programs and data files, has a significant problem associated with it. At least two memory references are needed to access a value in memory: One reference is to the page table to find the physical page frame, and another reference is for the actual data value. The **translation lookaside buffer** (TLB) is a solution to this problem.

The TLB is a small associative memory typically placed inside of the CPU that stores the most recent translations from virtual to physical address. The first time a given virtual address is translated into a physical address, this translation is stored in the TLB. Each time the CPU issues a virtual address, the TLB is searched for that virtual address. If the virtual page number exists in the TLB, the TLB returns the physical page number, which can be immediately sent to the main memory (but normally, the cache memory would intercept the reference to main memory and satisfy the reference out of the cache).

An example TLB is shown in Figure 7-27. The TLB holds 8 entries, for a system that has 32 pages and 16 page frames. The virtual page field is 5 bits wide because there are $2^5 = 32$ pages. Likewise, the physical page field is 4 bits wide because there are 2^4=16 page frames.

TLB misses are handled in much the same way as with other memory misses. Upon a TLB miss the virtual address is applied to the virtual memory system, where it is looked up in the page table in main memory. If it is found in the page table, then the TLB is updated, and the next reference to that page will thus result in a TLB hit.

Valid	Virtual page number	Physical page number
1	01001	1100
1	10111	1001
0	-----	----
0	-----	----
1	01110	0000
0	-----	----
1	00110	0111
0	-----	----

Figure 7-27 An example TLB that holds 8 entries for a system with 32 virtual pages and 16 page frames.

7.8 Advanced Topics

This section covers two topics that are of practical importance in designing memory systems: Tree decoders and content addressable memories. The former are required in large memories. The latter are required for associative caches, such as a TLB, or in other situations when data must be looked up at high speed based on its value rather than on the address of where it is stored.

7.8.1 *TREE DECODERS*

Decoders (see Appendix A) do not scale well to large sizes due to practical limitations on fan-in and fan-out. The decoder circuit shown in Figure 7-28 illustrates the problem. For N address bits, every AND gate has a fan-in of N. Each address line is fanned out to 2^N AND gates. The circuit depth is two gates.

The circuit shown in Figure 7-29a is a **tree decoder**, which reduces the fan-in and fan-out by increasing circuit depth. For this case, each AND gate has a fan-in of F (for this example, $F = 2$) and only the address line that is introduced at the deepest level (a_0 here) is fanned out to $2^N/2$ AND gates. The depth has now increased to $log_F(2^N)$. The large fan-out for the higher order address bits may be a problem, but this can be easily fixed without increasing the circuit depth by adding fan-out buffers in the earlier levels, as shown in Figure 7-29b.

Thus, the depth of a memory decoder tree is $log_F(2^N)$, the width is 2^N, and the maximum fan-in and fan-out of the logic gates within the decoder is F.

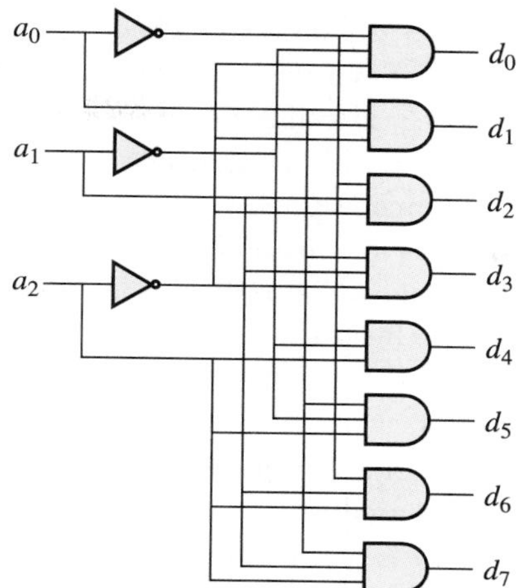

Figure 7-28 A conventional decoder.

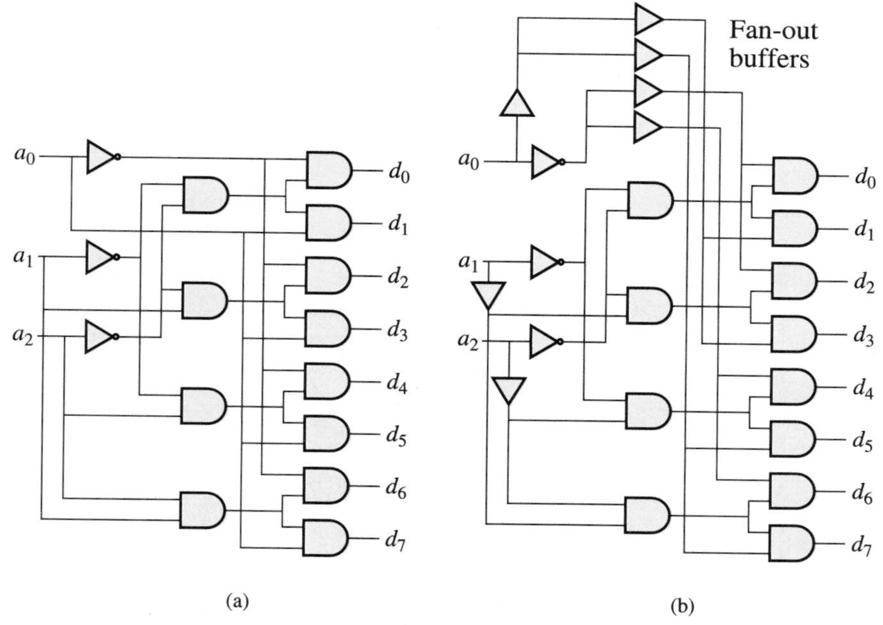

Figure 7-29 (a) A tree decoder; (b) a tree decoder with fan-ins and fan-outs of two.

7.8.2 *DECODERS FOR LARGE RAMS*

For very large RAMs, if the 2-1/2D decoding scheme is not used, tree decoders are employed to keep fan-in and fan-out to manageable levels. In a conventional RAM an M-bit-wide address uniquely identifies one memory location out of a memory space of 2^M locations. In order to access a particular location, an address is presented to the root of a decoder tree containing M levels and 2^M leaves. Starting with the root (the top level of the tree) a decision is made at each ith level of the tree, corresponding to the ith bit of the address. If the ith bit is 0 at the ith level, then the tree is traversed to the left, otherwise the tree is traversed to the right. The target leaf is at level $M - 1$ (counting starts at 0). There is exactly one leaf for each memory address.

The tree structure results in an access time that is logarithmic in the size of the memory. That is, if a RAM contains N words, then the memory can be accessed in $O\lceil log_F N \rceil$ time, where F is the fan-out of the logic gates in the decoder tree (here, we assume a fan-out of two). For a RAM of size $N, M = \lceil log_F N \rceil$ address bits are needed to identify each word uniquely. As the number of words in the memory grows, the length of the address grows logarithmically, so that one level of depth is added to the decoder tree each time the size of the memory doubles. As a practical example, consider a 128-megaword memory that requires 27 levels of decoding (2^{27} = 128 Mwords). If we assume that logic gates in the decoding tree switch in 2 ns, then an address can be decoded in 54 ns.

A four-level decoder tree for a 16-word RAM is shown in Figure 7-30. As an example of how the decoder tree works, the address 1011 is presented at the root node. The most significant bit in the address is a 1, so the right path is traversed at Level 0 as indicated by the arrow. The next most significant bit is a 0, so the left path is traversed at Level 1; the next bit is a 1, so the right path is traversed at Level 2; and the least significant bit is a 1, so the rightmost path is traversed next and the addressed leaf is then reached at Level 3.

7.8.3 *CONTENT-ADDRESSABLE (ASSOCIATIVE) MEMORIES*

In an ordinary RAM, an address is applied to the memory, and the contents of the given location are either read or written. In a **content-addressable memory** (CAM), also known as an associative memory, a word composed of **fields** is applied to the memory and the resulting address (or index) is returned if the word or field is present in the memory. The physical location of a CAM word is generally not as significant as the values contained in the fields of the word. Relationships between addresses, values, and fields for RAM and CAM are shown in Figure 7-31.

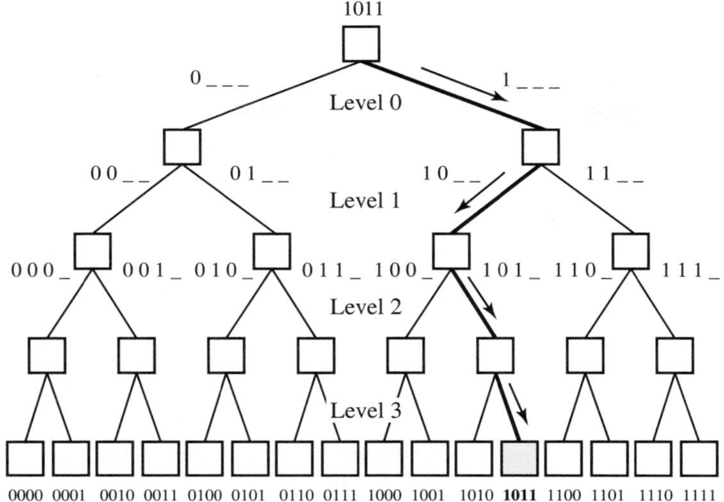

Figure 7-30 A decoding tree for a 16-word random access memory.

Random access memory

Address	Value
0000A000	0F0F0000
0000A004	186734F1
0000A008	0F000000
0000A00C	FE681022
0000A010	3152467C
0000A014	C3450917
0000A018	00392B11
0000A01C	10034561
← 32 bits →	← 32 bits →

Content addressable memory

Field1	Field2	Field3
000	A	9E
011	0	F0
149	7	01
091	4	00
000	E	FE
749	C	6E
000	0	50
575	1	84
← 12 bits →	← 4 bits →	← 8 bits →

Figure 7-31 Relationships between random access memory and content addressable memory.

Values are stored in sequential locations in a RAM, with an address acting as the key to locate a word. Four-byte address increments are used in this example, in which the word size is four bytes. Values are stored in fields in the CAM, and in principle any field of a word can be used to key on the rest of the word. If the CAM words are reordered, then the contents of the CAM are virtually unchanged since physical location has no bearing on the interpretation of the fields. A reordering of the RAM may change the meanings of its values entirely. This comparison suggests that CAM may be a preferred means for storing information when there is a significant cost in maintaining data in sorted order.

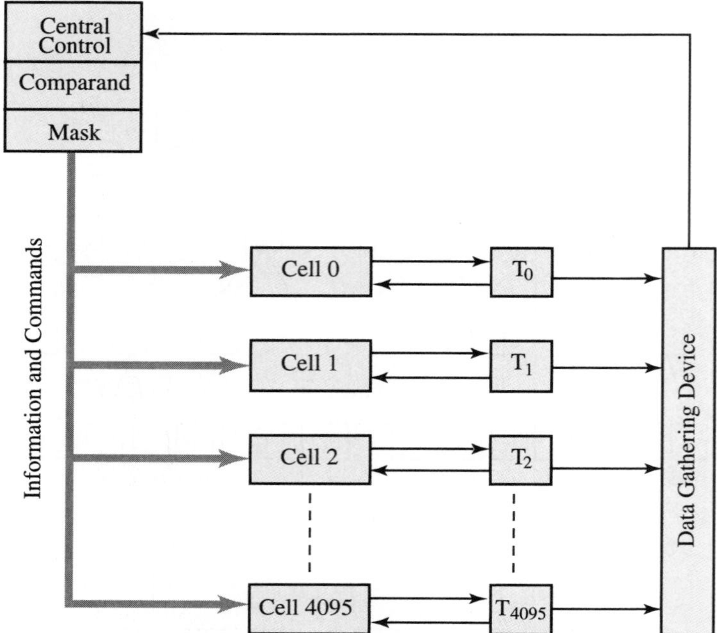

Figure 7-32 Overview of CAM (Adopted from Foster, 1976).

When a search is made through a RAM for a particular value, the entire memory may need to be searched, one word at a time, when the memory is not sorted. When the RAM is maintained in sorted order, a number of accesses may still be required to either find the value being searched or to determine the value is not stored in the memory. In a CAM, the value being searched is broadcast to all of the words simultaneously, and logic at each word makes a field comparison for membership, and in just a few steps the answer is known. A few additional steps may be needed to collect the results, but in general the time required to search a CAM is less than for a RAM in the same technology, for a number of applications.

Except for maintaining tags in cache memories and in translating among network addresses for routing applications (see Chapter 8), CAMs are not in common use largely due to the difficulty of implementing an efficient design with conventional technology. Consider the block diagram of a CAM shown in Figure 7-32. A central control unit sends a comparand to each of 4096 cells, where comparisons are made. The result is put in the tag bits T_i, which are collected by a data gathering device and sent to the central control unit (note that "tag" is

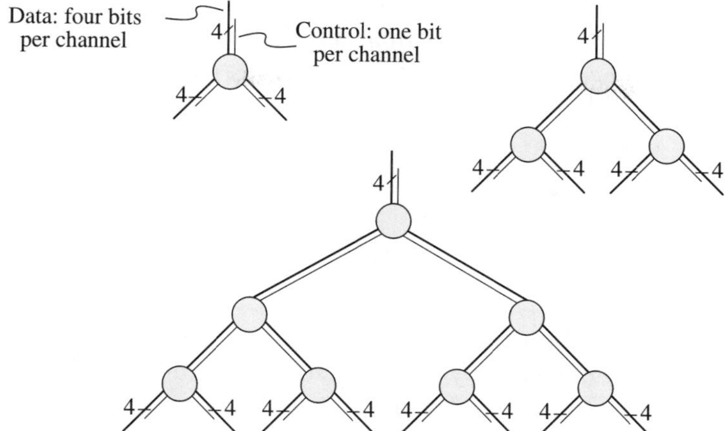

Figure 7-33 Addressing subtrees for a CAM.

used differently here than in cache memory). When the central control unit loads the value to be searched into the comparand register, it sets up a mask to block out fields that are not part of the value. A small local processor in each cell makes a comparison between its local word and the broadcast value and reports the result of the comparison to the data gathering device.

A number of problems arise when an attempt is made to implement this CAM architecture in a conventional technology such as **very large scale integration** (VLSI). The broadcast function that sends the comparand to the cells can be implemented with low latency if a tree structure is used. An H-tree (Mead and Conway, 1980) can be used for the tree layout if it will fit on a single IC. If the tree cannot be contained on a single chip, then connections must be made among a number of chips, which quickly limits chip density. For example, a node of a tree that has a single four-bit input and two four-bit outputs needs 12 input/output (I/O) pins and three control pins if only one node is placed on a chip. A three-node subtree needs 25 pins and a seven-node subtree needs 45 pins, as illustrated in Figure 7-33. A 63-node subtree requires 325 pins, excluding power and control pins, which is getting close to the limit of most present-day packaging technologies, which do not go much higher than 1000 pins per package. A useful CAM would contain thousands of such nodes with wider data paths, so the I/O bandwidth limit is realized early in the design of the CAM. Compromises can be made by multiplexing data onto the limited number of I/O connections, but this reduces effective speed, which is a major reason for using a CAM in the first place.

Although implementations of CAMs are difficult, they do find practical uses, such as in TLBs and in computer networks. One application is in a network controller, which receives data packets from several processors and then distributes those packets back to the processors or to other network controllers. Each processor has a unique address, which the CAM keys on to determine if the target processor for a packet is in its own network or if it must be forwarded to another network.

MEMORY DESIGN EXAMPLE: A DUAL-PORT RAM

A **dual-read**, or **dual-port**, RAM allows any two words to be read simultaneously from the same memory. As an example, we will design a 2^{20}-word by 8-bit dual-read RAM. For our design, any two words can be read at a time, but only one word can be written at a time. Our approach is to create two separate 2^{20}-word memories. When writing into the dual-read RAM, the address lines of both single-read RAMs are set identically and the same data is written to both single-read memories. During a read operation, the address lines of each single-read RAM are set independently, so that two different words can be simultaneously read.

Figure 7-34 shows a block diagram for the dual-read RAM. During a write operation, the A address is used for both single-read RAMs. Tri-state buffers at the B RAM address inputs are controlled by the $\overline{WR}$ line. When $WR = 0$, the A address is used at the B address input, otherwise, the B address is used at the B address input. The numbers that appear adjacent to the slashes indicate the number of individual lines that are represented by the single line. An 8 next to a slash indicates 8 lines, and a 20 next to a slash indicates 20 lines.

Each tri-state buffer has 20 input lines and 20 output lines, but Figure 7-34 uses a notation in which a single buffer represents 20 separate tri-state buffers that share the same control input. A buffer delay is inserted on the *WR* line in order to compensate for the delay on the complemented *WR* line, so that the A and B addresses are not unintentionally simultaneously enabled. ■

7.9 Case Study: Rambus Memory

There was a time when computer technology would be pushed from the laboratory into the marketplace. As the consumer marketplace for computing devices exploded, the "technology push" was replaced by "market pull," and consumer demand then dominated the preferences of technologists when it came to devel-

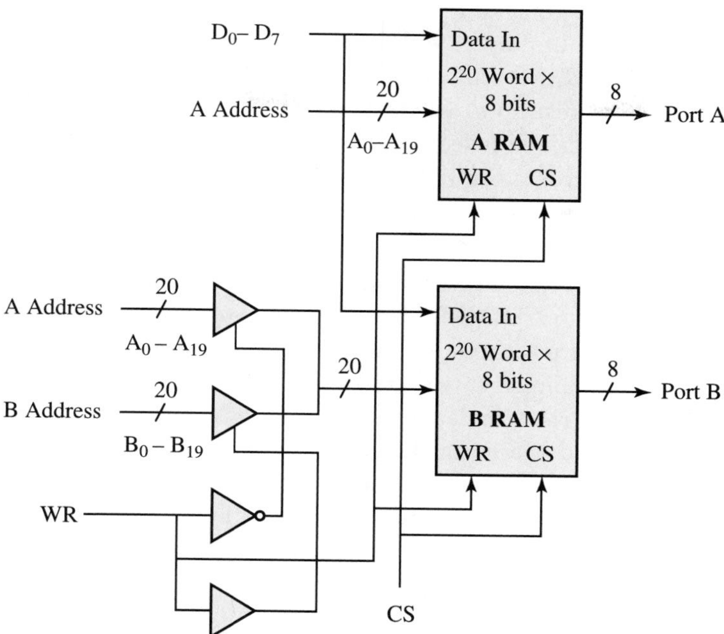

Figure 7-34 Block diagram of dual-read RAM.

oping a new memory technology. High-performance, expensive memory for high-end processors was displaced by high-density, low-cost memory for consumer electronics, such as videogames. It became more profitable for memory manufacturers to address the needs of high-volume consumer markets than to devote costly chip fabrication facilities to a comparatively small high-end market.

The consumer electronics industry now dominates the memory market, and even high-end, non consumer processors make heavy use of consumer electronics technology, exploiting architectural enhancements instead, or innovations in supporting technologies (such as high-speed interconnects) to compensate for the performance shortcomings of what we might call "videogame memory."

Videogame memory is not all that low end, however, and in fact makes use of extraordinary technology enhancements that squeeze the most performance out of ever denser, low-cost devices. A leading memory technology that is being introduced into Intel-based personal computers in 1999 was developed by Rambus, Inc. The Rambus DRAM (RDRAM) retrieves a block of 8 bytes internal to the DRAM chip on every access and multiplexes the 8 bytes onto a narrow 8-bit or 16-bit channel, operating at a rate of 800 MHz (or higher).

A typical DRAM core (that is, the storage portion of an ordinary DRAM) can store or retrieve a line of 8 bytes with a 100-MHz cycle. This is internal to the DRAM chip: Most DRAMs only deliver 1 byte per cycle, but the RDRAM technology can multiplex that up to 1 byte per cycle using a higher external clock of 800 MHz. That higher rate is fed to a memory controller (the "chipset" on an Intel machine), which demuxes it to a 32-bit-wide data stream at a lower rate, such as 200 MHz, going into a Pentium (or other processor chip).

The Rambus "RIMM" modules (Rambus Inline Memory Modules) look similar to ordinary SIMMs and DIMMs, but they operate differently. The Rambus memory uses **microstrip technology** (also known as **transmission lines**) on the motherboard, which implements a crude shield that reduces **radio frequency** (RF) effects that interfere with data traveling through wires on the motherboard, which are called board **traces**. In designing a printed circuit board (PCB) for Rambus technology, the critical parameters are (1) dielectric thickness of the PCB, (2) separation of the memory modules, and (3) trace width. There must be a ground plane (an electrical return path) beneath every signal line, with no vias (connections between board layers) along the path. All signals go on the top layer of the PCB. (A PCB can have a number of layers, but typically has no more than 8.) The memory controller and memory modules must all be equally spaced, such as .5 inches from the memory controller to the first RIMM, then .5 in to the next, etc.

The "Rambus Channel" is made up of transmission line traces. The trace widths end up being about twice as wide as ordinary traces, on the order of 12 mils (300 microns). Although 300 microns is relatively small for a board trace, if we want to send 128 signals over a PCB, using a 600-micron **pitch** (center-to-center spacing) with 300 microns between 300 micron traces, this corresponds to a footprint of 128 × 600 microns = 76 mm. This is a large footprint compared with lower-speed solutions that allow a much closer packing density.

In reality, the Rambus Channel only has 13 high-speed signals (the address is serialized onto a single line, there are 8 data lines, 1 parity line, 2 clock lines, and 1 command line) and so the seemingly large footprint is not a near-term problem. With a 16-bit version of the Rambus Channel on the horizon, the bandwidth problem appears to be in hand for a number of years using this technology. Extensibility to large word widths such as 64 bits or 128 bits will pose a significant challenge down the road, however, because the chipset will need to support that same word width—a formidable task with current packaging methods, which provide for over 500 pins on the chipset.

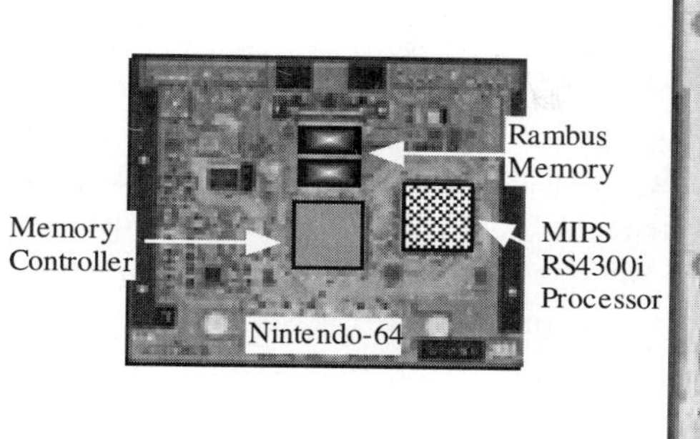

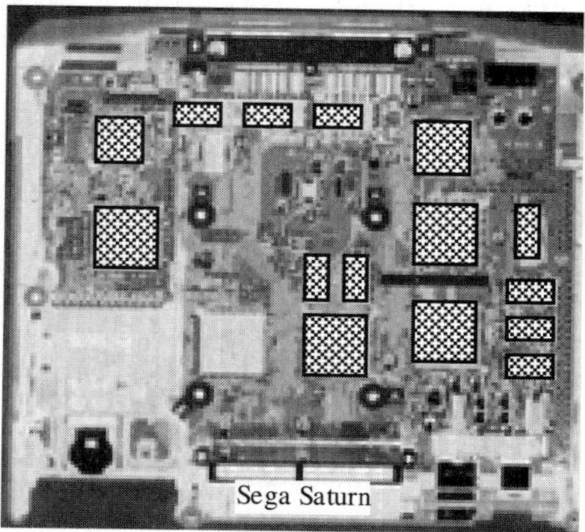

Figure 7-35 Rambus technology on the Nintendo 64 motherboard (top left) enables cost savings over the conventional Sega Saturn motherboard design (top right). The Nintendo 64 uses costlier plug-in cartridges (bottom), as opposed to inexpensive CD-ROMs used by the Sega Saturn.

Although Rambus memory of this type became available in 1998, the RIMM modules were not widely available until 1999, timed for the availability of a new memory controller (chipset) for the RIMMs. The memory controller is an important aspect of this type of memory because the view of memory that the CPU perceives is different from the physical memory.

Rambus memory is more expensive than conventional DRAM memory, but overall system cost can be reduced, which makes it attractive in low-cost, high-performance consumer electronics such as the Nintendo 64 video game console. The Nintendo 64 (see Figure 7-35) has four primary chips: A 64-bit MIPS RS4300i CPU; A Reality coprocessor, which integrates all graphics, audio, and memory management functions; and two Rambus memory chips.

The Rambus technology provides the Nintendo 64 with a bandwidth of 562.5 MB/s using a 31-pin interface to the memory controller. By comparison, a system using typical 64-bit-wide synchronous DRAMs (SDRAMs) requires a 110-pin interface to the memory controller. This reduction in pin count allows the memory controller to fit on the same **die** (the silicon chip) as the graphics and sound functions, in a relatively low-cost, 160-pin packaged chip.

The Rambus memory subsystem is made up of two memory chips that occupy 1.5 square inches of board space. An equivalent SDRAM design would require 6 square inches of board space. The space savings of using the Rambus approach enabled Nintendo to fit all of its components on a board measuring five by six inches, which is one quarter the size of the system board used in the competing Sega Saturn. In addition, Nintendo was able to use only a two-layer board instead of the four layers used in the Sega Saturn.

The cost savings Nintendo realized by choosing the Rambus solution over the 64-bit SDRAM approach are considerable but should be placed in perspective with the overall market. The ability to use a two-layer implementation saved Nintendo $5 per unit in manufacturing costs. Taken together, Nintendo estimates the total bill of materials cost savings over an equivalent SDRAM-based design was about 20%.

These cost savings need to be placed in perspective with the marketplace, however. The competing Sega Saturn and Sony Playstation use CD-ROMs for game storage, which cost under $2 each to mass produce. The Nintendo 64 uses a plug-in ROM cartridge that costs closer to $10 each to mass produce and can only store 1% of what can be stored on a CD-ROM. This choice of media may have a great impact on the overall system architecture, and so the Rambus approach may not benefit all systems to the same degree. Details matter a great deal when it comes to evaluating the impact of a new technology on a particular market, or even a segment of a market.

7.10 Case Study: The Intel Pentium Memory System

The Intel Pentium processor is typical of modern processors in its memory configurations. Figure 7-36 shows a simplified diagram of the memory elements and data paths. There are two L1 caches on board the actual Pentium chip, an instruction, or I-cache, and a data, or D-cache. Each cache has a 256 bit (32 byte) line size, with an equally sized data path to the CPU. The L1 caches are two-way set associative, and each way has a single LRU bit. The D-cache can be set to write-through or write-back on a per-line basis. The D cache is write no-allocate: Misses on writes do not result in a cache fill. Each cache is also

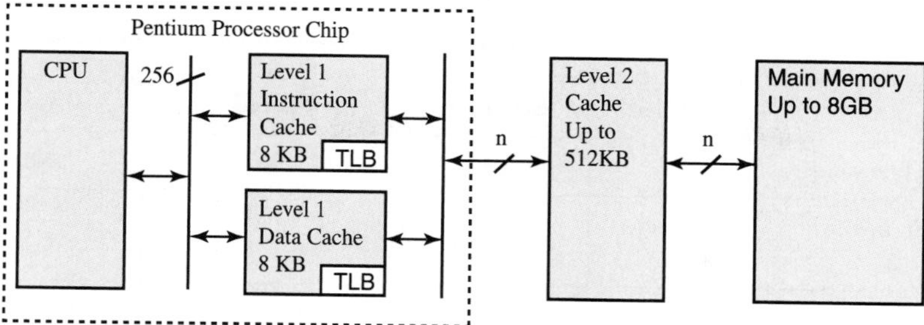

Figure 7-36 The Intel Pentium memory system.

equipped with a TLB that translates virtual to physical addresses. The D-cache TLB is four-way set associative, with 64 entries, and is dual ported, allowing two simultaneous data reference translations. The I-cache TLB is four-way set associative with 32 entries.

The L2 cache, if present, is two-way set associative and can be 256 KB or 512 KB in size. The data bus, shown as "*n*" in the figure, can be 32, 64, or 128 bits in size.

THE MESI PROTOCOL

The Pentium D cache, and the L2 cache if present, support the MESI cache coherency protocol for managing multiprocessor access to memory. Each D-cache line has two bits associated with it that store the MESI state. Each cache line will be in one of the four states:

- M—Modified. The contents of the cache line have been modified and are different from main memory.

- E—Exclusive. The contents of the cache line have not been modified and are the same as the line in main memory.

- S—Shared. The line is, or may be, shared with another cache line belonging to another processor.

- I—Invalid. The line is not in the cache. Reads to lines in the I state will result in cache misses.

Cache Line State	M Modified	E Exclusive	S Shared	I Invalid
Cache line valid?	Yes	Yes	Yes	No
Copy in memory is	out of date.	valid	valid	—
Copies exist in other caches?	No	No	Maybe	Maybe
A write to this line	does not go to the bus.	does not go to the bus.	goes to the bus and updates cache.	goes directly to the bus.

Table 7-2 MESI cache line states.

Table 7-2[1] shows the relationship between the MESI state, the cache line, and the equivalent line in main memory. The MESI protocol is becoming a standard way of dealing with cache coherency in multiprocessor systems.

The Pentium processor also supports up to six main memory segments (there can be several thousand segments, but no more than 6 can be referenced through the segment registers). As discussed in the chapter, each segment is a separate address space. Each segment has a base—a starting location within the 32-bit physical address space, and a limit, the maximum size of the segment. The limit may be either 2^{16} bytes or $2^{16} \times 2^{12}$ bytes in size. That is, the granularity of the limit may be one byte or 2^{12} bytes in size.

Paging and segmentation on the Pentium can be applied in any combination:

Unsegmented, unpaged memory. The virtual address space is the same as the physical address space. No page tables or mapping hardware is needed. This is good for high-performance applications that do not have a lot of complexity (that do not need to support growing tables, for example).

Unsegmented, paged memory. Same as for the unsegmented, unpaged memory, except that the linear address space is larger as a result of using disk storage. A page table is needed to translate between virtual and physical addresses. A trans-

[1]Taken from *Pentium Processor User's Manual, Volume 3, Architecture and Programming Manual,* © Intel Corporation, 1993.

lation lookaside buffer is needed on the Pentium core, working in conjunction with the L1 cache, to reduce the number of page table accesses.

Segmented, unpaged memory. Good for high-complexity applications that need to support growing data structures. This is also fast: Segments are fewer in number than pages in a virtual memory, and all of the segmentation mapping hardware typically fits on the CPU chip. There is no need for disk accesses as there would be for paging, and so access times are more predictable than when paging is used.

Segmented, paged memory. A page table, segment mapping registers, and TLB all work in conjunction to support multiple address spaces.

Segmentation on the Intel Pentium processor is quite powerful but is also quite complex. We only explore the basics here, and the interested reader is referred to (Intel, 1993) for a more complete description.

■ SUMMARY

Memory is organized in a hierarchy in which the densest memory offers the least performance, whereas the greatest performance is realized with the memory that has the least density. In order to bridge the gap between the two, the principle of locality is exploited in cache and virtual memories.

A cache memory maintains the most frequently used blocks in a small, fast memory that is local to the CPU. A paged virtual memory augments a main memory with disk storage. The physical memory serves as a window on the paged virtual memory, which is maintained in its entirety on a hard magnetic disk.

Cache and paged virtual memories are commonly used on the same computer, but for different reasons. A cache memory improves the average access time to the main memory, whereas a paged virtual memory extends the size of the main memory.

In an example memory architecture, the Intel Pentium has a split L1 cache and a TLB that reside on the Pentium core, and a unified L2 cache that resides in the same package as the Pentium although on a different silicon die. When paging is implemented, the page table is located in main memory, with the TLB reducing the number of times that the TLB is referenced. The L1 and L2 cache memories then reduce the number of times main memory is accessed for data. The Pentium also supports segmentation, which has its own set of mapping registers and control hardware that resides on the Pentium.

FURTHER READING

(Stallings, 1993) and (Mano, 1991) give readable explanations of RAM. A number of memory databooks [(Micron, 1992) and (Texas Instruments, 1991)] give practical examples of memory organization. (Foster, 1976) is the seminal reference on CAM. (Mead and Conway, 1980) describe the H-tree structure in the context of VLSI design. (Franklin et al., 1982) explores issues in partitioning chips, which arise in splitting an H-tree for a CAM. (Sedra and Smith, 1997) discuss the implementation of several kinds of static and dynamic RAM.

(Hamacher et al., 1990) gives a classic treatment of cache memory. (Tanenbaum, 1990) gives a readable explanation of virtual memory. (Hennessy and Patterson, 1995) and (Przybylski, 1990) cover issues relating to cache performance. Segmentation on the Intel Pentium processor is covered in (Intel, 1993). Kingston Technology gives a broad tutorial on memory technologies at http://www.kingston.com/king/mg0.htm.

Foster, C. C., *Content Addressable Parallel Processors*, Van Nostrand Reinhold Company (1976).

Franklin, M. A., D. F. Wann, and W. J. Thomas, "Pin Limitations and Partitioning of VLSI Interconnection Networks," *IEEE Trans Comp.*, **C-31**, 1109 (Nov. 1982).

Hamacher, V. C., Z. G. Vranesic, and S. G. Zaky, *Computer Organization*, 3/e, McGraw-Hill (1990).

Hennessy, J. L. and D. A. Patterson, *Computer Architecture: A Quantitative Approach*, 2/e, Morgan Kaufmann Publishers (1995).

Intel Corporation, *Pentium Processor User's Manual*, Volume 3: *Architecture and Programming Manual* (1993).

Knuth, D., *The Art of Computer Programming: Fundamental Algorithms*, vol. 1, 2/e, Addison-Wesley (1974).

Mano, M., *Digital Design*, 2/e, Prentice Hall (1991).

Mead, C. and L. Conway, *Introduction to VLSI Systems*, Addison-Wesley (1980).

Micron, *DRAM Data Book*, Micron Technologies, Inc., 2805 East Columbia Road, Boise, Idaho (1992).

Przybylski, S. A., *Cache and Memory Hierarchy Design*, Morgan Kaufmann Publishers (1990).

Sedra, A. and Smith, K., *Microelectronic Circuits*, 4/e, Oxford University Press (1997).

Stallings, W., *Computer Organization and Architecture*, 3/e, Macmillan (1993).

Tanenbaum, A., *Structured Computer Organization*, 3/e, Prentice Hall (1990).

Texas Instruments, *MOS Memory: Commercial and Military Specifications Data Book*, Texas Instruments, Literature Response Center, P.O. Box 172228, Denver, Colorado (1991).

■ PROBLEMS

7.1 A ROM lookup table and two D flip-flops implement a state machine as shown in the following diagram. Construct a state table that describes the machine.

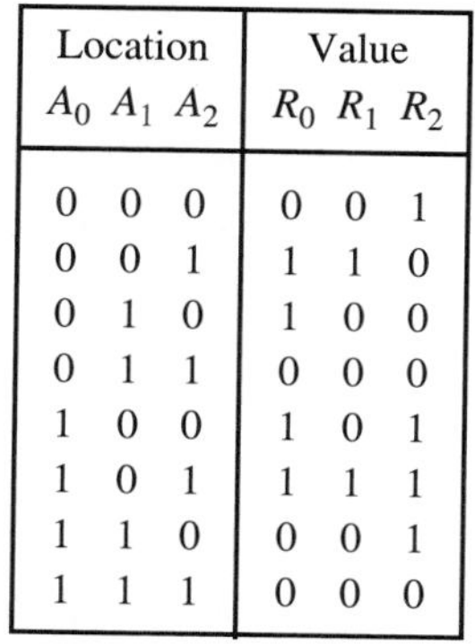

ROM contents

Location A_0 A_1 A_2	Value R_0 R_1 R_2
0 0 0	0 0 1
0 0 1	1 1 0
0 1 0	1 0 0
0 1 1	0 0 0
1 0 0	1 0 1
1 0 1	1 1 1
1 1 0	0 0 1
1 1 1	0 0 0

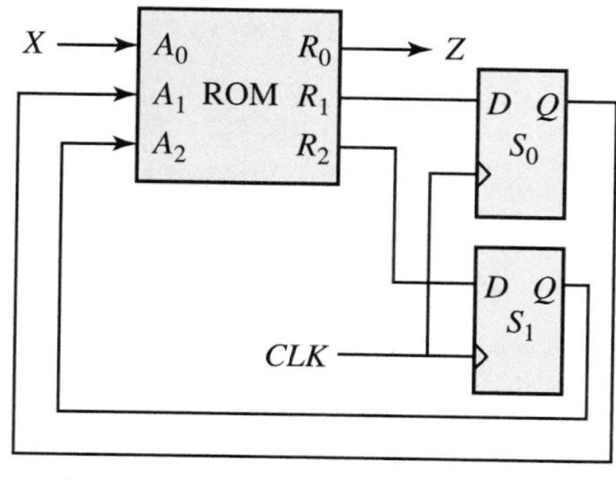

7.2 Fill in four memory locations for the lookup table shown in Figure 7-11 in which each of the four operations: add, subtract, multiply, and divide are performed on $A = 16$ and $B = 4$. Show the address and the value for each case.

7.3 Design an eight-word, 32-bit RAM using 8×8 RAMs.

7.4 Design a 16-word, four-bit RAM using 4×4 RAMs and a single external decoder.

7.5 Given a number of n-word by p-bit RAM chips,

(a) Show how to construct an n-word $\times$ $4p$-bit RAM using these chips. Use any other logic components that you have seen in the text that you feel are needed.

(b) Show how to construct a $4n$-word $\times$ p-bit RAM using these chips.

7.6 Draw the circuit for a 4-to-16 tree decoder, using a maximum fan-in and fan-out of two.

7.7 A direct mapped cache consists of 128 slots. Main memory contains 16K blocks of 16 words each. Access time of the cache is 10 ns, and the time required to fill a cache slot is 200 ns. Load-through is not used; that is, when an accessed word is not found in the cache, the entire block is brought into the cache, and the word is then accessed through the cache. Initially, the cache is empty. *Note*: When referring to memory, 1K = 1024.

(a) Show the format of the memory address.

(b) Compute the hit ratio for a program that loops 10 times from locations 15 to 200. Note that although the memory is accessed twice during a miss (once for the miss, and once again to satisfy the reference), a hit does not occur for this case. To a running program, only a single memory reference is observed.

(c) Compute the effective access time for this program.

7.8 A fully associative mapped cache has 16 blocks, with eight words per block. The size of main memory is 2^{16} words, and the cache is initially empty. Access time of the cache is 40 ns, and the time required to transfer eight words between main memory and the cache is 1 μs.

(a) Compute the sizes of the tag and word fields.

(b) Compute the hit ratio for a program that executes from 20 to 45, then loops four times from 28 to 45 before halting. Assume that when there is a miss, the entire cache slot is filled in 1 μs, and that the first word is not seen by the CPU until the entire slot is filled. That is, assume load-through is not used. Initially, the cache is empty.

(c) Compute the effective access time for the program described in part (b).

7.9 Compute the total number of bits of storage needed for the associative mapped cache shown in Figure 7-13 and the direct mapped cache shown in Figure 7-14. Include valid, dirty, and tag bits in your count. Assume that the word size is eight bits.

7.10 (a) How far apart do memory references need to be spaced to cause a miss on every cache access using the direct mapping parameters shown in Figure 7-14?

(b) Using your solution for part (a), compute the hit ratio and effective access time for that program with T_{Miss} = 1000 ns and T_{Hit} = 10 ns. Assume that load-through is used.

7.11 A computer has 16 pages of virtual address space but only four physical page frames. Initially the physical memory is empty. A program references the virtual pages in the order 0 2 4 5 2 4 3 11 2 10.

(a) Which references cause a page fault with the LRU page replacement policy?

(b) Which references cause a page fault with the FIFO page replacement policy?

7.12 On some computers, the page table is stored in memory. What would happen if the page table is swapped out to disk? Since the page table is used for every memory reference, is there a page replacement policy that guarantees that the page table will not get swapped out? Assume that the page table is small enough to fit into a single page (although usually it is not).

7.13 A virtual memory system has a page size of 1024 words, eight virtual pages, four physical page frames, and uses the LRU page replacement policy.

The page table is as follows:

Page #	Present bit	Disk address	Page frame field
0	0	01001011100	xx
1	0	11101110010	xx
2	1	10110010111	00
3	0	00001001111	xx
4	1	01011100101	01
5	0	10100111001	xx
6	1	00110101100	11
7	0	01010001011	xx

(a) What is the main memory address for virtual address 4096?

(b) What is the main memory address for virtual address 1024?

(c) A fault occurs on page 0. Which page frame will be used for virtual page 0?

7.14 When running a particular program with N memory accesses, a computer with a cache and paged virtual memory generates a total of M cache misses and F page faults. T_1 is the time for a cache hit; T_2 is the time for a main memory hit; and T_3 is the time to load a page into main memory from the disk.

(a) What is the cache hit ratio?

(b) What is the main memory hit ratio? That is, what percentage of main memory accesses do not generate a page fault?

(c) What is the overall effective access time for the system?

7.15 A computer contains both cache and paged virtual memories. The cache can hold either physical or virtual addresses, but not both. What are the issues involved in choosing between caching virtual or physical addresses? How can these problems be solved by using a single unit that manages all memory mapping functions?

7.16 How much storage is needed for the page table for a virtual memory that has 2^{32} bytes, with 2^{12} bytes per page and 8 bytes per page table entry?

7.17 Compute the gate input count for the decoder(s) of a 64 × 1-bit RAM for both the 2D and the 2-1/2D cases. Assume that an unlimited fan-in/fan-out is allowed. For both cases, use ordinary two-level decoders. For the 2-1/2D case, treat the column decoder as an ordinary MUX. That is, ignore its behavior as a DEMUX during a write operation.

7.18 How many levels of decoding are needed for a 2^{20}-word 2D memory if a fan-in of four and a fan-out of four are used in the decoder tree?

7.19 A video game cartridge needs to store 2^{20} bytes in a ROM.

(a) If a 2D organization is used, how many leaves will be at the deepest level of the decoder tree?

(b) How many leaves will there be at the deepest level of the decoder tree for a 2-1/2D organization?

7.20 The contents of a CAM are shown. Which set of words will respond if a key of 00A00020 is used on fields 1 and 3? Fields 1 and 3 of the key must match the corresponding fields of a CAM word in order for that word to respond. The remaining fields are ignored during the matching process but are included in the retrieved words.

Field → 4	3	2	1	0
F 1	A	0 0	0 2	8
0 4	2	9 D	1 F	0
3 2	A	1 1	0 3	E
D F	A	0 5	0 2	D
0 0	5	3 7	F 2	4

7.21 When the TLB shown in Figure 7-27 has a miss, it accesses the page table to resolve the reference. How many entries are in that page table?

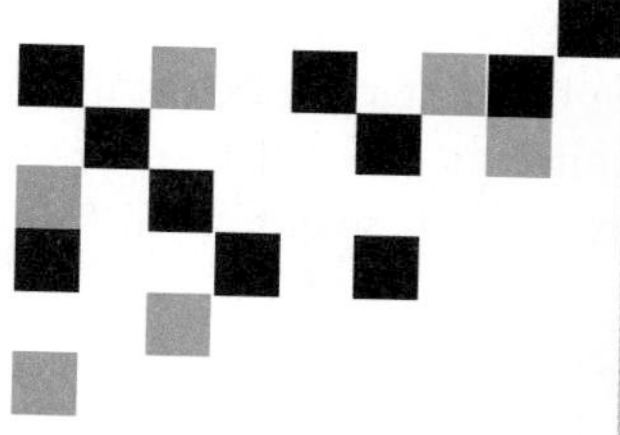

8 INPUT AND OUTPUT

In the earlier chapters, we considered how the CPU interacts with data that is accessed internal to the CPU or is accessed within the main memory, which may be extended to a hard magnetic disk through virtual memory. While the access speeds at the different levels of the memory hierarchy vary dramatically, for the most part the CPU sees the same response rate from one access to the next. The situation when accessing input/output (I/O) devices is very different.

- The speeds of I/O data transfers can range from extremely slow, such as reading data entered from a keyboard, to so fast that the CPU may not be able to keep up, as may be the case with data streaming from a fast disk drive or real-time graphics being written to a video monitor.
- I/O activities are **asynchronous**, that is, not synchronized to the CPU clock, as are memory data transfers. Additional signals, called **handshaking** signals, may need to be incorporated on a separate I/O bus to coordinate when the device is ready to have data read from it or written to it.
- The quality of the data may be suspect. For example, line noise during data transfers using the public switched telephone network, or errors caused by media defects on disk drives mean that error detection and correction strategies may be needed to ensure data integrity.
- Many I/O devices are mechanical and are in general more prone to failure than the CPU and main memory. A data transfer may be interrupted due to mechanical failure or special conditions such as a printer being out of paper.
- I/O software modules, referred to as **device drivers**, must be written in such a way as to address the aforementioned issues.

In this chapter, we discuss the nature of communicating using buses, starting first with simple bus fundamentals and then exploring multiple-bus architectures. We then take a look at some of the more common I/O devices that are connected to these buses.

In the next sections we discuss communications from the viewpoints of communications at the CPU and motherboard level and then branch out to the local area network.

8.1 Simple Bus Architectures

A computer system may contain many components that need to communicate with each other. In a worst-case scenario, all N components need to communicate simultaneously with every other component, in which $N^2/2$ links are needed for N components. The number of links becomes prohibitively large for even small values of N, but fortunately, as for long distance telecommunication, not all devices need to communicate simultaneously.

A **bus** is a common pathway that connects a number of devices. An example of a bus can be found on the **motherboard** (the main circuit board that contains the central processing unit) of a personal computer, as illustrated in simplified form in Figure 8-1. (For a look at a real motherboard, see Figure 1-6.) A typical motherboard contains **integrated circuits** (ICs) such as the CPU chip and memory chips, board **traces** (wires) that connect the chips, and a number of buses for

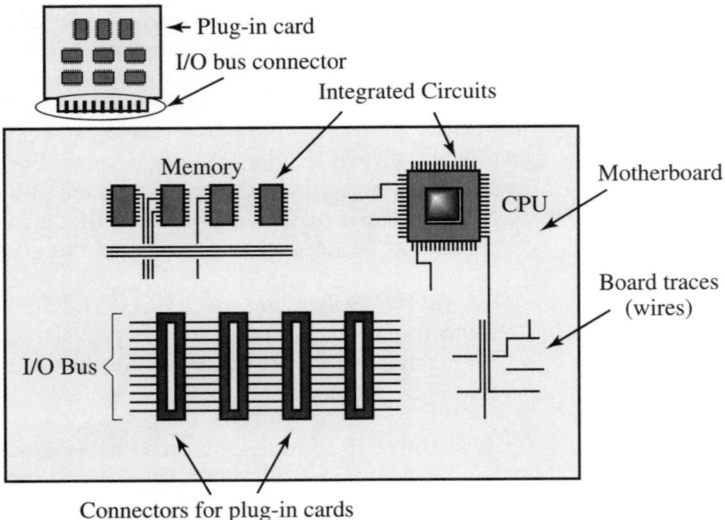

Figure 8-1 A simplified motherboard of a personal computer (top view).

chips or devices that need to communicate with each other. In Figure 8-1, an I/O bus is used for a number of cards that plug into the connectors, perpendicular to the motherboard in this example configuration.

8.1.1 *BUS STRUCTURE, PROTOCOL, AND CONTROL*

A bus consists of the physical parts, like connectors and wires, and a **bus protocol**. The wires can be partitioned into separate groups for control, address, data, and power, as illustrated in Figure 8-2. A single bus may have a few different power lines, and the example shown in Figure 8-2 has lines for ground (GND) at 0 V, and positive and negative voltages at +5 V, and –15 V, respectively.

The devices share a common set of wires, and only one device may send data at any one time. All devices simultaneously listen, but normally only one device receives. Only one device can be a **bus master**, and the remaining devices are then considered to be **slaves**. The master controls the bus and can be either a sender or a receiver.

An advantage of using a bus is to eliminate the need for connecting every device with every other device, which avoids the wiring complexity that would quickly dominate the cost of such a system. Disadvantages of using a bus include the slowdown introduced by the master/slave configuration, the time involved in implementing a protocol, and the lack of scalability to large sizes due to fan-out and timing constraints.

A bus can be classified as one of two types: **synchronous** or **asynchronous**. For a synchronous bus, one of the devices that is connected to the bus contains an oscillator (a clock) that sends out a sequence of 1's and 0's at timed intervals, as illustrated in Figure 8-3. The illustration shows a train of pulses that repeat at 10-ns intervals,

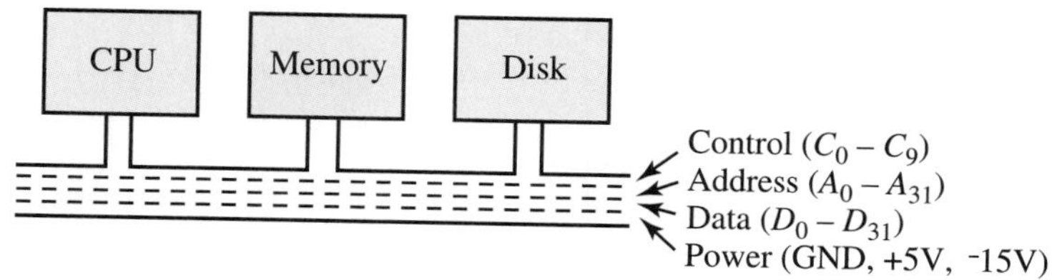

Figure 8-2 Simplified illustration of a bus.

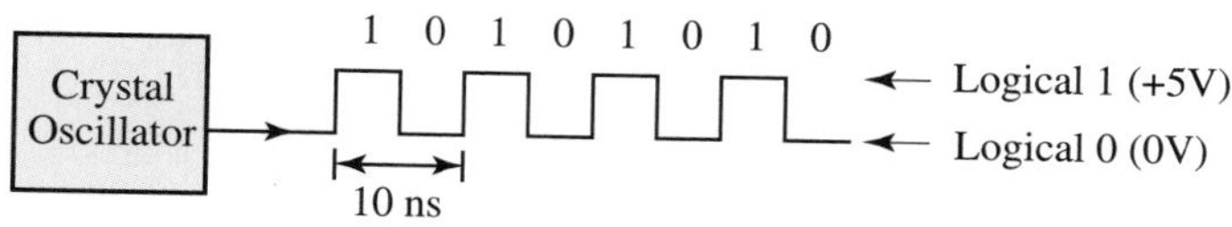

Figure 8-3 A 100-MHz bus clock.

which corresponds to a clock rate of 100 MHz. Ideally, the clock would be a perfect square wave (instantaneous rise and fall times) as shown in the figure. In practice, the rise and fall times are approximated by a rounded, trapezoidal shape.

8.1.2 *BUS CLOCKING*

For a synchronous bus, discussed in the following sections, a clock signal is used to synchronize bus operations. This bus clock is generally derived from the master system clock, but it may be slower than the master clock, especially in higher-speed CPUs. For example, one model of the Power Macintosh G3 computer has a system clock speed of 333 MHz but a bus clock speed of 66 MHz, which is slower by a factor of 5. This corresponds with memory access times that are much longer than internal CPU clock speeds. Typical cache memory has an access time of around 20 ns, compared to a 3-ns clock period for the processor described previously.

In addition to the bus clock running at a slower speed than the processor, several bus clock cycles are usually required to effect a bus transaction, referred to collectively as a single **bus cycle**. Typical bus cycles run from two to five bus clock periods in duration.

8.1.3 *THE SYNCHRONOUS BUS*

As an example of how communication takes place over a synchronous bus, consider the timing diagram shown in Figure 8-4, which is for a synchronous read of a word of memory by a CPU. At some point early in time interval T_1, while the clock is high, the CPU places the address of the location it wants to read onto the

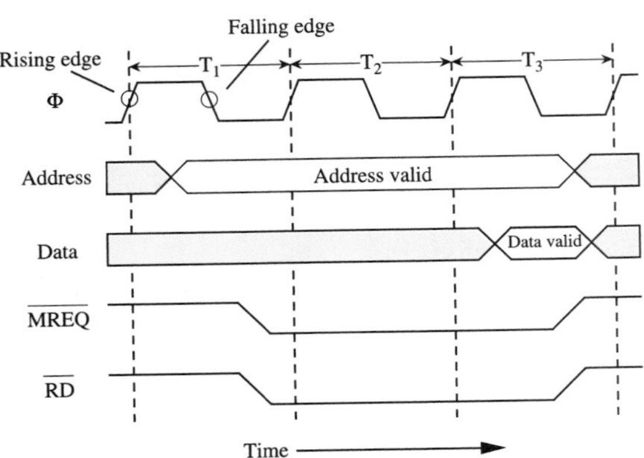

Figure 8-4 Timing diagram for a synchronous memory read (adapted from [Tanenbaum, 1999]).

address lines of the bus. At some later time during T_1, after the voltages on the address lines have become stable, or "settled," the $\overline{MREQ}$ and $\overline{RD}$ lines are asserted by the CPU. $\overline{MREQ}$ informs the memory that it is selected for the transfer (as opposed to another device, like a disk). The $\overline{RD}$ line informs the selected device to perform a read operation. The overbars on $\overline{MREQ}$ and $\overline{RD}$ indicate that a 0 must be placed on these lines in order to assert them.

The read time of memory is typically slower than the bus speed, and so all of time interval T_2 is spent performing the read, as well as part of T_3. The CPU assumes a fixed read time of three bus clocks, and so the data is taken from the bus by the CPU during the third cycle. The CPU then releases the bus by deasserting $\overline{MREQ}$ and $\overline{RD}$ in T_3. The shaded areas of the data and address portions of the timing diagram indicate that these signals are either invalid or unimportant at those times. The open areas, such as for the data lines during T_3, indicate valid signals. Open and shaded areas are used with crossed lines at either end to indicate that the levels of the individual lines may be different.

8.1.4 *THE ASYNCHRONOUS BUS*

If we replace the memory on a synchronous bus with a faster memory, then the memory access time will not improve because the bus clock is unchanged. If we increase the speed of the bus clock to match the faster speed of the memory, then slower devices that use the bus clock may not work properly.

An asynchronous bus solves this problem but is more complex because there is no bus clock. A master on an asynchronous bus puts everything that it needs on the bus (address, data, control) and then asserts $\overline{MSYN}$ (master synchronization). The slave then performs its job and then asserts $\overline{SSYN}$ (slave synchronization) when it is finished. The master then deasserts $\overline{MSYN}$, which signals the slave to deassert $\overline{SSYN}$. In this way, a fast master/slave combination responds more quickly than a slow master/slave combination.

As an example of how communication takes place over an asynchronous bus, consider the timing diagram shown in Figure 8-5. In order for a CPU to read a word from memory, it places an address on the bus, followed by asserting $\overline{MREQ}$ and $\overline{RD}$. After these lines settle, the CPU asserts $\overline{MSYN}$. This event triggers the memory to perform a read operation, which results in $\overline{SSYN}$ eventually being asserted by the memory. This is indicated by the **cause-and-effect** arrow between $\overline{MSYN}$ and $\overline{SSYN}$ shown in Figure 8-5. This method of synchronization is referred to as a "full handshake." In this particular implementa-

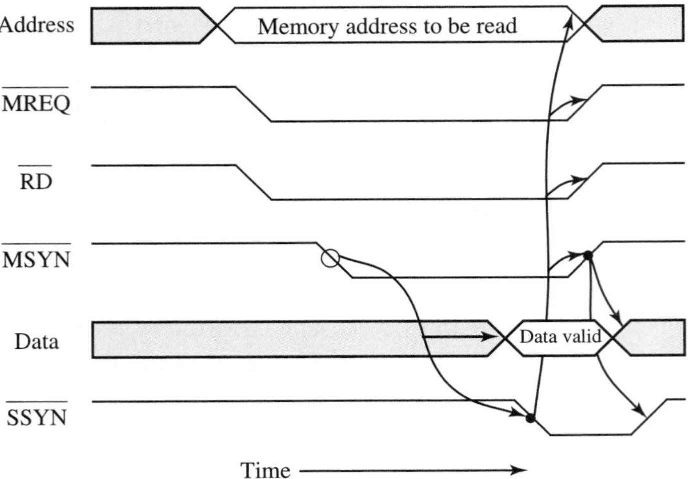

Figure 8-5 Timing diagram for asynchronous memory read (adapted from [Tanenbaum, 1999]).

tion of a full handshake, asserting $\overline{MSYN}$ initiates the transfer, followed by the slave asserting $\overline{SSYN}$, followed by the CPU deasserting $\overline{MSYN}$, followed by the memory deasserting $\overline{SSYN}$. Notice the absence of a bus clock signal.

Asynchronous buses can be more difficult to debug than synchronous buses when there is a problem, and interfaces for asynchronous buses can be more difficult to make. For these reasons, synchronous buses are very common, particularly in personal computers.

8.1.5 *BUS ARBITRATION—MASTERS AND SLAVES*

Suppose now that more than one device wants to be a bus master at the same time. How is a decision made as to who will be the bus master? This is the **bus arbitration** problem, and there are two basic schemes: **centralized** and **decentralized** (distributed). Figure 8-6 illustrates four organizations for these two schemes. In Figure 8-6a, a centralized arbitration scheme is used. Devices 0 through *n* are all attached to the same bus (not shown), and they also share a **bus request** line that goes into an **arbiter**. When a device wants to be a bus master, it asserts the bus request line. When the arbiter sees the bus request, it determines if a **bus grant** can be issued (it may be the case that the current bus master will not allow itself to be interrupted). If a bus grant can be issued, then the arbiter asserts the bus grant line. The bus grant line is **daisy chained** from one device to the next. The first device that sees the asserted bus grant and also wants to be the bus

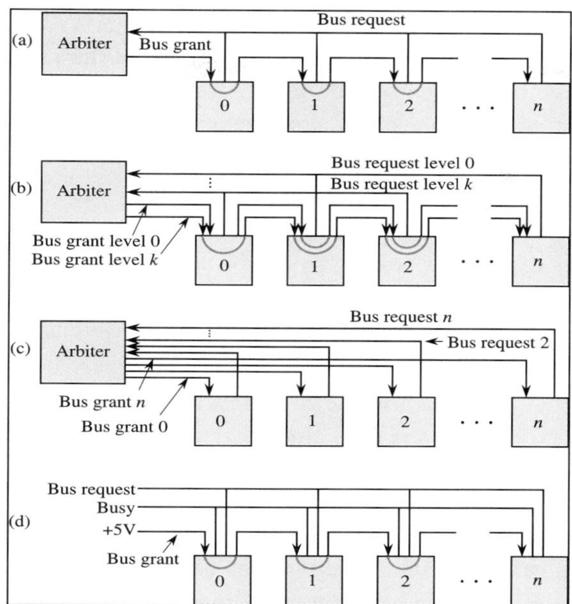

Figure 8-6 (a) Simple centralized bus arbitration; (b) centralized arbitration with priority levels; (c) fully centralized bus arbitration; (d) decentralized bus arbitration. (Adapted from [Tanenbaum, 1999]).

master takes control of the bus and does not propagate the bus grant to higher numbered devices. If a device does not want the bus, then it simply passes the bus grant to the next device. In this way, devices that are electrically closer to the arbiter have higher priorities than devices that are farther away.

Sometimes an absolute priority ordering is not appropriate and a number of bus request/bus grant lines are used as shown in Figure 8-6b. Lower numbered bus request lines have higher priorities than higher numbered bus request lines. In order to raise the priority of a device that is far from the arbiter, it can be assigned to a lower numbered bus request line. Priorities are assigned within a group on the same bus request level by electrical proximity to the arbiter.

Taking this to an extreme, each device can have its own bus request/bus grant line as shown in Figure 8-6c. This fully centralized approach is the most powerful from a logical standpoint, but from a practical standpoint, it is the least scalable of all of the approaches. A significant cost is the need for additional lines (a precious commodity) on the bus.

In a fourth approach, a decentralized bus arbitration scheme is used as illustrated in Figure 8-6d. Notice the lack of a central arbiter. A device that wants to become a bus master first asserts the bus request line and then it checks if the bus is busy. If the busy line is not asserted then the device sends a 0 to the next higher numbered device on the daisy chain, asserts the busy line, and deasserts the bus request line. If the bus is busy, or if a device does not want the bus, then it simply propagates the bus grant to the next device.

Arbitration needs to be a fast operation, and for that reason, a centralized scheme will only work well for a small number of devices (up to about eight). For a large number of devices, a decentralized scheme is more appropriate.

Given a system that makes use of one of these arbitration schemes, imagine a situation in which n card slots are used, and then card m is removed, where $m < n$. What happens? Since each bus request line is directly connected to all devices in a group, and the bus grant line is passed through each device in a group, a bus request from a device with an index greater than m will never see an asserted bus grant line, which can result in a system crash. This can be a frustrating problem to identify, because a system can run indefinitely with no problems until the higher numbered device is accessed.

When a card is removed, higher cards should be repositioned to fill in the missing slot, or a dummy card that continues the bus grant line should be inserted in place of the removed card. Fast devices (like disk controllers) should be given higher priority than slow devices (like terminals) and should thus be placed close to the arbiter in a centralized scheme, or close to the beginning of the bus grant line in a decentralized scheme. This is an imperfect solution given the opportunities for leaving gaps in the bus and getting the device ordering wrong. These days, it is more common for each device to have a separate path to the arbiter.

8.2 Bridge-Based Bus Architectures

From a logical viewpoint, all of the system components are connected directly to the system bus in the previous section. From an operational viewpoint, this approach is overly burdensome on the system bus because simultaneous transfers cannot take place among the various components. While every device is connected to the bus at the same time, several independent transfers may need to take place at any time. For example, a graphics component may be repainting a video screen at the same time that a cache line is being retrieved from main memory, while an I/O transfer is taking place over a network.

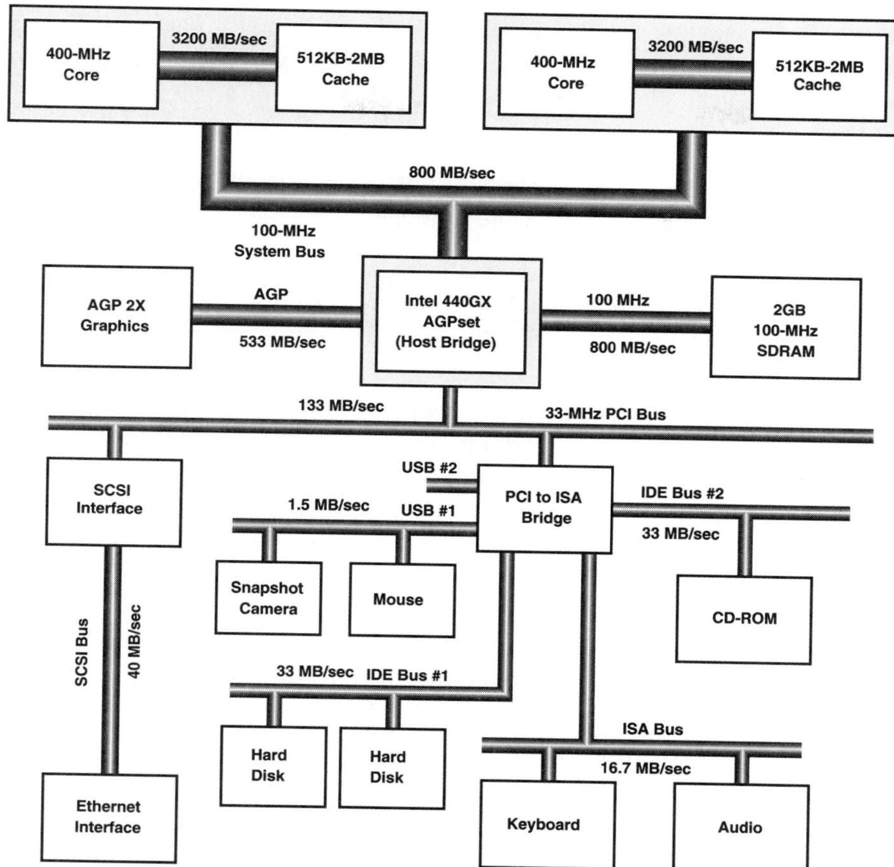

Figure 8-7 Bridging with dual Pentium II Xeon processors on Slot 2. (Source: http://www.intel.com)

These different transfers are typically segregated onto separate buses through the use of **bridges**. Figure 8-7 illustrates bridging with Intel's Pentium II Xeon processors. At the top of the diagram are two Pentium II processors, arranged in a **symmetric multiprocessor** (SMP) configuration. The operating system performs load balancing by selecting one processor over another when assigning tasks (this is different from parallel processing, discussed in Chapter 10, in which multiple processors work on a common problem). Each Pentium II processor has a "backside bus" to its own cache of 3200 MB/s (8 bytes wide × 400 MHz), thus segregating cache traffic from other bus traffic.

Working down from the top of the diagram, the two Pentium II processors converge on the system bus (sometimes called the "frontside bus"). The system bus is 32 bits wide and makes transfers on both the rising and falling edges of the 100-MHz bus clock, giving a total available bandwidth of 4 bytes × 2 edges × 100 MHz = 800 MB/s that is shared between the processors.

At the center of the diagram is the Intel 440GX AGPset "host bridge" which connects the system bus to the remaining buses. The host bridge acts as a go-between among the system bus, the main memory, the graphics processor, and a hierarchy of other buses. To the right of the host bridge is the main memory (synchronous DRAM), connected to the host bridge by an 800-MB/s bus.

In this particular example, a separate bus known as the advanced graphics port (AGP) is provided from the host bridge to the graphics processor over a 533-MB/s bus. Graphics rendering (that is, filling an object with color) commonly needs texture information that is too large to place economically on a graphics card. The AGP allows for a high speed path between the graphics processor and the main memory, where texture maps can now be effectively stored.

Below the host bridge is the 33-MHz peripheral component interconnect (PCI) bus, which connects the remaining buses to the host bridge. The PCI bus has a number of components connected to it, such as the small computer system interface (SCSI) controller, which is yet another bus, and which in this illustration accepts an Ethernet network interface card. Prior to the introduction of the AGP, graphics cards were placed on the PCI bus, which created a bottleneck for all of the other bus traffic.

Attached to the PCI bus is a PCI-to-ISA bridge, which actually provides bridging for two 1.5-MB/s universal serial bus (USB) buses, two 33-MB/s integrated drive electronics (IDE) buses, and a 16.7-MB/s industry standard architecture (ISA) bus. The IDE buses are generally used for disk drives, the ISA bus is generally used for moderate rate devices like printers and voice-band modems, and the USB buses are used for low bit rate devices like mice and snapshot digital cameras.

8.3 Communication Methodologies

Computer systems have a wide range of communication tasks. The CPU must communicate with memory and with a wide range of I/O devices, from extremely slow devices such as keyboards, to high-speed devices like disk drives and network interfaces. There may be multiple CPUs that communicate with one another either directly or through a shared memory, as described in the previous section for the dual Pentium II Xeon configuration.

Three methods for managing input and output are **programmed I/O** (also known as **polling**), **interrupt-driven I/O**, and **direct memory access** (DMA).

8.3.1 *PROGRAMMED I/O*

Consider reading a block of data from a disk. In programmed I/O, the CPU polls each device to see if it needs servicing. In a restaurant analogy, the host would approach the patron and ask if the patron is ready.

The operations that take place for programmed I/O are shown in the flowchart in Figure 8-8. The CPU first checks the status of the disk by reading a special register that can be accessed in the memory space or by issuing a special I/O instruction if this is how the architecture implements I/O. If the disk is not ready to be read or written, then the process loops back and checks the status continuously until the disk is ready. This is referred to as a **busy-wait**. When the disk is finally ready, then a transfer of data is made between the disk and the CPU.

After the transfer is completed, the CPU checks to see if there is another communication request for the disk. If there is, then the process repeats; otherwise the CPU continues with another task.

In programmed I/O the CPU wastes time polling devices. Another problem is that high-priority devices are not checked until the CPU is finished with its current I/O task, which may have a low priority. Programmed I/O is simple to implement, however, and so it has advantages in some applications.

8.3.2 *INTERRUPT-DRIVEN I/O*

With interrupt-driven I/O, the CPU does not access a device until it needs servicing, and so it does not get caught up in busy-waits. In interrupt-driven I/O, the device requests service through a special interrupt request line that goes directly to the CPU. The restaurant analogy would have the patron politely tapping silverware on a water glass, thus interrupting the waiter when service is required.

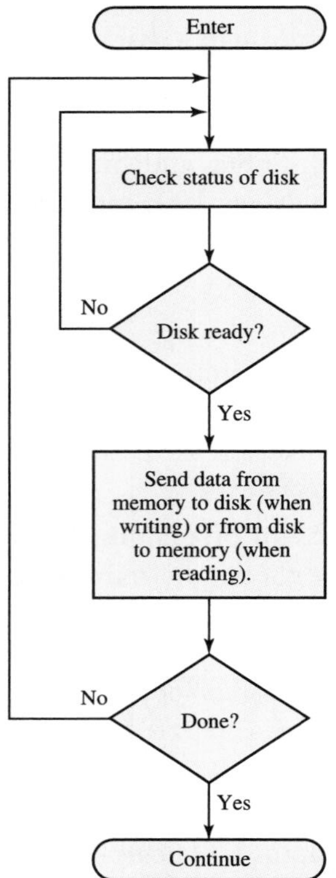

Figure 8-8 Programmed I/O flowchart for a disk transfer.

A flowchart for interrupt driven I/O is shown in Figure 8-9. The CPU issues a request to the disk for reading or for writing and then immediately resumes execution of another process. At some later time, when the disk is ready, it interrupts the CPU. The CPU then invokes an **interrupt service routine** (ISR) for the disk, and returns to normal execution when the interrupt service routine completes its task. The ISR is similar in structure to the procedure presented in Chapter 4, except that interrupts occur asynchronously with respect to the process being executed by the CPU: An interrupt can occur at any time during program execution.

There are times when a process being executed by the CPU should not be interrupted because some critical operation is taking place. For this reason, instruction sets include instructions to disable and enable interrupts under programmed control. (The waiter can ignore the patron at times.) Whether or not interrupts

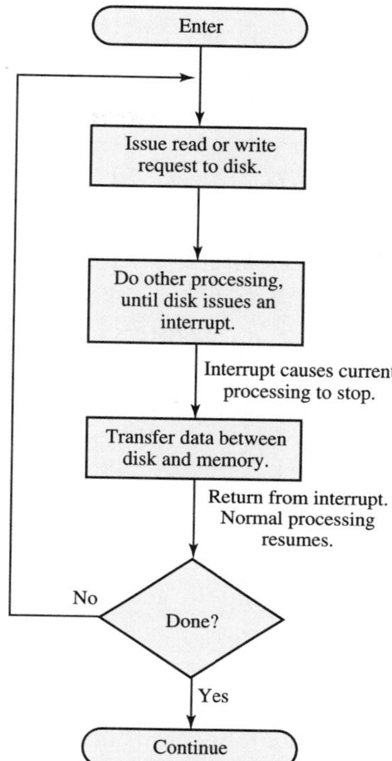

Figure 8-9 Interrupt-driven I/O flowchart for a disk transfer.

are accepted is generally determined by the state of the interrupt flag (IF), which is part of the processor status register. Furthermore, in most systems priorities are assigned to the interrupts, either enforced by the processor or by a **peripheral interrupt controller** (PIC). (The waiter may attend to the head table first.) At the top priority level in many systems, there is a **non maskable interrupt** (NMI), which, as the name implies, cannot be disabled. (The waiter will in all cases pay attention to the fire alarm!) The NMI is used for handling potentially catastrophic events such as power failures and more ordinary but crucially uninterruptible operations such as file system updates.

At the time when an interrupt occurs (which is sometimes loosely referred to as a **trap**, even though traps usually have a different meaning, as explained in Chapter 6), the processor status register and the program counter (`%psr` and `%pc` for the ARC) are automatically pushed onto the stack, and the Program Counter is loaded with the address of the appropriate interrupt service routine. The processor status register is pushed onto the stack because it contains the interrupt flag

(IF), and the processor must disable interrupts for at least the duration of the first instruction of the ISR. (See Problem 8.2.) Execution of the interrupt routine then begins. When the interrupt service routine finishes, execution of the interrupted program then resumes.

The ARC `jmpl` instruction (see Chapter 4) will not work properly for resuming execution of the interrupted routine, because in addition to restoring the program counter contents, the processor status register must be restored. Instead, the `rett` (return from trap) instruction is invoked, which reverses the interrupt process and restores the `%psr` and `%pc` registers to their values prior to the interrupt. In the ARC architecture, `rett` is an arithmetic format instruction with `op3 = 111001` and an unused `rd` field (all zeros).

8.3.3 *DIRECT MEMORY ACCESS*

Although interrupt driven I/O frees the CPU until the device requires service, the CPU is still responsible for making the actual data transfer. Figure 8-10 highlights the problem. In order to transfer a block of data between the memory and the disk using either programmed I/O or interrupt-driven I/O, every word travels over the system bus (or equivalently, through the host bridge) twice: first to the CPU, then again over the system bus to its destination.

A direct memory access (DMA) device can transfer data directly to and from memory rather than using the CPU as an intermediary, and can thus relieve congestion on the system bus. In keeping with the restaurant analogy, the host serves everyone at one table before serving anyone at another table. DMA services are usually provided by a DMA controller, which is itself a specialized processor whose specialty is transferring data directly to or from I/O devices and memory. Most DMA controllers can also be programmed to make memory-to-memory block moves. A DMA device thus takes over the job of the CPU during a transfer. In setting up the transfer, the CPU programs the DMA device with the start-

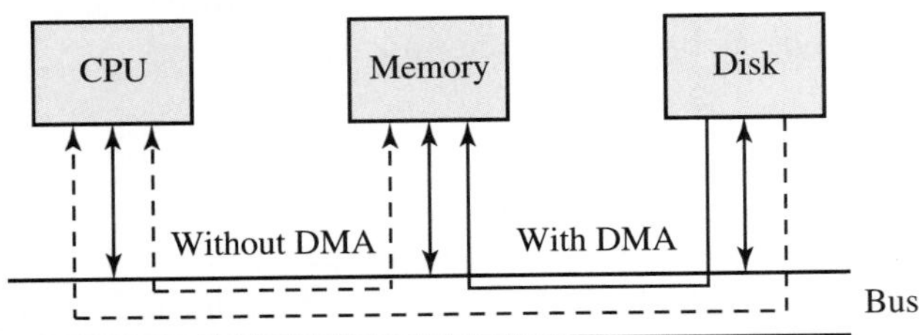

Figure 8-10 DMA transfer from disk to memory bypasses the CPU.

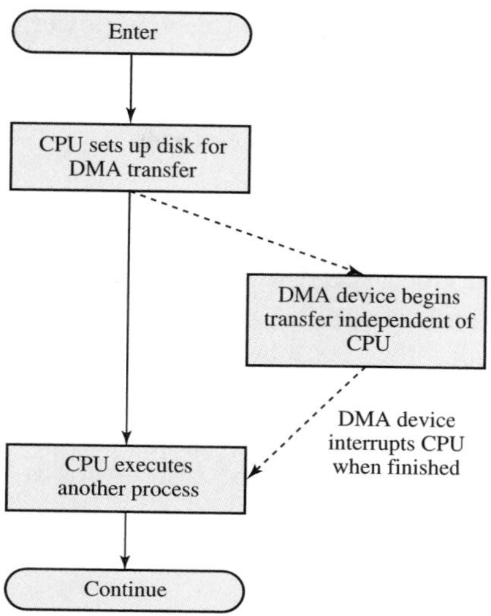

Figure 8-11 DMA flowchart for a disk transfer.

ing address in main memory, the starting address in the device, and the length of the block to be transferred.

Figure 8-11 illustrates the DMA process for a disk transfer. The CPU sets up the DMA device and then signals the device to start the transfer. While the transfer is taking place, the CPU continues execution of another process. When the DMA transfer is completed, the device informs the CPU through an interrupt. A system that implements DMA thus also implements interrupts as well.

If the DMA device transfers a large block of data without relinquishing the bus, the CPU may become starved for instructions or data, and thus its work is halted until the DMA transfer has completed. In order to alleviate this problem, DMA controllers usually have a "cycle-stealing" mode. In **cycle-stealing DMA** the controller acquires the bus, transfers a single byte or word, and then relinquishes the bus. This allows other devices, and in particular the CPU, to share the bus during DMA transfers. In the restaurant analogy, a patron can request a check while the host is serving another table.

8.4 Case Study: Communication on the Intel Pentium Architecture

The Intel Pentium processor family is Intel's current state-of-the art implementation of its venerable x86 family, which began with the Intel 8086, released in 1978. The Pentium is itself a processor family, with versions that emphasize high speed, multiprocessor environments, graphics, low power, etc. In this section we examine the common features that underlie the Pentium System Bus, which connects the Pentium to the host bridge (see Section 8.2).

8.4.1 *SYSTEM CLOCK, BUS CLOCK, AND BUS SPEEDS*

Interestingly, the system clock speed is set as a multiple of the bus clock. The value of the multiple is set by the processor whenever it is reset, according to the values on several of its pins. The possible values of the multiple vary across family members. For example, the Pentium Pro, a family member adapted for multiple CPU applications, can have multipliers ranging from 2 to 3-1/2. We mention again here that the reason for clocking the system bus at a slower rate than the CPU is that CPU operations can take place faster than memory access operations. A common bus clock frequency in Pentium systems is 66 MHz.

8.4.2 *ADDRESS, DATA, MEMORY, AND I/O CAPABILITIES*

The system bus effectively has 32 address lines and can thus address up to 4 GB of main memory. Its data bus is 64 bits wide; thus the processor is capable of transferring an 8-byte quadword in one bus cycle. (Intel x86 words are 16-bits long.) We say "effectively" because in fact the Pentium processor decodes the least significant three address lines, $A_2 - A_0$, into eight "byte enable" lines, *BE0#–BE7#*, prior to placing them on the system bus.[1] The values on these eight lines specify the byte, word, double word, or quad word that is to be transferred from the base address specified by $A_{31} - A_3$.

8.4.3 *DATA WORDS HAVE SOFT ALIGNMENT*

Data values have so-called **soft alignment**, meaning that words, double words, and quad words should be aligned on even word, double word, and quad word boundaries for maximum efficiency, but the processor can tolerate misaligned data items. The penalty for accessing misaligned words may be two bus cycles, which are required to access both halves of the datum.[2]

---

[1]The "#" symbol is Intel's notation for a bus line that is active low.

[2]Many systems require so-called hard alignment. Misaligned words are not allowed, and their detection causes a processor exception to be raised.

As a bow to the small address spaces of early family members, all Intel processors have separate address spaces for memory and I/O accesses. The address space to be selected is specified by the M/IO# bus line. A high value on this line selects the 4-GB memory address space, and low specifies the I/O address space. Separate opcodes, IN and OUT, are used to access this space. It is the responsibility of all devices on the bus to sample the M/IO# line at the beginning of each bus cycle to determine the address space to which the bus cycle is referring—memory or I/O. Figure 8-12 shows these address spaces graphically. I/O addresses in the x86 family are limited to 16 bits, allowing up to 64K I/O locations.

8.4.4 *BUS CYCLES IN THE PENTIUM FAMILY*

The Pentium processor has a total of 18 different bus cycles, to serve different needs. These include the standard memory read and write bus cycles, the bus hold cycle (used to allow other devices to become the bus master), an interrupt acknowledge cycle, various "burst" cache access cycles, and a number of other special-purpose bus cycles. In this case study we examine the read and write bus cycles, the "burst read" cycle, in which a burst of data can be transferred, and the bus hold/hold acknowledge cycle, which is used by devices that wish to become the bus master.

8.4.5 *MEMORY READ AND WRITE BUS CYCLES*

The "standard" read and write cycles are shown in Figure 8-13. By convention, the states of the Intel bus are referred to as "T states," where each T state is one clock cycle. There are three T states shown in the figure: T1, T2, and Ti, where Ti is the "idle" state, the state that occurs when the bus is not engaged in any specific activity and when no requests to use the bus are pending. Recall that a "#" following a signal name indicates that a signal is active low, in keeping with Intel

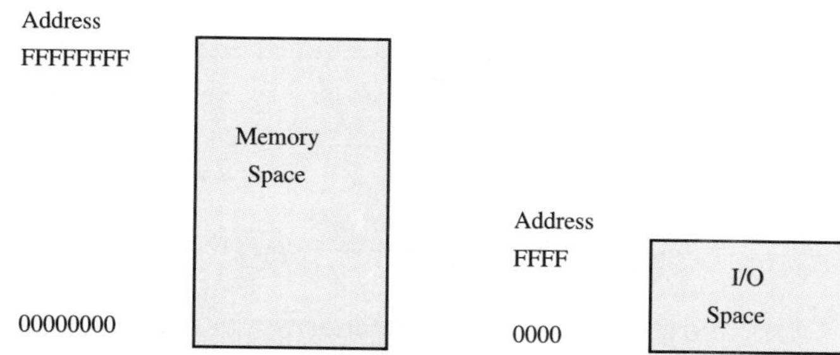

Figure 8-12 Intel memory and I/O address spaces.

conventions. Likewise we will use roman type for signal names when discussing Intel-specific signals.

Both read and write cycles require a minimum of two bus clocks, T1 and T2:

- The CPU signals the start of all new bus cycles by asserting the Address Status signal, ADS#. This signal both defines the start of a new bus cycle and signals to memory that a valid address is available on the address bus, ADDR. Note the transition of ADDR from invalid to valid as ADS# is asserted.
- The de-assertion of the cache load signal, CACHE#, indicates that the cycle will be a composed of a single read or write, as opposed to a burst read or write, covered later in this section.
- During a read cycle the CPU asserts read, W/R#, simultaneously with the assertion of ADS#. This signals the memory module that it should latch the address and read a value at the address specified.
- Upon a read, the memory module asserts the Burst Ready, BRDY#, signal as it places the data, DATA, on the bus, indicating that there is valid data on the data pins. The CPU uses BRDY# as a signal to latch the data values.
- Since CACHE# is deasserted, the assertion of a single BRDY# signifies the end of the bus cycle.
- In the write cycle, the memory module asserts BRDY# when it is ready to

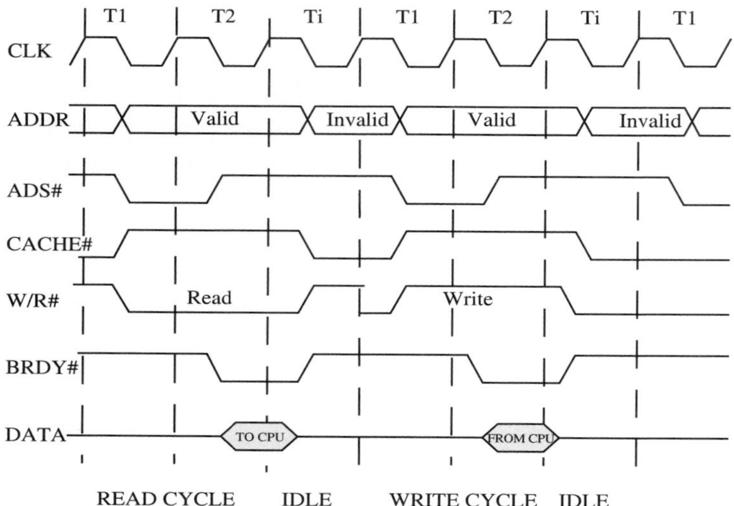

Figure 8-13 The standard Intel Pentium read and write bus cycles.

accept the data placed on the bus by the CPU. Thus BRDY# acts as a handshake between memory and the CPU.

- If memory is too slow to accept or drive data within the limits of two clock cycles, it can insert "wait" states by not asserting BRDY# until it is ready to respond.

8.4.6 *THE BURST READ BUS CYCLE*

Because of the critical need to supply the CPU with instructions and data from memory that is inherently slower than the CPU, Intel designed the burst read and write cycles. These cycles read and write four eight-byte quad words in a burst, from consecutive addresses. Figure 8-14 shows the Pentium burst read cycle.

The burst read cycle is initiated by the processor placing an address on the address lines and asserting ADS# as before, but now by asserting the CACHE# line the processor signals the beginning of a burst read cycle. In response the memory asserts BRDY# and places a sequence of four 8-byte quad words on the data bus, one quad word per clock, keeping BRDY# asserted until the entire transfer is complete.

There is an analogous cycle for burst writes. There is also a mechanism for coping with slower memory by slowing the burst transfer rate from one per clock to one per two clocks.

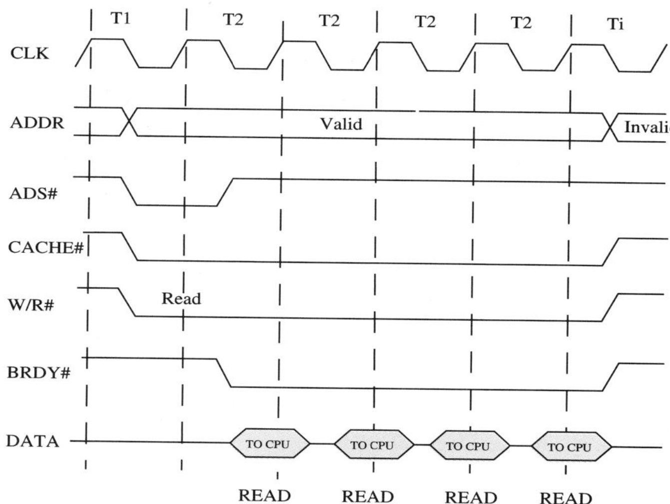

Figure 8-14 The Intel Pentium burst read bus cycle.

8.4.7 *BUS HOLD FOR REQUEST BY BUS MASTER*

There are two bus signals for use by devices requesting to become bus master: hold (HOLD) and hold acknowledge (HLDA). Figure 8-15 shows how the transactions work. The figure assumes that the processor is in the midst of a read cycle when the HOLD request signal arrives. The processor completes the current (read) cycle and inserts two idle cycles, Ti. During the falling edge of the second Ti cycle the processor floats all of its lines and asserts HLDA. It keeps HLDA asserted for two clocks. At the end of the second clock cycle the device asserting HLDA "owns" the bus, and it may begin a new bus operation at the following cycle, as shown at the far right end of the figure. In systems of any complexity there will be a separate bus controller chip to mediate among the several devices that may wish to become the bus master.

8.4.8 *DATA TRANSFER RATES*

Let us compute the data transfer rates for the read and burst read bus cycles. In the first case, 8 bytes are transferred in two clock cycles. If the bus clock speed is 66 MHz, this is a maximum transfer rate of

$$\frac{8}{2} \times 66 \times 10^6$$

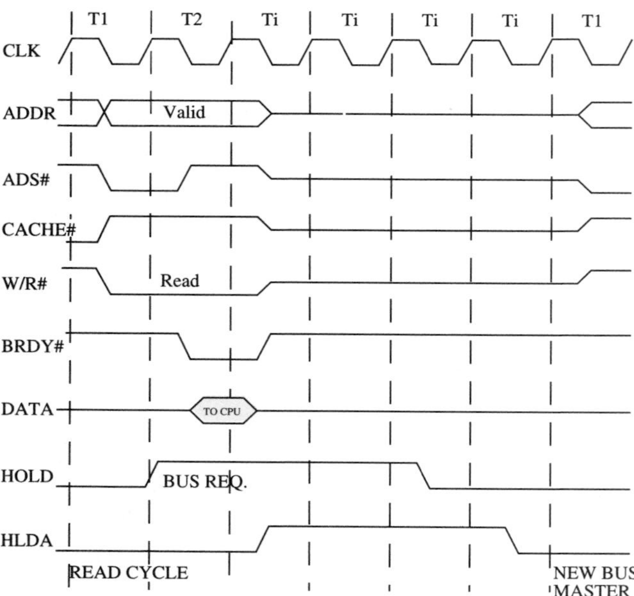

Figure 8-15 The Intel Pentium Hold-Hold Acknowledge bus cycle.

or 264 million bytes per second. In burst mode this rate increases to four 8-byte bursts in five clock cycles, for a transfer rate of

$$\frac{32}{5} \times 66 \times 10^6$$

or 422 million bytes per second. (Intel literature uses 4 cycles rather than 5 as the denominator, thus arriving at a burst rate of 528 million bytes per second. Take your pick.)

At the 422 million byte rate, with a bus clock multiplier of 3-1/2, the data transfer rate to the CPU is

$$\frac{422 \times 10^6}{3.5 \times 66 \times 10^6}$$

or about 2 bytes per clock cycle. Thus under optimum, or ideal conditions, the CPU is probably just barely kept supplied with bytes. In the event of a branch instruction or other interruption in memory activity, the CPU will become starved for instructions and data.

The Intel Pentium is typical of modern processors. It has a number of specialized bus cycles that support multiprocessors, cache memory transfers, and other special situations. Refer to the Intel literature (see Further Reading at the end of the chapter) for more details.

8.5 Mass Storage

In Chapter 7, we saw that computer memory is organized as a hierarchy, in which the fastest method of storing information (registers) is expensive and not very dense, and the slowest methods of storing information (tapes, disks, etc.) are inexpensive and are very dense. Registers and random access memories require continuous power to retain their stored data, whereas **media** such as magnetic tapes and magnetic disks retain information indefinitely after the power is removed, which is known as **indefinite persistence**. This type of storage is said to be **non volatile**. There are many kinds of non volatile storage, and only a few of the more common methods are described here. We start with one of the most prevalent forms: the **magnetic disk**.

8.5.1 *MAGNETIC DISKS*

A magnetic disk is a device for storing information that supports a large storage density and a relatively fast access time. A **moving head** magnetic disk is composed of a stack of one or more **platters** that are spaced several millimeters apart and are connected to a **spindle**, as shown in Figure 8-16. Each platter has two **surfaces** made of aluminum or glass (which expands less than aluminum as it heats up), which are coated with small particles of a magnetic material such as iron oxide, which is the essence of rust. This is why disk platters, floppy diskettes, audio tapes, and other magnetic media are brown. Binary 1's and 0's are stored by magnetizing small areas of the material.

A single **head** is dedicated to each surface. Six heads are used in the example shown in Figure 8-16, for the six surfaces. The top surface of the top platter and the bottom surface of the bottom platter are sometimes not used on multi platter disks because they are more susceptible to contamination than the inner surfaces. The heads are attached to a common **arm** (also known as a **comb**), which moves in and out to reach different portions of the surfaces.

In a hard disk drive, the platters rotate at a constant speed of typically 3600 to 10,000 revolutions per minute (RPM). The heads read or write data by magnetizing the magnetic material as it passes under the heads when writing or by sensing the magnetic fields when reading. Only a single head is used for reading or writing at any time, so data is stored in serial fashion even though the heads can

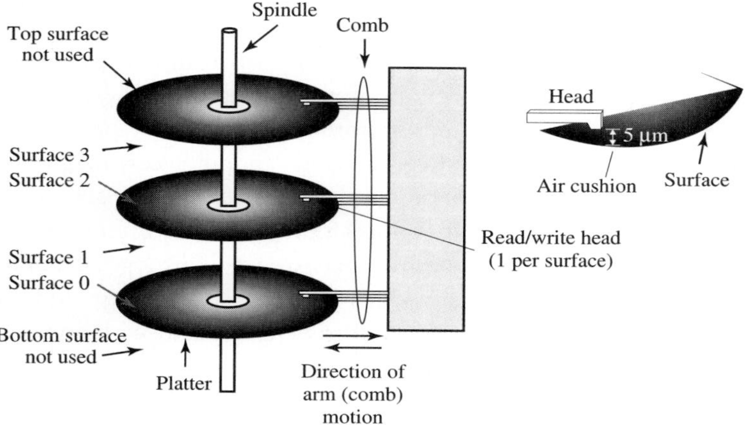

Figure 8-16 A magnetic disk with three platters.

in principle be used to read or write several bits in parallel. One reason that the parallel mode of operation is not normally used is that heads can become misaligned, which corrupts the way that data is read or written. A single surface is relatively insensitive to the alignment of the corresponding head because the head position is always accurately known with respect to reference markings on the disk.

Data Encoding

Only the transitions between magnetized areas are sensed when reading a disk, and so runs of 1's or 0's may not be accurately detected unless a method of encoding is used that embeds timing information into the data to identify the breaks between bits. **Manchester encoding** is one method that addresses this problem, and another method is **modified frequency modulation** (MFM). For comparison, Figure 8-17a shows an ASCII 'F' character encoded in the **non-return-to-zero** (NRZ) format, which is the way information is carried inside of a CPU. Figure 8-17b shows the same character encoded in the Manchester code. In Manchester encoding there is a transition between high and low signals on every bit, resulting in a transition at every bit time. A transition from low to high indicates a 1, whereas a transition from high to low indicates a 0. These transitions are used to recover the timing information.

A single surface contains several hundred concentric **tracks**, which in turn are composed of **sectors** of typically 512 bytes in size, stored serially, as shown in Figure 8-18. The sectors are spaced apart by **intersector gaps**, and the tracks are spaced apart by **intertrack gaps**, which simplify positioning of the head. A set of corresponding tracks on all of the surfaces forms a **cylinder**. For instance, track 0

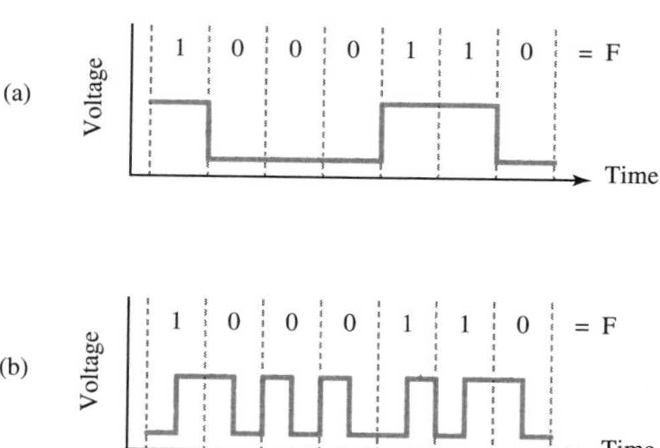

Figure 8-17 (a) Straight amplitude (NRZ) encoding of ASCII 'F'; (b) Manchester encoding of ASCII 'F'.

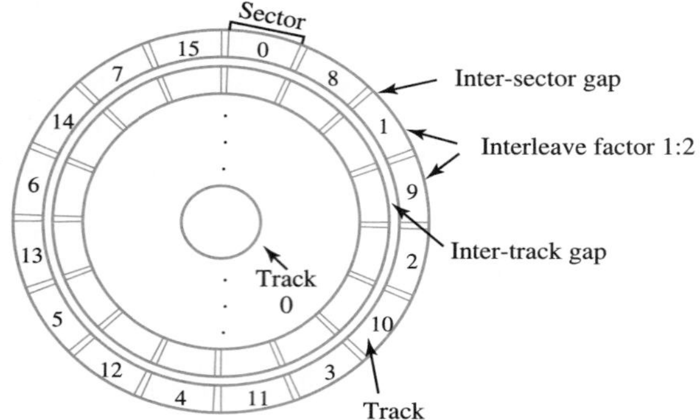

Figure 8-18 Organization of a disk platter with a 1:2 interleave factor.

on each of surfaces 0, 1, 2, 3, 4, and 5 in Figure 8-16 collectively form cylinder 0. The number of bytes per sector is generally invariant across the entire platter.

In modern disk drives the number of tracks per sector may vary in **zones**, where a zone is a group of tracks having the same number of sectors per track. Zones near the center of the platter where bits are spaced closely together have fewer sectors, while zones near the outside periphery of the platter, where bits are spaced farther apart, have more sectors per track. This technique for increasing the capacity of a disk drive is known as **zone-bit recording**.

Disk Drive Capacities and Speeds

If a disk has only a single zone, its storage capacity, C, can be computed from the number of bytes per sector, N, the number of sectors per track, S, the number of tracks per surface, T, and the number of platter surfaces that have data encoded in them, P, with the formula

$$C = N \times S \times T \times P$$

A high-capacity disk drive may have $N = 512$ bytes, $S = 1000$ sectors per track, $T = 5000$ tracks per surface, and $P = 8$ platters. The total capacity of this drive is $C =$ 512 bytes/sector × 1000 sectors/track × 5000 tracks/surface × 8 platters × 2 surfaces/platter or 38 GB.

Maximum data transfer speed is governed by three factors: the time to move the head to the desired track, referred to as the head **seek time**; the time for the desired sector to appear under the read/write head, known as the **rotational latency**; and the time to transfer the sector from the disk platter once the sector is positioned under the head, known as the **transfer time**. Transfers to and from a disk are always carried out in complete sectors. Partial sectors are never read or written.

Head seek time is the largest contributor to overall access time of a disk. Manufacturers usually specify an average seek time, which is roughly the time required for the head to travel half the distance across the disk. The rationale for this definition is that it is difficult to know, a priori, which track the data is on or where the head is positioned when the disk access request is made. Thus it is assumed that the head will, on average, be required to travel over half the surface before arriving at the correct track. On modern disk drives average seek time is approximately 10 ms.

Once the head is positioned at the correct track, it is again difficult to know ahead of time how long it will take for the desired sector to appear under the head. Therefore, the average rotational latency is taken to be 1/2 the time of one complete revolution, which is on the order of 4–8 ms. The sector transfer time is just the time for one complete revolution divided by the number of sectors per track. If large amounts of data are to be transferred, then after a complete track is transferred, the head must move to the next track. The parameter of interest here is the track-to-track access time, which is approximately 2 ms (notice that the time for the head to travel past multiple tracks is much less than 2 ms per track). An important parameter related to the sector transfer time is the **burst rate**, the rate at which data streams on or off the disk once the read/write operation has started. The burst rate equals the disk speed in revolutions per second times the capacity per track. This is not necessarily the same as the transfer rate, because there is a setup time needed to position the head and synchronize timing for each sector.

The maximum transfer rate computed from the factors above may not be realized in practice. The limiting factor may be the speed of the bus interconnecting the disk drive and its interface, or it may be the time required by the CPU to transfer the data between the disk and main memory. For example, disks that operate with the **small computer systems interface** (SCSI) standards have a transfer rate between the disk and a host computer of from 5 to 40 MB/s, which may be slower than the transfer rate between the head and the internal buffer on the disk. Disk drives contain internal buffers that help match the speed of the disk with the speed of transfer from the disk unit to the host computer.

Disk Drives are Delicate Mechanisms

The strength of a magnetic field drops off as the square of the distance from the source of the field, and for this reason it is important for the head of the disk to travel as close to the surface as possible. The distance between the head and the platter can be as small as 5 μm. The engineering and assembly of a disk do not have to adhere to such a tight tolerance—the head assembly is aerodynamically designed so that the spinning motion of the disk creates a cushion of air that maintains a distance between the heads and the platters. Particles in the air contained within the disk unit that are larger than 5 μm can come between the head assembly and the platter, which results in a **head crash**.

Smoke particles from cigarette ash are 10 μm or larger, and so smoking should not take place when disks are exposed to the environment. Disks are usually assembled into sealed units in **clean rooms**, so that virtually no large particles are introduced during assembly. Unfortunately, materials used in manufacturing (such as glue) that are internal to the unit can deteriorate over time and can generate particles large enough to cause a head crash. For this reason, sealed disks (formerly called **Winchester** disks) contain filters that remove particles generated within the unit and that prevent particulate matter from entering the drive from the external environment.

Floppy Disks

A **floppy disk**, or **diskette**, contains a flexible plastic platter coated with a magnetic material like iron oxide. Although only a single side is used on one surface of a floppy disk in many systems, both sides of the disks are coated with the same material in order to prevent warping. Access time is generally slower than a hard disk because a flexible disk cannot spin as quickly as a hard disk. The rotational speed of a typical floppy disk mechanism is only 300 RPM and may be varied as the head moves from track to track to optimize data transfer rates. Such slow rotational speeds mean that access times of floppy drives are 250–300 ms, roughly 10 times slower than hard drives. Capacities vary but range up to 1.44 MB.

Floppies are inexpensive because they can be removed from the drive mechanism and because of their small size. The head comes in physical contact with the floppy disk, but this does not result in a head crash. It does, however, place wear on the head and on the media. For this reason, floppies only spin when they are being accessed.

When floppies were first introduced, they were encased in flexible, thin plastic enclosures, which gave rise to their name. The flexible platters are currently encased in rigid plastic and are referred to as "diskettes."

Several high-capacity floppy-like disk drives have made their appearance in recent years. The Iomega Zip drive has a capacity of 100 MB and access times that are about twice those of hard drives, and the larger Iomega Jaz drive has a capacity of 2GB, with similar access times.

Another floppy-like drive recently introduced by Imation Corp., the SuperDisk, has floppy-like disks with 120 MB capacity and can also read and write ordinary 1.44-MB floppy disks.

Disk File Systems

A **file** is a collection of sectors that are linked together to form a single logical entity. A file that is stored on a disk can be organized in a number of ways. The most efficient method is to store a file in consecutive sectors so that the seek time and the rotational latency are minimized. A disk normally stores more than one file, and it is generally difficult to predict the maximum file size. Fixed file sizes are appropriate for some applications, though. For instance, satellite images may all have the same size in any one sampling.

An alternative method for organizing files is to assign sectors to a file on demand, as needed. With this method, files can grow to arbitrary sizes, but there may be many head movements involved in reading or writing a file. After a disk system has been in use for a period of time, the files on it may become **fragmented** (that is, the sectors that make up the files are scattered over the disk surfaces). Several vendors produce optimizers that will defragment a disk, reorganizing it so that each file is again stored on contiguous sectors and tracks.

A related facet in disk organization is **interleaving**. If the CPU and interface circuitry between the disk unit and the CPU all keep pace with the internal rate of the disk, then there may still be a hidden performance problem. After a sector is read and buffered, it is transferred to the CPU. If the CPU then requests the next contiguous sector, it may be too late to read the sector without waiting for another revolution. If the sectors are interleaved (for example, if a file is stored on alternate sectors, say 2, 4, 6, etc.), then the time required for the intermediate sectors to pass under the head may be enough time to set up the next transfer. In this scenario, two or more revolutions of the disk are required to read an entire track, but this is less than the revolution per sector that would otherwise be needed. If a single sector time is not long enough to set up the next read, than a greater interleave factor can be used, such as 1 : 3 or 1 : 4. In Figure 8-18, an interleave factor of 1 : 2 is used.

An operating system has the responsibility for allocating blocks (sectors) to a growing file and for reading the blocks that make up a file, and so it needs to know where to find the blocks. The **master control block** (MCB) is a reserved section of a disk that keeps track of the makeup of the rest of the disk. The MCB is normally stored in the same place on every disk for a particular type of computer system, such as the innermost track. In this way, an operating system does not have to guess at the size of a disk; it only needs to read the MCB in the innermost track.

Figure 8-19 shows one version of an MCB. Not all systems keep all of this information in the MCB, but it has to be kept *somewhere*, and some of it may even be kept in part of the file itself. There are four major components to the MCB. The preamble section specifies information relating to the physical layout of the disk, such as the number of surfaces, number of sectors per surface, etc. The files section cross references file names with the list of sectors of which they are composed and file attributes such as the file creation date, last modification date, the identification of

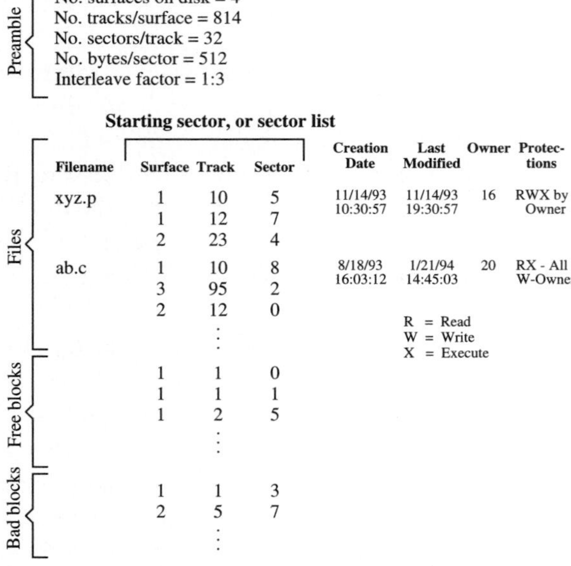

Figure 8-19 Simplified example of an MCB.

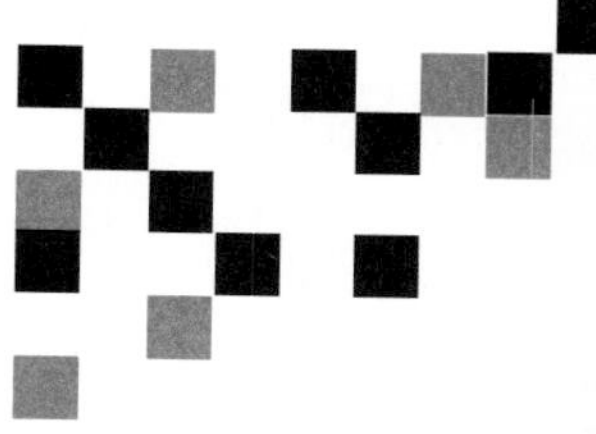

9 COMMUNICATION

Communication is the process of transferring information from a source to a destination. Communication systems for the most part cover distances between computers and may involve the public telephone system, radio, and television. Wide area communication systems have become very complex, with all combinations of voice, data, and video being transferred by wire, optical fiber, radio, and microwaves. Communication routes may traverse distances over land, under water, through local radio cells, and via satellite. Data that originates as analog voice signals may be converted to digital data streams for efficient routing over long distances and then converted back to an analog signal, without the awareness of those communicating.

In this chapter we focus on communication between entities located at distances ranging within a kilometer for a **local area network** (LAN) and across much larger distances for **wide area networks (WANs)**, as typified by the Internet. We start by discussing a few principles of communication.

9.1 Modems

People communicate over telephone lines by forming audible sounds that are converted to electrical signals, which are transmitted to a receiver, where they are converted back to audible sounds. This does not mean that people always need to speak and hear in order to communicate over a telephone line: This audible medium of communication can also be used to transmit nonaudible information that is converted to an audible form.

Figure 9-1 shows a configuration in which two computers communicate over a telephone line through the use of **modems** (which is a contraction of "modulator/demodulator"). A modem transforms an electrical signal from a computer into

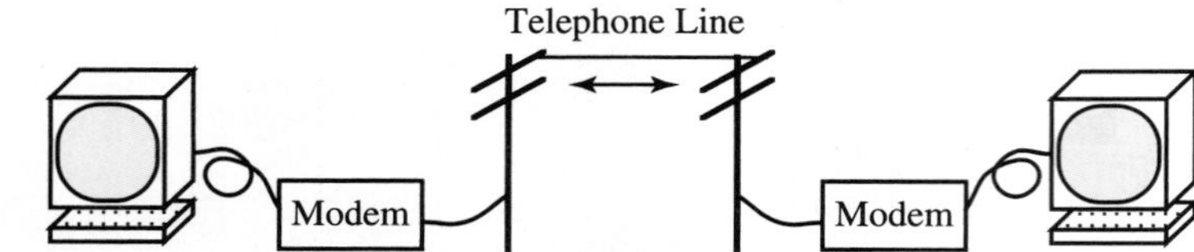

Figure 9-1 Communication over a telephone line with modems.

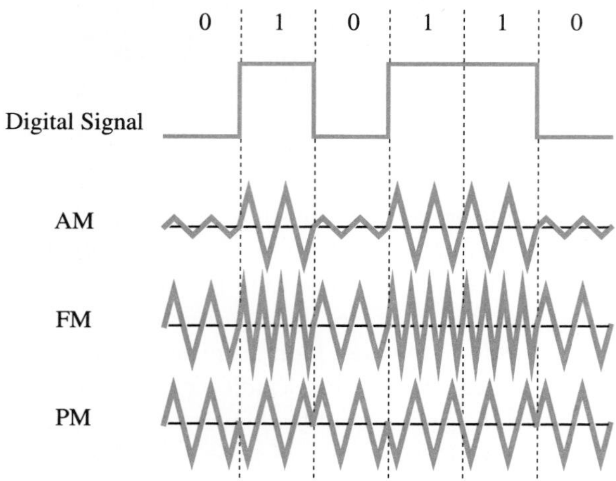

Figure 9-2 Three common forms of modulation.

an audible form for transmission and performs the reverse operation when receiving. (Modems are not only used for telephone communication; they are also used in other communication systems as well, such as data-over-cable TV networks.)

Modem communication over a telephone line is normally performed in serial fashion, a single bit at a time, in which the bits have an encoding that is appropriate for the transmission medium. There are a number of **modulation** schemes used in communication, which are encodings of data into the medium. Figure 9-2 illustrates three common forms of modulation.

Amplitude modulation (AM) uses the strength of the signal to encode 1's and 0's. AM lends itself to simple implementations that are inexpensive to build. However, since there is information in the amplitude of the signal, anything that changes the amplitude affects the signal. For an AM radio, a number of situations affect the amplitude of the signal (such as driving under a bridge or near electrical lines, lightning, etc.).

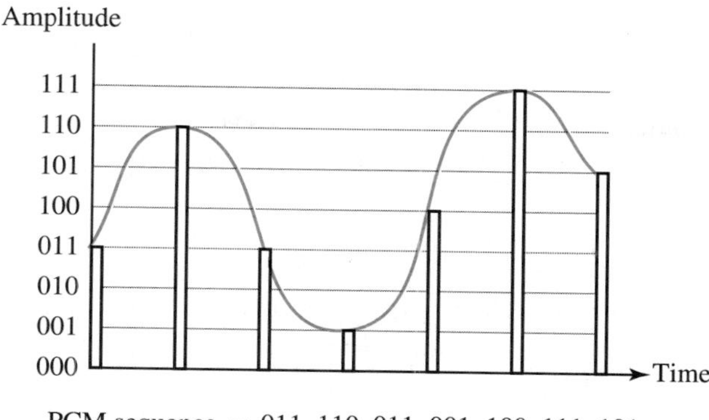

Figure 9-3 Conversion of an analog signal into a PCM binary sequence.

Frequency modulation (FM) is not nearly as sensitive to amplitude-related problems because information is encoded in the frequency of the signal rather than in the amplitude. The FM signal on a radio is relatively static free and does not diminish as the receiver passes under a bridge.

Phase modulation (PM) is most typically used in modems, where four phases (90 degrees apart) double the data bandwidth by transmitting two bits at a time (which are referred to as **dibits**). The use of phase offers a degree of freedom in addition to frequency and is appropriate when the number of available frequencies is restricted.

In **pulse code modulation** (PCM) an analog signal is sampled and converted into binary. Figure 9-3 shows the process of converting an analog signal into a PCM binary sequence. The original signal is sampled at twice the rate of the highest significant frequency, producing values at discrete intervals. The samples are encoded in binary and catenated to produce the PCM sequence.

PCM is a digital approach and has all of the advantages of digital information systems. By using repeaters at regular intervals the signal can be perfectly restored. By decreasing the distance between repeaters, the effective bandwidth of a channel can be significantly increased. Analog signals, however, can at best be guessed and can only be approximately restored. There is no good way to make analog signals perfect in a noisy environment.

Shannon's result about the data rate of a noisy channel applies here:

$$\textit{data rate} = \textit{bandwidth} \times \log(1 + S/N)$$

where S is the signal and N is the noise. Since a digital signal can be made to use arbitrarily noisy channels (in which S/N is large) because of its noise immunity, higher data rates can be achieved over the same channel. This is one of the driving forces in the move to digital technology in the telecommunications industry. The transition to all-digital has also been driven by the rapid drop in the cost of digital circuitry.

9.2 Transmission Media

In a geographically close environment, computers can be networked with private cables in a number of configurations. For geographically distant systems, the public switched telephone network (PSTN) can be used. Users connect to the PSTN with modems that convert logical bits into audible sounds. People can hear at frequencies up to about 20 KHz but only speak at frequencies up to about 4 KHz, which is approximately the bandwidth that traditional telephony will pass on a voice-grade line. An analog signal (such as voice) that is approximated with a digital signal needs to be sampled at least twice per cycle (to capture the high and low values), and so a sampling rate of 8 KHz is needed to digitize a voice-grade line. At 8 bits per sample, that gives a bit rate of 8 bits/cycle × 8 KHz = 64 Kbits/s which is what is available on an ordinary telephone line in North America. One sample out of every 8 is used by the telephone company to administer the line, and so the maximum bit rate possible on a voice-grade line is 56 Kbits/s.

A transmitted binary sequence is converted into high/low values, but the waveform gets attenuated and distorted, more so at high frequencies and long distances. Figure 9-4 illustrates the sampling problem. The binary pattern 01011001 is represented by an ideal wave, which is only approximated by a transmitted wave. The ideal wave contains discontinuities, which are difficult to produce with a real wave. In terms of analysis, we can think of the ideal wave as being approximated with a superposition of sinusoidal waves, with sharper edges achieved at higher frequencies.

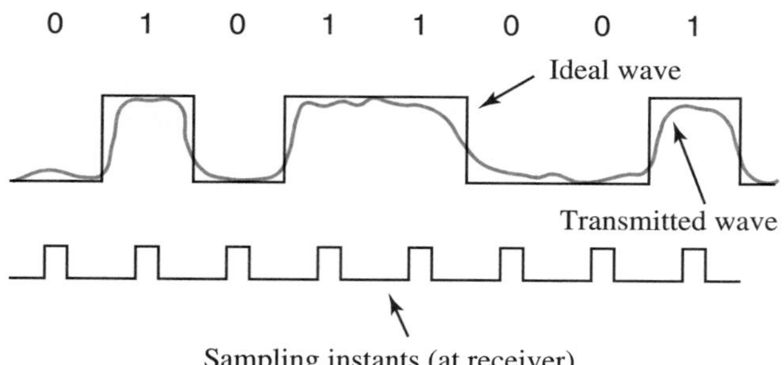

Figure 9-4 Ideal versus transmitted waves.

Unfortunately, high frequencies are attenuated more greatly than low frequencies in most media, and different frequencies propagate at different rates, which leads to distortions of the wave as it propagates. The degree of distortion varies with the transmission medium, several of which are described here.

9.2.1 *TWO-WIRE OPEN LINES*

In one of the simplest scenarios, a pair of wires, open to free space, carries a signal and a return (the "ground"). The two-wire open line configuration is shown in Figure 9-5a. The lines emit electromagnetic radiation, and they also pick up noise, not necessarily the same amount of noise for each line, which distorts the difference signal. The lines are also vulnerable to "capacitive coupling," which means they pick up unwanted signals from neighboring wires. The speed and distance for reliable transmission is limited to about 19.2 Kbps and 50 m.

9.2.2 *TWISTED-PAIR LINES*

If we twist the pair of lines in the two-wire open line configuration, then any spurious external noise that is introduced to the line affects both the signal and ground (reference) wires in the same way. Figure 9-5b shows the twisted-wire

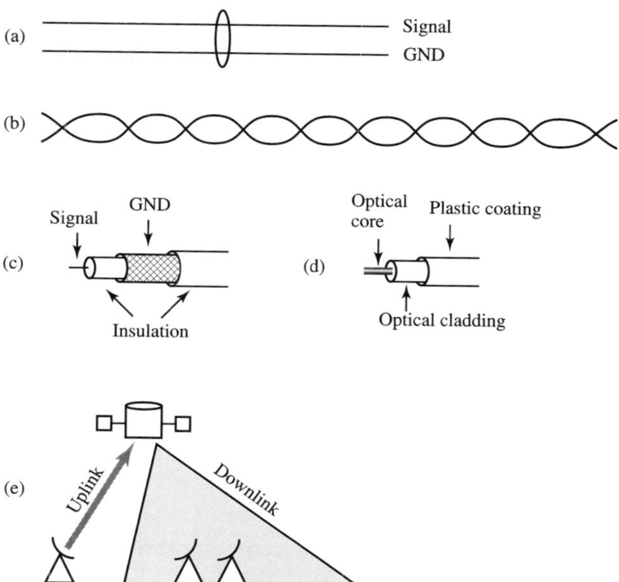

Figure 9-5 Transmission media. (a) Two-wire open lines; (b) twisted-pair lines; (c) ›axial cable; (d) optical fiber; (e)satellites.

configuration. The difference signal is thus unaffected, and reliable transmission can go up to 1 Mbps over 100 m.

9.2.3 *COAXIAL CABLE*

For higher speeds (10 Mbps) and longer distances (hundreds of meters), the signal wire is placed inside of the reference conductor (coaxially) with an insulator between the two, as shown in Figure 9-5c. (The braiding of the outer conductor makes the cable more flexible.) The idea is that the center conductor is effectively shielded from external interference and is also shielded from losses due to electromagnetic radiation.

9.2.4 *OPTICAL FIBER*

Optical communication is immune to electromagnetic interference and crosstalk and supports a much wider bandwidth. There is a need for optoelectronic conversions on each end, which is commercially available up to a few Gbps (using laser diodes.) Optical fiber consists of the optical core, optical cladding, and a plastic coating, as shown in Figure 9-5d.

A light emitting diode (LED) is a less expensive light source than a laser diode, but it emits light at various angles, and so a **multimode stepped index** fiber is used that reflects light less than the critical angle back into the core. Because the path lengths differ, the received pulse is wider, and only modest bit rates can be supported. The LEDs are inexpensive, however, and bending tolerances are a less significant issue than for laser diodes.

With a **multimode graded index** fiber, light is refracted more greatly as it moves away from the core, which narrows the pulse and reduces losses.

Single mode (monomode) fiber reduces the core diameter to a single wavelength so that light travels along a single dispersionless path. Laser diodes are commonly used as sources for single mode fiber and can operate up to several Gbps over tens of kilometers.

9.2.5 *SATELLITES*

Humanmade satellites that are launched into orbit around the Earth are used for communication when a broad area of coverage is needed at a lower cost than a wireline network (including optical fibers). Natural satellites, inside and outside of Earth orbits (such as the Moon and asteroids), can also be used for communication but are not generally in use for such purposes.

In satellite communication, a collimated microwave beam is transmitted from the ground to a satellite, where a transponder that covers a certain band of frequencies retransmits the signal to an area of coverage on the Earth. The satellite configuration is shown in Figure 9-5e.

A typical satellite has several transponders at 500 MHz per channel. A small area of coverage means that the transmitted signal is stronger and the receiving dishes can be smaller. This is typical for direct broadcast satellite (DBS) television, in which very small receiving dishes are used. The DBS satellites orbit the Earth at a low orbit, approximately 700 Km, and so a smaller collecting area is needed than for satellites that are placed in geosynchronous orbit (23,000 miles above the surface of the Earth), where the Earth's attractive gravitational force and the repelling centrifugal force are balanced, so that the satellite appears stationary over the ground when the orbit collocates with the equator. This is why large satellite dishes are aimed in the direction of the equator.

For two-way satellite network communication, the delay between the end user and the satellite needs to be tolerable. The uplink to the satellite is generally slower than the downlink. This matches the typical mode of operation for an end user on the Internet, since less than 10% of the network traffic goes from the end user to the Internet, and over 90% of the network traffic goes from the Internet to the end user. The speed of communication is limited by *c* (the speed of light in a vacuum), which is approximately 1 ns per foot or 5 μs per mile (5280 feet per mile). Over a distance of 23,000 miles, the free space delay is more than 100 ms to the satellite and another 100 ms back to the Earth, plus a processing delay. This is more than the acceptable average delay of 100 ms needed for a keystroke response. Low Earth orbit (LEO) is only 700 Km, and introduces a much smaller delay, on the order of spanning the distance of a few states in the United States, and is therefore better suited for interactive networking.

9.2.6 *TERRESTRIAL MICROWAVE*

Ground-based line-of-sight links are effective up to 50 Km, particularly for crossing difficult terrain, although they are prone to atmospheric disturbances, flocks of geese, etc.

9.2.7 *RADIO*

In cellular radio communication, a radio base station is placed in the middle of a **cell**, which is generally less than 20 Km in diameter. A restricted band of frequencies is used within a cell, for communication between roaming cellular devices and the base station. Neighboring cells use a different band of frequencies, so that there is no confusion at the cell boundary where a **handoff** is made as a roaming end user transits from one cell to another, which normally involves a frequency change.

Total available bandwidth in a cell is small, on the order of 2 MB/s, which is subdivided over the number of channels in use. In congested areas, cell sizes are smaller than in less densely populated areas, sometimes extending no farther than a single building.

9.3 Network Architecture: Local Area Networks

A **local area network** (LAN) is a communication medium that interconnects computers over a limited geographical distance of a few kilometers at most. A LAN allows a set of closely grouped computers and other devices to share common resources such as data, software applications, printers, and mass storage.

A LAN consists of hardware, software, and protocols. The hardware may be in the form of cables and interface circuitry. The software is typically embedded in an operating system and is responsible for connecting a user to the network. The protocols are sets of rules that govern format, timing, sequencing, and error control. Protocols are important for ensuring that data is packaged for injection into the network and is extracted from the network properly. The data to be transmitted is decomposed into pieces, each of which is prepended with a **header** that contains information about parameters such as the destination, the source, error protection bits, and a time stamp. The data, which is often referred to as the **payload**, is combined with the header to form a **packet** that is injected into the network. A receiver goes through the reverse process of extracting the data from the packet.

The process of communicating over a network is normally carried out in a hierarchy of steps, each of which has its own protocol. The steps must be followed in sequence for transmission and in the reverse sequence when receiving. This leads to the notion of a **protocol stack**, which isolates the protocol being used within the hierarchy.

9.3.1 *THE OSI MODEL*

The **Open System Interconnection** (OSI) model is a set of protocols established by the International Standards Organization (ISO) in an attempt to define and standardize data communications. The OSI model has been somewhat displaced

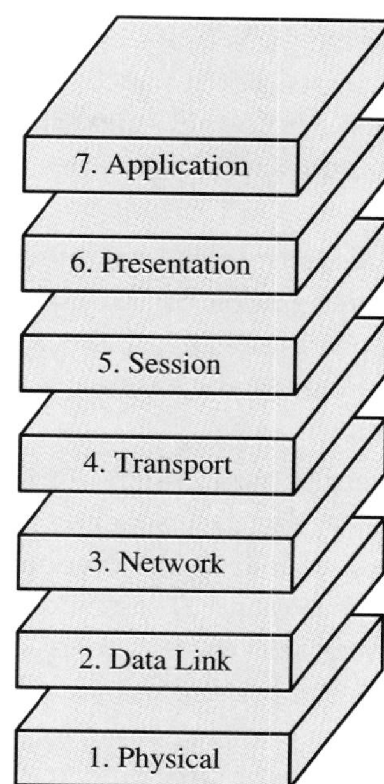

Figure 9-6 The seven layers of the OSI model.

by the Internet TCP/IP model (see Section 9.5) but still heavily influences network communication, particularly for the telecommunication industry.

In the OSI model the communication process is divided into seven layers: **application**, **presentation**, **session**, **transport**, **network**, **data link**, and **physical**, as summarized in Figure 9-6. As an aid in remembering the layers, the mnemonic is sometimes used: **A P**owered-down **S**ystem **T**ransmits **N**o **D**ata **P**ackets.

The OSI model does not give a single definition of how data communications actually take place. Instead, the OSI model serves as a reference for how the process should be divided and what protocols should be used at each layer. The concept is that equipment providers can select a protocol for each layer while ensuring compatibility with equipment from other providers that may use different protocols.

The highest level in the OSI model is the application layer, which provides an interface for allowing applications to communicate with each other over the network. It offers high-level support for applications that interact over the network, such as database services for network database programs, message handling for **electronic mail** (e-mail) programs, and file handling for file transfer programs.

The presentation layer ensures that information is presented to communication applications in a common format. This is necessary because different systems may use different internal data formats. For instance, some systems use a big-endian internal format while others use a little-endian internal format. The function of the presentation layer is to insulate the applications from these differences.

The session layer establishes and terminates communication sessions between host processes. The session layer is responsible for maintaining the integrity of communication even if the layers below it lose data. It also synchronizes the exchange and establishes reference points for continuing an interrupted communication.

The transport layer ensures reliable transmission from source to destination. It allocates communication resources so that data is transferred both quickly and cost effectively. The session layer makes requests to the transport layer, which prioritizes the requests and makes trade-offs among speed, cost, and capacity. For example, a transmission may be split into several packets, which are transmitted over a number of networks in order to obtain a faster communication time. Packets may thus arrive at the destination out of order, and it is the responsibility of the transport layer to ensure that the session layer receives data in the same order it is sent. The transport layer provides error recovery from source to destination and also provides flow control (that is, it ensures that the speeds of the sender and receiver are matched).

The network layer routes data through intermediate systems and subnetworks. Unlike the upper layers, the network layer is aware of the network **topology**, which is the connectivity among the network components. The network layer informs the transport layer of the status of potential and existing connections in the network in terms of speed, reliability, and availability. The network layer is typically implemented with **routers**, which connect different networks that use the same transport protocol.

The data link layer manages the direct connections between components on a network. This layer is divided into the **logical link control** (LLC), which is independent of the network topology, and the **media access control** (MAC), which is specific to the topology. In some networks the physical connections between devices are not permanent, and it is the responsibility of the data link layer to inform the physical layer when to make connections. This layer deals in units of **frames** (single packets, or collections of packets that may be interleaved), which contain addresses, data, and control information.

The physical layer ensures that raw data is transmitted from a source to a destination over the physical medium. It transmits and repeats signals across network boundaries. The physical layer does *not* include the hardware itself but includes methods of accessing the hardware.

9.3.2 *TOPOLOGIES*

There are three primary LAN organizations, as illustrated in Figure 9-7. The **bus** topology is the simplest of the three. Components are connected to a bus system by simply plugging them into the single cable that runs through the network or in the case of a wireless network, by simply emitting signals into a common medium. An advantage to this type of topology is that each component can communicate directly with any other component on the bus and that it is relatively simple to add another component to the network. Control is distributed among the components, and so there is no single network component that serves as an intermediary, which reduces the initial cost of this type of network. Disadvantages of this topology include a limit on the length of the cable from the bus to each network component (for a wireline network) and that a break in the cable may be needed in order to add another component to the network, which disrupts the rest of the network. An example of a bus-based network is Ethernet.

The **ring** topology uses a single cable, in which the ends are joined. Packets are passed around the ring through each network component until they reach their destinations. At the destinations, the packets are extracted from the network and are not passed farther along the ring. If a packet makes its way back to the originating system, then the transmission is unsuccessful, and so the packet is stopped and a new transmission can be attempted. An example of a ring-based LAN is IBM's token ring.

In a **star** topology, each component is connected to a central **hub**, which serves as an intermediary for all communication over the network. In a simple configu-

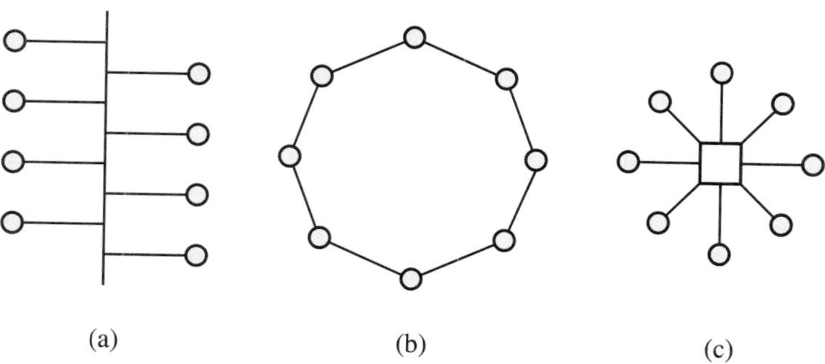

Figure 9-7 (a) Bus; (b) ring; and (c) star network topologies.

ration, the hub receives data from one component and forwards it to all of the other components, leaving it to the individual components to determine whether or not they are the intended target. In a more sophisticated configuration, the hub receives data and forwards it to a specific network component.

An advantage of a star topology is that most of the network service, troubleshooting, and wiring changes take place at the central hub. A disadvantage is that a problem with the hub affects the entire network. Another disadvantage is that geometrically, the star topology requires more cable than a bus or a ring because a separate cable connects each network component to the hub. An example of a star topology is ARCnet (although it is actually a bus-based network).

9.3.3 *DATA TRANSMISSION*

Communication within a computer is synchronized by a common clock, and so the transmission of a 1 or a 0 is signaled by a high or low voltage that is sampled at a time determined by the clock. This scheme is simple but does not work well over longer distances, as in a LAN. The problem is that there is no timing reference to signal the start or stop of a bit. When there is a long string of 1's or 0's, timing with respect to the sending and receiving clocks may drift because the clocks are not precisely synchronized. The distances over a LAN are too great to maintain both a global clock and high speed at the same time. LANs thus typically use the Manchester encoding scheme (see Section 8.5), in which timing is embedded in the data.

Manchester encoding is applied at the lowest level of transmission. At the next level, a data stream is decomposed into packets and frames that are transmitted over the network, not necessarily in order. The data link layer is responsible for decomposing a data stream into packets, forming packets into frames, and injecting frames into the network. When receiving frames, the data link layer extracts the packets and assembles them into a format that the higher-level network layers can use. The size of a data packet is commonly on the order of a kilobyte and requires a few microseconds for transmission at typical speeds and distances.

Ethernet is one of the most prevalent bus-based networks. Ethernet uses **carrier sense multiple access** with **collision detection** (CSMA/CD) for transmission. Under CSMA/CD, when a network component wants to transmit data, it first listens for a carrier. If there is a carrier present on the line, which is placed there by a transmitting device, then it transmits nothing and listens again after a random waiting period. The random waiting period is important in order to avoid a **deadlock** in which components that are trying to access the bus perpetually listen and wait in synchrony.

If there is no traffic on the line, then transmission can begin by placing a carrier on the line with the data. The source also listens for **collisions**, in which two or more components simultaneously transmit. A collision is detected by the presence of more than one carrier. Collisions can occur in a fully operational network as a result of the finite time it takes for a signal to travel the length of the bus. The propagation of signals on the bus is bounded by the speed of light over the length of the bus, which can be 500 m in a generic Ethernet installation. When a collision occurs, the transmitting components wait for a random interval before retransmitting.

Transmitted data moves in both directions over the bus. Every component sees every packet of data but only extracts those packets with corresponding destination addresses. After a packet is successfully delivered, the destination can generate an acknowledgment to the sender, typically at the transport layer. If the sender does not receive an acknowledgment after a fixed period of time (which must be greater than the round trip delay through the network), then it retransmits the message.

Collisions should occur infrequently in practice, and so the overhead of recovering from a collision is not very significant. A serious degradation in Ethernet performance does not occur until traffic increases to about 35% of network capacity.

9.3.4 *BRIDGES, ROUTERS, AND GATEWAYS*

As networks grow in size, they can be subdivided into smaller networks that are interconnected. The smaller **subnetworks** operate almost entirely independently of each other and can use different protocols and topologies.

If the subnetworks all use the same topology and the same protocols, then it may be the case that all that is needed to extend the network are **repeaters**. A repeater amplifies the signals on the network, which become attenuated in proportion to the distance traveled. The overall network is divided into subnetworks, in which each subnetwork operates somewhat independently with respect to the others. The subnetworks are not entirely independent because every subnetwork sees all of the traffic that occurs on the other subnetworks. A network with simple repeaters is not extensible to large sizes. Since noise is amplified as well as the signal, the noise will eventually dominate the signal if too many repeaters are used in succession.

A **bridge** (different from a bus bridge, introduced in Chapter 10) does more than simply amplify signal levels. A bridge restores the individual signal levels to logical 1 or 0, which prevents noise from accumulating. Bridges have some level of intelligence and can typically interpret the destination address of a packet and route it to the appropriate subnetwork. In this way, network traffic can be reduced, since the alternative method would be to blindly send each incoming packet to each subnetwork (as for a repeater-based network).

Although bridges have some level of intelligence in that they sense the incoming bits and make routing decisions based on destination addresses, they are unaware of protocols. A **router** operates at a higher level, in the network layer. Routers typically connect logically separate networks that use the same transport protocol.

A **gateway** translates packets up through the application layer of the OSI model (layers 4 through 7). Gateways connect dissimilar networks by performing protocol conversions, message format conversions, and other high-level functions.

9.4 Communication Errors and Error Correcting Codes

In situations involving communications between computers, and even inside of a computer system, there is a finite chance that the data is received in error, due to noise in the communication channel. The data representations we have considered up to this point make use of the binary symbols 1 and 0. In reality, the binary symbols take on physical forms such as voltages or electric current. The physical form is subject to noise that is introduced from the environment, such as atmospheric phenomena, gamma rays, and power fluctuations, to name just a few. The noise can cause errors, also known as **faults**, in which a 0 is turned into a 1 or a 1 is turned into a 0.

Suppose that the ASCII character 'b' is transmitted from a sender to a receiver, and during transmission, an error occurs, so that the least significant bit is inverted. The correct bit pattern for ASCII 'b' is 1100010. The bit pattern that the receiver sees is 1100011, which corresponds to the character 'c.' There is no way for the receiver to know that an error occurred simply by looking at the received character. The problem is that all of the possible 2^7 ASCII bit patterns represent valid characters, and if any of the bit patterns is transformed into another through an error, then the resulting bit pattern appears to be valid.

It is possible for the sender to transmit additional "check bits" along with the data bits. The receiver can examine these check bits and under certain conditions not only detect errors, but correct them as well. Two methods of computing these additional bits are described in the following sections. We start by introducing some preliminary information and definitions.

9.4.1 *BIT ERROR RATE DEFINED*

There are many different ways that errors can be introduced into a system, and those errors can take many different forms. For the moment, we will assume that the probability that a given bit is received in error is independent of the probability that other bits near it are received in error. In this case, we can define the **bit error rate** (BER) as the probability that a given bit is erroneous. Obviously this must be a small number and is usually less than 10^{-12} errors per bit examined for fiber networks. That means, loosely speaking, that as bits are examined, only one in every 10^{12} bits will be erroneous (in radio networks, as many as 1 in every 100 packets may contain an error.)

Inside of a computer system typical BERs may run 10^{-18} or less. As a rough estimate, if the clock rate of the computer is 500 MHz, and 32 bits are manipulated during each clock period, then the number of errors per second for that portion of the computer will be 10^{-18} errors/bit $\times$ 500 $\times$ 10^6 words/s $\times$ 32 bits/word or 1.6 $\times$ 10^{-8} errors per second, approximately one erroneous bit once every two years.

On the other hand, if one is receiving a bit stream from a serial communications line at, say, 1 million bits per second, and the BER is 10^{-10}, then the number of errors per second will be $1 \times 10^6 \times 10^{-10}$ or 10^{-4} errors per second, approximately 10 errors per day.

9.4.2 *ERROR DETECTION AND CORRECTION*

One of the simplest and oldest methods of error detection was used to detect errors in transmitting and receiving characters in telegraphy. A **parity bit**, 1 or 0, was added to each character to make the total number of 1's in the character even or odd, as agreed upon by sender and receiver. In our example of transmitting the ASCII character 'b,' 1100010, assuming even parity, a 1 would be attached as a parity bit to make the total number of 1's even, resulting in the bit pattern 11000101 being transmitted. The receiver could then examine the bit pattern, and if there was an even number of 1's, the receiver could assume that the character was received without error. (This method fails if there is a significant probability of two or more bits being received in error. In this case, other methods must be used, as discussed later in this section.) The intuition behind this approach is explored next.

Hamming Codes

If additional bits are added to the data, then it is possible not only to detect errors, but to correct them as well. Some of the most popular error correcting

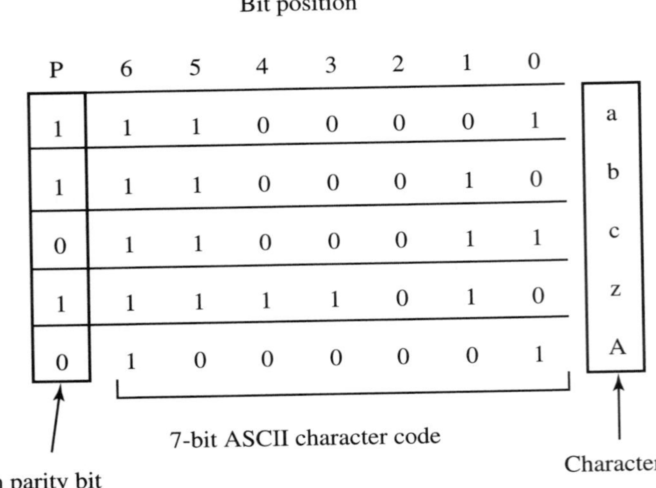

Figure 9-8 Even parity bits are assigned to a few ASCII characters.

codes are based on the work of Richard Hamming while at Bell Telephone Laboratories (now Lucent Technologies).

We can detect single-bit errors in the ASCII code by adding a redundant bit to each **codeword** (character). The **Hamming distance** defines the logical distance between two valid codewords, as measured by the number of digits that differ between the codewords. If a single bit changes in an ASCII character, then the resulting bit pattern represents a different ASCII character. The corresponding Hamming distance for this code is 1. If we recode the ASCII table so that there is a Hamming distance of 2 between valid codewords, then two bits must change in order to convert one character into another. We can then detect a single-bit error because the corrupted word will lie between valid codewords.

One way to recode ASCII for a Hamming distance of two is to assign a parity bit, which takes on a value of 0 or 1 to make the total number of 1's in a codeword odd or even. If we use **even parity**, then the parity bit for the character 'a' is 1 since there are three 1's in the bit pattern for 'a': 1100001 and assigning a parity bit of 1 (to the left of the codeword here) makes the total number of 1's in the recoded 'a' even: 11100001. This is illustrated in Figure 9-8. Similarly, the parity bit for 'c' is 0, which results in the recoded bit pattern 01100011. If we use **odd parity** instead, then the parity bits take on the opposite values: 0 for 'a' and 1 for 'c', which results in the recoded bit patterns 01100001 and 11100011, respectively.

The recoded ASCII table now has $2^8 = 256$ entries, of which half of the entries (the ones with an odd number of 1's) represent invalid codewords. If an invalid codeword is received, then the receiver knows that an error occurred and can request a retransmission.

A retransmission may not always be practical, and for these cases it would be helpful both to detect and correct an error. The use of a parity bit will detect an error but will not locate the position of an error. If the bit pattern 11100011 is received in a system that uses even parity, then the presence of an error is known because the parity of the received word is odd. There is not enough information from the parity bit alone to determine if the original pattern was 'a', 'b', or any of five other characters in the ASCII table. In fact, the original character might even be 'c' if the parity bit itself is in error.

In order to construct an error correcting code that is capable of detecting and correcting single-bit errors, we must add more redundancy than a single parity bit provides to the ASCII code by further extending the number of bits in each codeword. For instance, consider the bit pattern for 'a': 1100001. If we wish to detect and correct a single bit error in any position of the word, then we need to assign seven additional bit patterns to 'a' in which exactly one bit changes in the original 'a' codeword: 0100001, 1000001, 1110001, 1101001, 1100101, 1100011, and 1100000. We can do the same for 'b' and the remaining characters, but we must construct the code in such a way that no bit pattern is common to more than one ASCII character; otherwise we will have no means to determine unambiguously the original bit pattern.

A problem with using redundancy in this way is that we assign eight bit patterns to every character: one for the original bit pattern, and seven for the neighboring error patterns. Since there are 2^7 characters in the ASCII code, and since we need 2^3 bit patterns for every character, then we can only recode $2^7/2^3 = 2^4$ characters if we use only the original seven bits in the representation.

In order to recode all of the characters, we must add additional **redundant bits** (also referred to as **check bits**) to the codewords. Let us now determine how many bits we need. If we start with a k-bit word that we would like to recode, and we use r check bits, then the following relationship must hold:

$$2^k \times (k + r + 1) \leq 2^{k+r} \equiv k + r + 1 \leq 2^r \qquad (8.1)$$

Check bits C8 C4 C2 C1	Bit position checked
0 0 0 1	1
0 0 1 0	2
0 0 1 1	3
0 1 0 0	4
0 1 0 1	5
0 1 1 0	6
0 1 1 1	7
1 0 0 0	8
1 0 0 1	9
1 0 1 0	10
1 0 1 1	11

Figure 9-9 Check bits for a single error correcting ASCII code.

The reasoning behind this relationship is that for each of the 2^k original words, there are k bit patterns in which a single bit is corrupted in the original word, plus r bit patterns in which one of the check bits is in error, plus the original uncorrupted bit pattern. Thus, our error correcting code will have a total of $2^k \times (k + r + 1)$ bit patterns. In order to support all of these bit patterns, there must be enough bit patterns generated by $l + r$ bits; thus 2^{k+r} must be greater than or equal to the number of bit patterns in the error correcting code. There are $k = 7$ bits in the ASCII code, and so we must now solve for r. If we try a few successive values, starting at 1, we find that $r = 4$ is the smallest value that satisfies relation (8.1). The resulting codewords will thus have 7 + 4 = 11 bits.

We now consider how to recode the ASCII table into the 11-bit code. Our goal is to assign the redundant bits to the original words in such a way that any single-bit error can be identified. One way to make the assignment is shown in Figure 9-9. Each of the 11 bits in the recoded word are assigned a position in the table indexed from 1 to 11, and the 4-bit binary representations of the integers 1 through 11 are shown next to each index. With this assignment, reading across each of the 11 rows of four check bits, there is a unique positioning of the 1 bits in each row, and so no two rows are the same. For example, the top row has a single 1 in position C1, but no other row has only a single 1 in position C1 (other rows have a 1 in position C1, but they also have 1's in the other check bit positions).

Now, reading down each of the four check bit columns, the positions of the 1 bits tell us which bits, listed in the rightmost "Bit position checked" column, are

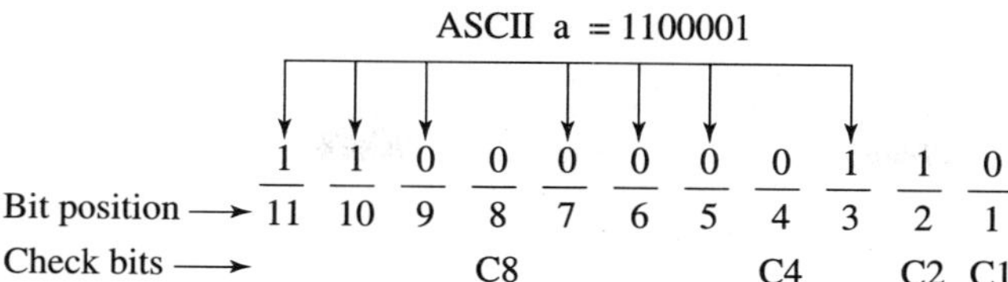

Figure 9-10 Format for a single error correcting ASCII code.

included in a group that must form even parity. For example, check bit C8 covers a group of 4 bits in positions 8, 9, 10, and 11, which collectively must form even parity. If this property is satisfied when the 11-bit word is transmitted, but an error in transmission causes this group of bits to have odd parity at the receiver, then the receiver will know that there must be an error in either position 8, 9, 10, or 11. The exact position can be determined by observing the remaining check bits, as we will see.

In more detail, each bit in the 11-bit encoded word, which includes the check bits, is assigned to a unique combination of the four check bits C1, C2, C4, and C8. The combinations are computed as the binary representation of the position of the bit being checked, starting at position 1. C1 is thus in bit position 1, C2 is in position 2, C4 is in position 4, etc. The check bits can appear anywhere in the word, but normally appear in positions that correspond to powers of 2 in order to simplify the process of locating an error. This particular code is known as a **single error correcting (SEC)** code.

Since the positions of the 1's in each of the check bit combinations is unique, we can locate an error by simply observing which of the check bits are in error. Consider the format shown in Figure 9-10 for the ASCII character 'a'. The values of the check bits are determined according to the table shown in Figure 9-9. Check bit C1 = 0 creates even parity for the bit group {1, 3, 5, 7, 9, 11}. The members in this group are taken from the positions that have 1's in the C1 column in Figure 9-9. Check bit C2 = 1 creates even parity for the bit group {2, 3, 6, 7, 10, 11}. Similarly, check bit C4 = 0 creates even parity for the bit group {4, 5, 6, 7}. Finally, check bit C8 = 0 creates even parity for the bit group {8, 9, 10, 11}.

As an alternative to looking up members of a parity group in a table, in general, bit n of the coded word is checked by those check bits in positions $b_1, b_2, \ldots b_j$, such that $b_1 + b_2 \ldots + b_j = n$. For example, bit 7 is checked by bits in positions 1, 2, and 4 because 1 + 2 + 4 = 7.

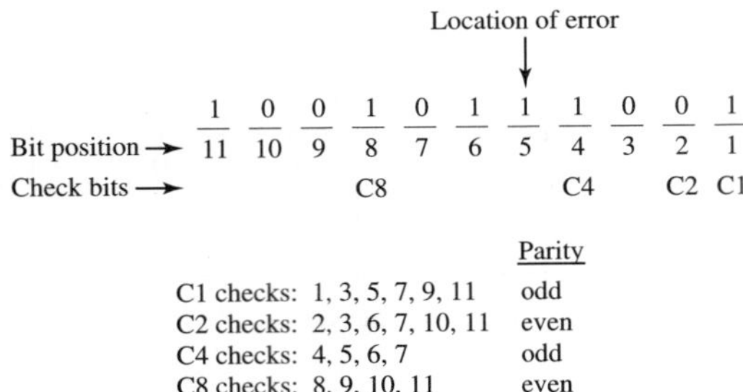

Figure 9-11 Parity computation for an ASCII character in an SEC code.

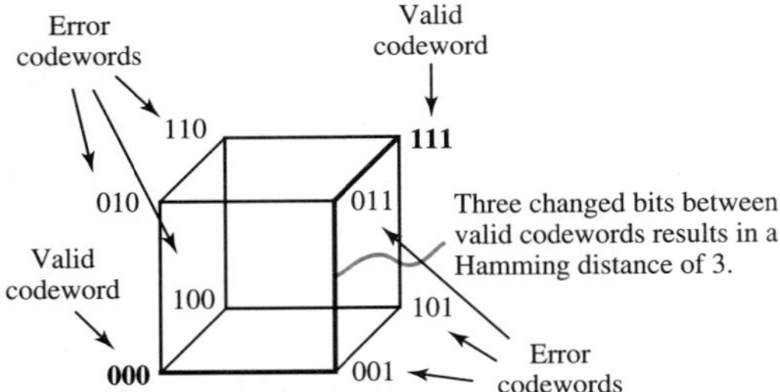

Figure 9-12 Hamming distance relationships among three-bit codewords. Valid codewords are 000 and 111. The remaining codewords represent errors.

Now suppose that a receiver sees the bit pattern 10010111001. Assuming that the SEC code for ASCII characters just described is used, what character was sent? We start by computing the parity for each of the check bits as shown in Figure 9-11. As shown in the figure, check bits C1 and C4 have odd parity. In order to locate the error, we simply add up the positions of the odd check bits. The error, then, is in position 1 + 4 = 5. The word that was sent is 10010101001. If we strip away the check bits, then we end up with the bit pattern 1000100, which corresponds to the ASCII character 'D'.

One way to think about an SEC code is that valid codewords are spaced far enough apart so that a single error places a corrupted codeword closer to one particular valid codeword than to any other valid codeword. For example, consider an SEC code for a set of just two symbols: {000, 111}. The Hamming distance relationships for all three-bit patterns are shown for this code in the cube in Figure 9-12. The cube has correspondingly higher dimensions for larger word sizes, resulting in what is called a **hypercube**. The two valid codewords are shown on opposing vertices. Any single bit error will locate an invalid codeword at a different vertex on the cube. Every error codeword has a closest valid codeword, which makes single error correction possible.

SECDED Encoding

If we now consider the case in which there are two errors, then we can see that the SEC code works for **double error detection** (**DED**) but not for **double error correction** (**DEC**). This is sometimes referred to as **SECDED** encoding. Since valid codewords are spaced at a Hamming distance of 3, two errors will locate an error codeword on the cube, and thus two errors can be detected. The original codeword cannot be determined unambiguously, however, since vertices that correspond to two errors from one codeword overlap vertices that correspond to a single error from another codeword. Thus, every SEC code is also a DED code, but every DED code is not necessarily a DEC code. In order to correct two errors, a Hamming distance of five must be maintained. In general, a Hamming distance of $p + 1$ must be maintained in order to detect p errors, and a Hamming distance of $2p + 1$ must be maintained to correct p errors.

9.4.3 *VERTICAL REDUNDANCY CHECKING*

The SEC code described in the previous section is used for detecting and correcting single bit errors in individual data words. Redundant bits are added to each data word, and each resulting codeword is treated independently. The recoding scheme is sometimes referred to as **horizontal** or **longitudinal redundancy checking** (LRC) because the width of the codeword is extended for the redundant bits.

An alternative approach is to use a **vertical redundancy checking** (VRC) code, in which a **checksum** word is added at the end of a group of words that are transmitted. In this case, parity is computed on a column by column basis, forming a checksum word that is appended to the message. The checksum word is computed and transmitted by the sender and is recomputed and compared to the transmitted checksum word by the receiver. If an error is detected, then the receiver must request a retransmission since there is not enough redundancy to identify the position of an error. The VRC and LRC codes can be combined to improve error checking, as shown for the ASCII characters 'A' through 'H' in Figure 9-13.

In some situations, errors are bursty and may corrupt several contiguous bits both horizontally and vertically. A more powerful scheme such as **cyclic redundancy checking** (CRC) is more appropriate for this situation, which is a variation of VRC checking in which the bits are grouped in a special way, as described in the next section.

P	Code	Character
0	1000001	A
0	1000010	B
1	1000011	C
0	1000100	D
1	1000101	E
1	1000110	F
0	1000111	G
0	1001000	H
1	0001000	Checksum

Figure 9-13 Combined LRC and VRC checking. Checksum bits form even parity for each column.

9.4.4 *CYCLIC REDUNDANCY CHECKING*

Cyclic redundancy checking (CRC) is a more powerful error detection and correction scheme that operates in the presence of **burst errors**, which each begin and end with a bit error, with zero or more intervening corrupted bits. The two endpoint corrupted bits are included in the burst error. If the length of a burst error is *B*, then there must be *B* or more uncorrupted bits between burst errors.

CRCs use **polynomial codes**, in which a frame to be transmitted is divided by a polynomial, and the remainder is appended to the frame as a **frame check sequence** (FCS), commonly known as the **CRC digits**. The frame is transmitted (or stored) along with the CRC digits. After receiving the frame, the receiver then goes through the same computation, using the same polynomial, and if the remainders agree then there are no detectable errors. There can be undetectable errors, and the goal in creating a CRC code is to select a polynomial that covers the statistically likely errors for a given fault model.

The basic approach starts with a *k*-bit message to be transmitted, $M(x)$, which is appended with *n* 0's in which *n* is the degree of the **generator polynomial,** $G(x)$, with $k > n$. This extended form of $M(x)$ is divided by $G(x)$ using modulo 2 arithmetic (in which carries and borrows are discarded), and then the remainder, $R(x)$, which is no more than *n* bits wide, forms the CRC digits for $M(x)$.

As an example, consider a frame to be transmitted:

$$M(x) = 1101011011$$

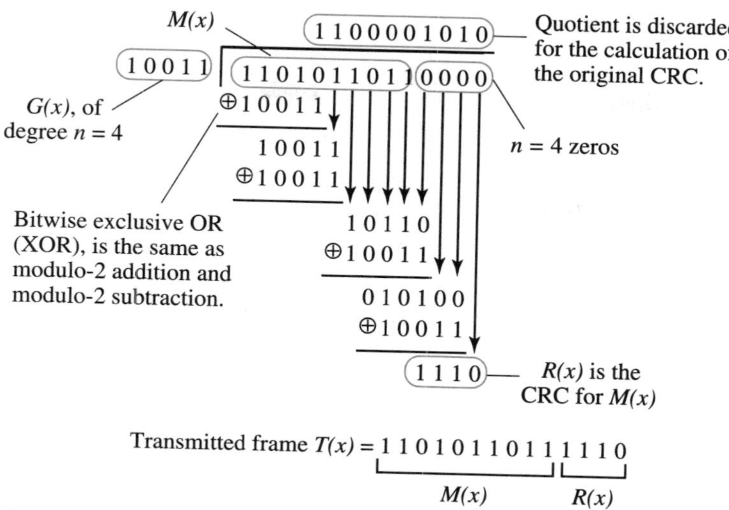

Figure 9-14 Calculation of the CRC digits.

and a generator polynomial $G(x) = x^4 + x + 1$. The **degree** of $G(x)$ (the highest exponent) is 4, and so we append 4 zeros to $M(x)$ to form the dividend of the computation.

The divisor is 10011, which corresponds to the coefficients in $G(x)$ written as:

$$G(x) = 1 \times x^4 + 0 \times x^3 + 0 \times x^2 + 1 \times x^1 + 1 \times x^0$$

Notice that $G(x)$ has a degree of $n = 4$ and that there are $n + 1 = 5$ coefficients. The CRC digits are then computed as shown in Figure 9-14. The divisor (10011) is divided into the dividend, but the magnitudes of the divisor and dividend do not play a role in determining whether the divisor "goes into" the dividend at the location of a particular digit. All that matters is that the number of bits in the divisor (which has no leading zeros) matches the same number of bits in the dividend (which also must not have leading zeros at the position being checked). Note that there are no borrows in modulo-2 subtraction and that a bit-by-bit exclusive-OR (XOR) operation between the divisor and the dividend achieves the same result.

Now suppose that the transmitted frame $T(x) = M(x) + R(x)$ gets corrupted during transmission. The receiver needs to detect that this has happened. The receiver divides the received frame by $G(x)$, and all burst errors that do not include $G(x)$ as a factor will be caught because there will be a nonzero remainder for these cases. That is, as long as the 1's in 10011 do not coincide with the positions of errors in the received frame, all errors will be caught. In general, a polynomial code of degree n will catch all burst errors of length $\leq n$.

Common polynomials that give good error coverage include

$$\text{CRC-16} = x^{16} + x^{15} + x^2 + 1$$

$$\text{CRC-CCITT} = x^{16} + x^{12} + x^5 + 1$$

$$\text{CRC-32} = x^{32} + x^{26} + x^{23} + x^{16} + x^{12} + x^{11} + x^{10} + x^8 + x^7 + x^5 + x^4 + x^2 + x + 1$$

A deeper analysis of CRC codes is beyond the scope of this book, and the reader is referred to (Hamming, 1986) for further details.

EXAMPLE: DOUBLE ERROR CORRECTION

Consider how many check bits are needed for a double error correcting ASCII code. There are $k = 7$ bits for each ASCII character, and we need to add r check bits to each codeword. For each of the 2^k ASCII characters there are $k + r$ possible one-bit error patterns, there are

$$\frac{(k+r)(k+r-1)}{2}$$

possible two-bit error patterns, and there is one bit pattern for the uncorrupted codeword. There are 2^{k+r} possible bit patterns, and so the following relation must hold:

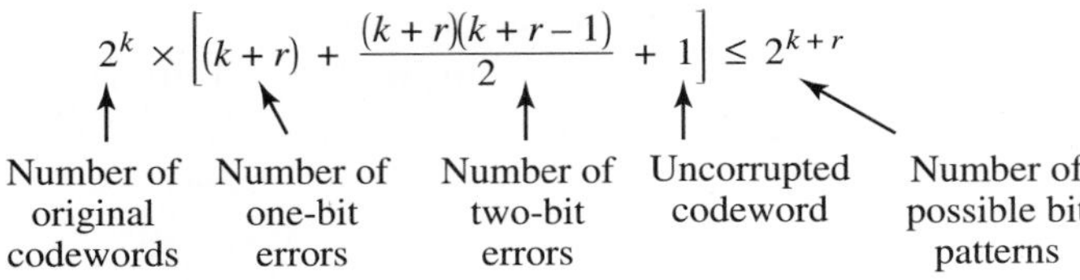

Simplifying, using $k = 7$, yields: $r^2 + 15r + 58 \le 2r + 1$ for which $r = 7$ is the smallest value that satisfies the relation.

Since a Hamming distance of $2p + 1$ must be maintained to correct p errors, the Hamming distance for this DEC code must be at least $2 \times 2 + 1 + 5$. If we use the same encoding for error detection instead, then we have $p + 1 = 5$, and since a Hamming distance of $p + 1$ must be maintained to detect p errors, then $p = 4$ errors can be detected. ■

9.5 Network Architecture: The Internet

In the early days of computing, computers were centralized facilities that contained most or all of the resources used by the populations they serviced. Data was transferred between computers via media (punched paper cards, paper tapes, magnetic tapes, and magnetic disks), hand-carried by an operator.

As the number of computers increased and costs shifted away from hardware and more toward labor, it became economical to link computers directly so that resources could be shared. This is what networking is about. We briefly explored local area networks in the context of the traditional seven-layer ISO model. Here we take a deeper look at architectural aspects of computer networks in the context of the Internet model.

9.5.1 *THE INTERNET MODEL*

In a telecommunication system there may be many sources and many destinations. An example of this form of communication is a long distance telephone network. For every telephone to be reachable from every other telephone, there must be a path, or **channel**, between each source and destination. If there are 10^7 telephones in New York City and 10^7 telephones in Chicago, then for everyone in one city to be able to call everyone in the other city, $10^7 \times 10^7 = 10^{14}$ channels must exist between the cities. Fortunately, not everyone in New York City wants to talk with everyone in Chicago at the same time, and a smaller number of channels between New York City and Chicago can be shared among all telephones in those cities. On the other hand, there must be at least one line from each telephone to the telephone company's central office, and there must be sufficient lines between central offices to handle the maximum number of simultaneously held conversations.

A small number of physical connections, on the order of a few to a few thousand depending on whether fibers or wires are used, are all that are needed to connect the cities because it is never the case that everyone in one city wants to call someone in the other city at the same time. The information carrying capacity of the connections (called **bandwidth**) is shared among all of the users so that a dramatic reduction in cost is realized. A control mechanism must be created, however, so that the bandwidth can be shared properly.

Layering in the TCP/IP Protocol Suite

An internet is a collection of interconnected networks. The Internet is probably the most well-known internet, using the TCP/IP protocol and IP addresses in what is known as the TCP/IP protocol suite (more on this later). The seven-layer OSI model has been simplified somewhat in the Internet, which can be thought of as having only four layers, as illustrated by the protocol stack shown in Figure 9-15. At the bottom of the protocol stack is the link layer, which is made up of the medium access control (MAC) and physical (PHY) sublayers. The link layer resolves contention for the medium when more than one device wants to transmit, manages the logical grouping of bits into frames, and implements error protection.

The link layer is responsible for simply getting a frame of bits from one machine to a directly connected machine. This is fine for point-to-point communication between two cooperating processes on different machines. In order for multiple processes to share the same link, however, a protocol is needed to coordinate which data goes to what process. This is the responsibility of the network layer, which is implemented with the Internet protocol (IP) for the Internet.

The network layer deals with hop-by-hop communication. The transport layer deals with end-to-end communication, in which there may be a number of intervening systems between the sender and receiver. The transport layer deals with retransmission (for errors, or packets dropped due to congestion), sequencing (packets may arrive out of order), flow control (applying back-pressure to the

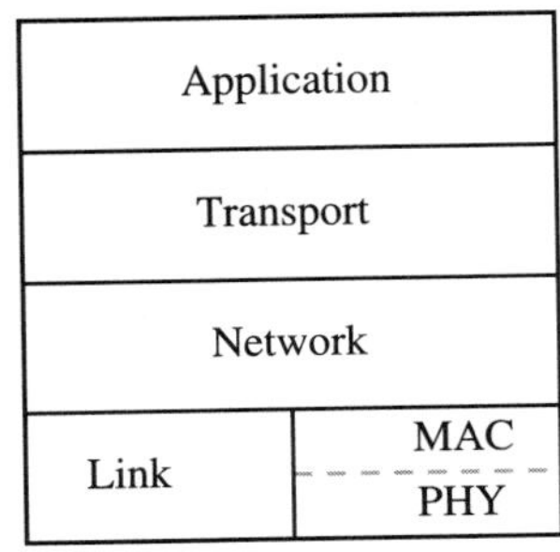

Figure 9-15 Internet protocol stack.

source to relieve congestion), and error protection (the link layer does not do enough error protection on its own). For the Internet, the transport layer is implemented with the transmission control protocol (TCP). The TCP/IP combination at the network and transport layers is the predominant Internet protocol suite. Any other appropriate protocols can be used at the link and application layers, and there are also other protocols used within the network and transport layers.

At the application layer, a process can exchange data with another process anywhere on the Internet and treat the connection as if it is a file on the local system, reading and writing bytes with ordinary read and write system calls, frequently implemented by **sockets**, which are pathways to the network through the operating system.

Internet Addresses

Every interface on the Internet has a unique IP address. Version 4 of the IP protocol, known as IPv4, is still widely used but is gradually being replaced by IPv6, which uses addresses that are four times larger and has several enhancements and simplifications to IPv4. An example of an IPv4 address, shown in "dotted decimal notation" is shown as follows:

```
165.230.140.67
```

Each number that is delimited by a dot is an unsigned byte in the range from 0 through 255. The equivalent bit pattern for the preceding IPv4 address is then

```
10100101.11100110.10001100.10000011
```

The leftmost bits determine the class of the address. Figure 9-16 shows the five IPv4 classes. Class A has 7 bits for the network identification (ID) and 24 bits for the host ID. There can thus be at most 2^7 class A networks and 2^{24} hosts on each class A network. A number of these addresses are reserved, and so the number of addresses that can be assigned to hosts is fewer than the number of possible addresses.

Class B addresses use 14 bits for the network ID and 16 bits for the host ID. Class C addresses use 21 bits for the network ID and 8 bits for the host ID. Class D addresses are used for **multicast** groups, to which an end system that has a class A, B, or C address subscribes and thereby receives all network traffic intended for that group. This is an efficient mechanism for sending the same packets to multiple subscribers, without flooding the network with broadcasts

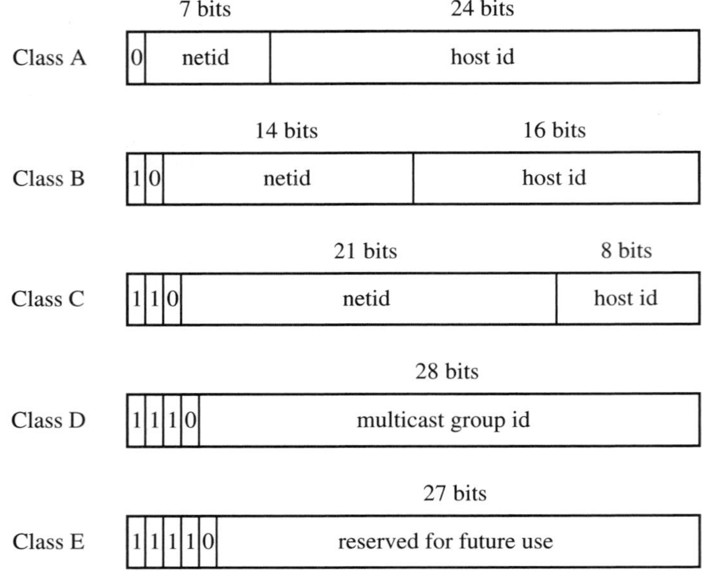

Figure 9-16 Five classes of IPv4 addresses.

and without the sender needing to keep track of all of the current subscribers. Class E addresses are unused.

The available supply of IPv4 addresses will run out soon after the year 2000, and so it is important that IPv6 be widely adopted soon. Already, many networks reuse IP addresses that are simultaneously in use elsewhere (using a protocol that allows for sharing of IP addresses), and others assign IP addresses only for the duration of a session (such as for a dialup line through a modem).

Ports

Loosely speaking, a **port** is how a process is known to the world. A port number identifies the source process, and a port number also identifies the destination process. Strictly speaking, the port identifies a network entry point for a process. Ports 0–1023 are **well-known ports** for server processes. For example, the `telnet` port is 23. On a Unix system, the command

```
% telnet cereal.rutgers.edu 23
```

will connect the user to system `cereal.rutgers.edu`. If the `23` is not present on the command line, then `23` is assumed. If `23` is replaced with another port, such as `13` for the daytime server, then a different process will be reached, with different resulting behavior.

Encapsulation

Network data is **encapsulated** as it passes through the network layers, as illustrated in Figure 9-17. The user data is sent to the network using similar read and write system calls that would be used for reading and writing files. The application layer sends user data to the transport layer, where the operating system adds a TCP header that identifies the source and destination ports, forming a TCP segment. The TCP segment is passed down to the network layer, where the TCP segment is repackaged into IP datagrams, each with an IP header identifying the source and destination systems. The IP datagrams are sent to the link layer, where the datagrams are encapsulated into Ethernet frames (for this example). The reverse process takes place on the receiving system.

A single TCP segment may be decomposed into a number of IP datagrams, which are independently routed through the Internet. Each IP datagram contains the source and destination IP addresses (in the IP header), the source and destination ports (in the TCP header), and the protocol at the next layer of encapsulation (in the IP header—TCP is only one of the transport layer protocols used in the Internet). Collectively, these five parameters uniquely identify each IP datagram as it traverses the Internet, which helps ensure that the datagrams arrive at the correct receiving process.

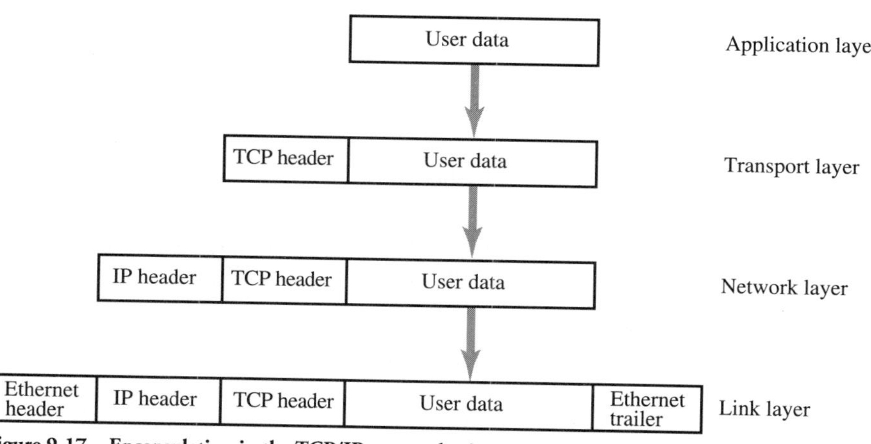

Figure 9-17 Encapsulation in the TCP/IP protocol suite.

The Domain Name System

The domain name systems (DNS) is a distributed database that maps between hostnames and IP addresses and provides mail routing information. For example, `cereal.rutgers.edu` maps to `165.230.140.67` (and vice versa), and all three names: `internet.rutgers.edu`, `www.internet.rutgers.edu`, and `mulder.rutgers.edu` map to `165.230.44.67`. The DNS is responsible for interacting with programs that need to map between names and addresses.

Each domain (like `rutgers.edu`) maintains its own database of information and runs a server that other systems across the Internet can query. Access to the DNS is provided through a **resolver**, which is embodied in library routines that are silently linked into high-level programs that access the network.

The network information center (NIC, also known as the InterNIC) manages the top-level domains and delegates authority for second-level domains. Within a **zone**, a local administrator maintains the name server database. There must be a primary name server, which loads its database from a file, and secondary name servers, which get their information from the primary name server. Caching is used, so that a query that causes other servers to be contacted does not cause future queries to cause additional contacts to other servers.

The World Wide Web

The World Wide Web (or simply, the Web) is made up of client processes (Web browsers) and Web servers running the HyperText Transport Protocol (HTTP) at the Application layer of the Internet. As distinctions get blurred in everyday usage, it is important to keep in mind that the Web is built on top of the Internet—the Web is not the Internet itself.

In 1989, Tim Berners-Lee at CERN (the European high-energy physics facility) developed a text-based Web, for exchanging technical documents among colleagues. In February 1993, the National Center for Supercomputing Applications (NCSA) at the University of Illinois at Urbana–Champaign released a graphical version of the Mosaic Web browser as well as an HTTP server, both free of charge, and the Web exploded to where it is today.

9.5.2 *BRIDGES AND ROUTERS REVISITED AND SWITCHES*

A **hub** is a central connection point for end systems. A hub is also known as a **bridge** when an end system is another hub. A hub simply copies packets from one network interface to all of the others, as illustrated in the configuration shown in Figure 9-18a. Hubs and bridges have modest intelligence these days, by isolating collisions on single network links (that is, if two packets collide on a span of the network, which is a normal but unwanted condition, the collision signal is not propagated to the other network links), and by limiting certain types of traffic from being sent to all other interfaces.

A **router** connects one network to another (see Figure 9-18b) and makes decisions with respect to forwarding packets across its boundaries. A router by defini-

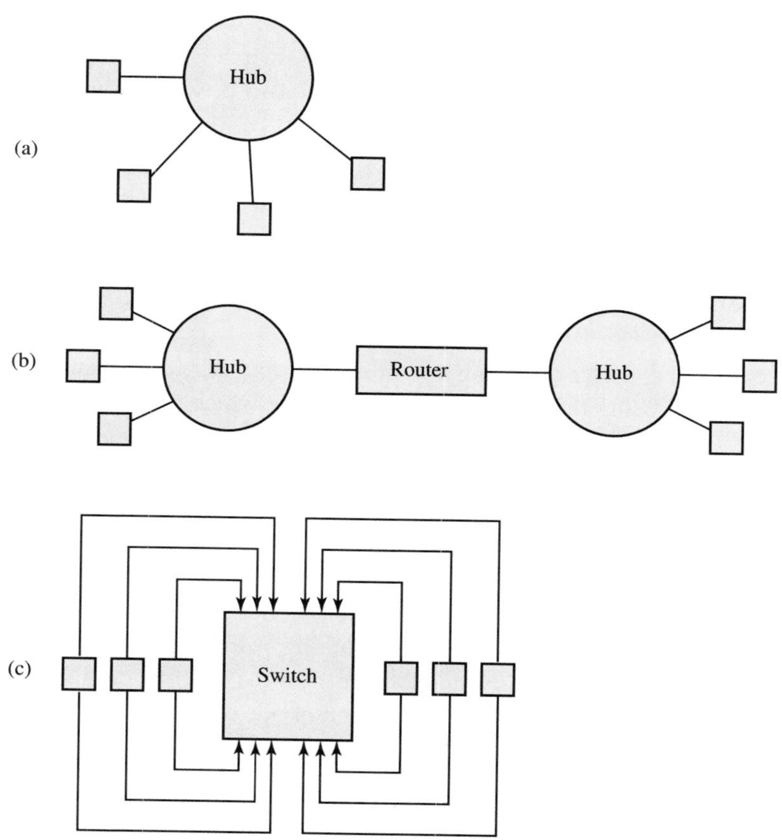

Figure 9-18 Configurations shown for (a) a hub; (b) a router; and (c) a switch.

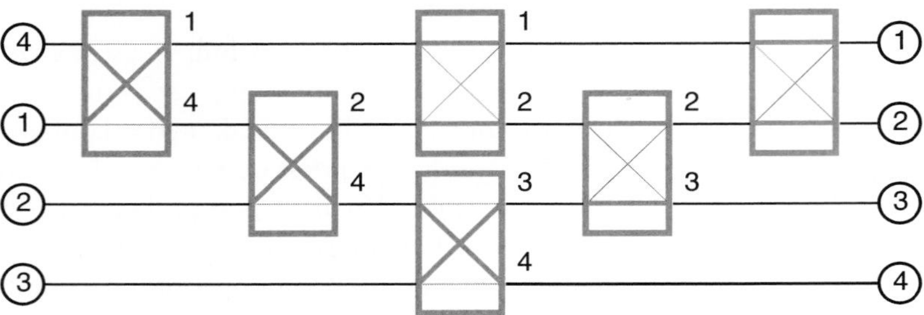

Figure 9-19 A 4 × 4 self-routing switch based on the bubblesort algorithm.

tion has more than one network interface and forwards packets between interfaces. The network protocols used on either side of a router can differ.

A router forwards packets based on the protocol, whereas a **switch** forwards packets based only on the destination address. A switch is a high-speed hub with no shared bandwidth, as illustrated in Figure 9-18c. A switch eliminates media access conflicts because there is no contention for the media.

An example of a switch is discussed in Section 10.9.2, in which an external controller sets up source-to-destination paths. An enhancement is a **self-routing network** that sets up source-to-destination connections on the fly, based on the destination addresses in the headers of packets traversing the network.

As an example, consider designing a 4-input, 4-output self-routing switch. We can accomplish this using the **bubblesort** algorithm, in which packets with the smallest addresses are bubbled to the top, by making pairwise exchanges starting from the top and working toward the bottom, dropping the packet with the largest address to the bottom on each pass. For n channels, there are $n(n-1)/2$ comparisons that need to be made. For this case, $n = 4$, and so $4(4-1)/2 = 6$ comparisons need to be made, which means that the switch needs 6 comparison boxes.

The corresponding 4-input, 4-output self-routing switch is shown in Figure 9-19. Unsorted packets enter at the left and emerge in sorted order by destination address on the right. (See Problem A-28 for the design of one of the comparison boxes.)

9.6 Case Study: Asynchronous Transfer Mode

Historically, there have been different networks that carry different types of information:

- Telex (old style teletypewriters, used for news feeds, stock quotes, etc.)
- "Plain old telephone service" (POTS) via the public switched telephone network (PSTN)
- Data, via the packet switched data network (PSDN)
- Television via: (1) ground based antennae; (2) community antennae TV (CATV known as cable TV); and (3) satellites
- Local data via local area networks (LANs)

Each network is separately planned, dimensioned, developed, and operated. This specialization results in independent worldwide networks. Bandwidth is not shared among the networks, yet when video traffic peaks at prime time, telephone traffic lulls. Although there may always be video programs available on a particular channel at all hours of the day, less expensive local programming may be used in the off-peak hours, reducing the need for video traffic via satellites or via long-distance wireline networks.

Each type of service needs to deal with peak traffic and bursty traffic on its own, although it would be more economical to share networks as long as the peaks and bursts do not coincide. An attempt at sharing is **Integrated Services Digital Network** (ISDN), which comes in two forms. **Narrowband-ISDN** (NISDN) is designed for 64 Kb/s telephone switching. NISDN allows voice and data traffic to be carried over the same network. **Broadband-ISDN** (BISDN) supports video traffic as well as voice and data traffic.

The ISDN **basic rate interface** (BRI) is used for NISDN. The BRI offers two Bearer (B) channels at 64 Kb/s per channel, for user data, and one Data (D) channel at 16 Kb/s, which is used for control and signaling. The total bit rate is 192 Kb/s when higher-level framing overhead is taken into account, but the maximum rate available to the user is 128 Kb/s when the two B channels are "bonded" into a single channel.

The ISDN **primary rate interface** (PRI) offers 23 B channels and one 64 Kb/s D channel and is commonly known as a "T1 line."

ISDN lines can be leased from telecommunication companies and can be configured to set up private networks. As a general rule of thumb, the monthly rate for leasing ten 64-Kb/s lines equals the rate for leasing a T1 line that supports twenty-three

64-Kb/s lines. A problem with the overall economics with ISDN is that the supported bit rates are service dependent (NISDN is an example of a service) as opposed to traffic dependent, which is needed by modern networks. Services must fall into even multiples of B and D channels in the offered ratios, or else they will not make efficient use of the available bandwidth. We may not know what bit rates future services will need, and so we need a service independent bit transport for a network to be extensible. The goal is to have a single network that can serve everyone, which is where **asynchronous transfer mode** (ATM) comes in.

9.6.1 *SYNCHRONOUS VERSUS ASYNCHRONOUS TRANSFER MODE*

With **synchronous transfer mode** (STM), also known as **time division multiplexing** (TDM), a data stream is made up of time slots that are assigned to channels in a round-robin fashion. Figure 9-20a illustrates TDM for four channels. A station can only send during a preassigned time slot. Other unused time slots may go by while a station waits for its preassigned time slot. (In the public switched telephone network, a time slot is 125 μs, which allows for 8000 samples per second at 8 bits per sample, resulting in 64 Kb/s for a voice-grade line.)

Figure 9-20b shows asynchronous transfer mode, which may still use 125 μs framing, but now any station can use any slot, and the network is used more efficiently. On the down side, operating an ATM network is much more complex than operating a simpler TDM network.

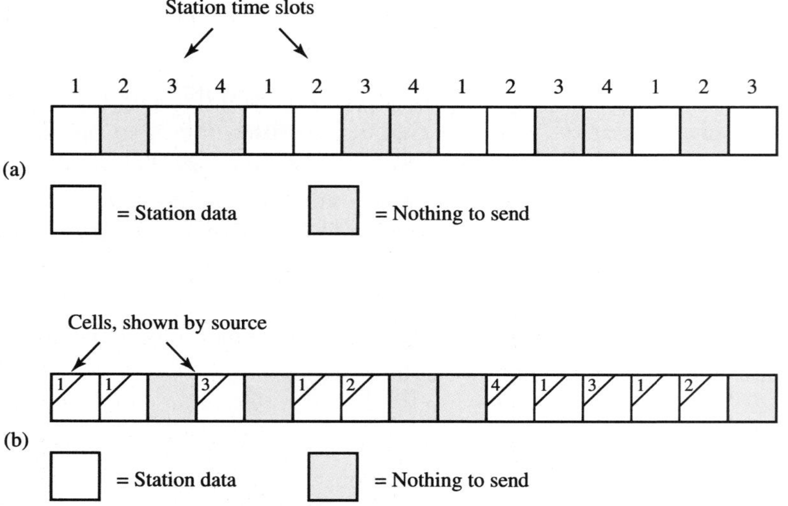

Figure 9-20 (a) Time division multiplexing versus (b) asynchronous transfer mode.

9.6.2 *WHAT IS ATM?*

ATM is a combination of hardware and a set of protocols that delivers a guaranteed bandwidth with a bounded low latency. Two enabling progress areas that make ATM possible are

1. Technology—The speed and density of VLSI allows network functionality to be pushed into the end systems rather than throughout the intermediary components. Error detection is only performed at the endpoints, for example, instead of at every intermediate router, as is common for the Internet. The development of high-bandwidth, low-bit-error-rate optical fiber is a supporting technology that makes this approach practical.

2. Systems—Fast packet switches that introduce a low latency into end-to-end communication enable the delivery of real-time services.

Typical speeds for ATM are in the range of 1 Gb/s to 2.5 Gb/s, with an average delay of only 450 μs for each switch that handles an ATM packet.

9.6.3 *ATM NETWORK ARCHITECTURE*

Before an ATM transfer takes place, a connection must be established by contacting a **signaling control point** (SCP), which is a network device that has the authority to configure ATM switches for the transfer. All packets are constrained to follow the path set up by the SCP, and all packets arrive in order.

The job of the switch is very simple: It simply looks at the destination address in the header and then it sends the packet on the path indicated in the header. A new destination address is placed in the header, as discussed next.

All ATM packets have the same fixed size of 53 bytes, as shown in Figure 9-21. The packet created by an end system for injection into the network, which is known as the **user-to-network interface** (UNI) format, is shown in Figure 9-21a, and the packet format used from that point onward, which is known as the **network-to-network interface** (NNI) format, is shown in Figure 9-21b.

The generic flow control (GFC) field is used at the network boundary to police how packets are allowed to enter the network. Once a packet is in the network, the GFC field of the UNI format is no longer needed and is then combined with the 8-bit virtual path identifier (VPI) field to form a 12-bit VPI field in the NNI format. The VPI field can be thought of as identifying one particular home for a cable that carries cable TV channels, whereas the virtual channel identifier (VCI) field identifies the specific channel. The payload type identifier (PTI) identifies whether the data field carries

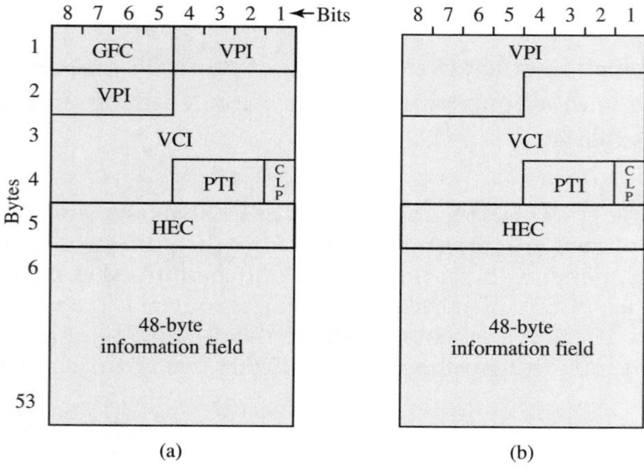

Figure 9-21 Format of an ATM packet. (a) User-to-network interface (UNI) format; and (b) network-to-network interface (NNI) format.

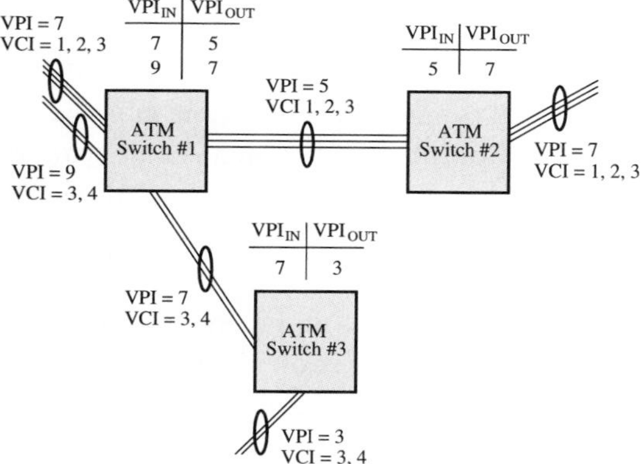

Figure 9-22 VPI switching in an ATM network. (Adapted from [dePrycker, 1993].)

user data or network data and other information. The cell loss priority (CLP) bit determines whether this cell can be dropped during times of congestion. The header error control (HEC) is a CRC over the header. The 48-byte payload field follows.

Figure 9-22 shows a simple ATM network that consists of three switches. Each switch has a symmetric routing table that can be driven in either direction. For example, at ATM Switch #1, an incoming packet (on the left) that has a VPI field of 7 is sent to the right after changing the VPI field to 5. Likewise, a packet that comes into ATM Switch #1 from the right with a VPI field of 5 is sent to the left after changing the VPI field to 7. This is referred to as virtual path switching because only the VPI field is used in routing the packet. The VCI field is unchanged. There can also be virtual channel switching in which routing is done based on the VCI field and the VPI field is left unchanged.

9.6.4 *OUTLOOK ON ATM*

Although ATM holds a great deal of promise for an extensible network that serves many user needs, economies of scale favor legacy networks such as Ethernet for end user systems. ATM appears mostly in backbone networks, with multiplexors and concentrators used for connecting legacy networks at the boundary of the backbone to the backbone itself. ATM continues its penetration into backbone networks and also to the desktop, which is currently the exception rather than the rule. Whether ATM makes it to the desktop pervasively, time will tell.

■ SUMMARY

Communication involves the transfer of information between systems. As a rule, data is transferred in bit-serial fashion because the time-of-flight delays dominate the transfer time for high speed networks. However, modulation schemes allow many bits to be encoded in a single sample, such as for a dibit. The choice of modulation scheme impacts the introduction of errors into the transmission of information. Error detection and correction are made possible through redundancy, in which there are more bit patterns possible than the number of valid bit patterns. If the error bit patterns do not have a single closest valid codeword, then error detection is possible but error correction is not possible. If every error bit pattern is reachable from only one valid bit pattern, then error correction is also possible.

Local area networks (LANs) manage complexity by using layering that is based on the OSI model. These days, LANs are typically connected to wide area networks (WANs), most notably the Internet. The Internet is based on the TCP/IP protocol suite. User data is encapsulated at the application, transport, network, and link layers and is sent through the Internet and de-encapsulated (demuxed) on the receiving system. As it is passed through the Internet, the data traverses various transmission media, which vary in bandwidth and distance capabilities.

■ FURTHER READING

(Shannon 1948) developed the basis for modern telecommucations theory. (Needleman, 1990) and (Schnaidt, 1990) give a thorough treatment of local area networks according to the OSI model, and (Tanenbaum, 1996) is a good reference on network communication in general. (Halsall, 1996) gives a thorough and readable treatment of network media types. (dePrycker, 1993) gives an in-depth account of ATM and its characteristics.

(Tanenbaum, 1999) and (Stallings, 1996) give readable explanations of Hamming encoding. (Hamming, 1986) and (Peterson and Weldon, 1972) give more detailed treatments of error correcting codes.

Halsall, F., *Data Communications, Computer Networks, and Open Systems*, 4/e, Addison-Wesley (1996).

Hamming, R. W., *Coding and Information Theory*, 2/e, Prentice Hall (1986).

Needleman, R., *Understanding Networks*, Simon and Schuster (1990).

Peterson, W. Wesley and E. J. Weldon, Jr., *Error-Correcting Codes*, 2/e, MIT Press (1972).

de Prycker, Martin, *Asynchronous Transfer Mode: Solution for Broadband ISDN*, 2/e, Ellis Horwood (1993).

Schnaidt, P., *LAN Tutorial*, Miller Freeman Publications (1990).

C. E. Shannon, *A mathematical theory of communication*, Bell System Technical Journal, **27**, 379-423 and 623-656, July and October (1948).

Stallings, W., *Computer Organization and Architecture: Designing for Performance*, 4/e, Prentice Hall (1996).

Tanenbaum, A., *Computer Networks*, 3/e, Prentice Hall (1996).

Tanenbaum, A., *Structured Computer Organization*, 4/e, Prentice Hall (1999).

■ PROBLEMS

9.1 What is the Hamming distance for the ASCII SEC code discussed in Section 9.4.2?

9.2 Construct the SEC code for the ASCII character 'Q' using even parity.

9.3 For parts (a) through (d), use a SEC code with even parity.

(a) How many check bits should be added to encode a six-bit word?

(b) Construct the SEC code for the six-bit word: 1 0 1 1 0 0. When constructing the code, number the bits from right to left starting with 1 as for the method described in Section 9.4.2.

(c) A receiver sees a two-bit SEC encoded word that looks like this: 1 1 1 0 0. What is the initial two-bit pattern?

(d) The 12-bit word 1 0 1 1 1 0 0 1 1 0 0 1, which includes an SEC code (even parity), is received. What 12-bit word was actually sent?

9.4 How many check bits are needed for a SEC code for an initial word size of 1024?

9.5 Construct a checksum word for EBCDIC characters 'V' through 'Z' using vertical redundancy checking with even parity. DO NOT use longitudinal redundancy checking.

9.6 Compare the number of bits used for parity in the SEC code with the simple parity VRC code, for 1024 eight-bit characters:

(a) Compute the number of check bits generated using SEC only (horizontally).

(b) Compute the number of checksum bits using VRC only.

9.7 The SEC code discussed in Section 9.4.2 can be turned into a double error detecting/SEC (DED/SEC) code by adding one more bit that creates even parity over the SEC code (which includes the parity bit being added.) Explain how double error detection works while also maintaining single error correction with this approach.

9.8 Compute the CRC for a message to be transmitted $M(x) = 101100110$ and a generator polynomial $G(x) = x^3 + x^2 + 1$.

9.9 What is the longest burst error that CRC-32 is sure to catch?

9.10 To which IPv4 class does address `165.230.140.67` belong?

9.11 How many networks (not hosts) can the IPv4 class A, B, and C addresses support? That is, how many distinct class A, B, and C network addresses can there be? Do not consider reserved addresses.

9.12 Network media always carry data in bit-serial fashion and virtually never in parallel. That is not to say that data could not be carried over a network in byte-parallel or word-parallel fashion; there simply is no advantage to doing it this way. To see why this is the case, calculate the time required to transmit a 32-bit word between two computers over a 32-foot network. The network speed is 1 Gbps per channel. The time-of-flight delay imposed by the distance is 1 ns per foot. Calculate the time to transmit the 32-bit word using a single channel (bit-serial fashion) and using 32 channels (word-parallel fashion).

9.13 An ATM network has two switches A and B that switch on the virtual path identifier only. The network topology and the routing tables for the switches are as follows:

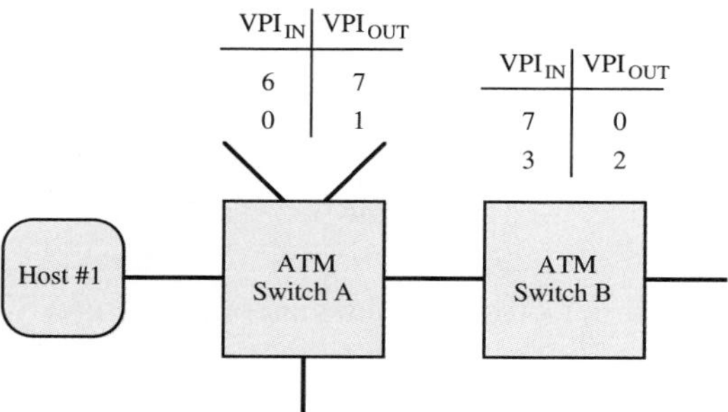

A cell comes into ATM switch A from Host #1 with the following UNI header (first 4 bytes):

Bytes \ Bits	8	7	6	5	4	3	2	1
1	1	1	0	0	0	0	0	0
2	0	1	1	0	0	0	0	0
3	0	0	0	0	0	1	0	1
4	0	0	0	0	0	0	0	0

Show the first four bytes of the outgoing NNI header.

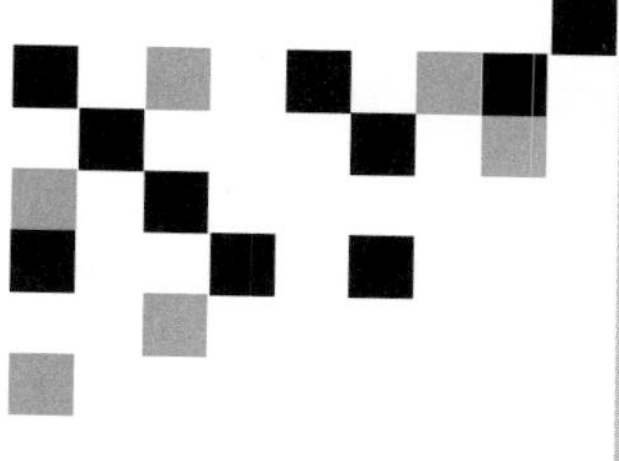

10 TRENDS IN COMPUTER ARCHITECTURE

In the earlier chapters, the fetch-execute cycle is described in the form "fetch an instruction, execute that instruction, fetch the next instruction, etc." This gives the impression of a straight-line linear progression of program execution. In fact, the processor architectures of today have many advanced features that go beyond this simple paradigm. These features include **pipelining**, in which several instructions sharing the same hardware can simultaneously be in various phases of execution; **superscalar execution**, in which several instructions are executed simultaneously using different portions of the hardware, with possibly only some of the results contributing to the overall computation; **very long instruction word** (VLIW) architectures, in which each instruction word specifies multiple instructions (of smaller widths) that are executed simultaneously; and **parallel processing**, in which multiple processors are coordinated to work on a single problem.

In this chapter we cover issues that relate to these features. The discussion begins with issues that led to the emergence of the reduced instruction set computer (RISC) and examples of RISC features and characteristics. Following that, we cover an advanced feature used specifically in SPARC architectures: **overlapping register windows**. We then cover two important architectural features: superscalar execution and VLIW architectures. We then move into the topic of parallel processing, touching both on parallel architectures and program decomposition. The chapter includes with case studies covering Intel's Merced architecture, the PowerPC 601, and an example of a pervasive parallel architecture that can be found in a home videogame system.

10.1 Quantitative Analyses of Program Execution

Prior to the late 1970s, computer architects exploited improvements in integrated circuit technology by increasing the complexity of instructions and addressing modes, as the benefits of such improvements were thought to be obvious. It became an effective selling strategy to have more complex instructions and

Statement	Average Percent of Time
Assignment	47
If	23
Call	15
Loop	6
Goto	3
Other	7

Figure 10-1 Frequency of occurrence of instruction types for a variety of languages. The percentages do not sum to 100 due to roundoff. (Adapted from [Knuth, 1991].)

more complex addressing modes than a competing processor. Increases in architectural complexity catered to the belief that a significant barrier to better machine performance was the **semantic gap**—the gap between the meanings of high-level language statements and the meanings of machine-level instructions.

Unfortunately, as computer architects attempted to close the semantic gap, they sometimes made it worse. The IBM 360 architecture has the `MVC` (move character) instruction that copies a string of up to 256 bytes between two arbitrary locations. If the source and destination strings overlap, then the overlapped portion is copied one byte at a time. The run-time analysis that determines the degree of overlap adds a significant overhead to the execution time of the `MVC` instruction. Measurements show that overlaps occur only a few percent of the time and that the average string size is only eight bytes. In general, faster execution results when the `MVC` instruction is entirely ignored, and instead its function is synthesized with simpler instructions. Although a greater number of instructions may be executed without the `MVC` instruction, on average fewer clock cycles are needed to implement the copy operation without using `MVC` than by using it.

Long-held views began to change in 1971, when Donald Knuth published a landmark analysis of typical Fortran programs, showing that most of the statements are simple assignments. Later research by John Hennessy at Stanford University and David Patterson at the University of California at Berkeley confirmed that most complex instructions and addressing modes went largely unused by compilers. These researchers popularized the use of program analysis and benchmark programs to evaluate the impact of architecture upon performance.

Figure 10-1, taken from (Knuth, 1971), summarizes the frequency of occurrence of instructions in a mix of programs written in a variety of languages. Nearly half of all instructions are assignment statements. Interestingly, arithmetic and other "more powerful" operations account for only 7% of all instructions. Thus, if we

	Percentage of Number of Terms in Assignments	Percentage of Number of Locals in Procedures	Percentage of Number of Parameters in Procedure Calls
0	–	22	41
1	80	17	19
2	15	20	15
3	3	14	9
4	2	8	7
≥ 5	0	20	8

Figure 10-2 Percentages showing complexity of assignments and procedure calls. (Adapted from [Tanenbaum, 1999].)

want to improve the performance of a computer, our efforts would be better spent optimizing instructions that account for the greatest percentage of execution time rather than focusing on instructions that are inherently complex but rarely occur.

Related metrics are shown in Figure 10-2. From the figure, the number of terms in an assignment statement is normally just a few. The most frequent case (80%) is the simple variable assignment, $X \leftarrow Y$. There are only a few local variables in each procedure, and only a few arguments are normally passed to a procedure.

We can see from these measurements that the bulk of computer programs are very simple at the instruction level, even though more complex programs could be created. This means that there may be little or no payoff in increasing the complexity of the instructions.

Discouragingly, analyses of compiled code showed that compilers usually did not take advantage of the complex instructions and addressing modes made available by computer architects eager to close the semantic gap. One important reason for this phenomenon is that it is difficult for a compiler to analyze the code in sufficient detail to locate areas where the new instructions can be used effectively, because of the great difference in meaning between most high-level language constructs and the expression of those constructs in assembly language. This observation, and the ever-increasing speed and capacity of integrated circuit technology, converged to bring about an evolution from complex instruction set computer (CISC) machines to RISC machines.

A basic tenet of current computer architecture is to make the frequent case fast, and this often means making it simple. Since the assignment statement happens so frequently, we should concentrate on making it fast (and simple, as a consequence). One way to simplify assignments is to force all communication with memory into just two commands: LOAD and STORE. The LOAD/STORE model is typical of RISC architectures. We see the LOAD/STORE concept in Chapter 4 with the `ld` and `st` instructions for the ARC.

By restricting memory accesses to LOAD/STORE instructions only, other instructions can only access data that is stored in registers. There are two consequences of this, both good and bad: (1) Accesses to memory can be easily overlapped, since there are fewer side effects that would occur if different instruction types could access memory (this is good); and (2) there is a need for a large number of registers (this seems bad, but read on).

A simpler instruction set results in a simpler and typically smaller CPU, which frees up space on a microprocessor to be used for something else, like registers. Thus, the need for more registers is balanced to a degree by the newly vacant circuit area, or chip **real estate** as it is sometimes called. A key problem lies in how to manage these registers, which is discussed in Section 10.4.

10.1.1 *QUANTITATIVE PERFORMANCE ANALYSIS*

When we estimate machine performance, the measure that is generally most important is execution time, *T*. When considering the impact of some performance improvement, the effect of the improvement is usually expressed in terms of the **speedup**, *S*, taken as the ratio of the execution time without the improvement (T_{wo}) to the execution time with the improvement (T_w):

$$S = \frac{T_{wo}}{T_w}$$

For example, if adding a 1 MB cache module to a computer system results in lowering the execution time of some benchmark program from 12 seconds to 8 seconds, then the speedup would be 12/8, = 1.5, or 50%. An equation to calculate speedup as a direct percent can be represented as

$$S = \frac{T_{wo} - T_w}{T_w} \times 100$$

We can develop a more fine-grained equation for estimating *T* if we have information about the machine's clock period, τ, the number of clock cycles per instruction, *CPI*, and a count of the number of instructions executed by the program during its execution, *IC*. In this case the total execution time for the program is given by

$$T = IC \times CPI \times \tau$$

CPI and *IC* can be expressed either as an average over the instruction set and total count, respectively, or summed over each kind and number of instructions in the instruction set and program. Substituting the latter equation into the former, we get

$$S = \frac{IC_{wo} \times CPI_{wo} \times \tau_{wo} - IC_w \times CPI_w \times \tau_w}{IC_w \times CPI_w \times \tau_w} \times 100$$

These equations and others derived from them are useful in computing and estimating the impact of changes in instructions and architecture upon performance.

EXAMPLE: CALCULATING SPEEDUP FOR A NEW INSTRUCTION SET

Suppose we wish to estimate the speedup obtained by replacing a CPU having an average *CPI* of 5 with another CPU having an average *CPI* of 3.5, with the clock period increased from 100 ns to 120 ns. The preceding equation becomes

$$S = \frac{5 \times 100 - 3.5 \times 120}{3.5 \times 120} \times 100 = 19\%$$

Thus, without actually running a benchmark program we can estimate the impact of an architectural change upon performance. ■

10.2 From CISC to RISC

Historically, when memory cycle times were very long and when memory prices were high, fewer, complicated instructions held an advantage over more, simpler instructions. There came a point, however, when memory became inexpensive enough and memory hierarchies became fast and large enough that computer architects began reexamining this advantage. One technology that affected this examination was **pipelining**—that is, keeping the execution unit more or less the same but allowing different instructions (which each require several clock cycles to execute) to use different parts of the execution unit on each clock cycle. For example, one instruction might be accessing operands in the register file while another is using the ALU.

We will cover pipelining in more detail later in the chapter, but the important point to make here is that computer architects learned that CISC instructions do not fit pipelined architectures very well. For pipelining to work effectively, each instruction needs to have similarities to other instructions, at least in terms of relative instruction complexity. The reason can be viewed in analogy to an assembly line that produces different models of an automobile. For efficiency, each "station" of the assembly line should do approximately the same amount and kind of work. If the amount or kind of work done at each station is radically different for different models, then periodically the assembly line will have to "stall" to accommodate the requirements of the given model.

CISC instruction sets have the disadvantage that some instructions, such as register-to-register moves, are inherently simple, whereas others, such as the MVC instruction and others like it, are complex and take many more clock cycles to execute.

The main philosophical underpinnings of the RISC approach are as follows:

- Prefetch instructions into an instruction queue in the CPU before they are needed. This has the effect of hiding the latency associated with the instruction fetch.
- With instruction fetch times no longer a penalty, and with cheap memory to hold a greater number of instructions, there is no real advantage to CISC instructions. All instructions should be composed of sequences of RISC instructions, even though the number of instructions needed may increase (typically by as much as 1/3 over a CISC approach).
- Moving operands between registers and memory is expensive and should be minimized.
- The RISC instruction set should be designed with pipelined architectures in mind.
- There is no requirement that CISC instructions be maintained as integrated wholes; they can be decomposed into sequences of simpler RISC instructions.

The result is that RISC architectures have characteristics that distinguish them from CISC architectures:

- All instructions are of fixed length, one machine word in size.
- All instructions perform simple operations that can be issued into the pipeline at a rate of one per clock cycle. Complex *operations* are now composed of simple *instructions* by the compiler.

- All operands must be in registers before being operated upon. There is a separate class of memory access instructions: LOAD and STORE. This is referred to as a LOAD-STORE architecture.

- Addressing modes are limited to simple ones. Complex addressing calculations are built up using sequences of simple operations.

- There should be a large number of general registers for arithmetic operations so that temporary variables can be stored in registers rather than on a stack in memory.

In the next few sections, we explore additional motivations for RISC architectures and special characteristics that make RISC architectures effective.

10.3 Pipelining the Datapath

The flow of instructions through a pipeline follows the steps normally taken when an instruction is executed. In the following discussion we consider how three classes of instructions—arithmetic, branch, and load-store—are executed, and then we relate this to how the instructions are pipelined.

10.3.1 *ARITHMETIC, BRANCH, AND LOAD-STORE INSTRUCTIONS*

Consider the "normal" sequence of events when an **arithmetic instruction** is executed in a load-store machine:

1. Fetch the instruction from memory.
2. Decode the instruction (it is an arithmetic instruction, but the CPU has to find that out through a decode operation).
3. Fetch the operands from the register file.
4. Apply the operands to the ALU.
5. Write the result back to the register file.

There are similar patterns for other instruction classes. For **branch instructions** the sequence is as follows:

1. Fetch the instruction from memory.
2. Decode the instruction (it is a branch instruction).

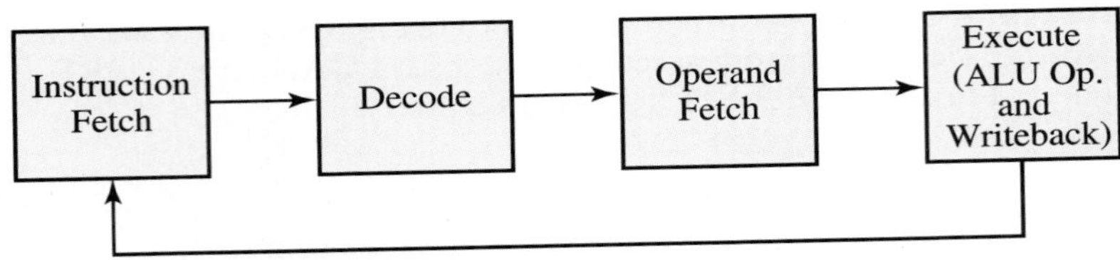

Figure 10-3 Four-stage instruction pipeline.

3. Fetch the components of the address from the instruction or register file.
4. Apply the components of the address to the ALU (address arithmetic).
5. Copy the resulting effective address into the PC, thus accomplishing the branch.

The sequence for **load and store instructions** is:

1. Fetch the instruction from memory.
2. Decode the instruction (it is a load or store instruction).
3. Fetch the components of the address from the instruction or register file.
4. Apply the components of the address to the ALU (address arithmetic).
5. Apply the resulting effective address to memory along with a read (load) or write (store) signal. If it is a write signal, the data item to be written must also be retrieved from the register file.

The three sequences show a high degree of similarity in what is done at each stage: (1) fetch, (2) decode, (3) operand fetch, (4) ALU operation, (5) result write-back.

These five phases are similar to the four phases discussed in Chapters 4 and 6 except that we have refined the fourth phase, "execute," into two sub-phases: ALU operation and write-back, as illustrated in Figure 10-3. A result write-back is not always needed, and one way to deal with this is to have two separate subphases (ALU and write-back) with a bypass path for situations when a write-back is not needed. For this discussion, we take a simpler approach and force all instructions to go entirely through each phase, whether or not that is actually needed.

10.3.2 *PIPELINING INSTRUCTIONS*

In practice, each CPU designer approaches the design of the pipeline from a different perspective, depending upon the particular design goals and instruction set. For example the original SPARC implementation had only four pipeline stages, while some floating point pipelines may have a dozen or more stages.

Each of the execution units performs a different operation in the fetch-execute cycle. After the instruction fetch unit finishes its task, the fetched instruction is handed off to the decode unit. At this point, the instruction fetch unit can begin fetching the *next* instruction, which overlaps with the decoding of the previous instruction. When the instruction fetch and decode units complete their tasks, they hand off the remaining tasks to the next units (operand fetch is the next unit for decode). The flow of control continues until all units are filled.

10.3.3 *KEEPING THE PIPELINE FILLED*

Notice an important point: Although it takes multiple steps to execute an instruction in this model, on average, one instruction can be executed per cycle as long as the pipeline stays filled. The pipeline does not stay filled, however, unless we are careful as to how instructions are ordered. We know from Figure 10-1 that approximately one in every four instructions is a branch. We cannot fetch the instruction that follows a branch until the branch completes execution. Thus, as soon as the pipeline fills, a branch is encountered, and then the pipeline has to be **flushed** by filling it with no-operations (NOPs). These NOPs are sometimes referred to as **pipeline bubbles**. A similar situation arises with the LOAD and STORE instructions. They generally require an additional clock cycle in which to access memory, which has the effect of expanding the execute phase from one cycle to two cycles at times. The "wait" cycles are filled with NOPs.

Figure 10-4 illustrates the pipeline behavior during a memory reference and also during a branch for the ARC instruction set. The `addcc` instruction enters the pipeline on time step (cycle) 1. On cycle 2, the `ld` instruction, which references

Time →	1	2	3	4	5	6	7	8
Instruction Fetch	addcc	ld	srl	subcc	be	nop	nop	nop
Decode		addcc	ld	srl	subcc	be	nop	nop
Operand Fetch			addcc	ld	srl	subcc	be	nop
Execute				addcc	ld	srl	subcc	be
Memory Reference						ld		

Figure 10-4 Pipeline behavior during a memory reference and a branch.

```
┌── srl    %r3, %r5
│   addcc %r1, 10, %r1
│   ld     %r1, %r2
└─▶ nop
    subcc %r2, %r4, %r4
    be     label
```

(a)

```
addcc %r1, 10, %r1
ld     %r1, %r2
srl    %r3, %r5
subcc %r2, %r4, %r4
be     label
```

(b)

Figure 10-5 SPARC code, (a) with a `nop` inserted, and (b) with `srl` migrated to `nop` position.

memory, enters the pipeline and `addcc` moves to the decode stage. The pipeline continues filling with the `srl` and `subcc` instructions on cycles 3 and 4, respectively. On cycle 4, the `addcc` instruction is executed and leaves the pipeline. On cycle 5, the `ld` instruction reaches the execute level but does not finish execution because an additional cycle is needed for memory references. The `ld` instruction finishes execution during cycle 6.

Branch and Load Delay Slots

The `ld` and `st` instructions both require five cycles, but the remaining instructions require only four. Thus, an instruction that follows an `ld` or `st` should not use the register that is being loaded or stored. A safe approach is to insert a NOP after an `ld` or an `st`, as shown in Figure 10-5a. The extra cycle (or cycles, depending on the architecture) for a load is known as a **delayed load**, since the data from the load is not immediately available on the next cycle. A **delayed branch** is similar, as shown for the `be` instruction in cycles 5 through 8 of Figure 10-4. The position occupied by this NOP instruction is known as a **load delay slot** or **branch delay slot**, respectively.

It is often possible for the compiler to find a nearby instruction to fill the delay slot. In Figure 10-5a, the `srl` instruction can be moved to the position of the `nop` since its register usage does not conflict with the surrounding code and reordering instructions this way does not impact the result. After replacing the `nop` line with the `srl` line, the code shown in Figure 10-5b is obtained. This is the code that is traced through the pipeline in Figure 10-4.

Speculative Execution of Instructions

An alternative approach to dealing with branch behavior in pipelines is simply to guess which way the branch will go and then undo any damage if the wrong path is taken. Statistically, loops are executed more often than not, and so it is usually a good guess to assume that a branch that exits a loop will not be taken. Thus, a processor can start processing the next instruction in anticipation of the direction of the branch. If the branch goes the wrong way, then the execution phase for the next instruction, and any subsequent instructions that enter the pipeline, can be stopped so that the pipeline can be flushed. This approach works well for a number of architectures, particularly those with slow cycle speeds or deep pipelines. For RISCs, however, the overhead of determining when a branch goes the wrong way and then cleaning up any side effects caused by wrong instructions entering the pipeline is generally too great. The `nop` instruction is normally used in RISC pipelines when something useful cannot be used to replace it.

EXAMPLE: ANALYSIS OF PIPELINE EFFICIENCY

In this example, we analyze the efficiency of a pipeline.

A processor has a five stage pipeline. If a branch is taken, then four cycles are needed to flush the pipeline. The branch penalty b is thus 4. The probability P_b that a particular instruction is a branch is .25. The probability P_t that the branch is taken is .5. We would like to compute the average number of cycles needed to execute an instruction, and the **execution efficiency**.

When the pipeline is filled and there are no branches, then the average number of cycles per instruction ($CPI_{\text{No\_Branch}}$) is 1. The average number of cycles per instruction when there are branches is then

$$\begin{aligned} CPI_{\text{Avg}} &= (1 - P_b)(CPI_{\text{No\_Branch}}) + P_b[P_t(1 + b) + (1 - P_t)(CPI_{\text{No\_Branch}})] \\ &= 1 + P_b P_t \end{aligned}$$

After making substitutions, we have

$$\begin{aligned} CPI_{\text{Avg}} &= (1 - .25)(1) + .25[.5(1 + 4) + (1 - .5)(1)] \\ &= 1.5 \text{ cycles} \end{aligned}$$

The execution efficiency is the ratio of the cycles per instruction when there are no branches to the cycles per instruction when there are branches. Thus we have:

Execution efficiency = $(CPI_{\text{No\_Branch}})/(CPI_{\text{Avg}}) = 1/1.5 = 67\%$.

The processor runs at 67% of its potential speed as a result of branches, but this is still much better than the five cycles per instruction that might be needed without pipelining.

There are techniques for improving the efficiency. As stated previously, we know that loops are usually executed more than once, so we can guess that a branch out of a loop will not be taken and be right most of the time. We can also run simulations on the nonloop branches, and get a statistical sampling of which branches are likely to be taken, and then guess the branches accordingly. As explained previously, this approach works best when the pipeline is deep or the clock rate is slow. ■

10.4 Overlapping Register Windows

One modern architectural feature that has not been as widely adopted as other features (such as pipelining) is **overlapping register windows**, which to date has only been adopted by the SPARC family. This feature is based upon studies that show typical programs spend much of their time dealing with procedure call-and-return overhead, which involves passing parameters on a stack located in main memory in traditional architectures. The SPARC architecture reduces much of this overhead by employing multiple register sets that overlap. These registers are used for passing parameters between procedures instead of using a stack in main memory.

Procedure calls may be deeply nested in an ordinary program, but for a given window of time the nesting depth fluctuates within a narrow band. Figure 10-6

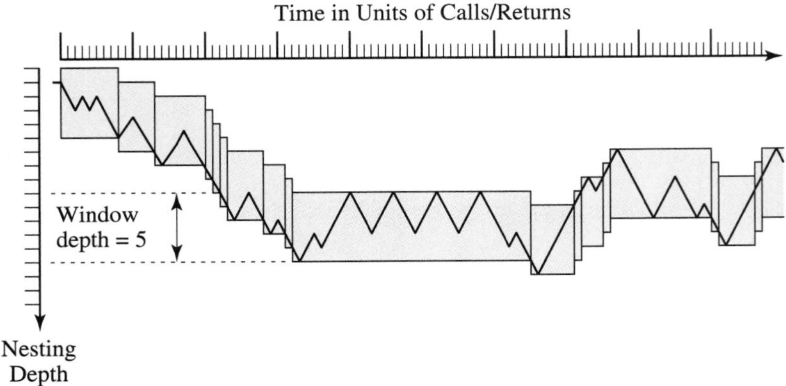

Figure 10-6 Call-return behavior as a function of nesting depth and time. (Adapted from [Stallings, 1996].)

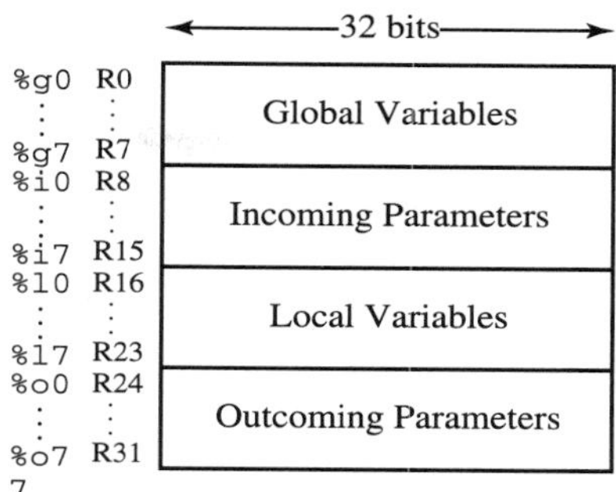

Figure 10-7 User's view of RISC I registers.

illustrates this behavior. For a nesting depth window size of five, the window moves only 18 times for 100 procedure calls. Results produced by a group at UC Berkeley (Tamir and Sequin, 1983) show that a window size of eight will shift on less than 1% of the calls or returns.

The small window size for nested calls is important for improving performance. For each procedure call, a stack frame is normally constructed in which parameters, a return address, and local variables are placed. There is thus a great deal of stack manipulation that takes place for procedure calls, but the complexity of the manipulation is not all that great. That is, stack references are highly localized within a small area.

The RISC I architecture exploits this locality by keeping the active portion of the stack in registers. Figure 10-7 shows the user's view of register usage for the RISC I. The user sees 32 registers in which each register is 32 bits wide. Registers R0–R7 are used for global variables. Registers R8–R15 are used for incoming parameters. Registers R16–R23 are used for local variables, and registers R24–R31 are used for outgoing parameters. The eight registers within each group are enough to satisfy the bulk of call/return activity, as evidenced by the frequency distribution in Figure 10-6.

Although the user sees 32 registers, there may be several hundred registers that overlap. Figure 10-8 illustrates the concept of overlapping register windows. The global registers are detached from the others and are continuously available as R0–R7. Registers R8–R31 make up the remaining 24 registers that the user sees, but this group of registers slides deeper into the **register file** (the entire set of registers) on each procedure call. Since the outgoing parameters for one procedure are the incoming parameters to another, these sets of registers can overlap. Registers

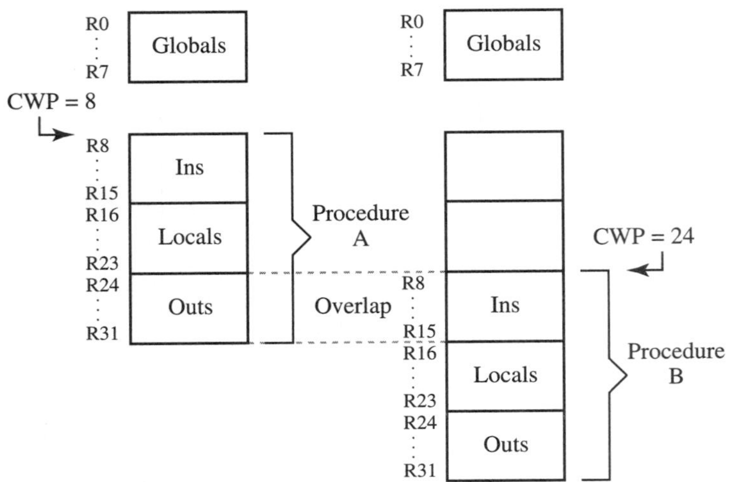

Figure 10-8 Overlapping register windows.

R8–R31 are referred to as a **window**. A **current window pointer** (CWP) points to the current window and increases or decreases for calls and returns, respectively.

In the statistically rare event when there are not enough registers for the level of nesting, then main memory is used. However, main memory is used for the *lowest* numbered window, so that the new current window still uses registers. The highest register location then wraps around to the lowest, forming a **circular buffer**. As returns are made, registers that were written to memory are restored to the register file. Thus, execution always takes place with registers and never directly with main memory.

EXAMPLE: COMPILED CODE FOR OVERLAPPING REGISTER WINDOWS AND DELAYED BRANCHES

In this section, we analyze a C compiler-produced SPARC assembly program that exploits features of the RISC concept. We start with the C program shown in Figure 10-9, in which the main routine passes two integers to a subroutine, which returns the sum of the integers to the main routine. The code produced by a Solaris Unix C compiler using the command line

```
gcc -S file.c
```

is shown in Figure 10-10.

```
/* Example C program to be compiled with gcc */

#include
<stdio.h>

main ()
{
    int a, b, c;

    a = 10;
    b = 4;
    c = add_two(a, b);

    printf("c = %d\n", c);
}

int add_two(a,b)
int a, b;
{
    int result;

    result = a + b;
    return(result);
}
```

Figure 10-9 Source code for C program to be compiled with gcc.

```
! Output produced by gcc compiler on Solaris (Sun UNIX)
! Annotations added by author

.file   add.c    ! Identifies the source program
.section        ".rodata"        ! Read-only data for routine main
        .align 8         ! Align read-only data for routine main on an
                         ! 8-byte boundary
.LLC0
        .asciz  "c = %d\n"       ! This is the read-only data
.section        "text"  ! Executable code starts here
        .align 4   ! Align executable code on a 4-byte (word) boundary
        .global main
        .type    main,#function
        .proc    04
main:            ! Beginning of executable code for routine main
        !#PROLOGUE#      0
        save %sp, -128, %sp  ! Create 128 byte stack frame. Advance
                             ! CWP (Current Window Pointer)
        !#PROLOGUE#      1
        mov 10, %o0   ! %o0 <- 10. Note that %o0 is the same as %r24.
    ! This is local variable a in main routine of C source program.
        st %o0, [%fp-20]     ! Store %o0 five words into stack frame.
        mov 4, %o0    ! %o0 <- 4. This is local variable b in main.
        st %o0, [%fp-24]     ! Store %o0 six words into stack frame.
        ld [%fp-20], %o0     ! Load %o0 and %o1 with parameters to
        ld [%fp-24], %o1     ! be passed to routine add_two.
        call add_two, 0      ! Call routine add_two
        nop     ! Pipeline flush needed after a transfer of control
        st %o0, [%fp-28]     ! Store result 67 words into stack frame.
                             ! This is local variable c in main.
        sethi %hi(.LLC0), %o1 ! This instruction and the next load
        or %o1, %lo(.LLC0), %o0 ! the 32-bit address .LLC0 into %o0
        ld [%fp-28], %o1   ! Load %o1 with parameter to pass to printf
```

Figure 10-10 gcc generated SPARC code (continued on next page).

```
        call printf, 0
        nop      ! A nop is needed here because of the pipeline flush
                 ! that follows a transfer of control.
.LL1
        ret      ! Return to calling routine (Solaris for this case)
        restore ! The complement to save. Although it follows the
            ! return, it is still in the pipeline and gets executed.
.LLfe1
        .size   main, .LLfe1-main ! Size of
        .align 4
        .global add_two
        .type   add_two, #function
        .proc 04
add_two:
         !#PROLOGUE# 0
         save %sp, -120, %sp
         !#PROLOGUE# 1
         st %i0, [%fp+68] !Same as %o0 in calling routine (variable a)
         st %i1, [%fp+72] !Same as %o1 in calling routine (variable b)
         ld [%fp+68], %o0
         ld [%fp+72], %o1
         add %o0, %o1, %o0 ! Perform the addition
         st %o0, [%fp-20]  ! Store result in stack frame
         ld [%fp-20], %i0  ! %i0 (result) is %o0 in called routine
         b .LL2
         nop
.LL2:
         ret
         restore
.LLfe2:
         .size   add_two, .LLfe2-add_two
         .ident  "GCC: (GNU) 2.5.8"
```

Figure 10-10 (continued).

An explanation of the more significant aspects of the assembled code is given in Figure 10-10, which includes a number of features found only in RISC code. There are a number of new instructions and pseudo-ops introduced in this code:

`.seg/.section` Unix executable programs have three segments for data, text (the instructions), and the stack. The `.seg` pseudo-op instructs the assembler to place the code that follows into one of these three segments. Some of the segments have different protections, which is why there is a `data` segment and also a `data1` segment. The `data1` segment contains constants and should be protected from writing. The `data` segment is both readable and writable and is therefore not protected against reading or writing (but it is protected from being executed, as is `data`). Newer versions of Unix allow more text and data areas to be used for different read, write, and execute protections.

`%hi` Same as ARC pseudo-op `.high22`.

`%lo` Same as ARC pseudo-op `.low10`.

add Same as addcc except that the condition codes are unaffected.

save Advances current window pointer and increments stack pointer to create space for local variables.

mov Same as
or %g0,register_or_immediate,destination_register. This differs from st because the destination is a register.

nop No-operation (the processor waits for one instruction cycle, while the branch finishes).

.ascii/.asciz Reserves space for an ASCII string.

set Sets a register to a value. This is a macro that expands to the sethi, %hi, and %lo constructs shown in #PROLOGUE# 1.

ret Return. Same as jmpl %i7+8, %g0. Notice that it seems like the return should only go 4 bytes past the calling instruction, not 8 bytes, as indicated previously. This is because the instruction that follows the call is a nop, inserted by the compiler to protect the integrity of the pipeline.

restore Decrements current window pointer.

b Same as ba.

.file Identifies the source file.

.align Forces the code that follows onto a boundary evenly divisible by its argument.

.type Associates a label with its type.

.size Computes the size of a segment.

.ident Identifies the compiler version.

We can see the positions of the delay slots, marked with nop instructions. (The optimizing feature of the compiler has not been applied yet.) Despite the availability of overlapping register windows in the SPARC architecture, the unoptimized code makes no use of this feature: Parameters to be passed to a routine are copied to the stack, and the called routine then retrieves these parameters from the stack. Again, the optimizing feature of the compiler has not yet been invoked (but read on).

Notice that the compiler does not seem to be consistent with its choice of registers for parameter passing. Prior to the call to `add_two`, the compiler uses `%o0` and `%o1` (`%r0` and `%r1`) for parameters passed to `add_two`. Then, `%r1` is used for the parameters passed to `printf`. Why did the compiler not start with `%r0` again, or choose the next available register (`%o2`)? This is the **register assignment problem**, which has been the object of a great deal of study. We will not go into details here,[1] as this is more appropriate for a course in compiler design, but suffice it to say that any logically correct assignment of variables to registers will work but that some assignments are better than others in terms of the number of registers used and the overall program execution time.

Why are the stack frames so large? We only need three words on the stack frame for local variables `a`, `b`, and `c` in `main`. We might also need a word to store the return address, although the compiler does not seem to generate code for that. There are no parameters passed to `main` by the operating system, and so the stack frame that `main` sees should only be four words (16 bytes) in size. Thus, the line at the beginning of routine main

```
save %sp, -128, %sp
```

should only be

```
save %sp, -16, %sp.
```

What is all of the extra space for? There are a number of runtime situations that may need stack space. For instance, if the nesting depth is greater than the number of windows, then the stack must be used for overflow. (See Figure D-2 in [SPARC, 1992].)

---

[1]Here are a few details, for the curious: `%r0` (`%o0`) is still in use (`add_two` is expecting the address of `LLC0` to show up in `%r0`), and `%r1` is no longer needed at this point, so it can be reassigned. But then why is `%r1` used in the `sethi` line? Would it have made sense to use `%r0` instead of introducing another register into the computation? See Problem 10.2 at the end of the chapter for more on this topic.

If a scalar is passed from one routine to another, then everything is fine. But if a callee refers to the address of a passed scalar (or aggregate), then the scalar (or aggregate) must be copied to the stack and be referenced from there for the lifetime of the pointer (or for the lifetime of the procedure, if the pointer lifetime is not known).

Why does the return statement `ret` cause a return to the code that is 8 bytes past the `call`, instead of 4 as we have been doing it? As mentioned previously, this is because there is a `nop` that follows `call` (the so-called delay-slot instruction).

Notice that routine labels that appear in the source code are prepended with an underscore in the assembly code, so that `main`, `add_two`, and `printf` in C become `_main`, `_add_two`, and `_printf` in `gcc` generated SPARC code. This means that if we want to write a C program that is linked to a `gcc` generated SPARC program, that the C calls should be made to routines that begin with underscores. For example, if `add_two` is compiled into SPARC code, and we invoke it from a C main program in another file, then the C program should make a call to `_add_two`, and *not* `add_two`, even though the routine started out as `add_two`. Further, the C program needs to declare `_add_two` as external.

If the compilation for `add_two` is continued down to an executable file, then there is no need to treat the labels differently. The `add_two` routine will still be labeled `_add_two`, but routine `main` will be compiled into code that expects to see `_add_two` and so everything will work OK. This is not the case, however, if a `gcc` program makes calls to a Fortran library.

Fortran is a commonly used language in the scientific community, and there are a number of significant Fortran libraries that are used for linear algebra, modeling and simulation, and parallel scientific applications. As programmers of language XYZ (whatever language that may be), we sometimes find ourselves wanting to write XYZ programs that make calls to Fortran routines. This is easy to do once we understand what is happening.

There are two significant issues that need to be addressed:

1. Differences in routine labels
2. Differences in subroutine linkage

In Fortran, the source code labels are prepended with two underscores in the assembly code. A C program (if C is language XYZ) that makes a call to Fortran routine `add_two` would then make a call to `__add_two`, which also must be declared as external in the C source code (and declared as global in the Fortran program).

If all of the parameters that are passed to the Fortran routines are pointers, then everything will work OK. If there are any scalars passed, then there will be trouble because C (like Java) uses call-by-value for scalars whereas Fortran uses call-by-reference. We need to "trick" the C compiler into using call-by-reference by making it explicit. Wherever a Fortran routine expects a scalar in its argument list, we use a pointer to the scalar in the C code.

As a practical consideration, the `gcc` compiler will compile Fortran programs. It knows what to do by observing the extension of the source file, which should be `.f` for Fortran.

Now let us take a look at how an optimizing compiler improves the code. Figure 10-11 shows the optimized code using the compiler's `-O` flag. Notice there is not a single `nop`, `ld`, or `st` instruction. Wasted cycles devoted to `nop` instructions have been reclaimed, and memory references devoted to stack manipulation have been eliminated.

10.5 Multiple Instruction Issue (Superscalar) Machines—The PowerPC 601

In the earlier pipelining discussion, we see how several instructions can be in various phases of execution at once. Here we look at superscalar architecture, where, with separate execution units, several instructions can be executed simultaneously. In a superscalar architecture, there might be one or more separate **integer units** (IUs), **floating point units** (FPUs), and **branch processing units** (BPUs). This implies that instructions need to be scheduled into the various execution units and, further, that instructions might be executed out of order.

Out-of-order execution means that instructions need to be examined prior to **dispatching** them to an execution unit, not only to determine which unit should execute them but also to determine whether executing them out of order would result in an incorrect program because of dependencies between the instructions. This in turn implies an **instruction unit**, IU, which can prefetch instructions into an instruction queue, determine the kinds of instructions and the dependence relations among them, and schedule them into the various execution units.

```
! Output produced by -O optimiziation for gcc compiler

.file   "add.c"
.section        ".rodata"
        .align 8
.LLC0:
        .asciz  "c = %d\n"
.section        ".text"
        .align 4
        .global main
        .type    main,#function
        .proc   04
main:
        !#PROLOGUE# 0
        save %sp,-112,%sp
        !#PROLOGUE# 1
        mov 10,%o0
        call add_two,0
        mov 4,%o1
        mov %o0,%o1
        sethi %hi(.LLC0),%o0
        call printf,0
        or %o0,%lo(.LLC0),%o0
        ret
        restore
.LLfe1:
        .size    main,.LLfe1-main
        .align 4
        .global add_two
        .type    add_two,#function
        .proc   04
add_two:
        !#PROLOGUE# 0
        !#PROLOGUE# 1
        retl
        add %o0,%o1,%o0
.LLfe2:
        .size    add_two,.LLfe2-add_two
        .ident  "GCC: (GNU) 2.7.2"
```

Figure 10-11 SPARC code generated with the `-O` **optimization flag.**

10.6 Case Study: The PowerPC™ 601 as a Superscalar Architecture

As an example of a modern superscalar architecture let us examine the Motorola PowerPC™ 601. The 601 has actually been superseded by more powerful members of the PowerPC family, but it will serve to illustrate the important features of superscalar architectures without introducing unnecessary complexity into our discussion.

10.6.1 *INSTRUCTION SET ARCHITECTURE OF THE POWERPC 601*

The 601 is a 32-bit general register RISC machine whose ISA includes:

- Thirty-two 32-bit general purpose integer registers (GPRs)
- Thirty-two 64-bit floating point registers (FPRs)

- Eight 4-bit condition code register
- Nearly 50 special-purpose 32-bit registers that are used to control various aspects of memory management and the operating system;
- Over 250 instructions (many of which are special purpose)

10.6.2 *HARDWARE ARCHITECTURE OF THE POWERPC 601*

Figure 10-12, adapted from the Motorola PowerPC 601 user's manual, shows the microarchitecture of the 601. The flow of instructions and data proceed via the system interface, shown at the bottom of the figure, into the 32-KByte cache. From there, instructions are fetched eight at a time into the instruction unit, shown at the top of the figure.The issue logic within the instruction unit examines the instructions in the queue for their kind and dependence and issues them into one of the three execution units: IU, BPU, or FPU.

The IU is shown as containing the GPR file and an integer exception register, XER, which holds information about exceptions that arise within the IU. The IU can execute most integer instructions in a single clock cycle, thus obviating the need for any kind of pipelining of integer instructions.

The FPU contains the FPRs and the floating point status and control register (FPSCR). The FPSCR contains information about floating point exceptions and the type of result produced by the FPR. The FPU is pipelined, and most FP instructions can be issued at a rate of one per clock.

As we mentioned in the section on pipelining, branch instructions, especially conditional branch instructions, pose a bottleneck when trying to overlap instruction execution. This is because the branch condition must first be ascertained to be true (for example, "branch on plus" must test the N flag to ascertain that it is cleared). The branch address must then be computed, which often involves address arithmetic. Only then can the PC be loaded with the branch address.

The 601 attacks this problem in several ways. First, as mentioned previously, there are eight 4-bit condition code registers instead of the usual one. This allows up to eight instructions to have separate condition code bits and therefore not interfere with each other's ability to set condition codes. The BPU looks in the instruction queue, and if it finds a conditional branch instruction it proceeds to compute the branch target address ahead of time and fetches instructions at the

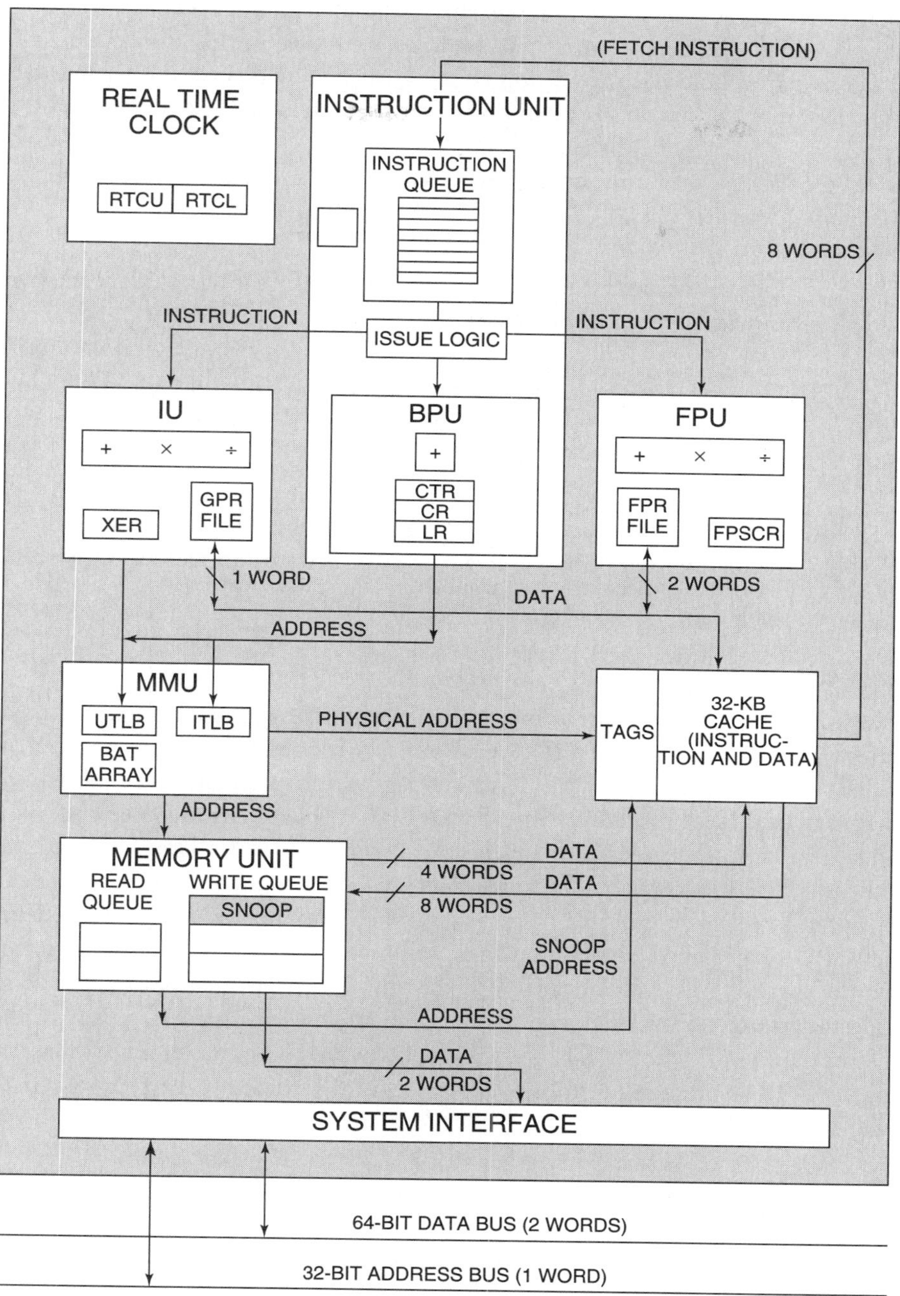

Figure 10-12 The PowerPC 601 architecture. (Adapted from the Motorola PowerPC 601 user's manual.)

branch target. If the branch is taken, this results in effectively a zero-cycle branch, since the instruction at the branch target has already been fetched in anticipation of the branch condition being satisfied. The BPU also has a link register (LR) in which it can store subroutine return addresses, thus saving one GPR as well as several other registers used for special purposes. Note that the BPU can issue its addresses over a separate bus directly to the MME and memory unit for prefetching instructions.

The RTC unit shown in the figure is a real-time clock that has a calendar range of 137 years, with an accuracy of 1 ns.

The MMU and memory unit assist in fetching both instructions and data. Note the separate path for data items that goes from the cache directly to the GPR and FPR register files.

The PowerPC 601 and its more powerful descendants are typical of the modern general-purpose microprocessor. Current microprocessor families are superscalar in design, often having several of each kind of execution unit.

10.7 VLIW Machines

There is an architecture that is in a sense competitive with superscalar architectures, referred to as the **VLIW** (Very Long Instruction Word) architecture. In VLIW machines, multiple operations are packed into a single instruction word that may be 128 or more bits wide. The VLIW machine has multiple execution units, similar to the superscalar machine. A typical VLIW CPU might have two IUs, two FPUs, two load/store units, and a BPU. It is the responsibility of the compiler to organize multiple operations into the instruction word. This relieves the CPU of the need to examine instructions for dependencies or to order or reorder instructions. A disadvantage is that the compiler must be pessimistic in its estimates of dependencies. If it cannot find enough instructions to fill the instruction word, it must fill the blank spots with NOP instructions. Furthermore, VLIW architectural improvements require software to be recompiled to take advantage of them.

There have been a number of attempts to market VLIW machines, but mainly, VLIW machines have fallen out of favor in recent years. Performance is the primary culprit, for the reasons just given, among others.

10.8 Case Study: The Intel IA-64 (Merced) Architecture

This section discusses a microprocessor family in development by an alliance between Intel and Hewlett-Packard, which is hoped will take the consortium into the twenty-first century. We first look into the background that led to the decision to develop a new architecture, and then we look at what is currently known about the architecture. (The information in this section is taken from various publications and Web sites and has not been confirmed by Intel or Hewlett-Packard.)

10.8.1 *BACKGROUND—THE 80X86 CISC ARCHITECTURE*

The current Intel 80x86 architecture, which runs on some 80% of desktop computers in the late 1990s, had its roots in the 8086 microprocessor, designed in the late 1970s. The architectural roots of the family go back to the original Intel 8080, designed in the early 1970s. Being a persistent advocate of upward compatibility, Intel has been in a sense hobbled by a CISC architecture that is over 20 years old. Other vendors such as Motorola abandoned hardware compatibility for modernization, relying upon emulators to ease the transition to a new ISA.

In any case, Intel and Hewlett-Packard decided several years ago that the x86 architecture would soon reach the end of its useful life, and they began joint research on a new architecture. Intel and Hewlett-Packard have been quoted as saying that RISC architectures have "run out of gas," so to speak, so their search led in other directions. The result of their research led to the IA-64, which stands for "Intel Architecture-64." The first of the IA-64 family is known by the code name **Merced**, after the Merced River, near San Jose, California.

10.8.2 *THE MERCED: AN EPIC ARCHITECTURE*

Although Intel has not released significant details of the Merced ISA, it refers to its architecture as Explicitly Parallel Instruction Computing, or **EPIC**. Intel takes pains to point out that it is *not* a VLIW or even an LIW machine, perhaps out of sensitivity to the bad reputation that VLIW machines have received; however, some industry analysts refer to it as "the VLIW-like EPIC architecture."

Features

While exact details are not publicly known as of this writing, published sources report that the Merced is expected to have the following characteristics:

- One hundred twenty-eight 64-bit GPRs and perhaps 128 80-bit FPRs.
- Sixty-four 1-bit predicate registers (explained later).
- Instruction words contain three instructions packed into one 128-bit parcel.
- Execution units, roughly equivalent to IU, FPU, and BPU, appear in multiples of three, and the IA-64 will be able to schedule instructions into these multiples.
- It will be the burden of the compiler to schedule the instructions to take advantage of the multiple execution units.
- Most of the instructions seem to be RISC-like, although it is rumored that the processor will (still!) execute 80x86 binary codes, in a dedicated execution unit, known as the DXU.
- Speculative loads. The processor will be able to load values from memory well in advance of when they are needed. Exceptions caused by the loads are postponed until execution has proceeded to the place where the loads would normally have occurred.
- Predication (*not* prediction), where both sides of a conditional branch instruction are executed and the results from the side not taken are discarded.

These latter two features are discussed in more detail later.

The Instruction Word

The 128-bit instruction word, shown in Figure 10-13, has three 40-bit instructions and an 8-bit template. The template is placed by the compiler to tell the CPU

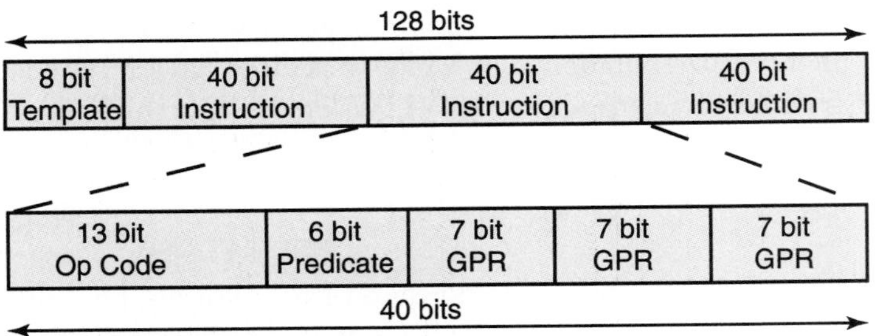

Figure 10-13 The 128-bit IA-64 instruction word.

which instructions in and near that instruction word can execute in parallel, thus the term "Explicit." The CPU need not analyze the code at run-time to expose instructions that can be executed in parallel because the compiler determines that ahead of time. Compilers for most VLIW machines must place NOP instructions in slots where instructions cannot be executed in parallel. In the IA-64 scheme, the presence of the template identifies those instructions in the word that can and cannot be executed in parallel, so the compiler is free to schedule instructions into all three slots, regardless of whether they can be executed in parallel.

The 6-bit predicate field in each instruction represents a tag placed there by the compiler to identify which leg of a conditional branch the instruction is part of and is used in branch predication.

Branch Predication

Rather than using branch prediction, the IA-64 architecture uses *branch predication* to remove penalties due to mispredicted branches. When the compiler encounters a conditional branch instruction that is a candidate for predication, it selects two unique labels and labels the instructions in each leg of the branch instruction with one of the two labels, identifying which leg they belong to. Both legs can then be executed in parallel. There are 64 one-bit predicate registers, one corresponding to each of the 64 possible predicate identifiers.

When the actual branch outcome is known, the corresponding one-bit predicate register is set if the branch outcome is TRUE, and the one-bit predicate register corresponding to the FALSE label is cleared. Then the results from instructions having the correct predicate label are kept, and results from instructions having the incorrect (mispredicted) label are discarded.

Speculative Loads

The architecture also employs **speculative loads** (that is, examining the instruction stream for upcoming load instructions and loading the value ahead of time, *speculating* that the value will actually be needed and will not have been altered by intervening operations). If successful, this eliminates the normal latency inherent in memory accesses. The compiler examines the instruction stream for candidate load operations that it can "hoist" to a location earlier in the instruction sequence. It inserts a *check* instruction at the point where the load instruction was originally located. The data value is thus available in the CPU when the check instruction is encountered.

The problem that is normally faced by speculative loads is that the load operation may generate an exception (for example, because the address is invalid). However, the exception may not be genuine, because the load may be beyond a branch instruction that is not taken and thus would never actually be executed. The IA-64 architecture postpones processing the exception until the check instruction is encountered. If the branch is not taken then the check instruction will not be executed, and thus the exception will not be processed.

All of this complexity places a heavy burden on the compiler, which must be clever about how it schedules operations into the instruction words.

80x86 Compatibility

Intel was recently granted a patent for a method, presumably to be used with IA-64, for supporting two instruction sets, one of which is the x86 instruction set. It describes instructions to allow switching between the two execution modes and for data sharing between them.

Estimated Performance

It has been estimated that the first Merced implementation will appear sometime in the year 2000 and will have an 800-MHz clock speed. Goals are for it to have performance several times that of current-generation processors when running in EPIC mode and that of a 500-MHz Pentium II in x86 mode. Intel has stated that initially the IA-64 microprocessor will be reserved for use in high-performance workstations and servers, and at an estimated initial price of $5000 each this will undoubtedly be the case.

On the other hand, skeptics, who seem to abound when new technology is announced, say that the technology is unlikely to meet expectations and that the IA-64 may never see the light of day. Time will tell.

10.9 Parallel Architecture

One method of improving the performance of a processor is to decrease the time needed to execute instructions. This will work up to a limit of about 400 MHz (Stone and Cocke, 1991), at which point an effect known as **ringing** on buses prohibits further speedup with conventional bus technology. This is not to say that higher clock speeds are not possible, because indeed current microprocessors have clock rates well above 400 MHz, but that "shared bus" approaches become impractical at these speeds. As conventional architectural approaches to improving performance wear thin, we need to consider alternative methods of improving performance.

One alternative approach to increasing bus speed is to increase the number of processors and decompose and distribute a single program onto the processors. This approach is known as **parallel processing**, in which a number of processors work collectively, in parallel, on a common problem. We see an example of parallel processing earlier in the chapter with pipelining. For that case, four processors are connected in series (Figure 10-3), each performing a different task, like an assembly line in a factory. The interleaved memory described in Chapter 7 is another example of pipelining.

A parallel architecture can be characterized in terms of three parameters: (1) the number of **processing elements** (PEs); (2) the interconnection network among the PEs; and (3) the organization of the memory. In the four-stage instruction pipeline of Figure 10-3, there are four PEs. The interconnection network among the PEs is a simple **ring**. The memory is an ordinary RAM that is external to the pipeline.

Characterizing the architecture of a parallel processor is a relatively easy task, but measuring the performance is not nearly so simple. Although we can easily measure the increased speed that a simple enhancement like a pipeline offers, the overall speedup is data dependent: Not all programs and data sets map well onto a pipelined architecture. Other performance considerations of pipelined architectures that are also data dependent are the cost of flushing a pipeline, the increased area cost, the latency (input to output delay) of the pipeline, etc.

A few common measures of performance are **parallel time**, **speedup**, **efficiency**, and **throughput**. The parallel time is simply the absolute time needed for a program to execute on a parallel processor. The speedup is the ratio of the time for a program to execute on a sequential (nonparallel, that is) processor to the time for that same program to execute on a parallel processor. In a simple form, we can represent speedup (S, now in the context of parallel processing) as

$$S = \frac{T_{\text{Sequential}}}{T_{\text{Parallel}}}$$

Since a sequential algorithm and a parallel version of the same algorithm may be programmed very differently for each machine, we need to qualify $T_{\text{Sequential}}$ and T_{Parallel} so that they apply to the best implementation for each machine.

There is more to the story. If we want to achieve a speedup of 100, it is not enough to simply distribute a single program over 100 processors. The problem is that not many computations are easily decomposed in a way that fully utilizes the available PEs. If there are even a small number of sequential operations in a parallel program, then the speedup can be significantly limited. This is summarized by **Amdahl's law**, in which speedup is expressed in terms of the number of processors p and the fraction of operations that must be performed sequentially f:

$$S = \frac{1}{f + \frac{1-f}{p}}$$

For example, if $f = 10\%$ of the operations must be performed sequentially, then speedup can be no greater than 10 regardless of how many processors are used:

$$S = \frac{1}{0.1 + \frac{0.9}{10}} \cong 5.3 \qquad S = \frac{1}{0.1 + \frac{0.9}{\infty}} = 10$$

$$p = 10 \text{ processors} \qquad p = \infty \text{ processors}$$

This brings us to measurements of **efficiency**. Efficiency is the ratio of speedup to the number of processors used. For a speedup of 5.3 with 10 processors, the efficiency is

$$\frac{5.3}{10} = .53, \text{ or } 53\%$$

If we double the number of processors to 20, then the speedup increases to 6.9 but the efficiency reduces to 34%. Thus, parallelizing an algorithm can improve performance to a limit that is determined by the amount of sequential operations. Efficiency is drastically reduced as speedup approaches its limit, and so it does not make sense to simply use more processors in a computation in the hope that a corresponding gain in performance will be achieved.

Throughput is a measure of how much computation is achieved over time and is of special concern for I/O bound and pipelined applications. For the case of a four-stage pipeline that remains filled, in which each pipeline stage completes its task in 10 ns, the average time to complete an operation is 10 ns even though it takes 40 ns to execute any one operation. The overall throughput for this situation is then

$$0.1\frac{\text{operation}}{\text{ns}} = 10^8 \text{ operations per second}$$

10.9.1 *THE FLYNN TAXONOMY*

Computer architectures can be classified in terms of their **instruction streams** and their **data streams**, using a taxonomy developed by M. J. Flynn (Flynn, 1972). A conventional sequential processor fits into the **single instruction stream, single data stream** (SISD) category, as illustrated in Figure 10-14a. Only a single instruction is executed at a time in a SISD processor, although

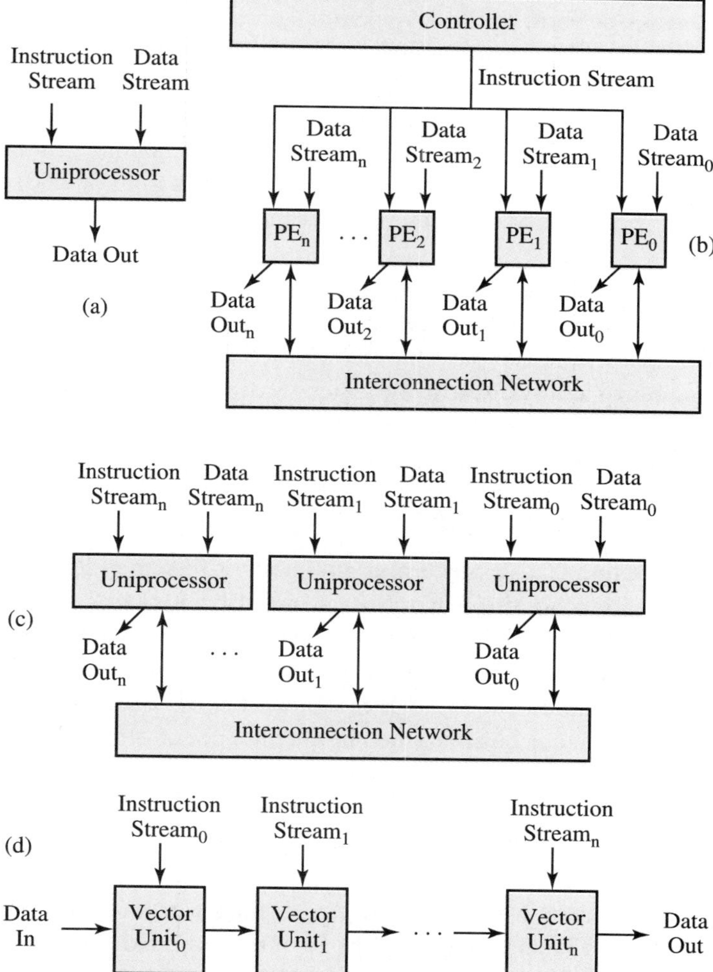

Figure 10-14 Classification of architectures according to the Flynn taxonomy: (a) SISD; (b) SIMD; (c) MIMD; (d) MISD.

pipelining may allow several instructions to be in different phases of execution at any given time.

In a **single instruction stream, multiple data stream** (SIMD) processor, several identical processors perform the same sequence of operations on different data sets, as illustrated in Figure 10-14b. A SIMD system can be thought of as a room filled with mail sorters, all sorting different pieces of mail into the same set of bins.

In a **multiple instruction stream, multiple data stream** (MIMD) processor, several processors perform different operations on different data sets, but are all coordinated to execute a single parallel program, as illustrated in Figure 10-14c. An example of a MIMD processor is the Sega home video entertainment system, which has four processors for (1) sound synthesis (a Yamaha synthesis processor); (2) sound filtering (a Texas Instruments programmable sound generator); (3) program execution (a 68000); and (4) background processing (a Z80). We will see more of the Sega Genesis in a case study at the end of the chapter.

In a **multiple instruction stream, single data stream** (MISD) processor, a single data stream is operated on by several functional units, as illustrated in Figure 10-14d. The data stream is typically a vector of several related streams. This configuration is known as a **systolic array**, which we see in Chapter 3 in the form of an array multiplier.

10.9.2 *INTERCONNECTION NETWORKS*

When a computation is distributed over a number of PEs, the PEs need to communicate with each other through an **interconnection network**. There is a host of topologies for interconnection networks, each with their own characteristics in terms of **crosspoint complexity** (an asymptotic measure of area), **diameter** (the length of the worst case path through the network), and **blocking** (whether or not a new connection can be established in the presence of other connections). A few representative topologies and control strategies for configuring networks are described in this section.

One of the most powerful network topologies is the **crossbar**, in which every PE is directly connected to every other PE. An abstract view of a crossbar is illustrated in Figure 10-15a, in which four PEs are interconnected. In a close-up view illustrated in Figure 10-16, the crossbar contains **crosspoint switches**, which are configurable devices that either connect or disconnect the lines that go through it. In general, for N PEs, the crosspoint complexity (the number of crosspoint

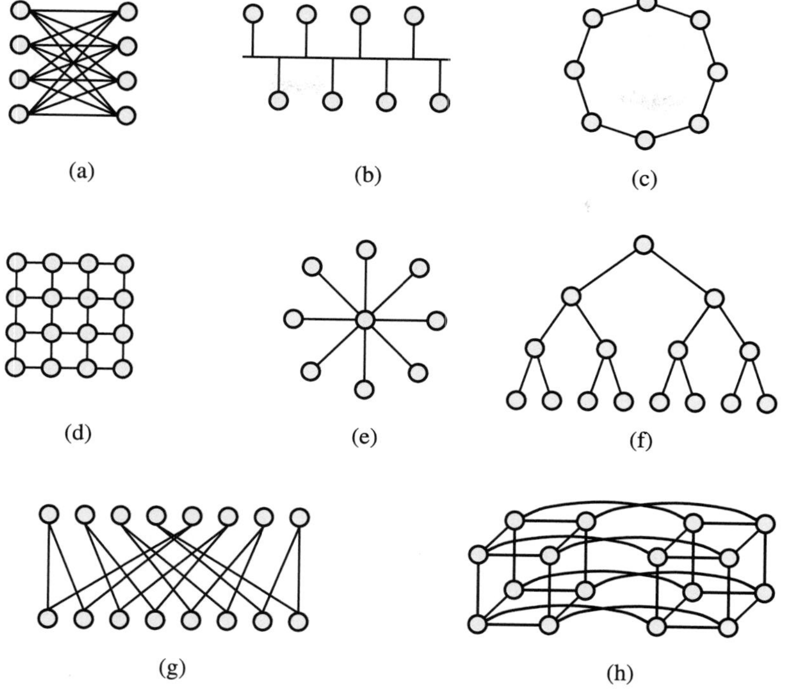

Figure 10-15 Network topologies: (a) crossbar; (b) bus; (c) ring; (d) mesh; (e) star; (f) tree; (g) perfect shuffle; (h) hypercube.

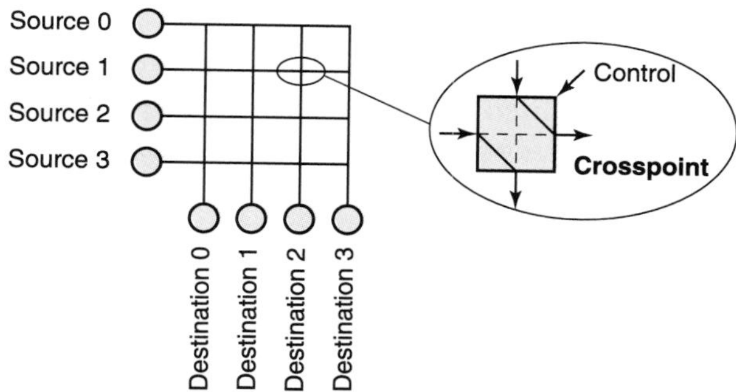

Figure 10-16 Internal organization of a crossbar.

switches) is N^2. In Figure 10-15a, $N = 4$ (not 8) because the output ports of the PEs on the left and the input ports of the PEs on the right belong to the same PEs. The crosspoint complexity is thus $4^2 = 16$. The network diameter is 1 since every PE can directly communicate with every other PE, with no intervening

PEs. The number of crosspoint switches that are traversed is not normally considered in evaluating the network diameter. The crossbar is **strictly nonblocking**, which means that there is always an available path between every input and output regardless of the configuration of existing paths.

At the other extreme of complexity is the bus topology, which is illustrated in Figure 10-15b. With the bus topology, a fixed amount of bus bandwidth is shared among the PEs. The crosspoint complexity is N for N PEs, and the network diameter is 1, so the bus grows more gracefully than the crossbar. There can only be one source at a time, and there is normally only one receiver, so blocking is a frequent situation for a bus.

In a ring topology, there are N crosspoints for N PEs, as shown in Figure 10-15c. As for the crossbar, each crosspoint is contained within a PE. The network diameter is $N/2$, but the collective bandwidth is N times greater than for the case of the bus. This is because adjacent PEs can communicate directly with each other over their common link without affecting the rest of the network.

In the mesh topology, there are N crosspoints for N PEs, but the diameter is only $2\sqrt{N}$, as shown in Figure 10-15d. All PEs can simultaneously communicate in just $3\sqrt{N}$ steps, as discussed in (Leighton, 1992) using an **off-line routing algorithm** (in which the crosspoint settings are determined external to the PEs).

In the star topology, there is a central hub through which all PEs communicate as shown in Figure 10-15e. Since all of the connection complexity is centralized, the star can only grow to sizes that are bounded by the technology, which is normally less than for decentralized topologies like the mesh. The crosspoint complexity within the hub varies according to the implementation, which can be anything from a bus to a crossbar.

In the tree topology, there are N crosspoints for N PEs, and the diameter is $2log_2N - 1$, as shown in Figure 10-15f. The tree is effective for applications in which there is a great deal of distributing and collecting of data.

In the perfect shuffle topology, there are N crosspoints for N PEs as shown in Figure 10-15g. The diameter is log_2N since it takes log_2N passes through the network to connect any PE with any other in the worst case. The perfect shuffle name comes from the property that if a deck of 2^N cards, in which N is an integer, is cut in half and interleaved N times, then the original configuration of the

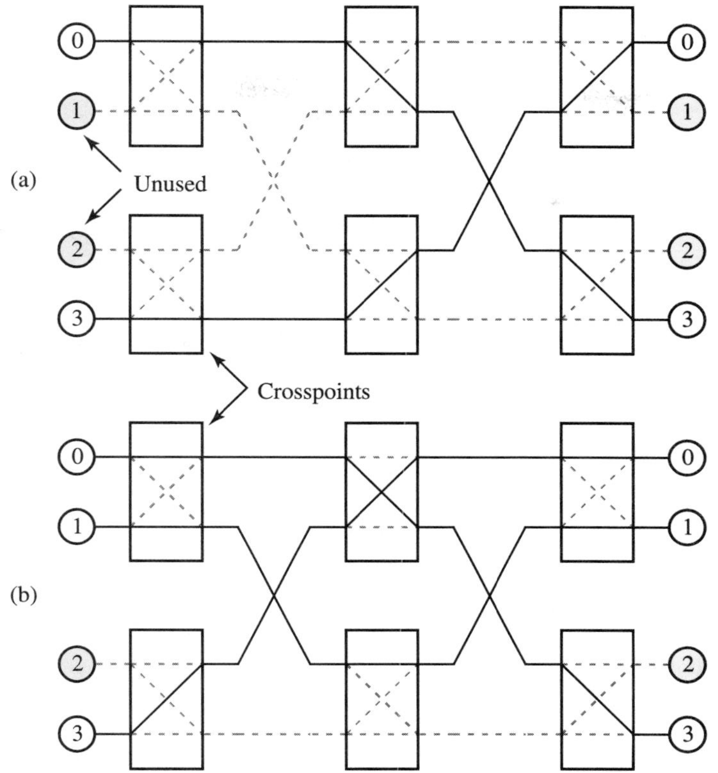

Figure 10-17 (a) Crosspoint settings for connections 0 → 3 and 3 → 0; (b) adjusted settings to accommodate connection 1 → 1.

deck is restored. All N PEs can simultaneously communicate in $3log_2N-1$ passes through the network as presented in (Wu and Feng, 1981).

Finally, the hypercube has N crosspoints for N PEs, with a diameter of log_2N-1, as shown in Figure 10-15h. The smaller number of crosspoints with respect to the perfect shuffle topology is balanced by a greater connection complexity in the PEs.

Let us now consider the behavior of blocking in interconnection networks. Figure 10-17a shows a configuration in which four processors are interconnected with a two-stage perfect shuffle network in which each crosspoint either passes both inputs straight through to the outputs or exchanges the inputs to the outputs. A path is enabled from processor 0 to processor 3, and another path is enabled from processor 3 to processor 0. Neither processor 1 nor processor 2

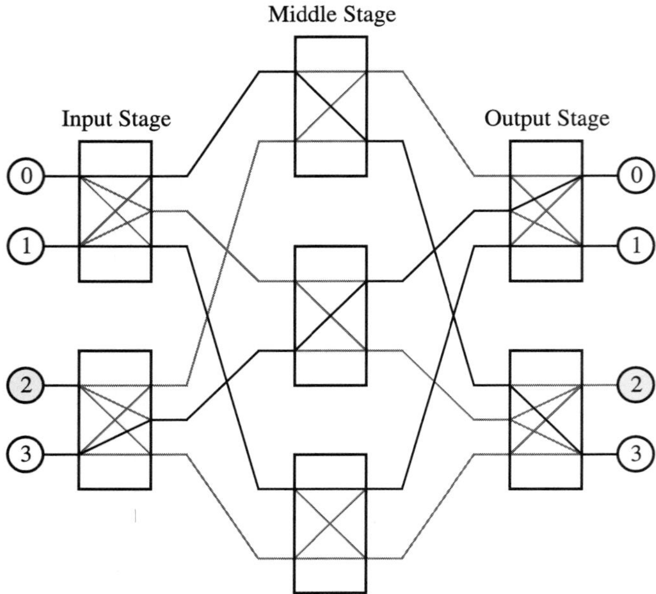

Figure 10-18 A three-stage Clos network for four PEs.

needs to communicate, but they participate in some arbitrary connections as a side effect of the crosspoint settings that are already specified.

Suppose that we want to add another connection, from processor 1 to processor 1. There is no way to adjust the unused crosspoints to accommodate this new connection because all of the crosspoints are already set, and the needed connection does not occur as a side effect of the current settings. Thus, connection 1 → 1 is now blocked.

If we are allowed to disturb the settings of the crosspoints that are currently in use, then we can accommodate all three connections, as illustrated in Figure 10-17b. An interconnection network that operates in this manner is referred to as a **rearrangeably nonblocking network**.

The three-stage **Clos network** is **strictly nonblocking**. That is, there is no need to disturb the existing settings of the crosspoints in order to add another connection. An example of a three stage Clos network is shown in Figure 10-18 for four PEs. In the input stage, each crosspoint is actually a crossbar that can make any connection of the two inputs to the three outputs. The crosspoints in the middle stage and the output stage are also small crossbars. The number of inputs to each input crosspoint and the number of outputs from each output crosspoint is selected according to the desired complexity of the crosspoints and the desired complexity of the middle stage.

The middle stage has three crosspoints in this example and, in general, there are $(n-1)+(p-1)+1 = n+p-1$ crosspoints in the middle stage, in which n is the number of inputs to each input crosspoint and p is the number of outputs from each output crosspoint. This is how the three-stage Clos network maintains a strictly nonblocking property. There are $n - 1$ ways that an input can be blocked at the output of an input stage crosspoint as a result of existing connections. Similarly, there are $p - 1$ ways that existing connections can block a desired connection into an output crosspoint. In order to ensure that every desired connection can be made between available input and output ports, there must be one more path available.

For this case, $n = 2$ and $p = 2$, and so we need $n+p-1 = 2+2-1 = 3$ paths from every input crosspoint to every output crosspoint. Architecturally, this relationship is satisfied with three crosspoints in the middle stage that each connect every input crosspoint to every output crosspoint.

EXAMPLE: STRICTLY NONBLOCKING NETWORK

For this example, we want to design a strictly nonblocking (three-stage Clos) network for 12 channels (12 inputs and 12 outputs to the network) while maintaining a low maximum complexity of any crosspoint in the network.

There are a number of ways that we can organize the network. For the input stage, we can have two input nodes with six inputs per node, or six input nodes with two inputs per node, to list just two possibilities. We have similar choices for the output stage. Let us start by looking at a configuration that has two nodes in the input stage and two nodes in the output stage, with six inputs for each node in the input stage and six outputs for each node in the output stage. For this case, $n = p = 6$, which means that $n+p-1 = 11$ nodes are needed in the middle stage, as shown in Figure 10-19. The maximum complexity of any node for this case is $6 \times 11 = 66$, for each of the input and output nodes.

Now let us try using six input nodes and six output nodes, with two inputs for each input node and two outputs for each output node. For this case, $n = p = 2$, which means that $n+p-1 = 3$ nodes are needed in the middle

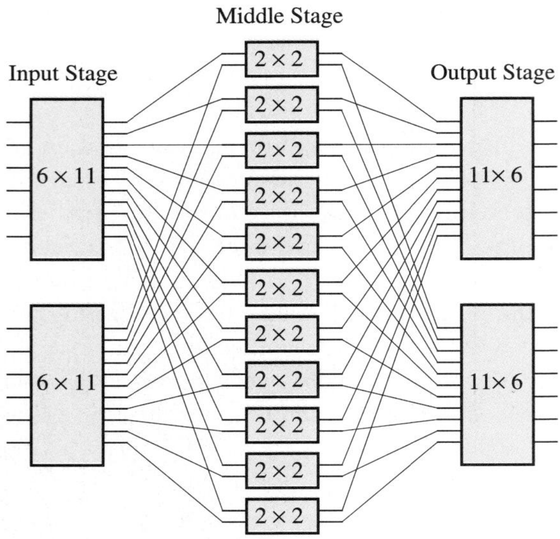

Figure 10-19 A 12-channel three-stage Clos network with $n = p = 6$.

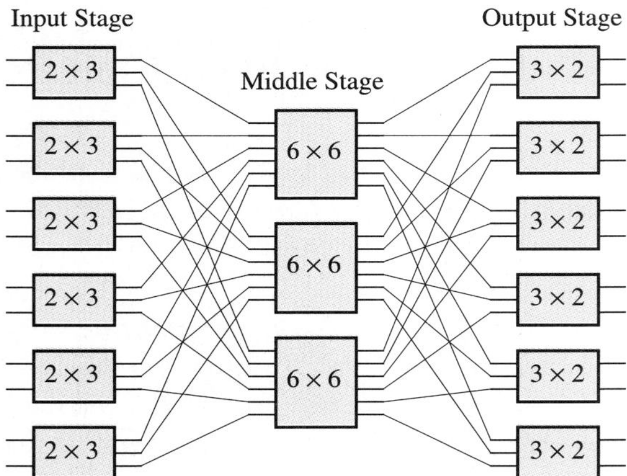

Figure 10-20 A 12-channel three-stage Clos network with $n = p = 2$.

stage, as shown in Figure 10-20. The maximum node complexity for this case is $6 \times 6 = 36$ for each of the middle stage nodes, which is better than the maximum node complexity of 66 for the previous case.

Similarly, networks for $n = p = 4$ and $n = p = 3$ are shown in Figures 10-21 and 10-22, respectively. The maximum node complexity for each of these net-

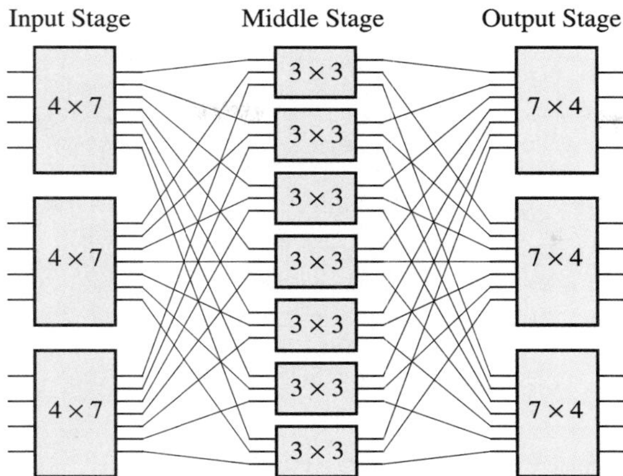

Figure 10-21 A 12-channel three-stage Clos network with $n = p = 4$.

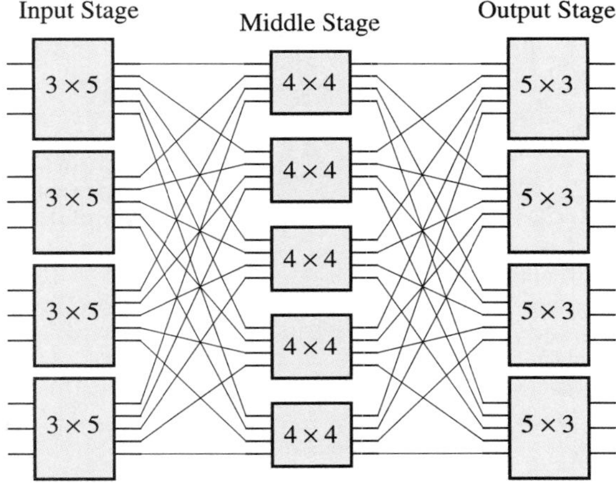

Figure 10-22 A 12-channel three-stage Clos network with $n = p = 3$.

works is $4 \times 7 = 28$ and $4 \times 4 = 16$, respectively. Among the four configurations studied here, $n = p = 3$ gives the lowest maximum node complexity.■

10.9.3 *MAPPING AN ALGORITHM ONTO A PARALLEL ARCHITECTURE*

The process of mapping an algorithm onto a parallel architecture begins with a **dependency analysis** in which data dependencies among the operations in a program are identified. Consider the C code shown in Figure 10-23. In an ordinary SISD processor, the four numbered statements require four time steps to complete, as illustrated in the control sequence of Figure 10-24a. The **depen-**

Operation numbers

```
    func(x, y)   /* Compute (x² + y²) × y² */
    int x, y;
    {
    int temp0, temp1, temp2, temp3;

0   temp0 = x * x;
1   temp1 = y * y;
2   temp2 = temp1 + temp2;
3   temp3 = temp1 * temp2;

    return(temp3);
    }
```

Figure 10-23 A C function computes $(x^2 + y^2) \times y^2$**.**

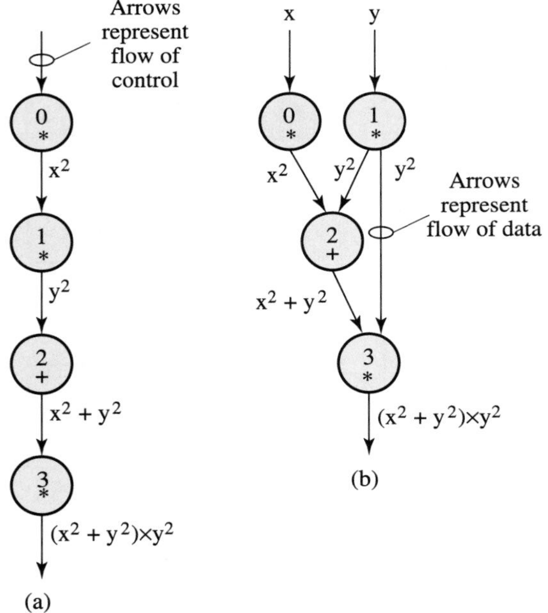

Figure 10-24 (a) Control sequence for C program; (b) dependency graph for C program.

dency graph shown in Figure 10-24b exposes the natural parallelism in the control sequence. The dependency graph is created by assigning each operation in the original program to a node in the graph and then drawing a directed arc from each node that produces a result to the node(s) that needs it.

(a)

$$\begin{bmatrix} a_{00} & a_{01} & a_{02} & a_{03} \\ a_{10} & a_{11} & a_{12} & a_{13} \\ a_{20} & a_{21} & a_{22} & a_{23} \\ a_{30} & a_{31} & a_{32} & a_{33} \end{bmatrix} \begin{bmatrix} x_0 \\ x_1 \\ x_2 \\ x_3 \end{bmatrix} = \begin{bmatrix} b_0 \\ b_1 \\ b_2 \\ b_3 \end{bmatrix}$$

(b)

$$b_0 = \overset{0}{\boxed{a_{00}x_0}} \overset{4}{+} \overset{1}{\boxed{a_{01}x_1}} \overset{6}{+} \overset{2}{\boxed{a_{02}x_2}} \overset{5}{+} \overset{3}{\boxed{a_{03}x_3}}$$

$$b_1 = \overset{7}{\boxed{a_{10}x_0}} \overset{11}{+} \overset{8}{\boxed{a_{11}x_1}} \overset{13}{+} \overset{9}{\boxed{a_{12}x_2}} \overset{12}{+} \overset{10}{\boxed{a_{13}x_3}}$$

$$b_2 = \overset{14}{\boxed{a_{20}x_0}} \overset{18}{+} \overset{15}{\boxed{a_{21}x_1}} \overset{20}{+} \overset{16}{\boxed{a_{22}x_2}} \overset{19}{+} \overset{17}{\boxed{a_{23}x_3}}$$

$$b_3 = \overset{21}{\boxed{a_{30}x_0}} \overset{25}{+} \overset{22}{\boxed{a_{31}x_1}} \overset{27}{+} \overset{23}{\boxed{a_{32}x_2}} \overset{26}{+} \overset{24}{\boxed{a_{33}x_3}}$$

Figure 10-25 (a) Problem setup for $Ax = x$; (b) equations for computing the b_i.

The control sequence requires four time steps to complete, but the dependency graph shows that the program can be completed in just three time steps, since operations 0 and 1 do not depend on each other and can be executed simultaneously (as long as there are two processors available.) The resulting speedup of

$$\frac{T_{\text{Sequential}}}{T_{\text{Parallel}}} = \frac{4}{3} = 1.\bar{3}$$

may not be very great, but for other programs, the opportunity for speedup can be substantial, as we will see.

Consider a matrix multiplication problem $Ax = b$ $A\mathbf{x} = \mathbf{b}$ in which A is a 4×4 matrix and x and b are both 4×1 matrices, as illustrated in Figure 10-25a. Our goal is to solve for the b_i, using the equations shown in Figure 10-25b. Every operation is assigned a number, starting from 0 and ending at 27. There are 28 operations, assuming that no operations can receive more than two operands. A program running on a SISD processor that computes the b_i requires 28 time steps to complete, if we make a simplifying assumption that additions and multiplications take the same amount of time.

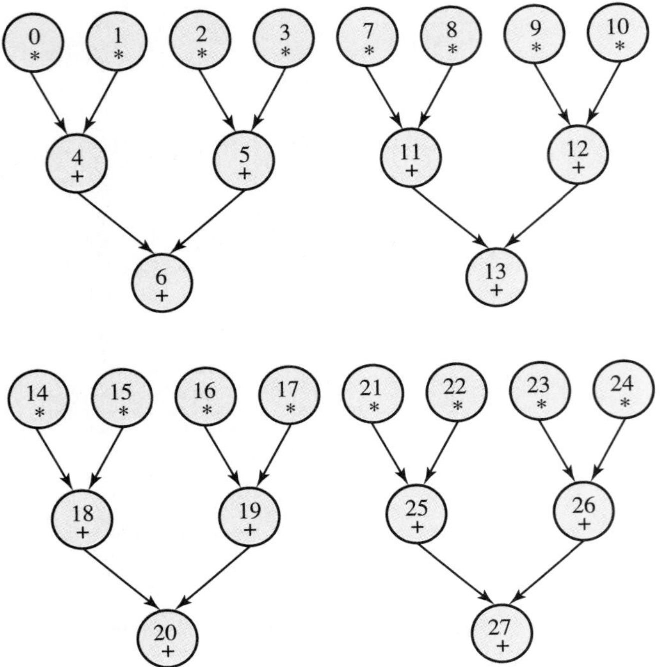

Figure 10-26 Dependency graph for matrix multiplication.

A dependency graph for this problem is shown in Figure 10-26. The worst case path from any input to any output traverses three nodes, and so the entire process can be completed in three time steps, resulting in a speedup of

$$\frac{T_{\text{Sequential}}}{T_{\text{Parallel}}} = \frac{28}{3} = 9.\bar{3}$$

Now that we know the structure of the data dependencies, we can plan a mapping of the nodes of the dependency graph to PEs in a parallel processor. Figure 10-27a shows a mapping in which each node of the dependency graph for b_0 is assigned to a unique PE. The time required to complete each addition is 10 ns, the time to complete each multiplication is 100 ns, and the time to communicate between PEs is 1000 ns. These numbers are for a fictitious processor, but the methods extend to real parallel processors.

As we can see from the parallel time of 2120 ns to execute the program using the mapping shown in Figure 10-27a, the time spent in communication dominates

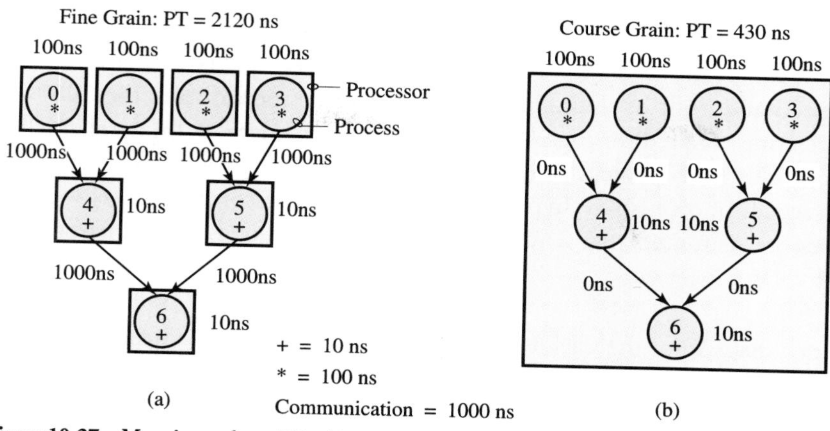

Figure 10-27 **Mapping tasks to PEs: (a) one PE per operation; (b) one PE per b_i.**

performance. This is worse than a SISD approach, since the 16 multiplications and the 12 additions would require 16 × 100 ns + 12 × 10 ns = 1720 ns. There is no processor-to-processor communication cost within a SISD processor, and so only the computation time is considered.

An alternative mapping is shown in Figure 10-27b, in which all of the operations needed to compute b_0 are clustered onto the same PE. We have thus increased the **granularity** of the computation, which is a measure of the number of operations assigned to each PE. A single PE is a sequential, SISD processor, and so none of the operations within a cluster can be executed in parallel, but the communication time among the operations is reduced to 0. As shown in the diagram, the parallel time for b_0 is now 430 ns, which is much better than either the previous parallel mapping or a straight SISD mapping. Since there are no dependencies among the b_i, they can all be computed in parallel, using one processor per b_i. The actual speedup is now

$$\frac{T_{\text{Sequential}}}{T_{\text{Parallel}}} = \frac{1720}{430} = 4$$

Communication is always a bottleneck in parallel processing, and so it is important that we maintain a proper balance. We should not be led astray into thinking that adding processors to a problem will speed it up when, in fact, adding processors can increase execution time as a result of communication time. In general, we want to maintain a ratio in which

$$\frac{T_{\text{Communication}}}{T_{\text{Computation}}} \leq 1$$

10.9.4 *FINE-GRAIN PARALLELISM—THE CONNECTION MACHINE CM-1*

The Connection Machine (CM-1) is a massively parallel SIMD processor designed and built by Thinking Machines Corporation during the 1980s. The architecture is noted for high connectivity between a large number of small processors. The CM-1 consists of a large number of one-bit processors arranged at the vertices of an *n*-space hypercube. Each processor communicates with other processors via routers that send and receive messages along each dimension of the hypercube.

A block diagram of the CM-1 is shown in Figure 10-28. The host computer is a conventional SISD machine such as a Symbolics computer (which was popular at the time) that runs a program written in a high-level language such as LISP or C. Parallelizeable parts of a high-level program are farmed out to 2^n processors (2^{16} processors is the size of a full CM-1) via a memory bus (for data) and a microcontroller (for instructions) and the results are collected via the memory bus. A separate high bandwidth datapath is provided for input and output directly to and from the hypercube.

The CM-1 makes use of a 12-space hypercube between the routers that send and receive data packets. The overall CM-1 prototype uses a 16-space hypercube, and so the difference between the 12-space router hypercube and the 16-space PE hypercube is made up by a crossbar that serves the 16 PEs attached to each

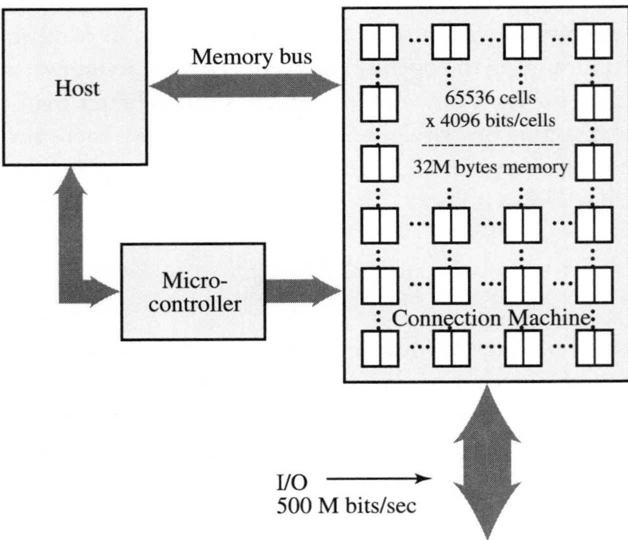

Figure 10-28 Block diagram of the CM-1. (Adapted from [Hillis, 1985].)

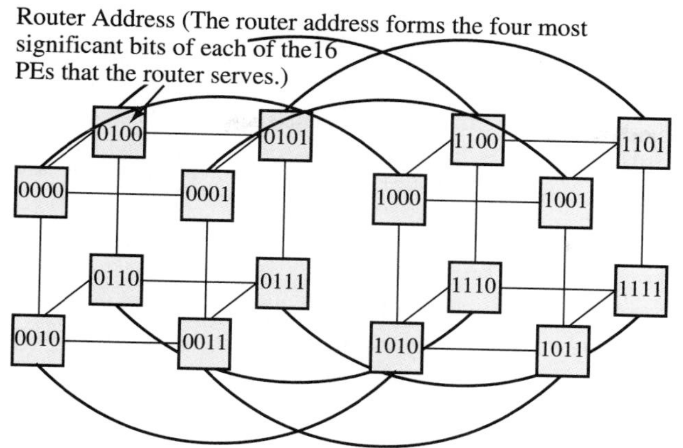

Figure 10-29 A four-space hypercube for the router network.

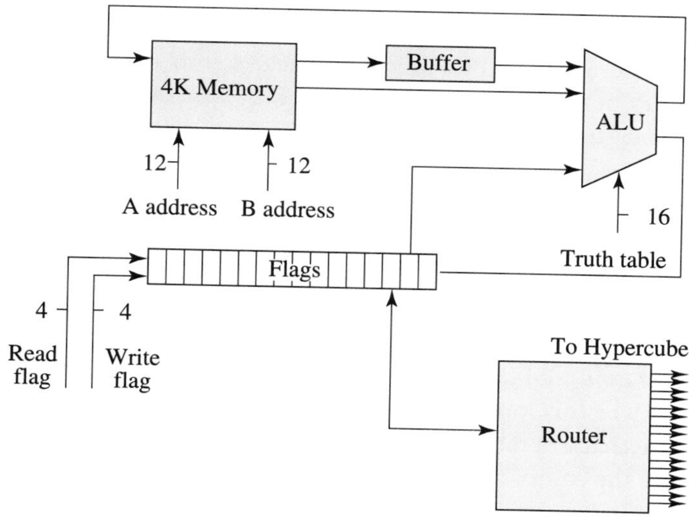

Figure 10-30 Block diagram of a CM-1 processing element

router. For the purpose of example, a four-space hypercube is shown in Figure 10-29 for the router network. Each vertex of the hypercube is a router with an attached group of 16 PEs, each of which has a unique binary address. The router hypercube shown in Figure 10-29 thus serves 256 PEs. Routers that are directly connected to other routers can be found by inverting any one of the four most significant bits in the address.

Each PE is made up of a 16-bit flag register, a three-input, two-output ALU, and a 4096-bit random access memory, as shown in Figure 10-30. During operation, an external controller (the microcontroller of Figure 10-28) selects two bits from memory via the A address and B address lines. Only one value can be read from memory at a time, so the A value is buffered while the B value is fetched. The controller selects a flag to read and feeds the flag and the A and B values into an ALU whose function it also selects. The result of the computation produces a new value for the A addressed location and one of the flags.

The ALU takes three one-bit data inputs, two from the memory and one from the flag register, and 16 control inputs from the microcontroller and produces two one-bit data outputs for the memory and flag registers. The ALU generates all $2^3 = 8$ combinations (minterms) of the input variables for each of the two outputs. Eight of the 16 control lines select the minterms that are needed in the sum-of-products form of each output.

PEs communicate with other PEs through routers. Each router services communication between a PE and the network by receiving packets from the network intended for the attached PEs, injecting packets into the network, buffering when necessary, and forwarding messages that use the router as an intermediary to get to their destinations.

The CM-1 is a landmark machine for the massive parallelism made available by the architecture. For scalable problems like **finite element analysis** (such as modeling heat flow through the use of partial differential equations), the available parallelism can be fully exploited. There is usually a need for floating point manipulation for this case, and so floating point processors augment the PEs in the next generation CM-2. A natural way to model heat flow is through a mesh interconnect, which is implemented as a hardwired bypass to the message-passing routing mechanism through the North-East-West-South (NEWS) grid. Thus we can reduce the cost of PE-to-PE communication for this application.

Not all problems scale so well, and there is a general trend moving away from fine-grain parallel processing. This is largely due to the difficulty of keeping the PEs busy doing useful work while also keeping the time spent in computation greater than the time spent in communication. In the next section, we look at a coarse-grain architecture: the CM-5.

10.9.5 *COURSE-GRAIN PARALLELISM: THE CM-5*

The CM-5 (Thinking Machines Corporation) combines properties of both SIMD and MIMD architectures and thereby provides greater flexibility for map-

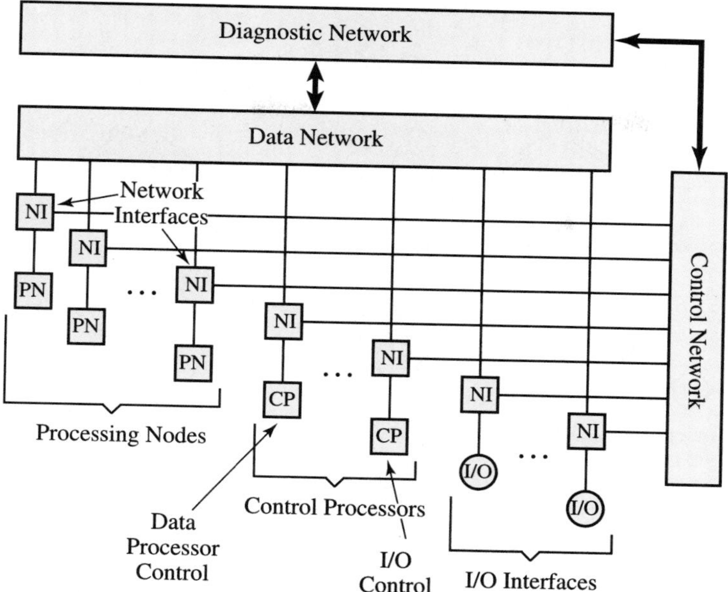

Figure 10-31 The CM-5 architecture.

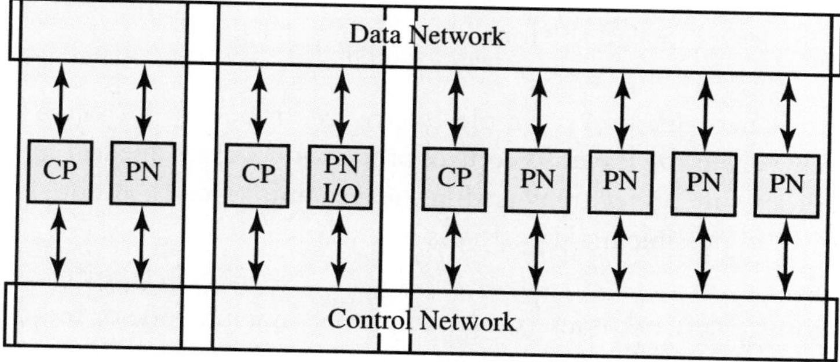

Figure 10-32 Partitions on the CM-5.

ping a parallel algorithm onto the architecture. The CM-5 is illustrated in Figure 10-31. There are three types of processors for data processing, control, and I/O. These processors are connected primarily by the data network and the control network, and to a lesser extent by the diagnostic network.

The processing nodes are assigned to control processors, which form **partitions**, as illustrated in Figure 10-32. A partition contains a control processor, a number of processing nodes, and dedicated portions of the control and data networks.

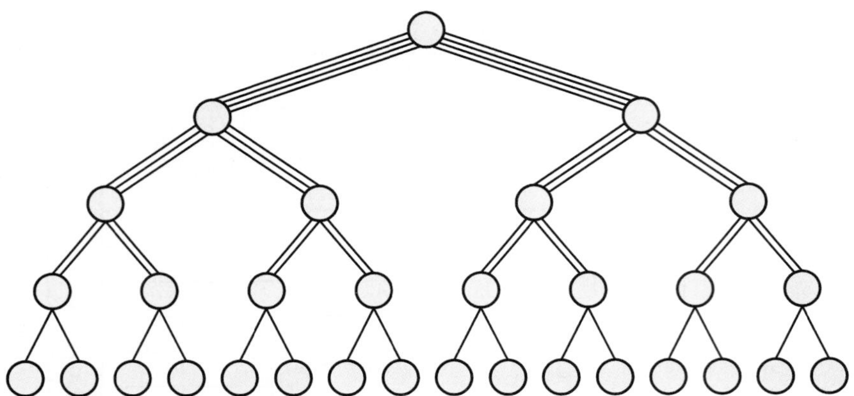

Figure 10-33 An example of a fat tree.

Note that there are both user partitions (where the data processing takes place) and I/O partitions.

The data network uses a **fat-tree** topology, as illustrated in Figure 10-33. The general idea is that the bandwidth from child nodes to parent nodes increases as the network approaches the root, to account for the increased traffic as data travels from the leaves toward the root.

The control network uses a simple binary tree topology in which the system components are at the leaves. A control processor occupies one leaf in a partition, and the processing nodes are placed in the remaining nodes, although not necessarily filling all possible node positions in a subtree.

The diagnostic network is a separate binary tree in which one or more diagnostic processors are at the root. At the leaves are physical components, such as circuit boards and backplanes, rather than logical components, such as processing nodes.

Each control processor is a self-contained system that is comparable in complexity to a workstation. A control processor contains a RISC microprocessor that serves as a CPU, a local memory, I/O that contains disks and Ethernet connections, and a CM-5 interface.

Each processing node is much smaller and contains a SPARC-based microprocessor, a memory controller for 8, 16, or 32 Mbytes of local memory, and a network interface to the control and data networks. In a full implementation of a CM-5, there can be up to 16,384 processing nodes, each performing 64-bit floating point and integer operations, operating at a clock rate of 32 MHz.

Overall, the CM-5 provides a true mix of SIMD and MIMD styles of processing and offers greater applicability than the stricter SIMD style of the CM-1 and CM-2 predecessors.

10.10 Case Study: Parallel Processing in the Sega Genesis

Home video game systems are examples of (nearly) full-featured computer architectures. They have all of the basic features of modern computer architectures and several advanced features. One notably lacking feature is permanent storage (like a hard disk) for saving information, although newer models even have that to a degree. One notably advanced feature, which we explore here, is the use of multiple processors in a MIMD configuration.

Three of the most prominent home video game platforms are manufactured by **Sony**, **Nintendo**, and **Sega**. For the purpose of this discussion, we will study the Sega Genesis, which exploits parallel processing for real-time performance.

10.10.1 *THE SEGA GENESIS ARCHITECTURE*

Figure 10-34 illustrates the external view of the Sega Genesis home video game system. The Sega Genesis consists of a motherboard (which contains electronic components such as the processor, memory, and interconnects) and also a few hand-held controllers and an interface to a television set.

Figure 10-34 External view of the Sega Genesis home video game system.

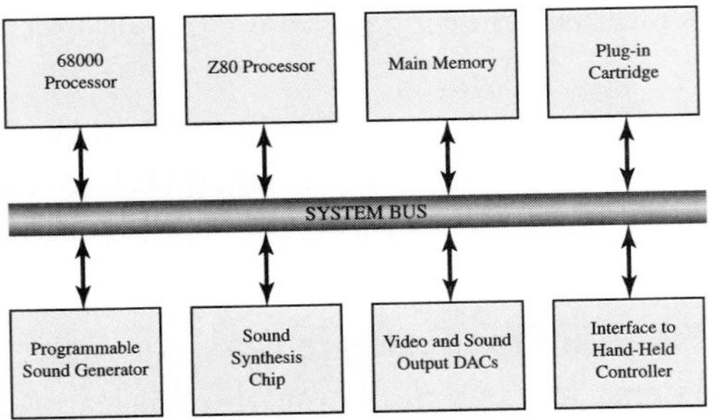

Figure 10-35 System bus model view of the Sega Genesis.

In terms of the conventional von Neumann model of a digital computer, the Sega Genesis has all of the basic parts: input (the controllers), output (the television set), arithmetic logic unit (inside of the processor), control unit (also inside the processor), and memory (which includes the internal memory and the plug-in game cartridges).

The system bus model captures the logical connectivity of the Sega architecture as well as some of the physical organization. Figure 10-35 illustrates the system bus model view of the Sega Genesis. The Genesis contains two general-purpose microprocessors, the Motorola 68000 and the Zilog Z80. These processors are older, low-cost processors that handle the general program execution. Video game systems must be able to generate a wide variety of sound effects, a process that is computationally intensive. In order to maintain game speed and quality during sound generation the Genesis off-loads sound effect computations to two special-purpose chips, the Texas Instruments programmable sound generator (TI PSG) and the Yamaha sound synthesis chip. There are also I/O interfaces for the video system and the hand-held controls.

The 68000 processor runs the main program and controls the rest of the machine. The 68000 accomplishes this by transferring data and instructions to the other components via the system bus. One of the components that the 68000 processor controls is the architecturally similar, but smaller Z80 processor, which can be loaded with a program that executes while the 68000 returns to execute its own program, using an arbitration mechanism that allows both processors to share the bus (but only one at a time).

The TI PSG has three square wave tones and one white noise tone. Each tone/noise can have its own frequency and volume.

The Yamaha synthesis chip is based on FM synthesis. There are six voices with four operators each. The chip is similar to those used in the Yamaha DX27 and DX100 synthesizers. By setting up registers within the chips, a rich variety of sounds can be created.

The plug-in game cartridges contain the programs, and there is additional run-time memory available in a separate unit (labeled "Main memory" in Figure 10-35). Additional components are provided for video output, sound output, and hand-held controllers.

10.10.2 *SEGA GENESIS OPERATION*

When the Sega Genesis is initially powered on, a RESET signal is enabled, which allows all of the electrical voltage levels to stabilize and initializes a number of runtime variables. The RESET signal is then automatically disabled, and the 68000 begins reading and executing instructions from the game cartridge.

During operation, the instructions in the game cartridge instruct the 68000 to load a program into the Z80 processor and to start the Z80 program execution while the 68000 returns to its own program. The Z80 program controls the sound chips, while the 68000 carries out graphical operations, probes the hand-held controllers for activity, and runs the overall game program.

10.10.3 *SEGA GENESIS PROGRAMMING*

[Note from Authors: This section is adapted from a contribution by David Ashley, dash@xdr.com.]

The Sega Genesis uses plug-in cartridges to store the game software. Blank cartridges can be purchased from third-party vendors, which can then be programmed using an inexpensive **PROM burner** card that be plugged into the card cage of a desktop computer. Games can be written in high-level languages and compiled into assembly language or, more commonly, programmed in assembly language directly (even today, assembly language is still heavily used for game programming). A suite of development tools translates the source code into object code that can then be burned directly into the cartridges (once per cartridge). As an alternative to burning cartridges during development, the cartridge can be replaced with a reprogrammable development card.

The Genesis contains two general-purpose microprocessors, the Motorola 68000 and the Zilog Z80. The 68000 runs at 8 MHz and has 64 KB of memory devoted to it. The ROM cartridge appears at memory location 0. The 68000 off-loads sound effect computations to the TI PSG and the Yamaha sound synthesis chip.

The Genesis graphics hardware consists of two scrollable planes. Each plane is made up of tiles. Each tile is an 8 × 8 pixel square with 4 bits per pixel. Each pixel can thus have 16 colors. Each tile can use 1 of 4 color tables, so on the screen there can be 64 colors at once, but only 16 different colors can be in any specific tile. Tiles require 32 bytes. There is 64 KB of graphics memory, which allows for 2048 unique tiles if memory is used for nothing else.

Each plane can be scrolled independently in various ways. Planes consist of tables of words, in which each word describes a tile. A word contains 11 bits for identifying the tile, 2 bits for "flip x" and "flip y," 2 bits for the selection of the color table, and 1 bit for a depth selector. Sprites are also composed of tiles. A sprite can be up to 4 tiles wide by four tiles high. Since the size of each tile is 8 × 8, this means sprites can be anywhere from 8 × 8 pixels to 32 × 32 pixels in size. There can be 80 sprites on the screen at one time. On a single scan line there can be 10 32-pixel-wide sprites or 20 16-pixel-wide sprites. Each sprite can only have 16 colors taken from the 4 different color tables. Colors are allocated 3 bits for each gun, and so 512 colors are possible. (Color 0 = transparent.)

There is a memory copier program that is resident in hardware that performs fast copies from the 68000 RAM into the graphics RAM. The Z80 also has 8KB of RAM. The Z80 can access the graphics chip or the sound chips, but usually these chips are controlled by the 68000.

The process of creating a game cartridge involves (1) writing the game program, (2) translating the program into object code (compiling, assembling, and linking the code into an executable object module; some parts of the program may be written in a high level language, and other parts, directly in assembly language), (3) testing the program on a reprogrammable development card (if a reprogrammable development card is available), and (4) burning the program into a blank game cartridge.

See "Further Reading" for more information on programming the Sega Genesis.

SUMMARY

In the RISC approach, the most frequently occurring instructions are optimized by eliminating or reducing the complexity of other instructions and addressing modes commonly found in CISC architectures. The performance of RISC architectures is further enhanced by pipelining and increasing the number of registers available to the CPU. Superscalar and VLIW architectures are examples of newer performance enhancements that extend, rather than replace, the RISC approach.

Parallel architectures can be classified as MISD, SIMD, or MIMD. The MISD approach is used for systolic array processing and is the least general architecture of the three. In a SIMD architecture, all PEs carry out the same operations on different data sets, in an "army of ants" approach to parallel processing. The MIMD approach can be characterized as "herd of elephants," because there are a small number of powerful processors, each with their own data and instruction streams.

The current trend is moving away from the fine grain-parallelism that is exemplified by the MISD and SIMD approaches and toward the MIMD approach. This trend is due to the high time cost of communicating among PEs, and the economy of using networks of workstations over tightly coupled parallel processors. The goal of the MIMD approach is to better balance the time spent in computation with the time spent in communication.

FURTHER READING

Three primary characteristics of RISC architectures enumerated in Section 10.2 originated at IBM's T. J. Watson Research Center, as summarized in (Ralston and Reilly, 1993, pp. 1165–1167). (Hennessy and Patterson, 1995) is a classic reference on much of the work that led to the RISC concept, although the word "RISC" does not appear in the title of their textbook. (Stallings, 1991) is a thorough reference on RISCs. (Tamir and Sequin, 1983) show that a window size of eight will shift on less than 1% of the calls or returns. (Tanenbaum, 1999) provides a readable introduction to the RISC concept. (Dulong, 1998) describes the IA-64. The PowerPC 601 architecture is described in (Motorola).

(Quinn, 1987) and (Hwang, 1993) overview the field of parallel processing in terms of architectures and algorithms. (Flynn, 1972) covers the Flynn taxonomy of architectures. (Yang and Gerasoulis, 1991) argue for maintaining a ratio of communication time to computation time of less than 1. (Hillis, 1985) and (Hillis and Tucker, 1993) describe the architectures of the CM-1 and CM-5, respectively. (Hui, 1990) covers interconnection networks, and (Leighton, 1992) covers routing algorithms for a few types of interconnection networks. (Wu and Feng, 1981) cover routing on a shuffle-exchange network.

Additional information can be found on programming the Sega Genesis at http://hiwaay.net/~jfrohwei/sega/genesis.html.

Dulong, C., "The IA-64 Architecture at Work," *IEEE Computer*, **31**, pp. 24–32 (July 1998).

Flynn, M. J., "Some Computer Organizations and Their Effectiveness," *IEEE Transactions on Computers,* **30**, no. 7, pp. 948–960 (1972).

Hennessy, J. L. and D. A. Patterson, *Computer Architecture: A Quantitative Approach*, 2/e, Morgan Kaufmann Publishers (1995).

Hillis, W. D. and L. W. Tucker, "The CM-5 Connection Machine: A Scalable Supercomputer," *Communications of the ACM*, **36**, no. 11, pp. 31–40 (Nov., 1993).

Hillis, W. D., *The Connection Machine*, MIT Press (1985).

Hui, J. Y., *Switching and Traffic Theory for Integrated Broadband Networks*, Kluwer Academic Publishers (1990).

Hwang, K., *Advanced Computer Architecture: Parallelism, Scalability, Programmability*, McGraw-Hill (1993).

Knuth, D. E., An Empirical Study of FORTRAN Programs, *Software—Practice and Experience*, **1**, pp. 105–133, 1971.

Leighton, F. T., *Introduction to Parallel Algorithms and Architectures: Arrays, Trees, Hypercubes*, Morgan Kaufmann (1992).

Motorola Inc., *PowerPC 601 RISC Microprocessor User's Manual*, Motorola Literature Distribution, P. O. Box 20912, Phoenix, AZ, 85036.

Quinn, M. J., *Designing Efficient Algorithms for Parallel Computers*, McGraw-Hill (1987).

Ralston, A. and E. D. Reilly, eds., *Encyclopedia of Computer Science*, 3/e, van Nostrand Reinhold (1993).

SPARC International, Inc., *The SPARC Architecture Manual: Version 8*, Prentice Hall (1992).

Stallings, W., *Computer Organization and Architecture: Designing for Performance*, 4/e, Prentice Hall (1996).

Stallings, W., *Reduced Instruction Set Computers*, 3/e, IEEE Computer Society Press (1991).

Stone, H. S. and J. Cocke, "Computer Architecture in the 1990s," *IEEE Computer*, **24**, no. 9, pp. 30–38 (Sept., 1991).

Tamir, Y., and C. Sequin, "Strategies for Managing the Register File in RISC," *IEEE Trans. Comp.* (Nov. 1983).

Tanenbaum, A., *Structured Computer Organization*, 4/e, Prentice Hall (1999).

Wu, C.-L. and T.-Y. Feng, "The Universality of the Shuffle-Exchange Network," *IEEE Transactions on Computers*, **C-30**, no. 5, pp. 324–332 (1981).

Yang, T. and A. Gerasoulis, "A Fast Static Scheduling Algorithm for DAGs on an Unbounded Number of Processors," *Proceedings of Supercomputing '91*, Albuquerque, New Mexico (Nov. 1991).

PROBLEMS

10.1 Increasing the number of cycles per instruction can sometimes improve the execution efficiency of a pipeline. If the time per cycle for the pipeline described in Section 10.3 is 20 ns, then CPI_{Avg} is 1.5 × 20 ns = 30 ns. Compute the execution efficiency for the same pipeline in which the pipeline depth increases from 5 to 6 and the cycle time decreases from 20 ns to 10 ns.

10.2 The following SPARC code is taken from the `gcc` generated code in Figure 10-10. Can `%r0` be used in all three lines instead of "wasting" `%r1` in the second line?

```
    ...
st    %o0, [%fp-28]
sethi %hi(.LLC0), %o1
or    %o1, %lo(.LLC0), %o1
    ...
```

10.3 Calculate the speedup that can be expected if a 200-MHz Pentium chip is replaced with a 300-MHz Pentium chip, if all other parameters remain unchanged.

10.4 What is the speedup that can be expected if the instruction set of a certain machine is changed so that the branch instruction takes one clock cycle instead of three clock cycles, if branch instructions account for 20% of all instructions executed by a certain program? Assume that other instructions average three clock cycles per instruction and that nothing else is altered by the change.

10.5 Create a dependency graph for the following expression:

$$f(x, y) = x^2 + 2xy + y^2$$

10.6 Given 100 processors for a computation with 5% of the code that cannot be parallelized, compute speedup and efficiency.

10.7 What is the diameter of a 16-space hypercube?

10.8 For the Example at the end of Section 10.9.2, compute the total crosspoint complexity over all three stages.

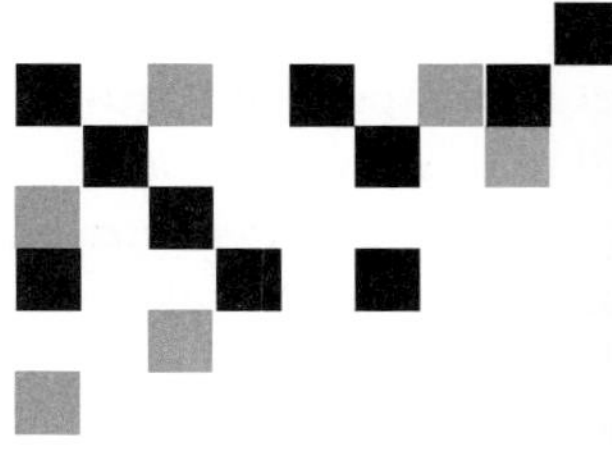

APPENDIX A: DIGITAL LOGIC

A

A.1 Introduction

In this appendix, we take a look at a few basic principles of digital logic that we can apply in the design of a digital computer. We start by studying **combinational logic**, in which logical decisions are made based only on combinations of the inputs. We then look at **sequential logic** in which decisions are made based on combinations of the current inputs as well as the past history of inputs. With an understanding of these underlying principles, we can design digital logic circuits from which an entire computer can be constructed. We begin with the fundamental building block of a digital computer, the **combinational logic unit (CLU)**.

A.2 Combinational Logic

A combinational logic unit translates a set of inputs into a set of outputs according to one or more mapping functions. The outputs of a CLU are strictly functions of the inputs, and the outputs are updated immediately after the inputs change. A basic model of a CLU is shown in Figure A-1. A set of inputs $i_0 - i_n$ is presented to the CLU, which produces a set of outputs according to mapping functions $f_0 - f_m$. There is no feedback from the outputs back to the inputs in a combinational logic circuit (we will study circuits with feedback in Section A.11).

Inputs and outputs for a CLU normally have two distinct values: high and low. When signals (values) are taken from a finite set, the circuits that use them are

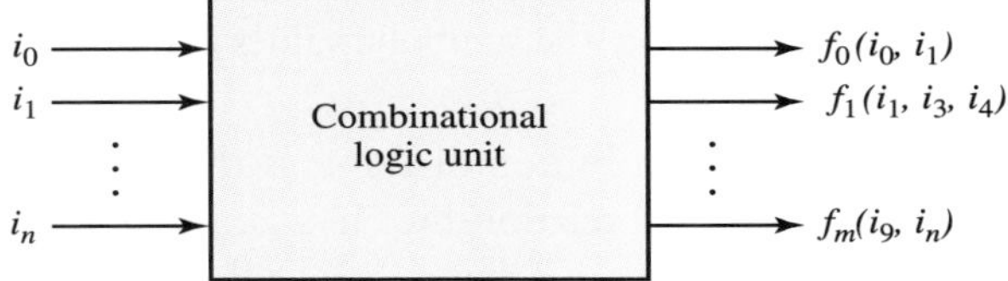

Figure A-1 External view of a combinational logic unit.

referred to as being **digital**. A digital electronic circuit receives inputs and produces outputs in which 0 volts (0 V) is typically considered to be a low value and +5 V is considered to be a high value. This convention is not used everywhere: High-speed circuits tend to use lower voltages; some computer circuits work in the **analog** domain, in which a continuum of values is allowed; and digital optical circuits might use phase or polarization, in which high or low values are no longer meaningful. An application in which analog circuitry is appropriate is in flight simulation, since the analog circuits more closely approximate the mechanics of an aircraft than do digital circuits.

Although the vast majority of digital computers are binary, **multi valued** circuits also exist. A wire that is capable of carrying more than two values can be more efficient at transmitting information than a wire that carries only two values. A digital multivalued circuit is different from an analog circuit in that a multivalued circuit deals with signals that take on one of a finite number of values, whereas an analog signal can take on a continuum of values. The use of multivalued circuits is theoretically valuable, but in practice it is difficult to create reliable circuitry that distinguishes between more than two values. For this reason, multivalued logic is currently in limited use.

In this text, we are primarily concerned with digital binary circuits, in which exactly two values are allowed for any input or output. Thus, we will consider only binary signals.

A.3 Truth Tables

In 1854 George Boole published his seminal work on an algebra for representing logic. Boole was interested in capturing the mathematics of thought and developed a representation for factual information such as "The door is open" or "The door is not open." Boole's algebra was further developed by Shannon into the form we use today. In Boolean algebra, we assume the existence of a basic postulate, that a binary variable takes on a single value of 0 or 1. This value corresponds to the 0 and +5 voltages mentioned in the previous section. The assignment can also be done in reverse order for 1 and 0, respectively. For purposes of understanding the behavior of digital circuits, we can abstract away the physical correspondence to voltages and consider only the symbolic values 0 and 1.

A key contribution of Boole is the development of the **truth table**, which captures logical relationships in a tabular form. Consider a room with two three-way switches A and B that control a light Z. Either switch can be up or down, or both

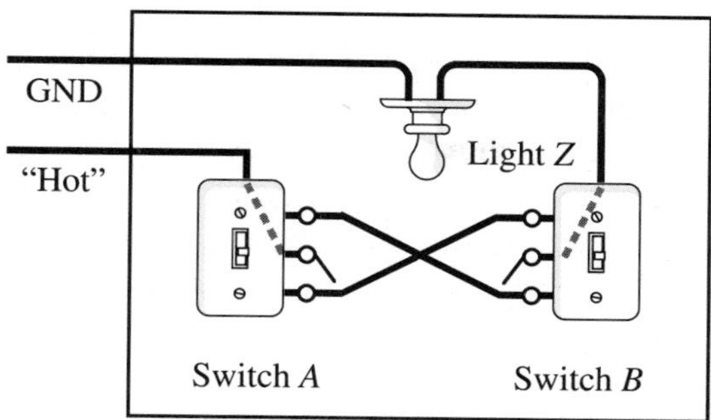

Inputs		Output
A	*B*	*Z*
0	0	0
0	1	1
1	0	1
1	1	0

Figure A-2 A truth table relates the states of three-way switches *A* and *B* to light *Z*.

Inputs		Output
A	*B*	*Z*
0	0	1
0	1	0
1	0	0
1	1	1

Figure A-3 Alternate assignments of outputs to switch settings.

switches can be up or down. When exactly one switch is up, the light is on. When both switches are up or down, the light is off. A truth table can be constructed that enumerates all possible settings of the switches as shown in Figure A-2. In the table, a switch is assigned the value 0 if it is down, otherwise it is assigned the value 1. The light is on when $Z = 1$.

In a truth table, all possible input combinations of binary variables are enumerated and a corresponding output value of 0 or 1 is assigned for each input combination. For the truth table shown in Figure A-2, the output function Z depends upon input variables A and B. For each combination of input variables there are two values that can be assigned to Z: 0 or 1. We can choose a different assignment for Figure A-2, in which the light is on only when both switches are up or both switches are down, in which case the truth table shown in Figure A-3 enumerates all possible states of the light for each switch setting. The wiring pattern would also need to be changed to correspond. For two input variables, there are $2^2 = 4$ input combinations and $2^4 = 16$ possible assignments of outputs to input combinations. In general, since there are 2^n input combinations for n inputs, there are $2^{\langle 2^n \rangle}$ possible assignments of output values to input combinations.

A.4 Logic Gates

If we enumerate all possible assignments of switch settings for two input variables, then we will obtain the 16 assignments shown in Figure A-4. We refer to these functions as **Boolean logic functions**. A number of assignments have special names. The *AND* function is true (produces a 1) only when A and B are 1, whereas the *OR* function is true when either A or B is 1 or when both A and B are 1. A function is false when its output is 0, and so the False function is always 0, whereas the True function is always 1. The plus signs '+' in the Boolean expressions denote logical *OR* and do not imply arithmetic addition. The juxtaposition of two variables, as in AB, denotes logical *AND* among the variables.

The A and B functions simply repeat the A and B inputs, respectively, whereas the $\overline{A}$ and $\overline{B}$ functions **complement** A and B, by producing a 0 where the uncomplemented function is a 1 and by producing a 1 where the uncomplemented function is a 0. In general, a bar over a term denotes the complement operation, and so the *NAND* and *NOR* functions are complements to *AND* and *OR*, respectively. The *XOR* function is true when either of its inputs, but not both, is true. The *XNOR* function is the complement to *XOR*. The remaining functions are interpreted similarly.

A **logic gate** is a physical device that implements a simple Boolean function. The functions that are listed in Figure A-4 have representations as logic gate symbols,

Inputs		Outputs							
A	B	*False*	*AND*	$A\overline{B}$	A	$\overline{A}B$	B	*XOR*	*OR*
0	0	0	0	0	0	0	0	0	0
0	1	0	0	0	0	1	1	1	1
1	0	0	0	1	1	0	0	1	1
1	1	0	1	0	1	0	1	0	1

Inputs		Outputs							
A	B	*NOR*	*XNOR*	$\overline{B}$	$A+\overline{B}$	$\overline{A}$	$\overline{A}+B$	*NAND*	*True*
0	0	1	1	1	1	1	1	1	1
0	1	0	0	0	0	1	1	1	1
1	0	0	0	1	1	0	0	1	1
1	1	0	1	0	1	0	1	0	1

Figure A-4 Truth tables showing all possible functions of two binary variables.

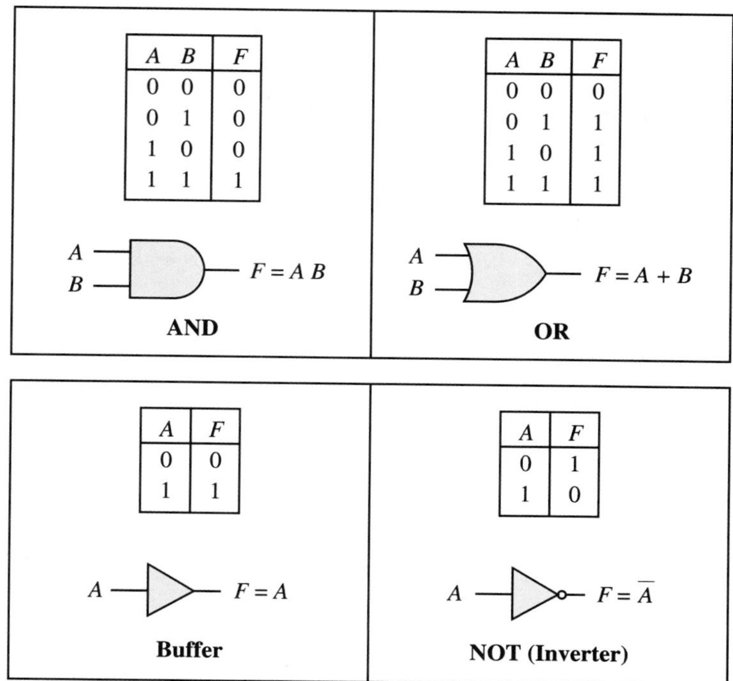

Figure A-5 Logic gate symbols for AND, OR, buffer, and NOT Boolean functions.

a few of which are shown in Figures A-5 and A-6. For each of the functions, *A* and *B* are binary inputs and *F* is the output.

In Figure A-5, the AND and OR gates behave as previously described. The output of the AND gate is true when both of its inputs are true and is false otherwise. The output of the OR gate is true when either or both of its inputs are true and is false otherwise. The buffer simply copies its input to its output. Although the buffer has no logical significance, it serves an important practical role as an amplifier, allowing a number of logic gates to be driven by a single signal. The NOT gate (also called an **inverter**) produces a 1 at its output for a 0 at its input and produces a 0 at its output for a 1 at its input. Again, the inverted output signal is referred to as the complement of the input. The circle at the output of the NOT gate denotes the complement operation.

In Figure A-6, the NAND and NOR gates produce complementary outputs to the AND and OR gates, respectively. The exclusive-OR (XOR) gate produces a 1 when either of its inputs, but not both, is 1. In general, XOR produces a 1 at its output

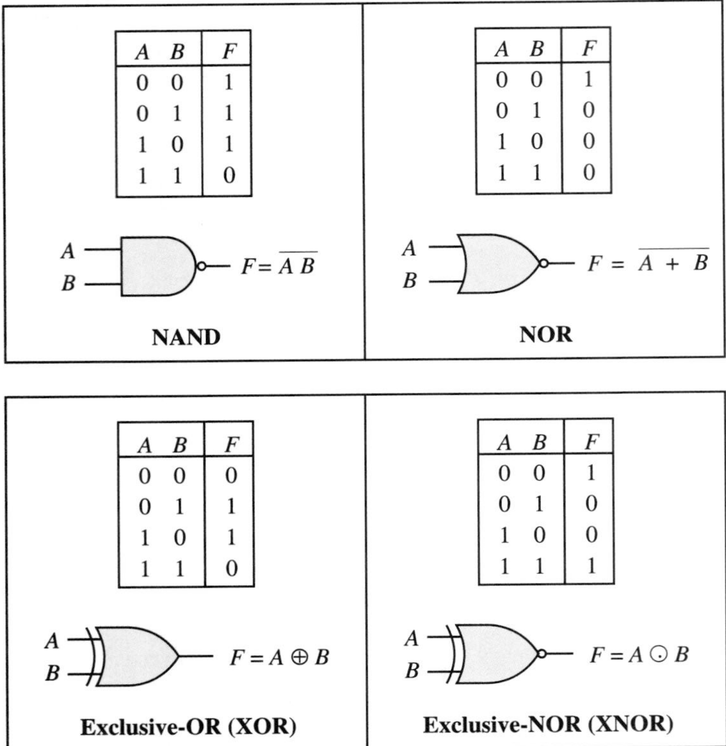

Figure A-6 Logic gate symbols for NAND, NOR, XOR, and XNOR Boolean functions.

whenever the number of 1's at its inputs is odd. This generalization is important in understanding how an XOR gate with more than two inputs behaves. The exclusive-NOR (XNOR) gate produces a complementary output to the XOR gate.

The logic symbols shown in Figures A-5 and A-6 are only the basic forms, and there are a number of variations that are often used. For example, there can be more inputs, as for the three-input AND gate shown in Figure A-7a. The circles at the outputs of the NOT, NOR, and XNOR gates denote the complement operation and can be placed at the inputs of logic gates to indicate that the inputs are inverted upon entering the gate, as shown in Figure A-7b. Depending on the technology used, some logic gates produce complementary outputs. The corresponding logic symbol for a complementary logic gate indicates both outputs, as illustrated in Figure A-7c.

Physically, logic gates are not magical, although it may seem that they are when a device like an inverter can produce a logical 1 (+5 V) at its output when a logical

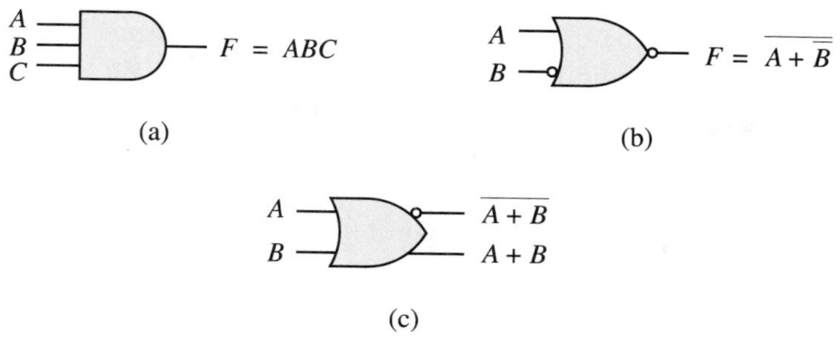

$F = ABC$

(a)

$F = \overline{A + \overline{B}}$

(b)

$\overline{A + B}$

$A + B$

(c)

Figure A-7 Variations of the basic logic gate symbols for (a) three inputs; (b) a negated output; and (c) complementary outputs.

0 (0 V) is provided at the input. The next section covers the underlying mechanism that makes electronic logic gates work.

A.4.1 *ELECTRONIC IMPLEMENTATION OF LOGIC*

Electrically, logic gates have power terminals that are not normally shown. Figure A-8a illustrates an inverter in which the +5 V and 0 V (GND) terminals are made visible. The +5 V signal is commonly referred to as V_{CC} for "voltage collector-collector." In a physical circuit, all of the V_{CC} and GND terminals are connected to the corresponding terminals of a power supply.

Logic gates are composed of electrical devices called **transistors**, which have a fundamental switching property that allows them to control a strong electrical signal with a weak signal. This supports the process of amplification, which is crucial for cascading logic gates. Without amplification, we would only be able to send a signal through a few logic gates before the signal deteriorates to the point that it is overcome by noise, which exists at every point in an electrical circuit to some degree.

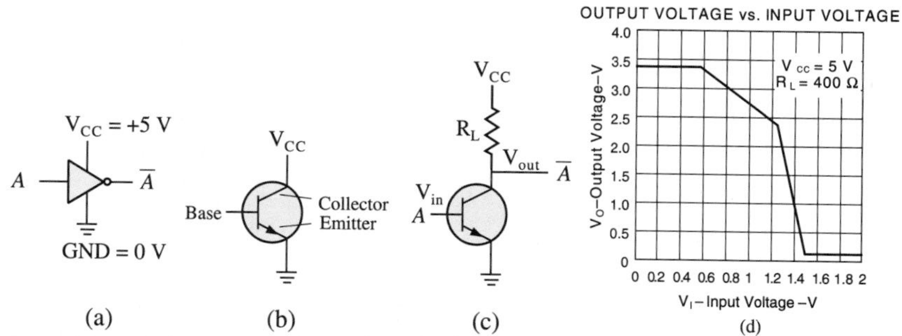

Figure A-8 (a) Power terminals for an inverter made visible; (b) schematic symbol for a transistor; (c) transistor circuit for an inverter; (d) static transfer function for an inverter.

The schematic symbol for a transistor is shown in Figure A-8b. When there is no positive voltage on the base, then a current will not flow from V_{CC} to GND. Thus, for an inverter, a logical 0 (0 V) on the base will produce a logical 1 (+5 V) at the collector terminal as illustrated in Figure A-8c. If, however, a positive voltage is applied to V_{in}, then a current will flow from V_{CC} to GND, which prevents V_{out} from producing enough signal for the inverter output to be a logical 1. In effect, when +5 V is applied to V_{in}, a logical 0 appears at V_{out}. The input-output relationship of a logic gate follows a nonlinear curve as shown in Figure A-8d for transistor-transistor logic (TTL). The nonlinearity is an important gain property that makes cascadable operation possible.

A useful paradigm is to think of current flowing through wires as water flowing through pipes. If we open a connection on a pipe from V_{CC} to GND, then the water flowing to V_{out} will be reduced to a great extent, although some water will still make it out. By choosing an appropriate value for the resistor R_L, the flow can be restricted in order to minimize this effect.

Since there will always be some current that flows even when we have a logical 0 at V_{out}, we need to assign logical 0 and 1 to voltages using safe margins. If we assign logical 0 to 0 V and logical 1 to +5 V, then our circuits may not work properly if .1 V appears at the output of an inverter instead of 0 V, which can happen in practice. For this reason, we design circuits in which assignments of logical 0 and 1 are made using **thresholds**. In Figure A-9a, logical 0 is assigned to the voltage range (0 V to 0.4 V) and logical 1 is assigned to the voltage range (2.4 V to +5 V). The ranges shown in Figure A-9a are for the output of a logic gate. There may be some attenuation (a reduction in voltage) introduced in the connection between the output of one logic gate and the input to another, and for that reason the thresholds are relaxed by 0.4 V at the input to a logic gate, as shown in Figure A-9b. These ranges can differ depending on the logic family.

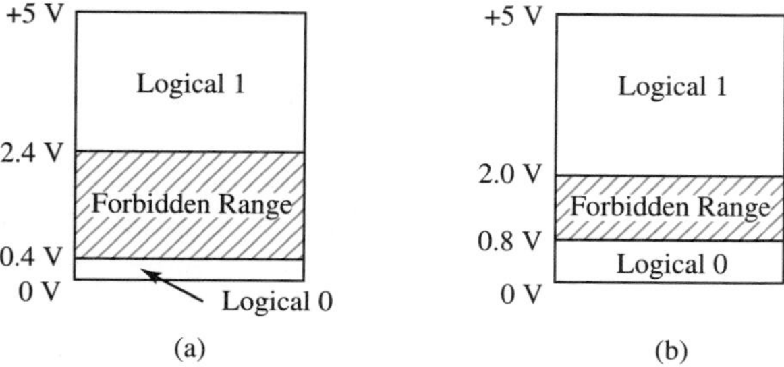

Figure A-9 Assignments of logical 0 and 1 to voltage ranges (a) at the output of a logic gates, and (b) at the input to a logic gate.

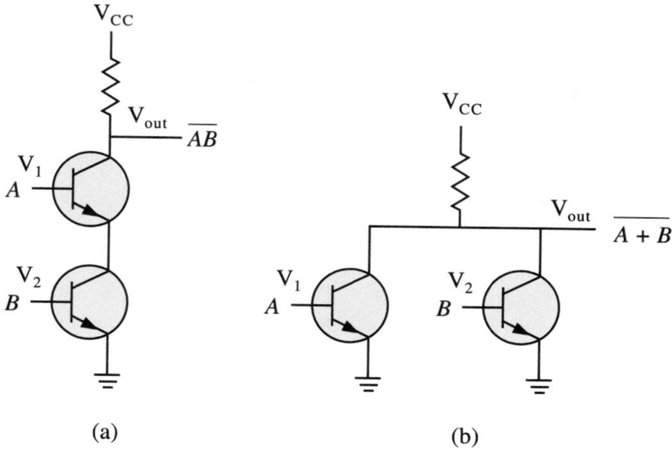

Figure A-10 Transistor circuits for (a) a two-input NAND gate and (b) a two-input NOR gate.

The output ranges only make sense, however, if the gate inputs settle into the logical 0 or 1 ranges at the input. For this reason, inputs to a logic gate should never be left "floating"—disconnected from a gate output, V_{CC}, or GND.

Figure A-10 shows transistor circuits for two-input NAND and NOR gates. For the NAND case, both of the V_1 and V_2 inputs must be in the logical 1 region in order to produce a voltage in the logical 0 region at V_{out}. For the NOR case, if either or both of the V_1 and V_2 inputs are in the logical 1 region, then a voltage in the logical 0 region will be produced at V_{out}.

A.4.2 *TRI-STATE BUFFERS*

A **tri-state buffer** behaves in a similar manner to the ordinary buffer that was introduced earlier in this appendix, except that a control input is available to disable the buffer. Depending on the value of the control input, the output is either 0, 1, or *disabled,* thus providing three output states. In Figure A-11, when the control input *C* is 1, the tri-state buffer behaves like an ordinary buffer. When *C* is 0, then the output is electrically disconnected and no output is produced. The ϕ's in the corresponding truth table entries mark the disabled (disconnected) states. The reader should note that the disabled state, ϕ, represents neither a 0 nor a 1, but rather the absence of a signal. In electrical circuit terms, the output is said to be in **high impedance**. The inverted control tri-state buffer is similar to the tri-state buffer, except that the control input *C* is complemented, as indicated by the bubble at the control input.

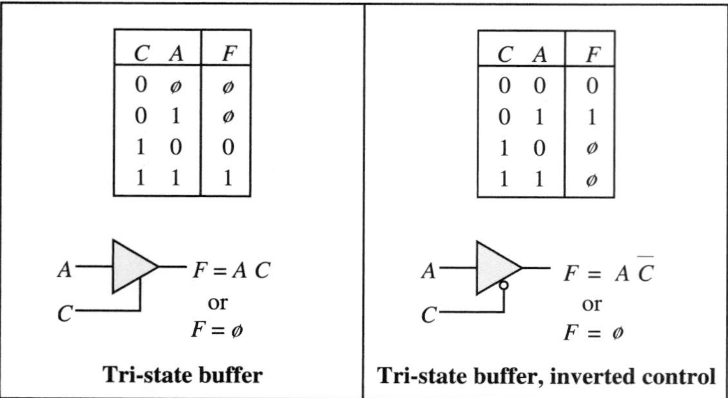

Figure A-11 Tri-state buffers.

An electrically disconnected output is different than an output that produces a 0, in that an electrically disconnected output behaves as if no output connection exists whereas a logical 0 at the output is still electrically connected to the circuit. The tri-state buffer allows the outputs from a number of logic gates to drive a common line without risking electrical shorts, provided that only one buffer is enabled at a time. The use of tri-state buffers is important in implementing **registers**, which are described later in this appendix.

A.5 Properties of Boolean Algebra

Table A-1 summarizes a few basic properties of Boolean algebra that can be applied to Boolean logic expressions. The postulates (known as Huntington's postulates) are basic axioms of Boolean algebra and therefore need no proofs. The theorems can be proven from the postulates. Each relationship shown in the table has both an AND and an OR form as a result of the **principle of duality**. The dual form is obtained by changing ANDs to ORs and changing ORs to ANDs.

The **commutative** property states that the order that two variables appear in an AND or OR function is not significant. By the principle of duality, the commutative property has an AND form ($AB = BA$) and an OR form ($A + B = B + A$). The **distributive** property shows how a variable is distributed over an expression with which it is ANDed. By the principle of duality, the dual form of the distributive property is obtained as shown.

The **identity** property states that a variable that is ANDed with 1 or is ORed with 0 produces the original variable. The **complement** property states that a variable that is ANDed with its complement is logically false (produces a 0, since at least one input is 0), and a variable that is ORed with its complement is logically true (produces a 1, since at least one input is 1).

The **zero** and **one** theorems state that a variable that is ANDed with 0 produces a 0, and a variable that is ORed with 1 produces a 1. The **idempotence** theorem states that a variable that is ANDed or ORed with itself produces the original variable. For instance, if the inputs to an AND gate have the same value or the inputs to an OR gate have the same value, then the output for each gate is the same as the input. The **associative** theorem states that the order of ANDing or ORing is logically of no consequence. The **involution** theorem states that the complement of a complement leaves the original variable (or expression) unchanged.

DeMorgan's theorem, the **consensus theorem**, and the **absorption theorem** may not be obvious, and so we prove DeMorgan's theorem for the two-variable case using perfect induction (enumerating all cases), and leave an algebraic proof of DeMorgan's theorem and an inductive proof of the consensus theorem as exercises (see Problems A.24 and A.25.) Figure A-12 shows a truth table for each expression that appears in either form of DeMorgan's theorem. The expressions that appear on the left and right sides of each form of DeMorgan's theorem produce equivalent outputs, which proves the theorem for two variables.

	Relationship	Dual	Property
Postulates	$AB = BA$	$A + B = B + A$	Commutative
	$A(B + C) = AB + AC$	$A + BC = (A + B)(A + C)$	Distributive
	$1A = A$	$0 + A = A$	Identity
	$A\overline{A} = 0$	$A + \overline{A} = 1$	Complement
Theorems	$0A = 0$	$1 + A = 1$	Zero and one theorems
	$AA = A$	$A + A = A$	Idempotence
	$A(BC) = (AB)C$	$A + (B + C) = (A + B) + C$	Associative
	$\overline{\overline{A}} = A$		Involution
	$\overline{AB} = \overline{A} + \overline{B}$	$\overline{A + B} = \overline{A}\,\overline{B}$	DeMorgan's Theorem
	$AB + \overline{A}C + BC = AB + \overline{A}C$	$(A + B)(\overline{A} + C)(B + C) = (A + B)(\overline{A} + C)$	Consensus Theorem
	$A(A + B) = A$	$A + AB = A$	Absorption Theorem

Table A-1 Basic properties of Boolean algebra.

A	B	$\overline{AB}$	$=\overline{A}+\overline{B}$	$\overline{A+B}$	$=\overline{A}\,\overline{B}$
0	0	1	1	1	1
0	1	1	1	0	0
1	0	1	1	0	0
1	1	0	0	0	0

Figure A-12 DeMorgan's theorem is proven for the two-variable case.

DeMorgan's theorem: $A + B = \overline{\overline{A + B}} = \overline{\overline{A}\,\overline{B}}$

$F = A + B \equiv F = \overline{\overline{A}\,\overline{B}}$

Figure A-13 DeMorgan's theorem is used in mapping an OR gate onto a NAND gate.

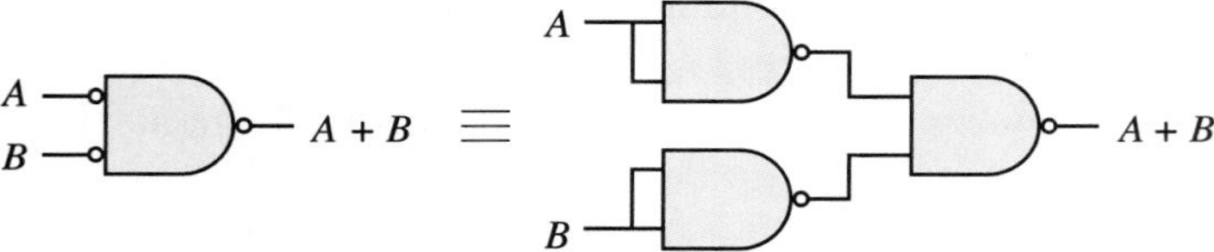

Figure A-14 Inverted inputs to a NAND gate implemented with NAND gates.

Not all of the logic gates discussed so far are necessary in order to achieve **computational completeness**, meaning that any digital logic circuit can be created from these gates. Three sets of logic gates that are computationally complete are {AND, OR, NOT}, {NAND}, and {NOR} (there are others as well).

As an example of how a computationally complete set of logic gates can implement other logic gates that are not part of the set, consider implementing the OR function with the {NAND} set. DeMorgan's theorem can be used to map an OR gate onto a NAND gate, as shown in Figure A-13. The original OR function $(A + B)$ is complemented twice, which leaves the function unchanged by the involution property. DeMorgan's theorem then changes OR to AND and distributes the innermost overbar over the terms A and B. The inverted inputs can also be implemented with NAND gates by the property of idempotence, as shown in Figure A-14. The OR function is thus implemented with NANDs. Functional equivalence among logic gates is important for practical considerations, because one type of logic gate may have better operating characteristics than another for a given technology.

A.6 The Sum-of-Products Form and Logic Diagrams

Suppose now that we need to implement a more complex function than just a simple logic gate, such as the three-input **majority** function described by the truth table shown in Figure A-15. The majority function is true whenever more than half of its inputs are true and can be thought of as a balance that tips to the left or right depending on whether there are more 0's or 1's at the input. This is a common operation used in fault recovery, in which the outputs of identical circuits operating on the same data are compared and the greatest number of similar values determine the output (also referred to as "voting" or "odd one out").

Since no single logic gate discussed up to this point implements the majority function directly, we transform the function into a two-level AND-OR equation and then implement the function with an arrangement of logic gates from the set {AND, OR, NOT} (for instance). The two levels come about because exactly one level of ANDed variables is followed by exactly one OR level. The Boolean equation that describes the majority function is true whenever F is true in the truth table. Thus, F is true when $A = 0$, $B = 1$, and $C = 1$, or when $A = 1$, $B = 0$, and $C = 1$, and so on for the remaining cases.

One way to represent logic equations is to use the **sum-of-products (SOP)** form, in which a collection of ANDed variables are ORed together. The Boolean logic equation that describes the majority function is shown in SOP form in Equation (A.1). Again, the '+' signs denote logical OR and do not imply arithmetic addition.

$$F = \bar{A}BC + A\bar{B}C + AB\bar{C} + ABC \qquad \text{(A.1)}$$

By inspecting the equation, we can determine that four three-input AND gates will implement the four **product terms** $\bar{A}BC$, $A\bar{B}C$, $AB\bar{C}$, and ABC, and

Minterm Index	A	B	C	F
0	0	0	0	0
1	0	0	1	0
2	0	1	0	0
3	0	1	1	1
4	1	0	0	0
5	1	0	1	1
6	1	1	0	1
7	1	1	1	1

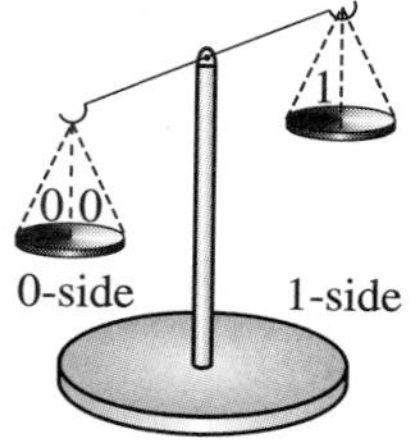

A balance tips to the left or right depending on whether there are more 0 s or 1 s.

Figure A-15 Truth table for the majority function.

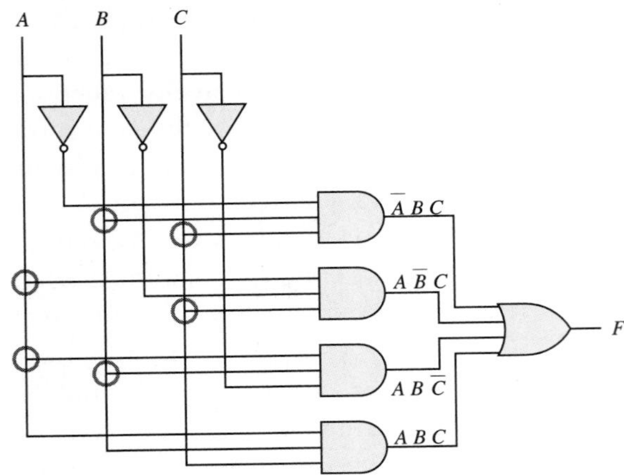

Figure A-16 A two-level AND-OR circuit implements the majority function. Inverters at the inputs are not included in the two-level count.

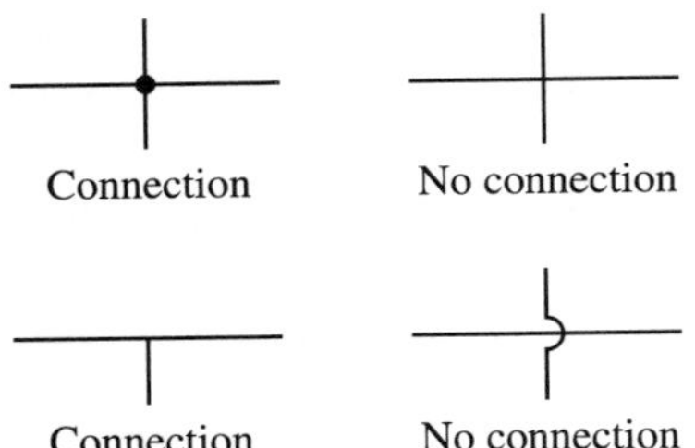

Figure A-17 Four notations used at circuit intersections.

then the outputs of these four AND gates can be connected to the inputs of a four-input OR gate, as shown in Figure A-16. This circuit performs the majority function, which we can verify by enumerating all eight input combinations and observing the output for each case.

The circuit diagram shows a commonly used notation that indicates the presence or absence of a connection, which is summarized in Figure A-17. Two lines that pass through each other do not connect unless a darkened circle is placed at the intersection point. Two lines that meet in a ⊤ are connected as indicated by the six highlighted intersections, and so darkened circles do not need to be placed over those intersection points.

When a product term contains exactly one instance of every variable, either in true or complemented form, it is called a **minterm**. A minterm has a value of 1 for exactly one of the entries in the truth table. That is, a *minimum* number of terms (one) will make the function true. As an alternative, the function is sometimes written as the logical sum over the true entries. Equation (A.1) can be rewritten as shown in Equation (A.2), in which the indices correspond to the minterm indices shown at the left in Figure A-15.

$$F = \sum \langle 3, 5, 6, 7 \rangle \tag{A.2}$$

This notation is appropriate for the **canonical** form of a Boolean equation, which contains only minterms. Equations (A.1) and (A.2) are both said to be in "canonical sum-of-products form."

A.7 The Product-of-Sums Form

As a dual to the sum-of-products form, a Boolean equation can be represented in the **product-of-sums (POS)** form. An equation that is in POS form contains a collection of ORed variables that are ANDed together. One method of obtaining the POS form is to start with the complement of the SOP form and then apply DeMorgan's theorem. For example, referring again to the truth table for the majority function shown in Figure A-15, the complement is obtained by selecting input terms that produce 0's at the output, as shown in Equation (A.3):

$$\overline{F} = \overline{A}\,\overline{B}\,\overline{C} + \overline{A}\,\overline{B}C + \overline{A}B\overline{C} + A\overline{B}\,\overline{C} \tag{A.3}$$

Complementing both sides yields Equation (A.4):

$$F = \overline{\overline{A}\,\overline{B}\,\overline{C} + \overline{A}\,\overline{B}C + \overline{A}B\overline{C} + A\overline{B}\,\overline{C}} \tag{A.4}$$

Applying DeMorgan's theorem in the form $\overline{W+X+Y+Z} = \overline{W}\,\overline{X}\,\overline{Y}\,\overline{Z}$ at the outermost level produces Equation (A.5):

$$F = (\overline{\overline{A}\,\overline{B}\,\overline{C}})(\overline{\overline{A}\,\overline{B}C})(\overline{\overline{A}B\overline{C}})(\overline{A\overline{B}\,\overline{C}}) \tag{A.5}$$

Applying DeMorgan's theorem in the form $\overline{WXYZ} = \overline{W} + \overline{X} + \overline{Y} + \overline{Z}$ to the parenthesized terms produces Equation (A.6):

$$F = (A + B + C)(A + B + \overline{C})(A + \overline{B} + C)(\overline{A} + B + C) \tag{A.6}$$

Equation (A.6) is in POS form and contains four **maxterms**, in which every variable appears exactly once in either true or complemented form. A maxterm, such

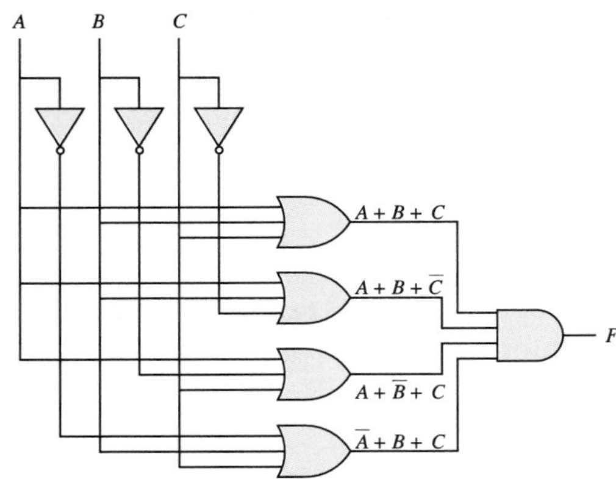

Figure A-18 A two-level OR-AND circuit that implements the majority function. Inverters are not included in the two-level count.

as $(A + B + C)$, has a value of 0 for only one entry in the truth table. That is, it is true for the *maximum* number of truth table entries without reducing to the trivial function of always being true. An equation that consists of only maxterms in POS form is said to be in canonical product-of-sums form. An OR-AND circuit that implements Equation (A.6) is shown in Figure A-18. The OR-AND form is logically equivalent to the AND-OR form shown in Figure A-16.

One motivation for using the POS form over the SOP form is that it may result in a smaller Boolean equation. A smaller Boolean equation may result in a simpler circuit, although this does not always hold true since there are a number of considerations that do not directly depend on the size of the Boolean equation, such as the complexity of the wiring topology.

The **gate count** is a measure of circuit complexity that is obtained by counting all of the logic gates. The **gate input count** is another measure of circuit complexity that is obtained by counting the number of inputs to all of the logic gates. For the circuits shown in Figures A-16 and A-18, a gate count of eight and a gate input count of 19 are obtained for both the SOP and POS forms. For this case, there is no difference in circuit complexity between the SOP and POS forms, but for other cases the differences can be significant. There is a variety of methods for reducing the complexity of digital circuits, a few of which are presented in Appendix B.

A.8 Positive versus Negative Logic

Up to this point we have assumed that high and low voltage levels correspond to logical 1 and 0, or TRUE and FALSE, respectively, which is known as **active**

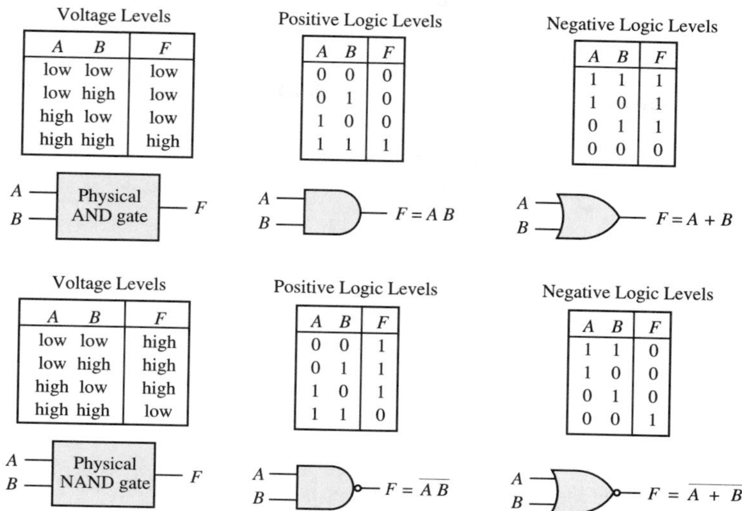

Voltage Levels

A	B	F
low	low	low
low	high	low
high	low	low
high	high	high

Positive Logic Levels

A	B	F
0	0	0
0	1	0
1	0	0
1	1	1

Negative Logic Levels

A	B	F
1	1	1
1	0	1
0	1	1
0	0	0

Voltage Levels

A	B	F
low	low	high
low	high	high
high	low	high
high	high	low

Positive Logic Levels

A	B	F
0	0	1
0	1	1
1	0	1
1	1	0

Negative Logic Levels

A	B	F
1	1	0
1	0	0
0	1	0
0	0	1

Figure A-19 Positive and negative logic assignments for AND-OR and NAND-NOR duals.

high or **positive logic**. We can make the reverse assignment instead: low voltage for logical 1 and high voltage for logical 0, which is known as **active low** or **negative logic**. The use of negative logic is sometimes preferred to positive logic for applications in which the logic inhibits an event rather than enabling an event.

Figure A-19 illustrates the behavior of AND-OR and NAND-NOR gate pairs for both positive and negative logic. The positive logic AND gate behaves as a negative logic OR gate. The physical logic gate is the same regardless of the positive or negative sense of the logic—only the interpretation of the signals is changed.

The mixing of positive and negative logic in the same system should be avoided to prevent confusion, but sometimes it cannot be avoided. For these cases, a technique known as "bubble matching" helps keep the proper logic sense correct. The idea is to assume that all logic is asserted high (positive logic) and to place a bubble (denoting logical inversion) at the inputs or outputs of any negative logic circuits. Note that these bubbles are the same in function as the bubbles that appear at the complemented outputs of logic gates such as NOR and NAND. That is, the signal that leaves a bubble is the complement of the signal that enters it.

Consider the circuit shown in Figure A-20a, in which the outputs of two positive logic circuits are combined through an AND gate that is connected to a positive

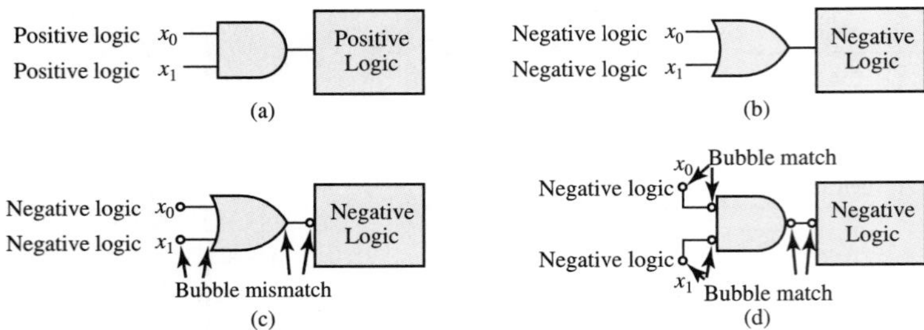

Figure A-20 The process of bubble matching.

logic system. A logically equivalent system for negative logic is shown in Figure A-20b. In the process of bubble matching, a bubble is placed on each active low input or output, as shown in Figure A-20c.

To simplify the process of analyzing the circuit, active low input bubbles need to be matched with active low output bubbles. In Figure A-20c there are bubble mismatches because there is only one bubble on each line. DeMorgan's theorem is used in converting the OR gate in Figure A-20c to the NAND gate with complemented inputs in Figure A-20d, in which the bubble mismatches have been fixed.

A.9 The Data Sheet

Logic gates and other logic components have a great deal of technical specifications that are relevant to the design and analysis of digital circuits. The **data sheet**, or "spec sheet," lists technical characteristics of a logic component. An example of a data sheet is shown in Figure A-21. The data sheet starts with a title for the component, which for this case is the SN7400 NAND gate. The description gives a functional description of the component in textual form.

The package section shows the pin layout and the pin assignments. There can be several package types for the same component. The function table enumerates the input-output behavior of the component from a functional perspective. The symbols "H" and "L" stand for "high" and "low" voltages, respectively, to avoid confusion with the sense of positive or negative logic. The symbol "X" indicates that the value at an input does not influence the output. The logic diagram describes the logical behavior of the component, using positive logic for this case. All four NAND gates are shown with their pin assignments.

The schematic shows the transistor level circuitry for each gate. In the text, we treat this low-level circuitry as an abstraction that is embodied in the logic gate symbols.

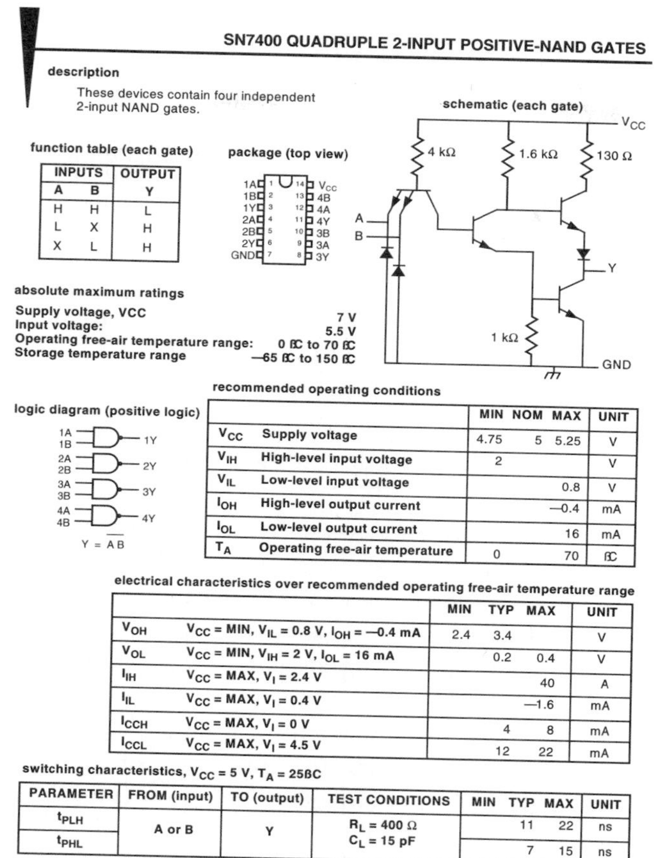

SN7400 QUADRUPLE 2-INPUT POSITIVE-NAND GATES

description

These devices contain four independent 2-input NAND gates.

function table (each gate)

INPUTS		OUTPUT
A	B	Y
H	H	L
L	X	H
X	L	H

absolute maximum ratings

Supply voltage, VCC	7 V
Input voltage:	5.5 V
Operating free-air temperature range:	0 ßC to 70 ßC
Storage temperature range	—65 ßC to 150 ßC

logic diagram (positive logic)

recommended operating conditions

		MIN	NOM	MAX	UNIT
V_{CC}	Supply voltage	4.75	5	5.25	V
V_{IH}	High-level input voltage	2			V
V_{IL}	Low-level input voltage			0.8	V
I_{OH}	High-level output current			—0.4	mA
I_{OL}	Low-level output current			16	mA
T_A	Operating free-air temperature	0		70	ßC

electrical characteristics over recommended operating free-air temperature range

		MIN	TYP	MAX	UNIT
V_{OH}	V_{CC} = MIN, V_{IL} = 0.8 V, I_{OH} = —0.4 mA	2.4	3.4		V
V_{OL}	V_{CC} = MIN, V_{IH} = 2 V, I_{OL} = 16 mA		0.2	0.4	V
I_{IH}	V_{CC} = MAX, V_I = 2.4 V			40	A
I_{IL}	V_{CC} = MAX, V_I = 0.4 V			—1.6	mA
I_{CCH}	V_{CC} = MAX, V_I = 0 V		4	8	mA
I_{CCL}	V_{CC} = MAX, V_I = 4.5 V		12	22	mA

switching characteristics, V_{CC} = 5 V, T_A = 25ßC

PARAMETER	FROM (input)	TO (output)	TEST CONDITIONS	MIN	TYP	MAX	UNIT
t_{PLH}	A or B	Y	R_L = 400 Ω, C_L = 15 pF		11	22	ns
t_{PHL}					7	15	ns

Figure A-21 Simplified data sheet for 7400 NAND gate (adapted from Texas Instruments *TTL Databook* [Texas Instruments, 1988]).

The "absolute maximum ratings" section lists the range of environmental conditions in which the component will safely operate. The supply voltage can go as high as 7 V and the input voltage can go up to 5.5 V. The ambient temperature should be between 0°C and 70°C during operation, but can vary between –65°C and 150°C when the component is not being used.

Despite the absolute maximum rating specifications, the recommended operating conditions should be used during operation. The recommended operating conditions are characterized by minimum (MIN), normal (NOM), and maximum (MAX) ratings.

The electrical characteristics describe the behavior of the component under certain operating conditions. V_{OH} and V_{OL} are the minimum output high voltage and the maximum output low voltage, respectively. I_{IH} and I_{IL} are the maximum currents into an input pin when the input is high or low, respectively. I_{CCH} and I_{CCL} are the package's power supply currents when all outputs are high or low, respectively.

This data can be used in determining maximum **fan-outs** under the given conditions. Fan-out is a measure of the number of inputs that a single output can drive, for logic gates implemented in the same technology. That is, a logic gate with a fan-out of 10 can drive the inputs of 10 other logic gates of the same type. Similarly, **fan-in** is a measure of the number of inputs that a logic gate can accept (simply, the number of input lines to that gate). The absolute value of I_{OH} must be greater than or equal to the sum of all I_{IH} currents that are being driven, and I_{OL} must be greater than or equal to the sum of all I_{IL} currents (absolute values) that are being driven. The absolute value of I_{OH} for a 7400 gate is .4 mA (or 400 μA), and so a 7400 gate output can thus drive ten 7400 inputs (I_{IH} = 40 μA per input).

The switching characteristics show the propagation delay to switch the output from a low to a high voltage (t_{PLH}) and the propagation delay to switch the output from a high to a low voltage (t_{PHL}). The maximum ratings show the worst cases. A circuit can be safely designed using the typical case as the worst case, but only if a test-and-select-the-best approach is used. That is, since t_{PLH} varies between 11 ns and 22 ns and t_{PHL} varies between 7 ns and 15 ns from one packaged component to the next, components can be individually tested to determine their true characteristics. Not all components of the same type behave identically, even under the most stringent fabrication controls, and the differences can be reduced by testing and selecting the best components.

A.10 Digital Components

High-level digital circuit designs are normally made using collections of logic gates referred to as **components** rather than using individual logic gates. This allows a degree of circuit complexity to be abstracted away and also simplifies the process of modeling the behavior of circuits and characterizing their performance. A few of the more common components are described in the sections that follow.

A.10.1 *LEVELS OF INTEGRATION*

Up to this point, we have focused on the design of combinational logic units. Since we have been working with individual logic gates, we have been working at the level of **small scale integration** (SSI), in which there are 10 to 100 components per chip. ("Components" has a different meaning in this context, referring to transistors and other discrete elements.) Although we sometimes need to work at this low level in practice, typically for high-performance circuits, the advent of microelectronics allows us to work at higher levels of integration. In **medium scale integration** (MSI), approximately 100 to 1000 components appear in a single chip. **Large scale integration** (LSI) deals with circuits that contain 1000 to 10,000 components per chip, and **very large scale integration** (VLSI) goes higher still. There are no sharp breaks between the classes of integration, but the distinctions are useful in comparing the relative complexity of circuits. In this section we deal primarily with MSI components.

A.10.2 *MULTIPLEXERS*

A **multiplexer** (MUX) is a component that connects a number of inputs to a single output. A block diagram and the corresponding truth table for a 4-to-1 MUX are shown in Figure A-22. The output *F* takes on the value of the data input that is selected by control lines *A* and *B*. For example, if $AB = 00$, then the value on line D_0 (a 0 or a 1) will appear at *F*. The corresponding AND-OR circuit is shown in Figure A-23.

When we design circuits with MUXes, we normally use the "black box" form shown in Figure A-22 rather than the more detailed form shown in Figure A-23. In this way, we can abstract away detail when designing complex circuits.

Multiplexers can be used to implement Boolean functions. In Figure A-24, an 8-to-1 MUX implements the majority function. The data inputs are taken directly from the truth table for the majority function, and the control inputs are assigned to the variables *A*, *B*, and *C*. The MUX implements the function by passing a 1 from the input of each true minterm to the output. The 0 inputs mark portions of the MUX that are not needed in implementing the function, and as a result, a number of logic gates are underutilized. Although portions of MUXes are almost always unused in implement-

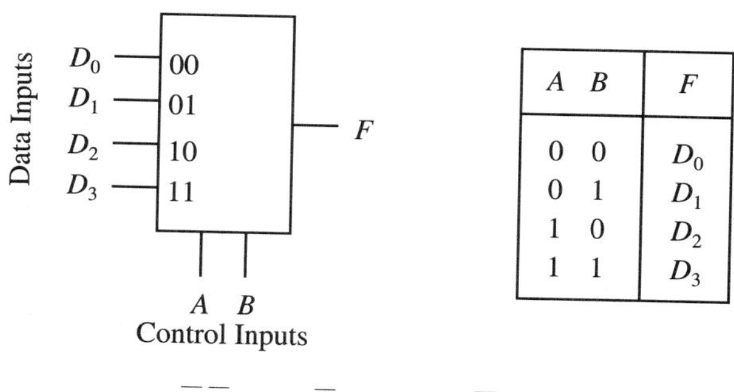

$$F = \overline{A}\,\overline{B}\,D_0 + \overline{A}\,B\,D_1 + A\,\overline{B}\,D_2 + A\,B\,D_3$$

Figure A-22 Block diagram and truth table for a 4-to-1 MUX.

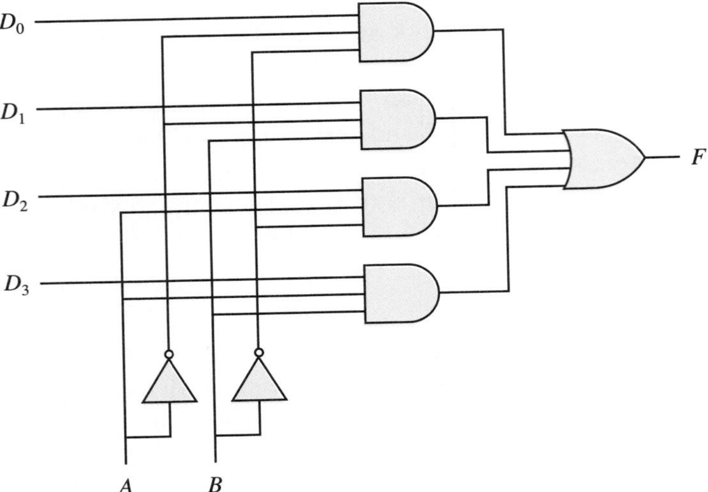

Figure A-23 An AND-OR circuit implements a 4-to-1 MUX.

A	B	C	M
0	0	0	0
0	0	1	0
0	1	0	0
0	1	1	1
1	0	0	0
1	0	1	1
1	1	0	1
1	1	1	1

0 — 000
0 — 001
0 — 010
1 — 011
0 — 100
1 — 101
1 — 110
1 — 111
F
A B C

Figure A-24 An 8-to-1 multiplexer implements the majority function.

ing Boolean functions, multiplexers are widely used because their generality simplifies the design process, and their modularity simplifies the implementation.

As another case, consider implementing a function of three variables using a 4-to-1 MUX. Figure A-25 shows a three-variable truth table and a 4-to-1 MUX that implements function F. We allow data inputs to be taken from the set $\{0, 1, C, \overline{C}\}$, and the groupings are obtained as shown in the truth table. When $AB = 00$, then $F = 0$ regardless of whether $C = 0$ or $C = 1$, and so a 0 is placed at the corresponding 00 data input line on the MUX. When $AB = 01$, then $F = 1$ regardless of whether $C = 0$ or $C = 1$,

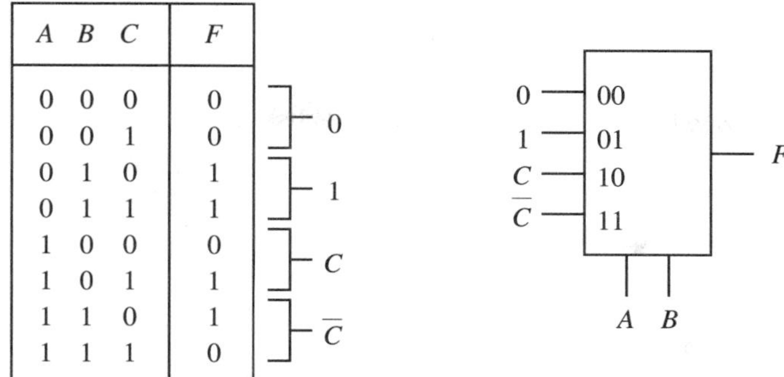

A	B	C	F
0	0	0	0
0	0	1	0
0	1	0	1
0	1	1	1
1	0	0	0
1	0	1	1
1	1	0	1
1	1	1	0

Figure A-25 A 4-to-1 MUX implements a three-variable function.

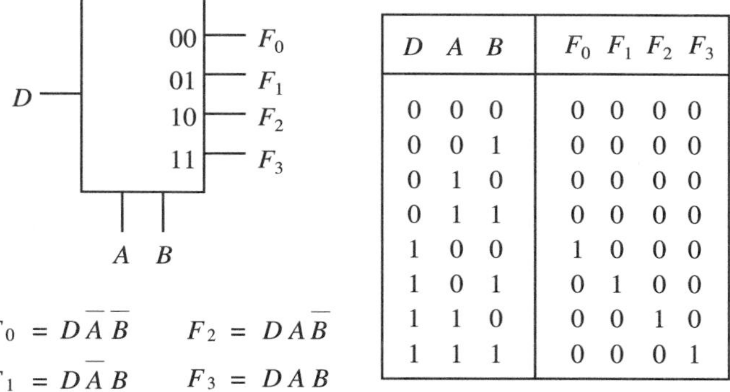

$F_0 = D\overline{A}\,\overline{B}$ $\quad F_2 = DA\overline{B}$

$F_1 = D\overline{A}B$ $\quad F_3 = DAB$

D	A	B	F_0	F_1	F_2	F_3
0	0	0	0	0	0	0
0	0	1	0	0	0	0
0	1	0	0	0	0	0
0	1	1	0	0	0	0
1	0	0	1	0	0	0
1	0	1	0	1	0	0
1	1	0	0	0	1	0
1	1	1	0	0	0	1

Figure A-26 Block diagram and truth table for a 1-to-4 DEMUX.

and so a 1 is placed at the 01 data input. When $AB = 10$, then $F = C$ since F is 0 when C is 0 and F is 1 when C is 1, and so C is placed at the 10 input. Finally, when $AB = 11$, then $F = \overline{C}$, and so $\overline{C}$ is placed at the 11 input. In this way, we can implement a three-variable function using a two-variable MUX.

A.10.3 *DEMULTIPLEXERS*

A **demultiplexer** (DEMUX) is the converse of a MUX. A block diagram of a 1-to-4 DEMUX with control inputs *A* and *B* and the corresponding truth table are shown in Figure A-26. A DEMUX sends its single data input *D* to one of its outputs F_i according to the settings of the control inputs. A circuit for a 1-to-4 DEMUX is shown in Figure A-27. An application for a DEMUX is to send data from a single source to one of a number of destinations, such as from a call request button for an elevator to the closest elevator car. The DEMUX is not normally used in implementing ordinary Boolean functions, although there are ways to do it (see Problem A.17).

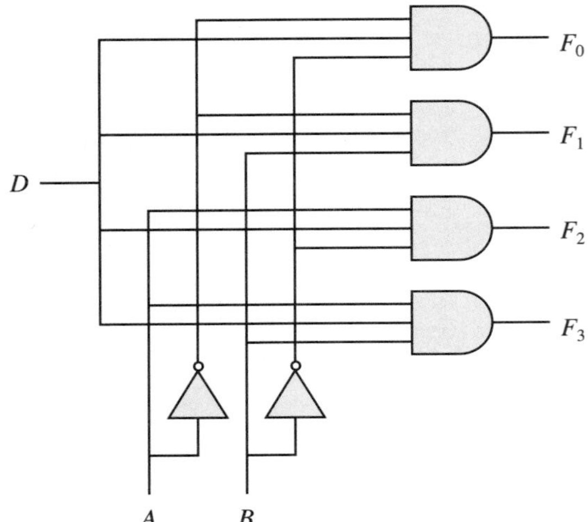

Figure A-27 A circuit for a 1-to-4 DEMUX.

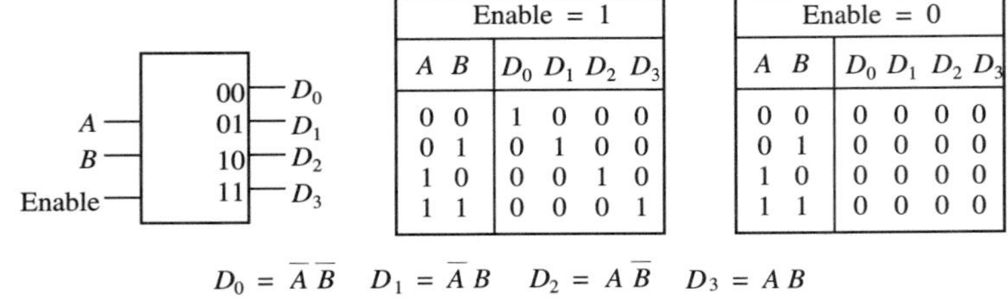

Enable = 1					
A	B	D_0	D_1	D_2	D_3
0	0	1	0	0	0
0	1	0	1	0	0
1	0	0	0	1	0
1	1	0	0	0	1

Enable = 0					
A	B	D_0	D_1	D_2	D_3
0	0	0	0	0	0
0	1	0	0	0	0
1	0	0	0	0	0
1	1	0	0	0	0

$D_0 = \overline{A}\,\overline{B}$ $D_1 = \overline{A}\,B$ $D_2 = A\,\overline{B}$ $D_3 = A\,B$

Figure A-28 Block diagram and truth table for a 2-to-4 decoder.

A.10.4 *DECODERS*

A **decoder** translates a logical encoding into a spatial location. Exactly one output of a decoder is high (logical 1) at any time, which is determined by the settings on the control inputs. A block diagram and a truth table for a 2-to-4 decoder with control inputs A and B are shown in Figure A-28. A corresponding logic diagram that implements the decoder is shown in Figure A-29. A decoder may be used to control other circuits, and at times it may be inappropriate to enable any of the other circuits. For that reason, we add an enable line to the decoder, which forces all outputs to 0 if a 0 is applied at its input. (Notice the logical equivalence between the DEMUX with an input of 1 and the decoder.)

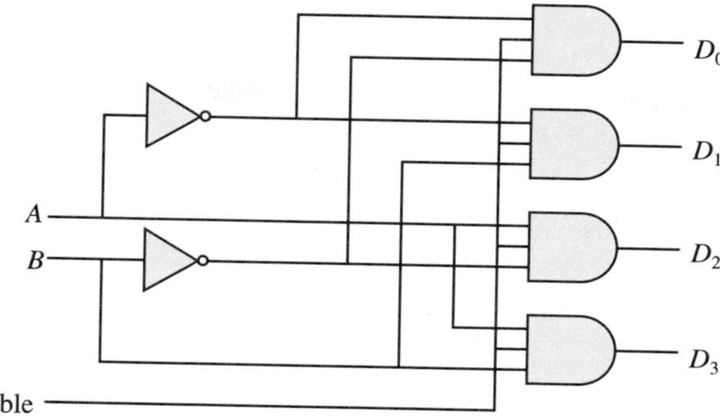

Figure A-29 An AND circuit for a 2-to-4 decoder.

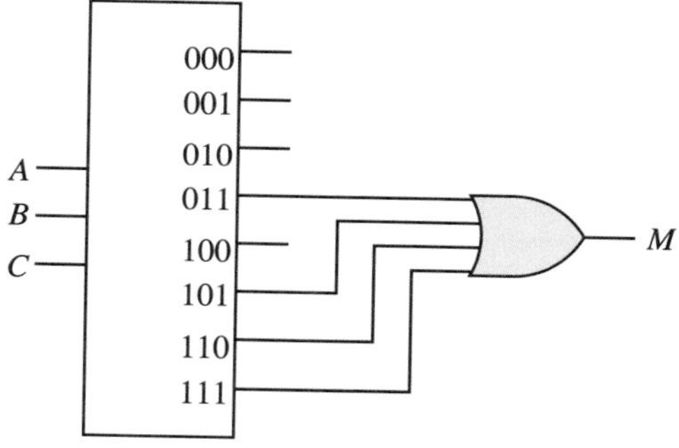

Figure A-30 A 3-to-8 decoder implements the majority function.

One application for a decoder is in translating memory addresses into physical locations. Decoders can also be used in implementing Boolean functions. Since each output line corresponds to a different minterm, a function can be implemented by logically ORing the outputs that correspond to the true minterms in the function. For example, in Figure A-30, a 3-to-8 decoder implements the majority function. Unused outputs remain disconnected.

A.10.5 *PRIORITY ENCODERS*

An **encoder** translates a set of inputs into a binary encoding and can be thought of as the converse of a decoder. A **priority encoder** is one type of an encoder, in which an ordering is imposed on the inputs. A block diagram and a corresponding truth table for a 4-to-2 priority encoder are shown in Figure A-31. A priority scheme is imposed on the inputs in which A_i has higher priority than A_{i+1}. The two-bit output takes on the value 00, 01, 10, or 11 depending on which inputs

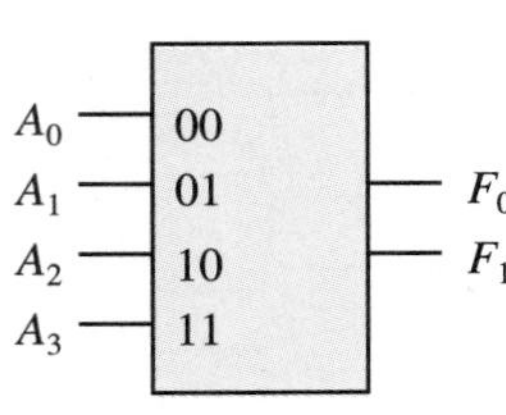

$$F_0 = \overline{A_0}\,\overline{A_1}A_3 + \overline{A_0}\,\overline{A_1}A_2$$
$$F_1 = \overline{A_0}\,\overline{A_2}A_3 + \overline{A_0}A_1$$

A_0	A_1	A_2	A_3	F_0	F_1
0	0	0	0	0	0
0	0	0	1	1	1
0	0	1	0	1	0
0	0	1	1	1	0
0	1	0	0	0	1
0	1	0	1	0	1
0	1	1	0	0	1
0	1	1	1	0	1
1	0	0	0	0	0
1	0	0	1	0	0
1	0	1	0	0	0
1	0	1	1	0	0
1	1	0	0	0	0
1	1	0	1	0	0
1	1	1	0	0	0
1	1	1	1	0	0

Figure A-31 Block diagram and truth table for a 4-to-2 priority encoder.

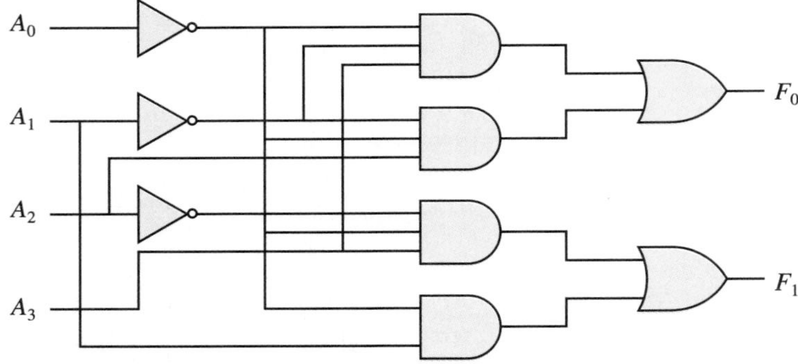

Figure A-32 Logic diagram for a 4-to-2 priority encoder.

are active (in the 1 state) and their relative priorities. When no inputs are active, then the output defaults to giving priority to A_0 ($F_0F_1 = 00$).

Priority encoders are used for arbitrating among a number of devices that compete for the same resource, as when a number of users simultaneously attempt to log on to a computer system. A circuit diagram for a 4-to-2 priority encoder is shown in Figure A-32. (The circuit has been reduced using methods described in Appendix B, but the input/output behavior can be verified without needing to know the reduction method.)

A.10.6 PROGRAMMABLE LOGIC ARRAYS

A **programmable logic array** (PLA) is a component that consists of a customizable AND matrix followed by a customizable OR matrix. A PLA with three inputs and two outputs is shown in Figure A-33. The three inputs *A*, *B*, and *C* and their complements are available at the inputs of each of eight AND gates that generate eight product terms. The outputs of the AND gates are available at the inputs of

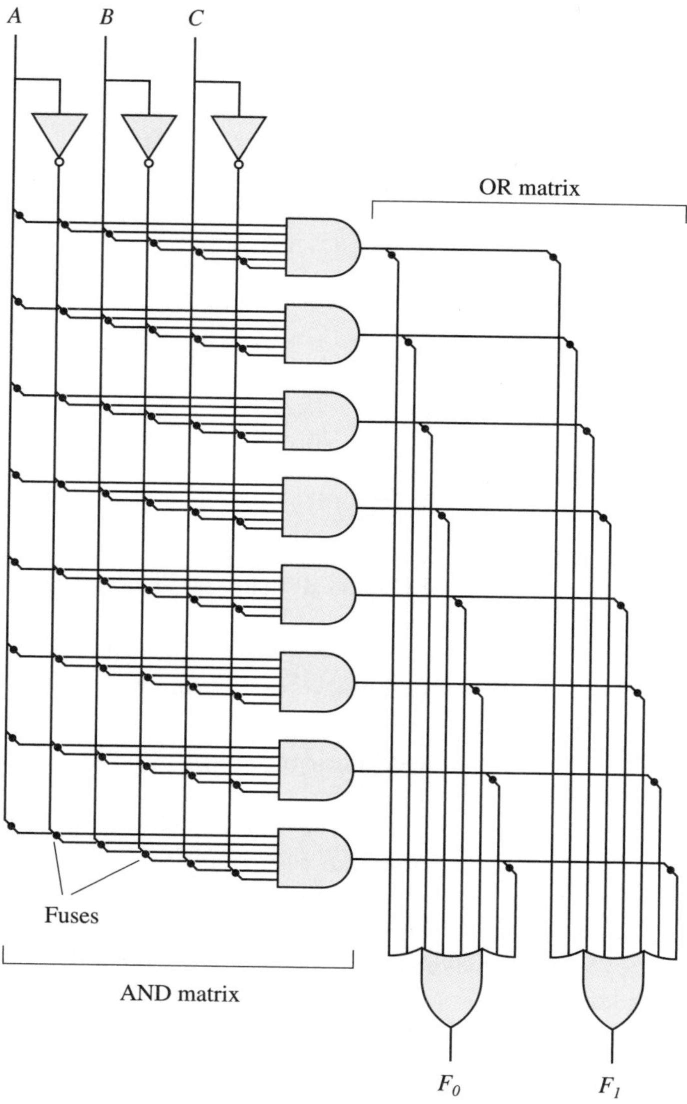

Figure A-33 A programmable logic array.

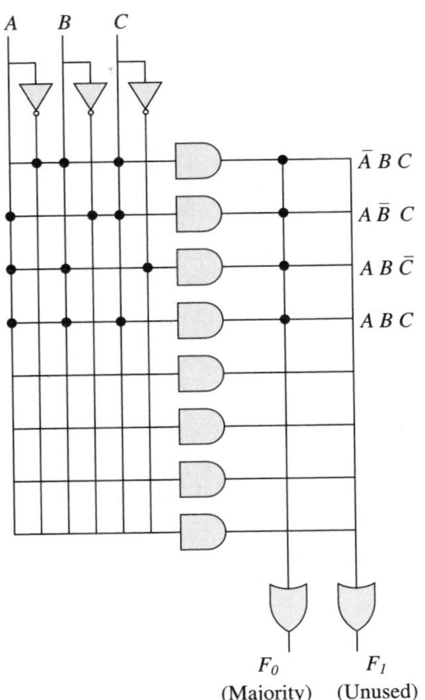

Figure A-34 Simplified representation of a PLA.

each of the OR gates that generate functions F_0 and F_1. A programmable fuse is placed at each crosspoint in the AND and OR matrices. The matrices are customized for specific functions by disabling fuses. When a fuse is disabled at an input to an AND gate, then the AND gate behaves as if the input is tied to a 1. Similarly, a disabled input to an OR gate in a PLA behaves as if the input is tied to a 0.

As an example of how a PLA is used, consider implementing the majority function on a 3×2 PLA (three input variables × two output functions). In order to simplify the illustrations, the form shown in Figure A-34 is used, in which it is understood that the single input line into each AND gate represents six input lines, and the single input line into each OR gate represents eight input lines. Darkened circles are placed at the crosspoints to indicate where connections are made. In Figure A-34, the majority function is implemented using just half of the PLA, which leaves the rest of the PLA available for another function.

PLAs are workhorse components that are used throughout digital circuits. An advantage of using PLAs is that there are only a few inputs and a few outputs, while there is a large number of logic gates between the inputs and outputs. It is

Figure A-35 Black box representation of a PLA.

important to minimize the number of connections at the circuit edges in order to modularize a system into discrete components that are designed and implemented separately. A PLA is ideal for this purpose, and a number of automated programs exist for designing PLAs from functional descriptions. In keeping with this concept of modularity, we will sometimes represent a PLA as a black box as shown in Figure A-35, and assume that we can safely leave the design of the internals of the PLA to an automated program.

EXAMPLE: A RIPPLE-CARRY ADDER

As an example of how PLAs are used in the design of a digital circuit, consider designing a circuit that adds two binary numbers. Binary addition is performed similar to the way we perform decimal addition by hand, as illustrated in Figure A-36. Two binary numbers *A* and *B* are added from right to left, creating a sum and a carry in each bit position. Two input bits and a carry-in must be summed at each bit position, so that a total of eight input combinations must be considered, as shown in the truth table in Figure A-37.

The truth table in Figure A-37 describes an element known as a **full adder**, which is shown schematically in the figure. A **half adder**, which could be used for the rightmost bit position, adds two bits and produces a sum and a carry, whereas a full adder adds two bits and a carry and produces a sum and a carry. The half adder is not used here in order to keep the number of different compo-

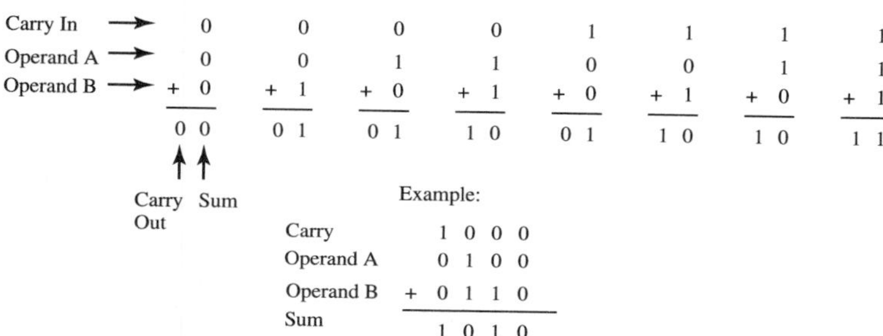

Figure A-36 Example of addition for two unsigned binary numbers.

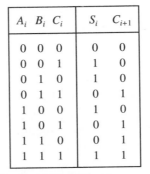

A_i	B_i	C_i	S_i	C_{i+1}
0	0	0	0	0
0	0	1	1	0
0	1	0	1	0
0	1	1	0	1
1	0	0	1	0
1	0	1	0	1
1	1	0	0	1
1	1	1	1	1

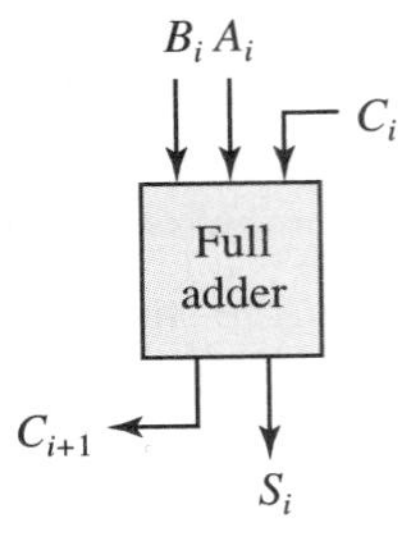

Figure A-37 Truth table for a full adder.

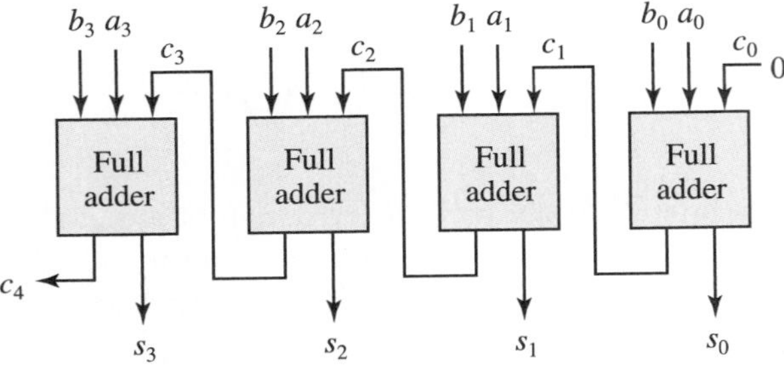

Figure A-38 A four-bit adder implemented with a cascade of full adders.

nents to a minimum. Four full adders can be cascaded to form an adder large enough to add the four-bit numbers used in the example of Figure A-36, as shown in Figure A-38. The rightmost full adder has a carry-in (c_0) of 0.

The reader will note that the value for a given sum bit cannot be computed until the carry-out from the previous full adder has been computed. The circuit is called a “ripple carry” adder because the correct values for the carry bits “ripple” through the circuit from right to left. The reader may also observe that even though the circuit looks “parallel,” in reality the sum bits are computed serially from right to left. This is a major disadvantage to the circuit. We discuss ways of speeding up addition in Chapter 3.

An approach to designing a full adder is to use a PLA, as shown in Figure A-39. The PLA approach is very general, and computer-aided design (CAD) tools for VLSI typically favor the use of PLAs over random logic or MUXes because of their generality. CAD tools typically reduce the sizes of the PLAs (we will see a few reduction techniques in Appendix B) and so the seemingly high gate count for the PLA is not actually so high in practice. ■

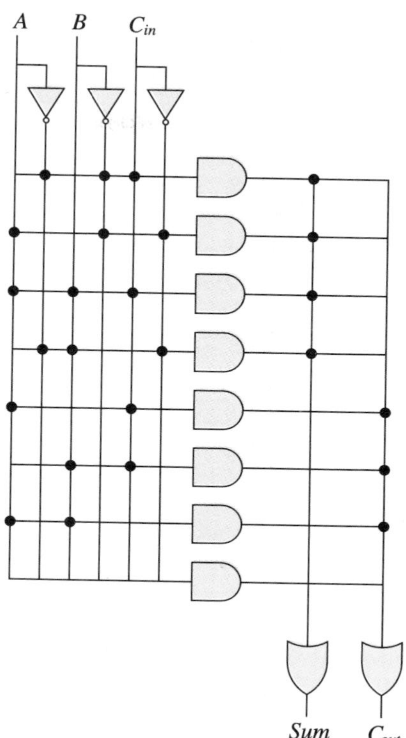

Figure A-39 PLA realization of a full adder.

A.11 Sequential Logic

In the earlier part of this appendix we explored combinational logic units, in which the outputs are completely determined by functions of the inputs. A sequential logic unit, commonly referred to as a **finite state machine** (FSM), takes an input and a current state and produces an output and a new state. An FSM is distinguished from a CLU in that the history of the inputs to the FSM influences its state and output. This is important for implementing memory circuits as well as control units in a computer.

The classical model of a finite state machine is shown in Figure A-40. A CLU takes inputs from lines $i_0 - i_k$, which are external to the FSM, and also takes inputs from state bits $ss_0 - s_n$, which are internal to the FSM. The CLU produces output bits $f_0 - f_m$ and new state bits. Delay elements maintain the current state of the FSM, until a synchronization signal causes the D_i values to be loaded into the s_i, which appear at Q_i as the new state bits.

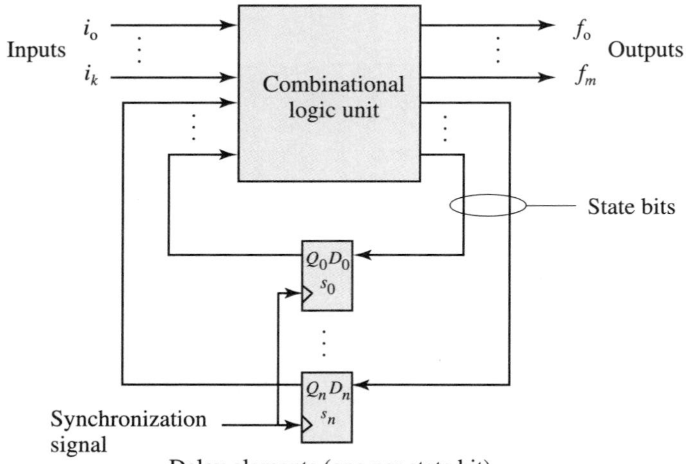

Figure A-40 Classical model of a finite state machine.

A.11.1 *THE S-R FLIP-FLOP*

A **flip-flop** is an arrangement of logic gates that maintains a stable output even after the inputs are made inactive. The output of a flip-flop is determined by both the current inputs and the history of inputs, and thus a combinational logic unit is not powerful enough to capture this behavior. A flip-flop can be used to store a single bit of information and serves as a building block for computer memory.

If either or both inputs of a two-input NOR gate is 1, then the output of the NOR gate is 0; otherwise the output is 1. As we saw earlier in this appendix, the time that it takes for a signal to propagate from the inputs of a logic gate to the output is not instantaneous, and there is some delay $\Delta\tau$ that represents the propagation delay through the gate. The delay is sometimes considered lumped at the output of the gate for purposes of analysis, as illustrated in Figure A-41. The lumped delay is not normally indicated in circuit diagrams but its presence is implied.

The propagation time through the NOR gate affects the operation of a flip-flop. Consider the **set-reset** (S-R) flip-flop shown in Figure A-42, which consists of two cross-coupled NOR gates. If we apply a 1 to S, then $\overline{Q}$ goes to 0 after a delay $\Delta\tau$, which causes Q to go to 1 (assuming R is initially 0) after a delay $2\Delta\tau$. As a result of the finite propagation time, there is a brief period of time $\Delta\tau$ when both the Q and $\overline{Q}$ outputs assume a value of 0, which is logically incorrect, but this condition will be fixed when the **master-slave** configuration is discussed later. If

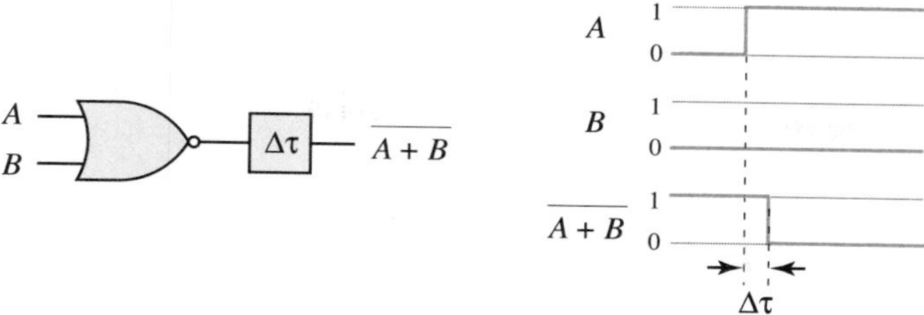

Figure A-41 A NOR gate with a lumped delay at its output.

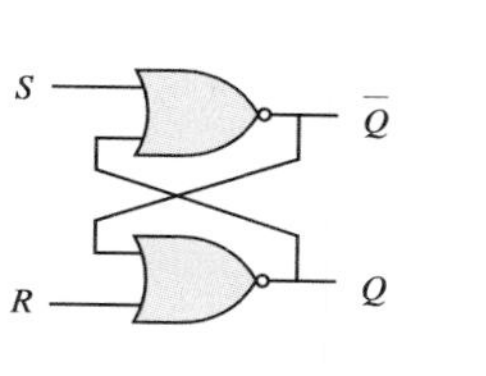

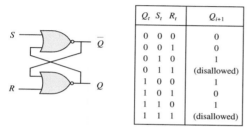

Q_t S_t R_t	Q_{t+1}
0 0 0	0
0 0 1	0
0 1 0	1
0 1 1	(disallowed)
1 0 0	1
1 0 1	0
1 1 0	1
1 1 1	(disallowed)

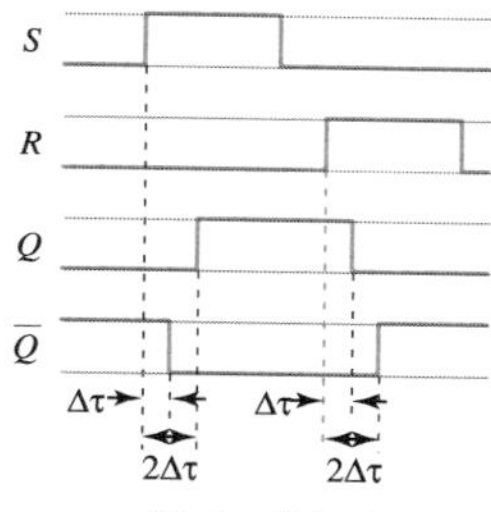

Figure A-42 An S-R flip-flop.

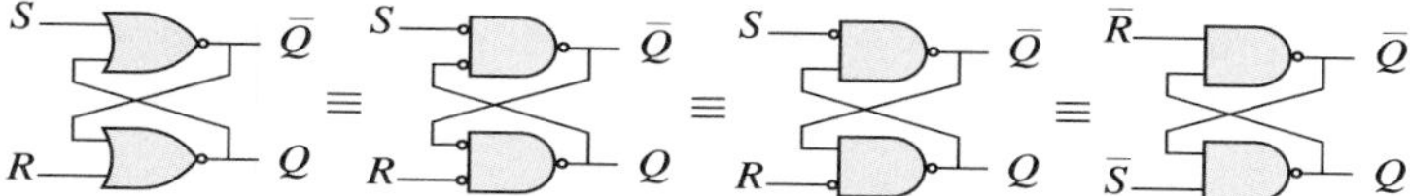

Figure A-43 A NOR implementation of an S-R flip-flop is converted into a NAND implementation.

we now apply a 0 to *S*, then *Q* retains its state until some later time when *R* goes to 1. The S-R flip-flop thus holds a single bit of information and serves as an elementary memory element.

There is more than one way to make an S-R flip-flop, and the use of cross-coupled NOR gates is just one configuration. Two cross-coupled NAND gates can also implement an S-R flip-flop, with $S = R = 1$ being the quiescent state. Making use of DeMorgan's theorem, we can convert the NOR gates of an S-R flip-flop into AND gates, as shown in Figure A-43. By "bubble pushing," we change the AND gates into NAND gates and then reverse the sense of *S* and *R* to remove the remaining input bubbles.

A.11.2 *THE CLOCKED S-R FLIP-FLOP*

Now consider that the inputs to the S-R flip-flop may originate from the outputs of some other circuits, whose inputs may originate from the outputs of other circuits, forming a cascade of logic circuits. This mirrors the form of conventional digital circuits. A problem with cascading circuits is that transitions may occur at times that are not desired.

Consider the circuit shown in Figure A-44. If signals *A*, *B*, and *C* all change from the 0 state to the 1 state, then signal *C* may reach the XOR gate before *A* and *B* propagate through the AND gate, which will momentarily produce a 1 output at *S*, which will revert to 0 when the output of the AND gate settles and is XORed with *C*. At this point it may be too late, however, since *S* may be in the 1 state long enough to set the flip-flop, destroying the integrity of the stored bit.

When the final state of a flip-flop is sensitive to the relative arrival times of signals, the result may be a **glitch**, which is an unwanted state or output. A circuit that can produce a glitch is said to have a **hazard**. The hazard may or may not manifest itself as a glitch, depending on the operating conditions of the circuit at a particular time.

In order to achieve synchronization in a controlled fashion, a **clock** signal is provided, to which every state-dependent circuit (such as a flip-flop) synchronizes itself by accepting inputs only at discrete times. A clock circuit produces a con-

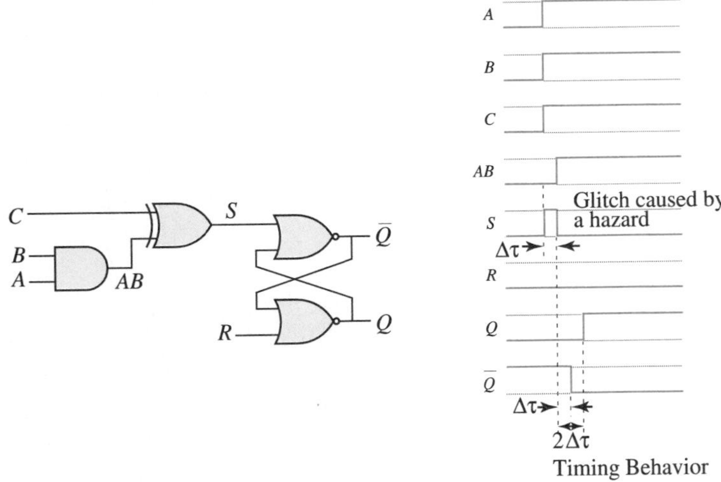

Figure A-44 A circuit with a hazard.

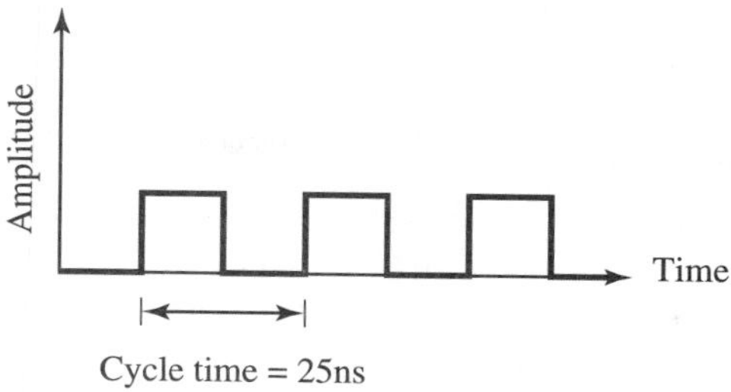

Figure A-45 A clock waveform.

Prefix	Abbrev.	Quantity	Prefix	Abbrev.	Quantity
milli	m	10^{-3}	Kilo	K	10^3
micro	μ	10^{-6}	Mega	M	10^6
nano	n	10^{-9}	Giga	G	10^9
pico	p	10^{-12}	Tera	T	10^{12}
femto	f	10^{-15}	Peta	P	10^{15}
atto	a	10^{-18}	Exa	E	10^{18}

Table A-2 Standard scientific prefixes for cycle times and clock rates.

tinuous stream of 1's and 0's, as indicated by the waveform shown in Figure A-45. The time required for the clock to rise, then fall, then begin to rise again is called the **cycle time**. The square edges that are shown in the waveform represent an ideal square wave. In practice, the edges are rounded because instantaneous rise and fall times do not occur.

The **clock rate** is taken as the inverse of the cycle time. For a cycle time of 25 ns/cycle, the corresponding clock rate is 1/25 cycles/ns, which corresponds to 40,000,000 cycles per second, or 40 MHz (for 40 megahertz). A list of other abbreviations that are commonly used to specify cycle times and clock rates is shown in Table A-2.

We can make use of the clock signal to eliminate the hazard by creating a **clocked S-R flip-flop**, which is shown in Figure A-46. The symbol *CLK* labels the clock input. Now *S* and *R* cannot change the state of the flip-flop until the clock is high. Thus, as long as *S* and *R* settle into stable states while the clock is low, then when the clock makes a transition to 1, the stable value will be stored in the flip-flop.

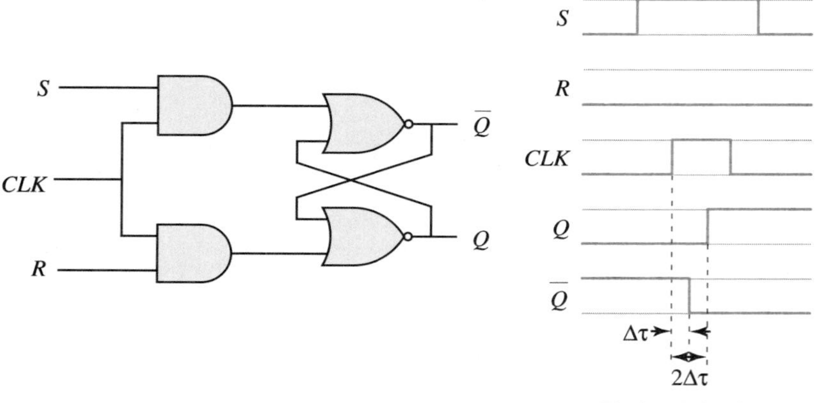

Figure A-46 A clocked S-R flip-flop.

A.11.3 *THE D FLIP-FLOP AND THE MASTER-SLAVE CONFIGURATION*

A disadvantage of the S-R flip-flop is that in order to store a 1 or a 0, we need to apply a 1 to a different input (*S* or *R*) depending on the value that we want to store. An alternative configuration that allows either a 0 or a 1 to be applied at the input is the **D flip-flop** which is shown in Figure A-47. The D flip-flop is constructed by placing an inverter across the *S* and *R* inputs of an S-R flip-flop. Now when the clock goes high, the value on the *D* line is stored in the flip-flop.

The D flip-flop is commonly used in situations where there is feedback from the output back to the input through some other circuitry, and this feedback can sometimes cause the flip-flop to change states more than once per clock cycle. In order to ensure that the flip-flop changes state just once per clock pulse, we break

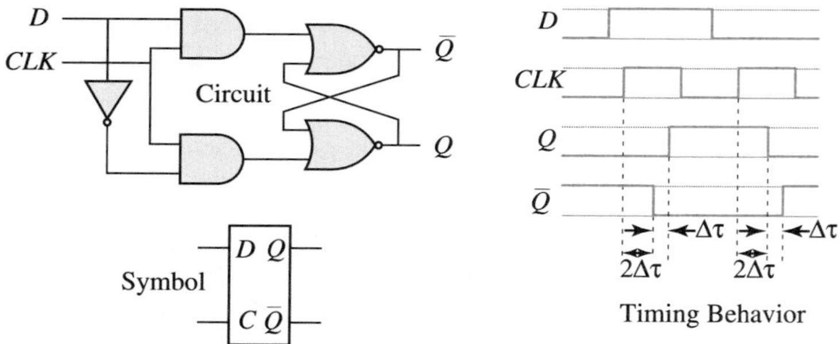

Figure A-47 A clocked D flip-flop. The letter 'C' denotes the clock input in the symbol form.

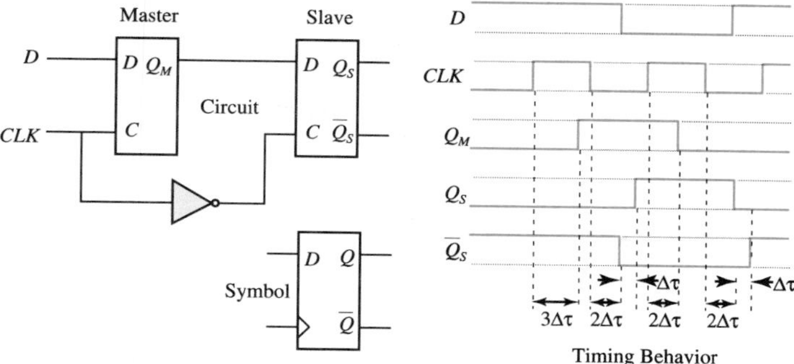

Figure A-48 A master-slave flip-flop.

the feedback loop by constructing a master-slave flip-flop, as shown in Figure A-48. The **master-slave flip-flop** consists of two flip-flops arranged in tandem, with an inverted clock used for the second flip-flop. The master flip-flop changes when the clock is high, but the slave flip-flop does not change until the clock is low; thus the clock must first go high and then go low before the input at D in the master is clocked through to Q_S in the slave. The triangle shown in the symbol for the master-slave flip-flop indicates that transitions at the output occur only on a rising (0 to 1 transition) or falling (1 to 0 transition) edge of the clock. Transitions at the output do not occur continuously during a high level of the clock as for the clocked S-R flip-flop. For the configuration shown in Figure A-48, the transition at the output occurs on the falling edge of the clock.

A **level-triggered** flip-flop changes state continuously while the clock is high (or low, depending on how the flip-flop is designed). An **edge-triggered** flip-flop changes only on a high-to-low or low-to-high clock transition. Some textbooks do not place a triangle at the clock input in order to distinguish between level-triggered and edge-triggered flip-flops and indicate one form or the other based on their usage or in some other way. In practice the notation is held somewhat loosely. Here we will use the triangle symbol and will also make the flip-flop type clear from the way it is used.

A.11.4 *J-K AND T FLIP-FLOPS*

In addition to the S-R and D flip-flops, the **J-K** and **T flip-flops** are very common. The J-K flip-flop behaves similarly to an S-R flip-flop, except that it flips its state when both inputs are set to 1. The T flip-flop (for "toggle") alternates states, as when the inputs to a J-K flip-flop are set to 1. Logic diagrams and symbols for

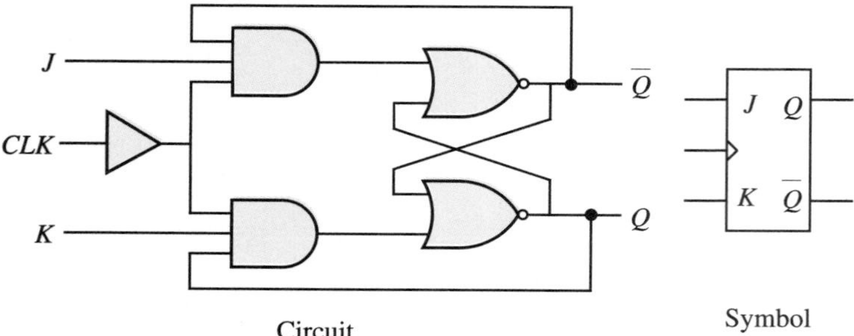

Figure A-49 Logic diagram and symbol for a basic J-K flip-flop.

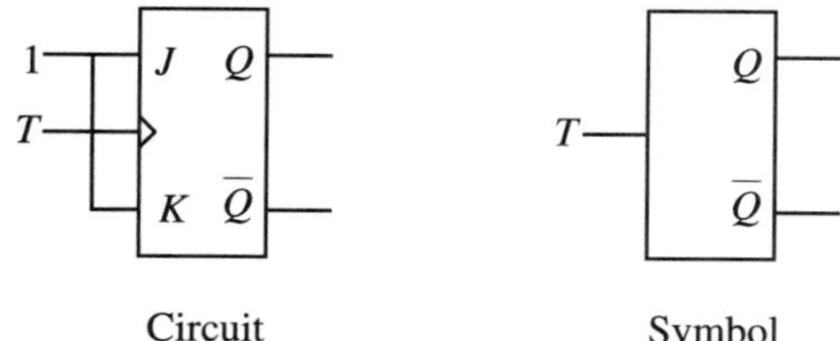

Figure A-50 Logic diagram and symbol for a T flip-flop.

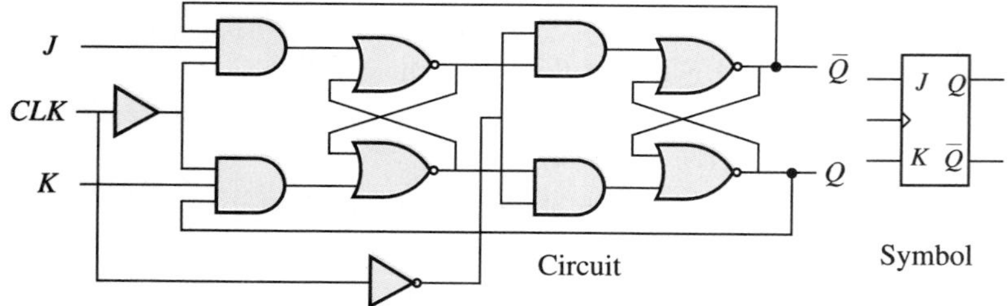

Figure A-51 Logic diagram and symbol for a master-slave J-K flip-flop.

the clocked J-K and T flip-flops are shown in Figures A-49 and A-50, respectively.

A problem with the toggle mode operation for the J-K flip-flop is that when *J* and *K* are both high when the clock is also high, the flip-flop may toggle more than once before the clock goes low. This is another situation in which a master-slave configuration is appropriate. A schematic diagram for a master-slave J-K flip-flop is shown in Figure A-51. The "endless toggle" problem is now fixed with this configuration, but there is a new problem of "ones catching." If an input is high for any time while the clock is high, and if the input is simply in a transition mode before settling, the flip-flop will "see" the 1 as if it was meant to be a valid

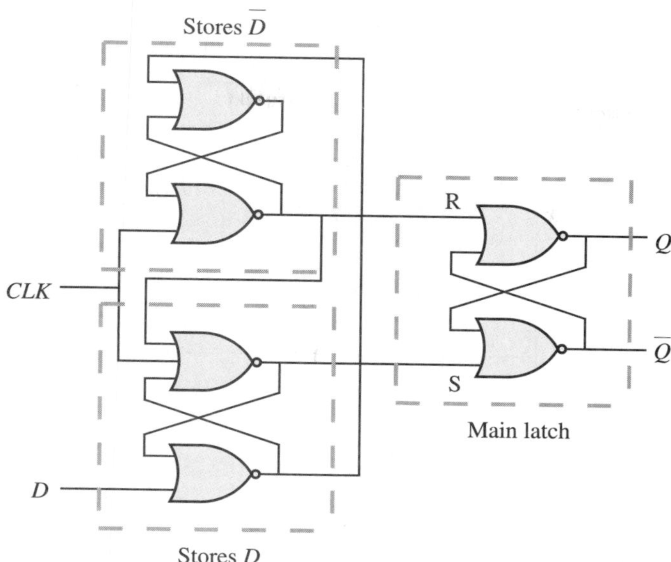

Figure A-52 Negative edge triggered D flip-flop.

input. The situation can be avoided if hazards are eliminated in the circuit that provides the inputs.

We can solve the ones catching problem by constructing edge triggered flip-flops in which only the transition of the clock (low to high for positive edge triggered and high to low for negative edge triggered) causes the inputs to be sampled, at which point the inputs should be stable.

Figure A-52 shows a configuration for a negative edge triggered D flip-flop. When the clock is high, the top and bottom latches output 0's to the main (output) S-R latch. The D input can change an arbitrary number of times while the clock is high without affecting the state of the main latch. When the clock goes low, only the settled values of the top and bottom latches affect the state of the main latch. While the clock is low, if the D input changes, the main flip-flop is not affected.

A.12 Design of Finite State Machines

Refer again to the classical model of an FSM shown in Figure A-40. The delay elements can be implemented with master-slave flip-flops, and the synchronization signal can be provided by the clock. In general, there should be a flip-flop on

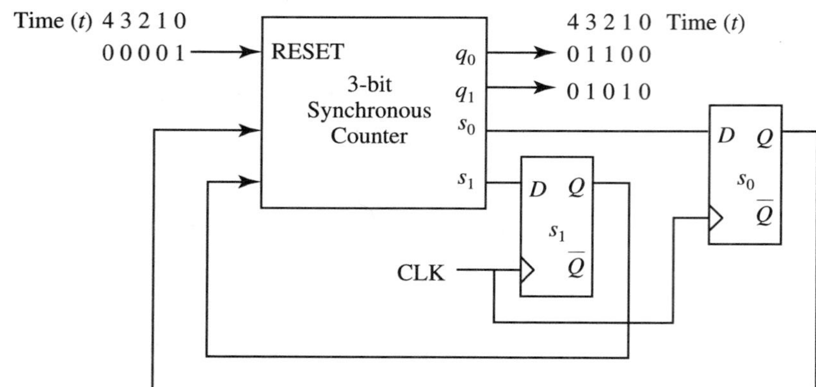

Figure A-53 A modulo(4) counter.

each feedback line. Notice that we can label the flip-flops in any convenient way as long as the meaning is clear. In Figure A-40, the positions of the inputs D_i and the outputs Q_i have been interchanged with respect to the flip-flop figures in the previous section.

Consider a modulo(4) synchronous counter FSM, which counts from 00 to 11 and then repeats. A block diagram of a synchronous counter FSM is shown in Figure A-53. The RESET (positive logic) function operates synchronously with respect to the clock. The outputs appear as a sequence of values on lines q_o and q_1 at time steps corresponding to the clock. As the outputs are generated, a new state s_1s_0 is generated that is fed back to the input.

We can consider designing the counter by enumerating all possible input conditions and then creating four functions for the output q_1q_0 and the state s_1s_0 . The corresponding functions can then be used to create a combinational logic circuit that implements the counter. Two flip-flops are used for the two state bits.

How do we know that two state bits are needed on the feedback path? The fact is, we may not know in advance how many state bits are needed, and so we would like to have a more general approach to designing a finite state machine. For the counter, we can start by constructing a **state transition diagram** as shown in Figure A-54, in which each state represents a count from 00 to 11, and the directed arcs represent transitions between states. State *A* represents the case in which the count is 00, and states *B*, *C*, and *D* represent counts 01, 10, and 11 respectively.

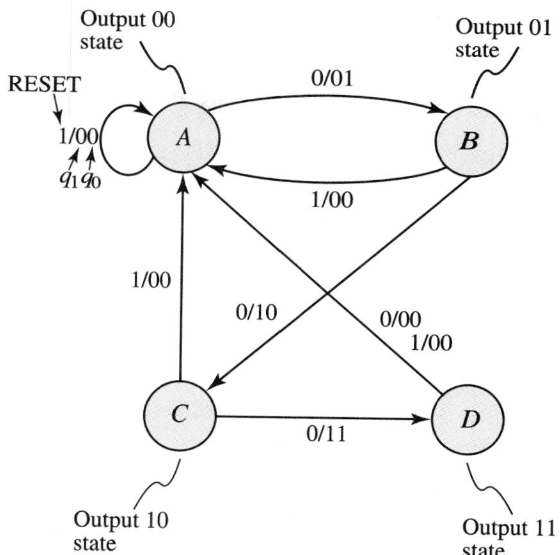

Figure A-54 State transition diagram for a modulo(4) counter.

Present state \ Input	*RESET* 0	*RESET* 1
A	*B*/01	*A*/00
B	*C*/10	*A*/00
C	*D*/11	*A*/00
D	*A*/00	*A*/00

Next state Output

Figure A-55 State table for a modulo(4) counter.

Assume the FSM is initially in state *A*. There are two possible input conditions: 0 or 1. If the input (RESET) line is 0, then the FSM advances to state *B* and outputs 01. If the RESET line is 1, then the FSM remains in state *A* and outputs 00. Similarly, when the FSM is in state *B*, the FSM advances to state *C* and outputs 10 if the RESET line is 0; otherwise the FSM returns to state *A* and outputs 00. Transitions from the remaining states are interpreted similarly.

Once we have created the state transition diagram, we can rewrite it in tabular form as a **state table**, as shown in Figure A-55. The present states are shown at the left, and the input conditions are shown at the top. The entries in the table

Present state (S_t) \ Input	RESET 0	RESET 1
A:00	01/01	00/00
B:01	10/10	00/00
C:10	11/11	00/00
D:11	00/00	00/00

Figure A-56 State table with state assignments for a modulo(4) counter.

RESET $r(t)$	$s_1(t)$	$s_0(t)$	$s_1s_0(t+1)$	$q_1q_0(t+1)$
0	0	0	01	01
0	0	1	10	10
0	1	0	11	11
0	1	1	00	00
1	0	0	00	00
1	0	1	00	00
1	1	0	00	00
1	1	1	00	00

$$s_0(t+1) = \overline{r(t)}\,\overline{s_1(t)}\,\overline{s_0(t)} + \overline{r(t)}s_1(t)\overline{s_0(t)}$$

$$s_1(t+1) = \overline{r(t)}\,\overline{s_1(t)}s_0(t) + \overline{r(t)}s_1(t)\overline{s_0(t)}$$

$$q_0(t+1) = \overline{r(t)}\,\overline{s_1(t)}\,\overline{s_0(t)} + \overline{r(t)}s_1(t)\overline{s_0(t)}$$

$$q_1(t+1) = \overline{r(t)}\,\overline{s_1(t)}s_0(t) + \overline{r(t)}s_1(t)\overline{s_0(t)}$$

Figure A-57 Truth table for the next state and output functions for a modulo(4) counter.

correspond to next state/output pairs, which are taken directly from the state transition diagram in Figure A-54. The highlighted entry corresponds to the case in which the present state is *B* and the input is 0. For this case, the next state is *C* and the next output is 10.

After we have created the state table, we encode the states in binary. Since there are four states, we need at least two bits to uniquely encode the states. We arbitrarily choose the encoding *A* = 00, *B* = 01, *C* = 10, and *D* = 11 and replace every occurrence of *A, B, C,* and *D* with their respective encodings, as shown in Figure A-56. In practice, the state encoding may affect the form of the resulting circuit, but the circuit will be logically correct regardless of the encoding.

From the state table, we can extract truth tables for the next state and output functions, as shown in Figure A-57. The subscripts for the state variables indicate timing relationships; s_t is the present state and s_{t+1} is the next state. The subscripts are commonly omitted since it is understood that the present signals appear on the right side of the equation and the next signals appear on the left side of the equation. Notice that $s_0(t+1) = q_0(t+1)$ and $s_1(t+1) = q_1(t+1)$,

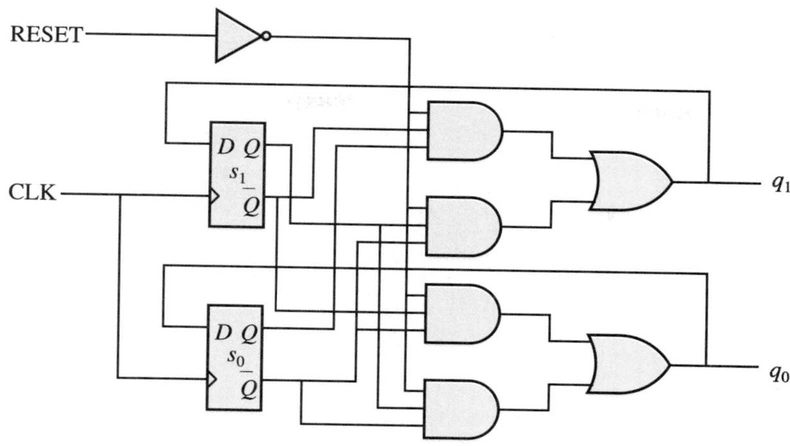

Figure A-58 Logic design for a modulo(4) counter.

so we only need to implement $s_0(t+1)$ and $s_1(t+1)$ and tap the outputs for $q_0(t+1)$ and $q_1(t+1)$.

Finally, we implement the next state and output functions using logic gates and master-slave D flip-flops for the state variables, as shown in Figure A-58.

EXAMPLE: A SEQUENCE DETECTOR

As another example, we would like to design a machine that outputs a 1 when exactly two of the last three inputs are 1. For example, an input sequence of 011011100 produces an output sequence of 001111010. There is a one-bit serial input line, and we can assume that initially no inputs have been seen. For this problem, we will use D flip-flops and 8-to-1 MUXes.

We start by constructing a state transition diagram, as shown in Figure A-59. There are eight possible three-bit sequences that our machine will observe: 000, 001, 010, 011, 100, 101, 110, and 111. State *A* is the initial state, in which we assume that no inputs have yet been seen. In states *B* and *C*, we have seen only one input, so we cannot output a 1 yet. In states *D*, *E*, *F*, and *G* we have only seen two inputs, so we cannot output a 1 yet, even though we have seen two 1's at the input when we enter state *G*. The machine makes all subsequent transitions among states *D*, *E*, *F*, and *G*. State *D* is visited when the last two inputs are 00. States *E*, *F*, and *G* are visited when the last two inputs are 01, 10, or 11, respectively.

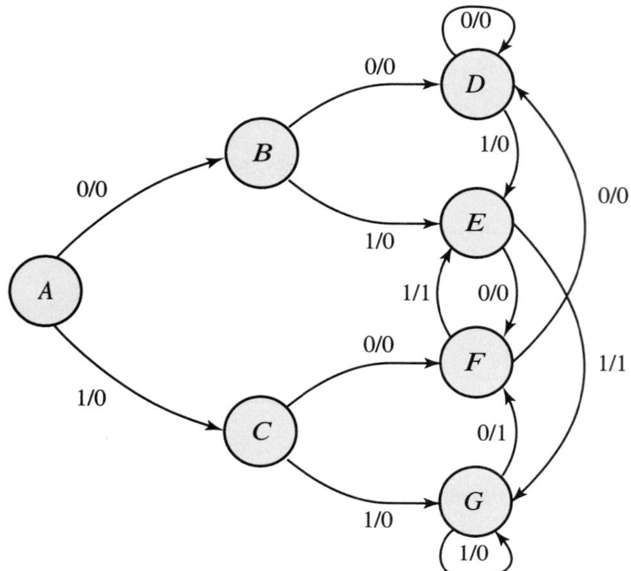

Figure A-59 State transition diagram for sequence detector.

Present state \ Input	X = 0	X = 1
A	*B*/0	*C*/0
B	*D*/0	*E*/0
C	*F*/0	*G*/0
D	*D*/0	*E*/0
E	*F*/0	*G*/1
F	*D*/0	*E*/1
G	*F*/1	*G*/0

Figure A-60 State table for sequence detector.

The next step is to create a state table, as shown in Figure A-60, which is taken directly from the state transition diagram. Next, we make a state assignment, as shown in Figure A-61a. We then use the state assignment to create a truth table for the next state and output functions, as shown in Figure Figure A-61b. The last two entries in the table correspond to state 111, which cannot arise in practice, according to the state table in Figure A-61a. Therefore, the next state and output entries do not matter and are labeled as 'd' for **don't care**.

Present state \ Input	X = 0	X = 1
$s_2 s_1 s_0$	$s_2 s_1 s_0 z$	$s_2 s_1 s_0 z$
A: 000	001/0	010/0
B: 001	011/0	100/0
C: 010	101/0	110/0
D: 011	011/0	100/0
E: 100	101/0	110/1
F: 101	011/0	100/1
G: 110	101/1	110/0

(a)

Input and state at time t				Next state and output at time t+1			
s_2	s_1	s_0	x	s_2	s_1	s_0	z
0	0	0	0	0	0	1	0
0	0	0	1	0	1	0	0
0	0	1	0	0	1	1	0
0	0	1	1	1	0	0	0
0	1	0	0	1	0	1	0
0	1	0	1	1	1	0	0
0	1	1	0	0	1	1	0
0	1	1	1	1	0	0	0
1	0	0	0	1	0	1	0
1	0	0	1	1	1	0	1
1	0	1	0	0	1	1	0
1	0	1	1	1	0	0	1
1	1	0	0	1	0	1	1
1	1	0	1	1	1	0	0
1	1	1	0	d	d	d	d
1	1	1	1	d	d	d	d

(b)

Figure A-61 State assignment and truth table for sequence detector.

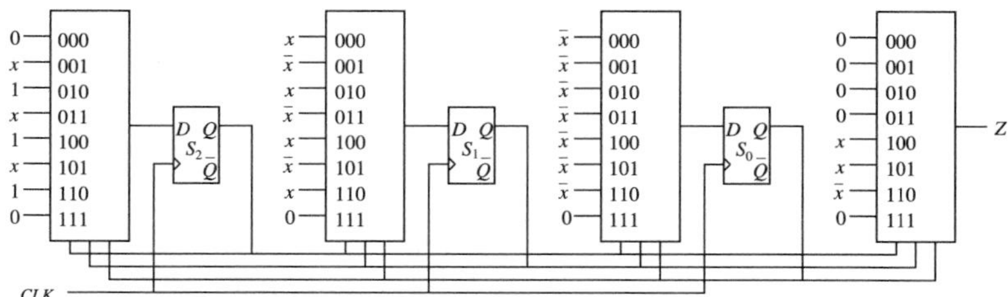

Figure A-62 Logic diagram for sequence detector.

Finally, we create the circuit, which is shown in Figure A-62. There is one flip-flop for each state variable, so there are a total of three flip-flops. There are three next state functions and one output function, so there are four MUXes. Notice that the choice of s_2, s_1, and s_0 for the MUX control inputs is arbitrary. Any other grouping or ordering will also work.

EXAMPLE: A VENDING MACHINE CONTROLLER

For this problem, we will design a vending machine controller using D flip-flops and a black box representation of a PLA (as in Figure A-35). The vending machine accepts three U.S. coins: the nickel (5¢), the dime (10¢), and the quarter (25¢). When the value of the inserted coins equals or exceeds 20¢, then the machine dispenses the merchandise, returns any excess money, and waits for the next transaction.

We begin by constructing a state transition diagram, as shown in Figure A-63. In state *A*, no coins have yet been inserted, and so the money credited is 0¢. If a nickel or dime is inserted when the machine is in state *A*, then the FSM makes a transition to state *B* or state *C*, respectively. If a quarter is inserted, then the money credited to the customer is 25¢. The controller dispenses the merchandise, returns a nickel in change, and remains in state *A*. This is indicated by the label "*Q*/110" on the state *A* self-loop. States *B* and *C* are then expanded, producing state *D*, which is also expanded, producing the complete FSM for the vending machine controller.

Notice the behavior that is specified by the state transition diagram when a quarter is inserted when the FSM is in state *D*. Rather than dispensing product, returning 20¢, and returning to state A, the machine dispenses product, returns 15¢, and makes a transition to state B. The machine keeps the 5¢ and awaits the

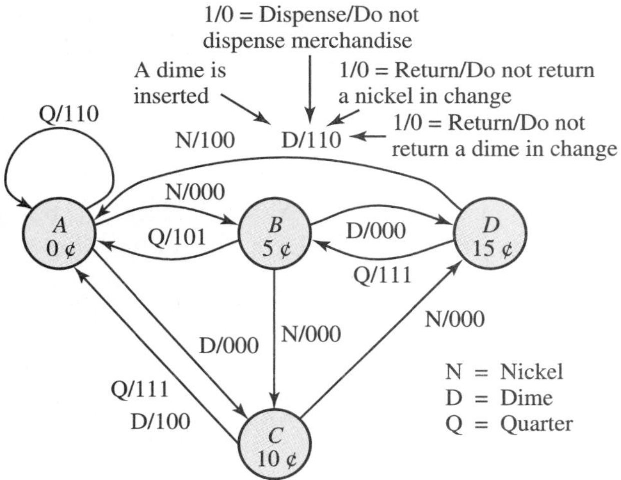

Figure A-63 State transition diagram for vending machine controller.

Input / P.S.	N 00	D 01	Q 10
A	*B*/000	*C*/000	*A*/110
B	*C*/000	*D*/000	*A*/101
C	*D*/000	*A*/100	*A*/111
D	*A*/100	*A*/110	*B*/111

(a)

Input / P.S.	N x_1x_0 00	D x_1x_0 01	Q x_1x_0 10
s_1s_0		s_1s_0 / $z_2z_1z_0$	
A:00	01/000	10/000	00/110
B:01	10/000	11/000	00/101
C:10	11/000	00/100	00/111
D:11	00/100	00/110	01/111

(b)

Figure A-64 (a) State table for vending machine controller; (b) state assignment for vending machine controller.

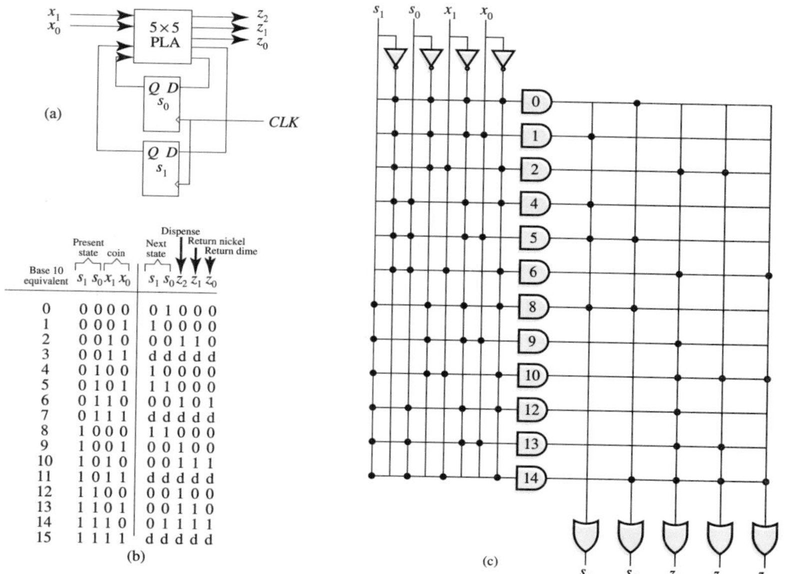

Base 10 equivalent	Present state s_1 s_0 / coin x_1 x_0	Next state s_1 s_0 / Dispense z_2 / Return nickel z_1 / Return dime z_0
0	0 0 0 0	0 1 0 0 0
1	0 0 0 1	1 0 0 0 0
2	0 0 1 0	0 0 1 1 0
3	0 0 1 1	d d d d d
4	0 1 0 0	1 0 0 0 0
5	0 1 0 1	1 1 0 0 0
6	0 1 1 0	0 0 1 0 1
7	0 1 1 1	d d d d d
8	1 0 0 0	1 1 0 0 0
9	1 0 0 1	0 0 1 0 0
10	1 0 1 0	0 0 1 1 1
11	1 0 1 1	d d d d d
12	1 1 0 0	0 0 1 0 0
13	1 1 0 1	0 0 1 1 0
14	1 1 1 0	0 1 1 1 1
15	1 1 1 1	d d d d d

(b)

Figure A-65 (a) FSM circuit, (b) truth table, and (c) PLA realization for vending machine controller.

insertion of more money! In this case, the authors allowed this behavior for the sake of simplicity, as it keeps the number of states down.

From the FSM we construct the state table shown in Figure A-64a. We then make an arbitrary state assignment and encode the symbols N, D, and Q in binary, as shown in Figure A-64b. Finally, we create a circuit diagram, which is shown in Figure A-65a. There are two state bits, so there are two D flip-flops.

The PLA takes four inputs for the present-state bits and the x_1x_0 coin bits. The PLA produces five outputs for the next-state bits and the dispense and return nickel/return dime bits. (We can assume that the clock input is asserted only on an event such as an inserted coin.)

Notice that we have not explicitly specified the design of the PLA itself in obtaining the FSM circuit in Figure A-65a. At this level of complexity, it is common to use a computer program to generate a truth table and then feed the truth table to a PLA design program. We could generate the truth table and PLA design by hand, of course, as shown in Figures A-65b and A-65c.

A.13 Mealy *versus* Moore Machines

The outputs of the FSM circuits we have studied so far are determined by the present states and the inputs. The states are maintained in falling edge triggered flip-flops, and so a state change can only occur on the falling edge of the clock. Any changes that occur at the inputs have no effect on the state as long as the clock is low. The inputs are fed directly through the output circuits, however, with no intervening flip-flops. Thus a change to an input at any time can cause a change in the output, regardless of whether the clock is high or low. In Figure A-65, a change at either the x_1 or x_0 inputs will propagate through to the $z_2z_1z_0$ outputs independent of the level of the clock. This organization is referred to as the **Mealy** model of an FSM.

In the Mealy model, the outputs change as soon as the inputs change, and so there is no delay introduced by the clock. In the **Moore** model of an FSM, the outputs are embedded in the state bits, and so a change at the outputs occurs on the clock pulse *after* a change at the inputs. Both models are used by circuit designers, and either model may be encountered outside of this textbook. In this section we simply highlight the differences through an example.

An example of a Moore FSM is shown in Figure A-66. The FSM counts from 0 to 3 in binary and then repeats, similar to the modulo(4) counter shown in Figure A-58. The machine only counts when $x = 1$; otherwise the FSM maintains its current state. Notice that the outputs are embedded in the state variables, and so there is no direct path from the input to the outputs without an intervening flip-flop.

The Mealy model might be considered to be more powerful than the Moore model because in a single clock cycle, a change in the output of one FSM can

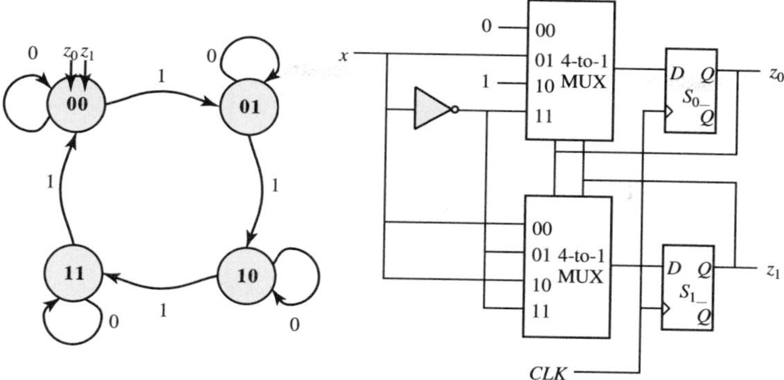

Figure A-66 A Moore binary counter FSM.

ripple to the input of another FSM, whose output then changes and ripples to the next FSM, and so on. In the Moore model, lock-step synchronization is strictly maintained, and so this ripple scenario does not occur. Spurious changes in the output of an FSM thus have less influence on the rest of the circuit in the Moore model. This simplifies circuit analysis and hardware debugging, and for these situations the Moore model may be preferred. In practice, both models are used.

A.14 Registers

A single bit of information is stored in a D flip-flop. A group of N bits, making up an N-bit word, can be stored in N D flip-flops organized as shown in Figure A-67 for a four-bit word. We refer to such an arrangement of flip-flops as a "register." In this particular configuration, the data at inputs D_i are loaded into the register when the Write and Enable lines are high, synchronous with the clock. The contents of the register can be read at outputs Q_i only if the Enable line is

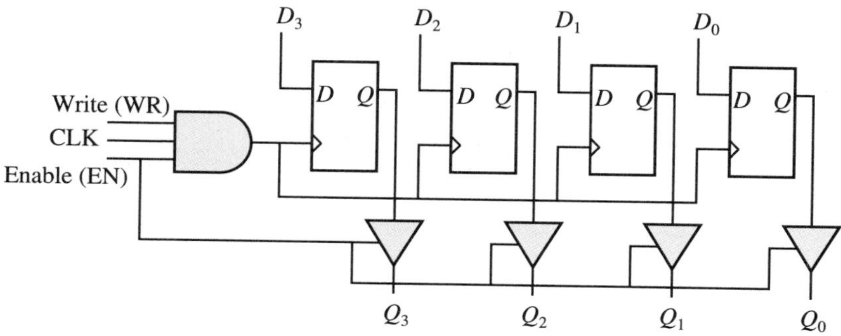

Figure A-67 A four-bit register.

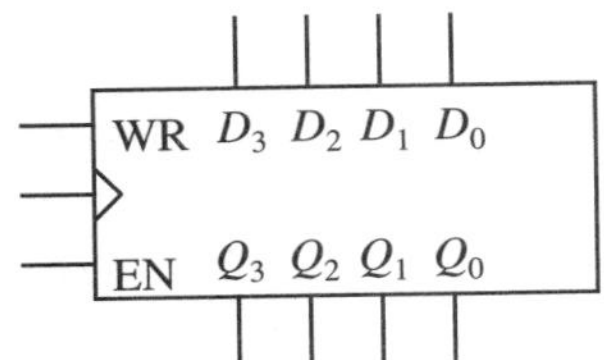

Figure A-68 Abstract representation of a four-bit register.

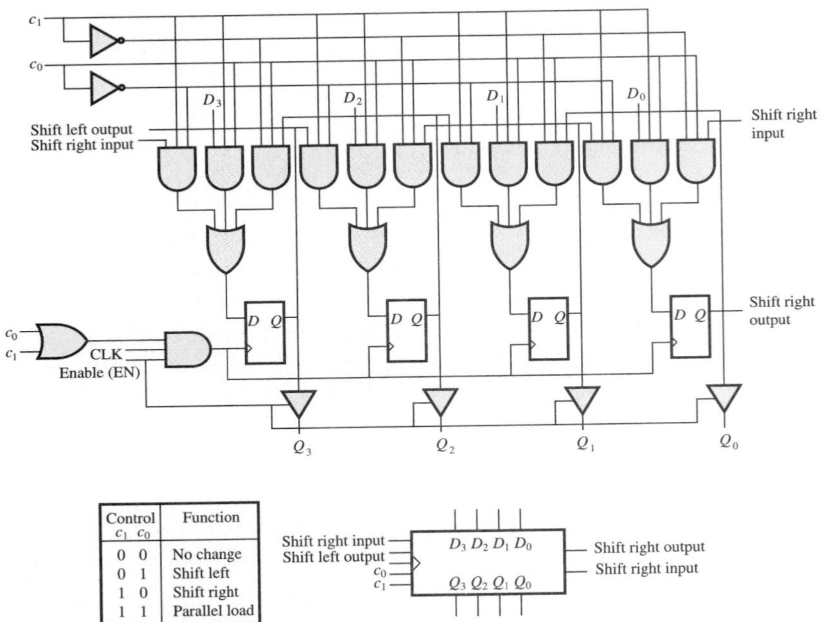

Control c_1 c_0	Function
0 0	No change
0 1	Shift left
1 0	Shift right
1 1	Parallel load

Figure A-69 Internal layout and block diagram for a left/right shifter with parallel read/write capabilities.

high, since the tri-state buffers are in the electrically disconnected state when the Enable line is low. We can simplify the illustration by just marking the inputs and outputs, as shown in Figure A-68.

A **shift register** copies the contents of each of its flip-flops to the next while accepting a new input at one end and "spilling" the contents at the other end, which makes cascading possible. Consider the shift register shown in Figure A-69. The register can shift to the left, shift to the right, accept a parallel load, or remain unchanged, all synchronous with the clock. The parallel load and parallel read capabilities allow the shift register to function as either a **serial-to-parallel converter** or as a **parallel-to-serial converter**.

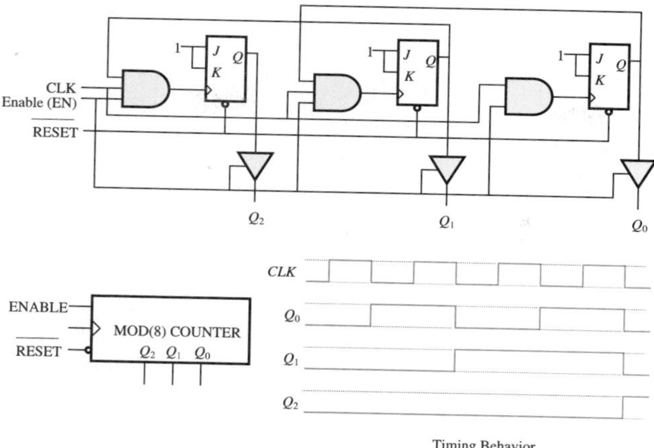

Figure A-70 A modulo(8) counter.

A.15 Counters

A **counter** is a different form of a register in which the output pattern sequences through a range of binary numbers. Figure A-70 shows a configuration for a modulo(8) counter that steps through the binary patterns 000, 001, 010, 011, 100, 101, 110, 111 and then repeats. Three J-K flip-flops are placed in toggle mode, and each clock input is ANDed with the Q output from the previous stage, which successively halves the clock frequency. The result is a progression of toggle flip-flops operating at rates that differ in powers of two, corresponding to the sequence of binary patterns from 000 to 111.

Notice that we have added an active low asynchronous RESET line to the counter, which resets it to 000, independent of the states of the clock or enable lines. Except for the flip-flop in the least significant position, the remaining flip-flops change state according to changes in states from their neighbors to the right rather than synchronous with respect to the clock. It is similar in function to the modulo(4) counter in Figure A-58 but is more easily extended to large sizes because it is not treated like an ordinary FSM for design purposes, in which all states are enumerated. It is, nevertheless, an FSM.

SUMMARY

In theory, any Boolean function can be represented as a truth table, which can then be transformed into a two-level Boolean equation and implemented with logic gates. In practice, collections of logic gates may be grouped together to form

MSI components, which contain on the order of a few to a few dozen logic gates. MUXes and PLAs are two types of MSI components that are used for implementing functions. Decoders are used for enabling a single output line based on the bit pattern at the input, which translates a logical encoding into a spatial location. There are several other types of MSI components as well. We find ourselves using MSI components in abstracting away the gate level complexity of a digital circuit. LSI and VLSI circuits abstract away the underlying circuit complexity at higher levels still.

A finite state machine (FSM) differs from a combinational logic unit (CLU) in that the outputs of a CLU at any time are strictly a function of the inputs at that time whereas the outputs of an FSM are a function of its past history of inputs.

Further Reading

Shannon's contributions to switching algebra (Shannon, 1938; Shannon, 1949) are based on the work of (Boole, 1854) and form the basis of switching theory as we now know it. There is a vast number of contributions to Boolean algebra that are too great to enumerate here. (Kohavi, 1978) is a good general reference for CLUs and FSMs. A contribution by (Davidson, 1979) covers a method of decomposing NAND-based circuits, which is of interest because some computers are composed entirely of NAND gates.

(Xilinx, 1992) covers the philosophy and practical aspects of the gate array approach and describes configurations of the Xilinx line of **field programmable gate arrays** (FPGAs).

Some texts distinguish between a flip-flop and a latch. (Tanenbaum, 1999) distinguishes between the two by defining a flip-flop to be edge triggered, whereas a latch is level triggered. This may be the correct definition, but in practice, the terms are frequently interchanged and any distinction between the two is obscured.

Boole, G., *An Investigation of the Laws of Thought*, Dover Publications, Inc. (1854).

Davidson, E. S., "An algorithm for NAND Decomposition under Network Constraints," *IEEE Trans. Comp.*, **C-18**, 1098 (1979).

Kohavi, Z., *Switching and Finite Automata Theory*, 2/e, McGraw-Hill (1978).

Shannon, C. E., "A Symbolic Analysis of Relay and Switching Circuits," *Trans. American Institute of Electrical Engineers*, **57**, pp. 713–723 (1938).

Shannon, C. E., "The Synthesis of Two-Terminal Switching Circuits," *Bell System Technical Journal*, **28**, pp. 59–98 (1949).

Tanenbaum, A., *Structured Computer Organization*, 4/e, Prentice Hall (1999).

Xilinx, *The Programmable Gate Array Data Book*, Xilinx, Inc., 2100 Logic Drive, San Jose, California (1992).

PROBLEMS

A.1 Figure A-13 shows an OR gate implemented with a NAND gate and inverters, and Figure A-14 shows inverters implemented with NAND gates. Show the logic diagram for an AND gate implemented entirely with NAND gates.

A.2 Draw logic diagrams for each member of the computationally complete set {AND, OR, NOT} using only the computationally complete set {NOR}.

A.3 Given the logic circuit shown, construct a truth table that describes its behavior.

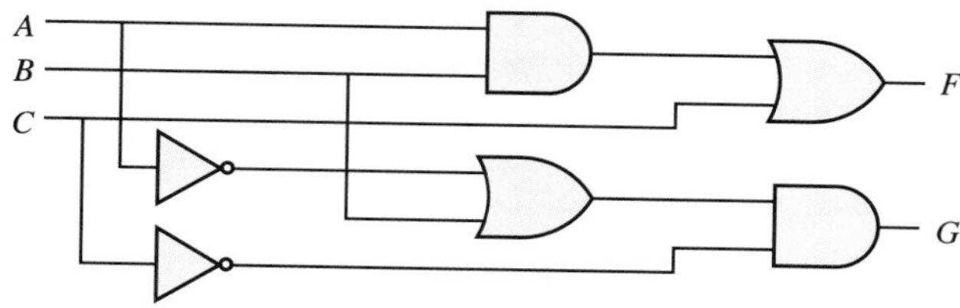

A.4 Construct a truth table for a three-input XOR gate.

A.5 Compute the gate input count of the 4-to-2 priority encoder shown in Figure A-32. Include the inverters in your count.

A.6 Design a circuit that implements function *f* below using AND, OR, and NOT gates. $f(A, B, C) = \bar{A}BC + \bar{A}\bar{B}\bar{C} + AB\bar{C}$

A.7 Design a circuit that implements function *g* below using AND, OR, and NOT gates. Do not attempt to change the form of the equation.

$$g(A, B, C, D, E) = A(BC + \overline{B}\overline{C}) + B(CD + E)$$

A.8 Are the following functions f and g equivalent? Show how you arrive at your answer.

$$f(A, B, C) = ABC + \overline{A}B\overline{C} \qquad g(A, B, C) = (A \oplus C)B$$

A.9 Write a Boolean equation that describes function F in the circuit shown.

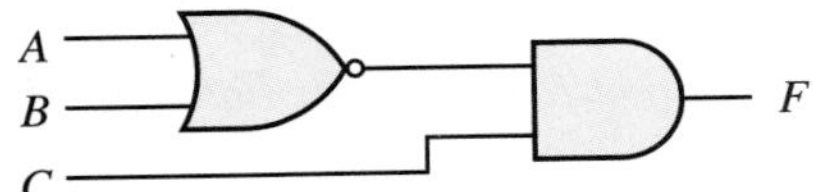

Put your answer in SOP form (without parentheses).

A.10 A four-bit **comparator** is a component that takes two four-bit words as inputs and produces a single bit of output. The output is a 0 if the words are identical and is a 1 otherwise. Design a four-bit comparator with any of the logic gates you have seen in this appendix. *Hint*: Think of the four-bit comparator as four one-bit comparators combined in some fashion.

A.11 Redraw the circuit shown so that the bubble matching is correct. The overbars on the variable and function names indicate active low logic.

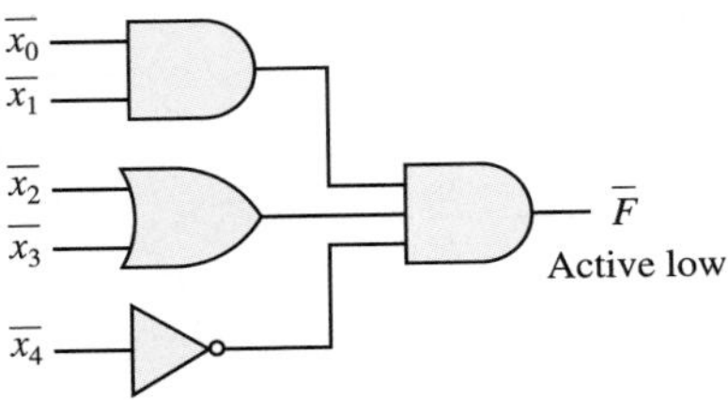

A.12 Use two 4-to-1 MUXes to implement the following functions:

A	B	F_0	F_1
0	0	0	0
0	1	1	0
1	0	1	0
1	1	0	1

A.13 Use one 4-to-1 MUX to implement the majority function.

A.14 Use a 2-to-4 decoder and an OR gate to implement the XOR of two inputs *A* and *B*.

A.15 Draw a logic diagram that uses a decoder and two OR gates to implement the following functions *F* and *G*. Be sure to label all lines in your diagram.

$$F(A, B, C) = \bar{A}B\bar{C} + \bar{A}\bar{B}C + A\bar{B}C + \bar{A}BC$$

$$G(A, B, C) = \bar{A}B\bar{C} + ABC$$

A.16 Design a circuit using only 2-to-1 multiplexers that implements the function of an 8-to-1 multiplexer. Show your design in the form of a logic diagram, and label all of the lines.

A.17 Since any combinational circuit can be constructed using only two-input NAND gates, the two-input NAND is called a universal logic gate. The two-input NOR is also a universal logic gate; however, AND and OR are not. Since a two-input NAND can be constructed using only 4-to-1 MUXes (it can be done with one 4-to-1 MUX), any combinational circuit can be constructed using only 4-to-1 MUXes. Consequently, the 4-to-1 MUX is also a universal device. Show that the 1-to-2 DEMUX is a universal device by constructing a two-input NAND using only 1-to-2 DEMUXes. Draw a logic diagram. *Hint*: Compose the NAND from an AND and an inverter each made from 1-to-2 DEMUXes.

A.18 A seven-segment display, like you might find in a calculator, is shown. The seven segments are labeled a through g. Design a circuit that takes as input a four-bit binary number and produces as output the control signal for just the b segment (not the letter 'b', which has the 1011 code). A 0 at the output turns the segment off, and a 1 turns the segment on. Show the truth table and an implementation using a single MUX, and no other logic components. Label all of the lines of the MUX.

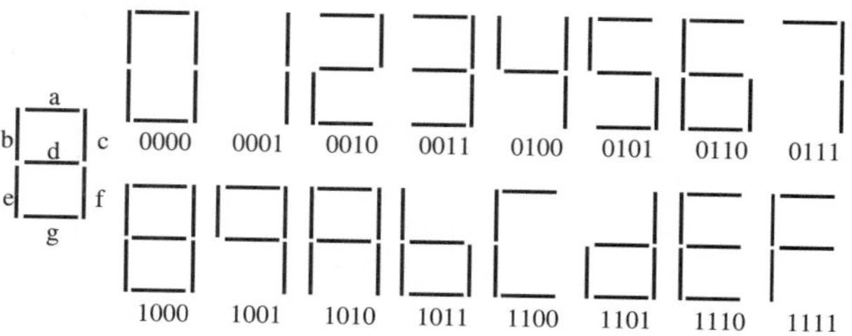

A.19 Implement function F shown in the following truth table using the 16-to-1 MUX shown. Label all of the lines, including the unmarked control line.

A	B	C	F
0	0	0	0
0	0	1	1
0	1	0	1
0	1	1	0
1	0	0	0
1	0	1	0
1	1	0	0
1	1	1	1

A.20 A **strict encoder** takes 2^N binary inputs, of which exactly one input is 1 at any time and the remaining inputs are 0, and produces an N-bit coded binary output that indicates which of the N inputs is high. For this problem, create a truth table for a 4-to-2 strict encoder in which there are four inputs: A, B, C, and D, and two outputs: X and Y. A and X are the most significant bits.

A.21 Consider a combinational logic circuit with three inputs a, b, and c, and six outputs u, v, w, x, y, and z. The input is an unsigned number between 0 and 7, and the output is the square of the input. The most significant bit of the input is a, and the most significant bit of the output is u. Create a truth table for the six functions.

A.22 Consider the function $f(a, b, c, d)$ that takes on the value 1 if and only if the number of 1's in b and c is greater than or equal to the number of 1's in a and d.

(a) Write the truth table for function f.

(b) Use an 8-to-1 multiplexer to implement function f.

A.23 Create a truth table for a single-digit ternary (base 3) comparator. The ternary inputs are A and B, which are each a single ternary digit wide. The output Z is 0 for $A < B$, 1 for $A = B$, and 2 for $A > B$. Using this truth table as a guide, rewrite the truth table in binary using the assignment $(0)_3 \rightarrow (00)_2$, $(1)_3 \rightarrow (01)_2$, and $(2)_3 \rightarrow (10)_2$.

A.24 Prove the consensus theorem for three variables using perfect induction.

A.25 Use the properties of Boolean algebra to prove DeMorgan's theorem algebraically.

A.26 Can an S-R flip-flop be constructed with two cross-coupled XOR gates? Explain your answer.

A.27 Modify the state transition diagram in the vending machine example to provide more realistic behavior (that is, it returns *all* excess money) when a quarter is inserted in state D.

A.28 Create a state transition diagram for an FSM that sorts two binary words A and B, most significant bit first, onto two binary outputs GE and LT. If A is greater than or equal to B, then A appears on the GE line and B appears on the LT line. If B is greater than A, then B appears on the GE line and A appears on the LT line.

A.29 Design a circuit that produces a 1 at the Z output when the input X changes from 0 to 1 or from 1 to 0, and produces a zero at all other times. For the initial state, assume a 0 was last seen at the input. For example, if the input sequence is 00110 (from left to right), then the output sequence is 00101. Show the state transition diagram, the state table, state assignment, and the final circuit using MUXes.

A.30 Design an FSM that outputs a 1 when the last three inputs are 011 or 110. Just show the state table. Do not draw a circuit.

A.31 Design a finite state machine that takes two binary words X and Y in serial form, least significant bit (LSB) first, and produces a 1-bit output Z that is true when $X > Y$ and is 0 for $X \leq Y$. When the machine starts, assume that $X = Y$. That is, Z produces 0's until $X > Y$. A sample input sequence and the corresponding output sequence are shown.

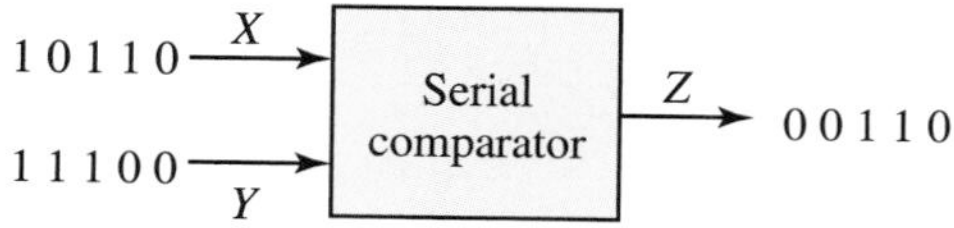

A.32 Create a state transition diagram for an FSM that sorts two ternary inputs, most significant digit first, onto two ternary outputs *GE* and *LT*. If *A* is greater than or equal to *B*, then *A* appears on the *GE* line and *B* appears on the *LT* line, otherwise *B* appears on the *GE* line and *A* appears on the *LT* line. A sample input/output sequence is shown. Use the ternary symbols 0, 1, and 2 when you label the arcs.

Input A:	0 2 1 1 2 0 1 2
Input B:	0 2 1 2 0 2 1 1
Output GE:	0 2 1 2 0 2 1 1
Output LT:	0 2 1 1 2 0 1 2
Time:	0 1 2 3 4 5 6 7

A.33 Create a state transition diagram for a machine that computes an even parity bit *z* for its two-bit input x_1x_0. The machine outputs a 0 when all of the previous two-bit inputs collectively have an even number of 1's, and outputs a 1 otherwise. For the initial state, assume that the machine starts with even parity.

A.34 Given the state transition diagram shown,

(a) Create a state table.

(b) Design a circuit for the state machine described by your state table using D flip-flop(s), a single decoder, and OR gates. For the state assignment, use the bit pattern that corresponds to the position of each letter in the alphabet, starting from 0. For example, *A* is at position 0, so the state assignment is 000; *B* is at position 1, so the state assignment is 001, and so on.

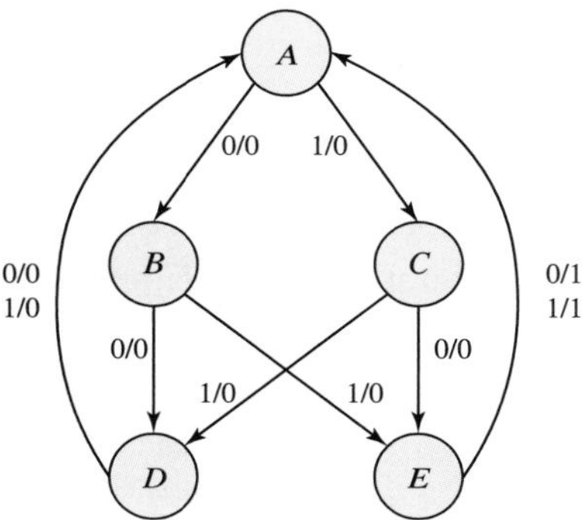

A.35 Redraw the circuit shown in Figure A-16 using AND and OR gates that have fan-in = 2.

A.36 Suppose that you need to implement an N-input AND gate using only three-input AND gates. What is the minimum number of gate delays required to implement the N-input AND gate? A single AND gate has a gate delay of 1; two cascaded AND gates have a combined gate delay of 2, etc.

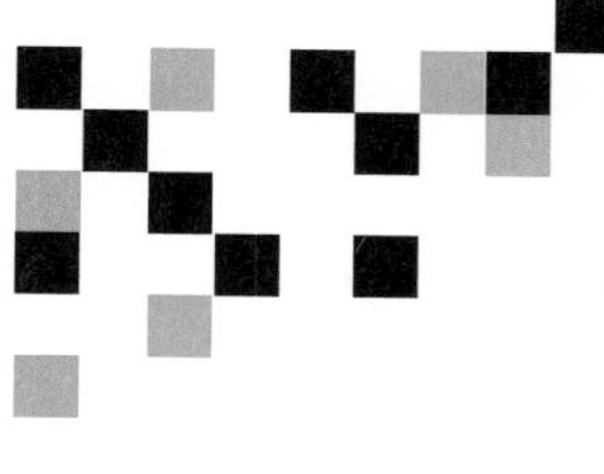

B

APPENDIX B: REDUCTION OF DIGITAL LOGIC

B.1 Reduction of Combinational Logic and Sequential Logic

In Appendix A, we focused primarily on the functional correctness of digital logic circuits. Only a small amount of consideration was given to the possibility that there may be more than one way to design a circuit, with some designs being better than others in terms of component count (that is, the numbers and sizes of the logic gates).

In this appendix, we take a systematic approach to reducing the numbers of components in a design. We first look at reducing the sizes of combinational logic expressions, which loosely correspond to the numbers and sizes of the logic gates in an implementation of a digital circuit. We then look at reducing the numbers of states in finite state machines (FSMs) and explore a few areas of FSM design that impact the numbers and sizes of logic gates in implementations of FSMs.

B.2 Reduction of Two-Level Expressions

It many cases the canonical **sum-of-products** (SOP) or **product-of-sums** (POS) forms are not minimal in terms of their number and size. Since a smaller Boolean equation translates to a lower gate input count in the target circuit, reduction of the equation is an important consideration when circuit complexity is an issue.

Three methods of reducing Boolean equations are described in the sections that follow: **algebraic reduction**, **Karnaugh map (K-map) reduction**, and **tabular reduction**. The algebraic method forms the basis for the other two methods. It is also the most abstract method, relying as it does on only the theorems of Boolean algebra.

The K-map and tabular methods are in fact pencil-and-paper implementations of the algebraic method. We discuss them because they allow the student to visualize the reduction process and thus to have a better intuition for how the process works. These manual processes can be used effectively to minimize functions that have (about) six or fewer variables. For larger functions, a computer-aided design (CAD) approach is generally more effective.

B.2.1 *THE ALGEBRAIC METHOD*

The algebraic method applies the properties of Boolean algebra that were introduced in Section A.5 in a systematic manner to reduce expression size. Consider the Boolean equation for the majority function, which is repeated from Appendix A:

$$F = \bar{A}BC + A\bar{B}C + AB\bar{C} + ABC \qquad \text{(B-1)}$$

The properties of Boolean algebra can be applied to reduce the equation to a simpler form, as shown in Equations (B-4) through (B-4):

$$F = \bar{A}BC + A\bar{B}C + AB(\bar{C} + C) \qquad \text{Distributive property} \qquad \text{(B-2)}$$

$$F = \bar{A}BC + A\bar{B}C + AB(1) \qquad \text{Complement property} \qquad \text{(B-3)}$$

$$F = \bar{A}BC + A\bar{B}C + AB \qquad \text{Identity property} \qquad \text{(B-4)}$$

The corresponding circuit for Equation (B-4) is shown in Figure B-1. In comparison with the majority circuit shown in Figure A-16, the gate count is reduced from 8 to 6 and the gate input count is reduced from 19 to 13.

We can reduce Equation (B-4) further. By applying the property of idempotence, we obtain Equation (B-5), in which we have reintroduced the minterm *ABC*.

$$F = \bar{A}BC + A\bar{B}C + AB + ABC \qquad \text{Idempotence property} \qquad \text{(B-5)}$$

We can then apply the distributive, complement, and identity properties again and obtain a simpler equation, as follows:

$$F = \bar{A}BC + AC(\bar{B} + B) + AB \qquad \text{Distributive property} \qquad \text{(B-6)}$$

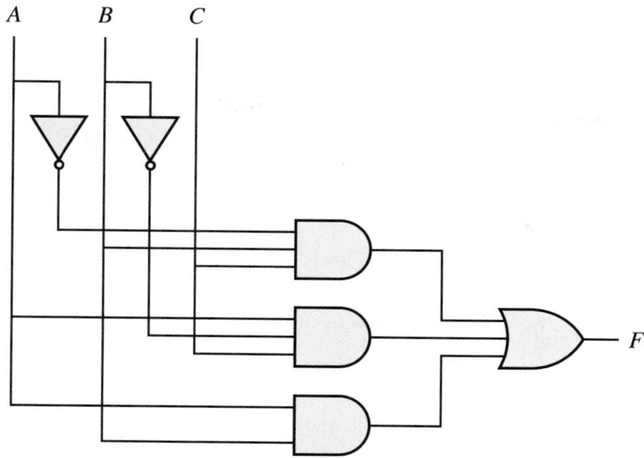

Figure B-1 Reduced circuit for the majority function.

$F = \bar{A}BC + AC(1) + AB$	Complement property	(B-7)
$F = \bar{A}BC + AC + AB$	Identity property	(B-8)

Equation (B-8) has a smaller gate input count of 11. We iterate this method one more time and reduce the equation further, as shown:

$F = \bar{A}BC + AC + AB + ABC$	Idempotence property	(B-9)
$F = BC(\bar{A} + A) + AC + AB$	Distributive property	(B-10)
$F = BC(1) + AC + AB$	Complement property	(B-11)
$F = BC + AC + AB$	Identity property	(B-12)

Equation (B-12) is now in its minimal two-level form and can be reduced no further.

B.2.2 *THE K-MAP METHOD*

The K-map method is, in effect, a graphical technique that can be used to visualize the minterms in a function along with variables that are common to them. Variables that are common to more than one minterm are candidates for elimi-

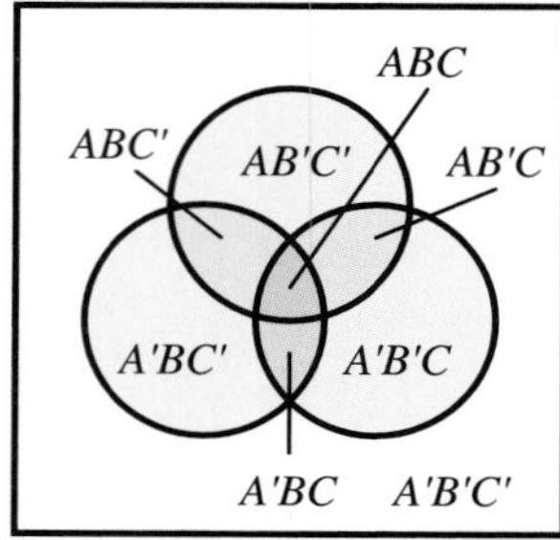

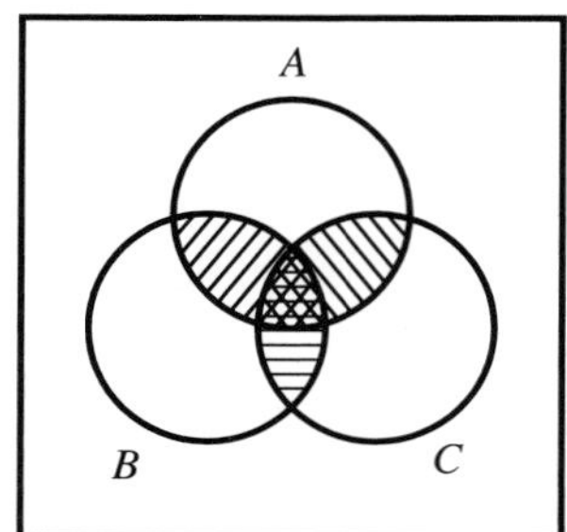

Figure B-2 A Venn diagram representation for three binary variables (left) and for the majority function (right).

C \ AB	00	01	11	10
0			1	
1		1	1	1

Figure B-3 A K-map for the majority function.

nation, as discussed previously. The basis of the K-map is the *Venn diagram*, which was originally devised to visualize concepts in set theory.

The Venn diagram for binary variables consists of a rectangle that represents the binary universe in SOP form. A Venn diagram for three variables *A*, *B*, and *C* is shown in Figure B-2. Within the universe is a circle for each variable. Within its circle a variable has the value 1, and outside of its circle a variable has the value 0. Intersections represent the minterms, as shown in the figure.

Adjacent shaded regions are candidates for reduction since they vary in exactly one variable. In the figure, region *ABC* can be combined with each of the three adjacent regions to produce a reduced form of the majority function. The K-map is just a topological, or relationship-preserving, transformation of the Venn diagram. As in the Venn diagram, in the K-map, minterms that differ in exactly one variable are placed next to each other.

A K-map for the majority function is shown in Figure B-3. Each cell in the K-map corresponds to an entry in the truth table for the function, and since there are eight entries in the truth table, there are eight cells in the corresponding K-map. A 1 is placed in each cell that corresponds to a true entry. A 0 is entered

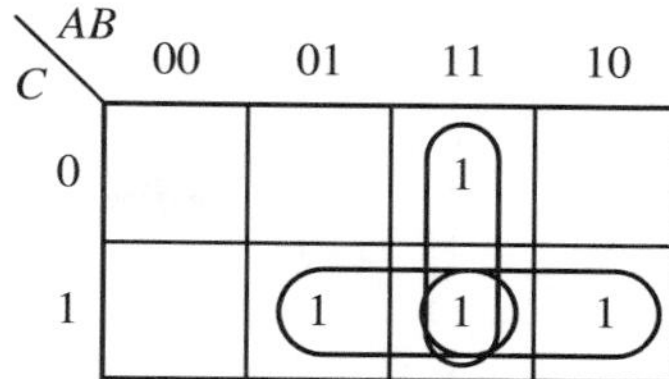

Figure B-4 Adjacency groupings for the majority function.

in each remaining cell but can be omitted from the K-map for clarity as it is here. The labeling along the top and left sides is arranged in a **Gray code**, in which exactly one variable changes between adjacent cells along each dimension.

Adjacent 1's in the K-map satisfy the condition needed to apply the complement property of Boolean algebra. Since there are adjacent 1's in the K-map shown in Figure B-3, a reduction is possible. Groupings of adjacent cells are made into rectangles in sizes that correspond to powers of 2, such as 1, 2, 4 and 8. These groups are referred to as **prime implicants**. As groups increase in size above a 1-group (a group with one member), more variables are eliminated from a Boolean expression, and so the largest groups that can be obtained are used. In order to maintain the adjacency property, the shapes of groups must always be rectangular, and each group must contain a number of cells that corresponds to an integral power of two.

We start the reduction process by creating groups for 1's *that can be contained in no larger group* and progress to larger groups until all cells with a 1 are covered at least once. The adjacency criterion is crucial, since we are looking for groups of minterms that differ in such a way that a reduction can be applied by using the complement and identity properties of Boolean algebra, as in Equation (B-13):

$$ABC + AB\overline{C} = AB(C + \overline{C}) = AB(1) = AB \tag{B-13}$$

For the majority function, three groups of size two are made, as shown in Figure B-4. Every cell with a 1 has at least one neighboring cell with a 1, and so there are no 1-groups. We look next at 2-groups and find that all of the 1-cells are covered by 2-groups. One of the cells is included in all three groups, which is allowed in the reduction process by the property of idempotence. The complement property eliminates the variable that differs between cells, and the resulting minimized equation is obtained [Equation (B-14)]:

$$M = BC + AC + AB \tag{B-14}$$

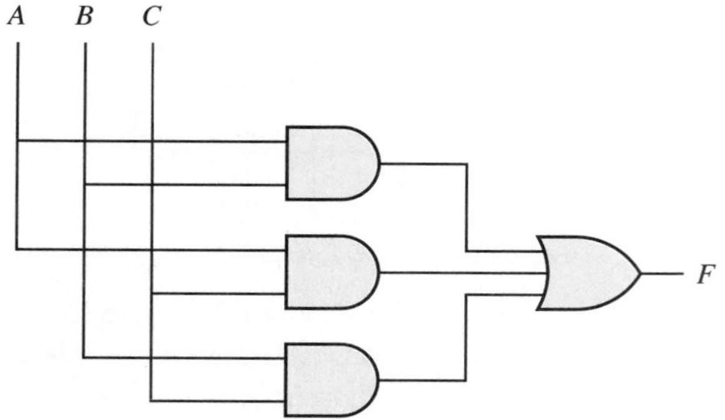

Figure B-5 Minimized AND-OR circuit for the majority function.

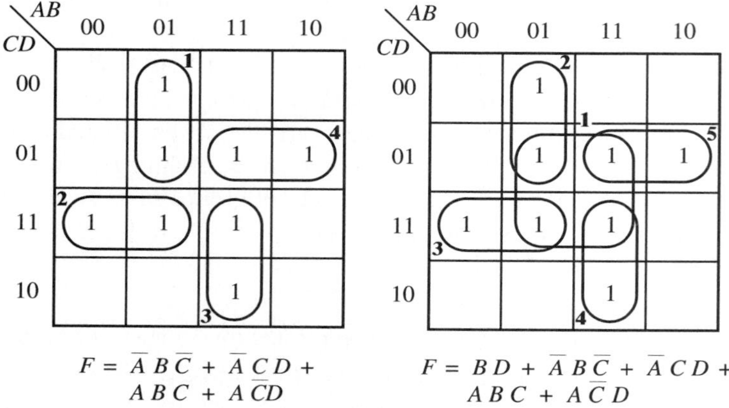

Figure B-6 Minimal K-map grouping (left) and K-map grouping that is not minimal (right) of a K-map.

The BC term is derived from the 2-group $(ABC + \bar{A}BC)$, which reduces to $BC(A + \bar{A})$ and then to BC. The AC term is similarly derived from the 2-group $(ABC + A\bar{B}C)$, and the AB term is similarly derived from the 2-group $(ABC + AB\bar{C})$. The corresponding circuit is shown in Figure B-5. The gate count is reduced from 8 to 4 as compared with the circuit shown in Figure A-16, and the gate input count is reduced from 19 to 9.

Looking more closely at the method of starting with 1-cells that can be included in no larger subgroups, consider what would happen if we started with the largest groups first. Figure B-6 shows both approaches applied to the same K-map. The reduction on the left is obtained by working with 1's that can be included in no

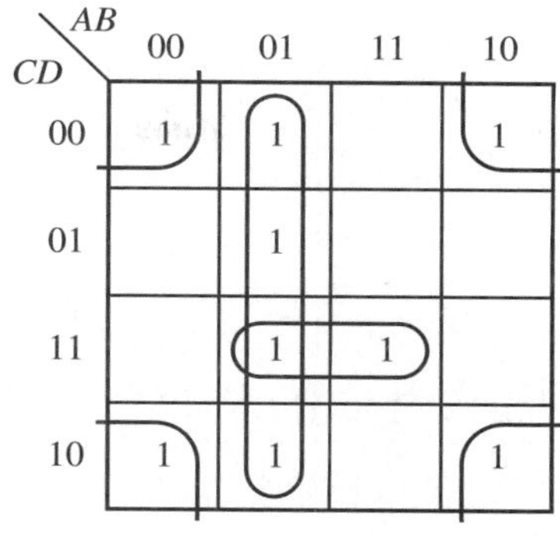

$$F = B\,C\,D + \overline{B}\,\overline{D} + \overline{A}\,B$$

Figure B-7 The corners of a K-map are logically adjacent.

larger subgroup, which is the method we have been using. Groupings are made in the order indicated by the numbers. A total of four groups are obtained, each of size two. The reduction on the right is obtained by starting with the largest groups first. Five groups are thus obtained, one of size four and four of size two. Thus, the minimal equation is not obtained if we start with the largest groups first. Both equations shown in Figure B-6 describe the same function, and a logically correct circuit will be obtained in either case; however, one circuit will not be produced from a minimized equation.

As another example, consider the K-map shown in Figure B-7. The edges of the K-map wrap around horizontally and vertically, and the four corners are logically adjacent. The corresponding minimized equation is shown in the figure.

Don't Cares

Now consider the K-maps shown in Figure B-8. The *d* entries denote *don't cares*, which can be treated as 0's or as 1's, at our convenience. A don't care represents a condition that cannot arise during operation. For example, if $X = 1$ represents the condition in which an elevator is on the ground floor and $Y = 1$ represents the condition in which the elevator is on the top floor, then X and Y will not both be 1 at the same time, although they may both be 0 at the same time. Thus, a truth table entry for an elevator function that corresponds to $X = Y = 1$ would be marked as a don't care.

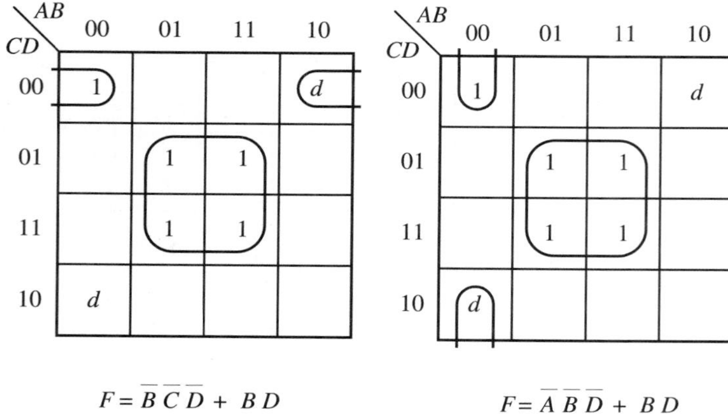

Figure B-8 Two different minimized equations are produced from the same K-map.

In Figure B-8, a more complex function is shown in which two different results are obtained from applying the same minimization process. The K-map on the left treats the top right don't care as a 1 and the bottom left don't care as a 0. The K-map on the right treats the top right don't care as a 0 and the bottom left don't care as a 1. Both K-maps result in minimized Boolean equations of the same size, and so it is possible to have more than one minimal expression for a Boolean function. In practice, one equation may be preferred over another, possibly in order to reduce the fan-out for one of the variables or to take advantage of sharing minterms with other functions.

Higher-Dimensional Maps

Figure B-9 shows a K-map in five variables. Each cell is adjacent to five others, and in order to maintain the inverse property for adjacent cells, the map on the left overlays the map on the right, creating a three-dimensional structure. Groupings are now made in three dimensions, as shown in the figure. Since the three-dimensional structure is mapped onto a two-dimensional page, some visualization is required on the part of the reader.

A six-variable K-map is shown in Figure B-10, in which the maps are overlaid four deep, in the order top-left, top-right, bottom-right, and bottom left. K-maps can be extended to higher dimensions for seven or more variables, but the visualization and the tedium tend to dominate the process. An algorithmic approach for more than four variables that lends itself to a simple implementation on a computer is described in Section B.2.3.

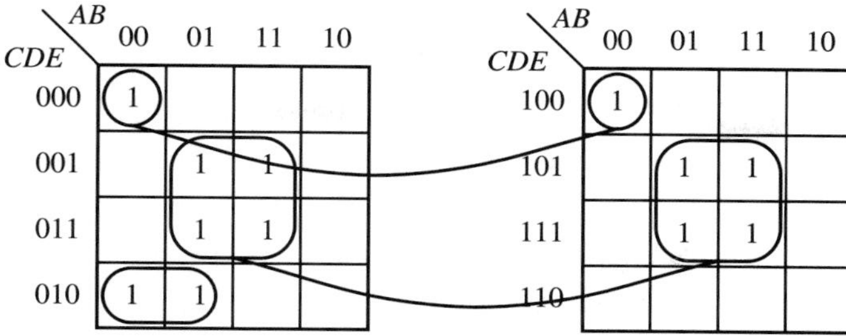

$$F = \overline{A}\,\overline{C}\,D\,\overline{E} + \overline{A}\,\overline{B}\,\overline{D}\,\overline{E} + B\,E$$

Figure B-9 A K-map in five variables.

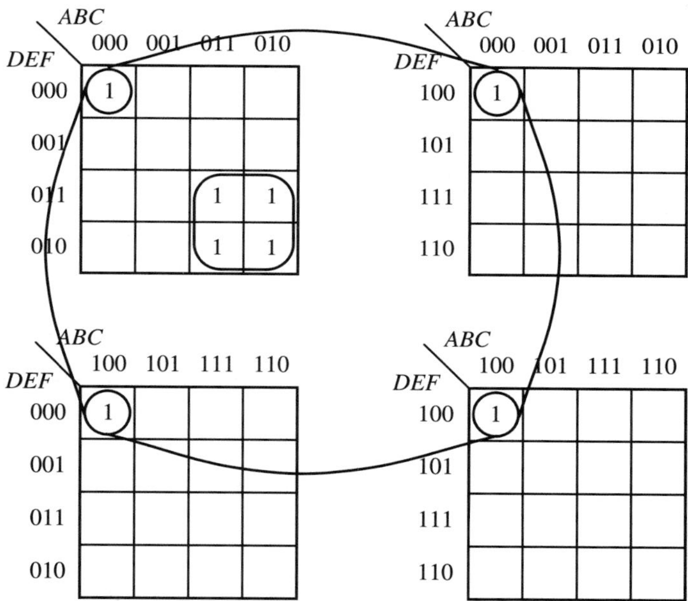

$$G = \overline{B}\,\overline{C}\,\overline{E}\,\overline{F} + \overline{A}\,B\,\overline{D}\,E$$

Figure B-10 A K-map in six variables.

Multilevel Circuits

It should be emphasized that a K-map reduces the size of a two-level expression, as measured by the number and sizes of the terms. This process does not neces-

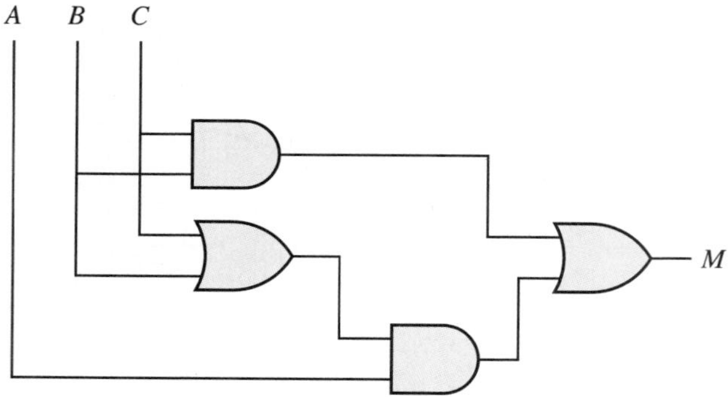

Figure B-11 A three-level circuit implements the majority function with a gate-input count of 8.

sarily produce a minimal form for multilevel circuits. For example, Equation B.14 is in its minimal two-level form, since only two levels of logic are used in its representation: three ANDed collections of variables (product terms) that are ORed together. The corresponding logic diagram that is shown in Figure B-5 has a gate-input count of 9. A three-level form can be created by factoring out one of the variables algebraically, such as A, as shown in Equation B.15:

$$M = BC + A(B + C) \qquad \text{(B-15)}$$

The corresponding logic diagram that is shown in Figure B-11 has a gate input count of 8, and thus a less complex circuit is realized by using a multilevel approach. There is now a greater delay between the inputs and the outputs, however, and so we might create another measure of circuit complexity: the **gate delay**. A two-level circuit has a gate delay of two because there are two logic gates on the longest path from an input to an output. The circuit shown in Figure B-11 has a gate delay of three.

Although there are techniques that aid the circuit designer in discovering trade-offs between circuit depth and gate input count, the development of algorithms that cover the space of possible alternatives in reasonable time is only a partially solved problem.

Map-Entered Variables

A simplified form for representing a function on a K-map is possible by allowing variables to be entered in the cells. For example, consider the four-variable K-map shown in Figure B-12. Only eight cells are used even though there are

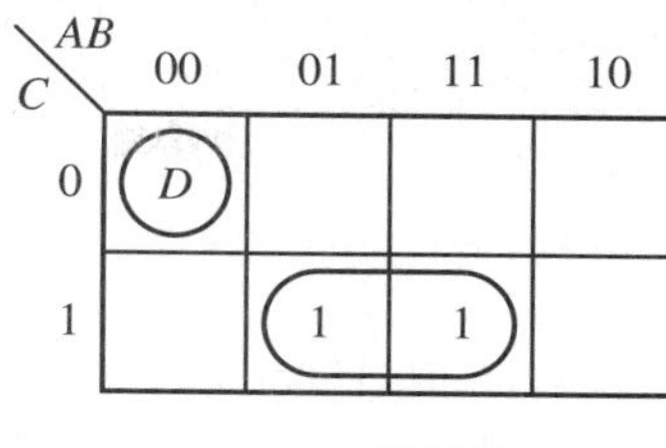

$$F = BC + \overline{A}\,\overline{B}\,\overline{C}D$$

Figure B-12 An example of a K-map with a map-entered variable *D*.

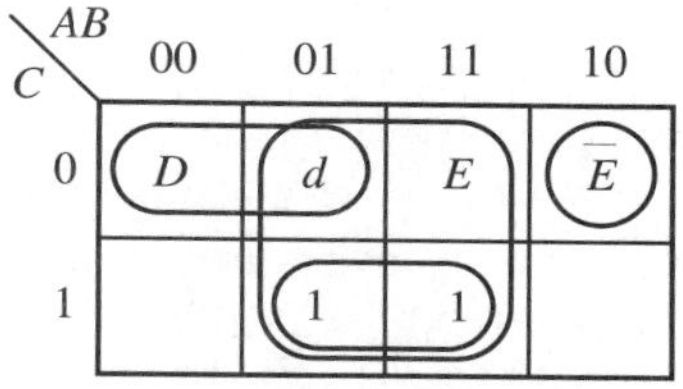

Figure B-13 A K-map with two map-entered variables *D* and *E*.

four variables, which would normally require $2^4 = 16$ cells. The **map-entered variable** *D* is treated as a 1 for the purpose of grouping, which for this case results in a 1-group since there are no adjacent 1's to the *D* cell. The resulting reduced equation is shown in the figure. Notice that the variable *D* appears in the minterm $\overline{A}\overline{B}\overline{C}D$, since *D* can assume a value of 0 or 1 even though we treated *D* as a 1 for the purpose of forming the 1-group.

The general procedure for producing a reduced expression from a K-map with map-entered variables is first to obtain an expression for the 1-cells while treating the map-entered variables as 0's. Minterms are then added for each variable while treating 1's as don't cares since the 1's have already been covered. The process continues until all variables are covered.

Consider the map shown in Figure B-13, in which *D*, *E*, and $\overline{E}$ are map-entered variables and *d* represents a don't care. The 1's are considered first, which produces the term *BC*. Variable *D* is considered next, which produces the term $\overline{A}\overline{C}D$. Variable *E* is considered next, which produces the term *BE*. Finally, variable $\overline{E}$ is considered, which produces the term $A\overline{B}\overline{C}\overline{E}$. Notice that a map-entered variable and its complement are considered separately, as for *E* in this example. Equation (B-16) shows the reduced form:

$$F = BC + \overline{A}\overline{C}D + BE + A\overline{B}\overline{C}\overline{E} \qquad \text{(B-16)}$$

B.2.3 *THE TABULAR METHOD*

An automated approach to reducing Boolean expressions is commonly used for single and multiple output functions. The tabular method, also known as the **Quine-McCluskey** method, successively forms Boolean cross products among groups of terms that differ in one variable and then uses the smallest set of reduced terms to cover the functions. This process is easier than the map method to implement on a computer, and an extension of the method allows terms to be shared among functions.

Reduction of Single Functions

The truth table shown in Figure B-14 describes a function *F* in four variables *A*, *B*, *C*, and *D*, and includes three don't cares. The tabular reduction process begins by grouping minterms for which *F* is nonzero according to the number of 1's in each minterm. Don't care conditions are considered to be nonzero for this process. Minterm 0000 contains no 1's and is in its own group, as shown in Figure B-15a. Minterms 0001, 0010, 0100, and 1000 all contain a single 1, but only minterm 0001 has a nonzero entry and so it forms another group.

The next group has two 1's in each minterm, and there are six possible minterms that can belong to this group. Only minterms 0011, 0101, 0110, and 1010 have nonzero entries, and so they comprise this group. There are three nonzero entries in the next group, which has three 1's in each minterm. The nonzero minterms are 0111, 1011, and 1110. Finally, there is one nonzero entry that contains four 1's, and the corre-

A	*B*	*C*	*D*	*F*
0	0	0	0	*d*
0	0	0	1	1
0	0	1	0	0
0	0	1	1	1
0	1	0	0	0
0	1	0	1	1
0	1	1	0	1
0	1	1	1	1
1	0	0	0	0
1	0	0	1	0
1	0	1	0	1
1	0	1	1	*d*
1	1	0	0	0
1	1	0	1	1
1	1	1	0	0
1	1	1	1	*d*

Figure B-14 A truth table representation of a function with don't cares.

Initial setup

A	B	C	D	
0	0	0	0	√
0	0	0	1	√
0	0	1	1	√
0	1	0	1	√
0	1	1	0	√
1	0	1	0	√
0	1	1	1	√
1	0	1	1	√
1	1	0	1	√
1	1	1	1	√

(a)

After first reduction

A	B	C	D	
0	0	0	_	*
0	0	_	1	√
0	_	0	1	√
0	_	1	1	√
_	0	1	1	√
0	1	_	1	√
_	1	0	1	√
0	1	1	_	*
1	0	1	_	*
_	1	1	1	√
1	_	1	1	√
1	1	_	1	√

(b)

After second reduction

A	B	C	D	
0	_	_	1	*
_	_	1	1	*
_	1	_	1	*

(c)

Figure B-15 The tabular reduction process.

sponding minterm makes up the last group. For larger truth tables, the process continues until all nonzero entries are covered. The groups are organized so that adjacent groups differ in the number of 1's by one, as shown in Figure B-15a.

The next step in the reduction process is to form a consensus (the logical form of a cross product) between each pair of adjacent groups for all terms that differ in only one variable. The general form of the consensus theorem is restated from Appendix A:

$$XY + \bar{X}Z + YZ = XY + \bar{X}Z \tag{B-17}$$

The term YZ is redundant, since it is covered by the remaining terms, and so it can be eliminated. Algebraically, we can prove the theorem as follows:

$$\begin{aligned} XY + \bar{X}Z + YZ &= XY + \bar{X}Z + YZ(X + \bar{X}) \\ &= XY + \bar{X}Z + XYZ + \bar{X}YZ \\ &= XY + XYZ + \bar{X}Z + \bar{X}YZ \\ &= XY(1 + Z) + \bar{X}Z(1 + Y) \\ &= XY + \bar{X}Z \end{aligned}$$

The consensus theorem also has a dual form:

$$(X+Y)(\bar{X}+Z)(Y+Z) = (X+Y)(\bar{X}+Z) \quad \text{(B-18)}$$

The idea of applying consensus in tabular reduction is to take advantage of the inverse property of Boolean algebra, similar to the way we did for K-maps in the previous section. For example, 0000 and 0001 differ in variable *D*, so 000_ is listed at the top of the reduced table shown in Figure B-15b. The underscore marks the position of the variable that has been eliminated, which is *D* for this case. Minterms 0000 and 0001 in Figure B-15a are marked with checks to indicate that they are now covered in the reduced table.

After every term in the first group is crossed with every term in the second group, we then move on to form a consensus between terms in the second and third groups. Note that it is possible that some terms cannot be combined into a smaller term because they differ in more than one variable. For example, terms 0001 and 0011 combine into the smaller term 00_1, as shown in the top of the second group in Figure B-15b, but terms 0001 and 0110 cannot be combined because they differ in three variables.

Once a term is marked with a check, it can still be used in the reduction process by the property of idempotence. The objective in this step of the process is to discover all of the possible reduced terms so that we can find the smallest set of terms that covers the function in a later step.

The process continues for the remaining groups. Any term that is not covered after all consensus groupings are made is marked with an asterisk to indicate that it is a prime implicant. After the first reduction is made for this example, all of the minterms shown in Figure B-15a are covered so there are no prime implicants at this point.

Now that the first reduction is made, we can start on the next reduction. In order for two reduced terms to be combined, they must again differ in exactly one variable. The underscores must line up, and only one of the remaining variables can differ. The first entry shown in Figure B-15b has an underscore in the rightmost field, which does not coincide with any term in the next group, so an asterisk is placed next to it, indicating that it can be reduced no further and is therefore a prime implicant. We continue by moving on to the second and third groups of Figure B-15b. Terms 00_1 and 01_1 combine to form reduced term 0_ _1 in the

Prime Implicants	Minterms						
	0001	0011	0101	0110	0111	1010	1101
000_	√						
*011_				√	√		
*101_						√	
0_ _1	√	√	√		√		
_ _11		√			√		
*_1_1			√		√		√

Figure B-16 Table of choice.

table shown in Figure B-15c. The process continues until the second reduction is completed, which is shown in Figure B-15c.

In constructing the reduced table shown in Figure B-15c, the prime implicants from the previously constructed table (Figure B-15b) are not included. The process continues for additional reductions until only prime implicants remain. For this example, the process stops after the second reduction when the three terms become prime implicants, as shown in Figure B-15c.

Taken as a whole, the prime implicants form a set that completely covers the function, although not necessarily minimally. In order to obtain a minimal covering set, a **table of choice** is constructed, as shown in Figure B-16. Each prime implicant has a row in the table of choice. The columns represent minterms in the original function that must be covered. Don't care conditions do not need to be covered and are not listed.

A check is placed in each box that corresponds to a prime implicant that covers a minterm. For example, prime implicant 000_ covers minterm 0001, so a check is placed in the corresponding box. Some prime implicants cover several minterms, as for 0_ _1, which covers four minterms. After all boxes are considered, columns that contain a single check are identified. A single check in a column means that only one prime implicant covers the minterm, and the corresponding prime implicant that covers the minterm is marked with an asterisk to indicate that it is **essential**.

Essential prime implicants cannot be eliminated, and they must be included in the reduced equation for the function. For this example, prime implicants 011_,

Eligible Set		Minterms	
		0001	0011
X	000_	√	
Y	0_ _1	√	√
Z	_ _11		√

Set 1	Set 2
000_	0_ _1
_ _11	

Figure B-17 Reduced table of choice.

101_, and _1_1 are essential. An essential prime implicant may cover more than one minterm, and so a **reduced table of choice** is created in which the essential prime implicants and the minterms they cover are removed, as shown in Figure B-17. The reduced table of choice may also have essential prime implicants, in which case a second reduced table of choice is created, and the process continues until the final reduced table of choice has only nonessential prime implicants.

The prime implicants that remain in the reduced table of choice form the **eligible set**, from which a minimal subset is obtained that covers the remaining minterms. As shown in Figure B-17, there are two sets of prime implicants that cover the two remaining minterms. Since Set 2 has the fewest terms, we choose that set and obtain a minimized equation for F, which is made up of essential prime implicants and the eligible prime implicants in Set 2:

$$F = \bar{A}BC + A\bar{B}C + BD + \bar{A}D \tag{B-19}$$

Instead of using visual inspection to obtain a covering set from the eligible set, the process can be carried out algorithmically. The process starts by assigning a variable to each of the prime implicants in the eligible, set as shown in Figure B-17. A logical expression is written for each column in the reduced table of choice as follows:

Column	Logical Sums
0001	$(X + Y)$
0011	$(Y + Z)$

In order to find a set that completely covers the function, prime implicants are grouped so that there is at least one check in each column. This means that the following relation must hold, in which G represents the terms in the reduced table of choice:

$$G = (X+Y)(Y+Z)$$

Applying the properties of Boolean algebra yields

$$G = (X+Y)(Y+Z) = XY+XZ+Y+YZ = XZ+Y$$

Each of the product terms in this equation represents a set of prime implicants that covers the terms in the reduced table of choice. The smallest product term (Y) represents the smallest set of prime implicants (0 _ _ 1) that covers the remaining terms. The same final equation is produced as before:

$$F = \bar{A}BC + A\bar{B}C + BD + \bar{A}D \qquad \text{(B-20)}$$

Reduction of Multiple Functions

The tabular reduction method reduces a single Boolean function. When there is more than one function that use the same variables, then it may be possible to share terms, resulting in a smaller collective size of the equations. The method described here forms an intersection among all possible combinations of shared terms and then selects the smallest set that covers all of the functions.

As an example, consider the truth table shown in Figure B-18, which represents three functions in three variables. The notation m_i denotes minterms according to the indexing shown in the table.

Minterm	A	B	C	F_0	F_1	F_2
m_0	0	0	0	1	0	0
m_1	0	0	1	0	1	0
m_2	0	1	0	0	0	1
m_3	0	1	1	1	1	1
m_4	1	0	0	0	1	0
m_5	1	0	1	0	0	0
m_6	1	1	0	0	1	1
m_7	1	1	1	1	1	1

Figure B-18 A truth table for three functions in three variables.

The canonical (unreduced) form of the Boolean equations is

$$F_0(A, B, C) = m_0 + m_3 + m_7$$

$$F_1(A, B, C) = m_1 + m_3 + m_4 + m_6 + m_7$$

$$F_2(A, B, C) = m_2 + m_3 + m_6 + m_7$$

An intersection is made for every combination of functions as follows:

$$F_{0,1}(A, B, C) = m_3 + m_7$$

$$F_{0,2}(A, B, C) = m_3 + m_7$$

$$F_{1,2}(A, B, C) = m_3 + m_6 + m_7$$

$$F_{0,1,2}(A, B, C) = m_3 + m_7$$

Using the tabular reduction method described in the previous section, the following prime implicants are obtained:

Function	Prime Implicant
F_0	000, _11
F_1	0_1, 1_0, _11, 11_
F_2	_1_
$F_{0,1}$	_11
$F_{0,2}$	_11
$F_{1,2}$	_11, 11_
$F_{0,1,2}$	_11

The list of prime implicants is reduced by eliminating those prime implicants in functions that are covered by higher order functions. For example, _11 appears in $F_{0,1,2}$, thus it does not need to be included in the remaining functions. Similarly, 11_ appears in $F_{1,2}$, and does not need to appear in F_1 or in F_2 (for this case, it does not appear as a prime implicant in F_2 anyway.) Continuing in this manner, a reduced set of prime implicants is obtained:

Function	Prime Implicant
F_0	000
F_1	0_1, 1_0

Prime Implicants \ Minterms		$F_0(A,B,C)$			$F_1(A,B,C)$					$F_2(A,B,C)$			
		m_0	m_3	m_7	m_1	m_3	m_4	m_6	m_7	m_2	m_3	m_6	m_7
F_0	*000	√											
F_1	*0_1				√	√							
F_1	*1_0						√	√					
F_2	*_1_									√	√	√	√
$F_{1,2}$	11_							√	√			√	√
$F_{0,1,2}$	*_11		√	√		√			√		√		√

Figure B-19 A multiple output table of choice.

F_2	_1_
$F_{0,1}$	none
$F_{0,2}$	none
$F_{1,2}$	11_
$F_{0,1,2}$	_11

A multiple output table of choice is then constructed, as shown in Figure B-19. The rows correspond to the prime implicants, and the columns correspond to the minterms that must be covered for each function. Portions of rows are blocked out where prime implicants from one function cannot be used to cover another. For example, prime implicant 000 was obtained from function F_0, and therefore cannot be used to cover a minterm in F_1 or F_2, and so these regions are blocked out. If, in fact, a prime implicant in F_0 can be used to cover a minterm in one of the remaining functions, then it will appear in a higher-order function such as $F_{0,1}$ or $F_{0,1,2}$.

The minimal form for the output equations is obtained in a manner similar to the tabular reduction process. We start by finding all of the essential prime implicants. For example, minterm m_0 in function F_0 is covered only by prime implicant 000, and thus 000 is essential. The row containing 000 is then removed from the table and all columns that contain a check mark in the row are also deleted. The process continues until either all functions are covered or until only nonessential prime implicants remain, in which case the smallest set of nonessential prime implicants that are needed to cover the remaining functions is obtained using the method described in the previous section.

The essential prime implicants are marked with asterisks in Figure B-19. For this case, only one nonessential prime implicant (11_) remains, but since all minterms are covered by the essential prime implicants, there is no need to construct a reduced table. The corresponding reduced equations are

$$F_0(A, B, C) = \overline{A}\overline{B}\overline{C} + BC$$

$$F_1(A, B, C) = AC + A\overline{C} + BC$$

$$F_2(A, B, C) = B$$

B.2.4 *LOGIC REDUCTION: EFFECT ON SPEED AND PERFORMANCE*

Up to this point, we have largely ignored physical characteristics that affect performance and have focused entirely on organizational issues such as circuit depth and gate count. In this section, we explore a few practical considerations of digital logic.

Switching Speed

The propagation delay (latency) between the inputs and output of a logic gate is a continuous effect, even though we considered propagation delay to be negligible in the early part of Appendix A. A change at an input to a logic gate is also a continuous effect. In Figure B-20, an input to a NOT gate has a finite transition time, which is measured as the time between the 10% and 90% points on the waveform. This is referred to as the *rise time* for a rising signal and the *fall time* for a falling signal.

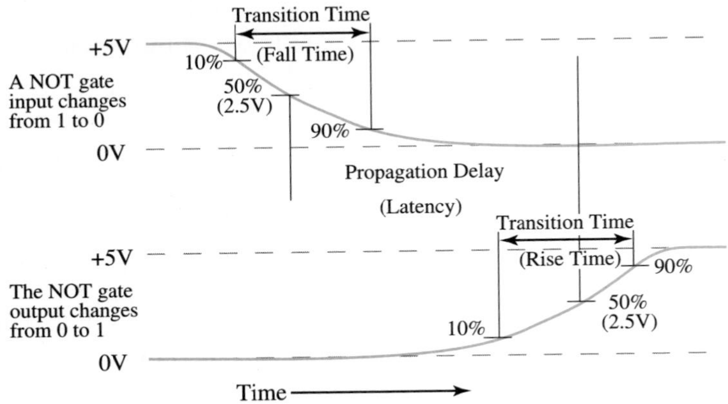

Figure B-20 Propagation delay for a NOT gate. (Adapted from [Hamacher et al., 1990].)

The propagation delay is the time between the 50% transitions on the input and output waveforms. The propagation delay is influenced by a number of parameters, and power is one parameter over which we have a good deal of control. As power consumption increases, propagation delay decreases, up to a limit. A rule of thumb is that the product of power consumption and the propagation delay for a logic gate stays roughly the same. Although we generally want fast logic, we do not want to operate with a high power dissipation because the consumed power manifests itself as heat that must be removed to maintain a safe and reliable operating condition.

In the complementary metal-oxide semiconductor (CMOS) logic family, power dissipation scales with speed. At a switching rate of 1 MHz, the power dissipation of a CMOS gate is about 1 mW. At this rate of power dissipation, 10,000 CMOS logic gates dissipate 10,000 gates $\times$ 1 mW/gate = 10 W, which is at the limit of heat removal for a single integrated circuit using conventional approaches (for a 1 cm^2 chip).

Single CMOS chips can have on the order of 10^7 logic gates, however, and operate at rates up to several hundred MHz. This gate count and speed are achieved partially by increasing the chip size, although this accounts for little more than a factor of 10. The key to achieving such a high component count and switching speed while managing power dissipation is to switch only a fraction of the logic gates at any time, which luckily is the most typical operating mode for an integrated circuit.

Circuit Depth

The latency between the inputs and outputs of a circuit is governed by the number of logic gates on the longest path from any input to any output. This is known as **circuit depth**. In general, a circuit with a small circuit depth operates more quickly than a circuit with a large circuit depth. There are a number of ways to reduce circuit depth that involve increasing the complexity of some other parameter. We look at one way of making this trade-off here.

In Appendix A, we used a MUX to implement the majority function. Now consider using a four-variable MUX to implement Equation (B-21). The equation is in two-level form, because only two levels of logic are used in its representation: six AND terms that are ORed together. A single MUX can implement this function,

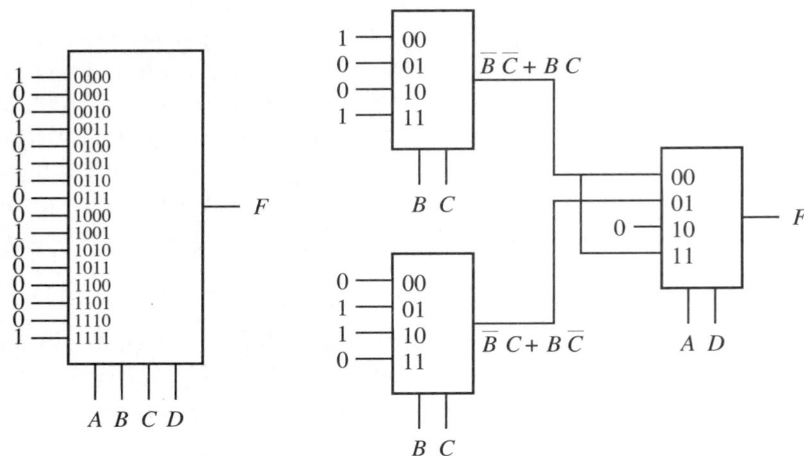

Figure B-21 A four-variable function implemented with a 16-to-1 MUX (left) and with 4-to-1 MUXes (right).

which is shown in the left side of Figure B-21. The corresponding circuit depth is two (that is, the gate-level configuration of the inside of the MUX has two gate delays). If we factor out A and B, then we obtain the four-level Equation (B-22) and the corresponding four-level circuit shown in the right side of Figure B-21.

$$F(A, B, C, D) = \overline{A}\overline{B}\overline{C}\overline{D} + \overline{A}\overline{B}CD + \overline{A}B\overline{C}D + \overline{A}BC\overline{D} + A\overline{B}\overline{C}D + ABCD \qquad \text{(B-21)}$$

$$F(A, B, C, D) = \overline{A}\overline{B}(\overline{C}\overline{D} + CD) + \overline{A}B(\overline{C}D + C\overline{D}) + A\overline{B}(\overline{C}D) + AB(CD) \qquad \text{(B-22)}$$

The gate input count of a 4-to-1 MUX is 18 as taken from Figure A-23 (including inverters), so the gate input count of the decomposed MUX circuit is $3 \times 18 = 54$. A single 16-to-1 MUX has a gate input count of 100. The 4-to-1 MUX implementation has a circuit depth of four (not including inverters) while the 16-to-1 MUX implementation has a circuit depth of two. We have thus reduced the overall circuit complexity at the expense of an increase in the circuit depth.

Although there are techniques that aid the circuit designer in discovering trade-offs between circuit complexity and circuit depth, the development of algorithms that cover the space of possible alternatives in reasonable time is only a partially solved problem.

Fan-in versus Circuit Depth

Suppose that we need a four-input OR gate as used in Figure A-23, but only two-input OR gates are available. What should we do? This is a common practical problem that is encountered in a variety of design situations. The associative property of Boolean algebra can be used to decompose the OR gate that has a fan-in of four into a configuration of OR gates that each have a fan-in of two, as shown in Figure B-22. In general, the decomposition of the four-input OR gate should be performed in balanced tree fashion in order to reduce circuit depth. A degenerate tree can also be used, as shown in Figure B-22, which produces a functionally equivalent circuit with the same number of logic gates as the balanced tree but results in a maximum circuit depth.

Although it is important to reduce circuit depth in order to decrease the latency between the inputs and the outputs, one reason for preferring the degenerate tree to the balanced tree is that the degenerate tree has a minimum cross sectional diameter at each stage, which makes it easy to split the tree into pieces that are spread over a number of separate circuits. This mirrors a practical situation encountered in packaging digital circuits. The depth of the balanced tree is $\lceil log_F(N) \rceil$ logic gates for an N-input gate mapped to logic gates with a fan-in of

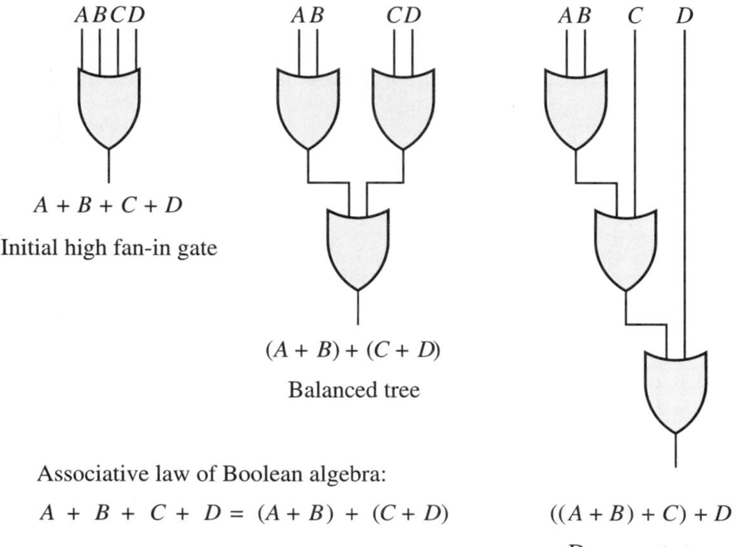

Figure B-22 A logic gate with a fan-in of four is decomposed into logically equivalent configurations of logic gates with fan-ins of two.

F, and the depth of the degenerate tree is $\left\lceil \frac{N-1}{F-1} \right\rceil$ logic gates for an N-input gate mapped to logic gates with a fan-in of F.

In theory, any binary function can be realized in two levels of logic gates given an arbitrarily large stage of AND gates followed by an arbitrarily large stage of OR gates, both having arbitrarily large fan-in and fan-out. For example, an entire computer program can be compiled in just two gate levels if it is presented in parallel to a Boolean circuit that has an AND stage followed by an OR stage that is designed to implement this function. Such a circuit would be prohibitively large, however, since every possible combination of inputs must be considered.

Fan-outs larger than about 10 are too costly to implement in many logic families due to the sacrifice in performance, as it is similar to filling 10 or more leaky buckets from a single faucet. Boolean algebra for two-level expressions is still used to describe complex digital circuits with high fan-outs, however, and then the two-level Boolean expressions are transformed into multilevel expressions that conform to the fan-in and fan-out limitations of the technology. Optimal fan-in and fan-out are argued to be $e \cong 2.7$ (Mead and Conway, 1980) in terms of transistor stepping size for bringing a signal from an integrated circuit (IC) to a pin of the IC package. The derivation of that result is based on capacitance of bonding pads, signal rise times, and other considerations. The result cannot be applied to all aspects of computing since it does not take into account overall performance, which may create local variations that violate the e rule dramatically. Electronic digital circuits typically use fan-ins and fan-outs of between 2 and 10.

B.3 State Reduction

In Appendix A, we explored a method of designing an FSM without considering that there may exist a functionally equivalent machine with fewer states. In this section, we focus on reducing the number of states. We begin with a description of an FSM that has some number of states, and then we hypothesize that a functionally equivalent machine exists that contains a single state. We apply all combinations of inputs to the hypothesized machine and observe the outputs. If the FSM produces a different output for the same input combination at different times, then there are at least two states that are distinguishable, which are therefore not equivalent. The distinguishable states are placed in separate groups, and the process continues until no further distinctions can be made. If any remaining groups have more than one state, then those states are equivalent and a smaller equivalent machine can be constructed in which each group is collapsed into a single state.

Present state \ Input	X: 0	X: 1
A	C/0	E/1
B	D/0	E/1
C	C/1	B/0
D	C/1	A/0
E	A/0	C/1

Figure B-23 Description of state machine M_0 to be reduced.

As an example, consider state machine M_0 described by the state table shown in Figure B-23. We begin the reduction process by hypothesizing that all five states can be reduced to a single state, obtaining partition P_0 for a new machine M_1:

$$P_0 = (ABCDE)$$

We then apply a single input to the original machine M_0 and observe the outputs. When M_0 is in state A and an input of 0 is applied, then the output is 0. When the machine is in state A and an input of 1 is applied, then the output is 1. States B and E behave similarly, but states C and D produce outputs of 1 and 0 for inputs of 0 and 1, respectively. Thus, we know that states A, B, and E can be distinguished from states C and D, and we obtain a new partition P_1:

$$P_1 = (ABE)(CD)$$

After a single input is applied to M_0, we know that the machine will be in either the ABE group or the CD group. We now need to observe the behavior of the machine from its new state. One way to do this is to enumerate the set of possible next states in a tree, as shown in Figure B-24. The process of constructing the tree begins by listing all of the states in the same partition. For machine M_0, the initial partition $(ABCDE)$ is shown at the root of the tree. After a 0 is applied at the input to M_0, the next state will be one of C, D, C, C, or A for an initial state of A, B, C, D, or E, respectively. This is shown as the $(CDA)(CC)$ partition in the 0 side of the tree, down one **ply** (one level) from the root. The output produced by the (CDA) group is different from the output produced by the (CC) group, and so their corresponding initial states are distinguishable. The corresponding states that are distinguished are the groups (ABE) and (CD), which form the partition $(ABE)(CD)$ as shown.

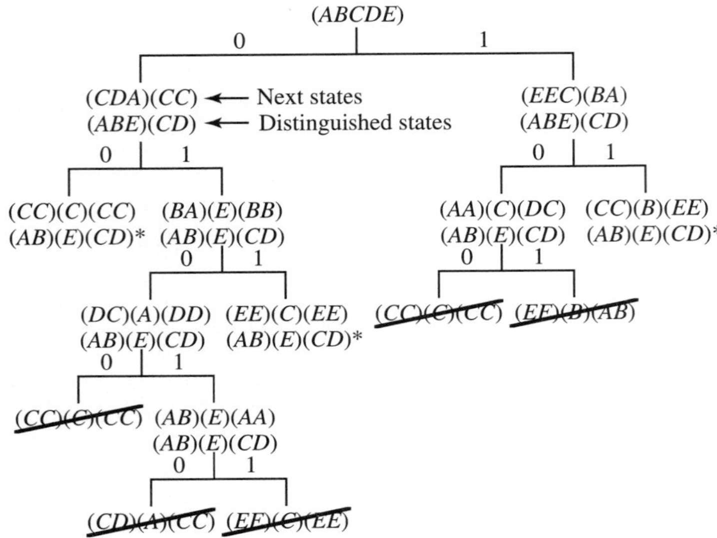

Figure B-24 A next state tree for M_0.

Similarly, after a 1 is applied at the input to M_0, the next state will be one of *E*, *E*, *B*, *A*, or *C* for an initial state of *A*, *B*, *C*, *D*, or *E*, respectively. This is shown on the right side of the tree. To form the next ply, we look at the (CDA) and (CC) groups separately. When a 0 is applied at the input when M_0 is in any of states *C*, *D*, or *A*, then the outputs will be the same for states *C* and *D* (the output is a 1, and the next states are *C* and *C*) but will be different for state *A* (the output is a 0, and the next state is *C*). This is shown as $(CC)(C)$ on the 0,0 path from the root.

Similarly, when a 0 is applied at the input when M_0 is in either of states *C* or *D*, then the outputs are the same, and the set of target states are $(CC)(C)(CC)$ on the 0,0 path from the root as shown, which corresponds to a partition on the initial states of $(AB)(E)(CD)$ if we trace back to the root. Thus, at this point, *A* is indistinguishable from *B*, and *C* is indistinguishable from *D*, but each parenthesized group can be distinguished from each other if we apply the sequence 0,0 to M_0 and observe the outputs, regardless of the initial state.

Continuing in this manner, the tree is expanded until no finer partitions can be created. For example, when a partition contains a group of states that can no longer be distinguished, as for $(CC)(C)(CC)$, then an asterisk is placed adjacent to the partition for the corresponding initial states and the tree is not expanded further from that point. The tree shown in Figure B-24 is expanded beyond this point only to illustrate various situations that can arise.

If a partition is created that is visited elsewhere in the tree, then a slash is drawn through it and the tree is not expanded from that point. For purposes of comparing similar partitions, $(CD)(A)(CC)$ is considered to be the same as $(CD)(A)(C)$, and $(AA)(C)(CD)$ is considered to be the same as $(A)(C)(CD)$, which is the same as $(DC)(A)(C)$ and $(CD)(A)(C)$. Thus the $(CD)(A)(CC)$ and $(AA)(C)(DC)$ partitions are considered to be the same. After the tree is constructed, the partitions with asterisks expose the indistinguishable states. Each group of parentheses in an asterisk partition identifies a group of indistinguishable states. For machine M_0, states A and B are indistinguishable, and states C and D are indistinguishable. Thus, we can construct a functionally equivalent machine to M_0 that contains only three states, in which A and B are combined into a single state and C and D are combined into a single state.

The process of constructing the next state tree is laborious because of its potential size, but we use it here in order to understand a simpler method. Rather than construct the entire tree, we can simply observe that once we have the first partition P_1, the next partition can be constructing by looking at the next states for each group and noting that if two states within a group have next states that are in different groups, then they are distinguishable since the resulting outputs will eventually differ. This can be shown by constructing the corresponding distinguishing tree. Starting with P_1 for M_0, we observe that states A and B have next states C and D for an input of 0 and have a next state of E for an input of 1, and so A and B are grouped together in the next partition. State E, however, has next states of A and C for inputs of 0 and 1, respectively, which differ from the next states for A and B, and thus state E is distinguishable from states A and B. Continuing for the (CD) group of P_1, the next partition is obtained as follows: After

$$P_2 = (AB)(CD)(E)$$

applying the method for another iteration, the partition repeats, which is a condition for stopping the process:

$$P_3 = (AB)(CD)(E)\surd$$

No further distinctions can be made at this point, and the resulting machine M_1 has three states in its reduced form. If we make the assignment $A' = AB$, $B' = CD$, and $C' = E$, in which the prime symbols mark the states for machine M_1, then a reduced state table can be created, as shown in Figure B-25.

Current state \ Input	X: 0	X: 1
AB: A'	*B'*/0	*C'*/1
CD: B'	*B'*/1	*A'*/0
E: C'	*A'*/0	*B'*/1

Figure B-25 A reduced state table for machine M_1.

B.3.1 *THE STATE ASSIGNMENT PROBLEM*

It may be the case that different state assignments for the same machine result in different implementations. For example, consider machine M_2 shown in the left side of Figure B-26. Two different state assignments are shown. State assignment SA_0 is a simple numerical ordering of $A \rightarrow 00$, $B \rightarrow 01$, $C \rightarrow 10$, and $D \rightarrow 11$. State assignment SA_1 is the same as SA_0 except that the assignments for C and D are interchanged. We consider an implementation of M_2 using state assignment SA_0 with AND, OR, and NOT gates, and apply K-map reduction to reduce the sizes of the equations. Figure B-27 shows the results of reducing the next state functions S_0 and S_1 and the output function Z. A corresponding circuit will have a gate input count of 29 as measured by counting the number of variables and the number of terms in the equations (note that one of the terms is shared and is counted just once). If we use state assignment SA_1 instead, then we will obtain a gate input count of 6, as shown in Figure B-28 (s_0 and s_1 do not contribute to the gate input count because they do not feed into logic gates).

State assignment SA_1 is clearly better than SA_0 in terms of gate input count but may not be better with regard to other criteria. For example, if an implementation is made with 8-to-1 MUXes, then the gate input count will be the same for

P.S. \ Input	X: 0	X: 1
A	*B*/1	*A*/1
B	*C*/0	*D*/1
C	*C*/0	*D*/0
D	*B*/1	*A*/0

Machine M_2

S_0S_1 \ Input	X: 0	X: 1
A: 00	01/1	00/1
B: 01	10/0	11/1
C: 10	10/0	11/0
D: 11	01/1	00/0

State assignment SA_0

S_0S_1 \ Input	X: 0	X: 1
A: 00	01/1	00/1
B: 01	11/0	10/1
C: 11	11/0	10/0
D: 10	01/1	00/0

State assignment SA_1

Figure B-26 Two state assignments for machine M_2.

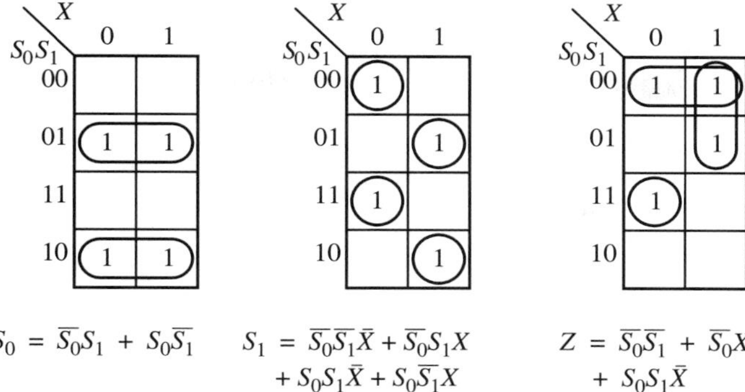

Figure B-27 Boolean equations for machine M_2 using state assignment SA_0.

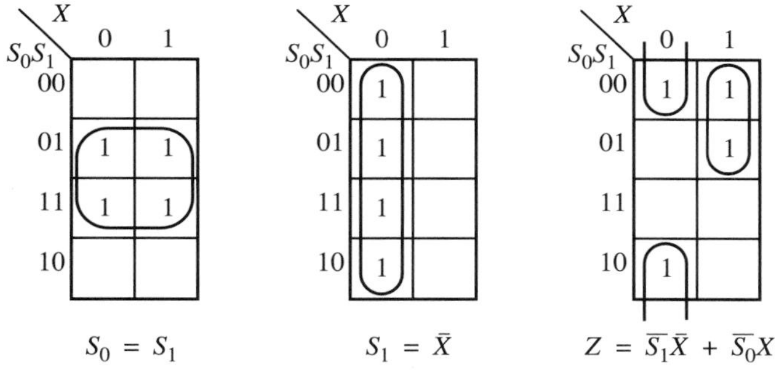

Figure B-28 Boolean equations for machine M_2 using state assignment SA_1.

SA_0 and SA_1. A further consideration is that it is not an easy process to find the best assignment for any one criterion. In fact, better gate input counts may be possible by increasing the number of state bits for some cases.

REDUCTION EXAMPLE: A SEQUENCE DETECTOR

In this section, we tie together the reduction methods described in the previous sections. The machine we would like to design outputs a 1 when exactly two of the last three inputs are 1 (this machine appeared in an example in Appendix A). An input sequence of 011011100 produces an output sequence of 001111010. There is one serial input line, and we can assume that initially no inputs have been seen.

We start by constructing a state transition diagram, as shown in Figure B-29. There are eight possible three-bit sequences that our machine will observe: 000, 001, 010,

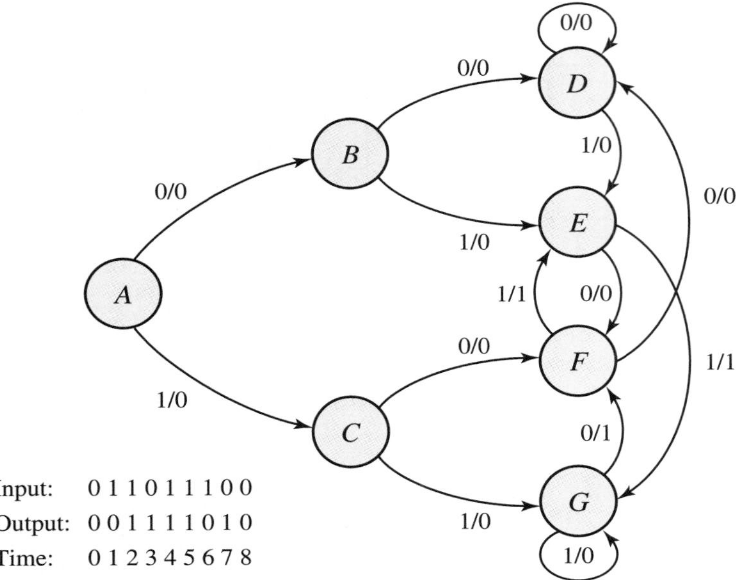

Figure B-29 State transition diagram for sequence detector.

011, 100, 101, 110, and 111. State *A* is the initial state, in which we assume that no inputs have yet been seen. In states *B* and *C*, we have seen only one input, so we cannot yet output a 1. In states *D*, *E*, *F*, and *G* we have only seen two inputs, so we cannot yet output a 1, even though we have seen two 1's at the input when we enter state *G*. The machine makes all subsequent transitions among states *D*, *E*, *F*, and *G*. State *D* is visited when the last two inputs are 00. States *E*, *F*, and *G* are visited when the last two inputs are 01, 10, or 11, respectively.

The next step is to create a state table and reduce the number of states. The state table shown in Figure B-30 is taken directly from the state transition diagram. We then apply the state reduction technique by hypothesizing that all states are equivalent and then refining our hypothesis. The process is as follows:

$$P_0 = (ABCDEFG)$$

$$P_1 = (ABCD)(EF)(G)$$

$$P_2 = (A)(BD)(C)(E)(F)(G)$$

$$P_3 = (A)(BD)(C)(E)(F)(G)\surd$$

Present state \ Input	X = 0	X = 1
A	*B*/0	*C*/0
B	*D*/0	*E*/0
C	*F*/0	*G*/0
D	*D*/0	*E*/0
E	*F*/0	*G*/1
F	*D*/0	*E*/1
G	*F*/1	*G*/0

Figure B-30 State table for sequence detector.

Present state \ Input	X = 0	X = 1
A: *A'*	*B'*/0	*C'*/0
BD: *B'*	*B'*/0	*D'*/0
C: *C'*	*E'*/0	*F'*/0
E: *D'*	*E'*/0	*F'*/1
F: *E'*	*B'*/0	*D'*/1
G: *F'*	*E'*/1	*F'*/0

Figure B-31 Reduced state table for sequence detector.

Present state \ Input	X = 0	X = 1
$S_2S_1S_0$	$S_2S_1S_0Z$	$S_2S_1S_0Z$
A': 000	001/0	010/0
B': 001	001/0	011/0
C': 010	100/0	101/0
D': 011	100/0	101/1
E': 100	001/0	011/1
F': 101	100/1	101/0

Figure B-32 State assignment for sequence detector.

States *B* and *D* along the 0,0,0 path in the state transition diagram are equivalent. We create a reduced table, using primed letters to denote the new states, as shown in Figure B-31.

Next, we make an arbitrary state assignment, as shown in Figure B-32. We then use the state assignment to create K-maps for the next state and output functions as shown in Figure B-33. Notice that there are four don't care conditions that

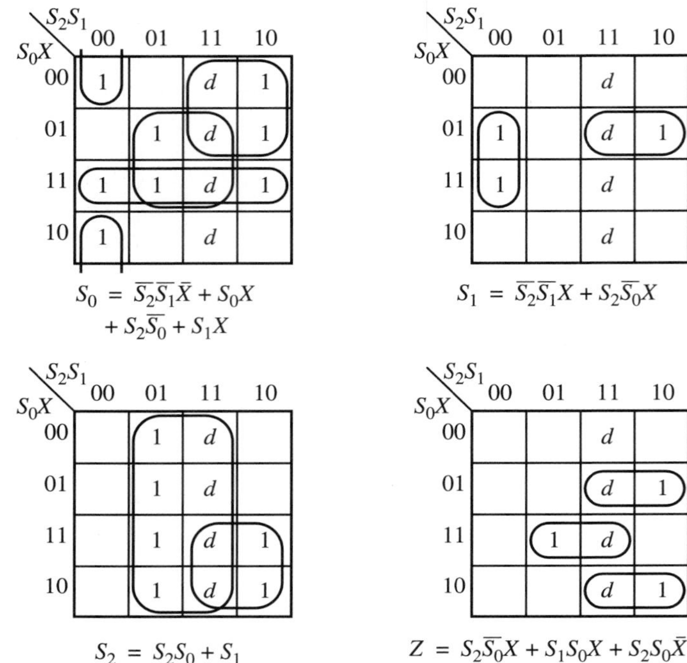

$S_0 = \overline{S_2}\overline{S_1}\overline{X} + S_0X + S_2\overline{S_0} + S_1X$
$S_1 = \overline{S_2}\overline{S_1}X + S_2\overline{S_0}X$
$S_2 = S_2S_0 + S_1$
$Z = S_2\overline{S_0}X + S_1S_0X + S_2S_0\overline{X}$

Figure B-33 K-map reduction of next state and output functions for sequence detector.

arise because the 110 and 111 state assignments are unused. Finally, we create the gate-level circuit, which is shown in Figure B-34. ■

B.3.2 *EXCITATION TABLES*

In addition to the S-R and D flip-flops, the **J-K** and **T flip-flops** (see Appendix A) are commonly used. The J-K flip-flop behaves similarly to an S-R flip-flop, except that it flips its state when both inputs are set to 1. The T flip-flop (for "toggle") alternates states, as when the inputs to a J-K flip-flop are set to 1. Logic diagrams and symbols for the J-K and T flip-flops are shown in Figures B-35 and B-36, respectively.

All of the flip-flops discussed up to this point as well as several variations are available as separate components, and in the past designers would choose one form or the other depending on characteristics such as cost, performance, availability, etc. These days, with the development of VLSI technology, the D flip-flop is typically used throughout a circuit. High-speed circuits making use of low-density logic, however, such as gallium arsenide (GaAs), may still find an

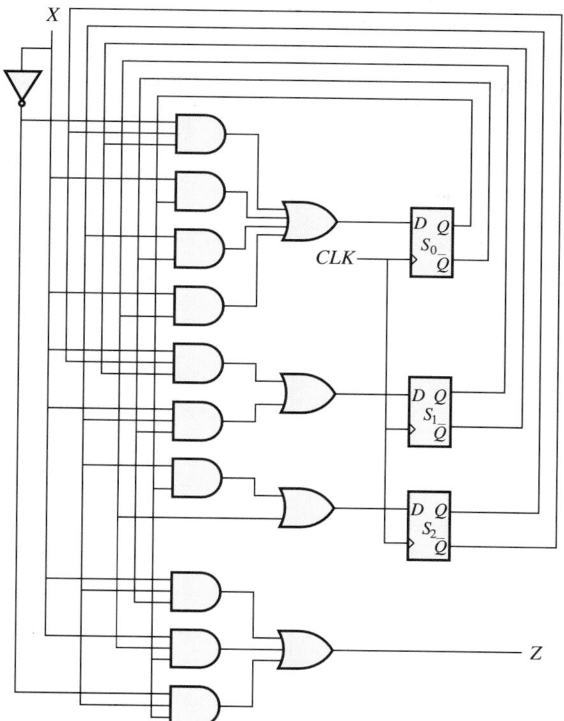

Figure B-34 Gate-level implementation of sequence detector.

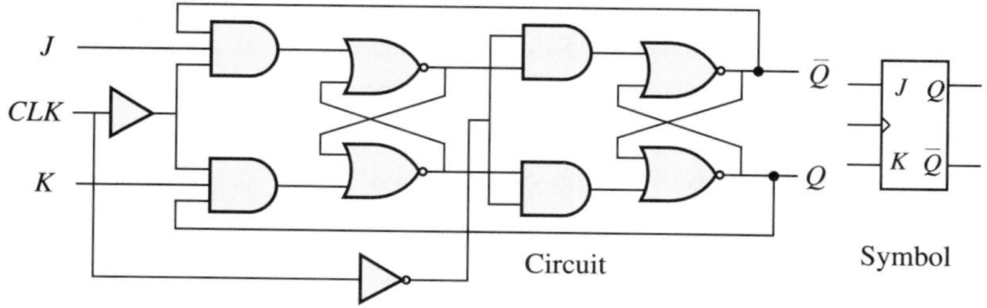

Figure B-35 Logic diagram and symbol for a J-K flip-flop.

application for the various forms. For situations such as this, we consider the problem of choosing a flip-flop that minimizes the total number of components in a circuit, in which a flip-flop is considered to be a single component.

The four flip-flops discussed up to this point can be described by **excitation tables**, as shown in Figure B-37. Each table shows the settings that must be applied at the inputs at time t in order to change the output at time $t + 1$.

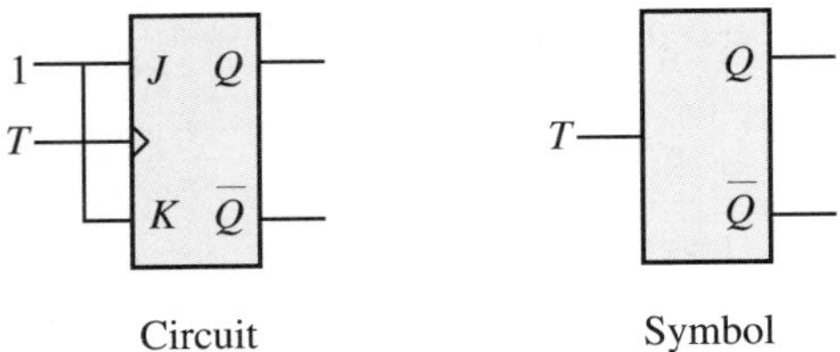

Figure B-36 Logic diagram and symbol for a T flip-flop.

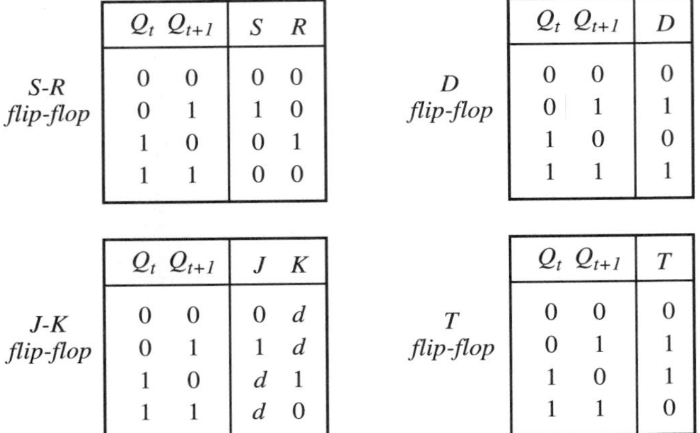

S-R flip-flop

Q_t	Q_{t+1}	S	R
0	0	0	0
0	1	1	0
1	0	0	1
1	1	0	0

D flip-flop

Q_t	Q_{t+1}	D
0	0	0
0	1	1
1	0	0
1	1	1

J-K flip-flop

Q_t	Q_{t+1}	J	K
0	0	0	*d*
0	1	1	*d*
1	0	*d*	1
1	1	*d*	0

T flip-flop

Q_t	Q_{t+1}	T
0	0	0
0	1	1
1	0	1
1	1	0

Figure B-37 Excitation tables for four flip-flops.

As an example of how excitation tables are used in the design of a finite state machine, consider using a J-K flip-flop in the design of a serial adder. We start with the serial adder shown in Figure B-38. State *A* represents the case in which there is no carry from the previous time step, and state *B* represents the case in which there is a carry from the previous time step.

We then create a truth table for the appropriate flip-flop. Figure B-39 shows a truth table that specifies functions for D, S-R, T, and J-K flip-flops as well as the output Z. We will only make use of the functions for the J-K flip-flop and the Z output here.

The way we construct the truth table is by first observing what the current state S_t is and then comparing it to what we want the next state to be. We then use the excitation tables to set the flip-flop inputs accordingly. For example, in the first line of the truth table shown in Figure B-39, when $X = Y = 0$ and the current state is 0, then the next state must be 0 as read from the state table of Figure B-38. In order to

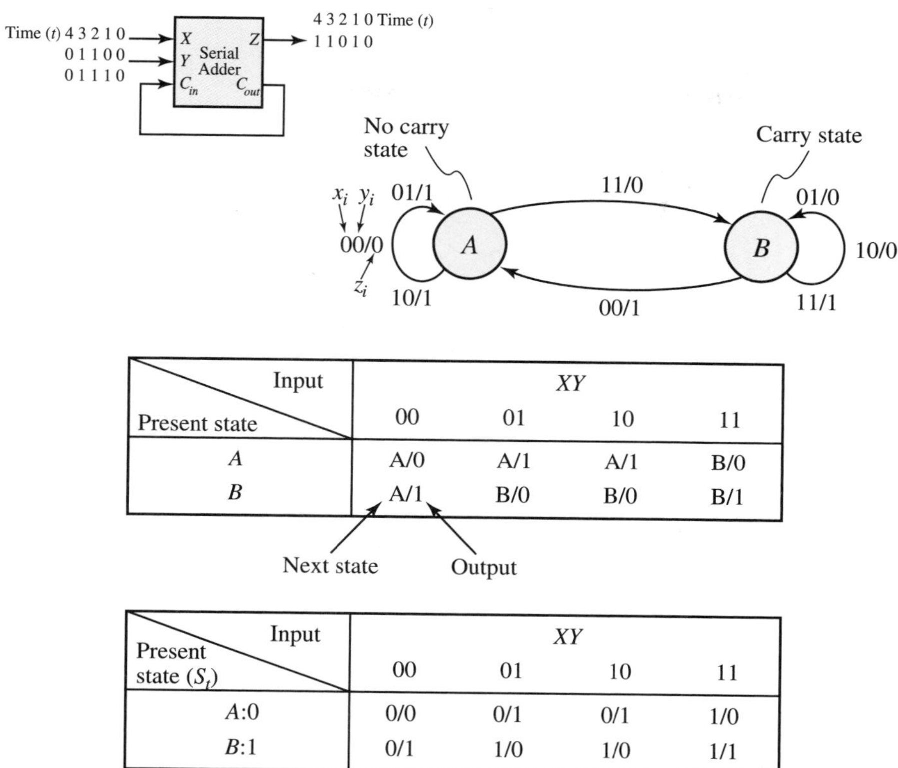

Present state \ Input	XY 00	01	10	11
A	A/0	A/1	A/1	B/0
B	A/1	B/0	B/0	B/1

Present state (S_t) \ Input	XY 00	01	10	11
A:0	0/0	0/1	0/1	1/0
B:1	0/1	1/0	1/0	1/1

Figure B-38 State transition diagram, state table, and state assignment for a serial adder.

X	*Y*	Present State S_t	*D*	(Set) *S*	(Reset) *R*	*T*	*J*	*K*	*Z*
0	0	0	0	0	0	0	0	*d*	0
0	0	1	0	0	1	1	*d*	1	1
0	1	0	0	0	0	0	0	*d*	1
0	1	1	1	0	0	0	*d*	0	0
1	0	0	0	0	0	0	0	*d*	1
1	0	1	1	0	0	0	*d*	0	0
1	1	0	1	1	0	1	1	*d*	0
1	1	1	1	0	0	0	*d*	0	1

Figure B-39 Truth table showing next-state functions for a serial adder for D, S-R, T, and J-K flip-flops. Shaded functions are used in the example.

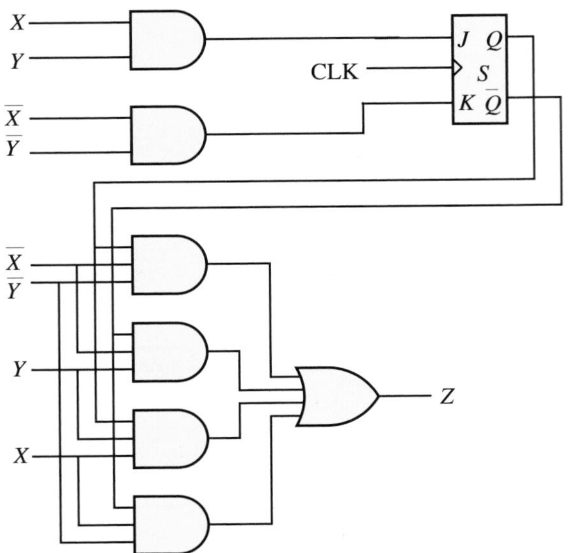

Figure B-40 Logic design for a serial adder using a J-K flip-flop.

achieve this for a J-K flip-flop, the J and K inputs must be 0 and d, respectively, as read from the J-K excitation table in Figure B-39. Continuing in this manner, the truth table is completed and the reduced Boolean equations are obtained as follows:

$$J = XY$$

$$K = \overline{X}\,\overline{Y}$$

$$Z = \overline{X}\,\overline{Y}S + \overline{X}Y\overline{S} + XYS + X\overline{Y}\,\overline{S}$$

The corresponding circuit is shown in Figure B-40. Notice that the design has a small gate input count (20), as compared with a gate input count of 25 for the logically equivalent circuit shown in Figure B-41, which uses a D flip-flop. Flip-flops are not included in the gate input count, although they do contribute to circuit complexity.

EXCITATION TABLE EXAMPLE: A MAJORITY CHECKER

For this example, we would like to design a circuit using T flip-flops and 8-to-1 MUXes that computes the majority function (see Figure A-15) for three inputs that are presented to an FSM in serial fashion. The circuit outputs a 0 until the third input is seen, at which point a 0 or a 1 is produced at the output according

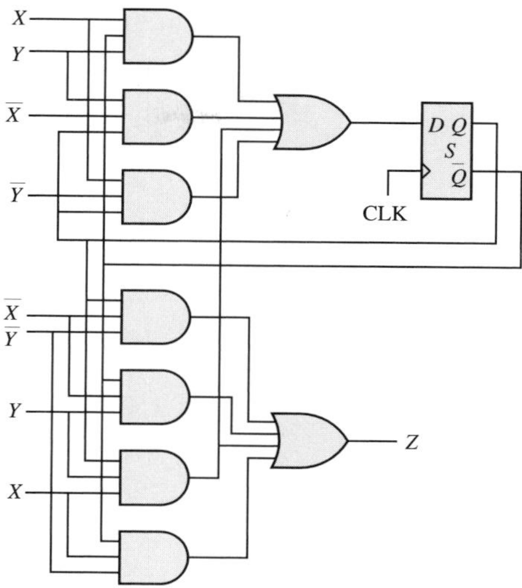

Figure B-41 Logic design for a serial adder using a D flip-flop.

to whether there are more 0's or 1's at the input, respectively. For example, an input of 011100101 produces an output of 001000001.

We start by creating a state transition diagram that enumerates all possible states of the FSM. In Figure B-42, a state transition diagram is shown in which the states are organized according to the number of inputs that have been seen. State *A* is the initial state in which no inputs have yet been seen. The three inputs are symbolized with the notation _ _ _. After the first input is seen, the FSM makes a transition to state *B* or state *C* for an input of 0 or 1, respectively. The input history is symbolized with the notation: 0_ _ and 1_ _ for states *B* and *C*, respectively. States *D*, *E*, *F*, and *G* enumerate all possible histories for two inputs, as symbolized by the notation 00_, 01_, 10_, and 11_, respectively.

The FSM outputs a 0 when making transitions to states *B* through *G*. On the third input, the FSM returns to state *A* and outputs a 0 or a 1 according to the majority function. A total of eight states are used in the FSM of Figure B-42, which are summarized in the state table shown in Figure B-43a.

The eight state FSM can be reduced to a seven state FSM. The reduction process is shown in Figure B-43b. States *E* and *F* can be combined, as shown in the reduced table of Figure B-43c. We use the reduced state table in creating a state assignment, which is shown in Figure B-44a for D flip-flops. We want to use T flip-flops and, keeping the same state assignment, obtain the state table shown in

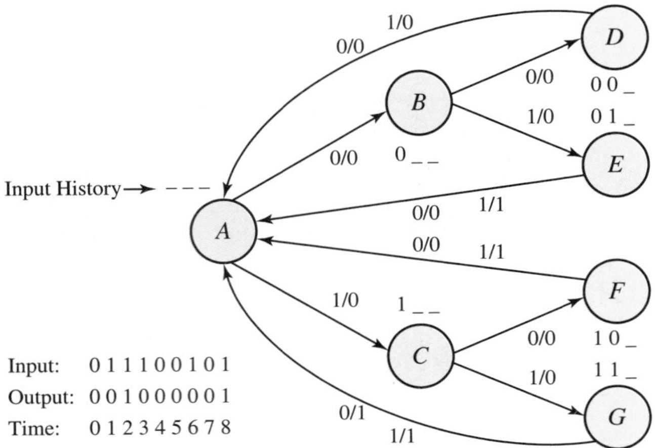

Figure B-42 State transition diagram for a majority FSM.

P.S. \ Input	X = 0	X = 1
A	B/0	C/0
B	D/0	E/0
C	F/0	G/0
D	A/0	A/0
E	A/0	A/1
F	A/0	A/1
G	A/1	A/1

(a)

$P_0 = (ABCDEFG)$
$P_1 = (ABCD)(EF)(G)$
$P_2 = (AD)(B)(C)(EF)(G)$
$P_3 = (A)(B)(C)(D)(EF)(G)$
$P_4 = (A)(B)(C)(D)(EF)(G)$ √

(b)

P.S. \ Input	X = 0	X = 1
A: A′	B′/0	C′/0
B: B′	D′/0	E′/0
C: C′	E′/0	F′/0
D: D′	A′/0	A′/0
EF: E′	A′/0	A′/1
G: F′	A′/1	A′/1

(c)

Figure B-43 (a) State table for majority FSM; (b) partitioning; (c) reduced state table.

P.S. $S_2S_1S_0$	X = 0 $S_2S_1S_0Z$	X = 1 $S_2S_1S_0Z$
A′: 000	001/0	010/0
B′: 001	011/0	100/0
C′: 010	100/0	101/0
D′: 011	000/0	000/0
E′: 100	000/0	000/1
F′: 101	000/1	000/1

(a)

P.S. $S_2S_1S_0$	X = 0 $T_2T_1T_0Z$	X = 1 $T_2T_1T_0Z$
A′: 000	001/0	010/0
B′: 001	000/0	010/0
C′: 010	110/0	111/0
D′: 011	011/0	011/0
E′: 100	100/0	100/1
F′: 101	101/1	101/1

(b)

Figure B-44 (a) State assignment for reduced majority FSM using D flip-flops; and (b) using T

Figure B-44b. The T flip-flop version is obtained by comparing the current state with the next state and following the excitation mapping for a T flip-flop shown in Figure B-37. The T flip-flop version has a 0 for the next state when the current and next states are the same in the D flip-flop version and has a 1 if the current and next states differ in the D flip-flop version. There are three bits used for the

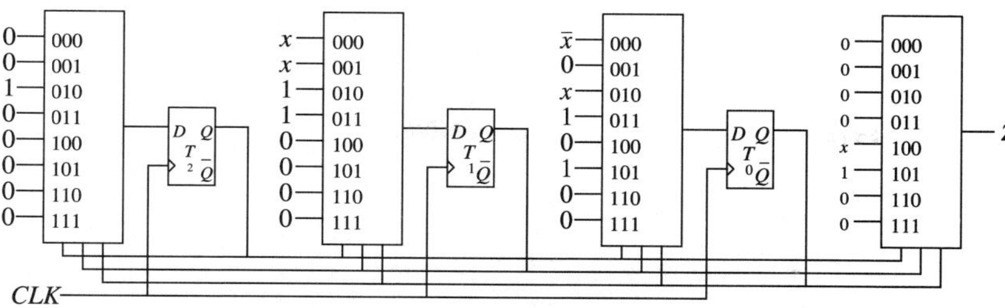

Figure B-45 Logic circuit for majority FSM.

binary coding of each state, and so there are three next state functions (s_0, s_1, and s_2) and an output function Z. The corresponding circuit using T flip-flops is shown in Figure B-45. Zeros are used for don't care states 110 and 111. ■

■ SUMMARY

Circuits that are generated from unreduced expressions may become very large, and so the expressions are reduced when possible into logically equivalent smaller expressions. One method of reducing expressions is to perform algebraic manipulation using the properties of Boolean algebra. This approach is powerful but involves trial and error, and it is tedious to carry out by hand. A simpler method is to apply K-map minimization. This is a more visual technique but becomes difficult to carry out for more than about six variables. The tabular method lends itself to automation and allows terms to be shared among functions.

An FSM can be in only one of a finite number of states at any time, but there are infinitely many FSMs that have the same external behavior. The number of flip-flops that are needed for an FSM may be reduced through the process of state reduction, and the complexity of the combinational logic in the FSM may be reduced by choosing an appropriate state assignment. The choice of flip-flop types also influences the complexity of the resulting circuit. The D flip-flop is commonly used for FSMs, but other flip-flops can be used such as the S-R, J-K, and T flip-flops.

■ FURTHER READING

(Booth, 1984) gives a good explanation of the Quine-McCluskey reduction process. (Kohavi, 1978) provides a thorough treatment of combinational logic reduction and state reduction. (Hamacher et al. 1990) have a good discussion of propagation delay and timing. (Mead and Conway, 1980) provide a concise description of VLSI design techniques. (Agrawal and Cheng, 1990) cover design for testability based on state assignments.

Agrawal, V. D. and K. T. Cheng, "Finite State Machine Synthesis with Embedded Test Function," *Journal of Electronic Testing: Theory and Applications*, **1**, pp. 221–228 (1990).

Booth, T. L., *Introduction to Computer Engineering: Hardware and Software Design*, 3/e, John Wiley & Sons (1984).

Hamacher, V. C., Z. G. Vranesic, and S. G. Zaky, *Computer Organization*, 3/e, McGraw-Hill (1990).

Mead, C. and Conway, L., Introduction to VLSI Systems, Addison-Wesley (1980).

Kohavi, Z., *Switching and Finite Automata Theory*, 2/e, McGraw-Hill (1978).

PROBLEMS

B.1 Given the following functions, construct K-maps and find minimal sum-of-products expressions for f and g.

$f(A, B, C, D) = 1$ when two or more inputs are 1, otherwise $f(A, B, C, D) = 0$.

$g(A, B, C, D) = 1$ when the number of inputs that are 1 is even (including the case when no inputs are 1), otherwise $g(A, B, C, D) = \overline{f(A, B, C, D)}$.

B.2 Use K-maps to simplify the following function f and its don't care condition below. Perform the reduction for (a) the sum-of-products form and (b) the product-of-sums form.

$$f(A, B, C, D) = \sum(2, 8, 10, 11) + \sum{}_d(0, 9)$$

B.3 Given a logic circuit, is it possible to generate a truth table that contains don't cares? Explain your answer.

B.4 The following K-map is formed incorrectly. Show the reduced equation that is produced by the incorrect map, and then form the K-map correctly and derive the reduced equation from the correct map. Note that both K-maps will produce functionally correct equations, but only the properly formed

K-map will produce a minimized two-level equation.

D \ ABC	000	001	011	010	110	111	101	100
0	1			1	1			1
1	1			1	1			1

B.5 A 4-to-1 multiplexer can be represented by the following truth table. Use map-entered variables to produce a reduced SOP Boolean equation.

A	B	F
0	0	D_0
0	1	D_1
1	0	D_2
1	1	D_3

B.6 Use the tabular method to reduce the function

$$f(A, B, C, D) = \sum(3, 5, 7, 10, 13, 15) + \sum{}_d(2, 6)$$

B.7 Use the tabular method to reduce the following three-output truth table:

Minterm	A	B	C	D	F_0	F_1	F_2
m_0	0	0	0	0	0	0	1
m_1	0	0	0	1	0	0	0
m_2	0	0	1	0	0	0	0
m_3	0	0	1	1	1	0	0
m_4	0	1	0	0	0	0	1
m_5	0	1	0	1	1	1	0
m_6	0	1	1	0	0	0	0
m_7	0	1	1	1	1	1	0
m_8	1	0	0	0	0	0	0
m_9	1	0	0	1	0	0	0
m_{10}	1	0	1	0	0	1	1
m_{11}	1	0	1	1	0	0	0
m_{12}	1	1	0	0	0	0	0
m_{13}	1	1	0	1	1	1	0
m_{14}	1	1	1	0	1	1	1
m_{15}	1	1	1	1	1	1	1

B.8 Reduce the following equation for F to its minimal two-level form, and implement the function using a three-input, one-output PLA.

$$F(A, B, C) = ABC + \bar{A}BC + A\bar{B}\bar{C} + \bar{A}\bar{B}C$$

B.9 Use function decomposition to implement the following function f with two 4-to-1 MUXes. Parenthesize the equation so that C and D are in the innermost level as in Equation B.22. Make sure that every input to each MUX is assigned to a value (0 or 1), to a variable, or to a function.

$$f(A, B, C, D) = ABCD + AB\overline{C}D + ABC\overline{D} + \overline{A}B$$

B.10 Reduce the following state table:

Present state \ Input	X = 0	X = 1
A	$D/0$	$G/1$
B	$C/0$	$G/0$
C	$A/0$	$D/1$
D	$B/0$	$C/1$
E	$A/1$	$E/0$
F	$C/1$	$F/0$
G	$E/1$	$G/1$

B.11 Reduce the following state table:

Present state \ Input	XY = 00	01	10	11
A	$A/0$	$B/0$	$C/0$	$D/0$
B	$A/0$	$B/1$	$D/0$	$D/1$
C	$E/1$	$B/0$	$B/0$	$E/1$
D	$A/0$	$D/1$	$D/0$	$B/1$
E	$C/1$	$D/0$	$D/0$	$E/1$

B.12 The following ternary state table may or may not reduce. Show the reduction process (the partitions) and the reduced state table.

Present state \ Input	x = 0	1	2
A	$B/0$	$E/2$	$G/1$
B	$D/2$	$A/1$	$D/0$
C	$D/2$	$G/1$	$B/0$
D	$B/2$	$F/1$	$C/0$
E	$A/0$	$E/2$	$C/1$
F	$C/0$	$E/2$	$F/1$
G	$D/0$	$E/2$	$A/1$

B.13 The following circuit has three master-slave J-K flip-flops. There is a single input CLK and three outputs Q_2, Q_1, and Q_0 that initially have the value 0. Complete the timing diagram by showing the values for Q_2, Q_1, and Q_0. Assume that there are no delays through the flip-flops.

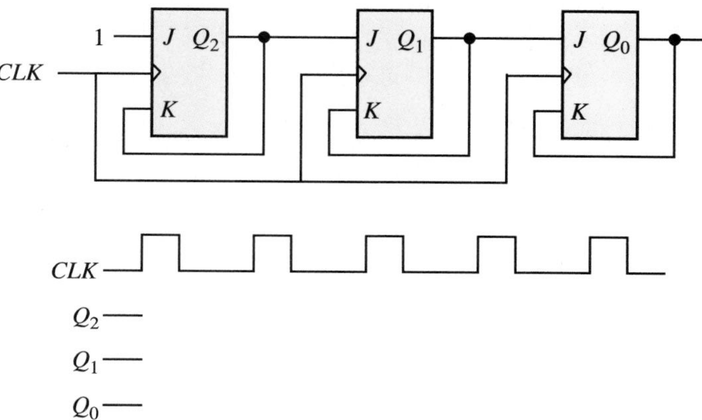

B.14 Use a T flip-flop to design a serial adder, using the approach described in Section B.3.2.

B.15 In the following reduced state table, the state assignments have already been made. Design the machine using D flip-flops, AND and OR gates. Use K-maps to reduce the expressions for the next state and output functions. Be careful to construct the K-maps correctly, since there are only three rows in the state table.

Present state \ Input	X = 0	X = 1
YZ		
A: 00	00/0	01/1
B: 01	10/1	00/1
C: 10	01/1	10/0

B.16 Draw a logic diagram that shows a J-K flip-flop can be created using a D flip-flop.

INDEX

C